COM 101

The World of Communication

The Human Storyteller

Boston University, College of Communication

Selected chapters from:

Media & Culture: Mass Communication in a Digital Age, Tenth Edition, 2016 Update
By Richard Campbell, Christopher R. Martin, and Bettina Fabos

Media in Society
By Richard Campbell, Joli Jensen, Douglas Gomery, Bettina Fabos, and Julie Frechette

Telling the Story: The Convergence of Print, Broadcast, and Online Media, Fifth Edition
By The Missouri Group, Brian S. Brooks, George Kennedy, Daryl R. Moen, and Don Ranly

The Film Experience, Fifth Edition
By Timothy Corrigan and Patricia White

Filmmaking in Action, First Edition
By Adam Leipzig, Barry S. Weiss, and Michael Goldman

News Reporting and Writing, Eleventh Edition
By The Missouri Group

macmillan learning
curriculum solutions

Content taken from:

Media & Culture: Mass Communication in a Digital Age, Tenth Edition, 2016 Update
By Richard Campbell, Christopher R. Martin, and Bettina Fabos

Media in Society
By Richard Campbell, Joli Jensen, Douglas Gomery, Bettina Fabos, and Julie Frechette

Telling the Story: The Convergence of Print, Broadcast, and Online Media, Fifth Edition
By The Missouri Group, Brian S. Brooks, George Kennedy, Daryl R. Moen, and Don Ranly

The Film Experience, Fifth Edition
By Timothy Corrigan and Patricia White

Filmmaking in Action, First Edition
By Adam Leipzig, Barry S. Weiss, and Michael Goldman

News Reporting and Writing, Eleventh Edition
By The Missouri Group

3 2 1

f e

Macmillan Learning Curriculum Solutions
14903 Pilot Drive
Plymouth, MI 48170
www.macmillanlearning.com

ISBN: 978-1-319-23352-5

Acknowledgments
Text acknowledgments and copyrights appear at the back of the book on page 619 which constitute an extension of the copyright page. Art acknowledgments and copyrights appear on the same page as the art selections they cover.

Table of Contents

Mass Communication

An Introduction to the Study of Communication

On the surface, studying communication is a fairly odd proposition. It would be like studying breathing, something we do every day without even thinking about it. Even when we think about studying some of the professional fields of communication, it may seem odd. Film, television, advertising, journalism and others are all things that we are exposed to on a daily basis. To study these things, therefore, is really to look at something that we already engage with every single day. However, because we are exposed to something every day does not necessarily mean we know how it works. Take breathing for example. We all know how to breathe, we all know when we're short of breath, and we all know that taking a deep breath can make us feel good sometimes. What we may not understand is the mechanics of breathing. We know that we breathe in and breathe out, and we know that we need to breathe, but how many of us really understand how breathing works? Are we experts on breathing? And now think about this, just because we know how to breathe and do it on a daily basis, it doesn't mean that we are qualified to serve as an anesthesiologist, or another type of doctor that might focus on how your lungs work.

Communication is very similar. We all communicate every day, whether it be person to person, over some mediated device, or even talking to ourselves. Each of us has myriad communication experience. But this experience does not mean that we necessarily understand communication. We may all know how to send a text message, or how to make a phone call, or even use emojis or other "new" ways of communication. But what is the meaning behind these things? It is this level of understanding that studying communication hopes to resolve.

There is a wise adage that says *in order to understand where we're going, we need to understand where we've been*. This is particularly true in understanding communication. For example, is the way in which we might use an emoji so very different from the way early Egyptians used hieroglyphics? Or perhaps the reasons we use social media so vastly different than the way humans once sat around a fire in the evening to share the day's events? Certainly the tools of communication have changed drastically, but the essence of human communication remains the same. Humans are, by nature, storytellers, and throughout this book and course, we will explore that very basic human need to communicate.

The book is meant to provide you with the basic information needed in order to pursue advanced study in the field of communication, but will only do so if you are purposeful in your use of it. Each of the selections has been carefully selected to provide you with a baseline on which to build your knowledge. In other words, this book is not the sum total of knowledge in communication, rather it is a doorway for your own discovery.

The Nature of This Course

Many students who sat in this course before you have viewed it as a rite of passage, or perhaps on the other end of the scale, a necessary evil. The goal of this course is to introduce you to Boston University's College of Communication, to the study of communication as a whole, and to inform you about the multitude of prospects that are available to you as you progress in your knowledge of communication. In other words, no small task awaits us.

However, while we will work towards the aforementioned goals, the true nature of this course is to help us understand communication better. To begin our journey of understanding how and why humans are driven to be storytellers, and in the end, to be able to better tell those stories which define us.

In addition to our text and class experience, each of you will also participate in a weekly discussion meant to assist you in focusing your knowledge. You will have a separate text for your discussion section, and will use each discussion meeting to further your knowledge by applying concepts we discuss in our larger gatherings.

At the end of the course, you will have been exposed to many (but not all!) of the fields of communication, and will be better positioned to answer *What kind of storyteller do I want to be? And, How will I tell those stories?* This is the nature of inquiry in the study and practice of communication.

Academic Conduct Code

Boston University's Academic Conduct Code is designed to assist in the development of a supportive and productive learning environment. It is both a description of the University's ethical expectations of students as well as a guarantee of students' rights and responsibilities as members of a learning community. The Code provides clarity related to policy and procedure regarding academic conduct.

For students, the Code establishes an environment of integrity and professionalism that helps to assure each individual of receiving appropriate recognition for his or her work. The ethical decisions that students face in an academic environment are similar to those they will encounter routinely in the professional world they will enter upon graduation or where they are currently employed. The Code allows faculty to conduct a fair and accurate evaluation of student performance and to maintain a supportive and just learning environment. Academic integrity is a critical component of such an environment, giving faculty the freedom to extend their role as educators to include serving as mentors and colleagues as well as instructors. For administrative staff, the Code gives them the ability to deal more effectively with students, and to work on a student's behalf both within the University and outside it.

This respect for universally recognized ethical values affects the University's reputation in both the academic and professional communities of which it is a part. This reputation is essential to the success of not only the current generation of students, but previous and future generations as well.

All students entering Boston University are expected to maintain high standards of academic honesty and integrity. It is the responsibility of every undergraduate student to be aware of the Academic Conduct Code's contents and to abide by its provisions. The Academic Conduct Committee of the individual School or College, which is composed of students, faculty and staff, has jurisdiction over all charges of academic misconduct brought against students.

In all charges of academic misconduct against a student, the student is entitled to full procedural fairness in any disciplinary proceedings. The Academic Conduct Code details the guidelines governing disciplinary proceedings. It also articulates the University's philosophy of discipline, defines violations of the code, and enumerates penalties applicable under the code.

I. Philosophy of Discipline

The objective of Boston University in enforcing academic rules is to promote a community atmosphere in which learning can best take place. Such an atmosphere can be maintained only so long as every student believes that his or her academic competence is being judged fairly and that he or she will not be put at a disadvantage because of someone else's dishonesty. Penalties should be carefully determined so as to be no more and no less than required to maintain the desired atmosphere. In defining violations of this code, the intent is to protect the integrity of the educational process.

II. Academic Misconduct

Academic misconduct is conduct by which a student misrepresents his or her academic accomplishments, or impedes other students' opportunities of being judged fairly for their academic work. Knowingly allowing others to represent your work as their own is as serious an offense as submitting another's work as your own.

III. Violations of This Code

Violations of this code comprise attempts to be dishonest or deceptive in the performance of academic work in or out of the classroom, alterations of academic records, alterations of official data on paper or electronic resumes, or unauthorized collaboration with another student or students. Violations include, but are not limited to:

A. **Cheating on examination**. Any attempt by a student to alter his or her performance on an examination in violation of that examination's stated or commonly understood ground rules.

B. **Plagiarism.** Representing the work of another as one's own. Plagiarism includes but is not limited to the following: copying the answers of another student on an examination, copying or restating the work or ideas of another person or persons in any oral or written work (printed or electronic) without citing the appropriate source, and collaborating with someone else in an academic endeavor without acknowledging his or her contribution. Plagiarism can consist of acts of commission—appropriating the words or ideas of another—or omission failing to acknowledge/document/credit the source or creator of words or ideas (see below for a detailed definition of plagiarism). It also includes colluding with someone else in an academic endeavor without acknowledging his or her contribution, using audio or video footage that comes from another source (including work done by another student) without permission and acknowledgement of that source.

C. **Misrepresentation or falsification of data** presented for surveys, experiments, reports, etc., which includes but is not limited to: citing authors that do not exist, citing interviews that never took place, or field work that was not completed.

D. **Theft of an examination**. Stealing or otherwise discovering and/or making known to others the contents of an examination that has not yet been administered.

E. **Unauthorized communication during examinations**. Any unauthorized communication may be considered prima facie evidence of cheating.

F. **Knowingly allowing another student to represent your work as his or her own.** This includes providing a copy of your paper or laboratory report to another student without the explicit permission of the instructor(s).

G. **Forgery, alteration, or knowing misuse of graded examinations, quizzes, grade lists, or official records of documents**, including but not limited to transcripts from any institution, letters of recommendation, degree certificates, examinations, quizzes, or other work after submission.

H. **Theft or destruction of examinations or papers** after submission.

I. **Submitting the same work in more than one course** without the consent of instructors.

J. **Altering or destroying another student's work or records**, altering records of any kind, removing materials from libraries or offices without consent, or in any way interfering with the work of others so as to impede their academic performance.

K. **Violation of the rules governing teamwork**. Unless the instructor of a course otherwise specifically provides instructions to the contrary, the following rules apply to teamwork: 1. No team member shall intentionally restrict or inhibit another team member's access to team meetings, team work-in-progress, or other team activities without the express authorization of the instructor. 2. All team members shall be held responsible for the content of all teamwork submitted for evaluation as if each team member had individually submitted the entire work product of their team as their own work.

L. **Failure to sit in a specifically assigned seat during examinations.**

M. **Conduct in a professional field assignment** that violates the policies and regulations of the host school or agency.

N. **Conduct in violation of public law occurring outside the University** that directly affects the academic and professional status of the student, after civil authorities have imposed sanctions.

O. **Attempting improperly to influence the award of any credit, grade, or honor.**

P. **Intentionally making false statements to the Academic Conduct Committee or intentionally presenting false information to the committee.**

Q. **Failure to comply with the sanctions imposed under the authority of this code.**

When an alleged Infraction occurs in a School/College other than the one in which the student is enrolled, the initial determination of misconduct will be made by the Academic Conduct Committee of the School/College where the alleged infraction occurred, while assessment of penalty will come from the student's School/College of enrollment, based upon recommendation of the Dean and committee from the School/College where the infraction took place.

IV. Action on Suspected Violations

Every School or College shall designate an Assistant or Associate Dean with responsibility for administering the procedures set forth in this Code.

As a general rule, faculty who have reason to believe that a student has violated this Code shall meet with the student, personally or through a designee, inform the student of the suspected violation, and document the student's response. Faculty members will then report suspected violations of the Code to the Assistant or Associate Dean using the "Faculty Report of Student Academic Misconduct." This form will be accompanied by a statement indicating the supporting evidence upon which the faculty member has relied as well as the student's response to the charges.

A. **Cases of undisputed academic misconduct by the first-time offenders** If the student has admitted to the academic misconduct and has never been found guilty of an academic conduct violation at Boston University, the faculty member may request the designated Dean's authorization to sanction the student by means of grading penalty. In such a case, a student who has admitted to academic misconduct may agree to a grading penalty as determined by the faculty, up to and including a failing grade in the course. The faculty member will inform the designated Dean of the proposed grading penalty.The designated Dean will ascertain whether the student has previously signed an Admission of Academic Misconduct Form or has any prior record of academic misconduct in any College or School in the University. If so, the designated Dean will refer the charges and supporting evidence to the Academic Conduct Committee, which shall then proceed with a hearing. If not, the designated Dean, at his or her discretion, and taking into account the nature of the infraction, may grant written permission to the faculty member to enter into an agreement with the student for a grading penalty in lieu of proceedings before the Academic Conduct Committee. If such permission is received, the faculty member will inform the student of the option to agree to a grading penalty. If the student chooses this option, the agreement between the faculty member and student must be formalized through the University's "Admission of Academic Misconduct" Form. An accused student is not compelled to sign such an agreement and may choose to exercise the right to have his or her case heard by the Academic Conduct Committee.

B. **Cases of disputed academic misconduct or cases of repeat offenders** If the student disputes the charge of Academic Misconduct or if the designated Dean denies permission for a grading penalty because the student is a repeat offender or because of the nature of the offense, the designated Dean shall then refer the charges and supporting evidence to the Academic Conduct Committee, which shall then proceed with a hearing.

V. Penalties

A. **Students who sign approved admission of academic misconduct forms** Students who sign Admission of Academic Misconduct Forms shall receive the grading penalty noted on the form. Students will also receive a letter of reprimand from the designated Dean. The form and the letter of reprimand will be retained in the student's file at the Dean's Office, but shall not be recorded on the student's permanent academic record. The reprimand will not be made public when records or transcripts are sent out. It may, however, be considered when reviewing the student's eligibility for University programs and when imposing sanctions for future offenses. It may also be reported in response to a direct question about past academic misconduct or disciplinary sanctions from an undergraduate, graduate, or professional school to which the student seeks admission or from other authorized entities.

B. **Students whose cases are referred to the committee** Students who are not allowed the option of a grading penalty or who elect to have their cases heard by the Academic Conduct Committee may receive the sanctions of Reprimand, Disciplinary Probation, Suspension, or Expulsion only through action of the Academic Conduct Committee. However, faculty members always retain the right to assign grades reflecting their principled and equitable assessment of students' work. If applicable, a faculty member may assign a grade of "I" in a course while a matter is pending before the Academic Conduct Committee. In a case in which the Academic Conduct Committee has found a violation of the Code, the ultimate grade assigned by the faculty member may also reflect the faculty member's determination of how seriously overall course goals and expectations of the academic discipline are compromised by work involved in an incident of academic misconduct, and how that work should in consequence contribute to the final course grade.

C. **Students who believe that a faculty member has penalized them for alleged acts of academic misconduct without having followed the procedures** set forth in this Code should make their concerns known as soon as possible to the designated Dean.

D. **If the accused is found by the committee** to have committed academic misconduct, the committee may recommend any reasonable appropriate penalty. The penalty will generally be one or more of those listed below. However, because it is impossible to anticipate all variables of misconduct, the committee has broad power to fashion a sanction that is fair to the student, suitable to the offense, and effective as a future deterrent. The committee may recommend such other appropriate sanction as it sees fit.

1. **No penalty for minor violations that do not warrant sanction.**

2. **Reprimand**

    a. For violations of a minor nature or mitigated by extenuating circumstances.

    b. A copy of the reprimand shall be placed in the student's file but shall not be recorded on the permanent academic record. Past reprimands may be considered in imposing sanctions for future offenses.

    c. Reprimands are not to be made public when records, transcripts, etc., are sent out, but may be reported in response to a direct question about past academic misconduct or disciplinary sanctions from an undergraduate, graduate, or professional school to which the student seeks admission or from other authorized entities.

    d. Reprimands place no restriction on the student's participation in academic or nonacademic School/College or all-University activities.

3. **Disciplinary probation**

    a. For violations deemed serious enough to warrant some abridgement of the student's rights and privileges.

    b. Given for a specified period of time.

    c. Recorded on the student's permanent internal record.

    d. Prohibits the student from being an officer in any recognized all-University or School/College student organization, and from participating in intercollegiate activities during the specified probation period.

4. **Suspension**

    a. For violations deemed serious enough to warrant separation of the student from the University community for a limited time, but not serious enough to warrant expulsion.

b. Given for a period of one to three semesters.

c. Recorded on the student's permanent internal record; the student's external record shall carry the statement "withdrawn."

d. The student must apply to the Dean of his or her School/College for readmission, making a satisfactory statement concerning his or her interim activities and his or her intended future conduct.

e. No academic coursework may be undertaken for Boston University credit, nor may any Boston University degree be conferred, during the period of suspension.

5. **Expulsion**

   a. For extremely serious academic misconduct.

   b. Recorded permanently on the student's academic record.

   c. Expulsion is permanent.

6. **Other sanctions**

   a. Removal from a Professional Program. For violations involving conduct that is considered serious enough to withdraw the student from a program leading to a professional endorsement from the University. Such conduct may take place within a professional field assignment as well as the University. Removal from a professional program does not, in itself, bar the student from graduation.

   b. For serious misconduct, including but not limited to misconduct that occurred while the student was enrolled at the University but was discovered after graduation or conduct involving fraudulent use of University transcripts or degree certificates after graduation, or similar serious misconduct, recommendation of the committee may include withholding of transcripts or revocation of the degree.

VI. Dissemination of Information

A. Notice of probation, suspension, or expulsion is sent to the parent or guardian of a student who has consented to the release of such information to his or her parents or guardians.

B. Dissemination of information is governed by the Family Educational Rights and Privacy Act of 1974. http://www.bu.edu/reg/ferpa/ferpa-policy.html

C. Penalties imposed through the Academic Conduct Code, including reprimands, may be reported to graduate and professional schools to which a student seeks admission, or to other authorized entities, notably in response to a question about past academic misconduct or disciplinary sanctions.

D. Efforts will be made to ensure that students receive a copy of the Academic Conduct Code at their first registration at the University. The URL to the code will be provided to students by their School/College.

Student Academic Conduct Committee

I. Procedure

A. **The designated Dean will institute proceedings** before the committee by forwarding the case to the Chair of the Academic Conduct Committee (committee). The committee shall consist of faculty and staff members appointed by the Dean and graduate students or advanced undergraduate students of not lower than junior-year standing, appointed by the Assistant or Associate Dean of the College. This committee has jurisdiction over every alleged act of academic misconduct on the part of (a) any student enrolled in the School/College, and (b) any student enrolled in a course taught in the School/College, whether that student is enrolled in that School/College or some other academic unit at the University or any other college or university. The committee will also have jurisdiction over every alleged act of misconduct pertaining to course credits earned in the School/College by any person. This shall include any person who has received a baccalaureate degree from the University.

B. **When students are called before academic conduct committees of another School/College in the University**, the designated Dean of the School or College holding the hearing shall inform the designated Dean of the School/College of enrollment of the nature of the charge and the time of the hearing. Whenever possible, a representative from the School/College of enrollment should be present at the hearing and deliberations.

C. **If the designated Dean refers the case to the Academic Conduct Committee**, the Dean's office shall inform the student (by hand-delivered or certified letter with return receipt, to be sent at least 12 days prior to the hearing) of the following matters:

1. The charges.

2. The date, time, and location of the hearing.

3. The fact that the student may request to reschedule the hearing, within a limited time period, for a valid reason.

4. The fact that the student may be accompanied by an advisor of his or her choice. At the discretion of the committee chair, the advisor may be allowed to make a brief statement on behalf of the student. The advisor may not participate directly in the hearing.

5. The fact that the student may also bring witnesses to provide additional information related to the alleged offense. The chair may limit or exclude the matters presented by any individual to the extent that such information is repetitive or is not probative of the guilt or innocence of the student.

6. The fact that he or she shall have the right to examine the person bringing the charges, to have access to all documents that have been introduced as evidence, to have copies of such documents prepared, and at the discretion of the chair and in a manner to be prescribed by the chair, to examine all witnesses.

7. The fact that the student may, but is not required, to submit a written statement and/or other documents for review by the Academic Conduct Committee, provided that any such written statement is prepared by the student (and not by his or her advisor), and provided that any statement or documents that student wishes the Academic Conduct Committee to review are received by the Dean's Office at least seven (7) days prior to the scheduled date of the hearing. The Academic Conduct Committee reserves the right not to accept or review any materials that are submitted after this deadline.

D. **Waiver of 12-day notice**. A student may waive the 12-day notice requirement. The committee may hold an expedited hearing when the Chair and student both believe that doing so is in the interest of fairness.

E. **Hearings**

1. Members of the committee may be excused if the case might involve a conflict of interest (e.g., kinship, teacher-student relationship, etc.).

2. The Dean may appoint pro tempore members to replace regular faculty members who are unable to attend, or who have been excused.

3. When students are called before Academic Conduct Committees of another School/College in the University, a representative from the home School/College student shall be invited to attend, but will not vote.

4. No student shall be found guilty except on the vote of a majority of the voting members present at a hearing.

5. The quorum for hearings shall be five voting members of the committee, at least three of whom shall be faculty members. Once the meeting is called to order, the departure or absence of one or more committee members shall not defeat the quorum and the meeting may continue to conclusion.

6. The chair shall be counted as a voting member, but shall cast his or her vote only in order to break a tie vote.

7. A hearing shall proceed in the absence of the accused student only if:

   a. The student waives the right to be present or

   b. The committee is satisfied that proper notice of the hearing was given to the student and that there is no legitimate cause for the absence.

8. The hearing shall be recorded by sound recording. The recordings are to be preserved for one year. Any participant in the hearing may obtain a copy of the recording or the transcript of the hearing (if one is made, though the University is under no obligation to produce a transcript) at actual cost. Deliberations are private and are not tape-recorded.

9. The Chair in his or her discretion shall administer the hearing to promote fairness. Subject to that discretion, the hearing shall include:

   a. Presentation of charges by the committee chair.

   b. Presentation and examination of material evidence and witnesses by the committee and by the accused student(s) but excluding material relevant to sanctions to be imposed. In appropriate circumstances the chair may take steps to protect a witness through actions such as sequestering, withholding a witness's identity, or taking testimony prior to a hearing.

   c. Statement by the accused student(s) and examination of the student(s) by the committee.

   d. Additional examination of witnesses if required.

   e. After excusing the accused student, and advisor, and witnesses, deliberation of the committee, which shall not be tape-recorded.

   f. Formulation of the judgment and assessment of any appropriate penalty by a majority vote of the members present.

10. The chair shall make the necessary determination of the scope of the inquiry with a view to according full and fair exploration of relevant material. It is in the discretion of the chair whether to accept additional documents prepared by any of the witnesses and first offered at the time of the hearing.

11. Because the hearing is not a court hearing, the committee is not bound by legal rules of evidence. However, every effort will be made to conduct hearings as fairly and expeditiously as possible.

12. The hearing shall not be public, and information gained at the hearing shall be treated as privileged information by all participants. This does not bar the disclosure of the findings and recommendations of the committee to those authorized to receive such information. Inasmuch as this provision is for the protection of the accused student, it does not bar him or her from disclosing information pertaining solely to him or herself, if he or she wishes to do so, provided, however that in proceedings involving multiple students, no student should disclose information learned about any other accused student to any persons not participating in the hearing.

13. At the request of the accused student, the chair of the Academic Conduct Committee may, at his or her discretion, elect to admit parents or legal guardians.

14. The hearing shall be conducted with proper decorum. The hearing may be recessed by the chair if:

    a. Additional evidence or witnesses are needed.

    b. It is apparent that a fair hearing cannot be held because of disturbances, illness, or similar causes.

15. The School/College may, from time to time, make public the facts and decisions of cases that come before the committee. However, such reports shall not reveal the name of any student, professor, or course involved in a case that has been heard by the committee.

F. **Recommendation**

1. **Cases involving student enrolled in the School/College where the infraction occurred.**

The committee shall write up its recommendation including a statement of the charges, evidence, judgment, and recommended penalty, which shall be transmitted to the designated Dean as soon as possible after the hearing at which the judgment was made. With regard to the judgment, the designated Dean shall review the evidence supporting the committee's findings. If necessary, the designated Dean may refer the matter back to the committee for further consideration and/or elaboration, or may request the transcript or recording of the hearing and/or copies of the evidence. However, the judgment of the committee shall not be replaced by a judgment more damaging to the student unless new evidence has been considered upon a rehearing. Similarly, with regard to the recommended penalty the designated Dean of the School or College conducting the hearing shall not impose more severe penalties than those recommended by the committee.

2. **Cases involving students enrolled in another School/College.**

If the accused student is not enrolled in the School/College where the infraction occurred, the designated Dean of the School/College conducting the hearing shall transmit the committee's judgment and recommended penalty to the designated Dean of the student's School/College. With regard to the judgment and recommended penalty, the designated Dean of the student's School/College shall review the evidence supporting the committee's findings. If necessary, the designated Dean may refer the matter back to the committee for further consideration and/or elaboration, or may request the transcript or recording of the hearing and/or copies of the evidence. However, the judgment of the committee shall not be replaced by a judgment more damaging to the student unless new evidence has been considered upon a rehearing. With regard to the recommended penalty, the designated Dean is not bound by the committee's recommendation, but shall make an independent determination of the appropriateness of the recommended penalty, and may impose a penalty that is greater or lesser than that recommended by the committee.

G. **The designated Dean of the student's School/College shall notify the student by certified or personally signed letter of the judgment and penalty imposed.** The student shall also be informed that there is a procedure for appeal.

II. Appeals

A. All decisions may be appealed to the designated Dean of the School/College in which the student is enrolled. Such appeals must be filed within 14 days of receipt of the judgment and penalty.

B. A student who is appealing is entitled to receive a copy of all materials considered by the committee, a copy of the tape recording of the hearing, and a copy of the committee's report.

C. When a student is enrolled in a School/College other than the School/College where the case was heard and is appealing both the judgment and penalty, the Dean of the student's School/College shall request that the Dean of the School/College where the case was heard render a decision on the appeal of the judgment. Thereafter, the Dean of the student's School/College of enrollment will render a decision on the appeal of the penalty.

D. Standard on Appeal: The decision of the designated Dean should be upheld unless it appears on appeal that the decision was unreasonable and unfair. The Dean will notify the student of the decision. The letter shall also inform the student of the procedure for appeal to the University Provost.

E. Within fourteen days of the receipt of the Dean's final response to appeals within the School/College, a student may appeal the judgment or the penalty to the University Provost. Appeals are to be in writing, setting forth the basis of the appeal and whether the student is appealing the judgment, the penalty, or both.

F. The Provost shall review the documentation, and when deemed necessary, may refer the appeal back to the original committee for clarification and comments.

G. Normally, a rehearing will be ordered only if new evidence is presented or a procedural error is identified. The procedure at a rehearing is the same.

H. After the hearing, a recommendation to the Provost is to be made, as described in section I. F. ("Recommendation"), above.

I. Before making a decision, the Provost may conduct his or her own investigation if he or she feels it is warranted.

J. The decision of the Provost is final [except that, in cases of degree revocation, in which instance, the student may appeal to the President, whose decision shall be final].

III. Reporting and Documenting Procedures

All evidence should be carefully documented using the guidelines set forth below:

A. The person originating the charges shall present them in writing, accompanied by suitable exhibits, to the Office of the Dean. That person shall make himself or herself available to the designated Dean for pre-hearing conferences if necessary, and shall appear at or be available for the student academic conduct hearing whenever possible. However, the Chair shall have the discretion to excuse the complainant's attendance if the absence will not prejudice the student.

B. Witnesses to the alleged infraction of the Student Academic Conduct Code may be requested to file a report on the incident and shall make themselves available for pre-hearing conferences and student academic conduct hearings.

C. The following are the guidelines for obtaining evidence of violations of the Student Academic Conduct Code in connection with:

1. Conduct during examinations. If an irregularity occurs during an examination, the person who originally notes the irregularity should attempt to have his or her observations corroborated by others who are also in the room (e.g., proctors). The person(s) making the report shall provide specific information such as the time of the observation, type or irregularity observed, number of times it took place, exactly which sections of the examination were affected by the infraction, the name of each individual participating in the irregularity, and the extent of participation by each individual.

2. Papers, reports, and examinations. If the misconduct is inferred from the appearance and/or content of a paper, examination, or other assignment where the professor or proctor has had no chance to observe the actual process, specific reference should be made to each section that gives evidence of misconduct. Where possible, copies of pertinent sections or answers and copies of any other pertinent material (original sources from which section or sections were allegedly plagiarized, and so on) should be submitted with the report to the Dean.

3. Other types of academic misconduct. Reports should be prepared using the same rules of careful observation and accurate documentation as outlined above.

Requirements

Boston University College of Communication

COM Foundation Requirements

Student Name: ______________________ BU ID: ______________

Semester/Year of BU Matriculation: ______________________ Today's Date: ______________

Use this sheet to keep track of when you completed each class and to make sure you satisfied all the requirements for graduation.

Information

- Enrollment in CO 201 during the second semester freshman year is contingent upon completion of WR 100 in the first semester. Students who take WR 097, WR 098 or WR 099 in the fall should consult with an academic counselor for advice on what to take in the spring.
- Students may be exempted from the foreign language requirement based on a score of 560 or higher on the SAT II, AP/IB or transfer credit or the Boston University language placement examination.
- Course offerings change and the listed classes are not available every semester. Be sure to check if the courses you select have any prerequisites.
- Students may not count a course for both a liberal arts requirement and the CAS Focus. Courses can not count for more than one requirement.
- Physical education or any one-credit music, art or officer's training program courses do not count toward the total number of credits needed to graduate.
- If you wish to fulfill a liberal arts requirement with a course not on this list, you MUST file a petition with Undergraduate Affairs BEFORE registering for that course.

Communication Core *(Two Courses)*

________ CO 101: The World of Communication *
Co-req: WR100
MUST receive C or higher.

________ CO 201: Introduction to Communication Writing**
Prereq: WR 100
*** Students entering BU Fall 2015 or later,majoring in Film & Television are not required to take CO 201 and should consult Film & Television curriculum guide*

History *(Two Courses)*

______ ______________ • ______ ______________

To be fulfilled by any two courses from the following: Any HI courses; Also any courses listed below.

AA 310: History of the Civil Rights Movement
AA 371: African American History
AA 382: Precolonial Africa
AA 385: Atlantic History
AA 395: African & Caribbean
AA 410: Blacks in Modern Europe
AA 480: History of Racial Thought
AN 368: Australian Culture and Society
AN 379: China: Tradition and Transition (area)
AM 301: Perspectives on the American Experience
AM 375: History of Women in the US
AR 100: Great Discoveries in Archaeology
AR 101: Introduction to Archaeology
AR 205: Origins of Civilization
AR 230: Archaeology of Classical Civilization
AR 232: Archaeology of Ancient Egypt
AR 251: Ancient Maya Civilization
AR 262: Asian Gods and Goddesses
CL 101: The Glory of Greece
CL 102: The Grandeur of Rome
CL 202: Warfare in Antiquity
CL 221: Greek History (formerly CL 321)
CL 222: Roman History
CL 300: The Age of Pericles
CL 302: The Age of Augustus
CL 303: Decline and Fall of the Roman Empire
CL 314: Women in Ancient Rome
CL 336: Roman Empire
EC 365: Economic Institutions in Historical Prospective
IR 303: Universal History
IR 365: Rise of China
IR 376: American Foreign Policy
PO 111: Intro to American Politics
RN 102: Sacred Journeys
RN 103: Religions of the World: Eastern
RN 104: World Religions
RN 111: US Religions
RN 214: Islam
RN 220: The Holy City
RN 242: Magic, Science and Religion
RN 312: Buddhism in America
RN 322: History of Judaism
RN 331: Zionism and the State of Israel
RN 384: The Holocaust
RN 385: Representations of the Holocaust in Literature and Film
CGS SS: Any CGS Social Science

Social Science *(Two Courses)*

______ ______________ • ______ ______________

To be fulfilled by any two courses from the following: Any EC, IR, PO, PS, or SO courses; Also any AN, AR, or GE courses except those listed as a natural science on the opposite side, unless listed below; Also any courses listed below.

AA 313: Politics of The Wire
AA 363: Race & Development of American Economy
AA 382: Precolonial Africa
AM 367: Material Culture
CC 112/203/204/211: Core Social Science
GE 100: Introduction to Environmental Science
GE 150: Sustainable Energy
GE 250 Fate of Nations
LC 286: Topics in Chinese Culture
PH 155: Politics and Philosophy
PH 241: Philosophy of Personality
PH 242: Human Nature
PH 253: Social Philosophy
PH 254: Political Philosophy
PH 255: Philosophy of Law
PH 256: Philosophy of Gender and Sexuality
SP 302: Contemporary Spanish Culture
SS 315: Aotearoa New Zealand
WS 101: Gender and Sexuality I
WS 102: Gender and Sexuality II
WS 213: Sexism in the 20th Century *(formerly WS 113)*
WS 214: Women in Arts and Culture *(formerly WS 114)*
WS 305: Critical Issues in Women's Studies
WS 340: Women, Race and Gender in Media
WS 342: Women, Law and Society
WS 348: Gender and International Development
WS 360: Global Feminism
CGS SS: Any CGS Social Science
SED PE 375: Psychology of Sport

06/15

FOUNDATION REQUIREMENTS Page 1 of 2

Writing and Literature *(Four Courses)*

________ WR 150: Writing and Research Seminar

________ ________________________ • ________ ________________________ • ________ ________________________

To be fulfilled by any three courses from the following: Any EN, WR, or XL courses; Also any courses listed below.

AA 304: African American Women Writers
AA305: Toni Morrison
AA 404: African American and Asian American Women Writers
CC 101, CC 102, CC 201, CC 202: Core Humanities
CL 102: The World of Rome
CL 213: Greek and Roman Mythology
CL 224: Greek Drama in Translation
CL 226: Ancient Epic in Translation
CL 262: Homeric Epic
CL 305: Themes in Literature and Film
CL 310: Classical Tradition in Modern Literature
CL 325: Greek Tragedy + Film
CL 350: Greek Short Story
PH 159: Philosophy and Film
PH 258: Philosophy and Literature
PH 259: Philosophy of the Arts
RN 101: The Bible
RN 102: Sacred Journeys
RN 201: The Hebrew Bible
RN 206: World Scriptures
RN 241: Topics in Religion and Evil
RN 340: The Quran
RN 385: Representations of the Holocaust in Literature and Film
RN 426: Topics in Religion and Literature in East Asia
WS 101: Gender and Sexuality I
WS 102: Gender and Sexuality II
WS 213: Sexism in the 20th Century *(formerly WS 113)*
WS 214: Creating Women *(formerly WS 114)*
WS 305: Critical Issues in Women's Studies
WS 344: Images of Women in Popular Culture
WS 346: Women in Film
CFA TH 101: Intro to Aesthetics & Dramatic Literature
CFA TH102: Dramatic Literature I
CFA TH 201: Dramatic Literature II
CFA TH 202: Dramatic Literature III
CFA DR 202: Modern Drama II
CGS HU: any CGS Humanities
CGS RH: any CGS Rhetoric

** Necessary prerequisites for WR 150 (WR 097, WR 098, WR 099, or WR 100) may fulfill the other three requirements. All literature courses in foreign languages can count toward WR requirement.*

Foreign Language *(Two Courses)*

________ ________________________ • ________ ________________________

Any foreign language including sign language. Second semester proficiency is required. Students exempt from language requirement must still satisfy credit requirements.

Liberal Arts Elective *(One Course)*

________ ________________________ Any four-credit CAS or CGS liberal arts course.

Philosophy *(One Course)*

________ ________________________ **To be fulfilled by any one course from the following: Any PH course; Also any course listed below.**

RN 100: Religion and Culture
RN 103: Religions of the World: Eastern
RN 104: World Religions
RN 106: Death and Mortality
RN 210: Buddhism
RN 211: Chinese Religions
RN 212: Christianity
RN 213: Hinduism
RN 214: Islam
RN 215: Japanese Religions
RN 216: Judaism
RN 397: Topics in Philosophy and Religion
SO 225: Law and Society
CGS HU 201: History of Western Ethics I
CGS HU202: History of Western Ethics II

Math, Natural Science and Computer Science *(One Course)*

________ ________________________ **To be fulfilled by any course from the following: Any AS, BI, CH, CS, ES, MA or PY courses; Also any courses listed below.**

AN 102: Human Behavioral Biology and Evolution
AN 210: Medical Anthropology
AN 234: Evolutionary Psychology
AN 263: Behavioral Biology of Women
AN 331: Human Origins
AN 332: Primate Behavior Adaptations
AN 333: Human Population Biology
AN 334: Human Behavior Evolution
AR 102: Introduction to Sciences in Archaeology
AR 381: Introduction to Paleoethnobotany
AR 382: Zooarchaeology
CC 105/106/111/212: Core Sciences
EC 171: Personal Lifestyle Economics
EC 305: Economic Statistics
GE 100: Intro to Environmental Science
GE 101: Natural Environment
GE 104: Natural Environments: The Physical Landscape
GE 110: Changing Planet: Perspectives from Space
GE 150: Sustainable Energy
GE 250: Fate of Nations
GE 309: Intro Environmental Analysis and Politics
HI/GE 394: Environmental History of Africa
PH 160: Reasoning and Argumentation
PH 251: Medical Ethics
PH 265: Minds and Machines
PH 266: Mind, Brain and Self
PH 270: Philosophy of Science
PH 271: History of Science
PH 272: Science, Technology and Values
PH 277: Philosophy & Methods in Human Science
PS 205: Memory and Brain
PS 231: Physiological & Psychology
PS 338: Neuropsychology
RN 239: Religion and Science
RN 242: Magic, Science and Religion
CGS NS: Any CGS Natural Science
SAR HS 201: Intro to Nutrition
SAR HS 251: Human Nutritional Science *Prereq: one semester of biology*
SMG QM 221: Probability & Statistics
SMG QM 222: Modeling Business Decisions and Market Outcomes

Statistics *(One Course)*

________ ________________________ **To be fullfilled by any one of the following courses:**

CS 109/MA 109: The Art and Science of Quantitative Reasoning
MA 113: Elementary Statistics
MA 115: Statistics I
MA 116: Statistics II
MA 213: Basic Statistics and Probability
MA 214: Applied Statistics
PS 211: Intro to Experimental Design in Psychology
CGS MA113: Elementary Statistics
CGS MA 115: Statistics
SMG QM 221: Probabilistic and Statistical Decision Making for Management
SMG QM 222: Model Business Decisions

FOUNDATION REQUIREMENTS Page 2 of 2

CINEMA & MEDIA STUDIES — GRADUATION REQUIREMENTS GUIDE

Use this guide to track when you complete each class and to make sure you satisfy graduation requirements.

Student Name:_______________________________ BU ID:_______________

Faculty Advisor Name:_______________________________ Date:_______________

ABOUT CINEMA & MEDIA STUDIES

The Cinema & Media Studies Program (CIMS) will offer students a rigorous and comprehensive education in the history, aesthetics, theory, formal practices, and sociocultural dimensions of moving-image media. The major is available to all undergraduate studies in COM or CAS. It is a Bachelor of Arts degree (BA). Students cannot double major with CIMS and any other major in COM.

Note: All CI courses may be offered in either CAS or COM, or in both. There is no distinction between a COM CI course and a CAS CI course.

The Cinema & Media Studies major at COM requires completing of all COM Foundation requirements as a part of the degree program. Please consult COM Student Services at room 123 for information about the COM Foundation Requirements.

FILM HISTORY CORE (2 courses)

_____CI101 History of Global Cinema

_____CI102 History of Global Cinema

FILM AESTHETICS (CHOOSE ONE)

_____CI201 Literature and Art of Film (meets with CAS EN175) **OR**

_____CI202 Understanding Film (meets with COM FT250, formerly FT360)

TV STUDIES (1 course)

_____CI303 Understanding Television (meets with COM FT303)

FILM THEORY/CRITICISM (1 course)

_____CI510 Film Theory (meets with COM FT536)

GENRE/MOVEMENT/NON-NARRATIVE REQUIREMENT (CHOOSE ONE)
One course in Film Genre, Movement, or Non-Narrative Structure. Course offerings include*:

_____CI420 Classical Hollywood Romantic Comedies/Melodramas
_____CI521 The American Independent Film Movement
_____CI522 The Documentary (meets with COM FT560)
_____CI523 Melodrama in Japanese Film (meets with CAS LJ451)
_____CI524 Film Noir (meets with CAS EN571)
_____CI525 The Horror Film (meets with CAS EN574)
_____CI526 The Gangster Film
_____CI527 The Musical
_____CI529 Hollywood Film Genres (meet with CAS EN594)
_____CI530 TV Genres
_____CI531 Special Topics in Non-Fiction Film
_____CI534 Avant-Garde Cinema (meets with COM FT547)
_____CI535 Topics in Avant-Garde
_____CI536 Global New Waves
_____CI535 French New Wave (meets with COM FT563)

Some may also meet with a COM Special Topics course, see Film Department for details.
Other Genre, Movement, and Non-Narrative Structure courses may be offered as CI320-329 or CI420-429. Other offerings may be listed as CI520-529.
*These offerings are not limited to what is listed here. Speak with a program director for more information.

FILMMAKER/AUTEUR REQUIREMENT (CHOOSE ONE)
One course in Filmmaker or Auteur subject. Course offerings include*:

_____CI540 Michael Haneke (meets with COM FT529)
_____CI541 Scorsese/Coppola/DePalma
_____CI 542 David Cronenberg (meets with Com FT511)
_____CI543 Hitchcock (meets with COM FT535)
_____CI544 Coen Brothers (Meets with CAS EN593)
_____CI545 Stanley Kubrick
_____CI546 Dark Dreams: Cinema of David Lynch
_____CI547 Godard (meets with COM FT577)
_____CI548-533 Study of a Major Auteur

Some may also meet with a COM Special Topics course, see Film Department for details.
Other Filmmaker/Auteur courses may be offered as CI340-359 or CI440-459. Other offerings may be listed as CI540-559.

*These offerings are not limited to what is listed here. Speak with a program director for more information

CINEMA & MEDIA STUDIES — GRADUATION REQUIREMENTS GUIDE

CINEMA & MEDIA ELECTIVES (CHOOSE FOUR)

Please note that any CI course not being used as a different requirement can count as a Cinema & Media Studies Elective. You may also choose from the list below. Students must choose a total of FOUR courses to fulfill this requirement.

_____CI261 Soviet/Russian Film (meets with CAS LR388)
_____CI262 Gender in East Asian Film (meets with CAS XL382)
_____CI361 German Cinema
_____CI367 Love in Indian Lit and Film (meets with CAS XL381)
_____CI461 New French Identities (meets with CAS LF469)
_____CI464 Topics in Comparative Literature
_____CAS AN397 Anthropological Photography in Film
_____CAS CL325 Greek Tragedy in Film
_____CAS LC287 Screening Modern China
_____CAS LF286 French Cinema
_____CAS LF369 Youth Migration in Literature & Film
_____CAS LF586 Reading French Narrative Film
_____CAS LG387 Weimar Cinema
_____CAS LI283 Italian Culture & Cinema
_____CAS LI473 Masters of Italian Cinema
_____CAS LJ283 Modern Japanese Culture in Cinema
_____CAS LK383 Modern Korean Culture in Cinema
_____CAS LN225 Tradition in Indian Film & Literature
_____CAS LP310 Brazilian Cinema
_____CAS LS308 Women, War, Violence in Spanish Film
_____CAS LS452 Latin American Cinema
_____CAS PH159 Philosophy & Film
_____CAS RN203 Religion & Film
_____CAS WS346 Women & Film
_____CAS XL382 Gender & Film
_____CAS XL386 Africa on Screen
_____COM FT310 Screenwriting I
_____COM FT316 British Film & TV Since 1960
_____COM FT317 British Cinema & Society
_____COM FT345 Cinema in Australia: Australian Film Festival
_____COM FT353 Production I
_____COM FT404 Asian Cinema
_____COM FT415 Film & TV Drama in Ireland
_____COM FT457 American Masterworks
_____COM FT458 International Masterworks
_____COM FT520 TV Theory & Criticism
_____COM FT524 The Golden Age of Television
_____COM FT 533 American Independent Film
_____COM FT 549 The Profane
_____COM FT 552 Special Topics*
_____COM FT553 Special Topics*
_____COM FT554 Special Topics*
_____CAS/COM CI491 or 492 Cinema & Media Studies Directed Study**
_____CAS/COM CI493 or 494 Cinema & Media Studies Internship**
_____CI497 or 498 Senior Honors Research

Some of these courses are offered through BU Study Abroad programs only. Some courses may meet with CAS or COM CI courses, as well.
*Topics will vary. Please check with Film & Television Department to discuss current and past offerings.
** Only four credits of either internship or directed study can count as Cinema & Media Electives. Four more credits of either can count as free elective credit. The maximum number of Internship and Directed Study credit a student can receive toward the degree is eight

OTHER REQUIREMENTS OF THE PROGRAM

Regional Requirement: At least three (3) of the courses chosen in the major must be from three distinct regions. These regions are: Africa, Asia, Europe, Latin America, the Middle East, and North America. The courses counting for this requirement may be taken with the Genre, Auteur, and Electives sections. Please consult the Program Director with any questions, or see website for list of courses for a different region.

Please check off your regional requirements as you complete (three must be checked):
_____AFRICA _____ASIA _____EUROPE _____LATIN AMERICA _____THE MIDDLE EAST _____NORTH AMERICA

Numbering Requirement: At least three (3) of the courses chosen in the major must be at the 400-599 level.

Grade Requirement: All courses toward the major must be completed with a grade of C or higher.

COM DEGREE REQUIREMENTS

- Students must finish with a minimum of a 2.0 overall GPA and a 2.0 GPA in COM.
- Students must complete a minimum of 128 total credits toward their degree.

NOTES

BU

Boston University College of Communication
Department of Film & Television

Updated May 2016

JOURNALISM — GRADUATION REQUIREMENTS GUIDE

Use this guide to track when you complete each class and to make sure you satisfy graduation requirements.

Student Name:______________________________ BU ID:______________

Faculty Advisor Name:______________________________ Date:______________

CORE REQUIREMENTS (Six Courses)

_____ JO 250 Fundamentals of Journalism [Prereq: CO 201]
_____JO 303 Visual Journalism
_____JO 304 Online Journalism [Prereqs: JO 303]
_____JO 310 Beat Reporting [Prereq. JO 250]
_____JO 357 History and Principles of Journalism
_____JO 525 Media Law and Ethics

RECOMMENDED FOCUS AREAS (Three Courses)
Focus areas are not required.

JOURNALISM

_____JO 309 Feature Writing [Prereq: JO 310]
_____JO 503 Journalism Research
_____JO 527 Narrative Journalism
_____JO 535 Investigative Reporting
_____JO 542 The Literature of Journalism

ONLINE JOURNALISM

_____JO 508 Copy Editing [Prereq: JO 301]
_____JO 520 Advanced Media Design [Prereq: JO 301, JO 512]
_____JO 550 Advanced Online Journalism [Prereq: JO 304]

PHOTOJOURNALISM

_____JO 312 Photojournalism I [Prereq: JO 303]
_____JO 513 Advanced Photojournalism [Prereq. JO 312]
_____JO 515 Multimedia Photojournalism
_____JO 522 Professional Portfolio

GENERAL COURSES

_____JO412, JO413 Internship*
_____JO490 Directed Study
_____JO502 Special Studies (varies by semester)

BROADCAST JOURNALISM

_____JO 351 Reporting with Audio and Video [Prereq: JO 250 or JO 303]
_____JO 431 Video Enterprise Reporting [Prereq: JO 351] [Recommended Prereq: JO 435 or JO 451]
_____JO 435 Online Radio Newsroom [Prereq: JO 351]
_____JO 451 Television Newsroom [Prereq: JO 351]
_____JO 519 Narrative Radio
_____JO 524 Broadcast Sports Journalism
_____FT 534 Documentary Production
_____FT 560 The Documentary

MAGAZINE JOURNALISM

_____JO 301 Editorial Design
_____JO 403 Magazine Journalism [Prereq: JO 310]
_____JO 408 Magazine Workshop [Prereq: JO 310]
_____JO 512 Editorial Design
_____JO 535 Investigative Reporting

Note: Journalism electives may also be used to fulfill this three course requirement. Journalism electives are any 300 level or higher Journalism class.

*Internship pre-requisites: Rising junior standing, 3.0 COM GPA, completion of JO250 and either JO303 or JO357.

ELECTIVES

- A total of 128 credits is required for graduation. Elective courses will be needed to satisfy this requirement. The number of electives may vary depending on previous course work.

JOURNALISM — GRADUATION REQUIREMENTS GUIDE

CAS FOCUS

- Three (3) courses in the same CAS department.*
- Each course must be junior (300) level or higher, except: 200 level or higher foreign language courses (not 200-level literature and civilization courses) will count (e.g. LS211, 212, and 303 will fulfill a focus).** As of Fall 2011, HI courses numbered 200 or higher can now count toward a CAS focus.
- One (and only one) 100 or 200 level course will count as long as it is a prerequisite for one of the other two 300-level courses in the focus.
- Any other exceptions, such as having three thematically related courses in different departments count, must be petitioned through your major department.
- A CAS minor will automatically fulfill the CAS focus requirement as long as three of the minor courses are not also counted as COM foundation requirements.
- The courses counting toward the focus cannot also count for the foundation requirements.
- Students wanting several Questrom or CFA courses should plan to use their electives to get desired courses in those areas rather than trying to substitute these for their CAS focus.

**The course prefix must be the same for the courses within the department, e.g., third semester Spanish, third semester French, and third semester Italian will not fulfill a focus even though they are all offered through the Department of Romance Studies.*

***For students who have placed out of the foreign language requirement or have otherwise fulfilled it may start a new language track and have the first and second semesters (e.g. LS111 and LS112) count toward the concentration in addition to what is stated above. This is only for students who have the language requirement fulfilled and are starting a new language.*

CAS FOCUS COURSES

Focus

Course no. and name | Course no. and name | Course no. and name

DEGREE REQUIREMENTS

- A total of 128 credits is required for graduation.
- Students are allowed to complete a maximum of six credits of internship registered through an internship coordinator. These six credits can be used towards the 128 required for graduation. In addition, students are allowed to complete a maximum of four credits registered through a Boston University internship based Study Abroad program. These four credits can be used towards the 128 required for graduation.
- Any additional internship credits above and beyond four credits completed through a BU Study Abroad program cannot count towards graduation. If a student completes a total of six internship credits through their internship coordinator and four credits of internship through a Boston University internship based Study Abroad program a total of ten credits can count towards the 128 required for graduation. Four of the credits can count towards the major requirements and six of those credits will be general electives.

SPECIAL OPPORTUNITIES FOR JOURNALISM MAJORS

The Department of Journalism offers several special programs which allow students to craft special areas of expertise within their degree. Any JO courses taken in these areas can count toward the JO program requirements on the front.

SPORTS JOURNALISM Courses in sports journalism allow students to not only craft a specialization in sports reporting but to further define themselves by following tracks in print and online media or in broadcast media.

STATE HOUSE PROGRAM This program offers real-world experience producing content for some 15 Massachusetts daily newspapers, websites and radio stations. Students gain experience and develop confidence in their abilities to produce content on state government and politics in a challenging, deadline environment. As the largest news operation in the Massachusetts State House, the program produces more than 200 byline pieces per semester along with blogs, radio reports, and video packages. By semester's end, students have amassed 20 to 30 byline clips, including many front-page displays, along with multimedia content including a page on the program's website. State House Program alumni have gone on to The Boston Globe, Boston.com, The Wall Street Journal, The Lowell Sun and The Eagle-Tribune, The Brockton Enterprise and a range of other suburban dailies and weeklies.

WASHINGTON D.C. PROGRAM This program offers Journalism students a rare opportunity: to work as professional reporters in our nation's capital, covering events that shape the world and preparing byline stories for daily newspapers, radio, and television stations. Participants cover Capitol Hill news conferences, congressional hearings, and other important events, then work with experienced editors to shape their stories for daily newspapers, radio/TV stations, and websites. Housing and classrooms are provided in the Boston University Washington Center on Connecticut Avenue. Newsroom facilities are located in the Center and in BU's state-of-the-art Center for Digital Imaging Arts in Georgetown. The program is offered to graduate students AND qualified seniors.

Updated May 2016

BU

Boston University College of Communication
Department of Journalism

FILM & TELEVISION — GRADUATION REQUIREMENTS GUIDE

THIS GUIDE IS MEANT FOR STUDENTS ENTERING BU IN FALL OF 2015 or later. STUDENTS WHO ENTERED PRIOR SHOULD USE THE OLD GUIDE. Use this guide to track when you complete each class and to make sure you satisfy graduation requirements.

Student Name:______________________ BU ID:______________

Faculty Advisor Name:______________________ Date:______________

PROGRAM REQUIREMENTS

_____FT 201 Screen Language

_____FT 250 Understanding Film (formerly FT360) **OR** FT 303 Understanding Television

_____FT 310 Storytelling for Film and Television

ONE ADDITIONAL STUDIES REQUIREMENT (can be either Foreign Cinema or Television Studies course, regardless of pre-req)

Students who choose to take both FT 303 AND FT 250 do NOT need to select this additional studies course.

FOREIGN CINEMA STUDIES [Prereq: FT 250 *(formerly FT360)*]
If you take FT250 (but not FT303): Choose one film studies course with an international focus.*

_____FT 316 The Impact of Film & Television in Modern Britain
_____FT 317 British Cinema and Society
_____FT 404 Asian Cinema
_____FT 458 International Masterworks
_____FT 511 It Came From Canada: The Films of David Cronenberg
_____FT 513 Three Polish Directors: Polanski, Wajda, Kieslowski
_____FT 547 History of the Avant-garde, Part I: International Avant-garde
_____FT 548 Antonioni/Bergman
_____FT 550 Scandinavian Cinema
_____FT 563 French New Wave
_____FT 576 Global New Waves

YOU DO NOT NEED THE REQUIRED PRE-REQUISITE TO HAVE ANY OF THESE COURSES COUNT FOR THIS REQUIREMENT.

TELEVISION STUDIES [Prereq: FT 303]
If you take FT303 (but not FT250): Choose one designated TV studies course.*

_____FT 520 TV Theory and Criticism
_____FT 524 Golden Age of Television
_____FT 543 Television Comedy
_____FT 552 Experimental TV
_____FT 561 Television Drama
_____FT 570 Uncensored TV

_____FT250 Understanding Film (formerly FT360) OR FT 303 Understanding Television (if the other has already been completed)

***For a list of other Foreign Cinema and TV Studies courses, visit website: http://www.bu.edu/com/current-students/film-tv/registration-information/current-film-television-studies-courses/. After you fulfill your studies requirement, you may take additional courses from this group toward your program electives.**

PROGRAM ELECTIVES (CHOOSE FIVE)

FILM & TV STUDIES *(Complete list available on department website)*

_____FT 401 Romantic Comedies and Melodramas [Prereq: FT 250]
_____FT 454 Special Topics
_____FT 457 American Masterworks [Prereq: FT 250]
_____FT 506 Digital Game Studies [Prereq: FT 250]
_____FT 552 Television Special Topics [Prereq: FT 303]
_____FT 554 Film Special Topics** [Prereq: FT 250]
_____FT 560 The Documentary [Prereq: FT 250]
_____FT 569 Holocaust on Film [Prereq: FT 250]

MANAGEMENT/PRODUCING

_____FT 304 Film Industry [Prereq: FT 250]
_____FT 325 Creative Producing I [Prereq: FT 303]
_____FT 503 TV to Tablets
_____FT 508 Line Producing [Prereq: FT 250]
_____FT 517 Television Management [Prereq: FT 303]
_____FT 518 Media Management Strategy [Prereq: FT517]
_____FT 525 Creative Producing II [Prereq: FT 325]
_____FT 566 A Business of Hollywood [LA]
_____FT 566 B Careers in Hollywood [LA]
_____FT 591 Media Business

WRITING [PREREQ: FT310]

_____FT 411 Screenwriting II
_____FT 412 Screenwriting III
_____FT 512 Episodic Drama
_____FT 514 Writing the Television Pilot [Prereq: FT 522 or 512]
_____FT 522 Situation Comedy
_____FT 542 Screenwriting IV
_____FT 552 Special Topics**
_____FT 582 Writing the Narrative Short

PRODUCTION

_____FT 352 Film-Style Video Production
_____FT 353 Production I
_____FT 402 Production II - Digital [B- or better FT 353]
_____FT 468 Production III [application required] [Prereq: FT 402]
_____FT 502 Sound Design [Prereq: FT 353]
_____FT 504 Post-Production FX Editing [Prereq: FT 353]
_____FT 505 Hothouse Productions [Prereq: FT 353]
_____FT 507 TV Studio Production [Prereq: FT 353]
_____FT 526 Directing [Application Required] [Prereq: FT 353]
_____FT 527 Lighting [Prereq: FT353]
_____FT 544 Documentary Production [Prereq: FT 353]
_____FT 551 Designing the Short Film
_____FT 552 Special Topic **
_____FT 553 Special Topic **
_____FT 555 Narrative Documentary Practicum
[Prereq: B+ in FT 402, FT 403 or FT 850 or consent]
_____FT 565 Motion Picture Editing [Prereq: FT 353]
_____FT 589 Advanced Production Workshop [Prereq: FT402 + FT526]
_____FT 590 2D Animation
_____FT 593 Cinematography [Prereq: FT 353]
_____FT 594 Advanced Cinematography [Prereq: FT593]

GENERAL

_____FT 456 Acting for Directors and Writers
_____FT 493/494 Internship [Prereq: Junior standing and minimum 3.0 GPA]
_____FT 491/492 Directed Study
_____FT 573/574 BUTV I and II

**Course topics change each semester. Check with Film & Television office for current descriptions.
Note: Any FT 300 or above course not listed may count toward a Film & Television program elective. Students are also required to attend two (2) Cinematheque events per semester.

FILM & TELEVISION GRADUATION REQUIREMENTS GUIDE

CAS FOCUS

- Three (3) courses in the same CAS department.*
- Each course must be junior (300) level or higher, except: 200 level or higher foreign language courses (not 200-level literature and civilization courses) will count (e.g. LS211, 212, and 303 will fulfill a focus).** As of Fall 2011, HI courses numbered 200 or higher can now count toward a CAS focus.
- One (and only one) 100 or 200 level course will count as long as it is a prerequisite for one of the other two 300-level courses in the focus.
- Any other exceptions, such as having three thematically related courses in different departments count, must be petitioned through your major department.
- A CAS minor will automatically fulfill the CAS focus requirement as long as three of the minor courses are not also counted as COM foundation requirements.
- The courses counting toward the focus cannot also count for the COM foundation requirements.
- Students wanting several Questrom or CFA courses should plan to use their electives to get desired courses in those areas rather than trying to substitute these for their CAS focus.

**The course prefix must be the same for the courses within the department, e.g., third semester Spanish, third semester French, and third semester Italian will not fulfill a focus even though they are all offered through the Department of Romance Studies.*

***For students who have placed out of the liberal arts foreign language requirement or have otherwise fulfilled it may start a new language track and have the first and second semesters (e.g. LS111 and LS112) count toward the focus in addition to what is stated above. This is only for students who have the language requirement fulfilled and are starting a new language.*

CAS FOCUS COURSES

Focus

Course no. and name   Course no. and name   Course no. and name

DEGREE REQUIREMENTS

- A total of 128 credits and 32 four-credit courses is required for graduation.
- A maximum of four internship credits can count as one Film & Television program elective. Students are limited to four total credits of internship domestically though the Film & Television Department's Internship Coordinator and an additional four credits through a Boston University Study Abroad program. No more than eight Film & Television internship credits can ever count towards a student's degree.

PRODUCTION AND FACILITIES USAGE POLICY

The equipment and facilities of Production Services are solely for the use of students who are enrolled in FilmTV production classes or butv10 and working on projects and assignments for these classes or butv10. Directed Studies are not considered production classes and may not be used for producing film or television projects.

Updated May 2016

BU

Boston University College of Communication
Department of Film & Television

MASS COMMUNICATION, ADVERTISING & PUBLIC RELATIONS — GRADUATION REQUIREMENTS GUIDE

Use this guide to track when you complete each class and to make sure you satisfy graduation requirements.

Student Name:____________________ BU ID:____________________

MC/ADV/PR Emphasis: ____________ Faculty Advisor Name:____________ Date:____________

MASS COMMUNICATION FOUNDATION REQUIREMENTS

_____CM 321 Mass Communication Research _____CM 331 Writing for Mass Communication [Prereq: CO 201] _____CM 380 Theory & Process of Communication

CHOOSE ONE OF THE FOLLOWING COURSES

_____CM 303 Organizational Structure & Behavior
_____CM 311 Professional Presentations
(Comm Studies students cannot count this class here)
_____CM 323 Design and New Media
_____CM 409 Persuasion and Public Opinion
_____CM 481 Law of Communication
(Comm Studies students cannot count this class here)

COM EMPHASIS (Choose five courses from one of the following areas: Communication Studies, Advertising, or Public Relations)

Courses displayed in bold are required.

COMMUNICATION STUDIES

_____**CM 311 Professional Presentations**
_____**CM 481 Law of Communication**
_____CM 301 Principles & Practices of PR
_____CM 303 Org Structure & Behavior
_____CM 317 Introduction to Advertising
_____CM 323 Design & New Media
_____CM 409 Persuasion & Public Opinion
_____CM 471 COM Internship* [Prereq: CM 331 & either CM 481 or CM 321, junior or senior status, and COM GPA of 3.0 or higher]
_____CM 510 Computers in Communication
_____CM 514 New Comm Technologies
_____CM 523 Design & Interactive Experiences [Prereq: CM 323 or CM 510]
_____CM 529 Design & New Media II [Prereq: CM 323]
_____CM 534 Negotiation & Conflict Res
_____CM 535 Political Campaigning
_____CM 555 Writing for Multimedia [Prereq: CM 331]
_____CM 557 Media Effects
_____CO 350 Mass Media in Australia (semester in Australia)

ADVERTISING

_____**CM 317 Introduction to Advertising**
_____**CM 417 Fund. Of Creative Development [Prereq: CM 317 & CM 331]**
_____CM 323 Design & New Media
_____CM 334 Advertising in the UK (in London)
_____CM 335 Seminar in Advertising, UK (in London)
_____CM 405 New & Trad Media Strategies [Prereq: CM 317]
_____CM 410 NSAC (4 cr. total required) [Prereg: CM317]
_____CM 411 Art Direction [Prereq: CM 317, CM 331, & CM 417]
_____CM 412 Cons. Insight & Acct Planning [Prereq: CM 317]
_____CM 416 Strategic Brand Solutions [Prereq: CM 317]
_____CM 419 Advertising Management [Prereq: CM 317]
_____CM 420 AdLab (4 cr. total required) [Prereq: CM 317]
_____CM 423 Portfolio Development for Ad [Prereq: CM 317, CM 331, & CM 417]
_____CM 425 Advanced Copywriting [Prereq: CM 317, CM 331, & CM 417]
_____CM 437 Portfolio Development II [Prereq: CM 317, CM 331, & CM 417]
_____CM 471 COM Internship* [Prereq: CM 317 & CM 331, junior or senior status, and COM GPA of 3.0 or higher
_____CM 508 Video Prod for Mktg Comm
_____CM 518 Creating Video Campaigns [Prereq: CM 317, CM 331, & CM 417]
_____CM 519 Interactive Mktg Comm [Prereq CM 317]
_____CM 521 British & European Marketing Strategy (semester in London)
_____CM 527 Strategic Creative Development [Prereq: CM 317, CM 331, & CM 417]
_____CM 529 Design & New Media II [Prereq: CM 323]
_____CM 555 Writing for Multimedia [Prereq: CM 331]
_____SMG SM131/FE101 Mgmt as a System (6 cr) (formerly SMG SM299)

PUBLIC RELATIONS

_____**CM 301 Principles & Practices of PR**
_____**CM 441 Media Relations (Prereq: CM301 & CM331**
_____CM 313 Corporate Communication (Prereq: CM301) **OR**
CM 345 PR in Non-Profit Settings (Prereq: CM301)
OR
CM 734 Governmental PR (Prereq. CM301) (offered only rarely)

-- AND EITHER --

_____CM 471 COM Internship* [Prereq: CM 301 & CM 331, junior or senior status, And COM GPA of 3.0 or higher
OR
CM 473 PR Lab (4 cr total required) [Prereq: CM 301 & CM 331]

-- AND EITHER --

_____CM 443 New Media & PR [Prereq: CM 301]
OR
CM 525 PR Ethics [Prereq: CM 301]
OR
CM 522 Managing Corporate Crises & Issues [Prereq: CM 301]

**Only four credits of internship can be used to satisfy an emphasis requirement.*

MASS COMMUNICATION, ADVERTISING & PUBLIC RELATIONS

GRADUATION REQUIREMENTS GUIDE

CAS FOCUS

- Three (3) courses in the same CAS department.*
- Each course must be junior (300) level or higher, except: 200 level or higher foreign language courses (not 200-level literature and civilization courses) will count (e.g. LS211, 212, and 303 will fulfill a focus).** As of Fall 2011, HI courses numbered 200 or higher can now count toward a CAS focus.
- One (and only one) 100 or 200 level course will count as long as it is a prerequisite for one of the other two 300-level courses in the focus.
- Any other exceptions, such as having three thematically related courses in different departments count, must be petitioned through your major department.
- A CAS minor will automatically fulfill the CAS focus requirement as long as three of the minor courses are not also counted as COM foundation requirements.
- The courses counting toward the focus cannot also count for the foundation requirements.
- Students wanting several Questrom or CFA courses should plan to use their electives to get desired courses in those areas rather than trying to substitute these for their CAS focus.

**The course prefix must be the same for the courses within the department, e.g., third semester Spanish, third semester French, and third semester Italian will not fulfill a focus even though they are all offered through the Department of Romance Studies.*

***For students who have placed out of the foreign language requirement or have otherwise fulfilled it may start a new language track and have the first and second semesters (e.g. LS111 and LS112) count toward the focus in addition to what is stated above. This is only for students who have the language requirement fulfilled and are starting a new language.*

CAS FOCUS COURSES

____
Focus

__________ Course no. and name | __________ Course no. and name | __________ Course no. and name

DEGREE REQUIREMENTS

- A total of 128 credits is required for graduation.
- A maximum of four internship credits can count as one Mass Communication program elective. Students are limited to four total credits of internship domestically though a departmental internship coordinator and an additional four credits through a Boston University Study Abroad program. No more than eight Mass Communication internship credits can ever count towards a student's degree.

NOTES:

Updated May 2016

BU

Boston University College of Communication
Department of Mass Communication, Advertising & Public Relations

B.S. Advertising

BU College of Communication

Department of Mass Communication, Advertising and Public Relations

This guide is meant for freshmen entering Boston University (BU) in Fall 2018 and forward, and transfer students entering BU Fall 2020 and forward.

Name: ______________ BU ID: ______________ Date: ______________

All courses listed below have a COM prefix unless otherwise noted. All courses require a minimum pre-req of sophomore standing unless otherwise noted.

College Requirements (4 total credits required plus CO 575)

- ☐ **CO 101** The Human Storyteller (open to freshmen, a minimum grade of a C or higher is required, CAS WR 120 co-req)
- ☐ **CO 575** COM Professional Experience (zero credits, repeatable)

Department Requirements (16 total credits required)

- ☐ **CO 201** Intro to Communication Writing (pre-req CAS WR 120, open to 2nd semester freshmen)
- ☐ **CM 180** Understanding Media (open to 2nd semester freshmen)
- ☐ **CM 321** Communication Research Methods (pre-req CM 180)
- ☐ **CM 331** Writing for Communication (pre-req CO 201)

Advertising Core (12 total credits required)

- ☐ **CM 217** Intro to Advertising (open to 2nd semester freshmen)

Choose **two** from:

- ☐ **CM 412** Consumer Insight & Acct Planning (pre-req CM 217)
- ☐ **CM 417** Fundamentals of Creative Development (pre-req CM 217)
- ☐ **CM 419** Advertising Management (pre-req CM 217)

Advertising Program Requirements (16 total credits required)

- ☐ **CM 211** Professional Presentations
- ☐ **CM 323** Design Strategy & Software
- ☐ **CM 405** Media Strategies (pre-req CM 217)
- ☐ **CM 411** Art Direction (pre-req CM 217 & CM 417)
- ☐ **CM 412** Consumer Insight & Acct Planning (pre-req CM 217)
- ☐ **CM 417** Fundamentals of Creative Development (pre-req CM 217)
- ☐ **CM 419** Advertising Management (pre-req CM 217)
- ☐ **CM 420** Ad Lab / **421** Ad Lab E-Board (pre-req Junior standing, CM 217) (only 4 credits total can count here)
- ☐ **CM 423** Portfolio Development (pre-req CM 217 & CM 417) (Repeatable, max of 8 credits can count here, but cannot be taken more than twice)
- ☐ **CM 425** Copywriting (pre-req CM 217 & CM 417)
- ☐ **CM 471** Internship (pre-req Junior standing, CM 217 & CM 331, good academic standing) (only 4 credits total can count here)
- ☐ **CM 518** Creative Video Development (pre-req CM 217 & CM 417)
- ☐ **CM 519** Interactive Marketing Strategies (pre-req CM 217)
- ☐ **CM 527** Brand Experience Marketing (pre-req CM 217 & CM 417)
- ☐ **CM 529** Advanced Design Strategy & Software (pre-req CM 323)
- ☐ **CM 535** Political Campaigns
- ☐ **CM 539** Health Campaigns
- ☐ **CM 334E** Advertising in the UK (London Abroad)
- ☐ **CM 335E** Seminar in Advertising Strategy (London Abroad)
- ☐ **CM 447E** International Brand Management (London Abroad)
- ☐ **CM 521E** British and European Marketing Strategy (London Abroad)
- ☐ **CM 563E** Entertainment Marketing (LA Abroad)
- ☐ **CM 564E** Entertainment Promotion Speakers Series (LA Abroad)

NOTE: A maximum of 12 credits of the six courses listed with an E designation may count as Advertising Program courses. These E courses are taught through BU Study Abroad programs.

DEGREE REQUIREMENT NOTES:

- A minimum of 128 credits is required for graduation.
- Students must also complete all BU Hub general education requirements.
- No one-credit courses, PDP courses, or ROTC courses can count towards graduation.
- Advertising students are limited to four total credits of internship domestically through a departmental internship coordinator and an additional four credits through a Boston University Study Abroad Program. No more than 8 credits of Advertising internship can count toward the degree. Only four credits of internship can count toward the Advertising Program Requirements, the other four credits will count as general electives.
- Only eight credits of each of the following courses can count toward the 128 required for a degree: COM CM 420/421, COM CM 423, COM CM 471, COM CM 474.
- Please note that students cannot double major or minor between Advertising, Media Science, and Public Relations, due to shared department requirements.
- A maximum of 52 credits (typically equivalent to 13 BU courses) from the Department of Mass Communication, Advertising, and Public Relations (including CO 201, but excluding CO 101 and CO 575) can be taken on the Charles River Campus.

BOSTON UNIVERSITY

Plan of Study

Name: ______________ College: __________ Major: ________________

	Fall Classes	Spring Classes
First Year		
Second Year		
Third Year		
Fourth Year		

Major, Minor, and College Requirements

BU Hub Requirements

Intellectual Toolkit:

Critical Thinking______/_______ ☐ ☐

Research & Info Literacy______/______ ☐ ☐

Creativity/Innovation______/______ ☐ ☐

Teamwork______/______ ☐ ☐

Life Skills__________

Philosophical, Aesthetic, Historical Interpretation

Philosophical Inquiry____________ ☐

Aesthetic Exploration___________ ☐

Historical Consciousness_________ ☐

Scientific & Social Inquiry

Scientific Inquiry I_________ ☐

Social Inquiry I_________ ☐

Scientific/Social Inquiry II_______ ☐

Quantitative Reasoning

Quantitative Reasoning I_________ ☐

Quantitative Reasoning II___________ ☐

Diversity, Civic Engagement, & Global Citizenship

Individual in Community_________ ☐

Global Cit./Intercultural Literacy______/______ ☐☐

Ethical Reasoning___________ ☐

Communication

First Year Writing Seminar________ ☐

Writing, Research, & Inquiry________ ☐

Writing Intensive Course____/____ ☐☐

Oral/Signed Communication_________ ☐

Digital/Multimedia Expression_______ ☐

B.S. Film and Television

Department of Film and Television

BU College of Communication

This guide is meant for freshmen entering Boston University (BU) in Fall 2018 and forward, and transfer students entering BU Fall 2020 and forward.

Name: ______ BU ID: ______ Date: ______

All courses listed below have a COM prefix unless otherwise noted. All courses require a minimum pre-req of sophomore standing unless otherwise noted.

College Requirements (4 total credits required plus CO 575)

- [ ] **CO 101** The Human Storyteller (open to freshmen, a minimum grade of a C or higher is required, CAS WR 120 co-req)
- [ ] **CO 575** COM Professional Experience (zero credits, repeatable)

Department Foreign Language Requirements (2nd semester proficiency in a foreign language or American Sign Language is required)

- [ ] ______ ______
- [ ] ______ ______

2nd semester proficiency can be displayed via college level course work, BU COM proctored language placement exam, AP, IB, or other advanced credit score, 560 or high SATII Score.

Department Requirements (12 total credits required)

- [ ] **FT 201** Screen Language (open to 2nd semester freshmen – highly encouraged to be first FT course taken)
- [ ] **FT 310** Storytelling for Film and Television (pre-req CAS WR 120)
- [ ] **FT 250** Understanding Film **OR** **FT 303** Understanding Television

Film and Television Studies Requirement (4 total credits required)

- [ ] ______ ______

Additional Film and Television Studies course. This may be the 2nd of FT 250 or FT 303 (if a student takes both); or it can be a TV Studies or Foreign Cinema Studies course. Courses offered for these requirements exist both in the COM Film & Television Department as well as the division of Cinema & Media Studies. Courses that will fulfill this requirement are listed at this website, which will be routinely updated and maintained with historical accuracy by the Film and Television Department. Additionally, other current semester courses that may fulfill this requirement can be found online here. Please note that all TV Studies courses require FT303 as a pre-requisite, whereas Foreign Cinema Studies courses may not require a pre-requisite.

Film and Television Program Requirements (28 total credits required)

The Film & Television Department has non-required tracks. While pathways are not required, they are encouraged. Sequencing of courses are listed here via pre-reqs and can be further expanded upon through meaningful conversation with a faculty advisor. Courses listed here do not include the full offerings.

PRODUCTION:

- [ ] **FT 353** Production I (pre-req FT 201)
- [ ] **FT 402** Production II (pre-req FT 201, FT 353 with B- or better, and either FT502, FT 526, FT 565, or FT 593)
- [ ] **FT 468** Production III (pre-req FT 402 & instructor consent)
- [ ] **FT 502** Sound Design (pre-req FT 201 & FT 353)
- [ ] **FT 504** Post Production FX Editing (pre-req FT 201 & FT 353)
- [ ] **FT 505** Hothouse Productions (pre-req FT 353 & instructor consent)
- [ ] **FT 507** TV Studio Production (pre-req FT 201 & FT 353)
- [ ] **FT 526** Directing (pre-req FT 201, FT 353 & & instructor consent)
- [ ] **FT 555** Narrative Documentary Production (pre-req FT 201 & FT 353)
- [ ] **FT 565** Motion Picture Editing (pre-req FT 201 & FT 353)
- [ ] **FT 589** Advanced Production Workshop (pre-req FT 201, FT 353, FT 402, & FT 526)
- [ ] **FT 544** Documentary Production (pre-req FT 201 & FT 353)
- [ ] **FT 592** Production Design (pre-req FT 201 & FT 353)
- [ ] **FT593** Cinematography (pre-req FT 201 & FT 353)
- [ ] **FT594** Advanced Cinematography (pre-req FT 201, FT 353, & FT 593)

WRITING:

- [ ] **FT 411** Screenwriting I (pre-req FT 310)
- [ ] **FT 412** Screenwriting II (pre-req FT 310 & FT 411)
- [ ] **FT 512** Writing the Episodic Drama (pre-req FT 310)
- [ ] **FT 514** Writing the Television Pilot (pre-req FT 310 & either FT 512 or FT 520)
- [ ] **FT 520** Writing the Situation Comedy (pre-req FT 310)
- [ ] **FT 542** Screenwriting III (pre-req FT 310, FT 411, & FT 412)
- [ ] **FT 582** Writing the Narrative Short (pre-req FT 310)

MANAGEMENT:

- [ ] **FT 304** Film Industry
- [ ] **FT 325** Creative Producing I (pre-req FT 303)
- [ ] **FT 525** Creative Producing II (pre-req FT 303 & FT 325)
- [ ] **FT 503** TV to Tablets (pre-req FT 303)
- [ ] **FT 508** Line Producing (pre-req FT 201 & FT 353)
- [ ] **FT 517** Television Management (pre-req FT 303)
- [ ] **FT 518** Media Money Trail (pre-reg FT 303)
- [ ] **FT 591** Media Business (pre-req FT 303)

FILM AND TELEVISION STUDIES:

- [ ] **FT 404** Asian Cinema
- [ ] **FT 437** American Masterworks
- [ ] **FT 458** International Masterworks
- [ ] **FT 500** Film and Television Criticism
- [ ] **FT 520** TV Theory and Criticism
- [ ] **FT 531** Feminist TV
- [ ] **FT 532** NBC: Anatomy of a Network
- [ ] **FT 536** Film Theory and Criticism
- [ ] **FT 549** The Profane
- [ ] **FT 563** French New Wave
- [ ] **FT 570** Uncensored TV

GENERAL:

- [ ] **FT491/FT492** Directed Study (pre-req instructor and departmental approval) (only 4 credits can count here)
- [ ] **FT493/FT494** COM Internship (pre-req FT 201 & FT 310, junior standing, 3.0 COM GPA or higher) (only 4 credits can count here)
- [ ] **FT573/FT574** BUTV10 1 and 2 (pre-req consent of instructor)

Note: Any COM FT course 300-level or above may count as a Film and Television Program Requirement.

DEGREE REQUIREMENT NOTES:

- A minimum of 128 credits is required for graduation.
- Students must also complete all BU Hub general education requirements.
- No one-credit courses, PDP courses, or ROTC courses can count toward graduation.
- Film and Television students are limited to four total credits of internship domestically through a departmental internship coordinator and an additional four credits through a Boston University Study Abroad Program. No more than eight credits of Film and Television internship can count toward the degree. Only four credits of internship can count toward the Film and Television Program Requirements, the other four credits will count as general electives
- Only eight credits of each of the following courses can count toward the 128 required for a degree: COM FT 493/FT 494, COM FT 491/FT 492.
- Please note that students cannot double major or minor between Film and Television and Cinema and Media Studies due to significant requirement overlap.
- A maximum of 52 credits (typically equivalent to 13 BU courses) from the Department of Film and Television (excluding CO 101 and CO 575) can be taken on the Charles River Campus.

BOSTON UNIVERSITY

Plan of Study

Name: ____________ College: ________ Major: ______________

	Fall Classes	Spring Classes
First Year		
Second Year	Fall Classes	Spring Classes
Third Year	Fall Classes	Spring Classes
Fourth Year	Fall Classes	Spring Classes

Major, Minor, and College Requirements

BU Hub Requirements

Intellectual Toolkit:

Critical Thinking_____/_____ ☐ ☐
Research & Info Literacy_____/_____ ☐ ☐
Creativity/Innovation_____/_____ ☐ ☐
Teamwork_____/_____ ☐ ☐
Life Skills________

Philosophical, Aesthetic, Historical Interpretation

Philosophical Inquiry__________ ☐
Aesthetic Exploration__________ ☐
Historical Consciousness________ ☐

Scientific & Social Inquiry

Scientific Inquiry I________ ☐
Social Inquiry I________ ☐
Scientific/Social Inquiry II______ ☐

Quantitative Reasoning

Quantitative Reasoning I________ ☐
Quantitative Reasoning II__________ ☐

Diversity, Civic Engagement, & Global Citizenship

Individual in Community________ ☐
Global Cit./Intercultural Literacy_____/_____ ☐☐
Ethical Reasoning__________ ☐

Communication

First Year Writing Seminar_______ ☐
Writing, Research, & Inquiry_______ ☐
Writing Intensive Course____/____ ☐☐
Oral/Signed Communication________ ☐
Digital/Multimedia Expression______ ☐

B.S. Journalism

BU College of Communication

Department of Journalism

This guide is meant for freshmen entering Boston University (BU) in Fall 2018 and forward, and transfer students entering BU Fall 2020 and forward.

Name: ____________ BU ID: ____________ Date: ____________

All courses listed below have a COM prefix unless otherwise noted. All courses require a minimum pre-req of sophomore standing unless otherwise noted.

College Requirements (4 total credits required plus CO 575)

- ☐ **CO 101** The Human Storyteller (open to freshmen, a minimum grade of a "C" is required, CAS WR 120 is a co-req)
- ☐ **CO 575** COM Professional Experience (zero credits, repeatable)

Department Requirements (24 total credits required)

- ☐ **CO 201** Intro to Communication Writing (pre-req CAS WR 120, open to 2nd semester freshmen)
- ☐ **JO 150** History and Principles of Journalism (open to 2nd semester freshmen)
- ☐ **JO 200** Newswriting (pre-req CO 201)
- ☐ **JO 205** Visual Storytelling
- ☐ **JO 210** Reporting in Depth (pre-req JO 200 & JO 205)
- ☐ **JO 350** Law and Ethics of Journalism

Journalism Professional Core Requirement (minimum of 4 total credits required)

Students must complete one of the following three courses:

- ☐ **JO 400** Newsroom (pre-req JO 150, JO 200, JO 205, JO 210, & JO 350) (course is repeatable & will be accompanied by a one-credit Innovation Lab – JO 401 – the one credit for JO 401 cannot count toward the 128 credits required for graduation)
- ☐ **JO 455** Professional Project (pre-req approval of faculty committee) (variable credit)
- ☐ **JO 546** Journalism Statehouse Program (pre-req approval of instructor) (8 credits)

Students who take more than one of the Journalism Professional Core courses can use the credits for the second or third course listed above toward Journalism Program Requirements.

Journalism Program Requirements (16 total credits required)

- ☐ **JO 301** Editorial Design (pre-req JO 205)
- ☐ **JO 309** Feature Writing (pre-req JO 200, JO 205, & JO 210)
- ☐ **JO 312** Photojournalism I (pre-req JO 205)
- ☐ **JO 351** Reporting with Audio and Video (pre-req JO 200 & JO 205)
- ☐ **JO 403** Magazine Writing and Editing (pre-req JO 200 & JO 210)
- ☐ **JO 404** Radio Station Management (pre-req instructor consent)
- ☐ **JO 412** COM Internship (variable credit) (pre-req JO 200 & JO 205, junior standing, good academic standing) (only 4 credits can count here)
- ☐ **JO 451** Television Newsroom (pre-req JO 200, JO 205, & JO 351)
- ☐ **JO 490** Directed Study (variable credit) (pre-req instructor and departmental consent) (only 4 credits can count here)
- ☐ **JO 500** Media Criticism
- ☐ **JO 501** Business and Economics Reporting (pre-req JO 200)
- ☐ **JO 502** Special Topics (variable credit, pre-reqs may vary by topic)
- ☐ **JO 504** Arts Criticism
- ☐ **JO 505** Race and Gender in Media
- ☐ **JO 508** Copyediting (pre-req JO 200)
- ☐ **JO 511** Covering Politics (only available as part of Statehouse program)
- ☐ **JO 513** Photojournalism II (pre-req JO 205 & JO 312)
- ☐ **JO 514** Sports Journalism (pre-req JO 200)
- ☐ **JO 519** Narrative Radio (pre-req JO 200, JO 205, JO 351, & JO 435)
- ☐ **JO 520** Advanced Editorial Design (pre-req JO 205 & JO 301)
- ☐ **JO 521** Data Journalism (pre-req JO 200)
- ☐ **JO 524** Sports Reporting and Production (pre-req JO 200, JO 205, & JO 351)
- ☐ **JO 527** Narrative Journalism (pre-req JO 200)
- ☐ **JO 532** Sports Seminar (pre-req JO 200)
- ☐ **JO 541** Art of the Interview (pre-req consent of instructor)
- ☐ **JO 542** Literature of Journalism (pre-req JO 150)
- ☐ **JO 543** Restoring Lost Stories (pre-req JO 150 & JO 200)

Students who take all three of JO 404, JO 412, and JO 490 must note that only 8 credits total from these three courses can count as Journalism Program Requirements. Students can only take a maximum of 12 credits from these toward the minimum credit total of 128 required for graduation.
Note: Any COM JO course 300-level or above may count as a Journalism Program Requirement. Recommended, but not required pathways are available through consultation with faculty advisors in the Journalism Department. The pathways will be updated routinely to mirror the ever-changing world of professional journalism.

DEGREE REQUIREMENT NOTES:

- A minimum of 128 credits is required for graduation.
- Students must also complete all BU Hub general education requirements.
- No one-credit courses, PDP courses, or ROTC courses can count toward graduation.
- Journalism students are limited to four total credits of internship domestically through a departmental internship coordinator and an additional four credits through a Boston University Study Abroad Program. No more than eight credits of Journalism internship can count toward the degree. Only four credits of internship can count toward the Journalism Program Requirements, the other four credits will count as general electives.
- Only eight credits of each of the following courses can count toward the 128 required for a degree: COM JO 400, COM JO 412, COM JO 490.
- A maximum of 52 credits (typically equivalent to 13 BU courses) from the Department of Journalism (including CO 201, but excluding CO 101 and CO 575) can be taken on the Charles River Campus.

BOSTON UNIVERSITY

Plan of Study

Name: ________ College: ________ Major: ________

	Fall Classes	Spring Classes	Major, Minor, and College Requirements
First Year			
Second Year	Fall Classes	Spring Classes	
Third Year	Fall Classes	Spring Classes	
Fourth Year	Fall Classes	Spring Classes	

BU Hub Requirements

Intellectual Toolkit:
Critical Thinking______/______ ☐ ☐
Research & Info Literacy______/______ ☐ ☐
Creativity/Innovation______/______ ☐ ☐
Teamwork______/______ ☐ ☐
Life Skills__________

Philosophical, Aesthetic, Historical Interpretation
Philosophical Inquiry__________ ☐
Aesthetic Exploration__________ ☐
Historical Consciousness__________ ☐
Scientific & Social Inquiry
Scientific Inquiry I__________ ☐
Social Inquiry I__________ ☐
Scientific/Social Inquiry II__________ ☐

Quantitative Reasoning
Quantitative Reasoning I__________ ☐
Quantitative Reasoning II__________ ☐
Diversity, Civic Engagement, & Global Citizenship
Individual in Community__________ ☐
Global Cit./Intercultural Literacy______/______ ☐☐
Ethical Reasoning__________ ☐

Communication
First Year Writing Seminar__________ ☐
Writing, Research, & Inquiry__________ ☐
Writing Intensive Course____/____ ☐☐
Oral/Signed Communication__________ ☐
Digital/Multimedia Expression__________ ☐

B.S. Media Science

Department of Mass Communication, Advertising and Public Relations

BU College of Communication

This guide is meant for freshmen entering Boston University (BU) in Fall 2018 and forward, and transfer students entering BU Fall 2020 and forward.

Name: ______ BU ID: ______ Date: ______

All courses listed below have a COM prefix unless otherwise noted. All courses require a minimum pre-req of sophomore standing unless otherwise noted.

College Requirements (4 total credits required plus CO 575)

- ☐ **CO 101** The Human Storyteller (open to freshmen, a minimum grade of a C or higher is required, CAS WR 120 co-req)
- ☐ **CO 575** COM Professional Experience (zero credits, repeatable)

Department Requirements (16 total credits required)

- ☐ **CO 201** Intro to Communication Writing (pre-req CAS WR 120, open to 2nd semester freshmen)
- ☐ **CM 180** Understanding Media (open to 2nd semester freshmen)
- ☐ **CM 321** Communication Research Methods (pre-req CM 180)
- ☐ **CM 331** Writing for Communication (pre-req CO 201)

Media Science Core (16 total credits required)

- ☐ **CM 280** Persuasion Theory (pre-req CM 180)
- ☐ **CM 481** Media Law and Policy
- ☐ **CM 535** Political Campaigns
- ☐ **CM 539** Health Campaigns

Media Science Program Requirements (12 total credits required)

- ☐ **CM 211** Professional Presentations
- ☐ **CM 323** Design Strategy & Software
- ☐ **CM 422** Advanced Communication Research Methods (pre-req CM 321)
- ☐ **CM 471** Internship (variable credit)(pre-req CM 280 & CM 331, junior standing, good academic standing)(only 4 credits can count here)
- ☐ **CM 510** Media Expression and Communication
- ☐ **CM 514** Communication Technologies
- ☐ **CM 520** The COMmunicator (2 credit course, a maximum of 4 credits can count here and toward graduation, pre-req CM 331)
- ☐ **CM 523** Design & Interactive Experiences (pre-req CM 323 or CM 510)
- ☐ **CM 526** Integrated Marketing Communication (pre-req CM 280)
- ☐ **CM 529** Advanced Design Strategy & Software (pre-req CM 323)
- ☐ **CM 555** Advanced Media Writing (pre-req CM 331)
- ☐ **CM 557** Media Effects (pre-req CM 180 & CM 321)

DEGREE REQUIREMENT NOTES:

- A minimum of 128 credits is required for graduation.
- Students must also complete all BU Hub general education requirements.
- No one-credit courses, PDP courses, or ROTC courses can count toward graduation.
- Media Science students are limited to four total credits of internship domestically through a departmental internship coordinator and an additional four credits through a Boston University Study Abroad Program. No more than eight credits of Media Science internship can count toward the degree. Only four credits of internship can count toward the Media Science Program Requirements, the other four credits will count as general electives.
- Only eight credits of each of the following courses can count toward the 128 required for a degree: COM CM 471, COM CM 474.
- Please note that students cannot double major or minor between Advertising, Media Science, and Public Relations, due to shared department requirements.
- A maximum of 52 credits (typically equivalent to 13 BU courses) from the Department of Mass Communication, Advertising, and Public Relations (including CO 201, but excluding CO 101 and CO 575) can be taken on the Charles River Campus.

BOSTON UNIVERSITY

Plan of Study

Name: ________ College: ________ Major: ________

	Fall Classes	Spring Classes
First Year		
Second Year		
Third Year		
Fourth Year		

Major, Minor, and College Requirements

BU Hub Requirements

Intellectual Toolkit:
Critical Thinking____/____ ☐ ☐
Research & Info Literacy____/____ ☐ ☐
Creativity/Innovation____/____ ☐ ☐
Teamwork____/____ ☐ ☐
Life Skills________

Philosophical, Aesthetic, Historical Interpretation
Philosophical Inquiry________ ☐
Aesthetic Exploration________ ☐
Historical Consciousness________ ☐
Scientific & Social Inquiry
Scientific Inquiry I________ ☐
Social Inquiry I________ ☐
Scientific/Social Inquiry II________ ☐

Quantitative Reasoning
Quantitative Reasoning I________ ☐
Quantitative Reasoning II________ ☐
Diversity, Civic Engagement, & Global Citizenship
Individual in Community________ ☐
Global Cit./Intercultural Literacy____/____ ☐☐
Ethical Reasoning________ ☐

Communication
First Year Writing Seminar________ ☐
Writing, Research, & Inquiry________ ☐
Writing Intensive Course____/____ ☐☐
Oral/Signed Communication________ ☐
Digital/Multimedia Expression________ ☐

B.S. Public Relations

BU College of Communication

Department of Mass Communication, Advertising and Public Relations

This guide is meant for freshmen entering Boston University (BU) in Fall 2018 and forward, and transfer students entering BU Fall 2020 and forward.

Name: ______________ BU ID: ______________ Date: ______________

All courses listed below have a COM prefix unless otherwise noted. All courses require a minimum pre-req of sophomore standing unless otherwise noted.

College Requirements (4 total credits required plus CO 575)

- ☐ **CO 101** The Human Storyteller (open to freshmen, a minimum grade of a C or higher is required, CAS WR 120 co-req)
- ☐ **CO 575** COM Professional Experience (zero credits, repeatable)

Department Requirements (16 total credits required)

- ☐ **CO 201** Intro to Communication Writing (pre-req CAS WR 120, open to 2nd semester freshmen)
- ☐ **CM 180** Understanding Media (open to 2nd semester freshmen)
- ☐ **CM 321** Communication Research Methods (pre-req CM 180)
- ☐ **CM 331** Writing for Communication (pre-req CO 201)

Public Relations Core (12 total credits required)

- ☐ **CM 215** Principles and Practice of Public Relations (open to 2nd semester freshmen)
- ☐ **CM 441** Media Strategies and Management (pre-req CM 215 & CM 331)
- ☐ **CM 442** Business Fundamentals for Public Relations (pre-req CM 215)

Public Relations Program Requirements (16 total credits required)

- ☐ **CM 211** Professional Presentations
- ☐ **CM 313** Corporate Communications (pre-req 215)
- ☐ **CM 323** Design Strategy & Software
- ☐ **CM 345** Non-Profit Public Relations (pre-req CM 215)
- ☐ **CM 412** Consumer Insight & Acct Planning (pre-req CM 217)
- ☐ **CM 443** Digital Media and Public Relations (pre-req CM 215)
- ☐ **CM 444** Governmental Public Affairs (pre-req CM 215)
- ☐ **CM 448** International Public Relations (pre-req CM 215)
- ☐ **CM 471** Internship (pre-req CM 215 & CM 331, junior standing, good academic standing) (only 4 credits can count here)
- ☐ **CM 473** PR Lab / **CM 475** PR Lab E-Board (pre-req CM 215 & CM 331, junior standing) (only 4 credits can count here)
- ☐ **CM 481** Media Law and Policy
- ☐ **CM 513** Investor Relations (pre-req CM 215)
- ☐ **CM 519** Interactive Marketing Strategies (pre-req CM 215 or CM 217)
- ☐ **CM 522** Crisis Communication (pre-req CM 215)
- ☐ **CM 524** Public Relations Career Management (pre-req CM 215)
- ☐ **CM 525** Public Relations Ethics (pre-req CM 215)
- ☐ **CM 526** Integrated Marketing Communication (pre-req CM 215)
- ☐ **CM 535** Political Campaigns
- ☐ **CM 539** Health Campaigns
- ☐ **CM 555** Advanced Media Writing (pre req CO 201 & CM 331)
- ☐ **SHA HF 375** Special Event Planning & Operations

DEGREE REQUIREMENT NOTES:

- A minimum of 128 credits is required for graduation.
- Students must also complete all BU Hub general education requirements.
- No one-credit courses, PDP courses, or ROTC courses can count toward graduation.
- Public Relations students are limited to four total credits of internship domestically through a departmental internship coordinator and an additional four credits through a Boston University Study Abroad Program. No more than eight credits of Public Relations internship can count toward the degree. Only four credits of internship can count toward the Public Relations Program Requirements, the other four credits will count as general electives
- Only eight credits of each of the following courses can count toward the 128 required for a degree: COM CM 471, COM CM 473/COM CM 475, COM CM 474.
- Please note that students cannot double major or minor between Advertising, Media Science, and Public Relations, due to shared department requirements.
- A maximum of 52 credits (typically equivalent to 13 BU courses) from the Department of Mass Communication, Advertising, and Public Relations (including CO 201, but excluding CO 101 and CO 575) can be taken on the Charles River Campus.

BOSTON UNIVERSITY

Plan of Study

Name: ____________ College: __________ Major: ______________

	Fall Classes	Spring Classes
First Year		
Second Year		
Third Year		
Fourth Year		

Major, Minor, and College Requirements

BU Hub Requirements

Intellectual Toolkit:

- Critical Thinking______/______ ☐ ☐
- Research & Info Literacy______/______ ☐ ☐
- Creativity/Innovation______/______ ☐ ☐
- Teamwork______/______ ☐ ☐
- Life Skills__________

Philosophical, Aesthetic, Historical Interpretation

- Philosophical Inquiry__________ ☐
- Aesthetic Exploration__________ ☐
- Historical Consciousness__________ ☐

Scientific & Social Inquiry

- Scientific Inquiry I__________ ☐
- Social Inquiry I__________ ☐
- Scientific/Social Inquiry II_______ ☐

Quantitative Reasoning

- Quantitative Reasoning I__________ ☐
- Quantitative Reasoning II__________ ☐

Diversity, Civic Engagement, & Global Citizenship

- Individual in Community__________ ☐
- Global Cit./Intercultural Literacy______/______ ☐ ☐
- Ethical Reasoning__________ ☐

Communication

- First Year Writing Seminar________ ☐
- Writing, Research, & Inquiry________ ☐
- Writing Intensive Course____/____ ☐ ☐
- Oral/Signed Communication________ ☐
- Digital/Multimedia Expression________ ☐

Section 1

Film and Television

Chapter 1

Film Studies, Fan Studies

"It's Just a Movie"

Why You Should Analyze Film and Television

Greg M. Smith

"'It's Just a Movie': A Teaching Essay for Introductory Media Classes" by Greg M. Smith, first published in *Cinema Journal*, Volume 41 Issue 1, pp. 127–134. Copyright (c) 2001 by the University of Texas Press. Reprinted with permission of the University of Texas Press.

The question arises almost every semester. My introductory media class and I will be hip deep in analyzing the details of a particular film, and then a hand will creep up, usually from the back: "Aren't we reading too much into this? After all, it's just a movie." Taking a deep breath, I then launch into a spirited defense of our analytic activity. After five or ten minutes of this, the student usually has a shell-shocked, what-did-I-do-to-deserve-this look on her face.

I've never been pleased with my spur-of-the-moment justifications of film and television analysis, which tend to come across as a bit defensive. Worst of all, they don't deal with the full complexity of the question, and I do believe that it is a very profound question. Why are we spending so much time finding new meanings in something as insignificant as a movie or a TV show? Aren't we just "reading into it"? The student's question deserves a fuller answer, or rather, it deserves several answers. As a way of finding those answers, this essay extends the dialogue started by that series of brave, inquiring students in my classes.

Nothing left to chance

"All right, do you really think that every little thing in film and TV is there for a reason?"

Lots of things in our everyday world are there by accident. If I trip over a stone that causes me to bump into someone, that jostling encounter is probably not part of a higher design. It's just a random occurrence of the sort that happens all the time with no enormous significance in the real world. There is a temptation to treat a film in a similar manner, as if spontaneous things occur by chance. Nothing could be further from the truth.

Hollywood films and network television are some of the most highly scrutinized, carefully constructed, least random works imaginable. Of course, we know this, having read *Entertainment Weekly*. We all know that it takes thousands of people to create mainstream media: directors and actors, grips and gaffers. We know that producing film and television is a highly coordinated effort by dedicated professionals, but to most people it's a bit of a mystery what all these people do. When we watch film and television, we are encouraged to forget about all that mysterious collective labor. A movie usually asks us to get caught up in the story being told, in the world that has been created for us, not to be aware of the behind-the-scenes effort that brought us this story and this world. We tend to forget the thousands of minute decisions that consciously construct this artificial world.

When I put on a shirt in the morning, I do so with very little thought (as my students will tell you). A movie character's shirt is chosen by a professional whose sole job is to think about what kind of shirt this character would wear. Similar decisions are made for props, sound, cutting, and so on. Most mediamakers work hard to exclude the random from their fictional worlds. Sets are built so that the mediamaker can have absolute control over the environment. The crew spends a great deal of time and expense between shots adjusting the lighting so that each shot will look as polished as possible. When mediamakers want something to seem to be random, they carefully choreograph this random-appearing behavior. For instance, extras who are merely walking by the main characters are told where to go and what to do to appear "natural." Even seemingly random events and minute details in a film/television program are chosen and staged.

But what about directors who don't sanitize the film set, who try to let bits of the real world into their work (from the Italian neorealists to Kevin Smith's *Clerks*)? What about actors, such as Dustin Hoffman and Robin Williams, who like to improvise? What about documentary mediamakers who don't script what happens in front of the camera? What about reality TV? Don't these let a little bit of chance creep into the film? Not really. One could say that these strategies let some chance occurrences make it onto the raw footage. However, the mediamaker and the editor watch the collected footage over and over, deciding which portions of which takes they will assemble into the final cut. They do so with the same scrutiny that was applied to the actual shooting. Even if they recorded something unplanned, they make a conscious choice to use that chance occurrence. What was chance in the filming becomes choice in the final editing.

Italian neorealism was a filmmaking movement that began in the physical and economic devastation of post-World War II Italy. Under these conditions the Italian film industry could not make films with the technical polish of their 1930s output, and so they turned their poverty into an advantage.

Beginning with Roberto Rossellini's *Rome, Open City*, the Italian neorealists used real locations in war-torn Italy (instead of tightly controlled sets); available lighting (instead of nuanced theatrical light); nonprofessional actors (alongside trained professionals); and a looser, more episodic way of telling stories (instead of tightly controlled plotting). Italian neorealism strikingly contrasted with Hollywood's slick studio output, making these films seem more grounded in the details of real life. Although the movement was short lived (ending in the early 1950s, when Italy became more affluent), its influence was enormous. Many "new waves" of filmmaking hark back to neorealism as a way to distinguish their look from the Hollywood norm. Hollywood itself incorporated some of neorealism's features (location shooting, episodic storytelling) beginning in the 1950s to give its films a more realistic feel. Key figures in the movement include Rossellini, Vittorio De Sica (*Bicycle Thieves, Umberto D*), and screenwriter/theorist Cesare Zavattini.

"Come on, do directors, editors, and set designers *really* spend all that time scrutinizing such details?" Think of it this way. A Hollywood blockbuster may cost up to $300 million. If you were to make something that costs that much, wouldn't you scrutinize every tiny detail? Even a "low budget" film can cost $30 million or so. With so much money riding on a film, the scrutiny is enormous, and it extends to all levels. Of course this process, like all human effort, is fallible; mistakes do sometimes creep in (for example, an extra in *Spartacus*—dry in ancient Rome—can be seen wearing a wristwatch). All too often, beginning media scholars have a tendency to assume that odd moments in the film/television program are mistakes, when the opposite assumption is more likely to be true. Nothing in a final film is there without having been examined by scores of professionals who have carefully chosen the components. You can trust that if something is in a film, it's there for a reason.

A movie is not a telegram

"Okay, so the director really cares about the details. But do you think your interpretation is what she really meant to say?"

In high school English classes you may have been taught to look for the meaning of a literary work, a single sentence that summarizes what the author was trying to convey. So you might have boiled Shakespeare's *Macbeth* down to a single sentence that reveals the moral lesson to be learned from the play (perhaps "Greed for power corrupts people"). One can reduce a literary work or film or television program to its message, which makes the game of interpretation a fairly simple one. All we have to do is figure out what the author/director was trying to say.

Some mediamakers have scoffed at the idea that their movies contain any such messages. Hollywood producer Samuel Goldwyn is alleged to have said, "If I wanted to send a message, I would've called Western Union" (the nineteenth/twentieth-century equivalent of text messaging). What is at issue here is the conception of what communication is. The traditional understanding of speech considers a sender trying to relay a message to a receiver (often called the S-M-R model). A sender has a clear intention of what she wants to get across to the receiver, but she may not present her message particularly clearly. The receiver tries to understand the message, but she can misunderstand the sender for a variety of reasons. By comparing the sender's intention with the receiver's understanding, one can discover how effective the communication was. For example, if a receiver gets a text message asking for bail money and then starts collecting the necessary cash, then a successful instance of communication has taken place.

The *sender-message-receiver (S-M-R)* model was proposed in 1949 by Claude Shannon and Warren Weaver as an outgrowth of their work with telephone companies to improve the accuracy/understanding of phone conversations. It has been expanded to become perhaps the most dominant framework for understanding communication. A more fully elaborated S-M-R model also includes an awareness that the channel/medium affects the overall communication; that there is "noise" on that channel that can interfere with the message; and that the receiver/audiences can communicate "feedback" to give the sender a sense of whether the message is getting through. Theorists have proposed numerous elaborations and expansions on the S-M-R model, but it still remains at its core a fairly one-way model of linear communication.

It is tempting to conceptualize film and television as communication in this way. To see how a movie is, one could compare the mediamaker's intentions with our interpretations and see if we "got it." If the audience member didn't receive the message, then perhaps the film is poorly made or perhaps the viewer is not very savvy.

Films, television shows, plays, and novels, however, are not telegrams or cell phone text messages; they are infinitely more complicated. One of the first traps that the budding critic should avoid is thinking that a film or TV program can be understood as having a single message which we either "get" or not. To do so is to treat it like a telegram. Cinema and television are richer forms of communication than can be conceptualized as sender-message-receiver.

"Okay, so perhaps the director isn't just sending a single message. Maybe she's sending several messages. If we can figure out what those messages are, then we've got it, yes?"

First of all, there's a big question concerning who the "author" of a film or television program is. Thousands of people put their work into a major media project. If all of them are trying to convey meaning, do we have to consider all their combined intentions? Or if some people's contributions are more important than others (actors, directors, cinematographers, producers), then can we understand a movie as the sum total of their intentions? The question of authorship in film and television is a much thornier one than the question of a book's authorship.

Let's make it easy on ourselves. Let's assume that the author of a movie is the person who is in charge of coordinating all decisions in the shooting process: the director.[1] If we can figure out what the director intends, then we've got it, right? If we could interview Hitchcock and gain an understanding of what was going through his mind when he made *Vertigo*, then we would have gained a pretty solid hold on the film, yes?

But can we reduce the film to what the director consciously intends? At times we all express the beliefs, attitudes, and assumptions of our era without necessarily being conscious of

1 In film and television, the director is usually in charge of the process of shooting, though she may not be in overall control of the final product. In some films, the producer has the right to the "final cut." In most television shows, the director of an individual episode is hired by the person in charge of the overall series, called the "show runner." In this situation, the director answers to the show runner.

doing so. Did Hitchcock fully understand his attitude toward blonde women, or was he propagating a widely held belief in his society? Sometimes the ideology of our day speaks through us with little awareness on our part. In addition, we can unconsciously express personal issues as well as social attitudes. Many believe that the unconscious seeks to express painful things that we have repressed and buried within ourselves. These tensions can emerge in our everyday lives through dreams or Freudian slips or the artwork that we make. Perhaps Hitchcock was unconsciously working through his own personal obsession with cool, aloof women in ways that he didn't even understand as he made *Vertigo*. Since human beings cannot be reduced to their conscious thoughts, films should not be reduced to the director's conscious intentions.

"Okay, okay, so if we get a sense of what the director's conscious intentions are, what ideological beliefs she gained from her socialization, and what her unconscious issues are (admittedly a difficult process), then we've arrived at a well-grounded, comprehensive description of what the film is trying to communicate, right?"

We have, if we stay within the sender-message-receiver model that works for text messaging. But let's step outside that model. Why should we limit the viewer to making only those meanings which come directly from the sender/mediamaker? If I get meaning from media and apply it to my life, why should I have to check with the mediamaker to see if that's the right meaning? In other words, why should the mediamaker have more authority over interpreting the film than I do?

"Because she's the director. It's her movie," you may reply. I would respond, "You're the audience. It's your movie, too." If you let go of the notion of a mediamaker trying to convey a message, then the audience's activity is to interpret the film according to their lives, their experiences, their tastes—not the director's. That activity is just as valid as the mediamaker's. A movie's meaning does not lie solely within the film itself but in the interaction of the film and the audience.

As we learn more and more about how audiences interpret media, we discover what a striking range of interpretations people make. If we consider those interpretations to be somehow less valid than the mediamaker's, then we lose much of the complexity of how movies work, make meaning, and give pleasure in our society.

"Reading into" the movie

"But those audiences are just reading things into the movie, right?"

Let's think about what "reading into" a movie is. "That's simple," you might reply. "It's when an audience puts things into the movie that aren't there." That certainly seems straightforward enough. But is it?

Picture yourself watching a horror film in which a group of teenagers are staying at a spooky cabin deep in the woods. It's midnight. A couple sneaks off to a back bedroom and have sex. The attractive young woman then gets up, decides that she's going to take a shower, and says that she'll be right back.

You know that this woman will be toast in a matter of minutes.

But how do you know? There's nothing in the film itself which says that this woman will die. The same incident (romantic rural location, sexy couple) could take place in a romantic film, and the shower would not raise any hackles. No, the knowledge of her imminent death comes from you, the experienced horror film viewer. You have "read into" the scene.

Like the characters in *Scream*, you know that horror operates according to a set of rules or conventions that have been established by previous members of the genre. The mediamaker depends on you knowing these conventions. She knows that by sending the woman to the shower, she can create tension in the audience. ("No! Don't go, you crazy girl!" Hopefully you don't advise your real-life friends not to shower.) The filmmaker can toy with the audience, delaying the inevitable, because she knows that we expect the girl to be slashed. It is our job as audience members to read into the scene; mediamakers count on that.

Film and television rely on the audience to supply information that is only hinted at, like the shower convention in horror films. This "reading into" even occurs at the simplest levels of mediamaking. When we see a shot of someone getting into a car and driving away, followed by a shot of the car pulling into another driveway, we understand that the driver drove from one place to another. We understand this without the film/TV show actually showing us the drive across town. If we were limited to what was explicitly laid out in the TV program, if we didn't read into the film, then we wouldn't be able to make basic sense out of the movie. There's not a choice of whether you read into film/television or not; audiences have to.

This is not to say that you can read media in any way you want. Certain pieces of information in a film/television show are established beyond dispute. If you don't think that *Seinfeld* is about friends hanging out in New York City, then you have missed something. If you believe that it is a television series about Arctic beekeeping, then you are doing a remarkably perverse bit of reading into.

Between the pedestrian kind of reading into (the driving-across-town example, which some would call an inference or expectation) and the ludicrous kind of reading into (*Seinfeld*-as-Arctic-beekeeping-film), there is a wide range of possible readings. Some of these you may find to be too much of a stretch. What I would ask is that you be open to the possibility that some of these readings may be interesting. Don't close down your mind simply because an interpretation involves "reading into" a movie, because all media viewing involves reading into. Instead, look at the film/television program with an open mind and see if there is evidence to support a particular interpretation. If someone says that *Seinfeld* is really about the search for God or about Freudian revenge on the father, look at the TV show to see if there is corroborating material. Based on the film/television program, decide if there is a case to be made for that particular interpretation.

Just a movie

"Okay, maybe I see the value of coming up with new interpretations of *Hamlet* or *Citizen Kane*, but *Seinfeld*? Or *Evil Dead 2*? *Rush Hour*? *Everybody Loves Raymond*? *Survivor*? Come on. Aren't you taking these a bit too seriously? After all, it's just a movie (or a TV show)."

You wouldn't say, "Why are you analyzing *Hamlet*? After all, it's just Shakespeare." Why is it okay to analyze Shakespeare and not *Evil Dead 2* or *Everybody Loves Raymond*? The answer has as much to do with the social status of these works as it does with the works themselves.

There was a time when the study of Shakespeare would have been questionable as being not serious enough. At first, scholars in the West didn't think that anything written in English was as worthy of study as the classics written in Greek. Homer, Sophocles, and Aristotle were the serious works which should be taught in school, not Shakespeare's plays or Dickens's novels. Lawrence Levine has traced how the status of Shakespeare's work has changed in America, from a rather lowbrow standing in vaudeville productions to its current highbrow connotation as Art-with-a-capital-A. Dickens's novels, now clearly considered classics, were serialized in newspapers as pulp fiction. In that day, to argue that Dickens's work should be taught in schools would seem almost scandalous. Such trash obviously could not withstand the scrutiny applied to great works like Homer's *Odyssey*, or so it must have seemed.

Instead of relying purely on our society's understanding of what kinds of artworks are good enough to be taken seriously, we should instead look to the artworks themselves. If we look for rich interpretations of a work, we may find them or we may not. The point is not to dismiss the process outright simply because it's "just a movie." The proof is in the pudding, as the old saying goes. If your analysis produces insightful, well-grounded interpretations in a film/TV program, then that media text is definitely fruitful for analyzing, even if it is titled something like *Evil Dead 2*.

No one will argue that all media works are equally rich for analysis. Probably *Hamlet* is a more complex text to examine than *Evil Dead 2* is. But that shouldn't lead us to neglect a text that is "just a movie" or "just a TV show." You should take insight where you can get it. And even if a certain media text is not particularly complex, it can still provide hints about the society that produced it. Events don't have to be overtly complicated to yield knowledge.

For example, Robert Darnton, in his essay "Workers Revolt: The Great Cat Massacre of the Rue Saint-Séverin," analyzes a particularly unpromising-sounding phenomenon: a mock trial and execution of some cats by the apprentices and journeymen in a Parisian printing shop in the 1730s. What could this bizarre, sadistic, and unusual ritual possibly tell us about French society of that time? Reading closely, Darnton shows how this odd ceremony can reveal much about the relationship between workers and bosses, the sexual and class structures of the society, and the tradition of a craft. His essay demonstrates that even the slightest cultural artifacts bear the imprint of the society that made them. Examining a film can give us clues about the meanings and assumptions that are shared by the members of a culture. If a mock trial of cats can reveal social interrelationships, then an uncomplicated film/TV show that doesn't bear much aesthetic scrutiny can be examined for its social insights. All cultural products carry cultural meaning.

Ruining the movie

Part of the resistance to applying analytic tools to *Evil Dead 2* or *Survivor* is the belief that such analysis will kill the pleasure we have in watching the film. After all, movies and television are intended to be "mere entertainment." We have already dealt with the question of the mediamaker's intention, so let's not deal further with whether or not we should be limited to the mediamaker's conception of their work as "mere entertainment." Instead, let's deal with the fear that analyzing a film or television program will destroy the simple pleasure of watching it.

Sometimes it seems that the surest way to ruin a good book is to have to read it for a class. English classes are supposed to make you read things that you wouldn't normally pick up yourself. They force you to read Chaucer or Joyce, and the process of analyzing these works hopefully gives you insight into your life. But that's a very different thing from reading Michael Crichton or John Grisham in the airport. There you're reading to escape. If we start thinking too hard about airport novels or mainstream films, doesn't it ruin them?

When people learn that I am a media studies academic, they frequently ask, "Are you ever able to just sit back and enjoy a movie, or are you always analyzing it?" The question never rings true to me because it's phrased as an either/or option. For me, it's not a matter of substituting cerebral analysis for visceral pleasure; I experience both simultaneously. I don't lose the pleasure of rooting for the good guy while I'm admiring a movie's editing and thinking about the plot's social ramifications. After taking media studies classes, I can add the pleasures of analysis to the pleasures of moviegoing and television viewing.

I realize that as you are taking an introductory media analysis class, it may not seem like there's much pleasure in analysis. It probably seems more like tedious, difficult work. At first it may seem that you're losing the pleasurable experience of film and television as you dissect it, but as you get better at analysis, you will be able to recombine those activities. The end result, I believe, is a richer kind of pleasure. I believe that I respond more fully to the movies and television than I did before I started analyzing them. I now feel joy at a well-composed shot, a tautly constructed narrative structure, and an innovative social commentary, as well as the simpler pleasure of finding out whodunnit. The outcome we hope for in a media analysis class is not to ruin film and television but to increase the complexity of your enjoyment.

Why do that? Why tinker with the simple pleasure of watching a movie? This question goes to the foundation of what education is. The basic faith underlying education is that an examined life is better, richer, fuller than an unexamined life. How do we really know that self-examination is better than the bliss of simple ignorance? Like most statements of faith, there's no way to prove it. But by being in a college classroom, you have allied yourself with those of us who believe that if you don't examine the forces in your life, you will become subject to them. You can go throughout your life merely responding to movies and television, but if you are an educated person, you will also think about them, about what they mean and how they are constructed. In so doing, you may gain pleasures and insights that you could not have obtained any other way. This is the promise of the educated life in reading, in living, and in watching movies.

An earlier version of this chapter appeared as "It's Just a Movie: A Teaching Essay for Introductory Media Classes" in *Cinema Journal* 41.1 (Fall 2001): 127–34.

Works Cited

Darnton, R. (1985) "Workers Revolt: The Great Cat Massacre of the Rue Saint-Séverin," in *The Great Cat Massacre and Other Episodes in French Cultural History*, New York: Random House.

Levine, L. (1990) *Highbrow/Lowbrow: The Emergence of a Cultural Hierarchy in America*, Cambridge, MA: Harvard University Press.

Encountering Film: From Preproduction to Exhibition

"Encountering Film: From Preproduction to Exhibition" from *The Film Experience*, Fifth Edition, by Timothy Corrigan and Patricia White, pp. 17–53 (Chapter 1, "Encountering Film: From Preproduction to Exhibition").

Between 2013 and 2015, Ryan Coogler directed two very different kinds of films—*Fruitvale Station* (2013), a small but intense drama about an African American man mistakenly shot and killed by a transit policeman on a subway platform, and *Creed* (2015), the seventh film in the Rocky franchise, about the bond between Rocky Balboa and Apollo Creed's son as he prepares for a championship fight. Although both feature rising star Michael B. Jordon, the production, distribution, and exhibition of the two films illustrate how films, even by the same director, can be shaped by extremely different institutional histories that in turn shape our understanding of them.

Based on actual events that occurred in 2008 in California, Ryan Coogler's *Fruitvale Station* generated extensive buzz at both the Sundance and Cannes film festivals. When its theatrical release in July 2013 coincided with the acquittal of accused murderer George Zimmerman for his "Stand your ground" shooting of a young, unarmed African American in Florida, *Frutivale Station* became not just an emotionally searing film but also part of larger conversations, still ongoing, about justice in the streets of America.

Coogler's 2015 *Creed* traveled a different path. This franchise film inherits the whole history of the *Rocky* series, which focused on star Sylvester Stallone's character as a boxer from the working-class neighborhoods of Philadelphia. In *Creed*, Rocky is an older and wiser man asked to train the son (Jordan) of his old rival. It's a more crowd-pleasing, formulaic film than *Fruitvale Station*, and a bigger box office success, but they both appeal to African American and broader audiences.

As these two disparate films suggest, film production, distribution, and exhibition shape our encounters with movies, and these aspects of film are in turn shaped by how movies are received by audiences.

Whether we follow movie news or not, we know that a great deal has taken place before we as viewers experience a film. The varied practices that go into moviemaking are artistic and commercial but also cultural and social, and they anticipate the moment of viewing, at which meaning and value are generated. Understanding the process that takes a film from an idea to its final form deepens an appreciation for film form and the labor and craft of filmmakers and reveals ways that culture and society influence filmmaking itself.

This chapter describes the process of production as well as the fate of a finished film as it is distributed, promoted, and exhibited. Such extrafilmic processes describe events that precede, surround, or follow the actual images we watch and are inseparable from the film experience.

As viewers, our response, enjoyment, and understanding are shaped by where and when we see a movie as much as by the film's form and content. The film experience now encompasses ever smaller viewing devices (including computers, iPads, and smartphones), changing social environments (from IMAX to home theaters), and multiple cultural activities designed to promote interest in individual films (reading about films, directors, and stars; playing video games; watching special DVD editions; or connecting to social media that support a film franchise). Waiting in line with friends for a Thursday night premiere and half-watching an edited in-flight movie are significantly different experiences that lead to different forms of appreciation and understanding. Overall, it is helpful to think of production and reception as a cycle rather than a one-way process: what goes into making and circulating a film anticipates the moment of viewing, and viewing tastes and habits influence film production and dissemination.

Production: How Films Are Made

The aim at each step of filmmaking is to create an artistic and commercial product that will engage, please, or provoke viewers. In short, film **production** is a multi-layered activity in which industry, art, technology, and imagination intertwine. It describes the different stages—from the financing and scripting of a film to its final edit and, fittingly, the addition of production **credits** naming the companies and individuals involved—that contribute to the construction of a movie. Production may not seem like a central part of our film experiences as viewers, but the making of a film anticipates an audience of one sort or another and implies a certain kind of viewer. Does the film showcase the work of the director or the screenwriter? The cinematographer or the composer of the musical score? How does the answer to this question affect our perspective on the film? Understanding contemporary filmmaking in its many dimensions contributes to our appreciation of and ability to analyze films.

Preproduction

Although the word *production* is used to define the entire process of making a film, a great deal happens—and often a long time passes—before a film begins to be shot. **Preproduction** designates the phase when a film project is in development, involving preparing the script, financing the project, casting, hiring crew, and securing locations. In **narrative** filmmaking (scripted films), the efforts of the screenwriter, producer, and sometimes director, often in the context of a studio or an independent production company, combine at this stage to conceive and refine an idea for a film in order to realize it onscreen. Funds are raised, rights are secured, a crew is assembled, casting decisions are made, and key aspects of the film's design, including location scouting and the construction of sets and costumes, are developed during the preproduction phase. Documentary filmmakers might conduct archival or location research, investigate their subject, and conduct interviews during this period.

Screenwriters

A **screenwriter** (or scriptwriter) is often the individual who generates the idea for a narrative film, either as an original concept or as an adaptation of another source (such as a novel, true story, or comic book character). The screenwriter presents that early concept or material in a **treatment**, a short prose description of the action of a film and major characters of the story, written before the screenplay. The treatment is then gradually expanded to a complete **screenplay** (or script)—the text from which a movie is made, including dialogue and information about action, settings, shots, and transitions. This undergoes several versions, from the temporary screenplay submitted by the screenwriter to the final shooting script that details exact scenes and camera setups. As these different scripts evolve, one writer may be responsible for every version, or different writers may be employed at each stage, resulting in minor and sometimes major changes along the way. Even with a finished and approved script, in the studio context an uncredited **script doctor** may be called in to do rewrites. From *Sunset Boulevard* (1950), about a struggling screenwriter trapped in the mansion of a fading silent film star, to *Adaptation* (2002), about (fictional) screenwriter Charlie Kaufman's torturous attempt to adapt Susan Orlean's book *The Orchid Thief*, numerous films have found drama in the process of screenwriting itself (Figure 1-1). One reason may be the dramatic shifts and instabilities in the process of moving from a concept to a completed screenplay to a produced film, a process that highlights the difficulties of trying to communicate an individual vision to an audience.

Figure 1-1. ***Adaptation*** (2002). As its title indicates, screenwriting is the topic of this inventive film, in which Charlie Kaufman, played by Nicolas Cage, is both a fictionalized character and the actual credited writer.

Producers and Studios

The key individuals in charge of movie production and finances are a film's producers. A **producer** oversees each step of a film project, especially the financial aspects, from development to postproduction and a distribution deal. At times, a producer may be fully involved with each step of film production from the selection and development of a script to the creation of an advertising campaign for the finished film. At other times, a producer may be an almost invisible partner who is responsible principally for the financing of a movie. Producers on a project also sometimes include filmmakers who are working on other areas of the film, such as the director, screenwriter, or actors.

Producers were extremely powerful in the heyday of the **studio system**, a term that describes the industrial practices of large production companies responsible for filmmaking in Hollywood or other national film industries. The Hollywood studio era extended from the 1920s through the 1950s. MGM was identified with the creative vision of the supervisor of production, Irving B. Thalberg, who as production head worked closely with studio mogul Louis B. Mayer from the mid-1920s until Thalberg's premature death in 1936. After leaving MGM to found his own studio, producer David O. Selznick controlled all stages of production, beginning with the identification of the primary material for the film. For instance, he acquired *Gone with the Wind* as a property even before the novel was published. Selznick supervised every aspect of the 1939 film version of the best-seller, even changing directors during production—a process documented in his famous production memos.

Since the rise of the independent film movement in the 1990s, independent producers have worked to facilitate the creative freedom of the writer and director, arranging the financing for the film as well as seeing the film through casting, hiring a crew, scheduling, shooting, **postproduction** (the period in the filmmaking process that occurs after principal photography has been completed, usually consisting of editing, sound, and visual effects work), and distribution sales. For example, producer James Schamus first worked with Ang Lee on the independent film *Eat Drink Man Woman* (1994) and cowrote the screenplays of *Sense and Sensibility* (1995), *Crouching Tiger, Hidden Dragon* (2000), and *Lust, Caution* (2007). As vice president of Focus Features (a specialty division of Universal), Schamus shepherded Lee's *Brokeback Mountain* (2005) through all stages of production.

Regardless of the size or type of film being made, distinctions among the tasks and roles of types of producers exist. An executive producer may be connected to a film primarily in name, playing a role in financing or facilitating a film deal and having little creative or technical involvement. On a documentary, an executive producer might work with the television channel commissioning the program. A coproducer credit may designate an investor or an executive with a particular production company partnering in the movie, someone who had no role in its actual production. The **line producer** is in charge of the daily business of tracking costs and maintaining the production schedule of a film, while a **unit production manager** is responsible for reporting and managing the details of receipts and purchases.

The budget of a film, whether big or minuscule, is handled by the producers. In budgeting, **above-the-line expenses** are the initial costs of contracting the major personnel, such as directors and stars, as well as administrative and organizational expenses in setting up a film production. **Below-the-line expenses** are the technical and material costs—costumes, sets, transportation, and so on—involved in the actual making of a film. Production values demonstrate how the quality of the film's images and sounds reflects the extent of these two expenses. In both subtle and not-so-subtle ways, production values often shape viewers' expectations about a film. High production values suggest a more spectacular or more professionally made movie. Low production values do not necessarily mean a poorly made film. In both cases, we need to adjust our expectations to the style associated with the budgeting.

Financing Film Production

Financing and managing production expenses is a critical ingredient in making a movie. Traditionally, studios and producers have worked with banks or large financial institutions to acquire this financing, and the term *bankable* has emerged as a way of indicating that a film has the necessary ingredients—such as a famous star or well-known literary source—to make that investment worth the risk. A mainstream action movie like *Suicide Squad* (2016), starring Will Smith, might cost well over $100 million to produce and over $50 million to market—a significant investment that assumes a significant financial return. Developed alongside the conception of a film, therefore, is a plan to find a large enough audience to return that investment and, ideally, a profit.

Some films follow a less typical financing path. Kevin Smith made *Clerks* (1994) by charging expenses to various credit cards. The 1990s saw a rise in independent film as financing strategies changed. Instead of relying on a single source such as a bank or a studio, independent filmmaking is financed by organized groups of individual investors or presales of distribution or broadcast rights in different markets. In the absence of studio backing, an independent film must appeal to potential investors with a known quantity, such as the director's reputation or the star's box-office clout. Although major star Julianne Moore was attached to Lisa Cholodenko's project *The Kids Are All Right* (2010) for five years, raising the film's $4 million budget was difficult (Figure 1-2). Filmmakers as successful as Spike Lee (*Do the Right Thing*, 1989) and Zach Braff (*Garden State*, 2004) have turned to the Kickstarter Web site to raise funding for recent projects.

Nonfiction films also require financing. Documentaries may be sponsored by an organization, produced by a television channel, or funded by a combination of individual donors and public funds. For instance, Jonathan Caouette's *Tarnation* (2003) recounts the filmmaker's childhood and adolescence through a collage of snapshots, Super-8 footage, answering machine messages, video diaries, and home movies (Figure 1-3). It does not use a conventional screenplay, and it was edited on a home computer with an alleged production budget of about $200. With John Cameron Mitchell and Gus Van Sant as executive producers, the film screened at the Sundance Film Festival. The publicity led to other festival invitations, a distribution deal for a limited theatrical release, and considerable critical attention.

Figure 1-2. ***The Kids Are All Right*** (2010). A modestly budgeted independent production usually requires name stars to attract financing. Even with cast members committed, however, Lisa Cholodenko's comedic drama about lesbian parents took years to produce.

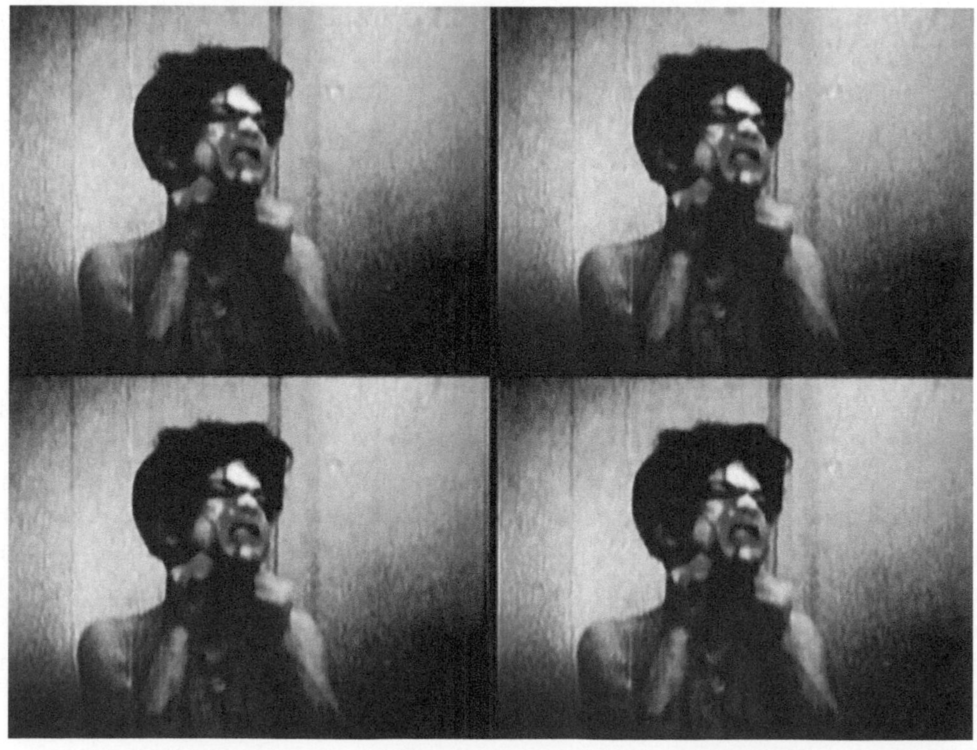

Figure 1-3. ***Tarnation*** (2003). As Jonathan Caouette's debut film shows, even an ultra-low-budget independent production can be released theatrically if it lands an adequate distribution deal.

Casting Directors and Agents

With the increasing costs of films and the necessity of attracting money with a bankable project, the roles of casting directors and agents have become more important. Traditionally the work of a **casting director**, the practice of identifying the actors who would work best in particular scripted roles emerged during the advent of the star system around 1910. Around this time, Florence Lawrence, the exceedingly popular star of Biograph Studio who was known as the "Biograph Girl," first demanded to be named and given a screen credit. Often in consultation with directors, producers, and writers, casting directors have since become bigger and more widely credited players in determining the look and scale of films as they revolve around the cast of stars and actors in those films.

Representing actors, directors, writers, and other major individuals in a film production, **agents** negotiate with writers, casting directors, and producers and enlist different personnel for a movie. The significance and power of the agent extends back at least to the 1930s, when talent agent Lew Wasserman, working as a publicist for the Music Corporation of America (MCA), began to create independent, multiple-movie deals for Bette Davis, Errol Flynn, James Stewart, and many others. By the mid-1950s, Wasserman and others had established a **package-unit approach** to film production whereby the agent, producer, and casting director determine a script, stars, and other major personnel as a key first step in a major production, establishing the production model that would dominate after the demise of the traditional studio system. By the mid-1970s, so-called superagents would sometimes predetermine a package of stars and other personnel from which the film must be constructed.

Locations, Production Design, Sets, and Costumes

In narrative films, the interaction between characters and the physical location of the action is often a central dimension of a film; hence, choices about location and set design are critical. Likewise, documentary filmmaking depends on location as well—from the record of a strike in *Harlan County, U.S.A.* (1976) to nature documentaries like *Planet Earth* (2006)—but it also uses sets for interviews.

Location scouts became commonplace in the early twentieth century. These individuals determine and secure places that provide the most suitable environment for shooting different movie scenes. Choosing a location is often determined by a series of pragmatic questions: Does the place fit the requirements of the script, and how expensive would it be to film at this location? Many films rely on constructed sets that recreate a specific place, but the desire for movie realism often results in the use of actual locations to invigorate a scene. Thus the *Lord of the Rings* (2001–2003) and *Hobbit* trilogies (2012–2014) take advantage of the lush and wild location filming in New Zealand, while *Only Lovers Left Alive* (2013) (Figure 1-4) makes the ravaged and vacated urban landscape of nighttime Detroit an important backdrop for its tale about two emotionally impoverished and disenchanted vampires. In recent decades, the cinematic task of re-creating real-seeming environments has shifted to computer-graphics technicians. These technicians design the models to be digitally transferred onto film, becoming, in a sense, a new kind of location scout.

Figure 1-4. ***Only Lovers Left Alive*** (2013). Cities like Tangiers and a decaying Detroit become distinctive backgrounds for Jim Jarmusch's moody, mordantly funny vampire story.

The **production designer** determines the film's overall look. **Art directors** are responsible for supervising the conception and construction of the physical environment in which actors appear, including sets, locations, props, and costumes. The set decorators complete the look of a set with the details. For example, in a movie set in a particular historical period and place, such as *Argo* (2012), the art department coordinated to create sets and locations that accurately reflect Tehran in 1980 and that also highlighted the suspenseful atmosphere surrounding the rescue of six Americans.

The role of **costume designers**, those who plan and prepare how actors will be dressed as their characters, greatly increased as the movie business expanded in the 1930s. Costume designers ensure the splendor, suitability, and sometimes the historical accuracy of the movie characters' appearances. Indeed, for those films in which costumes and settings are central to the story—films set in fantasy worlds or historical eras, such as *Pan's Labyrinth* (2006), which uses both kinds of settings—one could argue that the achievement of the film becomes inseparable from the decisions made about the art and costume design. In the end, successful films integrate all levels of the design, from the sets to the costumes, as in *The Grand Budapest Hotel* (2014), where the costumes re-create the 1930s in a luxurious hotel in Eastern Europe but have a zany excess and decadence that mirrors the plot and themes (Figure 1-5).

Figure 1-5. ***The Grand Budapest Hotel*** (2014). Wes Anderson clothes his characters in outfits that recall a 1930s sensibility but exaggerates those outfits to the point that they sometimes seem surreal.

Production

Most mythologized of all phases of moviemaking is production itself or **principal photography**, which is the majority of footage that is filmed. The weeks or months of actual shooting, on set or on location, are also known as a **film shoot**. Countless films, from *The Bad and the Beautiful* (1952) and *Irma Vep* (1996) to *Hitchcock* (2012), dramatize inspired or fraught interactions among cast, crew, and the person in charge of it all, the director (Figure 1-6 The reality of production varies greatly with the scale of the film and its budget, but the director, who has often been involved in all of the creative phases of preproduction, must now work closely with the actors and production personnel—most notably, the camera units headed by the cinematographer—to realize a collaborative vision.

Figure 1-6. ***Irma Vep*** (1996). Maggie Cheung stars in a film about making a film—starring Maggie Cheung.

The Director

The earliest films of the twentieth century involved very few people in the process of shooting a film, with the assumption that the cameraman was the de facto director. By 1907, however, a division of labor separated production roles, placing the director in charge of all others on the film set. Today the **director** is commonly regarded as the chief creative presence or the primary manager in film production, responsible for and overseeing virtually all the work of making a movie—guiding the actors, determining the position of the camera, and selecting which images appear in the finished film.

Directors have different methods and degrees of involvement. Alfred Hitchcock claimed he never needed to see the action through the camera viewfinder because his script directions were so precise that there would be only one way to compose the shot. Others are comfortable relinquishing important decisions to their assistant director (AD), cinematographer, or sound designer. Still others, like Woody Allen and Barbra Streisand, assume multiple roles (screenwriter, actor, and editor) in addition to that of director (Figures 1-7a and 1-7b).

In Hollywood during the studio era, when directors' visions often were subordinated to a "house style" or a producer's vision, directors worked so consistently and honed their craft with such skilled personnel that critics can detect a given director's signature style across routine assignments. This has elevated directors like Howard Hawks (*Bringing Up Baby*, 1938, and *His Girl Friday*, 1940) and Nicholas Ray (*Rebel Without a Cause*, 1955) to the status of **auteurs**—directors who are considered "authors" of films in which they express their own individual vision and experiences.

(a) (b)

Everett Collection, Inc.

Figure 1-7. Barbra Streisand. Stardom as a singer and actor gave Streisand the opportunity to turn to directing. In ***Yentl*** (1983), her first film as a director, her protagonist dresses as a boy to study the Torah.

Today a company backing a film will choose or approve a director for projects that seem to fit with his or her skills and talents. For example, Mexican director Alfonso Cuarón's success with films like *A Little Princess* (1995) and *Great Expectations* (1998) led to his early involvement with *Harry Potter and the Prisoner of Azkaban* (2004). Because of the control and assumed authority of the director, contemporary viewers often look for stylistic and thematic consistencies in films by the same director, and filmmakers like Quentin Tarantino have become celebrities. This follows a model prevalent in art cinema made outside Hollywood in which the vision of a director like Jean-Luc Godard or Tsai Ming-liang (*What Time Is It There?*, 2001) is supported by the producer and made manifest in virtually every aspect of the film.

The Cast, Cinematographer, and Other On-Set Personnel

The director works with the actors to bring out the desired performance, and these collaborations vary greatly. Because film scenes are shot out of order and in a variety of shot scales, the cast's performance must be delivered in bits and pieces. Some actors prepare a technical performance; others rely on the director's prompting or other, more spontaneous inspiration. Daniel Day-Lewis, the star of *Lincoln* (2012) and *There Will Be Blood* (2007), is known for immersing himself in every role to such an extent that he stays in character throughout the entire production, even when the cameras are not rolling. David Fincher's exacting directorial style requires scores of takes, or different versions of a shot, a grueling experience for *Zodiac* (2007) actors Jake Gyllenhaal and Robert Downey Jr. Some directors gravitate to particularly sympathetic and dynamic relations with actors—Tim Burton with Johnny Depp, Pedro Almodóvar with Penelope Cruz, and Martin Scorsese with Robert De Niro and Leonardo DiCaprio.

The **cinematographer**, also known as the director of photography (DP), selects the cameras, film stock, lighting, and lenses to be used as well as the camera setup or position. In consultation with the director, the cinematographer determines how the action will be shot, the images composed, and, later, the kind of exposure needed to print the takes. The cinematographer oversees a **camera operator** (who physically manipulates the camera) and other camera and lighting crew. Many films owe more to the cinematographer than to almost any other individual in the production. The scintillating *Days of Heaven* (1978) profits as much from the eye of cinematographer Néstor Almendros as from the direction of Terrence Malick, and the consistently stunning work of cinematographer Michael Ballhaus on films such as Rainer Werner Fassbinder's *The Marriage of Maria Braun* (1979) and Martin Scorsese's *The Departed* (2006) arguably displays the artistic singularity and vision that are usually assigned to film directors (Figure 1-8).

Figure 1-8. ***The Departed*** (2006). Cinematographer Michael Ballhaus suggests interpretations of the characters' motives through shot composition and lighting.

Other personnel are also on the set—including the **production sound mixer** (who is the sound engineer on the production set) and other sound crew, including the boom operator; the **grips** who install lighting and dollies; the special effects coordinator; the scenic, hair, and make-up artists; and the catering staff. A production coordinator helps this complex operation run smoothly. During the shoot, the director reviews **dailies** (footage shot that day) and begins to make **selects** (takes that are chosen to use in editing a scene). After principal photography is completed, sets are broken down, and the film "wraps," or completes production. A film shoot is an intense, concentrated effort in which the contributions of visionary artists and professional crew mesh with schedule and budget constraints.

Postproduction

Some of the most important aspects of a finished film—including editing, sound, and visual effects—are achieved after principal photography is completed and production is over. How definitive or efficient the process is depends on many factors. A documentary may be constructed almost entirely during this phase, or a commercial feature film may have to be recut in response to test screenings or the wishes of a new executive who has assumed authority over the project.

Editing and Sound

The director works closely with the editor and his or her staff during **editing**—the process of selecting and joining film footage and shots into a finished film with a distinctive style and rhythm. This process now is largely carried out with digital footage and computer-based editing. Editing is anticipated during preproduction of fiction films with the preparation of a shooting script, and in production it is recognized in the variety and number of takes provided. Only a fraction of the footage that is shot is included in the finished film, however, making editing crucial to its final form. In documentary production, editing may be the most important stage in shaping the film. When the editing is completed, the picture is said to be *locked*.

Postproduction also includes complex processes for editing sound and adding special effects. A sound editor oversees the work of **sound editing**—combining music, dialogue, and effects tracks to interact with the image track. Less apparent than the editing of images, sound editing can create noises that relate directly to the action of the image (such as matching the image of a dog barking), underpin those images and actions with music (such as the pounding beats that follow an army into battle), or insert sounds that counterpoint the images in ways that complicate their meanings (such as using a religious hymn to accompany the flight of a missile). In the **sound mixing** process, all of the elements of the soundtrack—music, effects, and dialogue—are combined and adjusted to their final levels.

Special Effects

Special effects are techniques that enhance a film's realism or surpass assumptions about realism with spectacle. Whereas some special effects are prepared in preproduction (such as the building of elaborate models of futuristic cities), others can be generated in production (with special camera filters or setups) or created on set (for example, by using pyrotechnics).

Today most special effects are created in postproduction and are distinguished by the term **visual effects**—imagery combined with live action footage by teams of computer technicians and artists. In the contemporary digital age, computer technicians have virtually boundless postproduction capabilities to enhance and transform an image. Fantastical scenes and characters (such as Andy Serkis as Gollum in *Lord of the Rings*) can be acted out using **green-screen technology**, in which actors perform in front of a plain green background, and **motion-capture technology**, which transfers the actors' physical movements to **computer-generated imagery (CGI)**. The settings of the *Star Wars* prequel trilogy

(1999–2005) were generated largely in postproduction (Figure 1-9). All of the personnel who work behind the scenes on these many levels of filmmaking are acknowledged when the titles and credits are added in the final stage of postproduction.

Figure 1-9. ***Star Wars: Episode III—Revenge of the Sith*** (2005). Although the original ***Star Wars*** films used multiple sets, models, and props, much of the prequel series was generated using state-of-the-art computer technology.

Distribution: What We Can See

The completed film reaches its audience through the process of **distribution**, in which films are provided to venues in which the public can see them. These include theaters and video stores, broadcast and cable television, Internet streaming and **video on demand (VOD)**, libraries and classrooms—even hotels and airlines. Despite these many outlets for distribution, many worthy films never find a distributor and are never seen. As avenues of distribution multiply, new questions about the role of film culture in our individual and collective experience arise. Our tastes, choices, and opportunities are shaped by aspects of the industry of which we may be unaware, and we, in turn, influence what we can see in the future.

The discussion that follows, which emphasizes the U.S. feature-film distribution system since it often controls even foreign theaters, addresses how viewers and views of movies are prepared by the social and economic machinery of distribution.

Distributors

A **distributor** is a company or an agency that acquires the rights to a movie from the filmmakers or producers (sometimes by contributing to the costs of producing the film) and makes the movie available to audiences by renting, selling, or licensing it to theaters or other exhibition outlets. Top-grossing distributors include Walt Disney, Warner Bros., Sony Pictures, 20th Century Fox, Universal, Paramount Pictures, and Lionsgate. Smaller companies include the Weinstein Company, Magnolia Pictures, and divisions of both Netflix and Amazon.

The supply of films for distribution depends on the films that are produced, but the inverse of that logic is central to the economics of mainstream movie culture: what is produced depends on what Hollywood and many other film cultures assume can be successfully distributed. Film history has accordingly been marked with regular battles and compromises between filmmakers and distributors about what audiences are willing to watch. United Artists was formed in 1919 by four prominent Hollywood stars—D. W. Griffith, Charlie Chaplin, Mary Pickford, and Douglas Fairbanks—to distribute their independently produced films and became a major company. Decades later, in 1979, the independent distributor Miramax used aggressive promotional campaigns to make foreign-produced and independent movies viable in wide theatrical release, thus changing the distribution landscape.

Evolution of the Feature Film

Consider the following examples of how the prospects for distributing and exhibiting a film can influence and even determine its content and form, including decisions about its length. From around 1911 to 1915, D. W. Griffith and other filmmakers struggled to convince movie studios to allow them to expand the length of a movie from roughly fifteen minutes to over 100 minutes. Although longer films imported from Europe achieved some success, most producers felt that it would be impossible to distribute longer movies because they believed audiences would not sit still for more than twenty minutes. Griffith persisted and continued to stretch the length of his films, insisting that new distribution and exhibition patterns would create and attract new audiences—those willing to accept more complex stories and to pay more for them. Griffith's controversial three-hour epic, *The Birth of a Nation* (1915), was distributed as a major cultural event comparable to a legitimate theatrical or operatic experience and was an enormous commercial and financial success (Figure 1-10). The film became a benchmark in overturning one distribution formula, which offered a continuous program of numerous short films, and establishing a new one, which concentrated on a single **feature film**, a longer narrative movie that is the primary attraction for audiences.

Everett Collection, Inc.

Figure 1-10. Advertisement for *The Birth of a Nation* (1915). The ambitious nature of D. W. Griffith's controversial epic was apparent in its advertisements and unprecedented three-hour running time.

After 1915, most films were distributed with ninety- to 120-minute running times rather than in their previous ten- to twenty-minute lengths, and this pattern for distribution has proved durable. The recent trend toward longer running times, especially for "prestige" or "epic" films, acknowledges the flexible contexts in which films are now viewed.

Our experience of a movie—its length, its choice of stars (over unknown actors, for example), its subject matter, and even its title—is determined partly by decisions made about distribution even before the film becomes available to viewers. Most movies are produced to be distributed to certain kinds of audiences. Distribution patterns—whether a movie is available everywhere for everyone at the same time, is released during the holiday season, or is available only in specialty video stores or on Internet sites—bring expectations that a particular film either fulfills or frustrates.

Release Strategies

As one of its primary functions, distribution determines the number of copies of a film that will be available and the number of locations at which the movie will be seen. During the heyday of the Hollywood studio system, studios either showed their films in their own theater chains or sold them to theaters in packages, a practice known as **block booking**. An exhibitor was required to show cheaper, less desirable films as a condition of booking the star-studded A pictures. This practice was the target of antitrust legislation and finally was outlawed in the 1948 *United States v. Paramount* decision, which divorced the studios from their theater chains and required that films be sold individually. Typically, a distribution strategy kicks off with a **premiere**—a red carpet event celebrating the opening night of a movie that is attended by stars and attracts press attention. A film's initial opening in a limited number of **first-run theaters** (theaters that show recently released movies) as exclusive engagements gradually was expanded, allowing for a series of premieres.

In 1975, Steven Spielberg's *Jaws* introduced the practice of **wide release**, opening in hundreds of theaters simultaneously. Since then, a film with a mass circulation of premieres—sometimes referred to as **saturation booking** or a saturated release—is screened in as many locations as possible in the United States (and increasingly abroad) as soon as possible. For a potential blockbuster such as *X-Men: Apocalypse* (2016), the distributors immediately release the movie in a maximum number of locations and theaters to attract large audiences before its novelty wears off (Figure 1-11). In these cases, distribution usually promises audiences a film that is easy to understand and appeals to most tastes (offering action sequences, breathtaking special effects, or a light romance rather than controversial topics).

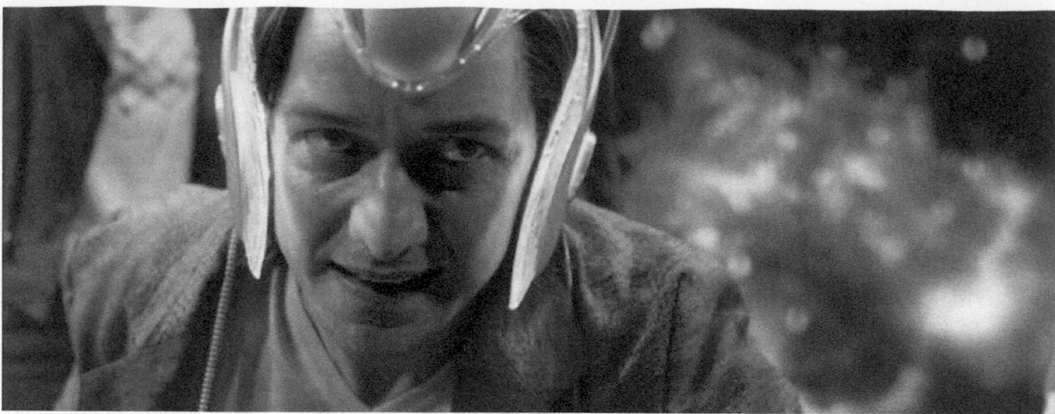

Figure 1-11. ***X-Men: Apocalypse*** (2016). As a major studio release and entry in the hugely successful Marvel series, the film received a saturated release, opening on around ten thousand screens in more than four thousand theaters.

A **limited release** may be distributed only to major cities—the cult comedy *Wet Hot American Summer* (2001) never played in more than thirty theaters—and then expand its distribution, depending on the film's initial success. Audience expectations for films following a limited release pattern are generally less fixed than for wide releases. They usually will be recognized in terms of the previous work of the director or an actor but will offer a certain novelty or experimentation (such as a controversial subject or a strange plot twist) that presumably will be better appreciated as the film is publicly debated and understood through the reviews and discussions that follow its initial release. The Weinstein Company's decision to limit the release of Todd Haynes's experimental biopic of *Bob Dylan, I'm Not There* (2007), to major cities was a strategic bid to maximize critical attention to the film's daring and the intriguing premise of its star performances, which include Cate Blanchett playing the 1960s Dylan (Figure 1-12).

Figure 1-12. ***I'm Not There*** (2007). Todd Haynes's experimental Bob Dylan biopic built up critical attention through a limited release pattern.

As part of these general practices, distribution strategies have developed over time to shape or respond to the interests and tastes of intended audiences. **Platforming** involves releasing a film in gradually widening markets and theaters so that it slowly builds its reputation and momentum through reviews and word of mouth. The strategy for expanding a release depends on box-office performance: if a film does well in its opening weekend, it will open in more cities on more screens. When the low-budget supernatural horror film *Paranormal Activity* (2007) was acquired and released by Paramount, audiences became directly involved in determining where the film would open by voting on director Oren Peli's Web site. A movie also can be distributed for special **exclusive release**, premiering in only one or two locations. A dramatic example of this strategy was seen with the restored version of Abel Gance's silent classic *Napoléon*, an epic tale of the life of the French emperor that periodically presents the action simultaneously on three screens. The original film premiered in April 1927. In 1981, the exclusive release of the restored film toured to one theater at a time, accompanied by a full orchestra; seeing it became a privileged event.

Target Audiences

Since the late twentieth century, movies also have been distributed with an eye toward reaching specific target audiences—viewers whom producers feel are most likely to want to see a particular film. Producers and distributors aimed *Shaft* (1971), an action film with a black hero, at African American audiences by distributing it primarily in large urban areas. Distributors positioned *Trainspotting* (1995), a hip tale of young heroin users in Edinburgh, to draw art-house and younger audiences in cities, some suburbs, and college and university towns. The *Nightmare on Elm Street* movies (1984–1994), a violent slasher series about the horrific Freddy Krueger, were aimed primarily at the male teenage audience who frequented cineplexes and, later, video stores.

The various distribution strategies all imply important issues about how movies should be viewed and understood. First, by controlling the scope of distribution, these strategies determine the quality and importance of an audience's interactions with a film. As a saturated release, the 2015 attempt to restart the *Fantastic Four* series aimed for swift gratification with a focus on special effects and action, before disappointed word of mouth could spread. Platformed gradually through expanding audiences, *Driving Miss Daisy* (1989) benefited from critical reflections on the relationship it depicts between an older white woman and her black chauffeur (Figure 1-13).

Figure 1-13. ***Driving Miss Daisy*** (1989). Platforming this modestly budgeted film cultivated audiences and critical responses.

Second, in targeting audiences, distribution can identify primary, intended responses to the film as well as secondary, unexpected ones. Movies from the Pixar animation studio might resonate the most with children and their parents, with stories in *Inside Out* (2015) (Figure 1-14), *Finding Dory* (2016), and *Toy Story 3* (2010) that address both childhood and the process of parenting, layering the animated adventures with inside jokes and references for adults. But as Pixar has established itself as a source of high-quality animation, their adult following has grown—including some former kids who may have grown up on the company's early movies and now will see follow-ups with their favorite characters even as they age out of the target audience. Awareness of these strategies of targeting indicates how our identification with and comprehension of films are as much a product of our social and cultural locations as they are a product of the film's subject matter and form.

Figure 1-14. ***Inside Out*** (2015). This computer-animated film is aimed principally at families, but childless audiences may still find plenty to identify with.

Ancillary Markets

Commercial cinema's reach has been expanding ever since studios began to take advantage of television's distribution potential in the mid-1950s. New technologies for watching movies continue to proliferate, and distribution has increasingly taken advantage of television, video, DVD, Blu-ray, and forms of video on demand (VOD). Today more of a film's revenue is generated by such **ancillary markets** than by its initial theatrical release.

Television Distribution

Historically, the motion picture industry competed with broadcasting, which distributed entertainment directly to the home through radio and later television. As television became popular in postwar America, the studios realized that the new medium provided an unprecedented distribution outlet. With the rise of cable television, studios were provided with even more lucrative opportunities to sell their vast libraries of films. Home video and the launch of dedicated movie channels like Turner Classic Movies (founded by Ted Turner to showcase his acquisition of MGM's collection) were a boon to cinema lovers as well.

With viewing options ranging from network to premium channels and from on-demand to subscription plans, more and more movies are presented through television distribution—the selection and programming, at carefully determined times, of films made for theaters and exclusively for television. Historically, there was a specific lag time between a theatrical release in a cinema and a cable or network release, but these relationships are changing. Some movies are distributed directly to video or cable, such as the ongoing series of follow-ups to *Bring It On* (2000). Whether a movie is released after its theatrical run or is made expressly for video and television, this type of distribution usually aims to reach the largest possible audience and thus to increase revenues. In an attempt to reach specialized audiences through subscription cable, distributors like IFC Films have made critically acclaimed foreign and U.S. independent films available on demand the same day they are released in art-house theaters in major cities, allowing television audiences in markets outside large cities access to such works as the Romanian *4 Months, 3 Weeks, 2 Days* (2007), winner of the Cannes Film Festival's top prize. Although the traditional wisdom is that such access will hurt the theatrical box office, the strategy allows such films to reach wider audiences, and positive word of mouth, for both the film and the distributor's "brand," might enhance overall theatrical revenue.

Guaranteed television distribution can reduce the financial risk for producers and filmmakers and thus, in some situations, allow for more experimentation or filmmaker control. In a fairly new trend, the flow between television and theatrical distribution is reversed. Premium (subscription) cable channels such as HBO increasingly produce their own films that include riskier subjects. Even though these films are presented on their networks, a theatrical window for the film to receive reviews and become eligible for awards is sometimes allowed.

Television distribution has both positive and negative implications. In some cases, films on television must adjust their style and content to suit constraints of both time and space: scenes might be cut to fit a time slot or be interrupted with commercial breaks (breaking up movies into miniseries events is less common today than it was in the past). For many years, the size and ratio of a widescreen film was changed to fit the traditionally square shape of the television monitor, thus altering the picture to suit the format. Now, widescreen ratios tend to be the default, sometimes distorting those films or other programming originally produced in the standard square format. In other cases, television distribution may expand the ways movies can communicate with audiences and experiment with different visual forms. *The Singing Detective* (1986) uses the long length of a television series watched within the home as the means to explore and think about the passage of time, the difficulty of memory, and the many levels of reality and consciousness woven into our daily lives.

Home Video, VOD, and Internet Distribution

Each new format for the public or private consumption of media—VHS (video home system), LaserDisc, DVD (digital video disk), Blu-ray—offers a new distribution challenge for media makers and a potential new revenue model for rights holders. Independent producers may find it difficult to transfer existing media to new formats or to make enough sales for a particular avenue of distribution to be viable. The home video era began with competition between Sony's Beta format and VHS. The VHS format won out, and with the widespread use of videocassette recorders (VCRs) in the 1980s, studios quickly released films in the VHS home video format, first for rental and increasingly for sales. There have been similar dueling interests in recent years, such as that between high-definition DVD (HD-DVD) and Blu-ray.

One of the most significant challenges to distributors posed by new formats is **piracy**, the unauthorized duplication and circulation of copyrighted material. Despite anti-copying software, the circulation of pirated films is widespread and can bypass social, cultural, and legal controls, bringing banned films to viewers in China, for example, or building subcultures and networks around otherwise hard-to-access films.

As with film distribution through cinema and television, distribution of consumer formats like video, DVD, and Blu-ray determines the availability of particular titles to audiences. A film may be made available for rental or purchase in stores, received by mail from companies like Netflix, or ordered from independent distributors such as Kino International.

Before the closing of many video stores caused by the shift to subscriber and on-demand services in the 2000s, the video store was a significant site of film culture. Because the selection in rental stores was based on a market perspective on local audiences as well as the tastes of individual proprietors, some films were distributed to certain cities or neighborhoods and excluded from other locations. The dominant chains (such as Blockbuster, which filed for bankruptcy in 2010) were likely to focus on high-concentration family-oriented shopping sites, offering numerous copies of current popular mainstream movies and excluding daring subject matter or older titles. Some local independent video stores specialized in art films, cult films, or movie classics (such as those released on DVD by the Criterion Collection). Still other local stores depended on X-rated films or video game rentals for their primary revenue. Sometimes distribution follows cultural as well as commercial logic. Bollywood films, available in video and even grocery stores in neighborhoods with large South Asian populations, provided a tie to cultural traditions and national stars and songs before access to such films became widespread.

For viewers, there were two clear consequences to these patterns of video distribution. The first is that video distribution can control and direct—perhaps more than theatrical distribution does—local responses, tastes, and expectations. As part of a community anchored by a particular video store, we see and learn to expect only certain kinds of movies when the store makes five or six copies of one blockbuster film available but only one or none of a less popular film. The second consequence highlights the sociological and cultural formations of film distribution. As a community outlet, video stores become part of the social fabric of a neighborhood. Viewers are consumers, and video stores can become forums in which the interests of a community of viewers—in children's film or art-house cinema, for instance—can determine which films are distributed. Michel Gondry's *Be Kind Rewind* (2008) shows an urban community coming together around the films made available at its locally owned video store after its employees begin to produce their own versions of rental titles to replace their demagnetized inventory (Figure 1-15). Such ties are less likely to be forged around recent alternatives to dedicated stores, such as DVD kiosks in grocery stores.

Figure 1-15. ***Be Kind Rewind*** (2008). The employees at a neighborhood video store attract a loyal local audience with their do-it-yourself inventory, like this re-created scene from Stanley Kubrick's *2001: A Space Odyssey* (1968).

The innovation in distribution of DVDs that was probably most responsible for the decline of the local video store is the rental-by-mail model launched by Netflix and followed by other companies. As part of a subscription system that offers viewers a steady stream of DVDs, Netflix members can select and return films as rapidly or as slowly as they wish. Because the DVDs arrive and are returned through the mail, this distribution arrangement emphasizes the rapidity of contemporary consumption of movies. And because a subscriber preselects DVDs that are then sent automatically, this kind of distribution lacks the kind of social interaction that used to exist in video stores.

But such models still involve a material object that is literally distributed to viewers. As high-speed Internet made downloading movies and live streaming a consumer option, many sites began to provide such opportunities, and distribution confronted yet another set of challenges. If a movie is rented on demand, how many times can it be watched? On how many different devices? Unauthorized downloading and sharing became even more difficult for distributors to regulate. At the same time, new opportunities for viewing and for forming social relations around cinema were generated. Netflix updated its own model to allow subscribers to stream titles to both computers and televisions—by far its largest section of the market today. With the success of streaming and downloading, viewers may feel that they finally have overcome the limits set by distribution, even though economic decisions still shape the circulation of film.

This new ease of film consumption raises different questions about changing viewing patterns and their implications, however. Do these new paradigms undermine the social and communal formations of the overall film experience? Does increased ease of access to film traditions remote in time or location make for a richer film culture? Do more platforms actually result in more viewing options, or do many of these services redivide smaller slices of the same pie? Finally, how might these patterns influence and change the kinds of movies that are made? The answers to these questions are not clear or certain. Indeed, these new viewing patterns may simply offer different ways for audiences to create different kinds of communities based on their own interests. Similarly, the more open access to periods of film history or foreign film cultures may broaden our sense of both but also may require more work and research into those discovered times and places.

Many kinds of films—such as artists' films, activist documentaries, alternative media, and medical or industrial films—are made without the intention of showing them for a profit. Although many of these films are shown publicly, they are not shown in a traditional theatrical context and do not necessarily have access to commercial video or Internet distribution methods. Some of these works serve a specific training or promotional purpose and are distributed directly to their intended professional or target audience. Others may find television or educational distributors from PBS to Women Make Movies. Still others may be uploaded to the Internet.

Distribution Timing

Distribution timing—when a movie is released for public viewing in certain locations or on certain platforms—is another prominent and changing feature of distribution. Adding significantly to our experience of movies, timing can take advantage of the social atmosphere, cultural connotations, or critical scrutiny associated with particular seasons and calendar periods. The summer season and the December holidays are the most important in the United States because audiences usually have more free time to see thrill rides like *Speed* (1994) (Figure 1-16).

Figure 1-16. ***Speed*** (1994). Action movies intended as summer amusements have become central to the release calendar.

Offering a temporary escape from hot weather, a summer release like *Jurassic World* (2015) offers the visual thrills and fun of rampaging dinosaurs, a bit like an old-fashioned sci-fi movie and a bit like the amusement park that the film's plot depicts. The Memorial Day release of *Pearl Harbor* (2001) immediately attracts the sentiments and memories that Americans have of World War II and other global conflicts. The film industry is calculating releases ever more carefully—for example, by holding a promising film for a November release so that it can vie for prestigious (and business-generating) award nominations.

Mistiming a film's release can prove to be a major problem, as was the case in the summer of 2013, when the DreamWorks cartoon *Turbo* followed too close on the heels of *Monsters University* and *Despicable Me 2* to gain much traction with the family audience that all three were targeting. Avoiding unwanted competition can be a key part of a distributor's timing. Recently, distributors moved up the opening of *The Shallows* (2016) to capitalize on positive buzz and avoid Fourth of July weekend competition (Figure 1-17).

Figure 1-17. ***The Shallows*** (2016). Just a few weeks before the scheduled June 2016 release of the shark thriller ***The Shallows***, the studio moved its date up by five days to capitalize on rising excitement over the film.

Multiple Releases

Of the several other variations on the tactics of timing, movies sometimes follow a first release or first run with a second release or second run. The first describes a movie's premiere engagement, and the second refers to the redistribution of that film months or years later. After its first release in 1982, for example, Ridley Scott's *Blade Runner* made a notable reappearance in 1992 as a longer director's cut (Figure 1-18). Although the first release had only modest success, the second (supported by a surprisingly large audience discovered in the home video market) appealed to viewers newly attuned to the visual and narrative complexity of the movie. Audiences wanted to see, think about, and see again oblique and obscure details in order to decide, for instance, whether Deckard, the protagonist, was a replicant or a human.

For *Blade Runner*'s twenty-fifth anniversary in 2007, a final cut was released theatrically but catered primarily to DVD customers. With multiple releases, financial reward is no doubt a primary goal, as the trend to reissue films in anticipation of or following major awards like the Oscars indicates.

Figure 1-18. ***Blade Runner*** (1982, 1992, 2007). Although its initial opening was disappointing, Ridley Scott's dystopian "future noir" was an early success on home video. Theatrical releases of a director's cut for its tenth anniversary and a final cut for its twenty-fifth make the question of the film's definitive identity as interesting as the questions of human versus replicant identity posed by its plot.

With a film that may have been unavailable to viewers during its first release or that simply may not have been popular, a re-release can lend it new life and reclaim viewers through a process of rediscovery. When a small movie achieves unexpected popular or critical success or a major award, for example, it can be redistributed with a much wider distribution circuit and to a more eager, sympathetic audience that is already prepared to like the movie. In a version of this practice, Mira Nair's *Salaam Bombay!* (1988) was re-released in 2013 to commemorate the twenty-fifth anniversary of the stunning debut by this now-celebrated Indian filmmaker. A re-release also may occur in the attempt to offer audiences a higher-quality picture or a 3-D repackaging of an older film or to clarify story lines by restoring cut scenes, as was done in 1989 with Columbia Pictures' re-release of the 1962 Academy Award–winning *Lawrence of Arabia*.

Similarly, television distribution can retime the release of a movie to promote certain attitudes toward it. *It's a Wonderful Life* did not generate much of an audience when it was first released in 1946. Gradually (and especially after its copyright expired in 1975), network and cable television began to run the film regularly, and the film became a Christmas classic shown often and everywhere during that season (Figure 1-19). In 1997, however, the NBC television network reclaimed the exclusive rights to the film's network broadcast in order to limit its television distribution and to try to make audiences see the movie as a special event.

Figure 1-19. ***It's a Wonderful Life*** (1946). A box-office disappointment when it initially was released, Frank Capra's film became a ubiquitous accompaniment to the holiday season on television. In recent years, NBC's broadcast restrictions attempted to restore the film's status as an annual family viewing event.

Day-and-Date Release

The **theatrical release window** of a film—the period of time before its availability on home video, video on demand, or television platforms, during which it plays in movie theaters—has traditionally been about three to six months to guarantee box-office revenue. This period is becoming shorter and shorter. **Day-and-date release** refers to a simultaneous-release strategy across different media and venues, such as a theatrical release and VOD availability. This practice is now routine for many smaller distributors. Sometimes films from Magnolia Pictures, like the recent *High-Rise* (2015) (Figure 1-20), will debut on VOD platforms before their theatrical release. In the future, day-and-date release may go further. Napster cofounder Sean Parker has discussed the introduction of a device that would play brand-new wide releases in customers' homes as soon as they are available in movie theaters. Some filmmakers such as Christopher Nolan and James Cameron have denounced this idea, while others like Steven Spielberg and Martin Scorsese have encouraged it.

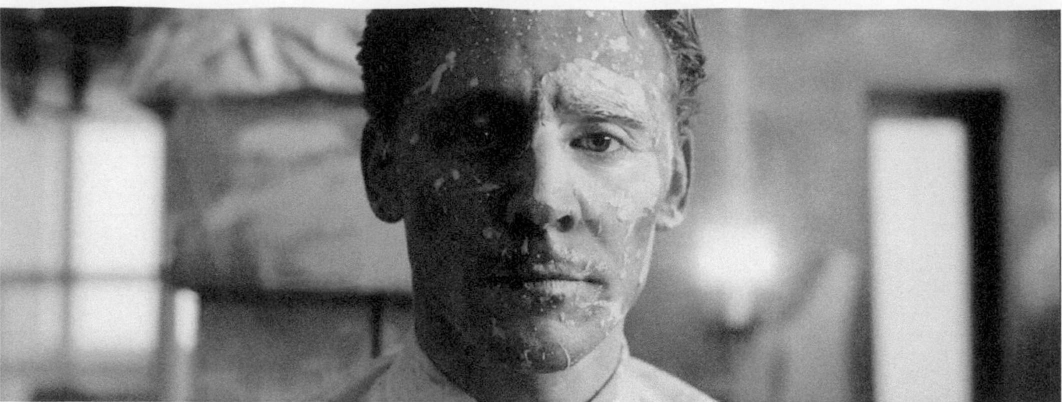

Figure 1-20. ***High-Rise*** (2015). Ben Wheatley's dystopian satire follows the inhabitants of an apartment building that is organized by class. Magnolia Pictures made the movie available both in select theaters and through video-on-demand outlets.

Whether or not this kind of distribution strategy actually announces a radical change in film distribution, it does signal the kinds of experimentation that digital production and distribution can allow and the inevitable changes and adjustments that will occur in the future in response to shifting markets, tastes, and technologies. Across the division between Nolan and Spielberg, it also suggests larger concerns about how these changes can affect our responses to films and the kinds of films that will be made.

Marketing and Promotion: What We Want to See

Why and how we are attracted to certain movies is directly shaped by the marketing and promotion that accompany distribution. A film might be advertised online as the work of a great director, for example, or it might be described as a steamy love story and illustrated with a sensational poster. A film trailer might emphasize the comedic aspect of an unusual or disturbing film like *The Lobster* (2016). Although these preliminary encounters with a film might seem marginally relevant to how we experience the film, promotional strategies, like distribution strategies, prepare us in important ways for how we will see and understand a film.

Generating Interest

Marketing and promotion aim to generate and direct interest in a movie. Film **marketing** identifies an audience for a specific product (in this case, a movie) and brings the product to its attention for consumption so that buyers will watch the product. Film **promotion** refers to the aspect of the industry through which audiences are exposed to and encouraged to see a particular film. It includes advertisements, trailers, publicity appearances, and product tie-ins. No doubt the **star system** is the most pervasive and potent component of the marketing and promotion of movies around the world. One or more well-known actors who are popular at a specific time and within a specific culture act as the advertising vehicle for the movie. The goal of the star system, like that of other marketing and promotional practices, is to create specific expectations that will draw an audience to a film. These marketing and promotional expectations—that Leonardo DiCaprio stars or that indie filmmaker Sarah Polley directs, for example—often become the view-finders through which an audience sees a movie.

The methods of marketing and promotion are many and creative. Viewers find themselves bombarded with newspaper and billboard advertisements, previews shown before the main feature, tie-in games featured on the official movie Web site, and trailers that appear when browsing the Internet. Stars make public appearances on radio and television talk shows and are profiled in fan magazines, and media critics attend early screenings and write reviews that are quoted in the ads for the film. All these actions contribute to movie promotion. In addition, although movies have long been promoted through prizes and gifts, modern distributors are especially adept at marketing films through **tie-ins**—ancillary products (such as soundtracks, toys, and other gimmicks made available at stores and restaurants) that advertise and promote a movie. *Minions* (2015), for example, was anticipated with an extensive line of toys and games that generated interest in the movie and vice versa.

Marketing campaigns for blockbuster films have become more and more extensive in recent years, with the promotion budget equaling and often even exceeding the film's production budget. A marketing blitz of note accompanied *Independence Day* (1996). Given its carefully timed release on July 3, 1996, following weeks of advertisements in newspapers and on television, it is difficult to analyze first-run viewers' feelings about this film without taking into account the influence of these promotions. Defining the film as a science fiction thriller, the advertisements and reviews drew attention to its status as the film event of the summer, its suitability for children, and its technological wizardry. Promoted and released to coincide with the Fourth of July holiday, *Independence Day* ads emphasized its patriotic American themes (Figure 1-21). In that light, many posters, advertisements, and publicity stills presented actor Will Smith together with Bill Pullman or Jeff Goldblum, not only to promote the film's stars but also to draw attention to the racial harmony achieved in the film and its appeal to both African American and white audiences. During the first month of its release, when U.S. scientists discovered a meteorite with fossils that suggested early life on Mars, promotion for the movie responded immediately with revised ads: "Last week, scientists found evidence of life on another planet. We're not going to say we told you so. . . ." In contrast, the 2016 sequel *Independence Day: Resurgence* never found a strong marketing hook and made far less money twenty years later.

Photofest, Inc.

Figure 1-21. ***Independence Day*** (1996). The film's massive promotional campaign for its Fourth of July weekend opening drew on blatant and subtle forms of patriotism, such as the multicultural appeal of its cast.

Some Hollywood promotions and advertisements emphasize the realism of movies, a strategy that promises audiences more accurate or more expansive reflections of the world and human experience. In *Silver Linings Playbook* (2012), a Bradley Cooper and Jennifer Lawrence film about a young man released from a mental institution, the struggle to cope with his bipolar disorder while living with his Philadelphia family was a reality that the film's promotions claimed had rarely before been presented in movies. A related marketing strategy is to claim textual novelty in a film, drawing attention to new features such as technical innovations, a rising star, or the acclaimed book on which the film is based. With early sound films like *The Jazz Singer* (1927), *The Gold Diggers of Broadway* (1929), and *Innocents of Paris* (1929), marketing advertisements directed audiences toward the abundance and quality of the singing and talking that added a dramatic new dimension to cinematic realism (Figure 1-22). Today promotions and advertisements frequently exploit new technologies. *Avatar*'s (2009) marketing campaign emphasized its new three-dimensional (3-D) technology. Marketers also can take advantage of current political events, as when they advertised the plot of Kathryn Bigelow's *Zero Dark Thirty* (2012), which told the story of the long international search for Osama bin Laden after September 11, 2001, by noting its timely encounter with debates and concerns around the use of torture and the killing of Osama bin Laden (Figure 1-23).

Figure 1-22. ***Innocents of Paris*** (1929). The marquee for the movie promotes the novelty of sound and song and this early musical's singing star.

As official promotion tactics, stars are booked to appear on talk shows and in other venues in conjunction with a film's release, but they may also bring unofficial publicity to a film. Brad Pitt and Angelina Jolie boosted audiences for the film *Mr. and Mrs. Smith* (2005) when they became a couple during its filming. Conversely, unwelcome publicity can cause an actor's contract to be canceled or raise concerns about the publicity's effect on ticket sales. Mel Gibson, for example, encountered difficulty finding big-studio work in Hollywood after his well-publicized personal troubles in 2010.

Figure 1-23. ***Zero Dark Thirty*** (2012). Topical interest in the hunt for Osama bin Laden, as well as the director's success with the similarly current ***The Hurt Locker*** (2008), fueled interest in Kathryn Bigelow's film.

Independent, art, revival, and foreign-language films have less access to the mechanisms of promotion than do current mainstream films, and social media have afforded new opportunities to spread the word to specialized audiences. In addition, audiences for these films are led to some extent by what we might call "cultural promotion"—academic or journalistic accounts that discuss and frequently value films as aesthetic objects or as especially important in movie history. A discussion of a movie in a film history book or a university film course thus could be seen as an act of marketing, which confirms that promotion is about urging viewers not just to see a film but also to see it with a particular point of view. Although these more measured kinds of promotion are usually underpinned by intellectual rather than financial motives, they also deserve our consideration and analysis.

How does a specific film history text, for instance, prepare you to see a film such as *Bonnie and Clyde* (1967)? Some books promote it as a modern gangster film. Others pitch it as an incisive reflection of the social history of the turbulent 1960s. Still other texts and essays may urge readers to see it because of its place in the oeuvre of a major U.S. director, Arthur Penn (Figure 1-24). Independent movies promote the artistic power and individuality of the director; associate themselves with big-name film festivals in Venice, Toronto, and Cannes; or call attention, through advertising, to what distinguishes them from mainstream Hollywood films. For a foreign film, a committed publicist can be crucial to its attaining distribution by attracting critical mention. Documentaries can be promoted in relation to the topical subject matter or controversy. In short, we do not experience any film with innocent eyes; consciously or not, we come prepared to see it in a certain way.

Figure 1-24. ***Bonnie and Clyde*** (1967). Critical accounts may position this film as an updated gangster film or as social commentary on the turbulent 1960s.

Advertising

Advertising is a central form of promotion that uses television, billboards, film trailers or previews, print ads, images and videos on Web sites, and other forms of display to bring a film to the attention of a potential audience. Advertising can use the facts in and issues surrounding a movie in various ways. Advertising often emphasizes connections with and differences from related or similar films or highlights the presence of a particularly popular actor or director. The poster for Charlie Chaplin's *The Kid* (1921), for example, proudly pronounces that it is "the great Film he has been working on for a whole year" (Figure 1-25). For different markets, *Prometheus* (2012) was promoted as a star vehicle for Sweden's Noomi Rapace or as the latest film from Ridley Scott, the director of *Alien* (1979), *Blade Runner* (1982), *Thelma & Louise* (1991), and *Black Hawk Down* (2001). It is conceivable that these two promotional tactics created different sets of expectations about the movie—one more attuned to tough female protagonists and the other to lavish sets and technological landscapes. As this example reveals, promotion tends both to draw us to a movie and also to suggest what we will concentrate on as a way of understanding its achievement.

Courtesy Everett Collection

Figure 1-25. ***The Kid*** (1921). Unlike posters for his well-known slapstick comedies, this poster shows Charlie Chaplin displaying a demeanor that suggests the serious themes of his first feature film.

Trailers

One of the most carefully crafted forms of promotional advertising is the **trailer**—a form of promotional advertising that previews edited images and scenes from a film in theaters before the main feature film, in television commercials, or on Web sites. In just a few minutes, the trailer provides a compact series of reasons that a viewer should see that movie. A trailer for Stanley Kubrick's *Eyes Wide Shut* (1999) is indicative of this form of advertising: it moves quickly to large bold titles announcing separately the names of Tom Cruise, Nicole Kidman, and Kubrick, foregrounding the collaboration of a star marriage and a celebrated director of daring films. Then, against the refrain from Chris Isaak's soundtrack song "Baby Did a Bad Bad Thing," a series of images condenses the progress of the film, including shots of Kidman undressing, Cruise sauntering with two beautiful women, the two stars sharing a passionate kiss, two ominous-looking men standing at the gate of an estate, and Cruise being enticed by a prostitute. Besides the provocative match of two, then-married star sex symbols with a controversial director, the trailer underlines the dark erotic mysteries of the film within an opulently decadent setting. It introduces intensely sexual characters and the alternately seedy and glamorous atmosphere of the film in a manner meant to draw fans of Cruise, Kidman, Kubrick, and erotic intrigue (Figure 1-26). That this promotion fails to communicate the stinging irony in the movie's eroticism may account for some of the disappointed reactions that followed its eager initial reception. The availability of trailers on the Internet has increased the novel approaches to this format, and trailers are now rated and scrutinized like theatrical releases.

Figure 1-26. ***Eyes Wide Shut*** (1999). Advertisements and trailers for Stanley Kubrick's last film emphasized the film's director, its stars—Tom Cruise and Nicole Kidman, who were married at the time—and its sexual content.

Media Convergence

Movie advertising has always targeted consumers' changing habits and has adapted strategies for this era of **media convergence**—the process by which formerly distinct media (such as cinema, television, the Internet, and video games) and viewing platforms (such as television, computers, and cell phones) become interdependent. A viewer might find and play an online game set in a film's fictional world on the film's Web site, read a comic-book tie-in, and watch an online promotion with the films' stars, all before viewing the movie in a theater. Indeed, the enormous sums spent on marketing a film's theatrical release are deemed worthwhile because they relate directly to the promotion of other media elements within the brand or franchise, such as video games, books, music, and DVD releases. Viewers understand these tactics and may participate in this convergence: a viewer who enjoys a film and its soundtrack might download a ringtone for her cell phone and place the title in her Netflix queue in anticipation of its release on DVD months later. But viewers may also decide to skip the theatrical release altogether and catch the film later on video on demand or DVD.

The enormous popularity of social networking sites has fostered the technique of **viral marketing**—a process of advertising that relies on existing social networks to spread a marketing message by word of mouth, electronic messaging, or other means. Because viral marketing works through networks of shared interest, it is less dependent than conventional promotional techniques on market research and can be a highly effective and informative indicator of audience preferences. Yet it is also less easily controlled than deliberately placed ads that are based on target demographics. In many ways, media convergence has allowed today's viewers to affect how films are understood and produced more than viewers did in years past.

The Hollywood studios made a production distinction between an **A picture** (a feature film with a large budget and prestigious source material or actors that has been historically promoted as a main attraction receiving top billing) and a **B picture** (a low-budget, non-prestigious movie that usually played on the bottom half of a double bill). Just as today the term **blockbuster** (a big-budget film intended for wide release, whose large investment in stars, special effects, and advertising attracts large audiences and big profits) prepares us for action, stars, and special effects, and **art film** (a film produced primarily for aesthetic rather than commercial or entertainment purposes, whose intellectual or formal challenges are often attributed to the vision of an auteur) suggests a more visually subtle, perhaps slower-paced or more intellectually demanding movie, the terminology used to define and promote a movie can become a potent force in framing our expectations.

The Rating System

Rating systems, which provide viewers with guidelines for movies (usually based on violent or sexual content), are a similarly important form of advertising that can be used in marketing and promotion. Whether they are wanted or unwanted by viewers, ratings are fundamentally about trying to control the kind of audience that sees a film and, to a certain extent, about advertising the content of that film.

In the United States, the current Motion Picture Association of America (MPAA) ratings system classifies movies as G (general audiences), PG (parental guidance suggested), PG-13 (parental guidance suggested and not recommended for audiences under thirteen years old), R (persons under age seventeen must be accompanied by an adult), and NC-17 (persons under age seventeen are not admitted). Films made outside the major studios are not required to obtain MPAA ratings, but exhibition and even advertising opportunities are closely tied to the system.

Other countries, as well as some religious organizations, have their own systems for rating films. Great Britain, for instance, uses these categories: U (universal), A (parental discretion), AA (persons under age fourteen are not admitted), and X (persons under age eighteen are not admitted). The age limit for X-rated films varies from country to country, the lowest being age fifteen in Sweden.

A project like *The Peanuts Movie* (2015), an animated adaptation of the famous comic strip, depends on its G rating to draw large family audiences, whereas sexually explicit films like Steve McQueen's *Shame* (2011), rated NC-17 for its explicit sexual content, and Nagisa Oshima's *In the Realm of the Senses* (1976), not rated and confiscated when it first came to many countries, can use the notoriety of their ratings to attract curious adult viewers. An NC-17 rating can damage a film's box-office prospects, however, because many outlets will not advertise such films. Many mainstream movies eagerly seek out a middle ground. Movies like *Ghostbusters* (2016) prefer a PG-13 rating because it attracts a young audience of eight-, nine-, and ten-year-olds who want movies with some adult language and action (Figure 1-27).

Figure 1-27. ***Ghostbusters*** (2016). A PG-13 rating can suggest a certain edge to a film that makes it attractive to preteens without alienating older viewers.

Word of Mouth and Fan Engagement

Our experiences when viewing a movie are shaped in advance in less evident and predictable ways as well. Word of mouth—the oral or written exchange of opinions and information sometimes referred to as the "buzz" around a movie—may seem to be an insignificant or vague area of promotion, yet our likes and dislikes are formed and given direction by the social groups we move in. Social networking sites that allow us to list or indicate our likes and dislikes with a click have expanded these social groups exponentially. We know that our friends like certain kinds of films, and we tend to enjoy and promote movies according to the values of our particular age group, cultural background, or other social determinant. When marketing experts promote a movie to a target audience, they intend to do so through word of mouth or "virally," knowing that viewers communicate with one another and recommend films to people who share their values and tastes (Figures 1-28a and 1-28b).

(a) (b)

Figure 1-28. ***Titanic*** (1997). Word of mouth anticipating the release of James Cameron's film focused on special effects. After the film's release, word of mouth among young female fans was appreciative of its star Leonardo DiCaprio and its romance plot.

Consider, for instance, how friends who enjoyed the novel might have discussed the making of the film *The Hunger Games* (2012). Would they be excited about the casting of rising star Jennifer Lawrence as the tough young heroine? About the genre of science fiction films set in a dystopian future and the potential for interesting visual effects? About other books by Suzanne Collins with which they are familiar? What would each of these word-of-mouth promotions indicate about the social or personal values of the person promoting the movie and the culture of taste influencing his or her views?

Fan magazines were an early extension of word of mouth as a form of movie promotion and have consistently shed light on the sociology of taste. Emerging in the 1910s and widely popular by the 1920s, such "fanzines" brought film culture home to audience members. Posing as objective accounts, many stories were actually produced by the studios' publicity departments. Those print fan magazines have evolved into Internet discussion groups, promotional and user-generated Web sites, social media accounts, and other fan activities, which have become an even bigger force in film promotion and culture. In fact, Web sites, often set up by a film's distributor, have become the most powerful contemporary form of the fanzine, allowing information about and enthusiasm for a movie to be efficiently exchanged and spread among potential viewers. Notoriously, the title *Snakes on a Plane* (2006) was so resonant with viewers in its very literalness that the Web activity around the film (even before its release) prompted changes to make the film more daring and campier. The subsequent box-office disappointment may have been a measure of viewers' reaction to marketing manipulations.

To encourage and develop individual interest in films, these fanzines and Web sites gather together readers and viewers who wish to read or chat about their ongoing interest in movies like the *Star Trek* films (1979–2016) or cult favorites like *Casablanca* (1942) or who wish to share fan productions. Here tastes about which movies to like and dislike and about how to see them are supported and promoted on a concrete social and commercial level. Information is offered or exchanged about specific movies, arguments are waged, and fan fiction or user-generated videos are developed around the film. Magazines may provide information about the signature song of *Casablanca*, "As Time Goes By," and the actor who sings it, Dooley Wilson. Message board participants may query each other about Mr. Spock's Vulcan history or fantasize about his personal life. The Internet promotes word of mouth about a film by offering potential audiences the possibility of some participation in the making of the film, an approach that is increasingly common today.

As they proliferate, promotional avenues like these deserve attention and analysis to try to determine how they add to or confuse our understanding of a film. Our different experiences of the movies take place within a complex cultural terrain where our personal interest in certain films intersects with specific historical and social forces to shape the meaning and value of those experiences. Here, too, the film experience extends well beyond the big screen.

Movie Exhibition: The Where, When, and How of Movie Experiences

Exhibition is the part of the industry that shows films to a paying public, usually in movie theaters. It may involve promotional elements like movie posters and publicity events in a theater lobby or be related to distribution through the calendar of film releasing. But exhibition, which is closely tied to **reception**—the process through which individual viewers or groups make sense of a film—is at the heart of the film experience. **Exhibitors** own individual theaters or theater chains and make decisions about programming and local promotion. They are responsible for the actual experience of moviegoing, including the concessions that make a night out at the movies different from one spent watching films at home and that bring in an estimated 40 percent of theater owners' revenue. Like distribution and promotion, we may take exhibition for granted, forgetting that the many ways we watch movies contribute a great deal to our feelings about, and our interpretations of, film. We watch movies within a cultural range of exhibition venues—in theaters, at home on video monitors, or on a plane or train on portable devices. Not surprisingly, these contexts and technologies anticipate and condition our responses to movies.

The Changing Contexts and Practices of Film Exhibition

Very different kinds of film response can be elicited by seeing the same movie at a cineplex or in a college classroom or by watching it uninterrupted for two hours on a big screen or in thirty-minute segments over four days on a computer. A viewer watching a film on an airplane monitor may be completely bored by it, but watching it later at home, he or she may find the film much more compelling and appreciate its visual surprises and interesting plot twists.

Movies have been distributed, exhibited, and seen in many different contexts historically. At the beginning of the twentieth century, movies rarely lasted more than twenty minutes and often were viewed in small, noisy **nickelodeons**—store-front theaters or arcade spaces where short films were shown continuously for a five-cent admission price to audiences passing in and out—or in carnival settings that assumed movies were a passing amusement comparable to other attractions. By the 1920s, as movies grew artistically, financially, and culturally, the exhibition of films moved to lavish **movie palaces** like Radio City Music Hall (which opened in 1932), with sumptuous seating for thousands amid ornate architecture. By the 1950s, city centers gave way to suburban sprawl, theaters lost their crowds of patrons, and drive-ins and widescreen and 3-D processes were introduced to distinguish the possibilities of film exhibition from its new rival, television at home. Soon television became a way to experience movies as special events in the flow of daily programming. In the 1980s, VCRs gave home audiences access to many movies and the ability to watch them when and how they wished, and the **multiplex**, a movie theater complex with many screens, became increasingly important as a way to integrate a choice of moviegoing experiences with an outing to the mall.

Today we commonly view movies at home on a disc player or computer screen, where we can watch them in the standard ninety- to 120-minute period, extend our viewing over many nights, or rewatch favorite or puzzling portions of them. Portable devices such as laptops, smartphones, and tablet computers give a new mobility to our viewing. As theaters continue to compete with home screens, film exhibitors have countered with so-called megaplexes—theaters with twenty or more screens, more than six thousand seats, and over a hundred showtimes per day. These new entertainment complexes may feature not just movies but also arcade games, restaurants, and coffee bars. Home exhibition has responded in turn with more elaborate digital picture and sound technologies and convergence between devices such as game consoles and television screens for streaming movies.

Figure 1-29. ***Zootopia*** (2016). Family films are distributed widely to theater chains and exhibited in early time slots, although some become crossover hits.

Technologies and Cultures of Exhibition

Viewing forums—the locations where we watch a movie—contribute to the wider culture of exhibition space and the social activities that surround and define moviegoing. Theatrical exhibition highlights a social dimension of watching movies because it gathers and organizes individuals as a specific audience at a specific place and time. Further, our shared participation in that social environment directs our attention and shapes our responses.

A movie such as *Zootopia* (2016) will be shown as a Saturday matinee in suburban theaters (as well as other places) to attract families with children to its talking-animal adventure (Figure 1-29). The time and place of the showing coordinate with a period when families can share recreation, making them more inclined to appreciate this empowering tale of societal harmony and self-confidence. Conversely, Peter Greenaway's *The Pillow Book* (1996), a complex film about a woman's passion for calligraphy, human flesh, poetry, and sex, would likely appear in a small urban theater frequented by individuals and young couples or groups of friends who also spend time in the theater's coffee bar (Figure 1-30). This movie probably would appeal to an urban crowd with experimental tastes and to those who like to watch intellectually stimulating and conversation-provoking films. Reversing the exhibition contexts of these two films would indicate how those contexts could generate wildly different reactions. The technological conditions of exhibition—that is, the industrial and mechanical vehicles through which movies are shown—shape the viewer's reaction as well, with screen sizes and locations varying widely from experience to experience.

Figure 1-30. ***The Pillow Book*** (1996). Art films, especially those that receive an NC-17 rating, are likely to be distributed primarily to specialty cinemas in urban locations.

Different technological features of exhibition are sometimes carefully calculated to add to both our enjoyment and our understanding of a movie. Cecil B. DeMille's epic film *The Ten Commandments* (1923) premiered in a movie palace, where the plush and grandiose surroundings, the biblical magnitude of the images, and the orchestral accompaniment supported the grand spiritual themes of the film. Thus the conditions for watching a film may parallel its ideas or formal practices. With the special projection techniques and 3-D glasses worn for *Creature from the Black Lagoon* (1954), the creature's appearance becomes even more startling. 3-D technology is an excellent example of changing exhibition technologies and cultures (Figure 1-31). Long regarded nostalgically as a gimmick of the 1950s, it made a comeback with state-of-the-art digital movie production and exhibition with the technology developed for *Avatar* (2009). Theater owners worldwide converted screens in order to show the film and to attract local audiences with the novelty of the spectacle. As a result, digital projection is now more prevalent than 35mm film.

Bettmann/Getty Images

Figure 1-31. 3-D exhibition. Viewers enjoy a screening with special 3-D glasses in the 1950s, the first heyday of the technology. As a technological innovation, 3-D brings the focus to exhibition contexts and offers a chance for theater owners to increase revenue.

In contrast to viewing technologies that attempt to enhance the spectacular nature of the big-screen experience are those that try to maximize (sometimes by literally minimizing) the uniquely personal encounter with the film image. Consumers have adapted quickly as distinct media (such as cinema, television, the Internet, and video games) and viewing platforms (such as television, computers, and cell phones) have become commercially, technologically, and culturally interdependent.

The Timing of Exhibition

Whereas distribution timing determines when a film is made available and in what format, the timing of exhibition is a more personal dimension of the movie experience. When and for how long we watch a film can shape how it affects us and what our attitude toward it is as much as where we see the film and with whom. Although it is common to see movies in the early evening, either before or after dinner, audiences watch movies of different kinds according to numerous rituals and in various time slots. Afternoon matinees, midnight movies, or in-flight movies on long plane rides give some indication of how the timing of a movie experience can vary and how that can influence other considerations about the movie. In each of these situations, our experience of the movies includes a commitment to spend time in a certain way. Instead of spending time reading, talking with others, sleeping, or working on a business project, we watch a movie. That time spent with a movie accordingly becomes an activity associated with relaxing, socializing, or even working in a different way.

Leisure Time

Traditionally, movie culture has emphasized film exhibition as leisure time, a time that is assumed to be less productive than time spent working and that reinforces assumptions about movies as the kind of enjoyment associated with play and pleasure. To some extent, leisure time is a relatively recent historical development. Since the nineteenth century, when motion pictures first appeared, modern society has aimed to organize experience so that work and leisure could be separated and defined in relation to each other. We generally identify leisure time as an "escape," "the relaxation of our mind and body," or "the acting out of a different self." Since the early twentieth century, movie exhibition has been associated with leisure time in these ways. Seeing a comedy on a Friday night promises relaxation at the end of a busy week. Playing a concert film on a DVD player while eating dinner may relieve mental fatigue. Watching a romantic film on television late at night may offer the passion missing from one's real life.

Productive Time

Besides leisure time, however, we can and should consider film exhibition as productive time—time used to gain information, material advantage, or knowledge. From the early years of the cinema, movies have been used to illustrate lectures or introduce audiences to Shakespearean performances. Educational films like those shown in health classes or driver education programs are less glamorous versions of this use of film. Although less widely acknowledged as part of film exhibition, productive time continues to shape certain kinds of film exhibition. For a movie reviewer or film producer, an early-morning screening may be about "financial value" because this use of time to evaluate a movie will presumably result in certain economic rewards. For another person, a week of films at an art museum represents "intellectual value" because it helps explain ideas about a different society or historical period. For a young American, an evening watching *Schindler's List* (1993) can be about "human value" because that film aims to make viewers more knowledgeable about the Holocaust and more sensitive to the suffering of other human beings.

The timing of exhibitions may frame and emphasize the film experience according to certain values. The Cannes Film Festival introduces a wide range of films and functions both as a business venue for buying and selling film and as a glamorous showcase for stars and parties. The May timing of this festival and its French Riviera location ensure that the movie experience will be about pleasure and the business of leisure time. In contrast, the New York Film Festival, featuring some of the same films, has a more intellectual or academic aura. It occurs in New York City during September and October, at the beginning of the academic year and the calendars of arts organizations, which associates this experience of the movies more with artistic value and productive time.

Classroom, library, and museum exhibitions tend to emphasize understanding and learning as much as enjoyment. When students watch films in these kinds of situations, they are asked to attend to them somewhat differently from the way they may view films on a Friday night at the movies. They watch more carefully, perhaps; they may consider the films as part of historical or artistic traditions; they may take notes as a logical part of this kind of exhibition. These conditions of film exhibition do not necessarily change the essential meaning of a movie; but in directing how we look at a film, they can certainly shade and even alter how we understand it. Exhibition asks us to engage and think about the film not as an isolated object but as part of the expectations established by the conditions in which we watch it.

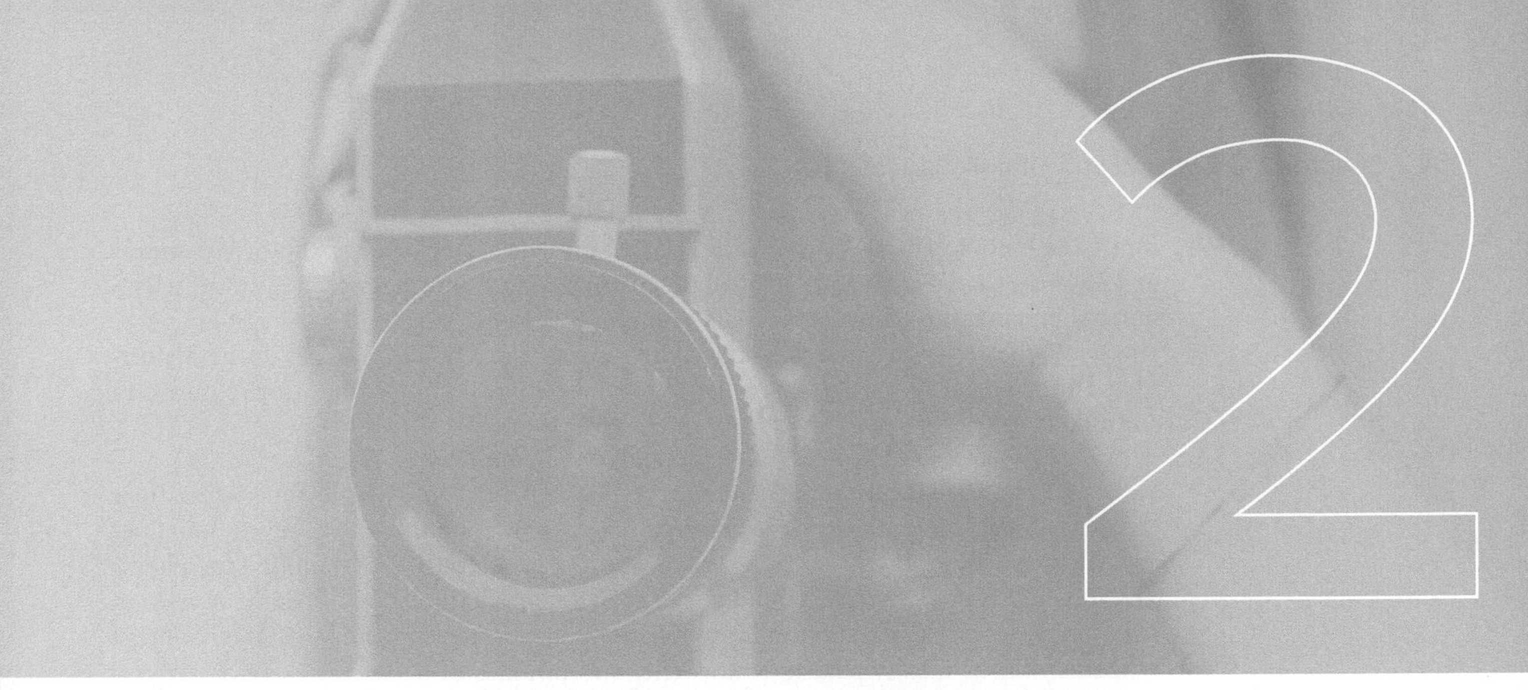

Chapter 2

Television and Film Management

The Blended Media Economy

"The Blended Economy" from *Media in Society,* by Richard Campbell, Joli Jensen, Douglas Gomery, Bettina Fabos, and Julie Frechette, pp. 165–190 (Chapter 7, "Media Economics").

Two days before Valentine's Day 2004, a battle for the Walt Disney Company—among the world's most well-known corporations—ensued that had wide ramifications for the future of media consolidation. Comcast, the largest cable provider in the United States, had put out a $66 billion unsolicited bid for Disney.[1] Michael Eisner, then Disney's chief operating officer, was under attack for the company's poor financial showing since 2000. He fought back for months to keep Disney a separate corporation. Although Eisner would eventually be forced out by Disney's unhappy board of directors in 2005, the company rebuffed Comcast's takeover plans.

But Comcast did not give up. In late 2009, Comcast paid more than $13 billion to General Electric for a 51 percent interest in NBC Universal. Then in 2013 Comcast bought the rest of NBC Universal for $16.7 billion. Comcast today earns the bulk of its revenue from television, Internet, and digital phone services offered in forty states; with eighteen million subscribers to its broadband Internet and cable services, it far outpaced second-place cable company Time Warner by 2013.

Who owns the media, how they operate these corporations—for profits—and how they fit institutionally into our democracy tell us that business takeover attempts matter. The Comcast/NBC Universal deal pushed to the forefront questions about how Disney, GE, and Comcast operate in cultural, political, and social arenas. Comcast owning NBC and the Universal movie studio means fewer owners controlling fewer companies. (Similarly, Comcast acquiring Disney would have changed not only Disney movies but also ABC-TV, ESPN, and all the other Disney and Comcast networks and properties.) Adding Comcast's control of NBC to Disney's ownership of ABC and New Corp.'s ownership of Fox means that fewer powerful companies control the distribution of information on network television—the place where most Americans still go for their national and international news. This could mean that negative news concerning a company's holdings might not get reported at a time when we need to know what corporate control of news and stories means in our digital age.

Mass media corporations are everywhere, and we spend considerable time using their products. For instance, the average home still has a TV set on more than seven hours per day. We measure the costs of creating media in millions of dollars: $500 million for a high-tech movie like *Avatar*, over $1 million per episode for Charlie Sheen when he starred in *Two and a Half Men*, and multimillion-dollar annual contracts for newscasters like Brian Williams, who is mainly paid to read twenty-two minutes of network news five nights a week, attracting about five to six million viewers each evening in 2013. For consumers, the media cost more and more to acquire—for example, $70 to $80 per month for a cable broadband connection, or $500 for a new high-definition TV set. To reach us, advertisers spend billions of dollars each year on television. The hardest of the corporations to analyze are media conglomerates—that is, many media under one corporate umbrella. For instance, various versions of *CSI*, the most popular TV franchise of the early to mid-2000s, were made by the Paramount Pictures studio in Hollywood, under a CBS productions unit, and shown on CBS. All of these units (and more) were owned and operated at the time by one media conglomerate: Viacom, Inc. But in late 2005, Viacom split into two separate companies, although Viacom chairman Sumner Redstone still held controlling interest in both companies in 2013. More intriguing, Viacom was actually created by CBS in 1970 when the Federal Communication Commission (FCC) made the network get rid of its syndication business. Viacom became that new business and made a fortune in the early 1990s syndicating old *Cosby Show* reruns, which helped it swallow (or at least control) its original parent—CBS.

In this chapter, we consider how to understand the economic aspects of mass media in society, primarily at the level of the corporation. Our goals are to understand what economic control and operation mean for the diversity of voices that speak to us all and for the operation of democracy, examining in particular who owns the corporations that provide us with the entertainment, news, and information; what is at stake when media operations change; and what forms of media ownership and operation consumers should expect in our mass mediated world. In examining media industries as collections of businesses, we pose questions to help understand how media companies—structured as money-making business enterprises—interact with our democratic and cultural interests. So why do corporations offer us, for example, particular types of television or music or movies or Web sites? Can media companies make a profit covering political events and key social issues related to the functioning of our democracy? And if not, who will report on these events and issues? And in the end, what kinds of media businesses would we like to have?

Media Corporations and Economic Analysis

Usually we see types of media corporations defined by their technology, such as the broadcast television corporation, the film company, or the music business. But that confuses the functions of the corporations. A more productive way of thinking about media corporations is to divide them by the three most common types of industry structures (i.e., collections of corporations offering similar products or services):

1. monopoly (domination by a single company)
2. oligopoly (domination by a few—usually four to seven—big corporations)
3. competition (many companies vying in the marketplace)

Over the post decade, mass media corporate power and influence have increased as fewer and fewer corporations face true competition; the most typical media market structure today is oligopoly. Local or regional monopolies exist, as in the one cable company (or newspaper) most of us have in our communities, but we must also consider other multichannel television services such as direct broadcast satellite or WiMax. How do we best go about analyzing the economics of the mass media industries? In this section, we offer three approaches to critiquing media business: Marxist analysis, free-market analysis, and industrial analysis. We find industrial analysis the most appropriate model, but discuss the other two for context.[2]

Marxist Analysis

Although Marxist forms of criticism have been adopted by many critics and meandered in many directions since the mid-nineteenth century, the basic idea is captured in the preface to Karl Marx's *A Contribution to the Critique of Political Economy*, first published in 1859: "The mode of production of material life conditions the social, political, and intellectual life process in general. It is not the consciousness of men that determines their being, but on the contrary, their social being that determines their consciousness."[3] To illustrate this, Marx created a "base/superstructure" model or metaphor to explain the idea that the quality of the social life of a people or nation is driven by their economic conditions. This economic foundation or "infrastructure" for Marx supports a "superstructure" that includes the ideas, laws, politics, religions, ethics, art, literature, and various media in a society. But according to Marx, the superstructure also houses "social consciousness," or what is most frequently referred to as **ideology**. As literary critic Terry Eagleton has explained: "The function of ideology . . . is to legitimize the power of the ruling class in society; in the last analysis, the dominant ideas of a society are the ideas of its ruling class."[4] All sorts of able critics have since deployed Marxist ideas and theories to study the ways dominant groups and ruling elites in any society maintain their power (and oppress subordinate groups) by controlling the "modes of production," or economic conditions.

Offering some of the most penetrating analyses of modern society, Marxist criticism has long viewed the influential cultural industry—that is, a collection of media corporations—as a classic example of monopolistic capitalism in which the economic control over media production determines the type of media any society gets. Many critics coming from this perspective, however, do not analyze or try to understand the full complexities of media corporations but simply assume they possess negative characteristics associated with the kind of capitalism that Marxists generally oppose (negative, in part, because capitalist managers, in order to sustain their control, conceal their machinations from their workers and the masses, who are exploited as the managers and bosses rake in profits). They focus on how these long-lived corporations have colluded to devise ways to maintain their economic power and cultural imperialism. So, for example, while capitalist corporate leaders and Hollywood celebrated Twentieth Century Fox and Paramount's co-financing of the blockbuster film *Titanic*, many Marxist critics saw this movie mega-hit as yet another example of studios working together—not competing—to best exploit their product and maximize profits, which they would share. So the film's producers cared not at all about the film's social, cultural, or democratic implications.

Marxist economists generally focus on the corporate propensity toward concentration of ownership that they consider central to monopoly capitalism. Marxist analysts stress the inevitable rise and continuation of giant corporations and how they seem to take over more mass media production, distribution, and use. They assume corporate stability and concentration and ignore that companies do fight for profits against one another: Think of the ongoing cable war that rages between Fox News (owned by News Corp.) and MSNBC (owned by Comcast). Look too at the recent fights between Fox and Time Warner over how much cable companies should be paying to carry regular local and network broadcast signals.

Traditional Marxist critics may also overlook that corporations seek to differentiate their offerings and to deploy new technologies in doing so. So, for example, Marxist thinking cannot easily reconcile the rise of Amazon.com or Google because such digital companies follow different, more complicated paths to industry domination than earlier media industries. Corporations also go in and out of business. RCA, for example, was once the most influential media company in the world but now exists only as a brand name leased by other companies. Similarly, AOL's 2001 takeover of Time Warner was ultimately a catastrophic failure and the powerful Tribune Media Company ended up in bankruptcy from late 2008 through 2012. Given these few examples, we need analytical approaches that can better explain the new possibilities for configuring media and the failure of old but once-strong capitalist models (some of which failed mightily without a workers revolt). We can't assume the continuing and ever-growing power of any media company.

Although Marxist analysis often demonstrates how media companies maintain their power while revealing very little of the production process to consumers and citizens, such analyses are not as strong in interpreting how a TV show or Hollywood film tells stories and makes sense to fans and audiences—who, first of all, may ignore these cultural products and, second, may interpret them in complex ways that the managers of media never intended. In addition, some Marxist analyses are not able to account for the high failure rate among new media products in the marketplace—as high as 80 and 90 percent in most years, a figure that does not support the stereotype of duped consumers buying everything that's heavily marketed but instead says that many consumers are discerning, not so easily seduced by the slick lure of advertising and promotion. Many of us resist buying what corporations are selling.

Free-Market Economics

Competition and choice lie at the heart of the second analysis model: free-market media economics. The free-market "bible" is Adam Smith's *An Inquiry into the Nature and Causes of the Wealth of Nations*, published in 1776.[5] Smith made the key point that under the right conditions free markets will produce the greatest wealth for nations that enable them. Later advocates of free-market competition have stressed that corporations offer a wide array of choices and that in an open and supposedly free marketplace, the media products that customers want will rise to the top while inferior products (and companies) will fail. For example, they might emphasize that no one was forced to go see *Avatar* and that the movie's producer-distributor, Twentieth Century Fox, created a superior media product that rose above the pack of inferior forms of mass culture when the film premiered in December 2009. The consumers had the choice to spend their money and time reading a book, magazine, or newspaper; watching programming on a hundred cable channels; listening to dozens of radio stations; cruising the Internet; or playing their favorite CD or DVD—but they chose to watch the film instead. Free-market economists assert as the very basis of their analysis this consumer sovereignty of choice and assume that no mass media company can force anyone to do or buy anything. Following Adam Smith, Alfred Marshall focused on the forces of supply and demand, seeing movie theater box office receipts or TV ratings as classic voting booths (i.e., customers "vote" with their dollars) where top films and TV programs win and unpopular movies or television stories fail to attract audiences.

What this analysis does not acknowledge is that this product diversity will often come from the same mass media conglomerate. One can see, for example, on a Time Warner channel such as TNT, CNN, or TCM, a variety of entertainment from science fiction to westerns, from reality shows to "infomercials," from dramas to comedies, from around-the-clock news to documentaries (all sometimes airing on a Time Warner cable system). But these choices all emerge from decisions made by a handful of corporate managers reporting to a corporate chief operating officer. Not recognizing this control, free marketers' overemphasis on choice reads like a predetermined pro-capitalist assumption, where profit trumps democracy and its concerns every time, in the same manner that many Marxist-based analyses start with the presumption that capitalism is essentially a bad or corrupt system. Instead of these two choices, we need analysis that starts with no predetermined answers.[6]

Industrial Economics

Industrial economists begin with neither pro- nor anticapitalistic assumptions, and instead seek to first define who owns the media, analyze what economic conduct emerges from that industrial structure, then examine how the industry performs given specified criteria, and finally recommend—if needed—possible public policy corrections to make the industry more accountable to consumers and citizens.

Industrial economists long have recognized, for example, the common tools mass media corporations use to maintain their considerable economic power and keep out competition. The key has been to use what companies refer to as **economies of scale**—spreading costs over many outlets and thereby reducing the price of a single unit or product. If, for example, a single local TV station produced one drama series for its own schedule, it would take on the whole cost of an expensive one-hour production. But a typical U.S. TV network—like ABC, CBS, NBC, or Fox—helps produce programs that air on 200-plus affiliated stations, spreading the costs around, harnessing the best talent at a central site (the network—which usually is a subsidiary in an entertainment conglomerate that also owns a giant film studio that can make TV shows), and commanding large national audiences for which advertisers

pay top dollar rather than much cheaper ad rates that the single local TV station could charge for its smaller local drama (which would also lack the high production values and top talent that a national network can attract).

Another argument maintains that media conglomerates—those that, like Time Warner or Disney, own units in every form of media production and distribution—can cross-subsidize, extracting profits from one thriving area to prop up another less financially successful area. Their film divisions—especially with a James Cameron movie like *Avatar* (as of 2013, the highest-grossing movie of all time, taking in $2.8 billion worldwide)[7]—might have a good year that offsets a poor performance in the music or publishing divisions within the same time frame. Single-line corporations (like an independent film company that makes a very small number of films each year) do not have this luxury. Thus, aspiring single-line corporate operations are invariably rare and even when they do succeed are usually bought up by larger companies. Corporations now *vertically integrate*, a process where, say, Time Warner and Disney make movies and, after the theatrical runs are finished, run them on their cable channels—thus "selling" to themselves. Another example would be the major TV networks (all now owned by companies with film studios) producing their own prime-time TV shows, running them on their own networks (or selling them to one another, as when Twentieth Century Fox produces *How I Met Your Mother* for air on CBS rather than the Fox network). These practices cut out the middle agent and save these large media corporations, who mostly just compete with each other, some major costs.

The objective of recommending industrial media economics is not to make us all into applied economists but rather to examine how economic forces determine what corporations own, how they operate, and how they control storytelling. This understanding allows us to make social and cultural judgments about how corporations are acting as players in society— and what kinds of stories they are telling and selling. The industrial media economists do not seek to value, as Marxists and free-market economists do, one form or another of corporate action. Instead, the industrial economist can suggest an array of public policy alternatives to correct identified deficiencies. Logically, the question industrial media economists turn to is how to judge the economic actions of media firms—from the largest, like Disney and Comcast, to the smallest, where a single individual runs an informational Web site.

Media Corporations and Performance Norms

In the end, industrial analysis of the ownership and operation of media corporations requires us to develop criteria for how corporations are performing in our economy, society, and culture. Developing explicit criteria helps us examine whether the media marketplace is working or not and to judge how corporations should behave in a democracy. If the industry is not performing well, we label this "market failure" and need to propose remedies to force better performance. Scholar Denis McQuail has suggested media performance norms that encompass most judgments. Some are easy to apply; others do not lend themselves to easy judgments. In the following section, the first criteria considered are easier to apply than those further down on the list. These are all value judgments, and the order does not reflect our priorities as authors—and perhaps not yours, as readers. We believe these values ought to promote democratic priorities, as much as possible, to work as well as possible.[8]

Facilitating Free Speech and Political Discussion

First, citizens in democracies ought to argue that media industries should facilitate free speech and political discussion. A democracy needs freedom of expression to make it work, and both noncommercial and commercial media ought to be open enough to promote debate of all points of view. The marketplace of ideas calls for criteria in which information and data are evidence-based, accurate, and comprehensive. But is this best done by letting media corporations pursue profits first and foremost—never considering noneconomic issues? Probably not. This is the cause of debate over the sensitive issue of government intervention in political speech supported by wealthy donors and companies versus the needs of a profit-maximizing economy.

For example, the ongoing loss of traditional reporting jobs and news companies led in 2010 to congressional hearings and major debates over the possible need of government support in subsidizing journalism at a time when the old advertising-based business models had broken down. Unlike toothpaste or Hollywood movies, good journalism is not just a product but an actual requirement for healthy democracy—and one that may not be able to sustain itself in a business world over the long term. The "press," in fact, is the only business that is specifically protected in the U.S. Constitution.

While political debate and excellent journalism are essential to any healthy democracy, they are not inexpensive to produce and raise a number of issues. Rules that encourage forums to which everyone can have equal access seem desirable. But today's political candidates spend more time raising money to advertise their stories on TV and the Internet than actually debating key social issues. Government subsidies for failing newspapers (or even bailing them out as we did with the auto industry and banks in 2009) might save some sectors of journalism, but such action would also raise questions about the danger of government interference in content. Early in our nation's history, though, the federal government heavily subsidized postal costs for newspapers and magazines, and since the late 1960s, the government has supported NPR and PBS, whose journalistic output and independence have usually been praised.

Our society could require government-licensed but commercially independent TV stations to provide free time to promote political debate. But free debate for all would limit our media institutions' ability to maximize profits, presenting a vexing problem that thus far has been resolved in favor of TV stations maintaining their right to charge for advertising. The next time a political debate airs on television, consider that the media enterprise broadcasting it is giving up profits at the expense of serving democracy (although some critics would argue that only the two main party candidates are taken seriously and allowed to participate in most national debates). It is a matter of debate as to whether they should be required to do this, if it should be left to their judgment, or if we should support government channels to broadcast all debates—paid for by our tax dollars.

Not Wasting Resources

Second, media corporations ought to avoid wasting resources; that is, they should be as efficient as possible. But monopolies do waste resources—they do not always care if they are

wasteful—in order to maintain their monopolistic position of power, which allows them to set prices for their products. Indeed, the wastefulness of monopolies is one characteristic on which all analysts agree. We see this waste in excessive salaries and benefits (especially for top managers and CEOs), excessive advertising, and excessive claims they make about their own benefit to society. How often in the past has a local media monopoly (which may have owned the top newspaper, radio, and TV stations in the same market) claimed to have its community at heart (even as it controlled much of the broadcast ad revenue and most classified advertising in its region) as it opposed any regulation that might affect its bottom line? But if a company controls a media industry in a region, citizens should be asking for alternatives. While free-market economists focus on only this performance criterion, Marxists take it for granted and assume as normal corporate neglect of democratic, social, and cultural concerns. Industrial economists, however, seek to determine whether a corporation is truly a monopoly. For example, in some small towns alternative or free advertising–supported newspapers have broken the monopoly hold; certainly, in many areas today, the Internet and the impact of craigslist, eBay, Monster.com, realtor.com, and auto trading Web sites have broken a regional media company's hold over classified ads.

Free-market economists might argue that regulation was never necessary because these new developments in the market—the Internet and other alternative media—checked the local media monopoly and eventually provided competition, and will continue to do so. However, this competition hasn't stopped the rapid decline of traditional print media and its commercial business model that had supported for so long much of the nation's best journalism. So key questions remain: Are the local news organizations still covering government and business in the region and doing the kinds of watchdog journalism that hold those in power accountable? If not, then should we be subsidizing journalism in particular areas to ensure that people are informed? These vexing questions lie at the heart of media economics and market failures—and urge a strong public policy response.

Facilitating Public Order

Third, media industries ought to facilitate public order, especially with regard to war, violence, and crime. For example, news media often report on crime and violence that threaten communities. Implicit in their coverage is that crime and violence disrupt order and the common good. War is trickier, often pitting citizens' need for information against a government's desire for secrecy. Governmental leaders often pressure the mass media to censor certain stories during wartime. In 2005 and 2006, for example, the Bush administration officials criticized major news organizations, particularly the *New York Times* and network news, for revealing that they were spying on U.S. citizens—without court approval—who may or may not have links to terrorist organizations. The administration had argued that they needed wide latitude in conducting a global war on terror. Indeed, war offers a classic example of how governments withhold information from media corporations in the name of national security. We need to come together as a society in times of war, but with how strict a set of restrictions on speech and communication? These restrictions are hotly debated as to where the line should be drawn.

Protecting and Maintaining Cultural Quality

Fourth, media corporations ought to protect and maintain cultural quality and offer diversity of opinion. This raises the question of whether companies that depend on advertising-generated revenue can develop quality programming—and not simply dish up one more season of worn-out formulaic rip-offs and assorted pandering—and if the government should force them to raise their standards (raising further questions about the subjectivity of the term "quality"). When government officials have sought to regulate content on television, radio, or film, they have run up against First Amendment protections. In 2006, the Bush administration served subpoenas to Internet search companies like Google and Yahoo! in order to perform random searches for individuals and companies trafficking in child pornography. We have rules and laws about obscenity, libel, and slander, but how should we regulate corporate and individual behavior to limit pornography and controversial speech when we have difficulty coming to a consensus over what constitutes obscenity and free expression?

Promoting New Technology

Fifth, media industries ought to bring new technologies to the marketplace as quickly as possible. Economists have long recognized that monopolies resist the innovation of new technologies in order to protect their highly profitable status quo positions. In fact, part of the problem in the decline of newspapers was how slow corporate executives and managers were to embrace the Internet and develop strategies that would have ensured a smoother transition into the Digital Age. If the newspaper industry itself had come up with ideas like craigslist, it might be in better financial shape today. It was, after all, fairly easy to see that classified advertising looked a lot better on the Internet without time and space restrictions than it did in the tiny typeface in most newspapers. In terms of television, should the government set and mandate standards, as the FCC actually did by mandating the end of analog television sets and signals in 2009? Or should buyers choose what is best for them individually, resulting in several standards and the higher costs of interchangeability these multiple standards set? Indeed, the media regulation approach in recent times in the United States—called deregulation—has usually left it to corporations to set the standards.

Applying these five criteria consistently, fairly, and equitably across all the mass media is difficult to do. We, as citizens, and our elected officials must make judgments. Consider, for example, the 1996 Telecommunications Act that promised more choice, more diversity, and more equity in the media. But instead this law led to concentrated ownership and higher prices. Although the growth of the Internet and the 2008–09 financial crisis has exposed many media corporations as **over-leveraged** (too much debt on top of the collapse of investment earnings, so not enough capital to pay the debt bills), these large companies still dominate the production and distribution of mainstream media content. With such corporations still seeking new and increased profits, they prompt questions about how we can best organize as a democracy to match the economic interests of big business with the coverage of different points of view in matters of politics and social affairs. This is why we must understand the ownership and operation of the mass media: So we can look for governmental support and civic strategies that make sense in making the media benefit society as a whole.

Media Corporations and Profit

Once we have established democratic criteria for media corporations, how do we balance the paramount goal of most corporations—profit maximization—with a plan to encourage democracy and diverse voices in the media marketplace? This is important because mass media are primarily organized as corporations; while, say, NPR may be many listeners' choice as the nation's most credible news service, it is supported by tax dollars and donations, and only a small portion of the radio audience listens to this noncommercial programming. On the other hand, in 2012, Clear Channel Corporation—a profit-making entity and the nation's largest radio conglomerate—owned 850 stations that reached roughly ninety million people. One of its subsidiaries, Premier Radio Networks, now produces syndicated radio content for more than five thousand stations, about half of the nation's commercial stations. (The company also owns 90 percent of Clear Channel Outdoor Holdings, among the world's largest billboard firms with nearly one million display ads worldwide.)

Before the 1996 Telecommunications Act removed most ownership restrictions, our government, operating on behalf of citizens and championing diversity of ownership, limited the number of radio stations one corporation could own to fewer than fifty. Clear Channel took advantage of the 1996 act and bought up hundreds more radio stations, and although they've struggled with debt since then (and resold more than 400 stations), the company still benefits from the economies of scale that earn them substantial profits—perhaps to the detriment of democratic interests and a diversity of owners in the marketplace. For example, Clear Channel offers a number of soundalike formats and prepackaged digital programming that it circulates on many of its stations, which undercuts local flavor and discourages individual radio stations from reflecting the unique characteristics of their particular communities in favor of maximized profits for the parent corporation.

Profit is defined as the difference between revenues taken in by the corporation and the costs it takes to produce a product or service. For example, a newspaper has traditionally made its money from what readers pay for street sales and subscriptions and what advertisers pay to have their ads run in the paper. These are the paper's revenues. On the other side, the newspaper counts as costs the salaries of reporters and editors, buildings to work in, computers, delivery trucks, paper, ink, and so forth. Managers hope that these costs add up to an amount less than the revenues; if so, the newspaper makes a profit. If there is no profit, the paper accepts a loss. No corporation can lose money too long or it will be sold or go out of business. In addition, as newspapers—at least the print versions—look more and more irrelevant in the Internet era, their stock prices can plummet even when they still make money. For example, in 2005 the *Los Angeles Times* made more than $1 billion in gross revenues and roughly $200 million in profits, yet its owner, the Tribune Company, declared bankruptcy late in 2008. This happened in part because few stockholders thought newspapers had a future following the decrease in (though not elimination of) many papers' profits.[9]

Costs can be high even in more potentially lucrative media, like film and television production. Brad Pitt can earn $20 million or more for one film role. Jerry Seinfeld, Ray Romano, Jennifer Aniston, and Charlie Sheen all became multimillionaires based on what they earned from their TV sitcoms. The stars of a hit TV show can make $100,000 to $1 million or more per episode, but if the revenues generated through advertising, cable fees, and international sales far exceed this, they are worth it to their corporate managers. A newspaper with less impressive profit margins might, theoretically, stay in business for the good of its community. But study after study has confirmed that corporations, when given the choice, choose to maximize their profits rather than seek what might best serve a community (or democracy as a whole). If benefits come along for society, they come as secondary effects. This is a problem with the profit-maximizing corporations that dominate the media world in a democratic society.

Still, profit maximization is the touchstone of our market economy. Like Michael Eisner and the attempted takeover of Disney by Comcast in 2004, shareholders who own the company will band together to oust managers or at least remind managers of what they want: profits. As such, they often ignore the effects on democracy, causing the friction and occasional public outrage over policy decisions that corporations make. It's worth noting, that journalists who might cover these issues are often employed by corporations whose profits could be threatened by revelations of daily business practices, high profit margins, and CEO incentives. On the upside, however, the economic crises of 2008–09 and their lingering effects have focused more attention on the business of media companies, their role in a depressed economy, and alternatives to doing business.

Indeed, profit maximization is not the only way to run mass media. There are many nonprofit media outlets, such as the radio and TV stations, newspapers, and Web sites run by colleges and universities. Florida's biggest newspaper, the *St. Petersburg Times*, is owned by a nonprofit company, the Poynter Institute. At the government-supported level, NPR and PBS do not seek to make a profit. They seek to simply—at the end of each year—make sure revenues from government funds, donors, and grants equal costs spent to produce their programming. In such nonprofit media, education, quality storytelling (especially stories that commercial media don't think are profitable), and public information are most often the goals, not maximizing profits. But in the twenty-first century, media companies remain primarily profit maximizers.

Direct and Indirect Revenue Streams

Although profits are the main goal of most commercial media corporations, not all revenues are the same. On the one hand, consumers pay directly for some products and services—whether going to a movie, purchasing a book, or buying a song online. This is called **direct revenue** and measures directly what books, movies, or music customers prefer.

But many media seem free. Buy a radio, plug it in, and there is no cost other than the electricity. Buy a computer, find a newspaper site—no charge. Advertisers pay the radio station and Google, and we get the music and news for "free." The advertisers must add in this advertising cost as part of their profit-making calculations, so in some ways it is more realistic to think that we pay for "free" broadcast radio and television when we buy the products and services that advertise on them. When a consumer sees a TV ad for a Ford SUV and that helps to spur the purchase of one, part of the price of the SUV is the cost that Ford has spent advertising. This is called **indirect revenue**, and it can confuse economic analysis because the media corporations are seeking to appeal to advertisers, not to customers. For an NFL game, a network media company's chief "product," then, is really the audience—both its overall size and its demographics (eighteen- to forty-nine-year-old males who might buy the beer that's advertised during the game being the most valuable in this case). In television, media corporations use data such as Nielsen ratings to determine the audience they can sell to advertisors.

Advertisers, of course, prefer audiences who might buy their products, and this preference involves two criteria that leave out a vast section of our population. First, advertisers prefer customers who will continue to buy new products and services; they have determined that those customers are part of the demographic group ages eighteen to forty-nine. This is why mainstream ads in mass media are generally not intended for the old and the very young—unless they're selling products like toys, sugared cereal, Viagra, or Life Alert. Secondly, advertisers exclude more of the population by targeting those customers who can afford to buy new products; this eliminates the lower-income populations. So we end up with, say, golf shows on weekends with ads for high-end sports cars because advertisers want to reach well-off men in the eighteen-to-forty-nine group who play golf. We see less news coverage of poverty or homelessness, or few sitcoms about working-class families, because this programming does not serve the audiences that advertisers want to reach. This hardly could be called helpful to a robust democracy.

Institutional Economic Model

In the end, we posit an **institutional economic model** with the mass media corporation at its center. We begin by recognizing that mass media corporations are not simple firms reducible to equations but large and complicated social, cultural, and political institutions. These mass media corporations rank among the most complex and important institutions in our lives. They do not simply make TV shows, magazines, or gadgets; they make and distribute the communication and culture that define and represent the major values of our society and democracy. Their status demands that we analyze the connections among society, culture, and these corporate institutions. Economic behavior and cultural actions are intertwined, and people are conditioned by culture and resist, change, or respond based in part upon the actions of corporations.

We should also acknowledge that the history of corporate institutions plays a central defining role in social life and that corporate institutions vary by ownership, market conditions, and technological possibilities. For example, the politically conservative Rupert Murdoch and his News Corp., in addition to the *Wall Street Journal*, own both the Fox TV network and Fox News cable channel—a news source that mostly champions a conservative point of view, even while claiming in its ad slogan to be "fair and balanced." The institutional output and goal are profit, but the corporate owners and managers also operate in a social context as well as an economic one, with key cultural and societal effects. Central are considerations of where social, economic, and political factors intertwine. As an example of this complexity, an episode of Fox series *The Simpsons* or *Family Guy* generates profits for Murdoch at the same time the cartoon often satirizes conservative politics and Fox's corporate culture or the poor working conditions under which an animated network series is produced. In other words, Murdoch has accepted certain kinds of resistance to his politics or criticism of his authority as long as his products generate revenue and help maximize News Corp.'s profits. In fact, he is *selling resistance* to his cultural influence and conservative values. One of the keys to the durability of capitalism is its ability to co-opt criticism and package it as a narrative product. Consider the long history of NBC's David Letterman and SNL criticizing and satirizing their corporate parents—first GE, then Comcast.

Media Corporations and Competition

The greatest corporate profits accrue when a company can dominate its competitors—or ultimately become a monopoly with no competition. One way for a firm to become dominant is to distinguish itself from its competitors. Beyond making desirable products, a firm may strive to win the hearts and minds of consumers by developing a distinct image for their entire product line—ensuring that the firm's identity or logo (and, by extension, its products or services) becomes synonymous with quality. This marketing strategy is known as **branding**. No one needs to know that ABC originally stood for American Broadcasting Company because ABC is a brand so well known to TV viewers that the logo and acronym are all that are needed. When that brand becomes synonymous with a media product audiences will enjoy, a company will do its best to portray that product as part of a larger brand from which consumers can expect similar quality or content. Following the success of shows like *Lost* and *Grey's Anatomy*, for example, ABC has branded subsequent programs in ads that refer to ABC's *The Bachelor* or ABC's *Revenge*.

To establish a brand, corporations try to become the first in the market and set up a vast network of outlets to reap economies of scale and thus make it harder for other players to compete. The corporation can recognize historical change and technical inventions and respond to the market demand they create by diversifying or **vertically integrating** (i.e., controlling production, distribution, and exhibition within the same company) or combining business strategies to continue industry domination and profit maximization over the long run. It is not easy to rate these elements in importance, but branding would seem to rank at the top of most lists.

Media Monopolies

Corporate owners and managers embrace monopoly because it has historically assured success and often secured vast profits, but true media monopolies, where a lone firm dominates a media industry, are rare. The single daily newspaper provides an example of media monopoly at a local level that many people will recognize—though with newspaper companies posting content online for free, even those monopolies have become less common. Newspaper readers in communities where one paper dominates often think back and ponder the "good old days" when cities as small as El Dorado, Kansas (population 10,000 in 1950) had three newspapers.

Monopolies obviously limit consumer choice. If a reader does not like the lone local newspaper owner's offerings, and local radio and television do not offer extensive or alternative coverage, then he or she gets little in the way of local news. A monopoly newspaper cannot always cover all subjects of interest to a community and thus makes choices—often for economic reasons—that some (or a lot) of the readers in its local area may not like. These choices may skew the paper's content to appeal to the well-off because advertisers like to

reach those who have the means to buy their products. For example, in 2007 the *Louisville Courier-Journal*, a Gannett company, shut its bureau coverage of poor mining counties in Kentucky and shifted resources to better serve Louisville's affluent suburbs. If low-income neighborhoods get mentioned in local news, this typically involves only crime stories because that's what consultants say sells and because it is inexpensive to do this kind of reporting. A monopoly paper may have built its reputation on strong coverage in certain areas of local news, but under contemporary economic conditions the diversity of coverage and viewpoints has decreased. A local monopoly paper may also be bought or owned by a larger company like Gannett, attracted to owning a profitable monopoly enterprise in the local market without much interest in fully serving the community.

Until about 2005 and 2006 when their stock values started dropping, most publicly owned monopoly newspapers were highly profitable—as is expected from a monopoly—often earning 20 percent pretax profits. So why didn't more people enter the newspaper business prior to the economic downturn? An analysis of economies of scale helps explain why most towns came to have only a single newspaper with a monopoly on the local-news audience. Critical here is understanding the notion of **first copy costs**, or **fixed costs**. All manufacturing operations can generally assign the costs of production to either fixed costs, which are needed for any level of production (e.g., printing presses)—or **variable costs**, which change as levels of production change (e.g., the need for more or fewer reporters).

In newspaper publishing, the fixed or first copy costs include the machinery, office building, and sales staff salaries, and all other costs associated with printing a basic number of words and photographs, including advertising copy. Before the presses roll each day, the publisher has incurred substantial baseline costs, which are most easily recouped if the paper is a monopoly. As a monopoly, the single owner can also choose to limit its variable costs, for example, by limiting coverage of local events or keeping fewer reporters on staff. As a monopoly, these owners can maximize profit, unafraid of a challenger, and offer a single news voice. Most monopoly newspapers have been subsidiaries of even larger media conglomerates, like Gannett or News Corp., companies that own many newspapers. Thus, local coverage can suffer because, as leading media economist Robert Picard has argued, "locally owned papers tend to do a better job of covering community controversies as news" than monopoly newspapers from out of town.[10] Chain-owned newspapers can simply take advantage of their monopoly position, creating larger profits with smaller staffs.

At the outset of the twenty-first century, cable TV providers also appeared to represent a media monopoly not particularly supportive of democratic ideals. In nearly 99 percent of communities, despite the threat of direct broadcast satellite (DBS) and other alternatives, the incumbent cable operators faced no real cable competition. In situations where DBS services, phone companies, or a second cable company do compete, the contrast is remarkable: A second competitor helps to lower prices and to provide more channels. But for consumers—even in limited competitive environments—rising monthly cable fees are simply a given. Up until the Internet started providing access to channels via cell phones, iPods, iPads, and other emerging technologies, we longed for more channels—and cheaper prices. But multiple-channel TV has not been cheap, nor do we get a voice as to which channels are available to us. Historically, decisions have most often been determined by a city's cable monopoly owner with a single goal in mind—profit maximization. Community access channels—free channels open to community programming—surfaced only because they were required by renewable franchise contract so that a cable company could maintain its fifteen-year (on average) legal monopoly.

Into the 2000s, Government Accountability Office studies reported the expected actions of a monopolist: that cable rates rise far faster than the core rate of inflation. The average yearly rise in overall prices was about 1 to 2 percent, but the average cable price increases came to 5 to 10 percent because consumers generally had just one choice for a cable provider. Providers also refused to allow consumers to select à la carte menus where they pay for only the channels they watch. In fact, in 2010 when consumer groups pressed for à la carte choices, cable companies suggested that they would raise the prices on these individual channels and that their current tiers of service menus would remain cheaper. Over the years, when monopoly cable companies in particular areas have added one or two channels, they then use that as an excuse to increase the basic consumer monthly bill by five to ten dollars.[11]

The two largest cable companies, Comcast and Time Warner, cover half the United States and together take advantage of significant economies of operation. Local monopoly corporations are collected under one larger corporate umbrella (similar to "chains" in the newspaper business), creating a **multiple system operator (MSO)**, where a number of cable franchises are group owned. An MSO can have a single accounting department, a single sales force, and a single repair division, for example, spreading these and other fixed costs across the various franchises to yield lower per franchise costs and higher profits. Thus, the illusion of multiple operations masks the truth of a single owner. And that single owner makes millions of dollars per year. That is why Comcast—the largest MSO in the United States by the mid-2000s—could make a serious offer to take over a larger, more famous company—the Walt Disney Corporation—and nearly succeed and then just a few years later purchase NBC Universal.

Corporate Competition

On the opposite end of the ownership scale sits corporate competition, where there are so many companies that no one really has an accurate list of which corporations are in business or not. Each is small relative to the others and there is constant changing of choice. These competitive industrial situations are, like media monopolies, quite rare. Currently, only two such media industries in the United States could boast a corporate competition model: magazines and the Internet. For example, while there have been a few large magazine chain owners like Meredith or Time Warner (which once owned more than seventy titles), there are so many magazines—in excess of 10,000 regularly published—that the precise number can only be estimated. The magazine industry ranges from hobbyist quarterlies to the *National Enquirer* to serious journalism to the *Progressive Farmer*. The range of topics and interests available via Internet publications (including online-only magazines, online versions of print titles, blogs, and more) is even more formidable. In terms of the magazine and Internet industries, consumers have real choice—a very different picture of the media than one in which the product and the storytelling are in the hands of an oligopoly or monopoly.

Yet choice is not always what corporate owners want. The magazines and Internet sites are rare examples of real choice in today's mediated society. Companies that run magazines, for

the most part, are far smaller (and easier for us to envision starting) than either of its print brethren—newspapers or book publishing—and much cheaper to start than television, music, or movies. Not many media conglomerates, which own media enterprises of various types, choose to operate magazines because there's little hope of gaining domination. Constantly, entrepreneurs start new magazines, usually around five to seven hundred per year, aimed at special interests or new niches. There is little overhead: The U.S. Postal Service handles delivery; design is done using digital desktop publishing programs; and freelance and part-time writers offer much of the content. The actual up-front investment in staff often consists of hiring a dozen people, renting a small amount of office space, investing in technology, and subcontracting the printing. Contrast this with the newspaper industry, where virtually no new daily print papers start up in a given year (although digital papers on the Internet are multiplying). There are today only about 1,400 daily newspapers in the United States (down from a high of 2,600 in 1910).

There are other advantages to corporate competition. Magazines and the Internet offer advertisers direct targeting of interested customers. Network television can supply national advertising, but often its reach is wasted on viewers with no interest in the products being hawked. In contrast, magazines and Web sites serve discrete interests and niche markets within the population. Specialization covers not just consumer concerns, but also the diverse information needs of business professions through a steady number of trade magazines and specialized Web sites. Consumer magazines, professional/business magazines, and Internet start-up companies serve the need of advertisers who wish to reach a smaller well-defined audience interested in specific products and services. In the magazine industry and on Web sites, individual voices can be easily accessed and specialized needs accommodated.

In following the magazine model, the Internet has evolved as an alternative delivery system for content currently published in magazines and many other media. Web sites like Hulu.com deliver network TV programs online. Recent developments like blogging and Twitter have become a popular way to easily publish content or interact with a community of readers. The Internet has exploded with services that provide a digest of articles and commentary circulated over e-mail or through comment boards, delivering added specialized features that no magazine can provide, including related links. One of the most profitable Web sites, eBay, includes many features previously found in magazines and newspapers but adds interactivity and real-time bidding—something older media can't offer. In addition, today one person can start a Web site cheaply about any one of her or his passions and update it daily by simply collecting messages from contributors who are also passionate about the subject. No advertising, no profit: just the will and time to assemble the messages day after day. If the site proves popular, advertising and profits may follow, as might interest from larger companies wanting a piece of the action.

While Web sites are not like traditional media, they are used for the entertainment and information functions we have long associated with older mass media such as newspapers and magazines. For example, eBay on the surface seems like an auction site, but many people consult it as if it were a magazine or newspaper simply composed of advertising; it offers more information for collectors than a single magazine could provide, with the added ability to purchase products instantly. While eBay seems to be creating and dominating a unique niche, Internet industries are changing so quickly that we can only speculate on the digital future and on how much online media will continue to transform older mass media forms. For now, though, it seems that, like magazines, there is no way for a handful of giant media companies to dominate the Internet's open architecture.

Typically, large media companies look for market power to help whittle down the number of other competitors so they can keep track of and react to new market trends. But in a competitive business environment this is not possible because, as with the 10,000-plus regularly published magazines or with nearly a half billion Web sites, there are too many to track to see what the competition is up to. In the end, however, real media economics are not represented by this competitive model, even if many citizens might prefer it for our democracy. The magazine and Internet models are exceptions. Under most economic arrangements in our mediated world, the typical media corporation faces but a handful of competitors. Still, the Internet is driving many changes in older business models and has proved to be the most difficult media enterprise in history to monopolize.

Media Oligopolies

Older media industries like film and music are in the hands of a few corporations; this environment is defined as an **oligopoly**. In an oligopoly, a handful of firms dominate a market or industry. One prominent example is the group of three major longtime U.S. television networks: NBC, ABC, and CBS (although this was later expanded to include Fox; the CW, which emerged from UPN and the WB; and Univision, the popular Hispanic network). Another example is the movie business, which is in the hands of the six commanding major Hollywood studios. Despite all of the choices available on cable and satellite TV, these six Hollywood companies—Disney, Time Warner, Sony, NBC Universal, Twentieth Century Fox, and Viacom/Paramount—produce and distribute most TV shows and movies. Given this landscape, we need to learn not only about the basic corporate institutions themselves but also about how they interact. The economic outcomes of oligopolistic corporate behavior depend on how many firms there are, how big they are in relationship to one another, past corporate histories, changing ownership structures, and sometimes the whims and politics of individual owners. At times this economic organization might help democracy; at other times it won't. As media consumers, we should study these arrangements corporation by corporation.

What makes this analysis so difficult is that corporations collude to monopolize some operations while competing in other agreed-upon arenas. For example, the five major corporations that controlled the music business—Viacom/Universal, Time Warner, EMI, Sony, and BMG/Bertlesmann—colluded to keep the price of CDs inflated. (Despite European Union opposition, Sony and BMG merged in the late 2000s.) The development of Internet file-sharing and illegal downloads and Apple's new business model (charging 99 cents, at the time, to download a song) put a dent in the old model, but the remaining four major music companies remain both in control and mutually interdependent, at least for now. When powerful corporations like these cooperate, they can act like monopolies, work together to lobby for positive governmental policies toward their industry, and thus thwart most potential competition. Nothing unites a media oligopoly more than a threat from the outside. Simply put, oligopolists tend to seek and agree upon an informal set of rules for "competition"—for instance, controlling the price of music downloads—thereby restricting the game of profit maximization to themselves. Since many media industries are controlled

primarily by oligopolies, it is hard to analyze monopolies or corporate competition models on their own. Analysis of oligopolies requires that we examine the historical development of the oligopoly and how the companies that make it up cooperate, or fail to.

Here is where we confront the media conglomerate, a media corporation that holds a number of subsidary media businesses. To maintain their positions of power in recent decades, these companies have diversified, both vertically and horizontally. **Vertical integration**, in the media industry, means a company owns the production, distribution, and public presentation or exhibition of its product. For example, Time Warner makes a movie, distributes it to theaters, and then later shows it on its wholly owned premium cable network—HBO. **Horizontal integration** means a conglomerate owns one kind of product or service in multiple markets. So, for example, the Disney movie studio demonstrates horizontal integration by producing not only Disney films, marketed at children, but films under brands it has developed for general audiences such as Touchstone Pictures, and former independent studios it has acquired, such as Miramax or Pixar.

Both vertical and horizontal integration seek to minimize the risk the company faces. Disney not only owns and operates a famous movie studio and set of theme parks but also a television network (ABC), a score of successful television and radio stations, the cable sports colossus ESPN and all its related channels, book and magazine holdings, and more. Because of this diversification, Disney is a classic media conglomerate that is not dependent on the business cycle of any single operation. Unprofitable subsidiaries can be reconstructed and repositioned with funds generated from other profitable ongoing businesses. Disney's only real competitors are a small number of media conglomerates, like News Corp. or Time Warner, with the resources to compete in the same markets and industries. This gives rise to an oligopoly that creates a high barrier for legitimate competitors trying to enter the same market. Many potential rivals lack these conglomerates' level of diversification that protects business operations across multiple media ventures.

The best way to predict the behavior of an oligopoly is to recognize that its members operate in reaction to one another. If these conglomerates were truly competitive, they could not acquire the information necessary to predict the behavior of their competitors; if they were a monopoly, they would not care. But an oligopoly is like a poker game with five or six players. Each player knows a great deal about what the others are up to but does not possess full knowledge. Take the case of the four dominant U.S. television networks. When NBC (owned by Comcast) offers a new comedy at a particular time on a particular day, its rivals counterprogram with, for example, a reality program or drama that might appeal to another large segment of the audience. This leads to some experimentation, but all too often only means a numbing generic sameness where similar program genres (for example, more of the same kinds of sitcoms, reality programs, or dramatic procedurals) face off against each other. Because media viewership is largely determined by fickle audiences with varied cultural tastes in search of their favorite kinds of narratives, no calculable, consistent, mathematical model predicts audience and consumer behavior. Indeed, economic theorists have a great deal of trouble modeling oligopolistic behavior and consumer response.

Despite potential unpredictability, the oligopoly has developed into the most common market structure for ownership in the mass media. For example, the Hollywood film industry remains an oligopoly of six. All compete to produce and release the top box office hits, but all cooperate to make sure the game remains primarily among themselves and that the price of movie tickets adjusts upwardly as audiences decline in the age of the Internet. The Big Six premiere the vast majority of possible blockbuster hits in multiplex theaters—and surely will continue to do this well into the future. Some may complain, but film fans generally don't seem to mind on a large scale; worldwide business at the box office has remained quite healthy since the dawn of the wide-release blockbuster in the late 1970s, with Paramount and Fox's co-production of *Titanic* in the 1990s having grossed more than $2.1 billion in ticket sales over the globe, and a dozen years later Fox's *Avatar* besting even these sizable numbers with $2.8 billion in sales.

Indeed, the Hollywood oligopoly is one of the tightest in the media business. We can most easily see this power in the activities of the Big Six's trade association—the Motion Picture Association of America (the MPAA)—where the six corporations deal with common concerns from rating films to smoothing the way for international distribution to protecting their valuable copyrights around the world. Here the collusion by corporations—an agreement about the best interests of all—helps shape the oligopoly of six more along the lines of a monopoly. And, as we have argued before, when one entity is the sole power and the sole voice, democracy and consumer choices may not be as well served. In such a system there may be little support for important films that might appeal to smaller audiences.

With the TV, music, and movie industries, as well as other oligopolies like them, the only real question at the close of each year is: Who ranked where in terms of revenues? Yet while this oligopoly is surely dominant, there does exist some room on the margins for minor companies. Strong examples arrived in 2004 with Mel Gibson's *Passion of the Christ* and Michael Moore's *Fahrenheit 9/11*, both rejected by the major Hollywood Six but both highly profitable. Both were considered too risky for Big Six backers; in these cases the media controversies surrounding the films led to higher revenues, but in many cases this kind of success does not happen. As such, the Hollywood oligopoly tolerates occasional success outside of the Big Six; if they permitted no independents on the margin, they would risk government antitrust action, which they want to avoid. The Big Six also need independent companies to develop new kinds of narratives that seem too risky, quirky, or innovative for the conventional industry. However, once an "independent" company (and even independents usually need the Big Six to distribute their film) has developed a track record of producing commercially successful films, a Big Six firm may buy them out or enter into a partnership. Because of their occasional outside-the-mainstream successes and distribution partnerships with independents, the MPAA and Big Six executives can preach to governmental officials that they have competition and thus do not break any antitrust laws.

Similarly, the music-business oligopoly tolerates a certain margin of independence and outsider work in order to gauge trends and innovation, and independently run music labels have seen increased success in the past decade (especially for the artists working for these labels) as the major-label system has been slow to adapt to technology changes and online opportunities in the industry. But the major music labels will still adopt musical acts or labels that began as independents or at least imitate them with the resources and power of the oligopoly structure to ensure higher success rates than less powerful independent companies.

The media consumer needs to pay close attention to changes in the oligopoly mix. That monopolies are bad for democracy is an easy case to make; but the claim that oligopolistic "competition" is not capable of serving both business's bottom line and democracy's ideals

is more problematic. Thus, media oligopolies are what we live with, but what we need are regulations that offer them incentives to act for the benefit of democracy—even as they go about their priority task of maximizing profits. The 2008–09 financial crisis is a good example in which the risky practices of a handful of giant banks, including Bank of America and Citigroup, considered "too big to fail," catapulted the world into an economic mess, with unenforced or missing oversight and lax regulations at the center of the debate. Even now, the big bank oligopoly continues to lobby against the very regulations that would have prevented the crisis in the first place.

Yet the oligopoly mix is constantly in flux. Mergers, break-ups, and over-leveraged corporations make the front page of the *Wall Street Journal*, the *New York Times*, and the evening network and daily cable news shows. The development of a successful oligopoly in a media industry or across media industries can mean greater profits for the players (though not as much as a monopoly) and more stability than a competitive media marketplace could offer—but at what cost? This is where the media consumer must be diligent. If service falters and choices become limited, it may be time to declare that an oligopoly is colluding and acting too much like a media monopoly. What to do? Seek help from government oversight groups that regulate nearly all mass media industries. Complain to the trade organizations that lobby on behalf of media oligopolies—such as the Recording Industry Association of America (RIAA) or the National Association of Broadcasting (NAB). Apply our media performance criteria. This means we have to carefully study media oligopolies, cite their failures, and then argue for antitrust action to break the conglomerates apart or regulations to prevent collusion among them. Citizen activism and the simple threat of government action can often change oligopoly behavior. But this requires us to pay attention, to hold our representatives (who are incessantly lobbied to and supported by media corporations) accountable, and to analyze media industry behavior corporation by corporation.

Production Planning and Management

"Production Planning and Management" from *Filmmaking in Action*, by Adam Leipzig, Barry S. Weiss, and Michael Goldman, pp. 97–118 (Chapter 5, "Production Planning and Management").[12]

"The execution of the initial plan and any backup scenarios should always follow the writer's words and the director's vision within the constraints of the budget."

—Tim Moore, veteran production manager and producer, whose films include *Flags of Our Fathers* (2006), *Gran Torino* (2008), *Invictus* (2009), and *American Sniper* (2014)

Figure 2-1. *The Climb* (2002).

By 2002, Tim Moore was a seasoned production manager, line producer, and producer of independent movies and television projects, but still about a year away from joining Clint Eastwood's team as a regular unit production manager and, later, co-producer. He was co-producing a small independent film called *The Climb* in Provo, Utah, responsible for setting up the schedule for a particularly grueling day of filming on the side of a snowy mountain in the middle of winter. By then, Moore was well-versed in the need to weave backup plans into his schedule, and it was a good thing.

"The first day, we built a camp on the side of the mountain in the snow, on a glacier," Moore recalls. He continues:

> The night before, it snowed, and when we tried to get up to our set, we couldn't even reach it, even with help from the ski patrol. So we took the crew and equipment down the mountain and set up to shoot the scene in the parking lot, and we tried to do it, but it started snowing again, and it was way too hard to shoot there. Luckily, we knew about a warehouse about three miles away and we took everything down there—it was a plan we had ready to go, just in case. That day, we went to three different locations, and ended up in the warehouse, putting tents up on a stage [in the warehouse], and shot the scenes inside [the tents]—about eight pages. We made our day, and later went back and got the outdoor coverage that we needed. Did we think we would ever need to use that plan? No, but you always have to have things ready to go.
>
> You have to think things out and not panic. There will always be an incident somewhere on every picture that will cause you to have to change your plans. It might be minor or it might be huge, but you have to be ready for it.

In Moore's case, he had experience, resources, and a team ready to help him execute his backup plans; the point, however, is that he had those backup plans to begin with. They were part of his schedule and, for that matter, part of his budget. His team had strategically developed a series of options for what they would do in certain situations that would allow them to complete their shooting days on time and on budget, and that made all the difference in the world on that particular project. In other words, they had a plan, and their plan worked. On that project, or on any project—be it professional or student—filmmakers' chances of success are directly linked to their ability to strategically plan and organize.

But what exactly does "plan and organize" mean when it comes to filmmaking, and what does it particularly mean at the student level, where resources are few and experience is limited?

"The lower the budget, the fewer the resources, the more important planning becomes," insists independent producer/director/writer Jon Gunn, whose directing credits include *My Date with Drew* (2004, as codirector) and *Like Dandelion Dust* (2009). "Lack of planning will limit you, and prevent you from accomplishing the things you need to make your movie everything you want it to be. So it's important to think ahead about various scenarios and possibilities—for instance, having a backup location in case it rains the day you are scheduled to shoot outside, or having a plan for consolidating 10 shots into three if you run out of time. These things are always smart, especially when you don't have money. Scheduling and budgeting are their own art forms, and they are particularly important when you are on a limited budget."[13]

Therefore, think of your schedule and budget combination as *the Plan*. The Plan is an initial realistic road map of how your movie will be brought to life—physically, technically, financially, and sensibly. It is far more than an estimating tool; it becomes the *practical definition* of how your story will be created. In effect, the Plan *becomes* your movie: the road, the car, the engine, the steering wheel, and even the finish line far off in the distance.

In this chapter, we will look at how a film's schedule and budget work in synergy as two sides of the same coin, and how they are created and managed. We'll examine what it will take to manage your production, including organizing production tasks and finding help and insight for organizing them; understanding the principles and technical aspects of creating, revising, and managing a shooting schedule; mastering the principles of building a movie budget and managing resources; and, perhaps most important of all, learning how to be personally *resourceful* along the way.

Key Concepts

- Organizing, tracking, reporting, and managing the schedule, budget, and logistics of a production often require bringing in others to assist you. This group will form the core of your *production management team*, handling tasks present on all projects, regardless of size.
- Movie schedules go through many drafts and variations. Each one is the product of exploring "what if" scenarios to find the most efficient ways to create your visual illusions.
- Similarly, your budget will be an evolving and organic document that will flow out of your schedule. At any level, there will be *hard costs* that you will need to find ways to pay for, and other costs that you will need to resolve with resources other than money. You will need to monitor your resources, how you are using them, and what the results are.

Management Overview

You may be the only person in charge of making and managing the Plan for your student film, or you may have help from friends, fellow students, family members, or even complete strangers eager to get experience. No matter what, production management tasks are plentiful at all levels of filmmaking, and strategies for dealing with them must be put into place. These tasks include creating and updating the aforementioned schedule and budget; managing the day-to-day logistical matters related to acquiring and moving cast, crew, and equipment from one location to the next; feeding people and getting expenses paid; solving problems as they arise; managing money; and answering to your professors or investors, if there are any.

In the professional world, these activities are handled by a seasoned production management team, which can include any number of producers who handle various executive, financial, management, or logistical tasks, in collaboration with more hands-on department heads on a day-to-day basis. As was discussed in Chapter 1, the lead producer is the ultimate manager and decision maker on a movie project, and on student projects, that person is you, no matter how you divide up the work or whom you bring in to collaborate with you. But from a basic, nuts-and-bolts, daily-grind point of view, the most crucial management authority on the production will be the **unit production manager**, or **UPM**, sometimes called the **line producer** or **co-producer,** although these exact titles have more rigid and official (and not always identical) meanings on professional productions and across different mediums, such as film as compared to television. This is because of how they are classified as union jobs by the Directors Guild of America. On union shows, the line producer will likely be more involved in creative matters, such as casting, actor contracts, and script changes, whereas the UPM will stay focused largely on physical production issues: crew hiring, transportation, permits, scouting, business matters, schedules, budgets, department heads, and so forth. For the student work you are doing right now, these job distinctions are not a significant concern, as they will likely be melded into a single position or split up based simply on what is feasible with few resources, but you should be aware such distinctions exist as you advance in your film career.

Software Can Help

One of the most commonly used management tools for most filmmakers at any level is Movie Magic Budgeting and Scheduling software, but there are many others, such as Microsoft Project, FastTrack Schedule 10, QuickBooks, not to mention common Excel spreadsheets.

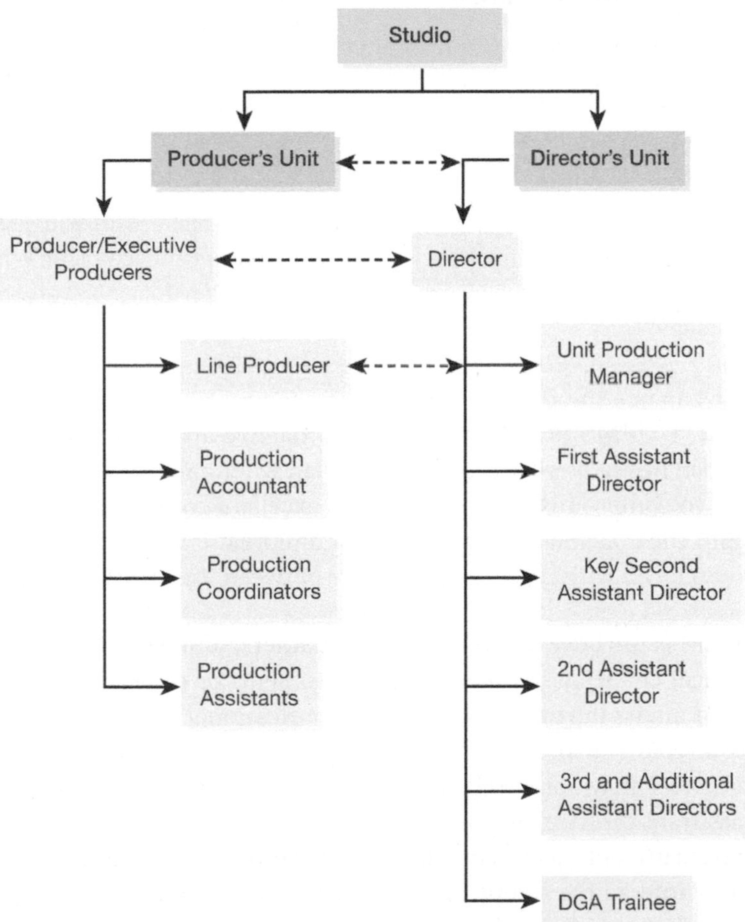

Figure 2-2. An organizational flow chart of a production management team.

In terms of basic duties, the UPM is the chief strategist/problem solver when it comes to day-to-day production management work. The person handling those duties will carry ultimate responsibility for making sure the project is completed on time and on budget. You

will likely be handling this job as well on most of your early student films, but you might eventually bring in others to assist you on some or all of the UPM's responsibilities—either formally or informally. But no matter how you split up the work, among the UPM's responsibilities will be the following:

- Organizing actor and crew contracts, if any
- Negotiating union contracts, if any
- Arranging location scouts and permits, if any
- Securing releases and interacting with local authorities for permissions and on safety issues
- Scheduling and budgets
- Interacting with department heads
- Organizing crew meals and transportation
- Solving logistical problems

You Can't Do It All

Aggressively seek help and delegate jobs—don't try to manage all details yourself. Much of producing a movie with few resources involves gathering your production management team in whatever form it takes each day and regularly distributing lists of action items to everyone, from crucial issues to the mundane.

The UPM must balance the intersection between money and the creative vision during production. Thus, a UPM not only needs to be proactive and anticipate problems before they arise, and then be ready with a contingency plan when they do, but also needs to know when and where to compromise. The job requires excellent communication skills, a gift for multitasking, and the conciliatory approach of a diplomat embarking on an international peace treaty when faced with issues that can arise between the creative team and the crew.

Typically, the UPM is too busy handling business matters, filling out paperwork, pondering upcoming logistical challenges, or dealing with problems or crises off-site to manage moment-by-moment affairs during production. On professional films, that job therefore falls to the assistant directors, with the first assistant director (first AD) serving as "the general on set," according to Tim Moore, and often two second assistant directors directly below the first AD. The assistant directors track each day's shooting schedule against the production schedule; prepare daily call sheets; and ensure that the set is running smoothly, moving the director and crew into all the setups planned for the day, with actors and crew positioned according to your plan and needs.

Again, you likely won't be hiring a team of people this extensive and structured for your student project, but even with limited resources, it's always a good idea to get help when you can, particularly where the business and management side of the project is concerned. Filmmaking is, after all, a collaborative art. You have to be honest about your strengths and weaknesses. If you do not have much business experience or are not an organized person, challenge yourself to find help filling in those gaps. As Jon Gunn advises, "If you know someone who is well organized, detail oriented, good at negotiating, or who has experience planning events, they could be very helpful on an independent film. A parent or family friend or neighbor might be able to arrange food or parking or negotiate for a location. There are a lot of tasks to be handled, and there are undoubtedly people you know who would be willing to help you, so don't be afraid to ask."

Practice

Building a Team

Presuming you have absolutely no funds to pay anyone for anything, take a student project you are developing or investigating, or one you would like to work on in the near future, and write a two-page description of how you would propose putting together a production management team for that project, and how you would delegate responsibilities. The proposal does not necessarily have to reflect what ends up being your final plan, though it could end up being a nice template, but it should be a realistic and logical description of the people you believe you could actually access and bring into the project to play specific managerial roles.

Business SMARTS

Business, Insurance, and Legal Requirements

Among the least enjoyable but most important aspects of filmmaking are certain business, insurance, and legal requirements, which may or may not apply to you as student filmmakers but which you need to know about in order to figure out if they will impact your work. Failing to do your due diligence in these areas, and to adequately fill out paperwork and keep proper records, could end up costing you money, involve you in legal entanglements, and delay or even ruin your project. Therefore, investigate and learn more about the following issues:

- **Releases.** These permit you to film and show certain individuals, places, and logos in your movie. Corporate logos, such as the famous Apple logo, are intellectual property. Someone owns them, and they only appear in movies when someone pays for the right or otherwise secures permission. If your movie is not a profit-making venture, it might not matter, but you need to be sure. What if your film later ends up on YouTube?
- **SAG-AFTRA (Screen Actors Guild–American Federation of Television and Radio Artists), other union considerations, and Workers' Comp.** Union agreements are needed to allow you to use union personnel on your project. Most likely, for a small, not-for-profit student film, you may not want to use union personnel, but you should still know the rules at your school and in your area, and the status of any actors you cast. If you cast an actor with a SAG-AFTRA card, you may end up having to pay that person union rates. Even for non-union individuals who aren't being paid, the law may require workers' compensation insurance or other types of coverage for anyone working on-set, depending on the state you're filming in. Various craft unions and guilds also define many

of the crew positions, as well as their respective pay rates, how many need to be hired, conditions of work, the number of hours they can work, required breaks, and so on. You need to understand what union requirements are in the area where you are filming in order to know if they will, or won't, impact your student production.

- **Permits.** As discussed elsewhere (see Chapter 4), you may need location permits from local authorities to film in certain places, but you might also need certain fire and safety permits for particular kinds of stunts or effects work, or to have certain kinds of crew or equipment or numbers of people in certain locations. You may need local authorities to authorize such things, and you may have to pay for a fire or police official to be present during filming of such sequences.

- **Damage protection insurance.** As the name implies, equipment and vehicle rental companies often require filmmakers to carry this kind of protection to cover damage to equipment rented from them. Location permits are frequently granted only on the condition that you also carry insurance to guarantee that any damage to property is covered. Sometimes companies that specialize in film production offer special entertainment packages that cover all forms of damage throughout principal photography for low-budget films.

- **Comprehensive general liability insurance.** Likewise, special coverage or signed waivers of coverage will often be required before you will be granted permits to stage dangerous or complicated stunts or pyrotechnic effects. This kind of insurance can be quite expensive, and students may not be able to easily purchase it or even acquire it through their film school policies. In any case, your school likely won't approve you moving ahead with stunts that are too dangerous—nor should they.

- **Copyrights.** This involves registering your work with the proper authorities, identifying you and any partners or financiers as the legal owners, so that no one can later copy or steal the work (see Chapter 3). Copyrights require paperwork and fees to be filed. But you also need to check with your school and find out who will own the copyright to your student film—you or the school?

- **Contractual responsibilities.** You need to read and understand all contracts before signing them, and most, if not all, may require legal advice. For instance, if you have anyone providing financing or offering distribution on the condition that you complete your movie by a particular date, you may be required to pay for a **completion bond**—another form of insurance—to guarantee your film will be finished.

- **Other Insurance.** On a film of even modest size, your insurance package may also include: *E&O*, or errors and omissions coverage, which provides protection in case you unintentionally infringe a known piece of copyrighted material; coverage for the budget of the film in case of the death or inability of an actor during production; and additional protections you may discuss with your insurance broker.

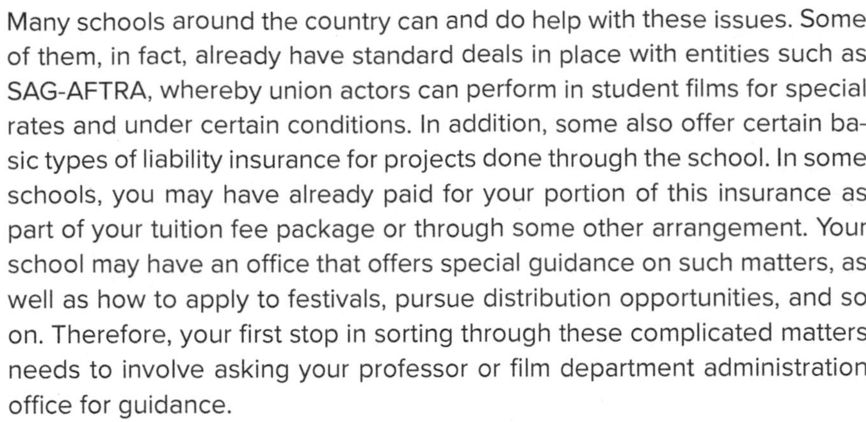

Many schools around the country can and do help with these issues. Some of them, in fact, already have standard deals in place with entities such as SAG-AFTRA, whereby union actors can perform in student films for special rates and under certain conditions. In addition, some also offer certain basic types of liability insurance for projects done through the school. In some schools, you may have already paid for your portion of this insurance as part of your tuition fee package or through some other arrangement. Your school may have an office that offers special guidance on such matters, as well as how to apply to festivals, pursue distribution opportunities, and so on. Therefore, your first stop in sorting through these complicated matters needs to involve asking your professor or film department administration office for guidance.

Network through this class, your professor, your film department, your school, your friends and family, and be aggressive about reading industry trade publications and going to industry events, trade shows, screenings, and panel discussions, where you can meet people, ask questions, and seek advice. It doesn't matter if these people have any previous experience or involvement in the film world. What matters is their skill set and whether or not you think they can help you manage your project.

Scheduling

The notion of any schedule is based on specific needs and goals, and is designed to permit you to move through your tasks as quickly and efficiently as possible. However, when it comes to making a movie, the schedule is the yin to the budget's yang; you can't design a reasonable budget until you have first created a logistically feasible schedule. And if you don't have a schedule and a budget, you can't make your movie—no matter how cool your idea is, how well written your script is, or how awesome the visuals in your head are.

This means that after finding a story and developing a script that you like, one of the first things you must do is sit down and break your script apart—far beyond any analysis work you or your departments heads, if any, might do to address specific aspects of a production, such as visual effects or production design. This is necessary because you need to make an initial overall estimate of the size, cost, and logistical needs of your entire production. Initially, these factors may be educated guesses, and may even be predetermined or guided by your instructor. In the professional world, they will be carefully calculated by professional producers and UPMs.

Once you have broken down the script, you will build a preliminary **shooting schedule**, which is essentially the plan for shooting particular scenes on particular days in particular places with particular people and in a particular order until you have the material you need to go into postproduction and edit it all together into a movie. Not only will you need to prepare the shooting schedule with backup scenarios and alternative options in mind, but you will need to take the time to analyze the schedule you have created and revise it multiple times before heading out and shooting anything.

Script Breakdown

In some respects, breaking down the script is similar to the art of marking up your script. In other ways it resembles how you or a department head concerned with one particular area of the production would analyze the script, as described in Chapter 4. Here, however, your job is global, not local, so to speak—it involves the entire production's needs and resources, and therefore, you have to go a lot further. Also, unlike how the director might mark up the script, this job is less of a creative one. Rather, it involves applying some cold, rational business considerations to your creative endeavor. In this case, your script evaluation work is all about scheduling and budgeting—finding affordable ways to move people and things where they need to be, when they need to be there in the most cost effective and logical order to give yourself the opportunity to make your creative vision a reality and not just a pipe dream.

Therefore, the overall **script breakdown** involves a series of formal steps in which you go through the script and identify key elements for each shot or scene. Key elements are, in essence, every person, place, or thing that you will need to schedule or otherwise allocate resources to in order to have them available and ready to go on your designated shooting day. Knowing these things, in turn, will help you ascertain how many shooting days you will likely need. Once you have this information, you can calculate what money and other resources you will need to spend, which will allow you to determine if your schedule is in fact feasible given your resources and timeline for completing the project. If it isn't, you will at least have a working foundation for scaling it back.

If, for example, you know you only have a 10-day window for production, and your breakdown and preliminary schedule tells you that you will need 20 days, it will immediately become obvious that something in your project needs to be scaled back. If you don't follow the basic procedures for breaking down your script, a problem of this sort might take you by surprise, causing you all sorts of complications in short order. The basic procedures to follow:

- **Line the script.** For this step, you literally mark up a physical script, or use specialized scheduling software, to call out key elements you will need to account for in your schedule: locations, actors, extras, vehicles, animals, makeup, props, costumes, visual effects, and so on. Pay attention to script notes about time of day and setting, and instructions about whether scenes must be interior (INT) or exterior (EXT)—and notice that we used the word *must*. As you go through the script, you need to calculate places where you might be able to change an interior to an exterior, night to day, or vice versa, in order to make the best use of your limited shooting days. Maintain the script instruction when the story *needs* you to, but when there is wiggle room, decide what is best for the schedule and resources and base your decision on those factors. Along the way, as we discuss in Chapter 4, these notations will indicate where and when you think a stage can replace a location, when one location can double for two or more locations, when you can use a visual effect or a simple camera or an optical technique to avoid a location or complicated set, and so on. This kind of thinking is crucial in schedule building.

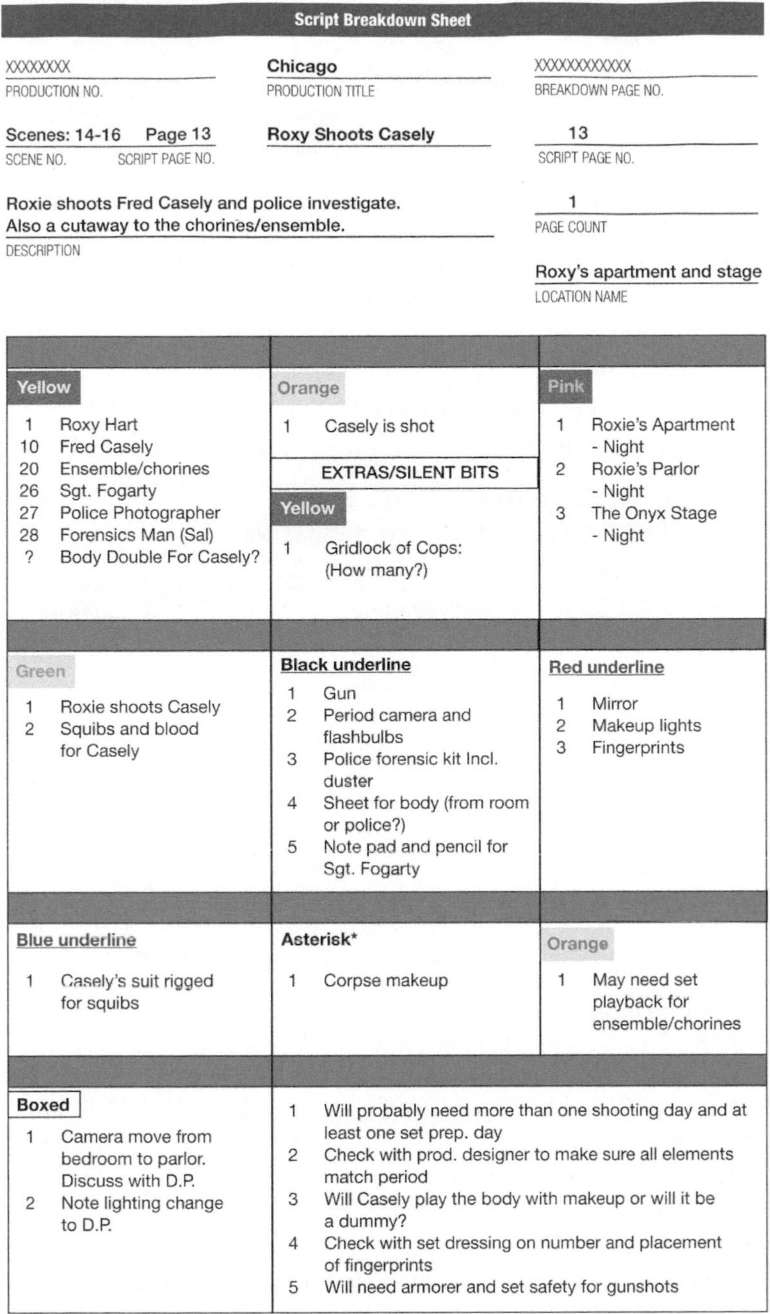

Script Breakdown Sheet

XXXXXXX	**Chicago**	XXXXXXXXXXX
PRODUCTION NO.	PRODUCTION TITLE	BREAKDOWN PAGE NO.
Scenes: 14-16 Page 13	**Roxy Shoots Casely**	**13**
SCENE NO. SCRIPT PAGE NO.		SCRIPT PAGE NO.
Roxie shoots Fred Casely and police investigate. Also a cutaway to the chorines/ensemble.		**1**
DESCRIPTION		PAGE COUNT
		Roxy's apartment and stage
		LOCATION NAME

Yellow 1 Roxy Hart 10 Fred Casely 20 Ensemble/chorines 26 Sgt. Fogarty 27 Police Photographer 28 Forensics Man (Sal) ? Body Double For Casely?	**Orange** 1 Casely is shot EXTRAS/SILENT BITS **Yellow** 1 Gridlock of Cops: (How many?)	**Pink** 1 Roxie's Apartment - Night 2 Roxie's Parlor - Night 3 The Onyx Stage - Night
Green 1 Roxie shoots Casely 2 Squibs and blood for Casely	**Black underline** 1 Gun 2 Period camera and flashbulbs 3 Police forensic kit Incl. duster 4 Sheet for body (from room or police?) 5 Note pad and pencil for Sgt. Fogarty	**Red underline** 1 Mirror 2 Makeup lights 3 Fingerprints
Blue underline 1 Casely's suit rigged for squibs	**Asterisk*** 1 Corpse makeup	**Orange** 1 May need set playback for ensemble/chorines

Boxed 1 Camera move from bedroom to parlor. Discuss with D.P. 2 Note lighting change to D.P.	1 Will probably need more than one shooting day and at least one set prep. day 2 Check with prod. designer to make sure all elements match period 3 Will Casely play the body with makeup or will it be a dummy? 4 Check with set dressing on number and placement of fingerprints 5 Will need armorer and set safety for gunshots

Figure 2-3. How a breakdown sheet might look, in this case using *Chicago* (2002) as an example.

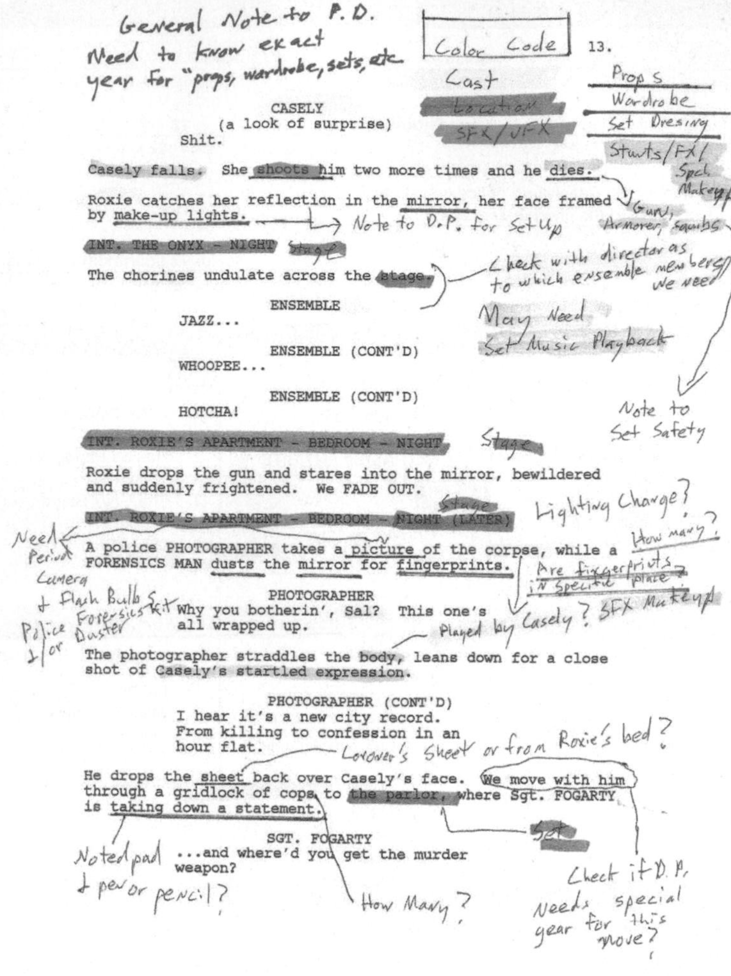

13.

CASELY
(a look of surprise)
Shit.

Casely falls. She shoots him two more times and he dies.

Roxie catches her reflection in the mirror, her face framed by make-up lights.

INT. THE ONYX - NIGHT

The chorines undulate across the stage.

ENSEMBLE
JAZZ...

ENSEMBLE (CONT'D)
WHOOPEE...

ENSEMBLE (CONT'D)
HOTCHA!

INT. ROXIE'S APARTMENT - BEDROOM - NIGHT

Roxie drops the gun and stares into the mirror, bewildered and suddenly frightened. We FADE OUT.

INT. ROXIE'S APARTMENT - BEDROOM - NIGHT (LATER)

A police PHOTOGRAPHER takes a picture of the corpse, while a FORENSICS MAN dusts the mirror for fingerprints.

PHOTOGRAPHER
Why you botherin', Sal? This one's all wrapped up.

The photographer straddles the body, leans down for a close shot of Casely's startled expression.

PHOTOGRAPHER (CONT'D)
I hear it's a new city record. From killing to confession in an hour flat.

He drops the sheet back over Casely's face. We move with him through a gridlock of cops to the parlor, where Sgt. FOGARTY is taking down a statement.

SGT. FOGARTY
...and where'd you get the murder weapon?

Courtesy of *Miramax*.

Figure 2-4. This page of the script for *Chicago* has been marked up with the kind of notes a production manager might use to keep track of various elements of the production.

- **Fill-in breakdown sheets.** Transfer the information you have broken out when you lined the script on a scene-by-scene basis to individual **breakdown sheets**, representing each scene in the movie. A professional breakdown sheet (such as Figure 2-3) features spreadsheet-style category boxes for each element, so that the data you port over from elements you flagged when you lined the script will ideally flow into appropriate categories—"cars" will end up listed under "vehicles," and "guns" will end up under "props," and so on. Depending on the software you use and your degree of sophistication, you can assign unique numbers for characters, scenes, props, and locations and then cross-reference them to make it easy for you to find elements and determine the frequency with which they appear in the story as you set out to budget for them. This provides you with the equivalent of a database that delineates elements for every scene, which you will need to take into consideration when creating a schedule.

Once you have breakdown sheets for every scene, you can easily calculate how many elements different scenes share in common, so that when you are ready to build your shooting schedule, you can make plans to shoot similar pieces of different scenes involving the same location, actors, props, or other elements at the same time, to make the best use of your resources. To be most efficient, assign headers to each breakdown sheet that include, at a minimum, the script page; the scene number or name; the number of pages; the location; and whether it is a day, night, interior, or exterior scene.

- **Create lists or boards.** This step involves sorting the information on the breakdown sheets to provide a visual representation of the different categories of elements so that an actual shooting schedule can begin to take shape. In the pre-digital era, this tool was known as the **production board**: a graphical display of breakdown-sheet information on a series of thin, color-coded cardboard charts, often called **production strips**, that the production manager would manually sort and mount on a large production board for the entire production management team to see and use, moving the strips around to form a rudimentary schedule. In some low-budget situations, independent filmmakers have even been known to use index cards. Today, scheduling software, such as affordable tools like Movie Magic Scheduling, have largely replaced physical boards or strips, but the idea is the same—to identify and arrange elements in such a way as to be able to build a shooting schedule. One of the beneficial things about today's online world is that you can easily create and inexpensively share simple spreadsheets and other documents online using Google Docs and other similar tools.

  Out of your breakdown sheets, especially if you use the right spreadsheet or scheduling software, it is fairly easy to sort and generate accurate and handy lists of related items, typically sorted in order of their expected cost. On professional productions, the most important lists are typically people and locations, since movie stars usually eat up the most money, and the availability of locations can frequently impact many aspects of your entire schedule. As a student filmmaker, you can evaluate which list will be most crucial and compile your lists according to your priorities. In any case, you will typically generate prop lists, wardrobe lists, vehicle lists, equipment lists, and other specialized lists, such as a list of visual or practical effects. These lists can be as detailed as you want or need them to be, and are a handy tool to help you both budget for particular items and, later, keep track of, and procure, those items. Essentially, you will be sorting out lists based on your project's needs. In a student production, virtually everyone will likely be volunteering his or her time. Therefore, although they might not be costing you much money, figuring out whom you will need—cast, crew, and support—and when, will be your biggest scheduling challenge. After all, in addition to scheduling around your project's needs, you will need to schedule around your *cast and crew's* limited availability, as well.

Shooting Schedule

There is no way around the fact that creating a shooting schedule is an art that takes time and experience to learn how to do skillfully. As we have already cautioned, a wide range of factors can impact it and force you to change it, often on the fly, requiring you to make as many contingency plans as possible when creating the schedule, as we will examine below. But if you boil things down, your basic *goals* for scheduling are as follows:

- Schedule so that you can capture what you absolutely must capture to complete your movie. Note that this is a far different thing than capturing everything you might *want* to capture. In other words: prioritize and make hard and often difficult choices along the way.
- Be as efficient and flexible as possible.
- Be as realistic as possible—don't attempt things that simply lie outside your resource capabilities.
- Always prepare as many backup options as you possibly can (see Action Steps: Be Prepared, below).

Action STEPS

Be Prepared

When scheduling a shoot, consider different scenarios and build various options into your schedule as backup plans should conditions require you to suddenly shift gears. Seasoned filmmakers recommend thinking about the following as you put your schedule together:

1. **Make sure any permits or releases have been identified and taken care of long *before* your shooting day.** Film history is littered with stories of shoots held up by union violations, fire or safety violations, or people showing up where they don't have permission to be. Have all paperwork in order before you go anywhere.
2. **Constantly analyze weather's potential impact on each of your exterior locations and schedule**, or at least make notes about what you would do on shooting days at those locations if you were rained out. Monitor the weather and stay in communication with your cast and crew, so that you can give them as much advance warning as possible if the time or location or scene to be shot the next morning will need to change.
3. **When feasible, arrange for what is known as a *cover set***—an accessible interior or covered location that you keep available to shoot at in the event bad weather or something else cancels shooting at an exterior location. Keep in mind that a cover set could be set up in a garage, a basement, your home, or in a location near your exterior location.
4. **If at all possible, schedule weather-dependent exterior shooting days early in your shooting schedule**, so that if you do get rained out, you might have time to return there, or at least to get exterior shots to combine with material you captured at your cover set.
5. **When scouting or arranging permission to shoot in a particular location, such as a restaurant, talk to your contact about an alternative day and time, beyond the agreed-upon day and time,** when it might be permissible for your team to show up with minimal notice. If you run into an exterior day ruined by weather and know you have permission to be in the restaurant that same day, you can save an entire day of shooting, but you won't know that if you haven't had that conversation well in advance.

Trim Your Shooting Script

Continually and dispassionately examine your script and schedule for scenes and shots you think your movie can live without—material that may be pretty or interesting, but that does not have a significant influence on your narrative. Schedule shooting for that material last, and cut it out if you fall behind schedule or need to switch to something else on a particular shooting day.

As you sort your strips or use your scheduling software, you need to plan what you calculate, not only the time it will take to shoot each scene but also the time it will take to set up and shoot on-set and, if necessary, to move from set to set or location to location. Obviously, you won't know precisely how long it will take to get each shot, capture each sequence, or finish each scene until you actually do it, because it will depend on how many takes and how much coverage you end up pursuing; how your equipment, cast, and crew perform; how well communication works on your set; what unforeseen circumstances you encounter; and how you deal with such things. However, as noted in Chapter 3, each page of a final, locked screenplay typically equates to about one minute of screen time; thus, roughly one-quarter of a script page is going to take up about 15 seconds of screen time. Therefore, in most cases, it won't be terribly efficient for you to spend an entire shooting day on a quarter page of your screenplay.

What *does* make sense is to plan your easiest-to-shoot scenes first, as a practical way to get your cast, crew, and sets ready before you segue into more complicated work later in the week. It's not unusual to schedule a day to prep a set and then shoot two or three quick scenes on the set on one day, and then schedule several rigorous pages to be shot on that same set the next day. The set will be prepped and ready on day two, and thus there is a natural progression between these two shooting days.

In fact, on low-budget films, you may shoot three or four pages over the course of 10 or 12 hours.[14] Generally, your pace is a function of your resources. The more money and time you have, the more deliberate you can afford to be. If you only have the luxury of a single day on a location, then logically everything your script says should be filmed in that location needs to be scheduled for that particular day. If all of those scenes won't fit into that one day, and there is no possibility of rearranging the schedule for returning there, then obviously you will need to cut something out. Therefore, your scheduled shot list should be a priority list, ranging from what is most important to what is least important, and not just in terms of shots but also in terms of coverage. Decide when you can live with one angle or less coverage or fewer takes and move on.

Here are some other logical guidelines to keep in mind when preparing your schedule and determining how to order your shoot:

- If your project's schedule allows formal rehearsal days during production, schedule them at the beginning of the week and start shooting on Wednesday, so that everyone comes into the first day of shooting fully prepared, and you leave yourself the following weekend to make changes if they are required.
- It is rarely a good idea to film your movie in linear script order, particularly at the low-budget level. You need to schedule your shoots around access to your locations, actors, and other resources; you can put it all together in the editing phase.

- If particular actors are only available on certain days, use your scheduling software to print out what is called a *day-out-of-days schedule* for that individual, and try to select days when you can shoot all material involving that actor, even if it is from different scenes.
- We suggest in Chapter 4 that there are many advantages to shooting in places you have access to. Among these advantages is the possibility of increased scheduling flexibility. If you have a family member or dear friend with a house on the beach that they will permit you to use, change scenes that take place in the country to the beach unless there is a strong creative reason that would prevent it. For student films in particular, much of a typical story can be told by shooting in places you already have access to and are quite familiar with. Working in places you know, or in places you have been given access to by people you know, will frequently mean you can get more time there, or at least be able to work more efficiently there, thus adding more options to your schedule.
- Schedule as much of the shoot to take place in one location, or in locations close to each other, as possible. The fewer moves there are between locations, the shorter time shooting will take, and the more you will be able to accomplish. If you have found a great old mansion in the country to shoot at, try to arrange to use the yard or surrounding grounds for your exterior work.
- Apply what you learned during location scouting (see Chapter 4). Learn everything you possibly can about where you are going and what typically goes on there at the time of day you will be there. For instance, if you have permission to shoot in the bleachers at a high school football field, and the bleachers are adjacent to a parking lot, know what time the parking lot starts filling up with noisy cars. If people start arriving at 9 a.m., schedule filming on the bleachers first thing, at 8 a.m., so that you can have a quieter environment and better sound for that scene before you move on to your scenes on the football field.
- Any time you can combine tasks, you will be ahead of the game. Be alert to identifying days when you can kill two birds with one stone, so to speak—shooting scenes you had initially pondered taking care of later in your schedule because you will have extra cameras available for other scenes on different days, or will already be at a comparable location. Plan sequences to be captured on particular days based on logistics and feasibility.
- Have a list of alternative shots or sequences or establishing material you could shoot at the same location, or other tasks you could take care of, if setup for a particularly complicated scene is taking too long—things you can get done while you are waiting to get other things done.

Keep Your Files

Even when your project is finished, organize and file away any important documents connected to it. If an injury or a legal dispute ever occurs related to the project, your records could prove useful. Therefore, it is always important, even on a small student film, to have an efficient record-keeping system during production, and a smart filing and archiving system afterward. On a studio project, you will be required to turn such documentation over to the studio on completion.

Practice

Creating a Backup Plan

Create two schedules for shooting what is supposed to be an exterior scene in your student film: one, the basic plan; and the other, the backup plan. Describe the scene, actors and crew needed, and location, and type up a simple morning shooting schedule. Then, presume there is a good possibility of rain that morning. Come up with a new schedule and plan for the same sequence. Will you have a cover set prepared? (If so, describe the details.) Will there be an available interior near the original exterior location and a creative way to move the scene inside and still make it work? Will you have an alternate scene that could be shot in the rain? Explain your plan, schedule, and justification for your decisions.

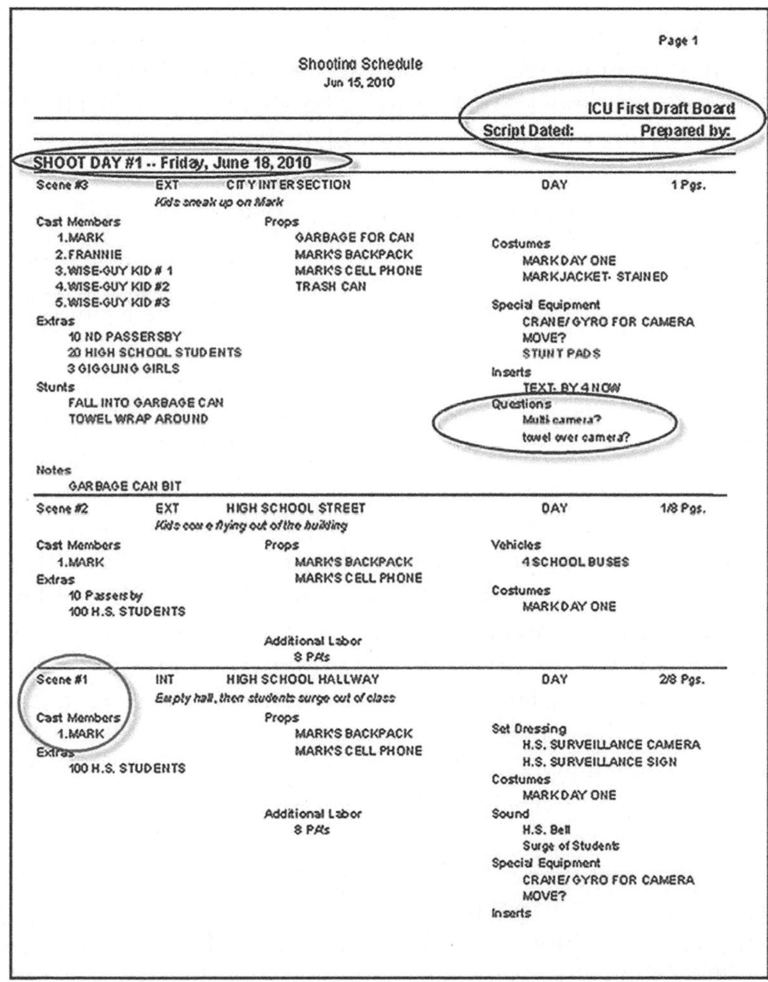

Page 1

Shootina Schedule
Jun 15, 2010

ICU First Draft Board
Script Dated: Prepared by:

SHOOT DAY #1 -- Friday, June 18, 2010

Scene #3 EXT CITY INTERSECTION DAY 1 Pgs.
Kids sneak up on Mark

Cast Members
1.MARK
2.FRANNIE
3.WISE-GUY KID # 1
4.WISE-GUY KID #2
5.WISE-GUY KID #3

Extras
10 ND PASSERSBY
20 HIGH SCHOOL STUDENTS
3 GIGGLING GIRLS

Stunts
FALL INTO GARBAGE CAN
TOWEL WRAP AROUND

Props
GARBAGE FOR CAN
MARK'S BACKPACK
MARK'S CELL PHONE
TRASH CAN

Costumes
MARK DAY ONE
MARK JACKET- STAINED

Special Equipment
CRANE/ GYRO FOR CAMERA MOVE?
STUNT PADS

Inserts
TEXT- BY 4 NOW

Questions
Multi camera?
towel over camera?

Notes
GARBAGE CAN BIT

Scene #2 EXT HIGH SCHOOL STREET DAY 1/8 Pgs.
Kids come flying out of the building

Cast Members
1.MARK

Extras
10 Passersby
100 H.S. STUDENTS

Props
MARK'S BACKPACK
MARK'S CELL PHONE

Additional Labor
8 PA's

Vehicles
4 SCHOOL BUSES

Costumes
MARK DAY ONE

Scene #1 INT HIGH SCHOOL HALLWAY DAY 2/8 Pgs.
Empty hall, then students surge out of class

Cast Members
1.MARK

Extras
100 H.S. STUDENTS

Props
MARK'S BACKPACK
MARK'S CELL PHONE

Additional Labor
8 PA's

Set Dressing
H.S. SURVEILLANCE CAMERA
H.S. SURVEILLANCE SIGN

Costumes
MARK DAY ONE

Sound
H.S. Bell
Surge of Students

Special Equipment
CRANE/ GYRO FOR CAMERA MOVE?

Inserts

Figure 2-5. In this example of a shooting schedule, you will see that many elements are specifically enumerated, including actors, props, costumes, and set dressing.

The shooting schedule will ultimately be used to generate the daily **call sheet**, a document that delineates each shooting day's operational plan in detail, informing everyone involved where they are supposed to be and when; what equipment, costumes, or props will be

needed; what scenes will be shot, and in what order; and so forth (see Figure 2-5). Additionally, a typical call sheet will list important ancillary information, like what the day's weather is expected to be like, parking information, emergency cell-phone numbers, meal times or options, and hospital or doctor information. Often, the first assistant director is responsible for generating each day's call sheet, subject to the producer's and the director's approval. Today, making call sheets is a relatively easy and inexpensive thing to do, thanks to several types of online and mobile apps now available, including Doddle, Pocket Call Sheet, and Shot Lister.[15]

Budgeting

As noted, you first need to create a preliminary schedule in order to construct a realistic budget for your production. A movie budget is essentially the financial representation of what you expect it will cost to execute that schedule and deliver the elements you are planning to create to make your movie. This is why we have emphasized that the two go together—if one changes, the other will likely change with it. That is why, like your schedule, your budget will evolve over time. And that is also why, in some cases, you may—as some studio productions do—initially design alternative budgets to account for different scenarios or possibilities that could come to fruition later.

As student filmmakers, your primary goal in making your movie is not (yet) the same as the primary goal of Hollywood studios: the almighty profit motive. However, at a foundational level, you still need to be able to figure out if you can afford to make the movie you have designed. But we have also emphasized what is obvious—that filmmaking is a creative endeavor. And you are students, with few resources. Therefore, many things in your screenplay will be left to a different sort of creativity to determine how you will execute them: creativity built around how cleverly you allocate and use scarce resources. As students, you will examine your resources, tailor the plan to what is feasible, and then budget for it. The creative importance of the scene and what you can afford to do with it will help you come to some budgetary conclusions about it.

It is crucial to remember: Your budget is not the creative *limiting* factor. It is the creative *defining* factor. Whether the budget is $100 or $100 million, it is still a finite number (exceeded by at least 10 percent in many cases). You and your team will have to figure out how to squeeze every penny out of whatever that finite number is to tell your story.

Whatever choices you make, there will be some kind of cost associated with them, even if those costs are bottom-of-the-barrel minimal. The cost of anything you might want to do, from getting a camera to clothing, transporting, or feeding actors, are all *potential* costs. As students, you will most likely be doing some of the jobs on the set yourself. Other jobs, such as acting and camera work, will be handled by volunteers. Even so, these volunteers will all need to be fed. Cars or trucks will need gas. If you don't have a camera, you will need to borrow, buy, or rent one. Anything that you actually spend money on—even pennies—will end up being a *hard* cost, which you will need to account for somehow. You will need to monitor these costs and adjust for them. Therefore, it is essential that you create a budget document in order to follow these costs and make sure that you don't spend more than you have—an eventuality that could grind your project to a halt, not to mention potentially land you in financial hot water. This budget document is not about making rough estimates; it is about notating *everything* you will need to make the movie, ascribing real costs to each element, and detailing how those costs are going to be covered. In this section, we will review how to make up such a budget document, how to resourcefully reduce costs or find work-arounds when you have no resources, and what the basic terminology and concepts are for movie budgeting.

Budget Document

Film budget documents generally have a standard format, and the important thing to remember is that the more detail included in your budget, the more accurate it will be and the better off the project will be. With basic skills, you can create a budget document using an Excel spreadsheet, but a wide range of budget template software tools are available at low or no cost across the Internet, including many tailored specifically for movie production. Whatever tool you use, the general format will look like this:

ICU
Student Name

DIRECTOR:
PRODUCER:

SCRIPT DATED:
START DATE:

LOCATION DAYS:
STAGE DAYS:
TOTAL SHOOT DAYS:
UNIONS:

Acct#	Category Description	Page	Orig	Total	Var
1100	STORY & SCREENPLAY	1	$0	$0	$0
1200	PRODUCERS	1	$580	$704	$124
1300	DIRECTOR	1	$780	$904	$124
1400	CAST	2	$1,272	$1,843	$571
1500	ATL TRAVEL & LIVING	3	$0	$0	$0
	Total Above-The-Line		**$2,632**	**$3,452**	**$820**
2100	PRODUCTION STAFF	3	$3,100	$4,426	$1,326
2200	BACKGROUND ACTORS	4	$696	$845	$149
2300	PRODUCTION DESIGN	5	$1,260	$1,509	$249
2400	SET CONSTRUCTION	6	$0	$0	$0
2500	SET DRESSING	6	$3,280	$3,404	$124
2600	PROPS	7	$7,695	$7,819	$124
2700	WARDROBE	9	$1,155	$1,279	$124
2800	MAKEUP & HAIR	10	$680	$804	$124
3100	SET OPERATIONS	11	$4,910	$5,159	$249
3200	SET LIGHTING	12	$3,710	$3,959	$249
3300	CAMERA	13	$24,261	$24,510	$249
3400	PRODUCTION SOUND	14	$3,310	$3,559	$249
3500	LOCATIONS	15	$6,625	$6,625	$0
3600	TRANSPORTATION	16	$5,315	$5,315	$0
3700	PROD FILM/ DATA MANAGEMENT	17	$800	$800	$0
3800	FACILITIES	17	$0	$0	$0
3900	SPECIAL EFFECTS	18	$0	$0	$0
4200	TESTS	18	$200	$200	$0
	Total Below-the-Line Production		**$66,997**	**$70,215**	**$3,218**
5100	EDITORIAL	18	$11,900	$12,522	$622
5200	MUSIC	19	$0	$0	$0
5300	POST PRODUCTION SOUND	19	$0	$0	$0
5400	POST FILM / DATA MANAGEMENT	20	$0	$0	$0
5500	TITLES & OPTICALS	20	$0	$0	$0
	Total Post Production		**$11,900**	**$12,522**	**$622**
6100	INSURANCE	20	$0	$0	$0
6300	LEGAL	20	$0	$0	$0
6400	GENERAL	21	$0	$0	$0
	Total Other		**$0**	**$0**	**$0**
	Grand Total		**$81,529**	**$86,189**	**$4,660**

Movie Magic Budgeting

Figure 2-6. Sample budget top sheet

- **Top sheet.** This is essentially a cover sheet that summarizes the budget document's major categories and lists the bottom line, or total cost of production. The **top sheet** is the first thing that financiers, studio heads, or—in your case—possibly your professor will review to get a sense of where your money is being allocated (see Figure 2-6). A complicated professional top sheet would likely list everything by department (camera, grip, transportation, office, second unit). As a student filmmaker, depending on the complexity of your project, you might also break things down that way. At a minimum, make your top sheet a fairly simple summary page that lists your **hard costs** (things you absolutely must find a way to pay for, such as gas, food, camera rental, and location fees), no-cost items, and all funding sources and amounts, thus providing a simple mathematical illustration of how much you need to spend juxtaposed with how much you are taking in. If there is money left over or an even zero at the bottom, you are in relatively good shape; if there is a negative amount resulting as your bottom line, you had better start revising your plans immediately.
- **Above-the-line costs.** Detailed breakdown pages will follow that will further delineate costs based on category, with above-the-line costs coming first. **Above-the-line (ATL) costs** refer to the generally more expensive costs of studio films—usually talent costs in the form of producers, actors, directors, writers, rights acquisition, and sometimes very highly paid craftspeople. On a student film, ATL costs may be minimal, since you are not typically paying much, if anything, to actors and are likely producing and directing yourself.
- **Below-the-line costs.** As you might expect, **below-the-line (BTL) costs** refer to the day-to-day costs of crew and equipment required for the physical production of the movie. These would include cameras, set construction, and tape or digital media. On a student film, if you have any extensive costs at all, they will likely come out of the BTL category.

In all budget documents, it is best to itemize your ATL and BTL costs. On the professional level, this can run on for thousands of lines and dozens—sometimes hundreds—of pages. Each line will account for one crew member, item to be rented or purchased, or supply to be consumed; the daily or weekly rate for the item; how many hours, days, or weeks it will be used; what scenes it will be used for, and the costs per scene or location in many cases; and the subtotal for that item. Each line of detail also ties to the schedule. Taxes (such as sales taxes) and *fringes* (such as Social Security payments, state disability insurance, union-mandated health and pension benefits) and other fees will have their own lines and sections; there will be categories for what currencies are being used or transferred, as well as a host of minute details that would be of interest only to studio or bank accountants. Also, in the modern era of digital filmmaking, visual effects can be so large and complex and eat up so many resources that they frequently go through their own, entirely separate scheduling and budgeting process.

Obviously, not all of this will apply to you right now. Still, this *approach* is the only real way that you, and anyone you are responsible to—your professor or school, financiers, family, partners, or friends—can know how your resources are being used; more importantly, since you are students, it is the only way you can possibly learn proper principles and procedures for motion picture budgeting. Though this may never become your passion as a filmmaker, if you ever hope to participate in producing your own work at any future level, having this knowledge will serve you well.

Remember Postproduction

When crafting a budget, don't shortchange postproduction, particularly sound effects. On low-budget projects in particular, it is likely that production sound will be far less than pristine and will need sweetening or looping and, more likely than not, sound effects added to make your illusions come to life. Prioritize limited resources based on the most essential things, and work backward from there. At the most rudimentary level, getting enough coverage and corresponding elements to tell your story well is what is absolutely essential, but you will need resources for post-production as well.

Be Resourceful

One of the positive things about making low-budget movies is that reality can lead to better creative choices, and not only where the on-screen narrative is concerned. As students, you have the opportunity—indeed, the requirement—to be ultra-resourceful on the business side of your project as well, and by definition, that resourcefulness requires a level of creativity and even panache. The better you get at figuring out ways to insert zeros into the "costs" column on your budget document, the more success you will eventually find at being an innovative and free-thinking, out-of-the-box filmmaker.

And when we say "resourceful," we mean in terms of finding ways to get jobs done and equipment and materials procured without spending money. There is an art to developing the skill of finding low- or no-cost labor, equipment, props, locations, costumes, and so on, and you will only get better at it over time. However, there are some tried-and-true shortcuts and tips that independent filmmakers have used for generations that you can consider, depending on your project's needs (see also Action Steps "Planning Crew Meals on a Tight Budget"). Among these are the following:

- Write or revise your script specifically to adhere to your budget and locations.
- Thoroughly research what your film school and other organizations offer students in terms of gear and resources, and inquire as to whether you can partner with the school or others on ownership of your film's copyright, as discussed earlier in this chapter. Your school or other "investors" may chip in equipment, funds, or other resources in return for an ownership stake in the movie (see Producer Smarts: "Finding Funding").
- To the degree you need to bring in crew in different disciplines, such as cinematography or editing, if you do not already have access to equipment, try to lure people who own their own equipment. This is particularly helpful with your cinematographer, editor, and location mixer.
- Inquire about discounts and free rentals of equipment for student filmmakers from equipment rental houses and local businesses. Some rental houses will also lower costs based on shorter-term rentals.
- Take advantage of free or low-cost cinematography, lighting, scheduling, and budgeting apps that are readily available to consumers, as well as specialized apps for other disciplines that are often low cost and tailored to the filmmaking community.

- Follow our advice in Chapter 4 and use furniture and set pieces from your own home and the homes of friends and family members.
- Use homes, property, and business locations of friends and family as shooting locations if available. Figure out if an area in your own home, your garage, or a warehouse or storage space that you have access to could be converted into a stage, if needed.
- Have cast, crew, classmates, friends, and family provide hair and makeup services—you already likely know people with good skills in these and similar areas.
- Trade credits and appearances of people, logos, businesses, and places for the right to shoot in locations or for labor, food, and equipment from locals in the town where you are shooting.
- Search for unsigned or unproduced local musicians in your school or community who are looking for exposure, and put their music in your film—and even get their help scoring the film—in return for exposing them to a wider audience and letting them promote your use of their work for their own needs.

Remember: all such items, even if coming to the project at no cost to you, need to be listed on your budget document and tracked. You may owe someone a credit in return for the resource or future revenue if the movie earns any money down the road, or you may need the information for tax purposes later on.

Track Your Spending

Run a weekly report to indicate whether your budget and spending is on track. On professional projects, a production accountant is assigned to monitor expenditures during production and feed the production management team up-to-date information on money being spent in the form of frequent cost reports that are generated every day, sometimes even multiple times during a day.

Producer SMARTS

Finding Funding

We have discussed how to be resourceful in terms of finding people, equipment, and services you won't have to pay much—if anything—to procure. However, a far more complex art involves the world of real film financing. There are certain pathways that exist for student filmmakers to find ethical methods to raise funds for projects under particular conditions. Obviously, the most feasible way for students to obtain funding is to enter a student competition or earn a scholarship or grant through their school or any of a number of national and international student film competitions.

Additionally, there is nothing to stop an enterprising student from holding fund-raising activities in the real world, or online through crowdfunding sites like Kickstarter. Thousands of student and independent film and video projects have raised funds and been produced this way. Also, you might offer a credit or equity stake in your movie to anyone who might want to give or lend you money to make your movie, but you should seek out competent legal and financial advice beyond the scope of this book before you go down the road of borrowing money. But what is a student filmmaker to do when winning a competition or raising large sums aren't feasible options?

While motion picture financing can be an arcane and confusing world, at a minimum you should strive to understand the basic concepts of how things work. Some of these often-used financing methods may not be viable for you yet. At your level, we are not urging you to seek out investors or borrow money, but rather to start learning how the financing game works for future reference if you are interested in continuing your filmmaking education. (Please remember that you must always have professional legal and financial advice before seeking financing on any film.) Well-established methods for financing major projects typically include the following:

- **Seed investors.** These people simply believe in a project and expect to get a return somehow. Typically, these investors provide "seed money," a small amount of up-front money to develop a project or to begin filming. Filmmakers might use that seed money to make a short trailer out of the early footage, often called a *sizzle piece*, for the express purpose of selling other investors on the project's potential. Though often risky for the investor, it is the most typical way students get outside funding help beyond the possibilities of grants or scholarships.
- **Nonprofit foundation and government grants.** Under certain conditions, these grants are sometimes applicable to student filmmakers.
- **Tax incentives and rebates.** If projects bring business to other states or countries, they can sometimes be given tax breaks or cash rebates in return for shooting there.
- **Presales.** This involves a method of providing financing in return for the right to distribute the film in different countries before it is even made (preselling the rights).
- **Debt financing.** This means getting a bank loan, to provide immediate cash the production can use. The loan will be paid back when tax incentives, rebates, or presales contracts are paid in full—plus interest to the bank, of course.
- **Co-productions.** These are collaborative productions, where two or more companies jointly produce the movie, with each company putting in financial and other resources.
- **Private equity financing.** This allows private individuals or organizations to invest cash in return for partial or full ownership of the film.

Action STEPS

Planning Crew Meals on a Tight Budget

Professional filmmakers say if there is one basic, logistical matter a young filmmaker should not overlook in scheduling and budgeting a movie shoot, it is the issue of food and meals for cast and crew. Although this may seem insignificant, in point of fact, even on a small production, food can turn into a major line item on a budget. And just as important, failure to schedule time for meals and provide a way to conveniently access food can directly impact efficiency—simply put, the old adage that an army (even a small one) moves on its stomach is true, particularly in filmmaking. This is especially true in the world of student filmmaking, in which most of the people helping you are volunteers. Feeding these people and thus keeping them content may well be the only tangible benefit you can provide them during production.

Therefore, here are some simple and basic tips about getting the crew fed in an affordable way, and scheduling meals in such a way as to improve efficiency on-set:

1. **Depending on conditions, try to schedule your shoot to begin after breakfast or end before dinner.**
2. **Strategically schedule only those actors and crew members you know you will need during mealtimes.** Even though your lead actors may be needed all day, your roomful of extras can be released before you need to feed them.
3. **Check with local restaurants and markets in the town and near the locations where you are filming**—some will provide deals or discounts for student productions if you approach them and make special requests, or negotiate to put their restaurant, market, sign, or logo in your movie.
4. **Keep snacks on-set.** Whereas the big studios have whole departments devoted to on-set food catering—craft services—affordable snacks, such as veggies, chips, and crackers, can be made readily available to large groups at very little expense when you buy in bulk at wholesalers such as Costco.
5. **Cook for your crew.** If you or a spouse, significant other, classmate, sibling, parent, friend, or colleague have great cooking skills and the time, it can frequently be far cheaper to whip up large batches of tasty dishes and cart them over to the set than to pay for restaurant or catered food.

Practice

Identify Hard Costs

Create a sample film budget for a short student film based on a simple three-day movie shoot using software you may already own or can easily acquire. The budget can be from a real project you are currently developing or an example of one using numbers for resources you think you could realistically access. The point of the exercise is to identify what absolute hard costs you think you would have to incur to make a short student film like the one you are envisioning. What expenses are there simply no way to avoid—food? gas? camera rentals? travel? location fees or permits?—and how much will those expenses cost you? Research such costs in detail.

UPM's Emergency Kit

- Budgeting and scheduling software tools
- Near-set office space for posting schedules and daily reports
- Petty cash
- Charged cell phone
- Extra batteries and chargers
- Walkie-talkies
- Readily available contact information for local police, fire, and permit authorities; local labor guilds; and medical facilities
- Fueled vehicle with navigation system

Chapter Essentials

- Organizing a movie project means putting on a producer's hat, creating a production management team, and delegating management tasks to that team. Someone acting in the capacity of unit production manager (UPM) will play essential roles in this process.
- The UPM will painstakingly line the script, identifying every element that needs to be scheduled or budgeted; organize those elements into detailed breakdown sheets; and create schedules and lists that allow you to efficiently figure out timelines and costs for each of those elements during the budgeting process. The UPM will also generate detailed shooting schedules, as well as call sheets that will serve as daily guides for every crew and cast member.
- Even with low resources, detailed budgets that delineate above-the-line and below-the-line costs are essential not only for business purposes but also creatively, in order to let you know what elements of your story are feasible to execute, and enable you to move your plan forward and avoid a stalled or derailed project. Resourceful independent filmmakers can reduce or eliminate costs, but they will still wind up with hard costs they will need to develop financing plans.

Chapter 3

Screenwriting

Start with the Script

"Start with the Script" from *Filmmaking in Action*, by Adam Leipzig, Barry S. Weiss, and Michael Goldman, pp. 19–42 (Chapter 2, "Start with the Script").

"The hardest part of any story is to figure out the point of entry where your story begins."

—Robert Towne, screenwriter of more than thirty-five films, including *Chinatown* (1974), *The Firm* (1993), and *Mission: Impossible* (1996)[1]

Figure 3-1. *Chinatown* (1974).

When Robert Towne began writing *Chinatown*, considered by many experts to be among the most finely structured screenplays of all time, he thought about the theme that would resonate in every scene. The story would be about Los Angeles's history, water rights, corruption, and power. At first Towne considered writing a detective movie. However, as his creative process deepened, he realized that a detective movie wasn't enough; he wanted to explore the theme of what crime really means. He would have his characters discover how land and community are destroyed as they encounter the disturbing, transgressive reality of modern cities springing into being.

He resolved to write a film far larger than a mere detective story, even though a detective would be its main character. Towne composed more than twenty outlines, each with thick, scene-by-scene descriptions. This gave him a view of most of the story. Then he scribbled one-sentence summaries of each scene on sheets of paper, so that he could cut them up and paste them on the door of the study where he and the director were working. They rearranged the scraps of paper over and over until they arrived at an order that worked. Towne then began crafting the scenes, fleshing out the characters and their actions through dialogue and dramatic moments.

Towne had turned down a lucrative studio job to write *Chinatown*; Paramount had offered him $175,000 to pen an adaptation of *The Great Gatsby*. Instead, Towne chose his passion project and grappled with the script for 10 months. He was rewarded when *Chinatown* won the Academy Award for Best Original Screenplay.

Towne's experience in writing *Chinatown* is a model for writing any film, big or small: build your idea; decide on your themes and characters; organize the structure; and work, work, work. The written word is the first road map for all successful movies, from 2-minute classroom projects to 15-minute thesis films, from 30-second commercials to epic-length features. Even documentaries begin with a written description of their subject matter. Completely visual films, including silent and animated movies, also begin with words.

Words are a way of describing your vision for the project, and they help make sure you and your collaborators are literally on the same page. Words are also the most cost effective way to test your storytelling and visual ideas, because it is always better to test your filmic imagination in a document, to make sure it is what you want and communicates that vision to others, before you start spending time and resources actively producing the movie.

In this chapter, you'll explore where stories come from, how to imagine characters, and the formats that work best to convey your ideas for the screen. You'll also discover the way scripts are refined until they are ready to be shot, a process that's called *development*. You'll learn how to do all this for your class project, which resembles the way many smaller, independent films are made, and also how writing operates in larger studio movies. No matter what scale you are working at, whether in school or on a Hollywood lot, good writing starts with a character the audience can identify with. As you begin, a blank canvas awaits your imagination; you are about to describe the movie you want to make. The suspense builds, and you ask yourself, What will happen next?

Key Concepts

- Good movies start with good ideas, and there are many ways to discover good ideas.
- Theme, story, and character are the building blocks of film narratives.

- When writing a screenplay, you need to follow a specific standard.
- Revising your script many times is a normal and necessary part of the process.

Where Do Ideas Come From?

An idea for a movie is more than just a thought: it must have at least one character, a conflict, and some kind of story. Like all narratives, movies have three elements: the teller of the tale, the tale itself, and the audience to whom the tale is told; in many ways, the audience is the real center of attention.

It's a good idea to begin by thinking about your audience, and yourself in relation to them. Who are you making the movie for—your class, people at your school, or perhaps a wider audience? Who are these people, and what will they enjoy? This isn't so much a matter of pandering to the audience, or putting your own deep passions on hold for the short-term gain of making something that will get a good grade or "sell," but acknowledging a fundamental principle of the entertainment enterprise: the word *entertainment* comes from the same word as *intertwine*, which means that bringing people together is a core value in what you are attempting. You must tell a story worth sharing, and care deeply about satisfying the people with whom you are sharing it.

There are two categories of ideas: those that come entirely from you, which are called original ideas, and those that are inspired by material you discover. Both are fertile ground for compelling movies.

Original Ideas

If you think of an idea for a movie yourself, it is called an **original idea.** That means it originated with you. This original idea can become the basis for all kinds of projects: movies, television shows, graphic novels, short videos, interactive games, books, and plays. An idea is just the beginning of something; how you choose to extend it creatively is based on your particular talents and your audience, what you are trying to communicate, and the medium that best suits the idea itself. In the case of your class project, you will be seeking a story that can be well told as a film, which means it should have strong characters, contain compelling visual elements, and be able to be told in a relatively few number of minutes.

As you come up with original ideas that you think may have screenplay potential, however, make sure you pause and take note of the difference between having an original idea for a story and how you specifically express the idea with your screenplay. As we will discuss later in this chapter, you will need to register and copyright your screenplays to protect them from being copied or stolen. But the raw conceptual idea itself, in most cases, is not what you will be trying to protect as much as the specific way in which you have expressed it with your story. For example, anyone is free to try and write a story about a historical event like the Iran hostage crisis or a mythical figure such as Hercules. But if your specific story comes anywhere close to the form or structure or characters, dialogue, or nature of the specific story owned by the studios that released *Argo* in 2012 or the *Hercules* action-adventure film of 2014, you may likely find yourself facing a lawsuit you would just as soon avoid. While it is not our place or purpose to give legal advice in this book, it is important that you be aware of this distinction.

The best original stories come from your own awareness—the people, relationships, and actions you have observed, lived, and taken. You need life experiences, sometimes deeply personal and emotional ones, to understand the story you want to tell and to be able to express it well. This doesn't mean you have to live everything in order to write about it: no screenwriter has ever lived in Renaissance England, but there are many movies that take place there. However, to write effectively about anything, you need to understand the human emotions and motivations of the characters, which means you need to be sensitive to your own life story and emotional responses.

Coming up with original ideas can seem difficult, and you will probably consider and reject several of them before settling on one that merits the time and effort you'll spend on your class film. There are many ways to explore movie stories—try some of the techniques in Action Steps: "Brainstorming Ideas"

Figure 3-2. ***Crash*** (2004), screenplay by Paul Haggis and Bobby Moresco, is based on Paul Haggis's original story. An unconventional film made outside the studio system, *Crash* won Academy Awards for Best Picture, Best Original Screenplay, and Best Editing.

Beginning with an original idea has several advantages. The first is that you are not relying on another person's work. You do not need to contact anybody to get permission to use an idea that is yours. (In any event, it would be unethical—and illegal—to use someone else's work and base your movie on it, unless the original author has given you permission.)

Another attribute of an original idea is that it can bring something new to the screen and be more fun for the audience. You have probably experienced movies that feel overly familiar, like a copy of something else. Audiences are bored with derivative work. They want and deserve something fresh, and they're looking to you to provide it for them. Even if your theme or setting is familiar, your actual plot and characters can bring a fresh take to that theme.

Action **STEPS**

Brainstorming Ideas

Sometimes it seems as though our minds are just filled with ideas—until we need to come up with one for a class project! Here are five effective ways to break through the brainstorming barrier.

1. **Create a mind map.** A movie-idea mind map is a diagram that begins with a character, incident, or place at the center, and then marks everything that comes off of it, like the spokes of a wheel. Each spoke can generate its own spokes as well. This puts your thoughts on paper, so you can look at it and discover the most valuable nuggets.

2. **Use the 10-minute trick.** It doesn't seem daunting if you don't have to do it for very long. Set your alarm for 10 minutes and write down as many movie ideas as you can in this short burst of time. You'll be amazed by how many you will come up with!

3. **Remember your best stories.** Is there a story you find yourself telling over and over because it's always funny or interesting or emotional? That story could be the basis for your class film; the fact that you tell it often means you probably already have a structure for the narrative.

4. **Keep a journal.** Always have a place to jot down thoughts as they come to you, and record at least one notable experience or character you meet every day. If you begin your journal now, at the beginning of the term, it will be filled with ideas by the time you need to select your project idea.

5. **Do it with friends.** Set a specific time (and a time limit, usually 30–60 minutes) to talk about ideas for a particular character or incident with your classmates. During the session, resist the urge to critique contributions in order to encourage creative flow, free from judgment or negativity. Make sure someone in the group makes an audio recording of what is said, as written notes can be incomplete and memories are not often accurate.

Source Material

If you base your film story on something that someone else has created, then it is called an **adapted screenplay**, and the place where the story came from is called **source material**. Source material can take many forms. It could be a graphic novel like *300* by Frank Miller; a comic book like *Spider-Man*; a work of literary fiction like *Winter's Bone*, *Slumdog Millionaire*, or the *Lord of the Rings* trilogy; a nonfiction history like *Band of Brothers*; a television show like *Star Trek* or *The A-Team*; or even another movie, like *The Ring*, which was adapted from a Japanese horror film. Source material can also come from newspaper or magazine articles; for example, *The Soloist* (2009) had its origin in a series of articles published in the *Los Angeles Times*.

Screenplays adapted from source material are among the most honored films in Oscar history. This is likely because the source material has already created the characters and the world in which the story takes place, endowing them with a multitude of interesting details, which makes the writer's job different if not easier. Even when a story is based on historical events, the screenwriter may be asked to adapt the work from a written history, because a book can bring together a great deal of research as well as a point of view on the material. Such was the case with the film *Captain Phillips* (2013), which was a true story with a screenplay based on an autobiographical book.

Adaptation, though, can be a tricky challenge for a writer. Books and interactive games—two popular sources for film adaptations—can take 40 hours or more to read or play to the end. How, then, to compact all that narrative into a feature film of two hours, or even a shorter movie? Obviously, in an adaptation, much material will need to be cut, but time constraints are only the most obvious of adaptation's challenges. The most fundamental difference between film and these other sources is that film storytelling inherently appears more *objective*, whereas novels and games are more *subjective*. In a novel or game, the reader or player can get inside the conscious experience of the main character—hear his or her thoughts and feel the interior monologue. In a film—even a film that has first-person voice-over narration—the main character is objectified because the audience sees him or her as an object of study.

Figure 3-3. Tom Hanks, as Captain Richard Phillips, faces off against the Somali pirate Muse, played by Barkhad Abdi, in ***Captain Phillips*** (2013). Billy Ray adapted the screenplay from Richard Phillips and Stephan Talty's autobiographical book, *A Captain's Duty: Somali Pirates, Navy SEALs, and Dangerous Days at Sea*.

A good example of this difference can be found in the novel *Push* by Sapphire and the film *Precious* (2009), adapted from it. The novel is written in the first person, in the voice of Clarice "Precious" Jones, an obese, 16-year-old African American girl who is pregnant with her second child. Although she is barely literate, Precious manages to convey her story, and the reader comes to know and empathize with her completely relatable desire to live her life with freedom, safety, and dignity, and to better herself against tragic odds. Of course, one of the literary tricks of the novel is that we never see Precious. Told in the first person and lacking images, readers are able to create their own mental image of what Precious looks like and make her relatable to their own experiences and viewpoints.

In the movie version, the filmmakers had to cast an actress in the lead role, creating a real image of Precious that wasn't available in the book. The challenge, then, was how to reconcile how the external world views Precious with her own internal life as described in the book. To allow viewers into Precious's head, screenwriter Geoffrey Fletcher invented fantasy sequences, providing a visual understanding for how Precious sees herself—graceful, beautiful, and empowered. The film screened at multiple festivals, did well at the box office, and won the Academy Award for Best Adapted Screenplay. Sometimes the key to adaptation is taking a completely unique creative approach—one not found in the original material.

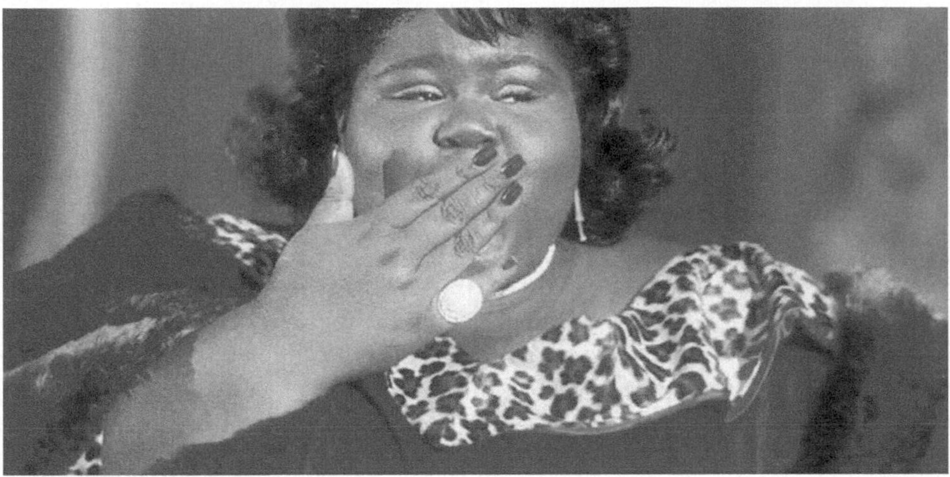

Figure 3-4. Precious, portrayed by Gabourey Sidibe, dances with flair in her first fantasy sequence in ***Precious*** (2009).

Intellectual Property

When dealing with any kind of adaptation, you must make sure you have the original creator's permission to adapt the underlying work. That's because all creative works are **intellectual property**—a legal term that means that creative works can be owned in the same way you can own a camera or a mobile phone. When you write a script in a professional setting, it is a best practice to make sure you can prove it is yours and when you wrote it, in the event someone later plagiarizes, or steals, your work. In the entertainment industry, this is done by either copyrighting your work or registering it with the Writers Guild of America, which is the professional organization for screenwriters, or both. (You don't need to be a member to register your work.)

Although it is important to protect yourself against plagiarism, it's also important to understand the concept of plagiarism. In order to prove plagiarism, you must prove that the offender had *access* to your work, which is why you must keep careful records about who has access to your material. Otherwise, it is quite possible that someone else came up with the same idea or story as you; indeed, many stories have strong similarities even though they were not stolen from someone else, especially adapted screenplays that often rely on different source material to tell the same story. All writers are describing versions of the same basic reality, so it is no surprise that stories often have common elements, albeit expressed differently.

Rights and Title

Just as you should care about protecting what is yours, other people will care about protecting what is theirs. For example, if you want to base your class film on a story someone else wrote, you need to ask permission. If you get permission, it is called a **grant of rights**. Any grant of rights should be written down and signed by both parties because memories are imperfect and friendships can easily fray. This is not a needless complication; in the Hollywood landscape, studios have spent millions of dollars to acquire rights to big franchise characters like Superman and the X-Men, and some rights holders have similarly spent millions of dollars going to court when they thought their rights were being infringed. In today's digital world this can apply to almost anything, even a landmark building, whose owners vigilantly will assert their rights to those iconic or trademarked images.

Register and Protect

You can protect your ideas, and prove that they originated with you, by registering them with the U.S. Copyright Office (www.copyright.gov) or with the Writers Guild of America (www.wga.org).

Because of digital distribution technologies, it is important to have all rights in a project in order to make a film—and in order to secure financing for the movie. "All rights" means everything: the right to make a movie, a television series, a series of books, interactive games, webisodes, and anything else. In fact, the legal language in rights contracts often contains a phrase that says the rights include "all rights now known or hereafter contemplated, for dissemination in all forms, on all devices, and in all media now known or hereafter devised, on Earth and throughout the Universe." No one can say the movie business doesn't think highly of itself!

When there is a clear link between the source material and works that derive from it, this is called the legal **chain of title**. "Title" simply means the right to do the work. For example, if you write a script, you own the title to it. If you give a director permission to make a movie of your script, you must also give the director title to make the movie, which is best done in a written document. Imagine a chain with many links, and you want to make sure the chain does not have any "broken links," or places where there is not a continuous flow of rights from one party to another; this is chain of title in action. Chain of title emphasizes that the act of writing is in fact the act of creating intellectual property—property that is real, needs to be protected, and has legal status.

Figure 3-5. ***Man of Steel***, Warner Bros.'s 2013 continuation of the Superman franchise, was subject to lengthy legal battles over rights. The courts decided in favor of the studio only eight weeks before the film opened. Studios spend tens of millions of dollars to acquire rights to well-known franchise characters—and millions more defending their rights in court.

Fair Use

Although you need to be cautious about using others' work, at times it is possible to do so under a legal doctrine called **fair use**. Fair use, which is actually written into U.S copyright law, means that you can use parts of other works in certain ways. For example, it is generally safe to do a parody or satire of another work—you can usually do a parody of a Hollywood movie as long as it is clear you are doing a parody.

It is also fair to quote short passages from other works when you are critiquing or commenting on them. Here's a fair quote: "The distinction between what is fair use and what is infringement in a particular case will not always be clear or easily defined. There is no specific number of words, lines, or notes that may safely be taken without permission." Here's the comment: That quote is from the Copyright Office's documents, and we're using it fairly. But the quote itself underlines the fact that the standards for fair use are hazy and vague, and may be applied on a case-by-case basis.

You or your friends may have had experiences in which you uploaded a video to YouTube only to have it taken down because it contained copyrighted music. It may seem fair to use the music, and maybe you only used it for a few seconds, but if the copyright holder complains, YouTube will take it down.

What are the best ways to deal with the uncertainties of fair use?

- Request and obtain written permission if you can.
- Learn your school's policy on fair use.
- Ask your teacher how the situation is usually handled in this class.

Practice

Comparing an Adapation

Choose a film that has been nominated for Best Adapted Screenplay. (You can find the most recent nominees at oscar.go.com/ nominees.) Familiarize yourself with the source material, then compare it to the film. Find five things the filmmakers changed when adapting the source material into a movie. What do you think about the changes? Would you have done anything differently?

Theme, Story, and Character

Effective movies command the audience's attention, compelling them to sit up in their seats and *want* to watch. That's because the best films view story and character with a thematic perspective, just as Robert Towne, in writing *Chinatown*, committed to an exploration of what crime means, not just a simple detective story.

How can you elevate your project to this level? Ask yourself why the movie exists—that is, what larger question is it trying to answer? Your response will reveal your film's **theme**: the big-picture thesis that illuminates something about the human condition and provides a universal take-away for the audience. A theme can be a statement or even a question.

Here are some examples of themes:

- Love conquers all.
- Is it possible to be a just person in an unjust world?
- Friendship matters more than money.

Themes sometimes sound trite, but you will find that all great movies have them.

As you consider your theme, make note of the amount of time you'll have to tell your story. Your class project may be two to five minutes. Theatrical films generally run about two hours. Television series on advertising-supported networks are 44 minutes for a one-hour episode and 22 minutes for a 30-minute episode after the time for commercials is deducted. YouTube's maximum upload is 11 hours, but users will often click away from a video in a few seconds if it doesn't capture and hold their interest.

Capturing audience interest from the first frame and holding it until the last is what will make a film entertaining, and the most effective way to accomplish this in such a highly focused medium is by telling the story of specific characters in a well-constructed *structure*.

"It's about Someone Who..."

> *When a woman, who has obsessively dedicated herself to the art of ballet, gets the chance of a lifetime to star in* Swan Lake, *she has to confront her inner demons . . .*
>
> *After two teenage kids, being raised by their lesbian moms, discover who their sperm-donor father is, they decide to arrange a meeting . . .*
>
> *Batman must emerge from a self-imposed exile to confront a masked terrorist bent on taking over Gotham City . . .*

All great films start with a character the audience can identify with, then present that character with a challenge or problem; these are the two factors that merit audience interest and can make a film entertaining. A character is the main person the story is about—or the main thing, as in the case of an animated movie like *Wall-E* (2008). The main character does not have to be likable—in the film *Captain Phillips* (2013), for example, the main character is gruff and abrasive—but must be someone the audience can relate to or, in other words, must be someone the audience will want to spend some time with.

A one-sentence description of the movie's story is called a **log line**. The preceding examples are log lines for, respectively, *Black Swan*, *The Kids Are All Right*, and *The Dark Knight Rises*. Log lines are used as shorthand in the entertainment industry to identify projects, and they closely mimic the way audiences will talk about a film. Ideally, a log line would be very similar to what you would tell a friend if the friend asked you, "What's that movie about?" In the preceding examples, the log lines describe the main characters and what they will encounter in less than 30 words. Let's pick them apart to see the four key aspects of a successful log line and film story.

1. The main characters: a woman; two teenage kids; Batman
2. The characters' context, or situation they find themselves in as the story begins: obsessively dedicated to the art of ballet; being raised by their lesbian moms; emerging from self-imposed exile
3. What triggers the story, also called the **inciting incident**: gets the chance of a lifetime to star in *Swan Lake*; discover who their sperm-donor father is; to confront a masked terrorist
4. What's going to happen: has to confront her inner demons; decide to arrange a meeting; protect Gotham City

The log line will be used to summarize your project if you enter it into competitions or film festivals, as the SEO (search engine optimization) description if you post it online, and to attract investors if one day you seek financing for it. You will also see log lines as the short descriptions of movies on services like Netflix, iTunes, and Hulu. If you can't boil your movie down to an efficient log line that accomplishes the four key elements, you probably need to do some more work crafting your story and thinking about your characters before you start writing.

TM & Copyright © Fox Searchlight/Courtesy Everett Collection

Figure 3-6a. ***Black Swan*** (2010)

b c

Figure 3-6. b. *The Kids Are All Right* (2010) **c. *The Dark Knight Rises*** (2012)

Structure

Because a film is a highly concentrated experience—a distillation of a story's key moments—storytelling *structure* plays a crucial role. **Structure**, when used to describe a story, means the order in which the story is told, or the way the scenes are set next to each other to form a coherent whole.

Structure is important for all films—especially short student films, in which following a formal storytelling structure often means the difference between an emotional and riveting experience and one that is boring and easily dismissed.

How to Start a Log Line

It's especially effective to begin a log line with "When," "After," or "During." These words lend a feeling of action.

The most frequently used structure in filmmaking is the three-act structure. The three-act structure is not a rule, and of course many dramatists have not followed it. Ancient Greek dramas have only one act. Shakespeare wrote his plays with five acts. But all successful stories, whether they are formally broken up into three acts or not, have the basic attributes of the three-act structure, which roughly translates into beginning, middle, and end. This is a fundamental necessity for class film projects, too.

The beginning, or setup, of your movie should introduce the main character, or **protagonist**, and the challenge or crisis he or she will face in order to achieve some specified goal or objective. Often the challenge is personified in another character, called the **antagonist**.

In the middle, the main character needs to engage in one or more actions that confront the antagonist and move in the direction of the goal. In a well-structured story, each action is more important and has higher stakes than the one before, but the main character doesn't achieve the goal yet; in fact, at the end of the middle, or second act, it often looks as if the antagonist will prevail.

In the third act, the main character must confront the greatest challenge; vanquish the antagonist once and for all (unless you are planning a sequel); and, in so doing, achieve the goal that was described in act one. Often the resolution in act three occurs because the protagonist realizes that he or she no longer wants what seemed so important in the first act; this movement in a character's desires or values is sometimes called the **character arc**. An example might be a story in which the protagonist wants fame and fortune in the first act, only to discover, in the third act, that love is what matters.

The third act carries a special burden: it is the key ingredient to a commercially successful film. Marketing research has shown that the last act of a movie is what audiences remember most, and if those final minutes fulfill the audience's expectations, they will have an overall positive impression of the movie. Of course, this doesn't mean that the film must finish with a happy ending, and that all issues must be resolved and "tied up with a bow," because life isn't like that; creatively and commercially successful films, however, conclude at a place of satisfying resolution and closure. This is often referred to as "what happens in the last reel"—a reference to the fact that movies literally used to be transported on separate film reels. Legendary film executive Louis B. Mayer, one of the founders of MGM studio, reportedly said, "There are only two things that are important in a movie—the first reel and the last reel. And the first reel doesn't matter so much."

Third-Act Problems Are First-Act Problems

If you have trouble figuring out the third act, it's probably because the first act isn't right yet. Go back to the first act and make sure you have spent enough time giving detail to characters and establishing the primary conflicts.

Tip

The three-act structure closely follows the form of the hero's journey described by mythologist and storyteller Joseph Campbell in his classic book *The Hero with a Thousand Faces*. In the hero's journey, he is often reluctantly called to take action to protect a kingdom or the entire world in the first act. When the hero begins his adventure, which is the beginning of the second act, he is involved in a series of battles, quests, or self-discoveries. At his lowest point, the hero suffers a crushing defeat and is killed either in fact or metaphorically, but his spirit rallies and he is resurrected (in the third act); he engages in a final battle with the antagonist and returns home with the world or the kingdom restored or rectified.

A typical feature-film screenplay is 120 pages long. The first act is in the first 30 pages, the second act is pages 31–90, and the third act is the last 30 pages. As you can see, the second act is the longest, and successful screenwriters often break the second act down into smaller sections to keep it manageable and exciting.

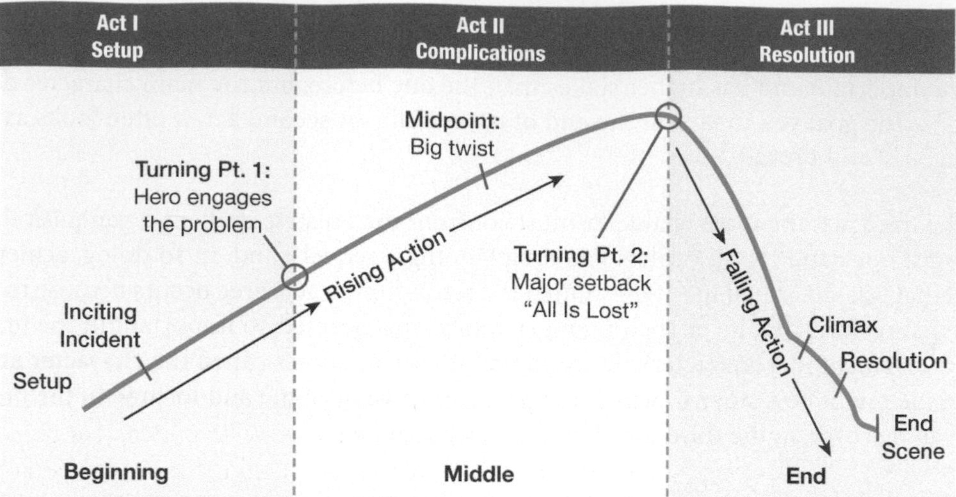

Figure 3-7. Three-act structure.

A five-minute student film might have a five-page script; the middle two to three pages will be the second act, and the first and last pages will be the first and third acts, respectively. In this compressed format, there is less time to flesh out complexities of theme, character, and plot. You will need to find efficient visual mechanisms to convey key information to the audience, and you should try to keep the plot simple and direct. In storytelling terms, short films most closely resemble the literary form of the short story, which announce their theme, quickly set up character and situation, and often rely on a plot twist or significant character transformation in the last paragraphs.

Although the three-act structure is a useful tool, and certainly a concept all screenwriters should be familiar with, it is by no means a strict requirement of good writing. For every writer who follows the three-act structure, there is another who passionately protests its programmatic efficiency, its substitution of creativity with formula, and its tendency for making movies predictable. Like most tools, it is best to think of the three-act structure as a valuable guide or starting point that can also be discarded when the demands of character and storytelling take over. In fact, in the best stories, the structure seems to take care of itself. (See Action Steps: How to Avoid Writing a *Bad* Student Film, below.)

Action **STEPS**

How to Avoid Writing a *Bad* Student Film

Some people say, "There are three kinds of student films: long, too long, and way too long." That's your first tip: be concise. The most successful student films embrace their brevity and do not overstay their welcome.

Here are six more tips you can use as you are crafting your screenplay to avoid making a bad student film:

1. **Don't tell a conventional love story, especially if it's about your recent breakup.** We've seen it before. If you're going to make a love story, make it *different*!

2. **Don't try to string together disconnected incidents or to tell a "slice of life" story—because those aren't stories.** A story has scenes that build on each other and move forward as the characters seek to achieve their goals.

3. **Don't strive for natural-sounding dialogue.** Great movie dialogue is made up of heightened and concentrated speech. Quentin Tarantino's films are a good example.

4. **Start each scene as late as possible, and get out of it as soon as possible.** Begin in the middle of the action, eliminate the fluff, and end with the audience wanting to know what happens in the next scene.

5. **Lose the music montages and dream sequences.** You won't have time for an effective montage in a short film, and dream sequences are overused. Concentrate on what the characters want, and show it in dialogue and action.

6. **Don't choose a story about making a movie, trying to make a movie, or otherwise trying to express yourself as an artist.** You are expressing yourself as an artist by making your movie—now go tell a great story.

Practice

Writing Log Lines

Log lines are notoriously difficult to write and perfect. The key is not to tell the movie's story. Instead, you need to do the following:

Engage the listener

Introduce the main character or characters and where the story takes place (also when the story takes place if not present day)

Tell what the big problem is going to be

Make it interesting—leave the listener curious about what happens next (Question: "And then what?" Answer: "You've gotta see the movie to find out!")

Try writing log lines for three movies you've seen, plus for three original ideas.

Writing and Screenplay Formats

It is an irony—comic or tragic, depending on your point of view—that almost all writers dislike writing. They like "having written"—but writing is often compared to purgatory. In fact, writers are well-known procrastinators, and they will do almost anything to avoid the act of putting words on the page. This is especially true in the film world, because writing is the loneliest profession in the industry. Every other filmmaking craft has strong elements of teamwork and collaboration, whereas the craft of writing is solitary. Many successful screenwriters work in teams, or have groups of other writers who form a core support

group, in an effort to ameliorate this inherent dilemma. You may be able to work with a writing partner in your class, but even if not, you can still cheer one another on as you work your way through the writing process.

Say It Out Loud

If something important happens in the action, refer to it in dialogue as well. That way, people who only read the dialogue will know what's going on.

Writer's block is a common term used to describe the difficulty of writing. Writers confront the blank page in different ways. Techniques include keeping a strict schedule of "writing hours" or requiring oneself to produce a certain number of pages each day. In addition, many writers develop a highly ritualized set of activities that allow them to get their writing to flow, whereas others adopt more prosaic approaches. More often than not, the best course is simply to jump in and start writing. A writer's draft is a purely personal experience until he or she chooses to share it with a reader—a thought that need not be foremost in anyone's mind when the writing process begins. Once a writer has produced a first draft, it is much easier to revise and turn it into a workable draft.

Each project has its own rhythms and writing requirements, which affect the writing process. Refer back to the number of pages in each act. Next time you watch a feature film, take a brief look at the time when you think each act ends. You will be surprised to see that the first act ends at about one half-hour into the film and the second act ends at about an hour and a half in to the film.

Screenplay Timing

One page of a screenplay = one minute of screen time

Always remember that writing is a craft that improves with practice and can be taught and studied. (See Action Steps: How to Get Started Writing Your Script, on the following page.) Though the "right" way to write is the way that works best for you, screenwriters over the years have developed a conventional formatting style that best expresses characters, dialogue, action, and visual descriptions. Because scripts are not ends in themselves—rather, they are like the architect's drawings that describe a building—these formal conventions help readers visualize what the writer imagines.

Practice

Screenplay Form

Watch a brief scene from a movie, and transcribe it using screenplay format. Notice what you put in dialogue and what you describe in action, setting, and so on.

Most screenwriters use free specialized writing software called Celtx, a free online program called Scripped, or Final Draft, which has a cost. These and other programs come with templates that automatically format for movies, television, animation, and other presentation requirements. However, since movies are a visual medium, and a good rule of writing is "show, don't tell," let's illustrate what the screenplay form looks like.

Action STEPS

How to Get Started Writing Your Script

Before you start writing scenes and dialogue, try these five action steps. They will help you stay focused and ensure that your first draft is a good starting place for further development.

1. **Pick a title.** You can always change it later, but having a title will make your movie feel more concrete.
2. **Decide on your theme, and write it down.** This will become your touchstone; every scene should relate to the theme, and if you're ever confused about what should happen next, or what a character should say, the theme will give you inspiration.
3. **Write your log line.** This will also focus you. If you have trouble writing the log line, take the time to make it clear and workable before you start to write.
4. **Write the outline.** Some writers like to make a graphic illustration of the story, with large boxes for each act, and smaller boxes for each scene. Others like to make bullet points or notes. But no matter where you begin with the outline, complete it with a formal outline document, listing each scene, who is in it, and what happens.
5. **Look at the outline to see if the structure works.** Reorder the scenes if necessary.

Now you're ready to start writing the script!

FADE IN:

A script typically starts with these words: FADE IN. Scripts are always written in 12-point Courier font, single-spaced. Margins are 1.5 inches on the left (to allow for 3-hole punching) and 1 inch on the right. Start with where we are:

EXT. LOCATION—NIGHT
That's called a "slug line." It is followed by a description of the location. EXT. means exterior. If it is an interior location, you would write INT. You always specify the time of day (NIGHT, DAY, EVENING, SUNRISE). These cues are important for the other departments in creating the look and feel you envision for the scene.

Descriptive actions are always separated with a double line space. There should rarely be more than two or three sentences in each paragraph, and each paragraph should only contain one descriptive idea.

Descriptions should be brief and direct. Write what you want the audience to see. Don't go into long, descriptive details—readers tend to skip over long descriptive sections like this one.

Each time you introduce a new CHARACTER, put the character's name in capital letters, followed by a brief description, such as ANNIE, a stunning brunette, running with her briefcase under her arm, trying to avoid SIMPSON (rakish, 30s), another pedestrian.

ANNIE
When a character has dialogue, the character's name is indented 3.5 inches from the left. Dialogue is 35 characters wide (3.5 inches in 12-point Courier font), indented 2.5 inches from the left, and left justified.

SIMPSON
(if there is action accompanying the dialogue, it is indented 3 inches from the left and is enclosed in parentheses)

And this is where the dialogue goes again.

ANNIE
Always refer to characters by the same name throughout the script. (if there is action in the middle of a character's dialogue, it goes here.) And then the dialogue resumes.

An action that follows the last line of dialogue in a scene is called putting a "button" on the scene. It gives the reader a sense of closure.

INT. LOCATION #2—DAY
Describe the new location.

Please note that you did not write CUT TO before the new scene. Cuts are always assumed and should not be written because they clutter the reading experience.

ANNIE

Now the characters talk again.

SIMPSON

Most of a screenplay's work is done in the dialogue.

ANNIE

The little, uh, natural kinds of things people say give away character.

SIMPSON

(waving his fingers in the air)

Like in the theater!

```
               ANNIE
          (pushing his fingers away)

          Thank you, Mr. Wikipedia.

               SIMPSON
          But there's another reason most of a
          screenplay's work is done in the dia-
          logue.

               ANNIE
          Why's that?

               SIMPSON
          It's easier to read. See how your eyes
          glide right down the page?

               ANNIE
          Yeah, it's not blocky and dense like all
          those description paragraphs up there.

               SIMPSON
          Not to mention that many people who read
          scripts—

               ANNIE
          (interrupting)

          Be nice ...

               SIMPSON
          —are generally lazy and skip the descrip-
          tive paragraphs anyway!

          (smiles)

          Nice? No. True? Yes.

     DISSOLVE TO:

     INT. SIMPSON'S BRAIN—GRAY AND MURKY—BUBBLING
     NOISES
```

Lightning sparks between the neurons! See how a screenplay can take you anywhere?

"Dissolve To:" is a transition line. It is indented 6.5 inches.

When you have reached the end of your screenplay, you write these words, also indented 6.5 inches:

FADE OUT.

Development

It's extremely rare for a first-draft screenplay to be ready to shoot; in fact, in your authors' collective careers, which span hundreds of movies, it has happened exactly once, and even then, the writer did revisions to attract casting and to customize the script to budget and location demands. Rather, scripts are written and rewritten, with input from constructive readers, directors, actors, and producers; this process is called **development**. The purpose of development is to refine the script so that it represents as precisely as possible the plan for shooting; even with a class project, good script development is the most essential element for ensuring a good movie.

Look for White Space

After you have finished your draft, look at it on page view. If you don't see a lot of white space, you have overwritten. Often times a writer may add white space to emphasize a key moment in the screenplay.

Developing Your Script

There are three great reasons to develop your script through several revisions to get it as polished as possible and to take development seriously. First, even though writing is hard, it requires far fewer resources than does shooting or editing. It is much cheaper—actually free!—to revise a page than to reshoot a scene. Second, a bad script never makes a good movie. Most films that fall short of excellence do so because their scripts were not good enough in the first place and did not go through sufficient independent scrutiny and feedback. Therefore, even if you are working on a project for yourself to direct (and produce and star in and write the songs for), you need to create a process for personal development to make your screenplay excellent. Such a process involves trusted friends and advisers who have experience reading scripts and commenting on them, who can be encouraging and give honest feedback, and who can be relied on to tell you the truth even when it is painful. Good writers are always helped by sensitive readers' responses, and all writing involves rewriting.

The third reason development needs to be taken seriously is because it involves business matters and intellectual property rights. Unfortunately, many first-time writers agree to work with writing partners, independent producers, and independent companies without a clear understanding of the business aspects of these relationships. In these instances, friendships are frequently damaged and projects, on the verge of getting made, get stopped dead in their tracks because of disputes over rights, ownership, and payment. It is always a good idea to have a written agreement about your project if you are working with anyone else, even if there is no money initially changing hands—and even if it is just for a class project and you memorialize your agreement by exchanging emails. For some of the elements typically found in a writer's contract, see Business Smarts: "A Writer's Contract". Remember: a verbal agreement is worth as much as the paper it is written on!

Business SMARTS

A Writer's Contract

If you're going to write for or with someone else, you need to have a contract—a written legal document that clearly explains what everyone has agreed to. Seek competent legal advice on any contract before you sign it, especially if it is a professional screenwriting contract, which usually runs 30 or more pages long and contains rather sophisticated provisions.

Following are some common points a contract will include:

- **If you are writing with someone else** (a writing partner). Who owns the material? If someone buys it, how will the money be split? How will writing credit be determined? If you come to a creative parting of ways in the future, what happens?
- **An option** (an agreement to purchase something in the future). For example, in independent films, a producer might option a script for one dollar for 12 months. (Producers and studios may option material for much more money, too.) That would mean the producer pays the writer one dollar and has the right to buy the screenplay sometime during the next 12 months. An option must specify the time period and the purchase price. Sometimes, options have a renewal built in, which means the option period can be extended for a pre-agreed-to time for a pre-agreed-to price.
- **Purchase price** (what the writer will be paid to sell rights to the script). The purchase price typically consists of immediate cash plus back-end money, or a percentage of future profits, *if any*. Note that most films don't make a profit.
- **What happens if the movie isn't made?** Do you get the project back? After what period of time? Would you have to repay some or all of the money in order to get your project back?
- **Writing steps.** If a writer is hired on an open assignment, the writer will be contracted for one or more writing steps. These steps may be a first draft, a revision, or a polish—levels of work defined by the Writers Guild. The writer will be paid some money on commencement of each step (at the start of writing) and the balance on delivery of the final step (when the script is turned in).
- **Credit.** If you are working on a non–Writers Guild movie, your contract should specify your writing credit and how you want to be credited on-screen, in posters, or in advertisements. Typically, the writer's credit is placed immediately before the director's credit, and the writer's contract will specify that the writer's name must be the same size, boldness, and typeface as the names of other people getting credit. If the Writers Guild is governing the project, it has the sole power to determine writing credit; the producers or the studio have no say in the matter.

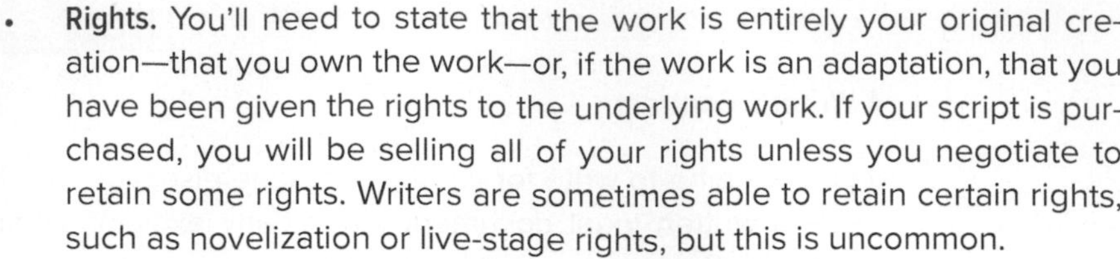

- **Rights.** You'll need to state that the work is entirely your original creation—that you own the work—or, if the work is an adaptation, that you have been given the rights to the underlying work. If your script is purchased, you will be selling all of your rights unless you negotiate to retain some rights. Writers are sometimes able to retain certain rights, such as novelization or live-stage rights, but this is uncommon.
- **Sequels and remakes.** Your contract may address whether or not you need to be offered the first crack at writing any projects based on your original work and if you will have any share in the profits from those projects regardless of your writing involvement. This stipulation is very important if your script ultimately becomes the basis for a hit studio franchise.

The Studio Development Cycle

Film studios have a much more formal and rigorous development process than you'll follow in class—a process that not only offers some perspective on what happens when millions of dollars are at stake, but also expands on why intellectual property rights, which you learned about earlier, are so important. Studios begin with a legal process of getting rights. Often, they will purchase, or **option**, the intellectual property rights in a given work (screenplays written independently, video games, or any other kind of intellectual property), which means the studio will pay a certain amount of money for the right to develop that project for a given period of time. When that time is up, the studio must either purchase the rights—in which case the studio will own the rights forever—or let the option go, in which case the rights will revert, or go back, to the original owner. This process is formally known as having your project put into **turn-around**.

Sometimes studios acquire rights to a story based on the writer's **pitch**. A pitch is a meeting in which the writer tells the film's story. The pitch generally has two forms—short and long. A short pitch, which may be given over the phone by the writer's agent or a producer, is two to three minutes and is enough to determine if there is interest. The long pitch, given in person by the writer, is 15 to 20 minutes and gives the whole story of the film. Although few projects sold as pitches ever get made into finished movies, studios still buy them occasionally, especially from established writers with whom the studio has a preexisting relationship, or if it is based on a recent, major worldwide event.

Another way studios obtain rights to a story is through script submissions, but these kinds of submissions can be tricky, as studios are often faced with lawsuits from people who believe the studios stole their idea. Studios will not even look at unsolicited submissions; you will get your screenplay back in the original sealed envelope that you sent it in, with a formal letter stating the studio's policy of not accepting unsolicited submissions. To give themselves some protection, studios accept script submissions only from recognized entertainment agents or attorneys, because these legally authorized writers' representatives understand the industry's business practices—especially the fact that many projects are similar to many other projects—and will counsel writers not to pursue unfounded plagiarism claims.

Write for Movies, Pitch for TV

Most successful studio movies are based on source material or scripts written independently by writers; very few start as pitches. In contrast, most television series start as pitches.

Even though studios restrict the ways they receive new material, they still face the daunting process of evaluating the 25,000 projects that are submitted to them each year. Because the volume of submitted screenplays is so large, studios employ teams of executives whose initial task is to determine whether each project is commercial and meets the studio's needs. These executives are assisted by *story analysts*, who read the projects and write *coverage*: a brief summary and commentary on each project. When executives decline a project, they say they are "passing" on it. The vast majority of scripts are rejected, both because of the sheer volume of them and because to say yes to a project entails a considerable commitment of time and finances.

If the executives believe the project should be acquired by the studio, they will pitch the project to upper management. If management concurs and a business arrangement or deal can be made, generally with a writer's agent or attorney, the studio will put the project into development; all studio business deals with writers are governed by the studios' contract with the Writers Guild. Each studio has between 100 and 200 projects in active development, and another two to three hundred projects that are inactive, or "on the shelf."

Studio development involves a close collaboration between the writer and the executives developing the project. Generally, there is an initial meeting during which the writer pitches a vision for writing or revising the project, and several meetings may follow in which the characters and story are discussed in greater detail. The executive may consult with upper studio management in an effort to ensure that the project's direction will ultimately be to their liking. (See Producer Smarts: "How to Work with the Writer")

When the writer turns in a draft of the script, the studio executives read it and decide if they are going to continue with the project and, if so, whether they will continue with the same writer. If the answer to both questions is yes, the executives will prepare **studio notes**, which provide a road map for the writer to follow in a script revision.

The studio may also decide to replace the writer, an event that happens frequently—especially on most films that eventually get made. In this case, the first writer's contract is terminated, and the project becomes an **open assignment**, meaning that the assignment is open for a new writer to work on it.

Practice

Short Pitching

This group exercise is best done with at least four people. Each of you should come up with a three-minute pitch for a full-length feature you might make one day. Then, for each pitch, the group should give reactions and notes on how to make it better. This process is a good model for what writers actually go through in studio notes/development sessions.

The studio may also decide to abandon the project entirely. Because studios have many projects in development even though they only make about 20 films per year, more than 80 percent of development projects are eventually abandoned. The average time a project is in development until it is either abandoned or given a green light (formally committed to production) is three years. Some projects move much more quickly, whereas others have been in development for 20 years or more before getting made. For this reason, studio development is often called "development hell" by writers, producers, and executives alike, with a knowing sense of irony about the arbitrary and lengthy nature of the process. On the other hand, it is a process that works best for the studios because it gives them security to know that a very large budget movie will have a script that the senior executives at the studio like.

Figure 3-8. ***Forrest Gump*** (1996)

Figure 3-9. ***On the Road*** (2012)

Forrest Gump was in development for nine years before it got made. Although that may seem like a long time, *On the Road*, the film adaptation of Jack Kerouac's landmark novel, was in development for more than 30 years.

Producer **SMARTS**

How to Work with the Writer

Producers play a crucial role in shaping screenplays, even if they may not write any of the words themselves. That's because producers often find and hire writers, and take the lead in giving notes to steer the development process. As a producer, when you're working with a writer, follow these constructive practices:

- Before writing commences, review the outline and offer feedback. The writer will be grateful if you can help ensure that the structure is sound.
- Offer to read scenes and give comments while the script is being written if the writer wants that kind of feedback.
- When the draft comes in, read it carefully and make notes. Pay attention to character, dialogue, plot, story structure, theme, rhythm, and flow, and also to whether the writer has called for any scenes that are beyond your project's budget or will be difficult to shoot. Then, meet with the writer to discuss the script and possible revisions. Always start with compliments and stress what is working well before delving into areas that need improvement.
- Afterward, it's helpful to follow up with a written memo summarizing the conversation and what the writer will do next. It is hard for writers to remember everything that is said during a development meeting; they're often focused on defending their first draft. The written memo will help them stay on course and remember what revisions they need to accomplish.

If the director has already been selected, make sure to include him or her in these steps, too.

Writer's Emergency Kit

- Pen and notepad, to record ideas as they occur and great bits of dialogue you hear in conversations, and an audio recording app for your mobile device to record meetings and thoughts on the fly
- A willingness to put your emotions and viewpoints out for public display
- A library card
- Screenplay software, and a way to back up your work with a hard drive or cloud-based storage
- Writing itself. When everything falls apart, the thing you can always fall back on is your craft. No one can take that away from you

Chapter Essentials

- Film ideas may either be original or come from source material; they are intellectual property, and your creative rights and those of others must be protected and respected.
- Well-made films are well structured, weaving theme, plot, and character into a compelling narrative.
- Easily accessible software programs will make your script look like a script by helping you with the proper format.
- Development—the process of revising the script with other stakeholders in the film—perfects the script and gets it ready for production.

Narrative Films: Telling Stories

"Narrative Films: Telling Stories" from *The Film Experience*, Fifth Edition, by Timothy Corrigan and Patricia White, pp. 243–281 (Chapter 7, "Narrative Films: Telling Stories").

Based on the book series by L. Frank Baum, *The Wizard of Oz* has been one of the most adapted and ubiquitous narratives in American history, including a 1925 silent version, the famous 1939 Technicolor film with Judy Garland, updates like Sam Raimi's 2013 *Oz the Great and Powerful*, and the modernized musical *The Wiz* (1978), performed decades later on TV as the holiday special *The Wiz Live!* (2015). With a sepia-tone frame questioning Dorothy's place in Kansas farm life, the Technicolor narrative of the 1939 classic catapults the heroine into a strange world where she meets the Scarecrow, the Tin Man, and the Cowardly Lion, who then accompany her as she encounters and overcomes a series of obstacles along her way and finally defeats the Wicked Witch of the West. Despite its fantastical elements, the narrative follows a cause-and-effect structure propelled by the protagonist's goal and eventually concludes in her return to her home and family. Indeed, the basic outline of this narrative might describe the shape of many very different stories, from *Finding Nemo* (2003) to *The Hurt Locker* (2008). At the same time, this particular narrative is also a fine example of how some narratives can approach the status of a cultural myth, shared by many different audiences.

Movies have thrived on the art and craft of **narrative**, a story with a particular plot and point of view. At its core, narrative maps the different ways we have learned to make sense of our place in history and the world as well as to communicate with others. Narrative film developed out of a long cultural, artistic, and literary tradition of storytelling that shows characters pursuing goals, confronting obstacles to those goals, and ultimately achieving some kind of closure. In general, narrative follows a three-part structure consisting of a beginning, a middle, and an ending. An established situation is disrupted, and events in the middle of the narrative lead to a restoration of order in the ending.

Storytelling has always been a central part of societies and cultures. Stories spring from both personal and communal memories and reconstruct the events, actions, and emotions of the past through the eyes of the present. They also offer explanations for events and features of the world that may otherwise seem beyond comprehension. In this way, stories strengthen both the memory and the imagination of a society. Many stories—Bible stories,

Hindu scriptures, Icelandic sagas, oral tales of indigenous cultures, and well-known stories of historical events (such as the Civil War) and people (such as Abraham Lincoln)—are all driven by these aims. In a sense, stories are both the historical center of a culture and the bonds of a community.

A Short History of Narrative Film

Over time, stories have appeared in a myriad of material forms and served innumerable purposes, many of which reappear in movie narratives. Some films, like *Little Big Man* (1970) and *Contempt* (1963), make explicit references to the narrative history that precedes them. *Little Big Man*, for instance, depicts the heritage of Native Americans gathered around the fire listening to storytellers recounting the history of their people. *Contempt*, in contrast, struggles with the narrative forms found in Homer's *Odyssey* and those demanded by commercial filmmaking—between telling a tale as an epic poem and as a Hollywood blockbuster (Figures 3-10a–3-10c).

To appreciate the richness of film narrative, viewers must keep in mind the unique cultural history of narrative itself. For example, oral narratives, which are spoken or recited aloud, represent a tradition that extends from the campfire to today's stage performance artists. Written narratives, such as Charles Dickens's *Bleak House* (1853), appear in printed form, while graphic narratives develop through a series of images, such as the stories told through lithographs in the eighteenth century and through modern comic books like *Deadpool* (Figure 3-11).

(a) Erich Lessing/Art Resource, NY

(b) © National Gallery, London/Art Resource, NY

Figure 3-10. ***The Odyssey.*** The history of narrative invariably reflects the historical pressures and conditions that determine how stories are told. **(a)** Ancient Greek epics, including the renowned *Odyssey*, often were depicted as visual narratives. **(b)** Since medieval times, the visual arts have incorporated stories and allegories into a single frame—for example, depicting multiple characters and events from the *Odyssey* in one sixteenth-century painting.

(c)

Figure 3-10. (c) More modern visual arts, like Jean-Luc Godard's *Contempt*, have engaged directly with the history of narrative. Godard's film is about the struggle to adapt the *Odyssey* to the screen.

Figure 3-11. ***Deadpool*** (2016). The transformation of visual narrative from comic-book page to big screen captures the imagination of fans and new viewers alike.

In these and other examples, the form and material through which a story is told affect aspects of the narrative, facilitating some characteristics of expression and prohibiting others. Oral narratives provide more direct and flexible contact with listeners, allowing a story to be tailored to an audience and to change from one telling to another. A visual narrative shows the appearance of characters more concretely than a literary one, whereas a literary narrative is able to present characters' thoughts more seamlessly than a visual narrative. A film narrative commonly draws from and combines these and other narrative traditions, and attending to how a particular film narrative employs the strategies of, say, oral narratives or operatic narratives illustrates the broad and complex history of storytelling embedded in cinematic form.

1900–1920s: Adaptations, Scriptwriters, and Screenplays

Although the first movies usually showed only simple moving images (such as a train arriving at a station), these images often referred to a story behind them. As film form developed, adaptations of well-known stories were a popular choice of filmmakers, much like today's adaptations of comic books and remakes of previous movies. Audiences' familiarity with the characters and plot helped them to follow emerging motion-picture narrative techniques. As early as 1896, the actor Joseph Jefferson represented Rip van Winkle in a brief short. By 1903, a variety of similar film tableaux—a story told through a single image—assumed that audiences would know the larger story behind what was shown on the screen, including Shakespeare's *King John* (1899), *Cinderella* (1900), *Robinson Crusoe* (1902), and *Ali Baba and the Forty Thieves* (1905) (Figure 3-12). *Uncle Tom's Cabin*, the most popular novel and stage play of the nineteenth century, was adapted for the screen numerous times in the silent film era, once by Edwin S. Porter in 1903 (Figure 3-13). Porter's films were among the first to use editing to tell stories, and by 1906 the movies were becoming a predominantly narrative medium.

Figure 3-12. ***Ali Baba and the Forty Thieves*** (1905). The tableaux of early films rely on imagery that assumes the audience knows the larger story behind the image.

Figure 3-13. ***Uncle Tom's Cabin*** (1903). Edwin S. Porter directed one of numerous silent film adaptations of the most popular nineteenth-century novel and stage play.

These early historical bonds between movies and stories served the development of what we call the *economics of leisure time*. In the first decades of the twentieth century, the budding movie industry recognized that stories take time to tell and that an audience's willingness to spend time watching stories makes money for the industry. In these early years, most individuals went to the movies to experience the novelty of "going to the movies" and spending an afternoon with friends or an hour away from work. By 1913, moviemakers recognized that by developing more complex stories they could attract larger audiences, keep them in their seats for longer periods, and charge more than a nickel for admission. Along with the growing cultural prestige of attending films that told serious stories, movies could now sell more time for more money through longer narratives. Quickly cinema established itself among the leading sources of cultural pleasures that included museums, art galleries, and traditional and vaudeville theaters. At the same time, cinema's own history came to be governed by the forms and aims of storytelling.

As narrative film developed, two important industrial events stand out—the introduction of screenplays and the advancement of narrative dialogue through sound. Whereas many early silent movies were produced with little advance preparation, the growing number and increasing length of movies from 1907 onward required the use of **screenwriters** (also called *scriptwriters*), who created the film's screenplay, either by beginning with an original treatment and developing the plot structure and dialogue over the span of several versions or by adapting short stories, novels, or other sources. As part of this historical shift, movies' narratives quickly became dependent on a **screenplay** (or film *script*), the text from which a movie is made, including dialogue and information about action, settings, shots, and transitions. It standardized the elements and structures of movie narratives. A copyright lawsuit regarding an early movie version of *Ben-Hur* (1907) immediately underlined the importance of scriptwriters who could develop original narratives.

1927–1950: Sound Technology, Dialogue, and Classical Hollywood Narrative

The introduction of sound technology and dialogue in the late 1920s proved to be one of the most significant advances in the history of film narrative. Sound affected the cinema in numerous ways, but perhaps most important was that it enabled film narratives to create and develop more intricate characters whose dialogue and vocal intonations added new psychological and social dimensions to film. More intricate characters were used to propel more complex movie plots. In many ways a product of the new narrative possibilities offered by sound, screwball comedies such as *Bringing Up Baby* (1938) feature fast-talking women and men whose verbal dexterity is a measure of their independence and wit (Figure 3-14). Other films of this period use sound devices, such as a whistled tune in Alfred Hitchcock's *The Man Who Knew Too Much* (1934), to make oblique connections between characters and events and to build more subtle kinds of suspense within the narrative.

Figure 3-14. ***Bringing Up Baby*** (1938). The coming of sound allowed for the witty dialogue of the fast-talking, independent heroines of screwball comedies. Such characters are epitomized by Susan Vance (played by Katharine Hepburn), whose "baby" in this film is a pet leopard.

The continuing evolution of the relation between sound and narrative helped to solidify and fine-tune the fundamental shape of classical Hollywood narrative in the 1930s and 1940s. During this period, the structure of this increasingly dominant narrative form became firmly established according to three basic features: (1) the narratives focus on one or two central characters, (2) these characters move a linear plot forward, and (3) the action develops according to a realistic cause-and-effect logic. A trio of movies produced in 1939, often heralded as Hollywood's golden year—*Gone with the Wind*, *Stagecoach*, and *The Wizard of Oz*—illustrate sound-era movie narratives as modern-age myths and, despite their many differences, describe narrative variations on this classical Hollywood structure. During these years, the Hollywood studio system grew in size and power, and it provided a labor force, a central producer system, and a global financial reach that created an extraordinarily efficient industrial system for storytelling. This system became increasingly identified with lucrative narrative genres, such as musicals and westerns.

Also during this period, the introduction and advancement of specific movie technologies—for example, deep-focus cinematography and Technicolor processes—offered ways to convey and complicate the narrative information provided by specific images. Although the plot structure of the classical narrative remained fully intact, these technologies allowed movies to explore new variations on narrative in the atmosphere of a scene or in the dramatic tensions between characters.

With growing pressure from the Motion Picture Producers and Distributors of America (headed by Will H. Hays from 1922 to 1945)—the U.S. organization that determined the guidelines for what was considered morally acceptable to depict in films and that adopted a strict Production Code in 1930—film narratives during the 1930s turned more conspicuously to literary classics for stories that could provide adult plots acceptable to censors. These classics included *Pride and Prejudice* (1938) and *Wuthering Heights* (1939). For an industry that needed more verbal narratives, Hollywood looked increasingly to New York and other places where literary figures like F. Scott Fitzgerald could be lured into writing new stories and scripts.

World War II (1939–1945) significantly jolted classical Hollywood narratives. The stark and often horrific events that occurred during the war raised questions about whether the classic narrative formulas of linear plots, clear-headed characters, and neat and logical endings could adequately capture the period's far messier and more confusing realities. If the narrative of *The Wizard of Oz* followed the yellow brick road that led a character home, the war-scarred narrative of *The Best Years of Our Lives* (1946) poignantly questioned what path to follow and even doubted whether one could ever go home again (Figure 3-15).

Figure 3-15. ***The Best Years of Our Lives*** (1946). This postwar narrative questions the happy ending and closure that a return home usually signifies.

1950–1980: Art Cinema

The global trauma of World War II not only challenged the formulaic Hollywood storytelling style of the time but also gave rise to an innovative art cinema that emerged in the 1950s and 1960s in Europe, Japan, India, Latin America, and elsewhere. This new form of cinema questioned many of the cultural perspectives and values that existed before the war. Produced by such directors as Ingmar Bergman, Federico Fellini, and Agnès Varda, European art cinema experimented with new narrative structures that typically subverted or overturned classical narrative models by featuring characters without direction, seemingly illogical actions, and sometimes surreal events. In *Cléo from 5 to 7* (1962), for instance, Varda restricts the narrative to two hours in the day of a singer, capturing the real-time details of her life. Although the protagonist fears a cancer diagnosis, the narrative eschews melodrama for the joys of wandering through the everyday (Figure 3-16).

Figure 3-16. ***Cléo from 5 to 7*** (1962). Agnès Varda's narrative restricts itself to two hours of real time as it documents an afternoon in the life of a young woman in Paris.

Influencing later new wave cinemas such as the New German Cinema of the 1970s and the New Hollywood cinema of the 1970s and 1980s, these films intentionally subverted traditional narrative forms such as linear progression of the plot and the centrality of a specific protagonist. In addition, these narratives often turned away from the objective point of view of realist narratives to create more individual styles and tell stories that were more personal than public. *Fellini's 8½* (1963), for instance, has an unmistakable autobiographical dimension as it recounts the struggles of a movie director wrestling with his anxieties about work and the memories that haunt him.

1980s–Present: From Narrative Reflexivity to Games

Contemporary movies represent a wide variety of narrative practices, but three can be identified as particularly significant and widespread in recent decades. Reflecting different technological, artistic, and industrial influences, these three narratives often reflect back on the process of making films, adapt the physical and psychological excitement of amusement parks, or mimic the interactivity of video and digital games.

In the practice of narrative reflexivity, filmmakers still tell stories but now call more attention to how they are telling those stories or how these stories are a product of certain narrative techniques and perspectives. *Adaptation* (2002) is thus a film about a screenwriter's struggles to adapt a *New Yorker* essay on orchids to the formulas of a Hollywood narrative. Meanwhile, replete with references to earlier films and narrative conventions, Quentin Tarantino's *Inglourious Basterds* (2009) is a self-conscious film fantasy about the killing of Nazi leaders during the screening of a film (Figure 3-17).

Figure 3-17. ***Inglourious Basterds*** (2009). Contemporary narratives like this film are highly self-conscious and reflexive about the historical sources and materials that construct their stories.

A second direction in movies of the last few decades is the appropriation of roller coaster–like narratives with soaring effects similar to amusement park rides and the physical and psychological thrills associated with them. The *Pirates of the Caribbean* movie series (2006–2017) is actually based on a Disneyland ride. Similarly, although the *Harry Potter* films (2001–2011) are based on J. K. Rowling's children's books rather than a theme park ride, they nonetheless seem to aspire, at least in part, to the narrative-ride model, complete with elaborate action sequences and IMAX- ready spectacle. In 2010, the Universal Studios theme parks opened extensive attractions called The Wizarding World of Harry Potter.

History CLOSE UP

Salt of the Earth

Turning actual events into a narrative often makes them more compelling. Characters with whom we can identify, sharply drawn conflict, and suspense about the outcome make *Salt of the Earth* (1954, above), based on a 1951 miners' strike in New Mexico, a gripping and deeply moving story. But despite these traditional narrative elements, the film broke with Hollywood convention in many ways. Shot on location with a mix of actors and Chicano/a community members, the story is told through the eyes of Esperanza, a young mother married to a striking miner. Initially meek, Esperanza learns to voice her concerns about issues affecting women in their company town, built on land that formerly belonged to Mexico. When the men are banned from picketing, the women walk the line instead. The story proceeds on both personal and political levels, as Esperanza and her husband, Juan, negotiate their roles and Esperanza takes a public role in the labor struggle. Both narrative threads rely on heroic acts by ordinary Americans about whom few Hollywood movies are made. Because the script was drafted in collaboration with the participants and directed by Herbert J. Biberman, one of the "Hollywood Ten" who were jailed for refusing to testify in congressional hearings into whether film industry professionals were current or former members of the American Communist Party, the film plays a role in another fraught narrative about American life—the history of

censorship. The set was threatened while the film was in production, and anti-Communist unions blocked laboratories from printing it and projectionists from showing it. Not until many years after the film was made did it become recognized as a deeply American narrative.

As films move into the digital age of the new millennium, a third tendency is to structure stories with the effects of video and digital gaming, making films (and their marketing campaigns) a kind of interactive game for audiences. Movies are increasingly implicitly or explicitly constructing stories as interactive explorations of space. In Doug Liman's *Edge of Tomorrow* (2014), the hero dies combating an alien invasion over and over, waking to attempt his mission again (Figure 3-18). Films no longer depict a linear plot that an audience simply follows in every instance. Indeed, as film narrative evolves in the twenty-first century, the convergences and exchanges between games and films may represent one of cinema's most interesting new directions.

Figure 3-18. ***Edge of Tomorrow*** (2014). The looping narrative of this science fiction film exemplifies the increasing influence of gaming on film narrative.

The Elements of Narrative Film

Narrative is universal, but it also is infinitely variable. The origins of cinema storytelling in other narrative forms and texts, the evolution of narrative strategies across film history, and the distinct narrative traditions across cultures give a sense of this variety. However, we can identify the common elements of narrative and some of the characteristic ways the film medium deploys them.

Stories and Plots

The main features of any kind of narrative are the story, characters, plot, and narration. A **story** is the subject matter or raw material of a narrative. In a story, actions and events (usually perceived in terms of a beginning, a middle, and an end) are ordered chronologically and focus on one or more **characters**—the individuals who motivate the events and perform the actions of the story. Stories tend to be summarized easily, as in "the tale of a man's frontier life on the Nebraska prairie" or "the story of a woman confronting the violence of her past in Pakistan." In the next section, we discuss characters in detail.

The **plot** is the narrative ordering of the events of the story as they appear in the actual work, selected and arranged according to particular temporal, spatial, generic, causal, or other patterns. In one story, the plot may include the smallest details in the life of a character; in another story, it may highlight only major, cataclysmic events. One plot may present a story as progressing forward step by step from the beginning to the end, and another may present the same story by moving backward in time. One plot may describe a story as the product of the desires and drives of a character, whereas another might suggest that events take place outside the control of that character. Although the story of John F. Kennedy's life and death are well known, movies depicting these events feature very different plots. Oliver Stone's *JFK* (1991) focuses on New Orleans district attorney Jim Garrison's investigation of conspiracy theories around the death, using a bewildering array of footage to unsettle our historical certainties. *Thirteen Days* (2001) is a telescopic narrative covering the 1962 Cuban missile crisis, creating drama by focusing on a president's character under pressure, even though the outcome is already known to viewers. Finally, *Jackie* (2016) shifts emphasis to the first lady, covering her life in the days after the assassination.

From early films like Edwin S. Porter's *Life of an American Fireman* (1903), regarded as one of the first significant narrative films, to modern movies like Christopher Nolan's *Memento* (2000), with its reverse chronology, movies have relied on the viewer's involvement in the narrative tension between story and plot to create suspense, mystery, and interest. Even in the short and simple rescue narrative of Porter's film (Figures 3-19a–3-19d), some incidental details are omitted, such as the actual raising of the ladders. To add to the urgency and energy of the narrative, the rescue is shown sequentially from two different camera setups, a practice that confused later audiences. In *Memento,* the tension between plot and story is more obvious and dramatic. This unusual plot, about a man without a short-term memory, begins with a murder and proceeds backward in time through a series of short episodes that unveil fragments of information about who the man is and why he committed the murder (Figure 3-20). In other films, we know the story; what interests us is discovering the particular ways the plot constructs that story.

(a) (b) (c) (d)

Photofest, Inc.

Figure 3-19. ***Life of an American Fireman*** (1903). This story proceeds from a fire alarm being sounded, to firefighters racing through the streets, to the rescue, with one event—the rescue of a woman via ladder—shown from two different perspectives.

Figure 3-20. ***Memento*** (2000). A crisis of memory becomes a crisis of plot in Christopher Nolan's innovative reverse narrative.

Characters

The first characters portrayed in films were principally bodies on display or in motion—a famous actor posing, a person running, a figure performing a menial task. When movies began to tell stories, however, characters became the central vehicle for the actions, and with the advent of the Hollywood star system around 1910, distinctions among characters developed rapidly. From the 1896 *Lone Fisherman* to the 1920 *Pollyanna* (featuring Mary Pickford), film characters evolved from amusing moving bodies to figures that had specific narrative functions and were portrayed by adored actors whose popularity made them nearly mythic figures. With the introduction of sound films in 1927, characters and their relationships were increasingly drawn according to traditions of literary realism and psychological complexity. Today the evolution of character presentation continues as the voices of real actors are adapted to animated figures and plots. Throughout all these historical incarnations, characters have remained one of the most immediate yet underanalyzed dimensions of the movies.

Character Roles

Characters are either central or minor figures who anchor the events in a film. They can propel the plot by fulfilling a particular character function, such as protagonist, antagonist, or helper—roles that recur across many plots. More complex characters motivate narrative events through specific situations or traits. Characters are commonly identified and understood through aspects of their appearance, gestures, actions, and dialogue; the comments of other characters; as well as such incidental but important features as their names or clothes.

In many narrative films, a character's inferred emotional and intellectual make-up motivates specific actions that consequently define that character. His or her stated or implied wishes and fears produce events that cause certain effects or other events to take place. Thus, the actions, behaviors, and desires of characters create the causal logic favored in **classical film narrative**, Hollywood's dominant style of narrative filmmaking in which characters' goals propel a linear plot toward closure. In *The Wizard of Oz* (1939), Dorothy's desire to "go

home"—to find her way back to Kansas—leads her through various encounters and dangers that create friendships and fears, and these events, in turn, lead to others, such as Dorothy's fight to retrieve the witch's broom. In the end, she returns home joyfully. The character of Dorothy is thus defined first by her emotional desire and will to go home and then by the persistence and resourcefulness that eventually allow her to achieve that goal (Figure 3-21).

Figure 3-21. ***The Wizard of Oz*** (1939). Narrative cause-and-effect logic finds Dorothy and her new companions on the yellow brick road, heading toward the Emerald City.

Most film characters are a combination of both ordinary and extraordinary features. This blend of fantasy and realism has always been an important movie formula: it creates characters that are recognizable in terms of our experiences and exceptional in ways that make them interesting to us. The complexities of certain film characters can be attributed to this blending and balancing. For example, the title characters of the biographical *Queen of Katwe* (2016), *Milk* (2008), and *Lincoln* (2012)—a young girl from one of Kampala's slums who became a chess champion, the activist who fought for gay rights in San Francisco, and the American president attempting to broker an antislavery legislation deal—all combine extraordinary and ordinary characteristics (Figures 3-22a–3-22c). Even when film characters belong to fantasy genres, as with the tough but vulnerable heroine of *Alien* (1979), understanding them means appreciating how that balance between the ordinary and the extraordinary is achieved.

(a)

(b)

(c)

Figure 3-22. Biographical film characters. These characters based on historical figures—from **(a)** ***Queen of Katwe*** (2016), **(b)** ***Milk*** (2008), and **(c)** ***Lincoln*** (2012)—represent a balance of the ordinary and the extraordinary.

Character Coherence, Depth, and Grouping

No matter how ordinary or extraordinary, unique or typical a character is, narrative traditions tend to require **character coherence**—consistency and coherence in a character's behaviors, emotions, and thoughts. Character coherence is the product of psychological, historical, or other expectations that see people (and thus characters in fictional narratives) as fundamentally consistent and unique. We usually evaluate a character's coherence according to one or more of the following three assumptions or models:

- *Values.* The character coheres in terms of one or more abstract values, such as when a character becomes defined through his or her overwhelming determination or treachery.
- *Actions.* The character acts out a logical relation between his or her implied inner or mental life and visible actions, as when a sensitive character acts in a remarkably generous way.
- *Behaviors.* The character reflects social and historical assumptions about normal or abnormal behavior, as when a fifteenth-century Chinese peasant woman acts submissively before a man with social power.

Defined within a realist tradition, the character Sergeant William James in Kathryn Bigelow's *The Hurt Locker* (2008) is part of a specialist bomb squad group in the Iraq War. His reckless behavior as he toys with mortal danger and death contrasts with his obsessive countdown of the days until he can return home. Questions about what drives and explains this character become part of the film's powerful depiction of war. When he finally returns home, only to quickly reenlist to return to Iraq, this complicated character seems revealed as one who coheres around a death wish of sorts or at least around the addictive excitement of risking death (Figure 3-23).

Figure 3-23. *The Hurt Locker* (2008). The contradictory behavior of Sergeant William James coheres around his addiction to danger and death.

Inconsistent, contradictory, or divided characters subvert one or more patterns of coherence. Although inconsistent characters occasionally may be the result of poor characterization, some films intentionally create an inconsistent or contradictory character as a way of challenging our sympathies and understanding. In films like *Desperately Seeking Susan* (1985)—about a bored suburban housewife, Roberta, who switches identities with an offbeat and mysterious New Yorker—characters complicate or subvert the expectation of coherence by taking on contradictory personalities. *Mulholland Dr.* (2001) dramatizes this instability when its two characters become mirror images of each other. In its tale of an amnesiac woman and a young actress who become entangled in a mysterious plot, fundamental notions about character coherence and stability are undermined (Figure 3-24).

Figure 3-24. ***Mulholland Dr.*** (2001). The double characters of the amnesiac and the young actress complicate character coherence.

Film characterization inevitably reflects certain historical and cultural values. The hero is overwhelmingly understood as male. In 2015, only 17 percent of the most successful Hollywood films had female leads. In Western cultures, movies promote the concept of the singular character, a unique individual distinguished by specific features and isolated from a social group. For example, the unique character of Jason Bourne in the series of *Bourne* films (2002–2016) is a product of a complex mixture of traits that reflect a modern notion of the advanced individual as one who is emotionally and intellectually complex and one of a kind. Character depth is the pattern of psychological and social features that distinguish a character as rounded and complex in a way that approximates realistic human personalities. It becomes a way of referring to personal mysteries and intricacies that deepen and layer the dimensions of a complicated personality. For example, the surface actions of Louise in *Thelma & Louise* (1991)—she refuses to drive through Texas to travel to Mexico—clearly hide a deep trauma (a presumed sexual assault) that she tries unsuccessfully to repress. The uniqueness of a character may be a product of one or two attributes—such as exceptional bravery, massive wealth, or superpowers—that separate him or her from all the other characters in the film. Sometimes we are led to question the value placed on singularity as a product of a social system that prizes individuality and psychological depth. After all, Hannibal Lecter in *The Silence of the Lambs* (1991) and its prequel and sequel is one of the most singular and exceptional characters in film history (Figure 3-25). Our troubling identification with him (at least in part) goes to the social heart of our admiration for such uniqueness.

Figure 3-25. *The Silence of the Lambs* (1991). Hannibal Lecter's dark depth of character is revealed.

Character grouping refers to the social arrangements of characters in relation to each other. Traditional narratives usually feature one or two **protagonists** (characters identified as the positive forces in a film) and one or two prominent **antagonists** (characters who oppose the protagonists as negative forces in a film). As with the sympathetic relationship between a German officer and a French prisoner in *Grand Illusion* (1937), this oppositional grouping of characters can sometimes be complicated or blurred.

In a film featuring an ensemble cast, such as *Crash* (2004), the conflicting relationships and competing interests among a group of interrelated characters provide much of the film's drama. Surrounding, contrasting with, and supporting the protagonists and antagonists, **minor characters** (also called *secondary characters*) are usually associated with specific character groups. In *Do the Right Thing* (1989), Da Mayor wanders around the edges of the central action throughout most of the film. Although he barely affects the events of the story, Da Mayor represents an older generation whose idealistic hopes have been dashed but whose fundamental compassion and wisdom stand out amid racial anger and strife.

Social hierarchies of class, gender, race, age, and geography, among other determinants, also come into play in the arrangements of film characters. Traditional movie narratives have focused on male protagonists and on heterosexual pairings in which males have claimed more power and activity than females. Another traditional character hierarchy places children and elderly individuals in subordinate positions. Especially with older or mainstream films, characters from racial minorities have existed on the fringes of the action and occupy social ranks markedly below those of the white protagonists. In *Gone with the Wind* (1939), for example, character hierarchy subordinates African Americans to whites. When social groupings are more important than individual characters, the collective character of the individuals in the group is defined primarily in terms of the group's action and personality. Sergei Eisenstein's *Battleship Potemkin* (1925) fashions a drama of collective characters, crafting a political showdown among czarist oppressors, rebellious sailors, and sympathetic civilians in Odessa. Modern films may shuffle those hierarchies noticeably so that groups like women, children, and the poor assume new power and position, as in *Winter's Bone* (2010), a story about a young female determined to find her lost father in a destitute Ozark Mountain region ravaged by a methamphetamine drug culture (Figure 3-26).

Figure 3-26. ***Winter's Bone*** (2010). The remarkable grit and determination of a young woman redefines both class and gender.

Character Types

Character types share distinguishing features with other similar characters and are prominent within particular narrative traditions such as fairy tales, genre films, and comic books. A single trait or multiple traits may define character types. These may be physical, psychological, or social traits. Tattoos and a shaved head may identify a character as a "skinhead" or punk, and another character's use of big words and a nasal accent may represent a New England socialite.

We might recognize the singularity of Warren Beatty's performance as Clyde in *Bonnie and Clyde* (1967), yet as we watch more movies and compare different protagonists, we can recognize him as a character type who—like James Cagney as gangster Tom Powers in *The Public Enemy* (1931) and Bruce Willis as John McClane in the *Die Hard* series (1988–2013)—can be described as a "tough yet sensitive outsider." By offering various emotional, intellectual, social, and psychological points of entry into a movie, character types include such figures as "the innocent," such as Elizabeth Taylor's Velvet Brown in *National Velvet* (1944); "the villain," such as Robert De Niro's Max Cady in Martin Scorsese's remake of

Cape Fear (1991); and the "heartless career woman," such as the imperious fashion editor played by Meryl Streep in *The Devil Wears Prada* (2006) (Figure 3-27). These and other character types can often be subclassified in even more specific terms—such as "the damsel in distress" or "the psychotic killer."

Figure 3-27. *The Devil Wears Prada* (2006). The "heartless career woman" character type is depicted by Meryl Streep in her role as imperious fashion editor Miranda Priestly.

Character types usually convey clear psychological or social connotations and imply cultural values about gender, race, social class, or age that a film engages and manipulates. In *Life Is Beautiful* (1997), the father (played by director Roberto Benigni) jokes and pirouettes in the tradition of comic clowns like Charlie Chaplin or Jacques Tati, outsiders whose physical games undermine the social and intellectual pretensions around them. In *Life Is Beautiful*, however, this comic type must live through the horrors of a Nazi concentration camp with his son, and in this context the character type becomes transformed into a different figure—a heroic type who physically and spiritually saves his child (Figure 3-28).

Figure 3-28. *Life Is Beautiful* (1997). The "comic" character type, depicted by Roberto Benigni in his role as a prisoner in a Nazi concentration camp, is transformed into the "hero" type.

Archetypes. Film characters also are presented as figurative types, characters so exaggerated or reduced that they no longer seem at all realistic and instead seem more like abstractions or emblems, like the white witch in *The Chronicles of Narnia: The Lion, the Witch, and the Wardrobe* (2006). In some movies, the figurative character appears as an **archetype**, a spiritual, psychological, or cultural model expressing certain virtues, values, or timeless realities—such as when a character represents evil or oppression. In *Battleship Potemkin* (1925), a military commander unmistakably represents social oppression, and a baby in a carriage becomes the emblem of innocence oppressed. In different ways, figurative types present characters as intentionally flat, without the traditional depth and complexity of realistically drawn characters, and often for a specific purpose—to create a comic effect, as with the absent-minded professor in *Back to the Future* (1985); to make an intellectual argument, as in *Battleship Potemkin*; or to populate a world of superheroes, as in *Batman v. Superman: Dawn of Justice* (2016).

Stereotypes. Sometimes a film reduces an otherwise realistic character to a set of static traits that identify him or her in terms of a social, physical, or cultural category—such as the "mammy" character in *Imitation of Life* (1934) (Figure 3-29) or the vicious and inhuman Vietnamese in *The Deer Hunter* (1978). This figurative type becomes a **stereotype**—a character type that simplifies and standardizes perceptions that one group holds about another, often less numerous, powerful, or privileged group. Although Louise Beavers's role and performance as Annie Johnson in *Imitation of Life* are substantive enough to complicate the way the role is written, it is still an example of how stereotypes can offend even when not overtly negative because they tend to be applied to marginalized social groups who are not represented by a range of character types.

Figure 3-29. ***Imitation of Life*** (1934). The "mammy" stereotype is identified by the black housekeeper's subservient role and dowdy costumes.

The relationship between film stars and character types has been a central part of film history and practice. For over a hundred years, the construction of character in film has interacted with the personae of recognizable movie stars. Rudolph Valentino played exotic romantic heroes in *The Sheik* (1921) and *Son of the Sheik* (1926), and his offscreen image was similarly molded to make him appear more exotic, with his enthusiastic female fans differentiating little between character and star. In *Meet the Parents* (2000) and its sequels, Robert De Niro's character draws on familiar aspects of the actor's tough-guy persona—for example, his role as a young Vito Corleone in *The Godfather: Part II* (1974) or as Travis Bickle in *Taxi Driver* (1976)—to humorous effect. Our experience of stars—garnered through publicity and promotion, television appearances, and criticism—resembles the process by which characters are positioned in narratives. Elements of characterization—clothing, personal relationships, perceptions of coherence or development—factor into our interest in stars and, in turn, into the ways that aspects of stars' offscreen images affect their film portrayals. One way to contemplate the effects of star image on character types is to imagine a familiar film cast differently. Would *Cast Away*'s (2000) story of everyman encountering his environment be the same if, instead of Tom Hanks, Jack Nicholson or Beyoncé Knowles played the lead?

Character Development

Finally, film characters usually change over the course of a realist film and thus require us to evaluate and revise our understanding of them as they develop. In a conventional story, characters are often understood or measured by the degree to which they change and learn from their experiences. Both the changes and a character's reaction to them determine much about the character and the narrative as a whole. We follow characters through this process of **character development**, which is shown in the patterns through which characters in a film move from one mental, physical, or social state to another. In Hitchcock's *Rear Window* (1954), the beautiful Lisa changes from a seemingly passive socialite to an active detective under the stress of investigating a murder mystery. In *Juno* (2007), the drama of a bright, sardonic sixteen-year-old's newly discovered pregnancy becomes less about a social or moral crisis in the community and more about her own self-discovery of the meaning of love, family, and friendship. The out-of-wedlock son of champion boxer Apollo Creed, Donnie Johnson, trains with and becomes a key support for his father's former rival Rocky Balboa, making a legacy for himself even as he is persuaded to take on his father's name (Figure 3-30).

Figure 3-30. ***Creed*** (2015). With a familiar plot about an underdog boxer, this new take on the *Rocky* series (1976–2015) engages the viewer through character development.

Character development follows four general schemes—external and internal changes and progressive and regressive development.

External Change. External change is typically a physical alteration, as when we watch a character grow taller or gray with age. Commonly overlooked as merely a realistic description of a character's growth, exterior change can signal other key changes in the meaning of a character. Similar to the female protagonist in *Pygmalion* (1938) and *My Fair Lady* (1964), the main character in *The Devil Wears Prada* (2006), Andy, is a naive recent college graduate who struggles with her first job at a fashion magazine, and her personal and social growth and maturation can be measured by her increasingly fashionable outfits.

Internal Change. Internal change measures the character's internal transformation, such as when a character slowly becomes bitter after experiencing numerous hardships or becomes less materially ambitious after gaining more of a spiritual sense of the world. In *Mildred Pierce* (1945), there is minimal external change in the appearance of the main character besides her costumes, but her consciousness about her identity dramatically changes—from a submissive housewife, to a bold businesswoman, and finally to a confused, if not contrite, socialite.

Progressive and Regressive Development. As part of these external and internal developments, progressive character development occurs with an improvement or advancement in some quality of the character. Regressive character development indicates a loss of or return to some previous state or a deterioration from the present state. For most viewers of *The Devil Wears Prada*, Andy grows into a more complex and more admirable woman. Mildred Pierce's path resembles for many a return to her originally submissive role.

Using these four schemes to understand character development can be a complex and sometimes even contradictory process. Some characters may seem to progress materially but regress spiritually, for instance. Other characters may not develop at all or may resist development throughout a film. Character development is frequently symptomatic of the larger society in which characters live. When the boy Oskar in Volker Schlöndorff's *The Tin Drum* (1979) suddenly refuses to grow at all, his distorted physical and mental development reflects the new Nazi society that then was developing in Germany (Figure 3-31).

Figure 3-31. ***The Tin Drum*** (1979). Oskar's arrested character development is a symptom of the new Nazi society.

Diegetic and Nondiegetic Elements

Most narratives involve two kinds of materials—those related to the story and those not related to the story. The film's **diegesis** is the world of the film's story (its characters, places, and events), including what is shown and what is implied to have taken place. The diegesis of Steven Spielberg's *Lincoln* (2012) includes characters and events explicitly revealed in the narrative, such as Abraham Lincoln's negotiations with lawmakers to pass an antislavery bill. However, the film's diegesis also includes viewers' knowledge of other unseen figures and events from American history, including the final battles of the Civil War and Lincoln's impending assassination. The extent to which we find the film realistic or convincing, creative or manipulative, depends on our recognition of the richness and coherence of the diegetic world surrounding the story.

The notion of diegesis is critical to our understanding of film narrative because it forces us to consider those elements of the story that the narration chooses to include or not include in the plot—and to consider *why* these elements are included or excluded. Despite the similarity of information in a plot and a story, plot selection and omission describe the exchange by which plot constructs and shapes a story from its diegesis. Consider a film about social unrest and revolution in Russia at the beginning of the twentieth century. Because the diegesis of that event includes a number of events and many characters, what should be selected, and what should be omitted? Faced with this question for his film on the 1905 revolution, Sergei Eisenstein reduced the diegesis to a single uprising on a battleship near the Odessa steps and called the film *Battleship Potemkin* (1925).

Information in the narrative can be nondiegetic. A **nondiegetic insert** is an insert that depicts an action, an object, or a title originating outside of the space and time of the narrative world. It includes material used to tell the story that does not relate to the diegesis and its world, such as background music and credits. These dimensions of a narrative indirectly add to a story and affect how viewers participate in or understand it. With silent films, nondiegetic information is sometimes part of the intertitles—those frames that usually print the dialogue of the characters but occasionally comment on the action—as when D. W. Griffith inserts a line from Walt Whitman ("Out of the cradle endlessly rocking") into his complex narrative *Intolerance* (1916).

Diegetic soundtracks include sound sources that can be located in the story, whereas nondiegetic soundtracks are commonly musical scores or other arrangements of noise and sound whose source is not found in the story. Most moviegoers are familiar with the ominously thumping soundtrack of *Jaws* (1975) that announces the unseen presence of the great white shark. In this way, the story punctuates its development to quicken our attention and create suspenseful anticipation of the next event (Figure 3-32).

Figure 3-32. ***Jaws*** (1975). In the opening sequence, Chrissie goes swimming during a late-night beach party. At first, all is tranquil, but the ominous thumping in the soundtrack foreshadows her violent death. This sound is used throughout the film to signal the presence of the shark.

Credits—a list at the end of a film of all the personnel involved in a film production, including cast, crew, and executives—are another nondiegetic element of the narrative. Sometimes seen at the beginning and sometimes at the end of a movie, credits introduce the actors, producers, technicians, and other individuals who have worked on the film. Hollywood movies today open with the names of famous stars, the director, and the producers, and their closing credits identify the secondary players and technicians. How this information is presented, especially in the opening credits, can suggest ways of looking at the story and its themes. In *Se7en* (1995), for instance, the celebrated opening credits graphically anticipate a dark story about the efforts of two detectives to track down a diabolical serial killer. Filmed in a suitably grainy and fragmented style and set to the sounds of a pulsating industrial soundtrack, the opening credits depict the obsessive mind of a maniac as he crafts morbid scrapbooks, providing both atmosphere and expository narrative information (Figure 3-33).

Figure 3-33. ***Se7en*** (1995). The presentation of the credits in a film can suggest ways for viewing its story and its unfolding themes.

Narrative Patterns of Time

Narrative films have experimented with new ways of telling stories since around 1900, the beginning of movie history. One of the first such films, Edwin S. Porter's *The Great Train Robbery* (1903), manipulated time and place by shifting from one action to another and coordinated different spaces by jumping between exterior and interior scenes. Since then, movie narratives have contracted and expanded times and places according to ever-varying patterns and well-established formulas, spanning centuries and traveling the world in *Cloud Atlas* (2012) or confining the tale to two hours in one town in Agnès Varda's *Cléo from 5 to 7* (1962). For more than a hundred years and through different cultures around the world, the art of storytelling on film has been developed and altered by intricate temporal organizations and spatial shapes that respond to changing cultural and historical pressures.

Linear Chronology

A narrative can be organized according to a variety of temporal patterns. Individuals and societies create patterns of time as ways of measuring and valuing experience. Repeating holidays once a year, marking births and deaths with symbolic rituals, and rewarding work for time invested are some of the ways we organize and value time. Similarly, narrative films develop a variety of temporal patterns as a way of creating meaning and value in the stories and experiences they recount.

Most commonly, plots follow a **linear chronology**—the arrangement of plot events and actions that follow each other in time. The logic and direction of the plot commonly follow a central character's motivation—that is, the ideas or emotions that make that person tick. In these cases, a character pursues an object, a belief, or a goal of some sort, and the events in the plot show how that character's motivating desire affects or creates new situations or actions. Put simply, past actions generate present situations, and decisions made in the present create future events. The narrative of *Little Miss Sunshine* (2006) has a linear structure. A family of offbeat and dysfunctional characters travels from New Mexico to California to participate in a beauty pageant, and on their drive toward this single goal, over the course of several days, they must overcome many sometimes hilarious predicaments, obstacles, and personalities in order to complete their narrative journey and ultimately discover themselves anew. Although journeys are obvious examples of linear plots, many film genres rely on this chronology. In a romantic comedy like *Trainwreck* (2015), the bad behavior of the heroine and the mistrust of her love interest lead to complications and misunderstandings, but these only delay the obvious resolution of the couple getting together (Figure 3-34).

Figure 3-34. ***Trainwreck*** (2015). The poor choices of Amy Schumer's character may seem to lead away from the desired goal but ultimately prove that the romantic pair are right for each other.

Linear narratives most commonly structure their stories in terms of beginnings, middles, and ends. As a product of this structure, the relationship between the narrative opening and closing is central to the temporal logic of a plot. How a movie begins and ends and what relationship exists between those two poles explain much about a film. Sometimes this relation can create a sense of closure or completion, as happens when a romance ends with a couple united or with a journey finally concluded. Other plots provide less certain relations between openings and closings.

In Ang Lee's *Life of Pi* (2012), Pi Patel's story begins with his childhood in a zoo and a dramatic shipwreck that leaves him drifting the seas in a lifeboat with a zebra, an orangutan, a hyena, and a male Bengal tiger nicknamed Richard Parker. At the conclusion, the reality of what actually happened (and what was fantasy) is brought into question (Figure 3-35).

Figure 3-35. ***Life of Pi*** (2012). In Ang Lee's magical film, the protagonist's fantastic adventure concludes with a dramatic ambiguity.

Plot Chronologies: Flashback and Flashforward

Despite the dominance of linear chronologies in movie narratives, many films deviate, to some extent, to create different perspectives on events. Such deviations may lead viewers toward an understanding of what is or is not important in a story or disrupt or challenge notions of the film as a realistic re-creation of events. Plot order describes how events and actions are arranged in relation to each other. Actions may appear out of chronological order, as when a later event precedes an earlier one in the plot.

One of the most common nonlinear plot devices is the narrative flashback, whereby a story shifts dramatically to an earlier time in the story. When a flashback describes the whole story, it creates a retrospective plot that tells of past events from the perspective of the present or future. In *The Godfather: Part II* (1974), the modern story of mobster Michael Corleone periodically alternates with the flashback story of his father, Vito, many decades earlier. This comparison of two different histories draws parallels and suggests differences between the father's formation of his Mafia family and the son's later destruction of that family in the name of the Mafia business (Figures 3-36a and 3-36b).

(a) (b)

Figure 3-36. ***The Godfather: Part II*** (1974). A retrospective plot of a father's formation of his Mafia family is woven into a contemporary tale of the son's later destruction of it.

Conversely but less frequently, a film may employ a narrative flashforward, leaping ahead of the normal cause-and-effect order to a future incident. A film narrative may show a man in an office and then flash forward to his plane leaving an airport before returning to the moment in the plot when he sits at his desk. In *They Shoot Horses, Don't They?* (1969), the plot flashes forward to a time when Robert, an unsuccessful Hollywood director during the Depression, is on trial. The unexplained scene creates a mysterious suspense that is not resolved until much later in the film.

Other nonlinear chronological orders might interweave past, present, and future events in less predictable or logical patterns. In *Eternal Sunshine of the Spotless Mind* (2004), the two main characters, Joel and Clementine, struggle to resurrect a romantic past that has been intentionally erased from their memories. The flashbacks here appear not as natural remembrances but as dramatic struggles to re-create a part of the personal narrative they have lost (Figure 3-37). *Hiroshima mon amour* (1959) mixes documentary photos of the nuclear destruction of Hiroshima at the end of World War II, a modern story of a love affair between a French actress and a Japanese architect, and flashback images of the woman growing up in France during the war, when she had a relationship with a German soldier (Figure 3-38). Gradually, and not in chronological order, the story of her past is revealed. Conversations with her lover and images of Japan during World War II seem to provoke leaps in her memory. As the film narrative follows these flashbacks, we become involved in the difficulty of memory as it attempts to reconstruct an identity across a historical trauma. When a narrative violates linear chronology in these ways, the film may be demonstrating how subjective memories interact with the real world. At other times, as with *Hiroshima mon amour*, these violations may be ways of questioning the very notion of linear progress in life and civilization.

Figure 3-37. *Eternal Sunshine of the Spotless Mind* (2004). The film's chronology attempts to recover what has been lost from the couple's story.

Figure 3-38. *Hiroshima mon amour* (1959). The nonlinear mix of past and present engages us in the main character's attempt to reconstruct an identity across a historical trauma.

The Deadline Structure

One of the most common temporal schemes in narrative films is the **deadline structure**—a narrative structured around a central event or action that must be accomplished by a certain time. This structure adds to the tension and excitement of a plot by accelerating the action toward that certain moment, hour, day, or year. These narrative rhythms can create suspense and anticipation that define the entire narrative and the characters who motivate it. In *The Graduate* (1967), Benjamin must race to the church in time to declare his love for Elaine and stop her from marrying his rival. In the German film *Run Lola Run* (1998), Lola has twenty minutes to find 100,000 deutsche marks to save her boyfriend. This tight deadline results in three different versions of the same race across town in which, like a game, Lola's rapid-fire choices result in three different conclusions (Figure 3-39).

Figure 3-39. ***Run Lola Run*** (1998). In three different versions of the same race against time, Lola is forced to make different choices.

Parallel Plots

The deadline structure points to another common temporal pattern in film narrative—the doubled or parallel plotline. In parallel plots, there is an implied simultaneity of or connection between two different plotlines, usually with their intersection at one or more points. Many movies alternate between actions or subplots that take place at roughly the same time and that may be bound together in some way, such as by the relationship of two or more characters. One standard formula in a parallel plot is to intertwine a private story with a public story. *Jerry Maguire* (1996) develops the story of Jerry's efforts to succeed as an agent in the cutthroat world of professional sports, and concurrently it follows the ups and downs of his romance with Dorothy, a single mother, and his bond with her son, Ray. In some crime or caper films, such as *Ocean's Eleven* (2001), a murder or heist plot (in this case, involving a complicated casino robbery) parallels and entwines with an equally complicated love story (here between Danny and Tess Ocean) (Figure 3-40). In addition to recognizing parallel plots, we need to consider the relationship between them.

Figure 3-40. ***Ocean's Eleven*** (2001). The weaving together of the plot to rob a casino and a love story creates thematic and formal connections.

Narrative Duration and Frequency

Movie narratives also rely on various other temporal patterns through which events in a story are constructed according to different time schemes. Not surprisingly, these narrative temporalities overlap with and rely on similar temporal patterns developed as editing strategies. Narrative duration refers to the length of time used to present an event or action in a plot. *Die Hard: With a Vengeance* (1995) features a now-standard digital countdown for a bomb that threatens to blow up New York City. The narrative suspense is, in large part, the amount of time the plot spends on this scene, dwelling on the bomb mechanism. The drawn-out time devoted to defusing the bomb, much longer than thirty real seconds, shows how the temporal duration can represent not simply a real but also an extended, in this case psychological, time.

At the other end of the spectrum, a plot may include only a temporal flash of an action that really endures for a much longer period. In *Secretariat* (2010), a rapid montage of images condenses many months of victories during which the renowned racehorse of the title rises to fame. Instead of representing the many details that extend an actual duration of one or more events, the plot condenses these actions into a much shorter temporal sequence. Both examples call attention to the difference between story time and plot time. Story events that take years—such as a character growing up—may be condensed into a brief montage in a film's plot.

In a linear plot, each event occurs once. But **narrative frequency**—the number of times a plot element is repeated throughout a narrative—can be manipulated as an important storytelling tool. For example, in the narrative of an investigation, a crime may be depicted many times as more pieces of the story are put together.

Narrative Space

Along with narrative patterns of time, plot constructions also involve a variety of spatial schemes constructed through the course of the narrative. These narrative locations—indoors, outdoors, natural spaces, artificial spaces, outer space—define more than just the

background for stories. Stories and their characters explore these spaces, contrast them, conquer them, inhabit them, leave them, build on them, and transform them. As a consequence, both the characters and the stories usually change and develop not only as part of the formal shape of these places but also as part of their cultural and social significance and connotations. Michael Haneke's *Amour* (2012) takes place almost exclusively in the apartment where a couple in their eighties have spent their married life (Figure 3-41). After Anne suffers a stroke, the drama of this single mise-en-scène generates layers and layers of shared emotions and memories as the husband and wife struggle with the climactic crisis they now face. The complex temporality of *Interstellar*'s (2014) science fiction plot—involving wormholes and characters traveling in space who age at different rates than people on earth—is stabilized to some extent by its narrative spaces, which depict vivid planetary environments. A fundamental narrative of betrayal is set on a frozen planet with a toxic atmosphere (Figure 3-42).

Figure 3-41. ***Amour*** (2012). The film takes place in an apartment where the confined space intensifies the residents' memories, experiences, emotions, and decisions.

Figure 3-42. ***Interstellar*** (2014). The temporal abstractions of outer space are countered by human struggles that occur in planetary spaces.

In conjunction with narrative action and characters, the cultural and social resonances of narrative spaces may be developed in four different ways—historically, ideologically, psychologically, and symbolically. Whether actual or constructed, the **historical location**—the recognized marker of a historical setting that can carry meanings and connotations important to the narrative—abounds in film narratives. For example, in *Roman Holiday* (1953), a character visits the monuments of Rome, where she discovers a sense of human history and a romantic glory missing from her own life (Figure 3-43). Films from *Ben-Hur* (1925) to *Gladiator* (2000) use the historical connotations of Rome to infuse the narrative with grandeur and wonder.

Figure 3-43. ***Roman Holiday*** (1953). During a character's exploration of Rome, a sense of human history emerges.

An **ideological location** is a space or place inscribed with distinctive social values or ideologies in a narrative. Sometimes these narrative spaces have unmistakable political or philosophical significance, such as Folsom State Prison, where Johnny Cash bonds with prisoners in *Walk the Line* (2005) (Figure 3-44), or the oppressive grandeur of the czar's palace in Eisenstein's *October* (1927). The politics of gender also can underpin the locations of a film narrative in crucial ideological ways. In *9 to 5* (1980), the plot focuses on the ways that three working women transform the patriarchal office space of their jobs into a place where the needs of women are met (Figure 3-45).

Figure 3-44. ***Walk the Line*** (2005). When Johnny Cash bonds with the inmates, the ideological significance of Folsom State Prison emerges.

Figure 3-45. ***9 to 5*** (1980). Three women transform the gendered politics of office space.

Psychological location in a film narrative suggests an important correlation between a character's state of mind and the physical place he or she inhabits in the story. In Sofia Coppola's *Lost in Translation* (2003), an American actor (played by Bill Murray) experiences confusion and communication difficulties while visiting contemporary Tokyo. These, along with his isolation in an expensive hotel, connect to deeper feelings of disaffection and disillusionment with his life back home (Figure 3-46). Less common, symbolic space is a space transformed through spiritual or other abstract means related to the narrative. In different versions of the Robinson Crusoe story—from Luis Buñuel's *The Adventures of Robinson Crusoe* (1954) to *Robinson Crusoe on Mars* (1964) and *Cast Away* (2000)—the space of an island might become emblematic of the providential ways of life or of the absurdity of the human condition (Figure 3-47).

Figure 3-46. ***Lost in Translation*** (2003). The isolation of an American actor in Tokyo suggests a disaffected psychological space.

Figure 3-47. ***Cast Away*** (2000). The island as symbolic space becomes emblematic of the absurdity of the human condition.

Complex narratives often develop and transform the significance of one or more locations, making this transformation of specific places central to the meaning of the movie. In Martin Scorsese's *Gangs of New York* (2002), the Five Points neighborhood of New York City in 1863 becomes a site of historical realism as an infamous gangland territory, a psychological place of terror and violence, the ideological location of emerging American social classes, and a symbol of American culture. In Jim Jarmusch's anthology film *Mystery Train* (1989), the narrative interweaves the stories of two Japanese tourists, an Italian woman on her way home to bury her husband, and three drifters who hold up a liquor store (Figure 3-48). All happen to seek refuge in a run-down Memphis hotel. Although they never meet, they infuse the narrative location of the hotel with the meanings of their individual dramas. For the Japanese couple, the hotel becomes a place of historical nostalgia for 1950s America and blues music; for the Italian woman, a comically ritualistic and spiritual location where she eventually meets Elvis Presley's ghost; and for the three drifters, a weird debating hall where they discuss contemporary social violence.

Figure 3-48. ***Mystery Train*** (1989). Japanese tourists, the ghost of Elvis, and bungling drifters transform the space of a run-down Memphis hotel into an offbeat carnival of loss and desire.

Narrative Perspectives

Plots are organized by the perspectives that inform them. Whether this perspective is explicit or implicit, we refer to this dimension of narrative as **narration**—the telling of a story or description of a situation. It is the emotional, physical, or intellectual perspective through which the characters, events, and action of the plot are conveyed. It shapes how plot materials appear and what is or is not revealed about them. Narration carries and creates attitudes, values, and aims that are central to understanding any movie. A **narrator** is a character or other person whose voice and perspective describe the action of a film, either in voiceover or through a particular point of view. It may be clearly designated in a film by direct address to the viewer. However, the term *narration* is not restricted to a single character or to verbalization within a movie about the plot but also can refer to how movies organize plot elements. The most common narrative perspectives are first-person, omniscient, and restricted. One tactic for drawing us into a story is a narrative frame. Frames and other devices direct the arrangement of the plot and indicate certain cultural, social, or psychological perspectives on the events of the story.

First-Person Narrative and Narrative Frames

Signaled by the pronoun *I* in written or spoken texts, a **first-person narration** in film may be attributed to a single character using voiceover commentary or to camera techniques and optical effects that mark an individual's perspective. However, movie images can usually only approximate a subjective point of view, in which the film frame re-creates what a single character sees for a limited period without appearing contrived. *Lady in the Lake* (1947), filmed from the point of view of detective Philip Marlowe, is a famous instance of cinematic first person and is considered by many to be a failed experiment.

Appearing at the beginning and end of a film, a **narrative frame** designates a context or person positioned outside the principal narrative of a film, such as bracketing scenes in which a character in the story's present begins to relate events of the past and later concludes her or his tale. This kind of narrative frame can help define a film's terms and meaning. Sometimes signaled by a voiceover, this frame may indicate the story's audience, the social context, or the period from which the story is understood. The frame may, for instance, indicate that the story is a tale for children, as in *The Blue Bird* (1940); that it is being told to a detective in a police station, as in *The Usual Suspects* (1995); or that it is the memory of a elderly woman, as in *Titanic* (1997). In each case, the film's frame indicates the crucial perspective and logic that define the narration.

In *Sunset Boulevard* (1950), the presence of the narrator is announced through the voice-over of the screenwriter-protagonist who introduces the setting and circumstances of the story. His voice and death become the frame for the story. Throughout the course of the film, his voiceover disappears and reappears, but we are aware from the start that the story is a product of his perspective.

Ang Lee's *The Ice Storm* (1997) also uses a narrative frame. In this case, the perspective of the frame is that of a young man whose commuter train has stopped en route to his home because of a heavy ice storm (Figure 3-49). The film begins as he waits in the night for the tracks to be cleared of ice and debris and reflects on his family. This isolated moment and compartment frame the flashback that follows. Although he, too, disappears as a narrator until we return to the train and his voice at the end of the movie, his role makes clear that this tale of a dysfunctional family in the 1970s is about this young man at a turning point in his life. Indeed, both these examples suggest a question to ask about narrators: does it make a difference if they are seen as part of the story?

Figure 3-49. ***The Ice Storm*** (1997). When a storm stops his train, a young man's thoughts on his past become the film's narrative frame.

Third-Person Narrative: Omniscient and Restricted

The perspective of a film may adopt **third-person narration**—a narration that assumes an objective and detached stance toward the plot and characters by describing events from outside the story. With third-person narratives like *Gravity* (2013), it still may be possible to describe a specific kind of attitude or point of view. Far from being staid and detached, the organizing perspective of this film is forceful and dynamic, with camera movements that observe the main character's plight (Figure 3-50).

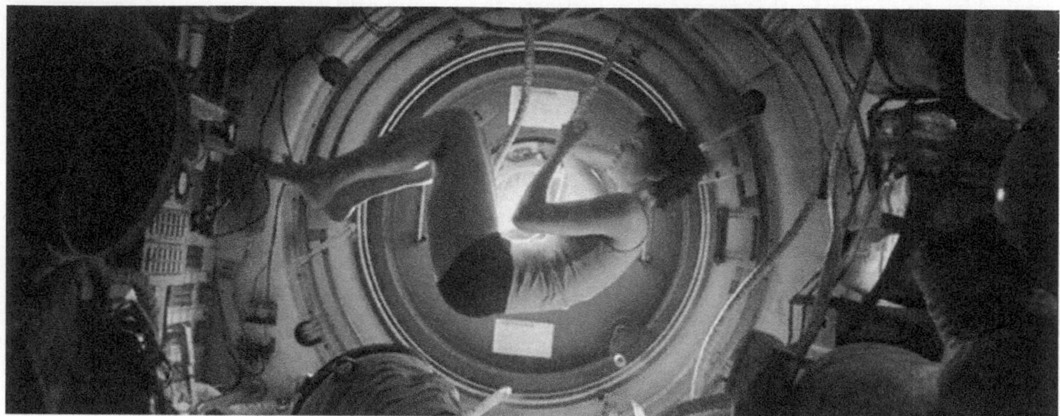

Figure 3-50. ***Gravity*** (2013). Although third-person narratives maintain objectivity, they also can create dynamic characters and action.

The standard form of classical movies is **omniscient narration**—narration that presents all elements of the plot, exceeding the perspective of any one character (a version of third-person narration). All elements of the plot are presented from many or all potential angles. An omniscient perspective knows all, knows what is important, and knows how to arrange events to reveal the truth about a life or a history. Although the four films in the *Bourne* series (2002–2016), for example, employ omniscient perspectives that follow Jason Bourne's flight through multiple cities around the world, the story itself contrasts the attempt of a covert American agency's surveillance mechanism to approximate that omniscient perspective in its pursuit of Bourne, while he constantly attempts to escape it.

A limited third-person perspective, or **restricted narration**—a narrative in which our knowledge is limited to that of a particular character—organizes stories by focusing on one or two characters. Even though this perspective on a story also assumes objectivity and is able to present events and characters outside the range of those primary characters, it confines itself largely to the experiences and thoughts of the major characters.

The historical source of restricted narration is the novel and short story. Its emphasis on one or two individuals reflects a relatively modern view of the world that is concerned mostly with the progress of individuals. Limiting the narration in this way allows the movie to attend to large historical events and actions (battles or family meetings, for instance) while also prioritizing the main character's problems and desires. Buster Keaton's *The General* (1927), set in Georgia and Tennessee during the Civil War, follows this pattern. Johnny Gray's ingenuity becomes apparent and seems much more honorable, and funny, than the grand epic of war that stays in the background of the narrative (Figure 3-51). With these and other restricted narratives, some characters receive more or less attention from the limited narrative point of view.

Figure 3-51. ***The General*** (1927). Restricted narration limits the plot to the experiences of the main character, Johnny Gray, as he rescues his locomotive and his girlfriend from the Union army during the Civil War.

Reflexive, Unreliable, and Multiple Narration

Omniscient narration and restricted narration are the most common kinds of classical narration, but some films use variations on these models. Reflexive narration is a mode of narration that calls attention to the narrative point of view of the story in order to complicate or subvert the movie's narrative authority as an objective perspective on the world. Robert Wiene's *The Cabinet of Dr. Caligari* (1920) is a well-known early example of reflexive narration that fractures the veracity and reliability of its point of view when, at the film's conclusion, we discover that the narrator is a madman. In *About a Boy* (2002), the main character often comments reflexively on his own behavior as he pretends to be a father in order to meet women.

Contemporary and experimental films commonly question the very process of narration at the same time that they construct the narrative. **Unreliable narration** is a type of narration that raises questions about the truth of the story being told (it is sometimes called *manipulative narration*). In *Fight Club* (1999), the bottom falls out of the narration when, toward the conclusion of the film, it becomes clear that the first-person narrator has been hallucinating the entire existence of a central character around whom the plot develops (Figure 3-52).

Figure 3-52. ***Fight Club*** (1999). This is a dramatic example of a film whose narration suddenly appears to be the questionable fantasy of the film's narrator.

Multiple narrations are found in films that use several different narrative perspectives for a single story or for different stories in a movie that loosely fits these perspectives together. The 1916 movie *Intolerance* weaves four stories about prejudice and hate from different historical periods ("the modern story," "the Judean story," "the French story," and "the Babylonian story") and could be considered a precursor to the tradition of multiple narration. Woody Allen's comedy *Zelig* (1983) parodies the objectivity proposed by many narratives by presenting the life of Leonard Zelig in the 1920s and 1930s through the onscreen narrations of numerous fictional and real persons (such as Saul Bellow and Susan Sontag). Contemporary films like *Crash* (2004) and *Babel* (2006) weave together different stories from around a city or even the world, coincidentally linked by major events in the characters' lives (Figure 3-53).

Figure 3-53. ***Babel*** (2006). Overlapping multiple narratives are woven together in a film about the search for a common humanity.

Compilation films (also called **anthology films**) are films comprised of various segments, often by different filmmakers—such as *Germany in Autumn* (1978), *Two Evil Eyes* (1990), *Four Rooms* (1995), and *Paris, je t'aime* (2006). They are more extreme versions of multiple narratives. Although the stories may share a common theme or issue—a political crisis in Germany, adaptations of Edgar Allan Poe stories, or zany guests staying in a decaying hotel—they intentionally replace a singular narrative perspective with smaller narratives that establish their own distinctive perspectives.

Making Sense of Film Narrative

In their reflections of time, change, and loss, film narratives engage viewers in ways that make time meaningful. From historical epics like *The Birth of a Nation* (1915) to the less plot-driven drama of teenage life on the run *American Honey* (2016), narrative movies have been prized as both public and private histories—as records of celebrated events, personal memories, and daily routines. Film, video, and computer narratives today saturate our lives with flashes of insight or events repeated again and again from different angles and at different speeds. Film narratives are thus significant for two reasons: they describe the different temporal experiences of individuals, and they reflect and reveal the shapes and patterns of larger social histories of nations, communities, and cultures.

The significance of film narrative never functions independently of historical, cultural, and industrial issues. Many narratives in Western cultures are more inward, centering on individuals, their fates, and their self-knowledge. Individual heroes are frequently male, with female characters participating in their quest or growth primarily through marriage—a pervasive form of narrative resolution.

Moreover, Western narrative models, such as the Judeo-Christian one that assumes a progressive movement from a fall to redemption, reflect a basic cultural belief in individual and social development. Certainly, cultural alternatives to this popular logic of progression and forward movement exist, and in some cultures individual characters may be less central to the story than the give-and-take movements of the community or the passing of the seasons. In *Xala* (1975), for instance, by Senegalese filmmaker Ousmane Sembène, the narration is influenced by oral tradition, and the central character's plight—he has been placed under a curse of impotence—is linked to a whole community. This tradition is associated with the griot, the storyteller in some West African cultures who recounts at public gatherings the many tales that bind the community together.

Shaping Memory, Making History

Film narratives shape memory by describing individual temporal experiences. In other words, they commonly portray the changes in a day, a year, or the life of a character or community. These narratives are not necessarily actual real-time experiences, as is partly the case in the single-shot film *Russian Ark* (2002). However, they do aim to approximate the patterns through which different individuals experience and shape time—time as endurance, time as growth, time as loss. In Lee Daniels' *The Butler* (2013), the narrative describes the life of Cecil Gaines, the butler for eight U.S. presidents, and intertwines his personal

struggles and achievements as a White House servant and the major historical events surrounding him, such as the civil rights movement and the Vietnam War. The often strained interactions between his personal experiences and public events celebrate how individual memory participates in the shape of history. In the virtually dialogue-free Italian film *Le Quattro Volte* (*The Four Times*) (2010), time is refracted in four episodes showing interrelated cycles of human, plant, and animal life (Figure 3-54).

Figure 3-54. ***Le Quattro Volte* (*The Four Times*)** (2010). One narrative told in this contemplative and often funny film is shaped by the observations of a baby goat.

Through their reflections on and revelations of social history, film narratives make history. Narratives order the various dimensions of time—past, present, and future events—in ways that are similar to models of history used by nations or other communities. Consequently, narratives create public perceptions of and ways of understanding those histories. The extent to which narratives and public histories are bound together can be seen by noting how many historical events—such as the U.S. civil rights movement or the first landing on the moon—become the subject for narrative films. But narrative films also can reveal public history in smaller events, where personal crisis or success becomes representative of a larger national or world history. The tale of a heroic African American Union army regiment, *Glory* (1989) (Figure 3-55) tells a history of the Civil War left out of narratives like *The Birth of a Nation* (1915) and *Gone with the Wind* (1939). By concentrating on the personal life of Mark Zuckerberg during his college years, *The Social Network* (2010) also reveals key dimensions of the social networking site Facebook and the cultural history of the digital revolution (Figure 3-56). In these cases, film narratives are about cultural origins, historical losses, and national myths.

Figure 3-55. ***Glory*** (1989). A narrative of the heroic African American Union army regiment that fought during the Civil War tells a different history of that war.

Narrative Traditions

Based on how movies can both shape memory and make history, two prominent styles of film narrative have emerged. The classical film narrative usually presents a close relationship between individual lives and social history, whereas the alternative film narrative often dramatizes the disjunction between how individuals live their lives according to personal temporal patterns and how those patterns conflict with those of the social history that intersects with their lives.

Classical Film Narrative

Three primary features characterize the classical film narrative:

- It centers on one or more central characters who propel the plot with a cause-and-effect logic, whereby an action generates a reaction.
- Its plots develop with linear chronologies directed at certain goals, even when flashbacks are integrated into that linearity.
- It employs an omniscient or a restricted narration that suggests some degree of realism.

Classical narrative often appears as a three-part structure: (1) a situation or circumstance is presented; (2) the situation is disrupted, often with a crisis or confrontation; and (3) the disruption is resolved. Its narrative point of view is usually objective and realistic, including most information necessary to understand the characters and their world.

Figure 3-56. ***The Social Network*** (2010). Here the personal history of the founder of Facebook reflects a much broader transformation in the social history of technology.

Since the 1910s, most U.S. films have followed the **classical Hollywood narrative**—the dominant form of classical film narrative associated with the Hollywood studio system from the end of the 1910s to the end of the 1950s—but there have been many historical and cultural variations on this narrative model. Both the 1925 and 1959 films of *Ben-Hur* develop their plots around the heroic motivations of the title character and follow his struggles and triumphs as a former citizen who becomes a slave, rebel, and gladiator, fighting against the cruelties of the Roman empire. Both movies spent great amounts of money on large casts of characters and on details and locations that attempt to seem as realistic as possible. Yet even if both these Hollywood films can be classified as classical narratives, they also can be distinguished by their variations on this narrative formula. Besides some differences in the details of the story, the first version attends more to grand spectacles (such as sea battles) and places greater emphasis on the plight of the Jews as a social group. The second version concentrates significantly more on the individual drama of Charlton Heston as Ben-Hur, on his search to find his lost family, and on Christian salvation through personal faith (Figure 3-57).

Figure 3-57. ***Ben-Hur*** (1959). As the different versions of this film demonstrate, classical Hollywood narrative can vary significantly through history—even when the story is fundamentally the same.

An important variation on the classical narrative tradition is the **postclassical narrative**—the form and content of films after the decline of the Hollywood studio system around 1960, including formerly taboo subject matter and narratives and formal techniques influenced by European cinema. This global body of films began to appear in the decades after World War II and remains visible to the present day. The postclassical model frequently undermines the power of a protagonist to control and drive the narrative forward in a clear direction. As a postclassical narrative, Martin Scorsese's *Taxi Driver* (1976) works with a plot much like that of *The Searchers* (1956), in which an alienated and troubled Civil War veteran searches the frontier for a lost girl, but in Travis Bickle's strange quest to rescue a New York City prostitute from her pimp, he wanders with even less direction, identity, and control than his predecessor, Ethan. Bickle, a dark hero, becomes lost in his own fantasies (Figure 3-58).

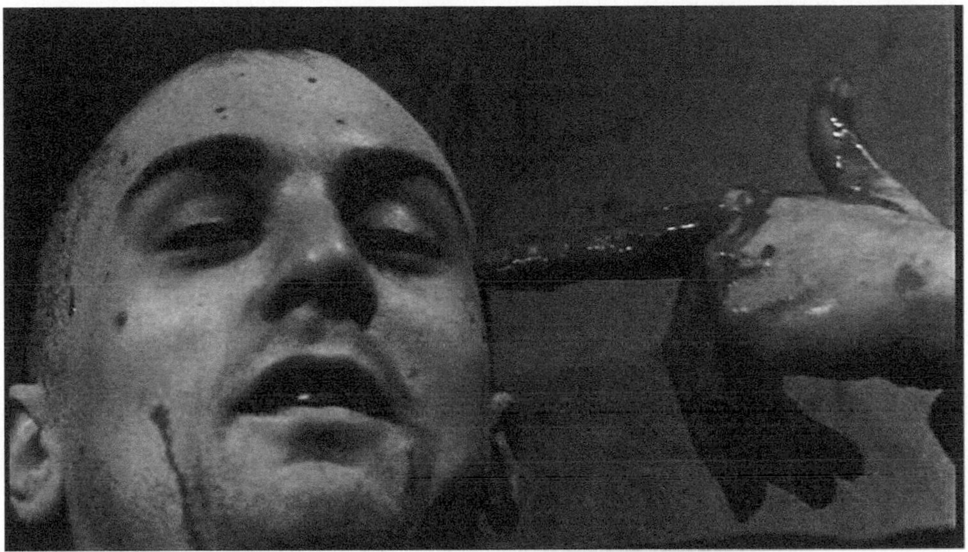

Figure 3-58. ***Taxi Driver*** (1976). Robert De Niro's character erupts into senseless violence and seems bent on his own destruction, significantly challenging classical narrative codes.

Alternative Film Narrative

Foreign and independent films may reveal information or perspectives traditionally excluded from classical narratives in order to unsettle audience expectations, provoke new thinking, or differentiate themselves from more common narrative structures. Generally, the **alternative film narrative** deviates from or challenges the linearity of classical film narrative, often undermining the centrality of the main character, the continuity of the plot, or the verisimilitude of the narration.

Both the predominance and motivational control of characters in moving a plot come into question with alternative films. Instead of the one or two central characters we see in classical narratives, alternative films may put a multitude of characters into play, and their stories may not even be connected. In Jean-Luc Godard's *La Chinoise* (1967), the narrative shifts among three young people—a student, an economist, a philosopher—whose tales appear like a series of debates about politics and revolution in the streets of Paris.

A visually stunning film from Iran, Abbas Kiarostami's *Taste of Cherry* (1997) contains only the shadow of a story and plot: the middle-aged Mr. Badii wishes to commit suicide for no clear reason. After witnessing a series of random encounters and requests, we remain uncertain about his fate at the conclusion. Freed of the determining motivations of classical characters, the plots of alternative film narratives tend to break apart, omit links in a cause-and-effect logic, or proliferate plotlines well beyond the classical parallel plot.

Many alternative film narratives question, in various ways, the classical narrative assumptions about an objective narrative point of view and about the power of a narrative to reflect universally true experiences. In *Rashomon* (1950), four people, including the ghost of a dead man, recount a tale of robbery, murder, and rape in four different ways, as four different narratives (Figure 3-59). Ultimately, the group that hears these tales (as the frame of the narrative) realizes that it is impossible to know the true story.

Figure 3-59. *Rashomon* (1950). Four different narrative perspectives tell a grisly tale that brings into question the possibility of narrative objectivity, especially when recounted by people deeply, and differently, affected by events.

By employing one or more of their defining characteristics, alternative film narratives also have fostered more specific cultural variations and traditions, including non-Western narratives and new wave narratives. Alternative, non-Western narratives swerve from classical Western narrative by drawing on indigenous forms of storytelling with culturally distinctive themes, characters, plots, and narrative points of view. Indian filmmaker Satyajit Ray, for example, adapts a famous work of Bengali fiction for his 1955 *Pather Panchali* and its sequels, *Aparajito* (1956) and *The World of Apu* (1959), to render the story of a boy named Apu and his impoverished family. Although Ray was influenced by European filmmakers—he served as assistant to Jean Renoir on *The River* (1951), filmed in India—his work is suffused with the symbols and slow-paced plot of the original novel and of village life, as it rediscovers Indian history from inside India (Figure 3-60a and Figure 3-60b).

(a)

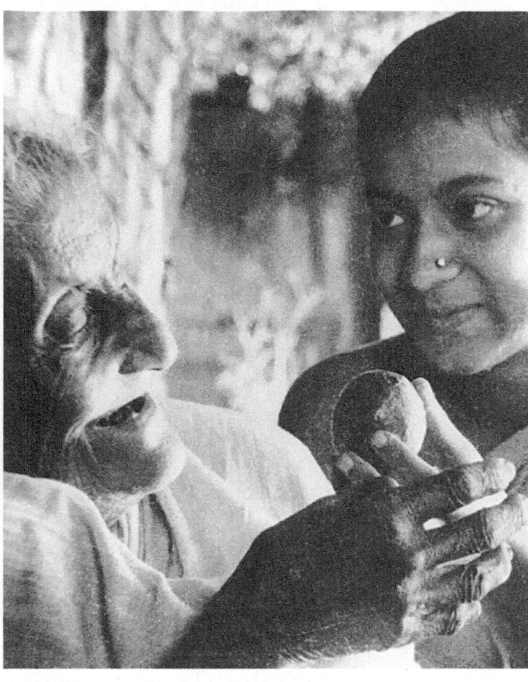

(b)

Figure 3-60. Alternative film narratives. (a) Jean Renoir's *The River* (1951) influenced the work of Satyajit Ray, but **(b)** Ray's ***Pather Panchali*** (1955), an adaptation of a famous Bengali novel, is suffused with the symbols and slow-paced plot that are indicative of the original work and Indian culture.

New wave narratives describe the proliferation of narrative forms that have appeared around the world since the 1950s. Often experimental and disorienting, these narratives interrogate the political assumptions of classical narratives by overturning their formal assumptions. Italian New Wave director Bernardo Bertolucci's *The Conformist* (1970) is an example. It creates a sensually vague and dreamy landscape where reality and nightmares overlap. Through the mixed-up motivations of its central character, Marcello Clerici, the film explores the historical roots of Italian fascism, a viciously decadent world of sex and politics rarely depicted in the histories of classical narrative (Figure 3-61).

Figure 3-61. ***The Conformist*** (1970). In this film by Italian New Wave director Bernardo Bertolucci, the historical roots of Italian fascism are imagined in an alternative narrative set within a dreamy landscape where reality and nightmares overlap.

Both these broad categories draw on many narrative cultures that differ sharply from each other, and both suggest not so much a complete opposition to classical narrative as much as a dialogue with that tradition. In this context, Indian film narratives are very different from African film narratives, and the new waves of Greece and Spain represent divergent issues and narrative strategies. All, however, might be said to confront, in one way or another, the classical narrative paradigm.

Chapter 4

Production

The Big Picture

"The Big Picture" from *Filmmaking in Action*, by Adam Leipzig, Barry S. Weiss, and Michael Goldman, pp. 1–16 (Chapter 1, "The Big Picture").

"Making a film is a bit like switching off the light in the room and trying to navigate around by touch and feel and smell."

—Steve McQueen, director of *12 Years a Slave* (2013), *Shame* (2011), and *Hunger* (2008)[1]

Figure 4-1. *Amreeka* (2009).

Cherien Dabis made her presence felt even before she came up to the stage. Ninety-seven minutes earlier, the house lights had dimmed and her first feature film, *Amreeka*, began its premiere screening. Starting in Palestine's West Bank and moving to suburban Chicago, *Amreeka* tells the story of an immigrant mother and son finding their way in a new land, America. As the final credits rolled, the audience rose to its feet with wild cheering as Cherien stepped to the microphone. She could barely contain her emotion as applause echoed through the theater.

Amreeka's crowd-pleasing premiere took place at the 2009 Sundance Film Festival, an annual event in Park City, Utah, that has come to represent the epicenter of independent movies. Each year, Sundance screens more than 100 feature films and more than 50 shorts, selected from over 12,000 submissions by filmmakers worldwide. To be selected by Sundance is a high honor; to be seen by an even wider audience is an achievement reserved for only a few Sundance films.

Amreeka cleared that hurdle as well. It went on to achieve national theatrical distribution—the first film by a Palestinian American director to attain this milestone—and was nominated for numerous awards worldwide, winning many of them. Cherien herself collected the coveted International Federation of Film Critics Prize during the world-renowned Cannes Film Festival, following an eight-minute standing ovation for *Amreeka* when it screened there.

How did this happen? Just a few years before, Cherien had been in a class like yours. Born and raised in Omaha, Nebraska, she studied creative writing and communication at the University of Cincinnati, and then applied to the master's program at Columbia University's School of the Arts. There, Cherien began the first draft of the screenplay that would become *Amreeka*. She worked on it tirelessly for five years before she acquired the necessary skills and garnered the financing and production support to finally get the movie made.

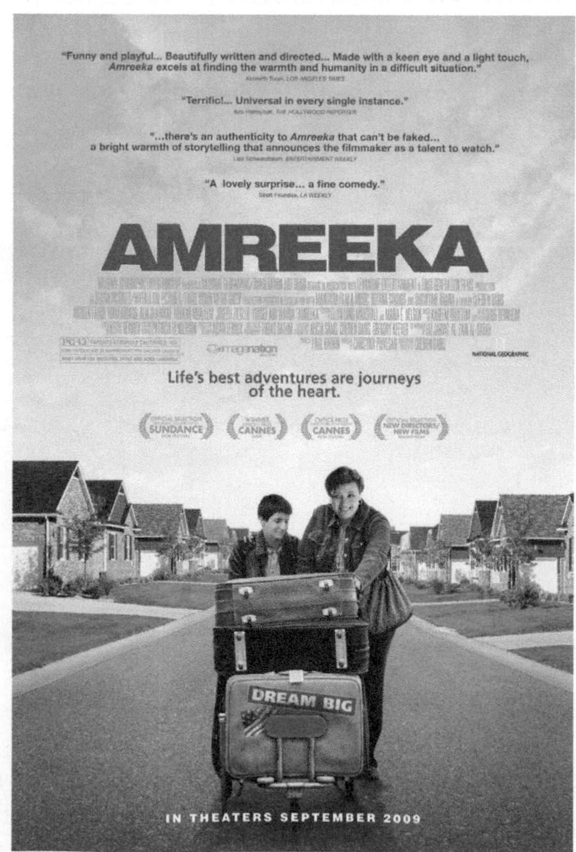

© National Geographic/Courtesy Everett Collection.

Amreeka is an immigrant story—a tale of people exploring a world that is new to them and somehow, against great odds, finding their way. In similar fashion, filmmakers at all levels—and all film projects—must navigate a path through what is, initially, an undiscovered country. This is even truer in your case, as filmmaking students launching into the journey for the first time. Without guidance, examples, and study, the terrain is forbidding, and a place where you may easily lose your way. Informed with knowledge, practice, and mentoring, however, it can be a rich and exciting universe, full of the most creative people on the planet, sharing stories in their richest incarnations with audiences that hunger to be enlightened and entertained.

Along the way, every person's path will be different, and Cherien's path won't be yours. As you will discover from the many people who tell their stories in this book, everyone follows a different muse and takes his or her own uniquely personal filmmaking journey. But that is one of the great attractions of a filmmaking career—those many paths, and the collaborators you can join forces with to create a cinematic sum greater than any single part along the way. If you get lost on one road, there are many others you can try. Eventually, if you work hard enough and maintain your focus, you will find an opportunity to move in the direction of your greatest skills and areas of interest. But first you need to learn about the possibilities that exist, and ground yourself with some core fundamentals you can use as a compass when the waters get choppy, as they certainly will. That is the purpose of this course and textbook: to provide a wide understanding of the filmmaking process, so that you can begin to discover for yourself which path you will want to continue on once you embark on the next phase of your journey.

Key Concepts

- A film, or movie, is an art form whereby a series of moving images are strategically created and linked together for the purpose of telling a particular story both to entertain and to inform an audience of the filmmaker's point of view and, in turn, evoke reactions and emotions.
- All filmmaking involves collaboration, attention to story and character, and problem solving.
- Because many skills are important for filmmaking, exploring the viewpoints of each key skill will help you understand the process.
- Movies are made step by step.

Why Make a Film?

In the history of human communication, no method of sharing information has spread as quickly or has had the ability to reach more people than the video revolution of the last decade or so. Suddenly, with the democratizing impact of consumer-affordable digital tools—video cameras on people's phones, for instance—and the groundbreaking development of YouTube in 2005 in concert with the broadband revolution that made it possible not only to make content formally and informally but also to share it with virtually everyone at the

click of a few buttons, anyone could make a video and share it. Today, in fact, more than one billion people visit YouTube each month.[2]

Figure 4-2. A popular YouTube video re-creates a musical number from ***Frozen*** (2013).

These realities don't make all those millions of people shooting and uploading videos "filmmakers," of course, but they do give you the opportunity to become one if you want it badly enough. Unlike what filmmaking students of generations past faced, the tools are largely affordable and within your grasp, as are the means to collaborate on the work and share it, too. And because you are fortunate enough to be in this course, you now have the opportunity to gain a solid foundation for doing these things using methods and techniques that have been used for generations to produce thought-provoking and escapist cinema in any and all genres.

Read the Industry

To expose yourself to how the world's leading filmmakers and their collaborators work, communicate, and interrelate, read industry trade publications in as many different disciplines as you can. Virtually every major discipline has one or more major trade publications for industry craftspeople, and the industry guilds often publish their own, as well.

But none of that will answer the question of why you would *want* to make movies. Everyone's personal motivations are his or hers alone; however, one fundamental reason shared by many great filmmakers is fairly straightforward: you have a story, something to say, and the best way for you to do that is through filmmaking. It might be something artistic, avant-garde, humorous, political, thought provoking, breathtaking, terrifying, or courageous, but whatever the message, the use of moving images is a particularly compelling way to say it. You may wish to tell a story, document a piece of history, bare your soul, or reveal the mysteries of someone's character. Or perhaps you simply want to make people laugh, make them cry, freak them out, or titillate them. The artistic, creative, and emotional reasons for wanting to make films are endless, but there is no doubt that moving images are the most boundless, unrestricted way to go about expressing whatever it is you want to express. Your film, for example, may be only 15 seconds, so you can upload it to Instagram in a heartbeat, or it may be 24 hours long, as was Christian Marclay's art movie about movies, *The Clock* (2010). Your movie may be in black and white or color, composed of typical moving images, as in most films you've seen, or made up of still pictures, as was Chris Marker's *La Jetée* (1962). Your film may be full of music, talking, sound and fury, or silence, like *La Fée aux Choux*, which was the first narrative movie, directed by Alice Guy-Blaché in 1896.

Figure 4-3. ***La Jetée*** (1962).

Figure 4-4. ***La Fée aux Choux*** (1896).

The point is, moving imagery is the one medium that allows you to cross boundaries, combine formats, create the visually stunning, experiment liberally, and follow classical patterns all at the same time; to follow strict rules and break others from one moment to the next; to raise a ruckus and silence a room; to blind your audience and make them strain to see what is going on; to offer them a clear vision of what you are trying to say, or to leave them scratching their heads, interpreting your work. In this respect, moving images can be more impactful than novels because they take you to two, three, and sometimes four dimensions of vision, sight, and interpretation. Therefore, if you are interested in visual storytelling and artistry, making a film is an excellent and compelling way to express yourself at a minimum, not to mention the fact that it involves a suite of artistic disciplines that might just land you a career along the way—or, at the very least, greatly improve your artistic and intellectual understanding of both storytelling and the world around you. In other words, filmmaking is unique, and a lot of fun besides. Of course, it is also something that is extremely hard to do well, as we shall discuss throughout this book.

Before we get to that, however, what, exactly, do we mean by the word *film*? The precise word *film* originally referred to strips of celluloid on which images were recorded; in the past decade, as you will learn, these celluloid strips have largely been replaced by digital cards and hard drives. However, we think of *film* as the product of your work, not the medium on which it was recorded. For the purposes of this book, and for the entertainment industry at large, we define a **film** quite simply and generically as a series of moving images intentionally constructed to tell a story. Whereas *film*, *movie*, or *video* are words now often used interchangeably, in this book we will be somewhat traditional and mostly refer to the product as *films* or *movies*—terms that we feel imply greater ambition and intention than *videos*, which refers to products generated both by those with artistic intent in today's digital world and by those without.

Thus, there are, as we have suggested, myriad reasons to make a film. But are there reasons *not* to make a film? Yes, indeed. As you will learn, if you do not know what you want to say, do not know who your audience is, or have no interest in or patience for collaborating and trusting others to help you achieve your vision, you should put down your camera and think seriously about what you are doing. Making a movie requires considerable effort from, ideally, a team of people with diverse talents, and if your purpose and ultimate viewers are not clear at the outset, it's likely that the work will go to waste because no one will see it. Fortunately, with this book, you will learn how to avoid this circumstance.

Get Out There and Network

Attend film festivals, local screenings, panel discussions, and trade shows whenever you can. Don't underestimate the educational and networking value of attending events, meeting industry people, and making it clear that you would like to tap their brains. Your film education will take place as much outside this classroom as inside it.

Beyond the conventional way we think about movies—as stories we watch for a few minutes or a few hours—the principles you will learn in this course will be essential for your success in any career you choose. Film communication now permeates every aspect of our lives, from corporate communications and television commercials to music videos, interactive games, educational materials, and much more. In any job you will have, your ability to make a film will make you a more valued employee; and if you choose to become an entrepreneur and work for yourself, filmmaking skills will be great assets for communicating your vision to colleagues.

In other words, filmmaking, one way or another, is going to be a part of your future, so you might as well learn how to do it right. (See Action Steps: Getting Started—What You Need to Make a Short Film Right Now, below.)

Practice

Where Are the Movies?

As you just read, film communication can happen anywhere. Find three examples of film communication in everyday life that do not come from traditional television, movies, computers, or mobile devices. Share them with your classmates, and explain how the moving images you encountered were used to influence and communicate. Note how many different examples the class came up with.

Action STEPS

Getting Started—What You Need to Make a Short Film Right Now

Don't want to wait? Go make a short movie to develop some fundamental experience right away. Don't worry about technical details, your lack of experience, or final quality. No matter the outcome, you only learn this craft by doing it. Here's how to get started in eight basic action steps:

1. Know what story you want to tell. Who is the main character? What will happen?

2. Write it down. Every movie needs a script, even if the script is only one page. Develop your main story as simple bullet points in the form of a basic treatment, and then evolve that into a short script.

3. Make a plan. Evaluate your script. Who will the actors be? What will they wear? Do they need any props? Where will you shoot? How many people do you need to help you? Make a list of things you will need, and then formulate a strategy for making sure you have everyone and everything you need.

4. Get your gear. For most basic short pieces, you can shoot with your mobile phone if necessary. Because you have limited resources and training, try to shoot outdoors or in interiors that can be lit from the outside to avoid worrying about lighting and other complexities, which we will discuss later in the book. In any case, figure out what you will need equipment-wise, whether it's a mobile phone or gear your school may provide, and organize it.

5. Shoot the scenes. Follow the script and make sure you have captured all the scenes and parts of scenes—close-ups of your main characters, wider shots to reveal where they are, and sound so you can hear what they are saying.

6. Edit it together. First, edit each scene internally, stringing together the different shots so that they clearly communicate what is happening. Then, edit the scenes in their story order. Use the most rudimentary consumer-based editing software that you can access on your mobile device, your personal computer, or that your school or friends can supply.

7. Add finishing touches. Is the dialogue clear? If not, perhaps you need to rerecord a line. Does your movie need music? titles?

8. Show it to your friends. How do they react? Do they understand the story and relate to the characters? Don't be afraid to adopt their notes, if they make sense to you. Is the movie you made similar to the movie you imagined?

Three Filmmaking Principles

As you have learned, at its core, filmmaking is about getting your message and story across to your audience. It is not about the equipment you are using, such as cameras and microphones; it is about your approach to your work, regardless of the tools. As technology advances, equipment changes, yet the approach to filmmaking has remained remarkably constant in its 120-year history.

For this reason, we do not overly emphasize specific makes and models of gear. That information is readily available from your instructor, across the web, and from the various industry resources we are recommending you investigate. The reality is that as you begin your filmmaking career, you will use whatever equipment you can get your hands on. As previously suggested, the greatest technological breakthrough of the digital era is the simple fact that it is, by its nature, democratizing—there is no reason not to attempt to make a movie as a student based on lack of access to technology. Consumer, "prosumer," quasi-professional, and high-end gear all exist in the same universe now, and from the phone in your pocket to the finest digital cameras on the market today, there are tools you will be able to procure for your early efforts.

Therefore, it makes sense for you to first focus on foundational principles: collaboration, emphasis on story and character, and problem solving.

Collaboration

Every film is a team effort. British director Paul Greengrass (*Captain Phillips*) calls filmmaking "a group activity" that requires "a common purpose" from everyone participating in its creation.[3] No movie of any length or consequence is made entirely by just one person. Even if it were possible for one individual to write the script, hold the camera, record the sound, act the roles, edit the images, and output the movie, there would still be the interaction between the filmmaker and his or her audience. A movie, in a sense, isn't fully a movie until it has been viewed and an emotional connection to the audience has been established. Therefore, there is no such thing as a solitary filmmaking experience—you have to involve, rely on, and consider other people's talents and viewpoints throughout the process.

Practice with Shorts

As you launch into learning the basics of filmmaking, don't underestimate the value of short films, experimental pieces, and technique practice, even above and beyond official class assignments. As with any endeavor, practice makes perfect, whether you are attempting to shoot, light, design, edit, or do any of a number of other functions.

Even in their construction, films comprise the greatest collaborative art form the world has ever known, involving layers of multiple elements, woven together at different times and in different ways to create a greater whole, much like a puzzle. Movies can't be thought of in the same way as books (author and paper) or paintings (artist, paint, and canvas). Filmmaking is a more layered art form. Actors and set painters, costumers and writers, drivers and choreographers, stuntmen and technicians, photographers and electricians, carpenters and fact checkers, musicians and editors, directors and producers, and many others—these folks in endless configurations are required to produce movies.

You, of course, are students, with little in the way of resources, and huge demands on you to take on more roles than would be the case on a professional production, both out of necessity and as part of your learning process. Still, even in your situation, you will need to find help when you can. In this class, even with fewer overall collaborators, you will rapidly come to understand and appreciate the benefits of teamwork to realize your film.

Because so many people and skills are involved, good filmmaking requires excellent communication skills and sensitivity to the talents and requirements of every craft involved. In this course, you will learn about the many collaborators who make a movie, explore their skill sets, and develop a useful vocabulary to use when working with them.

Find Your Collaborators

In your hunt for filmmaking collaborators, your first route should be through this class and your school's resources. Additionally, keep in mind that there are various websites that cater specifically to the independent filmmaking community, including some that try to connect students and young people in search of filmmaking experience on real projects, such as www.spidvid.com, www.filmzu.com, and www.filmsourcing.com.

Emphasis on Story and Character

Movies are, by their basic nature, about something. As you learned in Chapter 3, most films can be summarized with a log line that starts, "It's about . . ." Therefore, as we will emphasize more than once, every choice you make as a filmmaker must be in service to the main characters and their story. This principle will allow you to make wise decisions when you are under the pressured realities of production.

Figure 4-5. Writer-director Cherien Dabis collaborates with cast members Haim Abbas (seated, left) and Nisreen Faour (right) during production of ***Amreeka*** (2009).

For example: If you have time to capture only one shot, should it be of a beautiful sunset or of your main character's face at an emotional moment? Correct choice: The character's emotional reaction.

If you have a choice between making the story absolutely clear and leaving it to chance whether the audience will understand what's going on, what should you do? Correct answer: Make the story clear.

If you can afford either to shoot for one extra day or to rent a fancy camera with lots of special features, what should you pay for? Correct decision: The extra shooting day.

Your primary obligation to your audience is to communicate the story well, so they will be able to understand and empathize with your characters. If you do that, the audience will forgive technical imperfections. Plus, you'll be doing better than many first-time filmmakers! In this book, we frequently return to the importance of story and character to make sure your movie meets your audience's needs.

Problem Solving

Two things are certain on every movie project: there will be uncertainty, and things will periodically change from your original plan. Even if you only have a few hours to shoot your class project, something will eventually go wrong, and it will not always be what you expect. The level of uncertainty and unexpected problems increase with the scale of your film, and bigger films always face bigger problems.

In this book, we focus heavily on ingenuity and problem solving. We cannot teach you how to solve every problem, because problems, by their nature, are unpredictable. However, we can teach you how to deploy a mental attitude, generosity of spirit, and certain flexibility that will make the problems you encounter solvable, or at least allow you to formulate alternatives when circumstances require you to move in a different direction from where you were expecting to go.

Practice

Collaboration and Story

Work in three teams to build basic elements of a movie story. Team One must create two characters and invent a relationship between them. Team Two must take those characters and come up with a basic conflict or issue that impacts their relationship as a central plot point. Team Three must take these elements and choose two environments or settings in which the events take place. Then, bring the teams together to hone, massage, and integrate all these elements into one movie story. The idea is not to write a perfect story but to learn how to work with others to achieve your creative goal. What did you learn about collaboration in this exercise? What does it reveal about the creative process?

Six Filmmaking Viewpoints

The three core principles of filmmaking (collaboration, emphasis on story and character, and problem solving) might be thought of as the superstructure of the filmmaking process: no movie happens without them. Now let's turn to the "construction crew"—the people who actually get the movie made. These are the people you don't see, the people who are not the actors, yet it is these people whose viewpoints and actions determine the overall experience that filmgoers will enjoy—or not enjoy, as the case may be.

As student filmmakers, you will frequently have no choice but to take on many of these jobs yourself. On most of your initial projects, you will certainly handle multiple creative, managerial, and logistical roles simultaneously. Still, the *viewpoints* brought to the filmmaking whole from these distinct spots on the horizon remain and are crucial to the final product. You will need to learn what these roles are and either how to assume them yourself—by thinking the way these craftspeople think when working on a production—or how to collaborate successfully with those who do. Most likely, you will end up with a combination of the two.

With that said, here is a look at the important filmmaking roles and the corresponding viewpoints that go along with them.

Read, Read, Read

Read biographies and autobiographies about famous filmmakers to learn about the mind-set, creativity, and unique and fascinating conditions that formed their filmmaking viewpoints and helped them achieve their cinematic success.

Producer

The **producer** brings all the elements of a film together and supervises all the people. Producers are responsible for the creative outcome of the movie and for accomplishing it on time and on budget. In your school, you may be your own producer, or a classmate may take on the job. In the professional world, major productions frequently have multiple producers due to the complexity of the work and the responsibility of raising money for the film. Indeed, it is difficult for any one producer to have the expertise, time, and resources to manage all the many complex areas of a multimillion-dollar production by him- or herself. But even at that level, there are usually one or two producers responsible for the entire endeavor. No matter who is filling this role, the producer's viewpoint is wide, encompassing everything in the five basic phases of any movie's life cycle: development, preproduction, production, postproduction, and distribution/marketing. (See Producer Smarts: "Congratulations, You Are a Movie Producer!").

Writer

The **writer** imagines the story and its characters, and transforms them from mere ideas into a tangible, physical screenplay that can be shared with others. You might be your own screenwriter, or you might work with a classmate in crafting the script. The writer's viewpoint is all about the people on-screen and what happens to them: the narrative and its actors. A well-written screenplay is the lodestone from which all creative ideas will flow when producing a movie.

Director

The **director** is the most important single individual on a film set, as it is primarily the director's vision that is represented in the final product. Directors select the script they want to shoot; choose the actors and primary creative collaborators; and make countless key creative, technical, and logistical decisions during the filmmaking process. The director's viewpoint is both immediate and long term: it's about making minute-by-minute choices that achieve the best result in service of what the completed movie will look like.

Editor

The **editor** assembles the film that has been shot, finding the best way to tell the story and convey character by selecting images and sounds and placing them in a specific order designed to enhance the emotional impact of the director's creative intent for the material. Editing is the only craft that is unique to movies; it had to be invented for filmmaking to take place. The editor may be thought of as the "second writer" of the movie, after the screenwriter, and is frequently considered the director's single closest collaborator on movie productions. The editor's viewpoint is immensely practical; he or she must work with what images and sounds are available, crafting the best film story possible.

Image and Sound Crew

The artists who create what you see and hear belong to many different professions: directors of photography, production designers, sound designers, camera and sound crew, visual effects designers and supervisors, animators, music composers and supervisors, and many others. Although their specific tasks and how they are executed vary, their overall agenda is uniform: to design, capture, and create the visual imagery and sound experience of the movie. Their viewpoint begins at the conception stage—What should this look and sound like?—and extends through the actual accomplishment of the look-and-sound vision, down to the finest details.

Watch Lots of Movies

Tip

Watch at least one classic film a week every month for the entire term of this class. (The American Film Institute publishes a list of the "100 Greatest American Films" at www.afi.com/100years/movies10.aspx.) Watch with a critical eye, paying attention to the discipline or disciplines you are studying at the time: directing, cinematography, editing, production design, and so on. Take notes about the things that catch your eye, or tricks and techniques that you would like to emulate or at least learn more about. Why do you think these films have stood the test of time to be recognized as "classics"?

The Audience

The difference between this course and a media studies or film theory course is that we are guiding you to make movies that people will want to see. We believe that you are always making your movie for an audience, not for yourself. No matter what your role on the film, you must always think about the audience and how you are communicating with them: Will they understand what you are trying to say? Will they relate to the characters? Will the story make sense? In a professional production, the audience will watch the movie on screens across the world; for this class, your audience may be your instructor or your fellow students. The audience's viewpoint is the prevailing one in all filmmaking, and the audience's judgment is the ultimate arbiter of a film's success. Therefore, although your audience may have nothing specific to do with the physical production of your movie, they are included in this section to remind you that their viewpoint and emotional response are important things for you to evaluate while you are making your film—very possibly the most important.

Practice

Comparing Viewpoints

As you read about the different viewpoints involved in filmmaking, some of them may have seemed familiar to you. That's because these viewpoints have analogies in other aspects of life. Have you directed a group of people? written a story? edited or commented on someone else's work? Certainly, you have sat in an audience and been impacted by moving images or live performances. Practice thinking about these filmmaking viewpoints by selecting one or two that you have experienced at some point in the recent past, and share, discuss, and compare those experiences in small groups.

Beyond the six key viewpoints, every film has certain limitations imposed by the context in which it is being made. For this course, your limitations will be set primarily by your instructor: you will have a deadline, and you may have to make your film in black and white or color, obey a time limit, use only certain equipment, or be limited on whom you are allowed to ask for help. Even at the movie-studio level there are restrictions, which frequently involve running time, rating, casting, release date, and budget. We'll call these limitations, collectively, **oversight**. At the same time, oversight provides you with guidance, expertise, and resources; without the benefit of your school, for example, you might not have the camera or lights with which to make your movie. The point of oversight is to set boundaries and allocate resources for any production within the context of those boundaries.

Producer SMARTS

Congratulations, You Are a Movie Producer!

If you glance at the table of contents, you will see there is no separate chapter on producing. Although we discuss many of the producer's managerial tasks throughout the book and in these Producer Smarts sections, we do not focus specifically on this one job alone. Why not? Our reasoning is that a producer needs to know about every aspect of filmmaking; thus, every chapter in this book is, to a degree, a producing chapter. At the end of the day, the producer bears final responsibility for all business and creative aspects of a movie. In this class, although you may not have anyone who is officially credited as a "producer," the functions that a producer handles must still get done, whether you are making a one-minute class assignment, a short film, or a full-length feature. Here are some basic considerations:

- Calculate your limitations. How long can the film be? What resources are available in terms of time, budget, equipment, actors, locations, costumes, and props?
- Plan the production carefully to achieve the best creative outcome by making sure that the script is in good shape, that everyone involved is properly suited for his or her role, and that there is a reasonable schedule.
- Manage the day-to-day, or minute-by-minute, operation of the shoot by making sure that everything—and everyone—is ready and that there is a list of priorities, so that if something needs to be cut or plans change, the movie will still work without it, and if something needs to be added, you will have a plan for how you are going to do it.
- Be a supportive friend in the editorial and finishing process by verifying that there are resources at hand and by being an adviser on creative decisions.
- Share the film with a representative sample of the audience as early as possible, to get an objective reaction, so that the director and editor still have time to improve it before the deadline.

- Make sure the film is screened under optimum conditions—in an appropriate setting and for the right audience.
- Support your team creatively and emotionally throughout the process.

The Filmmaking Path

Whether you are accomplishing your class project in two days for no budget or spending two years and $200 million making a studio blockbuster, you will need to follow the same basic path in taking your initial idea from your brain to the printed page to a polished movie that an audience can watch and, if you did your job right, relate to. Logistics, details, and nuances will grow and shrink in importance during a project and from project to project depending on a host of factors (see Business Smarts: "Taking Care of Business"), but this basic filmmaking process will be the key to getting you where you want to go.

This journey is the focus of this textbook—not only identifying the steps you need to take but also examining how you can logically go about taking them in a creative and meaningful way. Loosely speaking, the basic components of a movie include recording and combining for eventual display the following elements:

- Images, including the use and manipulation of light and darkness
- Movement
- Sound
- Passage of time
- Sequences positioned in strategic order to tell the filmmaker's intended story
- Composition of the images with additional elements and manipulation to enhance emotion, create worlds, increase attention, please the senses, and improve continuity of the story[4]

The Wolf of Wall Street (2013)

Training video

Promotional video

Figure 4-6. You might work in the film industry in any number of capacities throughout your career: on a major motion picture, training video, or promotional video, among other possibilities.

As you have probably guessed, however, there is a lot more to it than these simple descriptions indicate, which is why we have broken down these lessons in the following ways, designed to direct you down this creative path. You will need to stop at various way stations along the road and plant your flag before you can move safely and effectively to your next milestone.

- **Concept and Preparation:** Once you've figured out what story you want to tell, you need to develop the idea, develop the characters and plot points, and transform it into a workable screenplay. After that, you need to learn the basic skills of directing and managing a production so that you can launch into *preproduction* and beyond, starting with the crucial phases of conceptualizing and designing the movie you want to make, and determining an action plan and budget of how you are going to make it.
- **Image and Sound:** You will need to learn the basic technical and creative skills you will need to launch the project into *production*, so that you can capture the images and sounds necessary to tell your story. Note that we use the word *necessary*—it will not be enough to simply learn how to use a camera or sound recording system. You will need to learn to use those skills strategically to tell your story. That means developing a keen understanding of how to use your camera, lighting tools, and sound capture tools to acquire the specific elements required for your story.
- **Production Glue:** Learn about the crucial postproduction process of editing: the myriad of technical skills necessary to be a good editor and, more importantly, the many ways you can advance your storytelling agenda by creatively weaving together the elements you have filmed or otherwise created to make a seamless whole. In the modern digital-filmmaking world, postproduction processes involving visual effects and animation continue to grow in importance, adding new and improved ways for filmmakers to combine real and synthetic elements with image and sound capture, as well as the editing process.
- **Filmmaking and Beyond:** Your filmmaking job is not done once your film has been edited. You will need to explore options you might pursue to get your film in front of audiences so that you can establish that core relationship that makes your movie a success: the bond between your story and the audience watching it. To do this, you need a level of understanding of film marketing and distribution, as well as a look at the many resources available to you for learning more about filmmaking and the people, tools, skills, and career options within this unique industry.

Start a Library

Start a film library—but don't just include films. Actively search for, analyze, learn from, and seek to be influenced by any form of moving-image media that impresses you: movies, television shows, commercials, music videos, web videos, industrial videos, animation, ride films, museum pieces, montages, and so on. Collect this material when you can, organize it into a library, and use your growing library as a tool to both inspire and teach you techniques or concepts as you launch your filmmaking career. You may find yourself turning back to this library to find inspiration when your creative process stalls.

On the subject of careers, it is worthwhile as you go through this course to understand that there are a myriad of potential career choices within the larger film industry, and only a small percentage of them directly involve making movies. There are commercials, music videos, corporate videos, training videos, web videos, interactive videos, video games, apps for mobile devices, and lots more to choose from. And within these areas, there are disciplines and subdisciplines and related and semirelated areas.

Practice

What Made the Movie?

What was the last film you saw? Using it as an example, select one particular aspect of the filmmaking work, such as editing, music, cinematography, costume design, or location choices. In a short paper, give your opinion on how this particular discipline contributed, or did not contribute, to the overall success of the film, and why. Later, after going through the specific chapter and corresponding lessons in class on that discipline, revisit your essay, and see if your views have either changed or evolved.

But whatever direction you choose to go in, having a solid overview of the entire filmmaking path can only help you. These are highly transferrable skills that can fit into various aspects of your life. Enjoy the journey that begins when you turn the first page on the path we have discussed. The cool thing about filmmaking is that you never know exactly what you will discover when you get to the end of the path—with one exception: whatever it is, it will be your own creation.

Business SMARTS

Taking Care of Business

As you dive into your film education, we will continually emphasize the joys of this creative form of expression. However, as previously noted, we will also be covering a host of managerial tasks. Now is a good time to take note of the fact that linked inexorably to these managerial tasks are various business-related issues that pertain to film productions of all sizes and shapes.

Even those business-related tasks that will not particularly impact your early student efforts are ones that, at some point in your film education, you will need to have a basic awareness about. If you move on to work in some capacity in the film industry, one or more of these issues could become central to your work. Therefore, periodically in this book we will address some of these business issues; explain why they are important; and discuss the fundamentals of what you need to know to make sure to protect yourself, your work, your crew, your equipment, and the environment in which you will be working.

For now, we want you to have a heads-up that this course is not only about your creative vision, making your masterpiece, and following your filmmaking dreams. That certainly can be the place you end up if you pursue your film education with the right mix of brains and passion, but the business side of this creative work needs your attention also. Indeed, one of the most important immediate challenges you will face as film students involves figuring out ways to separate and balance the creative and business sections of your brain so that both get proper attention and work in harmony to achieve the greater goal that lies before you: learning the fundamentals of filmmaking.

Filmmaker's Emergency Kit

- A good set of headphones. Speakers on a laptop or mobile device are not very good. To experience any movie well, you need to hear it in its full glory, and so you need quality headphones.
- Still cameras and audio and video recorders. Whether on your phone or separate devices, these allow you to record reference images and sounds wherever you go as you begin to develop student films.
- A subscription to a streaming service like Netflix or a DVD movie collection. "Classics" are classic for a reason; they contain a creative storehouse of filmmaking knowledge. The more you experience the vast creative library of movies, the better you will be as a filmmaker yourself, as you discover your own preferences.
- IMDB.com and other informational and movie websites. IMDB lists credits for almost every movie that has ever been released in the United States. Likewise, the-numbers.com or boxofficemojo.com provides box office performance information.

Chapter Essentials

- Moving images and the modern digital technology and workflows used to create, combine, edit, and distribute such imagery make filmmaking the most liberating and open of all art forms. This offers you the opportunity to express your creativity in literally endless ways, learning skills and techniques that will benefit you in many fields, whether or not you end up in a filmmaking career.
- The foundational principles on which all filmmaking endeavors are based are collaboration, emphasizing story and character above all else, and developing an ability to problem-solve in multiple scenarios.
- There are six viewpoints that collectively bring a film story together. Those viewpoints involve the perspective of the producer, the writer, the director, the editor, the image and sound crew, and the audience, which must connect emotionally with the filmmaker's efforts to make the movie experience complete.
- All movies, no matter how simple or complex, must follow a basic filmmaking path on their way to completion. That path includes a process of designing, capturing, manipulating, editing, and finalizing images, sounds, and other elements, to tell a story that incorporates characters, the passage of time, conflict, and more in order to link a filmmaker's point of view with an audience's emotional response.

Conceptualization and Design

"Conceptualization and Design" from *Filmmaking in Action*, by Adam Leipzig, Barry S. Weiss, and Michael Goldman, pp. 69–96 (Chapter 4, "Conceptualization and Design").

"There is no such thing as a paint- and construction- and decoration-free narrative film. If you do that, it's a documentary."

—Jeannine Oppewall, veteran production designer, whose films include *The Bridges of Madison County* (1995), *L.A. Confidential* (1997), *Pleasantville* (1998), *Catch Me If You Can* (2002), and *Seabiscuit (2003)*[5]

CHAPTER

Figure 4-7. ***Catch Me If You Can*** (2002).

When Jeannine Oppewall discussed production design concepts with Steven Spielberg for his 2002 film *Catch Me If You Can*, it didn't take long to realize her principal challenge would involve designing what she calls "a color arc" to help Spielberg tell the story of a con man's rise and fall through the film's narrative sections.

"Steven talked a lot about how the character Frank [Leonardo DiCaprio] started off ignorant and inexperienced, and then through a series of events, he learned how to practice his craft of passing false checks, got better at it, and then his life got more lively," says Oppewall, a Hollywood production designer with over 35 major feature films to her credit. "Then, he was caught, and his life became dull again. To interpret that visually, I decided to have him start out in a relatively monochromatic world, without many wild colors. Slowly, we would build up color and put more life into his environments, and then when he is at the top of his game, having the most fun of his life, that is where we would have the brightest colors in the movie. Later, when he is caught and in prison or in FBI custody, the colors become monochromatic and predictable again. It was a particularly controlled color arc to match what was going on in the story."

In production designer Jack Taylor's case, an initial examination of the script for the low-budget, independent film *Atlas Shrugged: Who Is John Galt?* quickly made clear that his principal challenge would be the issue of how to balance ambitious locations described in the script—the final movie in a trilogy based on the controversial Ayn Rand novel—and an extremely limited budget. Among the complex locations that the script required, for example, were an airplane crash site in a mountain forest, a mining cave, a mysterious energy-generating motor that lies at the heart of the plot, and a helicopter pad overlooking a glittering nighttime cityscape.

Taylor—a protégé of legendary production designer Henry Bumstead, who has worked for Clint Eastwood and Martin Scorsese, among others—says budget and logistics required the production to film on 71 location sets in just 18 grueling days, exclusively in the Los Angeles area. After some calculations, he quickly concluded that he would need to find an average of four workable location settings per day that could be transformed into different places, while also accommodating equipment and catering trucks, base camp, and crew. Thanks to his experience and exhaustive hours of research, Taylor eventually decided he could group the aforementioned four illusions together in a single location to be shot on a single day—at the Griffith Park forest area in the middle of Greater Los Angeles.

"I realized Griffith Park could be made to look like it was anywhere in the Colorado Rockies, so it became the area we made into the crash site,"[6] Taylor explains.

> A few steps away, under some cedar branches along a hiking trail, we were able to place the "Motor Generator Monolith Temple" as described in the script [and Ayn Rand's novel], and just up the nearby Park Service access road was the Forestry Department's Helipad that they use to land water-dropping helicopters. Wouldn't you know it, the helipad overlooks the sprawling Los Angeles basin for the night shot we needed with the towering buildings of downtown Los Angeles as a backdrop. And not far away, within company shuttling distance, were the Bronson Canyon caves, which were a perfect location for laying rail track for mining carts, as the script also required. [The same caves can be seen in the final sequence of John Ford's *The Searchers* and were used as the entrance to the Batcave on TV's *Batman*.]

The point of these examples is that both designers, above all else, dedicated themselves to meticulous analysis of their respective scripts, detailed research, location scouting, and a keen understanding of the role physical space and color play in telling cinematic stories. Taylor emphasizes that the production designer typically must, in low-budget filmmaking, "wear many hats. I had to be deeply involved in location selection and be responsible not only for the look and world environment that the characters of the picture inhabited, but also for the physical ability of the production company to be able to make the product on time, and within reasonable budget parameters."

In other words, it is not enough to be an accomplished artist, as Oppewall and Taylor are. You also need to emulate their considerable skill at pounding the pavement, strategically examining nooks and crannies of all sizes and descriptions, and constantly seeking out ways to balance what is aesthetically pleasing with what is efficient and both logistically and financially feasible.

Though your individual circumstances and skill level may be different, design will prove crucial for your first student film and your wider film education. Author Vincent LoBrutto describes production design as a discipline that "renders the screenplay in visual metaphors, a color palette, architectural and period specifics, locations, designs, and sets."[7] More simply, we might say that production design is about creating the environments necessary to tell your story.

In truth, however, production conceptualization and design is the most collaborative of the crafts. It involves, to one degree or another, the need to incorporate construction, props, locations, costumes, cinematography, lighting, sound, visual effects, graphic design, and even hair and makeup—or at least it interrelates with these departments over time. Learning the fundamentals of design will also help you understand what it takes for different craftspeople to do their jobs successfully, and how to think creatively and logistically at the same time. If you take the basic principles and strategies we will now discuss, and combine them with a proactive effort to widen your own education about art and design, train yourself to become more research oriented, and dedicate yourself to serving your story's advancement with every visual decision you make, you will achieve viable sets and locales for your films.

Key Concepts

- You will need to learn the basic principles of design and composition, and the concepts behind properly placing elements in a frame to best serve the story. This includes shapes, textures, size, scale, color, and more.
- Break down your screenplay and examine your resources to identify basic factors that will impact decisions about locations, sets, props, set pieces, and more. Among the most important of these will be the story's time period, geography, and locations, as well as the nature of your characters.
- A major tool will be previsualization techniques, ranging from simple sketches or storyboards to detailed digital animation to illustrate placement of elements, actors, cameras, and lights.

The Principles of Design

This is not an art class, and you are not reading an art textbook; why, then, is it useful to pause and learn some of the basic, art-related principles of production design, many of which emanate from the theatrical world?

Primarily, it's because a baseline goal when producing a movie is to ensure that all the things you want to be seen by viewers will, in fact, be seen as you intended, and anything you want hidden will be invisible. At the foundational level, then, you are attempting to figure out three things: how to use the physical space you have available to you, how to design sets for that space, and how to arrange elements on those sets to maximize creative success. Even when you are making a 3D movie, you are essentially conceptualizing and composing a 3D image on a two-dimensional surface. Where you place people and elements, where you want to draw the viewer's eye, where you want light and where you want darkness—these are all directly related to how you want the viewer to react, and the mood you want to evoke. These goals seem fairly simple and straightforward, but in fact, the more fundamentals of design you can master, complicated though they may be, the more success you will have in reaching such goals. Indeed, understanding these principles will help make you a better filmmaker in the long run, even if you have no desire to go into production design specifically, simply because you will have a better sense of how to use space and collaborate with other artists.

To be sure, you will need to do some exploration in other disciplines to get this education. Art, photography, theater, and literature are all areas in which you will learn about proportion, scale, composition, depth, color, and so on. But the basic fundamentals we will now discuss will serve you well as a solid foundation for those ongoing lessons.

Design Composition Elements

Later, in this chapter, we will analyze elements of good composition as they relate to cinematography—strategies and principles for positioning people and objects for the purpose of framing images through the lens for maximum balance and impact. This essentially involves how two-dimensional space will be organized in the frame. Before we get to that lesson, though, you need to think about composition as it relates to production design. Not surprisingly, the two areas in which composition is crucial—cinematography and production design—are interrelated. A key part of the production designer's job is to make sure elements are designed and arranged in such a way that the director and cinematographer can position or reposition people, objects, crew, and equipment to execute their visual plan for framing and executing shots. Without proper placement and spacing of elements on a set, filmmakers will have a hard time getting composition right.

Thus, from a design point of view, *composition* involves the proper design of spaces for filming, and the design and placement of elements on sets and locations behind—and all around—actors and other principal focal points. Keep in mind that the actor is typically the most important element in a frame—anything that competes with or dilutes the presence of your actors is usually to be avoided. The notion of designing a space to aid composition is subtly different from the notion of *arranging* elements in particular ways for particular shots—that is a subject we will discuss in the next section. Meanwhile, you may hear other terms that refer to the same concept as composition—*form* or *ordering*, for example. But whatever term you use, the point is, you need to get a plan together for how you want to structure spaces in every scene in your movie.

Remember that many important compositional concepts come out of the art and theatrical worlds, but their essential roles, in most cases, are similar or even identical when applied to moving-picture imagery. The most important concept of them all is the idea of *space* and how to use it. How you give the illusion of physical space or space between elements impacts how depth, size, and proportion are perceived by the viewer, and thus plays a direct role in the emotional impact of scenes. Cinematography and lighting are crucial to representing space in movies, but so is production design. In design, the term *positive space* refers to space that is filled with objects of some type. *Negative space*, as we will elaborate later in this chapter, refers to wide, open space that remains empty until used by actors as they move from one position to another. There are also the concepts of *shallow space* and *deep space* in design. When two objects are placed on a set and photographed with very little depth, whereby elements or people occupy almost the same positions, it is called shallow space, resulting in a flatter image. When one element is in the foreground and the other is in the distance, it is called deep space because that juxtaposition gives the illusion of distance.

Beyond those basic definitions, however, you need to think about how your use of space is helping, or hurting, the story. Usually, if you have competing ideas or are undecided about how to use a space, your best bet is to simplify things—strip away clutter and only use colors that invoke the intended mood.

Other important compositional categories for you to understand as you strive to properly execute design include the following:

- **Center of interest.** This is sometimes called "point of emphasis." As either name implies, the idea revolves around the notion that every frame in a motion picture has a specific area where the filmmaker wants your attention directed. In this sense, it's the most important part of the frame. Therefore, your design must accommodate what you want to emphasize in each shot. This might mean adding certain elements, like color or contrast or *props* or *set pieces* (see p. 199), or avoiding things that would distract from an actor or some other non-design-related element. Every element must have a purpose in adding to the characters or the story.
- **Harmony and contrast.** Similarly, these concepts out of the art world involve composing frames with matching or similarly shaped elements to avoid a distracting contrast, unless, of course, such contrast is a creative choice. Thus, you would want pieces of furniture to match or be similarly shaped or textured to achieve harmony, and you would mismatch them if you wanted to achieve contrast.
- **Value.** This refers to the differences between light and dark in a design—that is, the contrast between black and white elements: the larger the value, the wider the contrast in shots.
- **Balance.** This characteristic involves achieving some form of equality in terms of shapes, forms, colors, and so on, in a frame. Production design can be crucial in helping to achieve balance, so that the viewer's attention is not unintentionally directed to one part of a shot over another.
- **Line.** In frames, this term refers to shapes that essentially create a visual path for the eye to follow, usually toward the main focal point of a frame. Lines can therefore be patterns on walls, run in any number of directions, be of different thicknesses or textures, or not even be physical at all. Deliberately choreographed movement or blur can create lines, and visual illusions that mimic movement can also be incorporated.
- **Shape.** In design, shape is exactly what you think it is—two-dimensional areas with specific edges to them, generally classified as either geometric shapes or organic shapes. In either case, with good design, shape can be used strategically. If a table is shaped like an oval or an octagon in a particular scene, it is because filmmakers decided that the shape would work best in terms of drawing the viewer's eye to the primary element in the frame.
- **Color.** The foundation for all color-related goals, even those finalized in post-production, begins on-set, because color is a major tool in implying or enhancing different moods and emotions in cinematic stories. Thus, for production design, the term color refers primarily to specific hues and other properties, such as temperature, brightness, and saturation. (See Action Steps: "Choosing a Color Palette"and "Tech Talk: Color Theory in Design" for more on choosing a color palette and understanding the properties of color.)
- **Form.** In design, this term refers to three-dimensional objects that have a certain volume and thickness to them, and that can be lit or shaded in particular ways to create three-dimensional effects from certain angles.
- **Texture.** Although viewers can't physically enter movies and feel textures, they can subtly see them when elements are correctly designed. Texture is all about the quality or

feel—smooth, rough, jagged—of object surfaces. Remember, it only matters how the set looks on screen. If your set calls for granite floors, you don't necessarily need real granite. Very often, expensive materials and textures can be replaced with paint.

Use Paints

You can learn a great deal about color combinations simply and inexpensively by purchasing a set of watercolors or acrylic paints, blending them together in various ways, and then painting simple blocks of different colors and shades, or degrees of the same color, on a piece of paper. Pick a basic mood, such as joy or sadness, and try to create colors that express those feelings. This exercise will come in handy when you are trying to match mood and colors while designing sets.

Avoid Pure White

Generally, with digital cameras, it is not a good idea to film characters against pure white walls, as clothing and certain colors can cause artifacts (undesired changes in the way an image looks) against white backgrounds. If you have a creative reason to use a white wall, take that into consideration when costuming your actors, and make sure you do not use a flat lighting scheme.

- **Size/Scale.** Different sizes or differences in scale can evoke moods and emotions in viewers; therefore, size variations among elements are frequently used in production design. Keeping with the theme of simplification, you should typically apply scale in accordance to the theme or mood of the scene or the character's situation. If the character is lonely, lost, or overwhelmed, consider using a very large space to dwarf the actor. If the character feels trapped or claustrophobic or eager to escape a situation, think about including low ceilings to make the space feel more oppressive.
- **Rhythm.** In design parlance, rhythm refers to making certain elements recur or show up in some kind of regular pattern.

Mise-en-Scène

The specific arrangement of elements on a set goes hand in hand with the overall design and use of the space itself. The French term **mise-en-scène** has been brought over from the theatrical world to express this concept. Mise-en-scène refers to the display of every visible element in a frame—from the architectural structure to the paint on the walls down to the smallest props, and everything in between—with the notion being that everything visible has a purpose and is there to reinforce the point of the scene or aid viewers in figuring out, or contextualizing, the story's details based on what they see and how it's arranged.

Courtesy Everett Collection.

Figure 4-8. ***Out of the Past*** (1947) uses noir-style lighting as part of its mise-en-scène.

Do Your Homework

Watch movies and study film history. The best way to learn production design is to examine the work of leading directors and designers; the world of film is chock-full of this kind of work.

In that regard, there are certain factors you need to think about in terms of how elements will be arranged. These include the following:

- What or who will be dominant in the shot?
- What type of shot and camera angle will be used—wide shot? close shot? .
- How will you be framing the shot?
- What should be the dominant color in the scene?
- Form—will the set be open or closed? Will actors or elements be framed within a window? a door? an archway?
- Where will characters be placed, and how will they be moving—in other words, how will you be blocking the scene? Will they be facing the camera? each other?
- Depth—what kind of space will you want between characters and major elements? Will you need to emphasize any particular background elements?

These and other factors are reasons why storyboarding or digital previsualization, as we discuss on page 212, can be valuable in helping filmmakers visualize elements in relationship to one another and in relationship to the camera and lights, even helping to block out basic camera moves and angles. But no matter what method you use to "see" these elements coming together, you need to understand the function of each of these design-related elements:

- **Decor and props**. On a professional project, a separate **art director**, working for the production designer, will handle the creation of decorations, or **set pieces** (items that are not actually used but are part of the environment in which events take place), and **props** (items that characters will be physically interacting with and using). In this class, you will be figuring these things out for yourself. To accomplish your own mise-en-scène, move your thinking beyond simply "finding stuff that looks good" to thinking about each element's significance and usefulness. Will a decorative item reflect a character's life-style or beliefs, such as a crucifix on the wall if the character is religious? Will another decoration indicate the character's economic status or environment he or she is confined in? Will it indicate conditions or events, such as bars on windows or bullet holes in walls?
- **Costumes and makeup.** Logically, the purpose of a costume is to clothe a character according to that character's specific characteristics in order to enhance believability. In professional productions, costume design, makeup, and hair design are all separate disciplines, whereas you will have to handle these issues yourself. In either case, costumes, makeup, and hair eventually all need to be integrated with production design. Thus, the nature, color, patterns, texture, and placement of clothing on the actor are part of mise-en-scène—part of the larger arrangement of visual elements on your set. Therefore, you need to think about your overall design when considering costumes and makeup, rather than addressing them independently.
- **Lighting.** Lighting sits at the heart of successful cinematography because of how its skillful use can contribute to emotional reactions from the audience. Lighting impacts numerous other disciplines—production design, in particular. Simply put, light and design need each other. Design can help enhance or obstruct or manipulate light on-set, and light can help display or enhance designs or, alternatively, hide flaws, among other things. Along these lines, veteran director and production designer Catherine Hardwicke strongly urges students to study lighting in paintings and photographs. "What direction does the light come from?" she suggests you contemplate. "Don't forget, light can expand space—even small sources of light at the far end of a room, or deep in the distance, can add great depth and production value." *High-key light* and *low-key light* are important complements to design. High-key lighting reduces shadow and thus reduces tension; therefore, it is used in environments that are designed for those moods. Low-key lighting, by contrast, is a strong-contrast lighting approach designed to heighten tension with darkness and shadows. Orson Welles's *Touch of Evil* (1958) and Carol Reed's 1949 *The Third Man* (which starred Welles) perfectly illustrate how light and design can be united in tense stories. Having a close synergy between design, lighting, and camera positioning can also help you save time and money in the design process by eliminating elements that will never be seen in the frame.

Tech TALK

Color Theory in Design

Various aspects of color's role in cinematic presentations include such general notions as the idea that the more colorful an environment, the warmer it appears, and the less colorful, the colder or more sterile it appears. Color theory represents an entire academic discipline beyond this book's scope, and you will benefit from educating yourself about it in more detail beyond this course. From a production design point of view, focus not only on how to create or select particular colors for particular elements but also on how other elements will impact or be impacted by those choices. What factors influence or change colors or cause them to clash, contrast, or match up nicely with one another?

The principles of color theory can assist you with these questions. *Hues* (predominant color attributes), *luminance* (brightness), and *saturation* (intensity) are terms you should familiarize yourself with, because you will be considering them as you make color selections. Colors you choose can grow brighter, duller, distracting, more appealing, or confusing to the eye depending on various factors. In terms of filmmaking considerations, here are a few areas that directly impact color on-set:

- Lighting directly affects how color and physical elements appear to the camera and recording medium you are using.
- Smooth surfaces tend to make colors more saturated, and dull surfaces tend to make them less saturated.
- Dark backgrounds make foreground colors appear lighter, white backgrounds make foreground colors appear darker, and background and foreground colors can have a visual impact on the intensity of one another on the big screen.
- Warmer colors (reds, oranges, and yellows) tend to translate to more upbeat emotional responses from viewers. They also tend to make objects appear smaller and thus are often used closer to the camera. Cooler colors (blues, greens, and purples) tend to evoke less empathetic emotional responses and make objects look larger; therefore, they are often used for objects meant to be perceived as being far away.
- Some colors can evoke specific emotions, such as sexuality or anger in the case of red. White often suggests calm and simplicity, black often suggests evil or fear or deep mystery, and so on.

- **Human beings.** Besides the larger discussion of how to direct and use actors for maximum effect, and how costuming has an impact on design, the physical attributes of your actors and how they are placed and moved in scenes is also part of the mise-en-scène paradigm. In this respect, the concepts of **typage** and **frontality** come into play. Typage involves using actors based on facial or body features, almost a stereotype of sorts, but not only for purposes of story points. Typage can also be used to enhance design ideas—people with Asian features to enhance Asian environments, short or tall people to fit properly into certain fantasy environments, and so on. Frontality refers to the idea of staging an actor so that he or she faces the camera directly. This might be done if the actor is in a scene meant to make viewers feel they are part of the same world as the events they are seeing on the screen. If the actor is facing the camera, elements around him or her may need to be specially arranged.

- **Depth.** Earlier, we defined the term *space* as it relates to production design. Visual elements can be arranged to form shallow space or deep space. Those decisions connect directly to mise-en-scène considerations; the placement of elements will obviously be very different if your major points of focus are far away from one another in the frame rather than extremely close together.

Action STEPS

Choosing a Color Palette

It is important to remember that the more you get right in the design phase, the less digital color manipulations you will need to worry about postproduction. As you design your film, keep in mind that color is one of the designer's primary tools in helping to convey various aspects of a story's time frame, location, character traits, emotions, moods, and motivations.

Also, remember cinematography as you choose a color scheme. Study what colors will look good when captured in the light you plan to use with the cameras you plan to use, and keep in mind that certain colors will render differently depending on the film stock or digital camera system you use, how you light the scene, and what format you are outputting the images to. For example, any form of water can take on any color based on how it is lit, time of day, or the filter choices by the cinematographer. The design choice of the water's color will greatly influence the emotion of the shot.

Here are some tips for choosing and working with a color palette:

- **Select a general color palette.** This is not a hard-and-fast conceptual rule, nor is it about executing perfect color coordination. Rather, it is a useful guideline—a way of making sure everything captured by the camera stays within your story's world. When thinking about your palette, pay attention to colors used in photos, movies, magazine articles, and other materials. If they relate to the era and story themes you are putting together, evaluate if those color schemes would be applicable to your material.

- **Keep color choices consistent.** Be sure that they support the characters and environments you are photographing. If your movie is based on comic book material, you might use a comic-strip-inspired color palette. If you are making a film noir piece, you will probably gravitate to blacks, browns, grays, and anything else that looks good in low light.

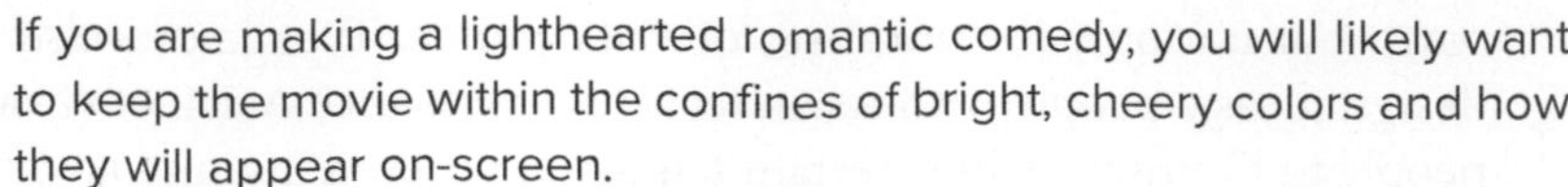

If you are making a lighthearted romantic comedy, you will likely want to keep the movie within the confines of bright, cheery colors and how they will appear on-screen.

- **Do color tests.** Use paint and fabric swatches, actual paint, or colored markers to experiment with combinations, examine options, and study various colors.
- **Create a color script.** A color script is a series of color drawings that show the design arc of the story from the perspective of color. Simply by looking at where the "cool colors" and the "warm colors" are placed, you can see the ups and downs of the story arc as visualized by the production designer.

Design Plan

With the aforementioned design principles in mind, formulate a workable plan for how you will go about designing your film's locations, sets, backgrounds, and other environments. Similar to other aspects of filmmaking, this starts with breaking down your script (see Action Steps: "Design Analysis"). During that process, you will reach conclusions about what scenes will require locations to shoot in, and which ones you will either need or want to build sets for. Then, you will dig deeper and decide what locations should be dressed up or altered in some way, and what set pieces and props you will need.

Practice

Analyze a Scene

Watch William Wyler's classic 1959 film, *Ben-Hur*, with special attention to the important four-minute "The Race Goes On . . ." scene, which takes place following the film's famous chariot race, when the dying Messala meets his vanquisher, Judah, as he lies on his deathbed. (You may also be able to find the specific scene on YouTube or elsewhere online.)

In the scene, take note of the production design in general, and the concept of mise- en-scène in particular. Write an essay describing in as much detail as you can how production design concepts came together to advance the emotional impact of the scene, from the smallest props and decorations to the colors, use of light and shadow, and so on. Note that there is no perfect description for all of this, but the sequence exemplifies how a set can be physically designed and a space used and lit so that the grand total of all the elements is far greater than the sum of the individual parts, which is, of course, the whole point of the mise-en-scène concept.

After you evaluate your story, think about which of these choices are realistic and which are not—what you *can* and *can't* actually do—and how you can either tailor your resources for what is on the written page of your script or strategically write something that you know will fit your resources. For example, if you know you will have no crew, and you have no construction experience or funds for buying materials, then obviously you will need to focus on finding existing locations rather than building sets. On a professional production, you would make these types of decisions in partnership with a production manager—the person responsible for evaluating proposed locations from a logistical standpoint. For now, at the student level, you will likely be solely responsible for considering the balance of your creative needs with your logistical limitations while evaluating this delicate location versus sets paradigm.

In fact, because of resource limitations, student filmmakers most typically film on location, rather than trying to afford stages and build sets. However, even if that is the case, you will almost certainly still need to build, paint, or otherwise change *something*. Thus, the fundamentals of figuring out and allocating resources, scouting locations and dressing them, and building sets or set pieces are just as important for you to learn as are the principles of art and composition.

Action STEPS

Design Analysis

The screenplay is the first indicator of what the foundation for your production design needs will be. Following is a rundown of basic factors in your screenplay that will directly impact your design plan. It's important for you to develop an awareness of these factors within your story before you can properly move on to the research phase and then begin designing sequences, because some, if not all of them, will influence virtually **every** design decision you make:

1. **Time and Place.** These are probably the most obvious considerations when you first review your screenplay. If your story is a period piece or takes place in a unique locale, that will directly influence many design parameters, from costumes to architecture to colors to doorknobs. But keep in mind that the trick is in the details: you will need to make notations about the kind of details you must research for the era and locations your story requires.

2. **Define Characters.** A character's personality, lifestyle, and personal needs directly impact, as they would in real life, that character's living, working, or recreational space. Evaluate and make notations about each character's personality, economic situation, age, and so on. Think of what kind of residence that character could logically afford or have access to.

3. **Light.** When evaluating your script, think *practically* about what kind of lighting the story will require. We have already discussed the value light can have in aiding production design, both generally and creatively, but you also need to think about light with specificity, as it relates to your story. On page 212 we examine previsualization, which can include particular lighting setups when feasible, but before you get to that point, breaking down your screenplay can help you determine what your overall lighting needs will be. After all, every locale other than a pitch-black room needs to have some kind of illumination. Scenes can be lit naturally, by sunlight, moonlight, or ambient light

through windows; by source lights built into the set; or by movie lights. Movie lights can be expensive and are not always feasible, particularly for student productions. So examine the script to start understanding what *kind* of lighting each scene might require and how you might fulfill those requirements. Will you need rooms with big windows? Can you illuminate scenes with practical lamps that are part of the design, forgoing movie lights? These are things you can notate when you first evaluate your script, long before you get into detailed research and design work.

4. **Color Palette.** On page 201, we discussed issues related to choosing a color palette in detail. Keep that discussion in mind as you break down your script, and search for the mood of every scene to help your design plan along; the mood of the events in the story will help you determine colors, so make notations about those sorts of things as you analyze the script.

5. **Dynamic Space.** As you read the script and make general notes about locations and sets, consider specific ways that you could make them as dynamic, interesting, and logistically feasible as possible. A boxed-in, four-wall room limits possibilities and actor movement, and should therefore only be used if the story demands it. If your options are limited, consider whether a certain space would allow you to establish depth with windows or glass doors. (See pp. 198–201 for more on the arrangement of people and elements within a particular space.)

6. **Feasibility Factors.** As you break down the script, think about resources and what is—and is not—practical. Are the locations or sets described in the screenplay even feasible? Will some of the elements called for require permits or bring about other complications? Should you consider rewriting scenes to ease some of these limitations? We discuss some of these logistical matters in more detail shortly, but you should start thinking about their impact on your design agenda as you begin to break down your script.

Research and References

After you have broken down your script to determine your overall project needs, you will begin meticulous research to find elements and solutions for strategically executing the design. As we have urged, you can, and should, do constant general research, and labor always to train your eye to notice light, shadows, textures, shades, fabrics, and other subtle things in the world around you and in great art and photographs; this kind of training will inform your decision-making process when you begin to design a particular set or location.

But general research isn't enough. You need to get specific—we want you to research potential visual qualities of every scene, location, interior, and environment. By "researching" them, we mean going out into the world and attempting to find direct or indirect visual references that evoke the environment in question. If you are shooting a scene at a circus, head to a real circus. If you have a sequence in a parking garage, study parking garages.

And by "going out," we mean exactly that—go out and study, and don't default to relying exclusively on the Internet. The web is a valuable and free research tool that students of earlier eras did not have access to. Yet veteran production designers insist that if you rely too heavily on it, and do not go out and physically examine real-world colors, fabrics, materials, and textures yourself, you will not be nearly as informed as you should be in making quality design decisions (see Producer Smarts: "Dumpster Diving").

Therefore, strategically collect and organize reference photos, magazine and book clippings, drawings, paint and fabric swatches, and so on. You should also create sketches or take photographs that relate to the types of environments you will be featuring in your film. If you have locations picked out, walk those locations, and take photos and room measurements, and draw sketches to keep a fresh frame of reference about each space.

As you collect this material, you must organize it. Some designers organize it into alphabetized files, others into binders or reference books that apply to each scene or location in a movie. Catherine Hardwicke calls these "look books"—essentially organized files or binders of relevant visuals and data that apply to all the locations in your film. These become your template for figuring out a final design for each location.

Keep in mind, however, that your binder or files may consist of more than just photos and sketches. They could also contain color options, swatches, paint chips, diagrams, notes, comparison imagery from different eras and sites, close-up photos of props and furniture, pieces of wood or fabric, and so on. Once you get the hang of it, you will be able to boil things down even further and collect reference material with more specificity. For example, you could look for the following:

- Different versions of similar places (restaurants, office lobbies, kitchens, parks); perhaps later you will prefer one over the other, or perhaps you will mix and match elements from the different versions you have studied
- Different exteriors visible in windows, depending on whether your setting is urban, rural, domestic, or foreign
- Reference materials of similar locations that are lit differently—with more or less exterior light or interior light only
- Examples of different kinds of furniture—more modern or more vintage, in good or bad shape, in a wide range of colors, and so on
- Comparisons or before/after imagery of the same place, or side-by-side comparisons between photos and drawings or paintings
- Imagery of locations empty and with people in them, so that you can study how people will interact with props and set pieces and impact the configuration of the space

These are just a handful of examples. There is no limit to what you can collect or how you can organize it, as long as your organizational method is efficient. Remember, as a bonus, these types of look books will outlive your project and eventually join a personal research library that you will likely find useful if you pursue filmmaking in the future.

Locations

Detailed script analysis and extensive research should lead you to a general understanding of when and why you would be best served shooting on location, and when you would ideally want to build sets to achieve particular shots. When all factors are equal, for most movies, the notion of reality, or at least believability, is central to connecting with audiences. This is one reason location shooting is often ideal; a real location, when dressed and shot properly, almost always feels more realistic than a fabricated set. Of course, all factors are not always equal, particularly when it comes to resources. Regardless of what level on the filmmaking hierarchy you are on, location shooting can be, in many cases, more affordable than renting a stage and building elaborate sets, at least when extensive travel is not involved. The complications of building sets and working on sound stages are a high bar for you to clear with few resources as film students. Therefore, as you pursue a filmmaking education, you are likely to be shooting on lots of real locations over time. Keep in mind, however, that a "location" could be your backyard or classroom or driveway. Such everyday places close to home are sites you should seriously consider if they can be made to fit with your story. Don't discount them—you can radically alter and highlight even the most mundane patch of grass if you need to.

To get started, you first need to know what to look for when scouting locations that will work practically and creatively. In the professional world, **location managers** take the lead in this effort, but they do so in close collaboration with the director, production manager, and production designer, who frequently join them on location scouts.

As student filmmakers, take extensive notes when you scout locations. One glaringly obvious factor does not need much elaboration: investigate from the outset whether it is even possible to get permission, or an official permit if required, to shoot there. Although it is true that many students and independent filmmakers shoot "guerrilla style" in public locations—simply showing up with camcorders, filming with minimal setup or crew, and departing as quickly as they came—understand that operating that way can be disrespectful to the general public frequenting that area at best, and downright illegal at worst. And creatively, shooting in that style may end up giving your narrative material a documentary feel that is not intended. Get permission or go somewhere else.

Producer SMARTS

Dumpster Diving

Many of the most important furnishings seen in the apartment of the Lynn Bracken character (played by Kim Basinger) in the 1997 noir classic *L.A. Confidential* were found in a consignment store in Palm Springs, according to Jeannine Oppewall, the film's production designer. She likewise found the dining room table featured in certain scenes of *The Bridges of Madison County* (1995) "in the front window of a used furniture store maybe an hour from the set"—a table Oppewall used again for a particular set in *L.A. Confidential*. Over the years, Oppewall has even put her own furniture, and the furniture and possessions of friends and crewmates, into feature films she has designed.

In that respect, Oppewall says, "production design is a shameless profession—we will beg, borrow, steal, and go anywhere to find something useful." In other words, even professional productions severely limit resources and require ingenuity on the part of the production designer and his or her team to find appropriate set pieces. That's good news for you, the film student, since you will likely have no budget of substance to work with, and yet, like professionals, you will need props and set pieces that fit your stories like a glove.

Therefore, as many designers suggest, go anywhere to find what you need, bargain hunt, and innovate. Think like a producer—you need not spend a sizable amount of money to furnish typical sets. This is an area in which you can most likely find what you need within the confines of your budget. Flea markets, garage sales, pawn shops, antique shops, estate auctions, consignment stores, junkyards, online sites like Craigslist where you can find used goods, neighbors' houses, and even your own home most likely contain most, if not all, of what you need. Jack Taylor freely admits to having gone dumpster diving in his career, even loading discarded items on street corners into his vehicle if he felt they had cinematic use.

Additionally, you will find that many prop and costume shops that normally service the entertainment and theater industries will offer special deals, discounts, and even free items to student productions out of a desire to promote their businesses and lure the next generation of potential customers.

Courtesy of Jeannine Oppewall.

Figure 4-9. This overhead shot of a living room set from *L.A. Confidential* (1997) shows a variety of props and set pieces.

With that said, here are other fundamental factors to consider:

- **Tweak your script to match what's available.** If resources dictate that you will only be able to shoot on campus or at your home, then there is no sense searching for a medieval castle to shoot in. You will either have to create that element with *stock elements* (images you can purchase from somewhere else) or visual effects, or go without it. If you're preparing your story and you learn that there is a gym on campus you think you can shoot in as well as a local public park, set scenes in similar locations, so you can use what you have at your disposal.
- **Consider large spaces.** For interior work, select large spaces with high ceilings and multiple doors or windows when you can, even if you are designing a small space. The advantages of shooting in a spacious environment are great, the cinematic tricks available to make the space look smaller on-screen are plentiful, and you will likely have opportunities to repurpose the space. Among its advantages: high ceilings and doors and windows you can maneuver through make it easier to fit people and equipment in and out of the space, and they enhance options for moving your camera.
- **Environments change.** As you examine locations, keep in mind season, time of day, weather, and that human or animal activity can change the look or structure of an exterior environment. Study the location at the approximate time of year and time of day when you would expect to be shooting. Find out if construction or seasonal events will change the environment in any way before you will be able to shoot there. Also, examine and measure natural or artificial light when scouting the environment, take pictures, and shoot test footage if you can. You must be certain that you will be able to do what you need to do when you return there days, weeks, or months later. In particular, for exteriors, spend enough time at the location to track the sun: take note of when the area is in full sunlight, part sunlight, and total shade. This will help you plan what time of day to use the location.
- **Hear the location.** Because you will likely be recording audio in the location, you need to study ambient noise there. Test levels and learn about local traffic patterns, whether animals or children frequent the area, and so on. Test echo patterns and record test sound there with the same equipment you will be using when shooting. Also, if you are planning to use wireless microphones, make sure there is no signal interference in the area.
- **Logistics.** The first, most basic thing to check is whether enough power supplies are readily available in the area for you to use freely, or if you will need to bring generators or extra batteries to the site. While you are at it, test some potential setups of how you would like to position cameras and microphones. You should also determine whether an exterior location is too grueling for your equipment, since electronic cameras and audio technology can be sensitive to moisture, wind, dirt, sand, and heat. Other logistical issues include parking; walk-up accessibility; access to food, shelter, and bathroom facilities; Internet or cell-phone connectivity; cooperation of the neighbors; and security.

There is one other factor to consider in deciding whether or not to shoot on location and, if so, how to go about finding those locations: time. It can be time-consuming and laborious to drive or fly, even if resources permit it, to various locations for hours, days, even weeks on end, to find spots that work best for you. Once again, think like a producer: if what you are looking for is exceedingly rare or unusual, and you expect it won't be easy to find, you will need to calculate the time and resource benefits of searching for that location versus coming up with a plan for building a set for it.

Carry a Logbook

When ramping up a production, carry a design logbook and routinely make notations in it of design elements in the real world, in your own environment, or in movies or other media that you encounter. Examine buildings, rooms, and furniture, and either make notes about interesting characteristics or take photographs.

Sets

There are many reasons to build sets rather than shoot exclusively on location, particularly when there is no accessible location available to you. Another reason might be when complete control of lighting is needed for a visual effects scene. It can sometimes be more cost effective to shoot on a stage rather than risk the vagaries of a location shoot, as light control is a dominating factor for that kind of material. More generally, you typically have more control over light, weather, power, and other logistical issues on a set.

Predesign When You Can

Predesign for technical requirements whenever possible, particularly electrical needs. Sometimes—when building walls, for example—you will need holes strategically cut to permit power cord access.

As noted earlier, one of the drawbacks is that you may have a hard time achieving the same level of realism that you would on location. Another obstacle revolves around resources. To build sets, you first need to find a place to build them—a sound stage usually, although you can creatively employ warehouses, basements, airline hangars, or garages for low-budget projects. Procuring permission and affording the cost of renting a sound stage can be difficult. Second, you need raw materials and proper equipment. Third, you must possess the design, construction, and paint skills necessary to build sets, as well as the ability to get the work done in a safe and efficient manner.

Sketch courtesy of Jeannine Oppewall.

Figure 4-10. A sketch of a set for *L.A. Confidential* (1997, *left*) and its final, live version (*right*).

Still, one way or another, you will eventually have to build a set of some type. Let's look at a handful of foundational issues you need to address when planning sets:

- **General design.** Using sketches, storyboards, or digital tools to previsualize your set (see p. 212), design not only what you generally want it to look like but also how you want it to function—where cameras and lights will go, for example. Depending on your tools, skill level, and experience, your design may be a full-on blueprint. But even if your skills don't permit that, be as specific as you can in terms of noting the size of the space you think you will need, remembering to include space for any important creative or logistical elements. Ideally, you will eventually create a **floorplan**—a map of the stage from above, so that you will be able to see all elements and their locations before you build anything.

Make a Strike Plan

Think about cleanup: Have a strategic plan in mind to strike, or dismantle, the set efficiently, and neatly dispose of all elements when you are done shooting. Certain materials can be stored and reused, others returned, others thrown away, and still others recycled. You need to research what, if anything, you are required to do with materials, especially with regard to possible hazardous waste, when you are done with them, and to plan the logistics of their removal early on, not just when you are done shooting your movie. In Hollywood and around the country, there are many companies that specialize in doing just this.

- **Finding a stage.** This can be tricky, because renting a stage or studio space is often expensive. However, your school may offer facilities in the cinema or theatrical departments that you can arrange to use. Likewise, community centers and religious institutions may have space you can "borrow" during off hours, as long as you sign liability waivers and clean up when you are done. Or, in some cases, depending on the size and scale of your movie and sets, you can build in a garage, on a porch, in a field, in a barn, on a blacktop, and so on.

- **Construction plan.** On a professional project, a **construction manager** puts together a construction team and builds sets for major projects. Construction managers have reams of specialists to assist, ranging from carpenters, stagehands, painters, plasterers, grips, **set decorators** or **dressers** (tasked with procuring and placing all props and pieces that are not connected physically to a set), **prop masters** (in charge of finding and preparing all primary props), and **greenspeople** (who handle all plants on the set). You may need to head up some or all of these tasks yourself, but unless you have a lot of time to prep or very little to build, you'll need a crew of some type. Turn to classmates and friends for help building key elements (see Tech Talk: "Common Set Structures"). In addition, it's a great idea to consult with a construction expert or professional at some point about the finer technical details of building sets. Obviously, keep safety in mind at all times, and understand that certain types of work in certain types of locations—and certain equipment—require permits and/or licensed experts to handle.

Tech TALK

Common Set Structures

Certain structures are commonplace on film sets and actually derive from the theatrical world. It is useful to familiarize yourself with these basic elements and nomenclature:

- **Flats.** This term refers to two-dimensional pieces of scenery you will be painting. Often, flats are little more than a material, like canvas, stretched over wooden frames. They can be anchored to the floor, lashed together, and used in all sorts of combinations. Flats can be kept standing straight up with various methods, including those as simple and inexpensive as weighting them on the bottom of the outside portion of the wall with sandbags. Keep in mind that this form of construction likely won't work for scenes in which people or objects need to interact directly with the wall, as the fabric on a flat may not be strong enough.
- **Platforms.** These are simple layers of wood used to add height to an area of the stage, such as when depicting one room being a few steps higher than another in a house or giving the illusion of having gone up steps.
- **Wagons.** These are platforms with wheels attached for purposes of moving them, as needed, around a stage. Wagons can be elaborate, even motorized, and run on tracks.
- **Turntables.** Sometimes called revolves, turntables consist of a circular platform designed to spin. Actors, entire sets, or portions of sets can be placed on them.
- **Cutouts.** These are thin pieces of material cut in such a way as to mimic a pattern or outline on an object, a wall, or a building. Often, cutouts are attached to flats to represent patterns of a design or element meant to be seen on a set.
- **Drops.** These are made from painted canvas or other material hung from above, and they are often used to create the illusion of a distant background element, such as a cityscape or night sky.
- **Scrims.** These are a form of a drop—large, typically unpainted, and often loosely woven or opaque so that they alter the properties of light when photographed from particular angles.
- **Cycloramas.** These are curved walls frequently built out of plaster but sometimes made of large pieces of fabric painted, hung, and lit in a particular way to give the illusion of a night sky or another wide, open space. "Cycs," as they are often called, can also be giant green screens or blue screens for visual effects purposes.
- **Projections.** As the name suggests, still or moving images projected live onto a background, such as a cyclorama or a flat, can be used to conjure background or distance illusions on set.

- **Building only what's necessary.** Think economically when figuring out what sets you will need, and keep in mind that a wealth of cinematic tricks exist that may permit you to film on partial sets—a wall or door frame, for instance. If a scene is extremely brief, it doesn't make sense to spend a lot of time or money on an elaborate set. For scenes in which you will be shooting in only one direction, you might be able to get away with not building a complete set, if portions of the set will not be captured on camera. If that is the case, only build or decorate the portion of the set from the direction you will be filming. For example, if you are using camera angles that never show the ceiling, then the ceiling does not need to be realistic—or even finished. Conversely, if a lengthy scene absolutely requires 360-degree coverage, apply what resources you have for set design and construction to those scenes above all others. Reuse sets when you can. You might be amazed how a few props and some paint can transform a hotel lobby into a business office.

Practice

Finding Elements

Read and evaluate a complete scene from any screenplay, compile a list of set pieces and props you would need to film the scene, and explain why each of them is necessary or at least useful to advancing the cause of the story and achieving the emotions intended by the writer. Then, put together a miniature "look book"—photographs, sketches, paintings, books, other movies, color swatches—that you would use as reference material for designing the look of that particular scene.

Predesign When You Can

When searching for locations, keep in mind the likely limitations of your shooting schedule and resources. If you find two locations for two separate scenes that you love but they are two hours apart, will you have time to schedule different days to shoot at each? Traveling between the two will eat up a large chunk of a shooting day. A better idea is to find your most complex or important location first, and then hunt for related locations nearby. Alternatively, see if you can dress one location in different ways, to stand in for different places. If you need to show interiors of two different homes, for instance, try to find one home in which you can use different rooms for different characters.

Previsualization

We have discussed the principles of good design; how to make a design plan; your options for finding and using locations; and planning and building sets. However, at some point during all these stages—and even after them, as you enter production and are actively planning specific shots—you will benefit from doing some kind of **previsualization**, or **previs**, work. The term *previsualization* can refer to state-of-the-art 3D computer animation, hand-drawn storyboards, simple sketches, paintings, simple models, stick figures drawn on napkins, and just about any other kind of conceptual art you can manufacture to help visualize individual elements, designs, themes, shots, camera moves, camera angles, complex visual effects, and any other images you will eventually need to create. The idea is to give yourself and collaborators a clear guide, or template, for what those elements will look like in the end and if they will physically fit in the space you are using.

Thus, in filmmaking, we often use the term *previs* loosely—it is not a linear process that takes place at one particular point during a project's life. Rather, it is a process that is used whenever it can be helpful. It helps production designers certainly, but it also helps directors, cinematographers, visual effects artists, and many others as they plan their work, while they do their work, and when they are trying to solve problems during those stages. In this sense, previs has become in recent years an important component of making big-budget films containing significant effects and stunts. Entire companies have emerged dedicated solely to the idea of helping filmmakers use computer animation and other visual effects' techniques to conceptualize complicated sequences.

Student filmmakers will have a hard time hiring previsualization companies or doing complex computer graphics previs work in most cases, but with affordable off-the-shelf tools available, even simple digital previs is within your grasp. You can use techniques such as storyboarding, sketching, and making concept art to help you design sets and elements, but over time, you will learn to use these digital tools throughout the entire filmmaking process. For production design, in particular, they will be most helpful to you only after you have a firm understanding of the basic design principles, planning, requirements, and options that we have examined earlier in this chapter. That is why we have saved the previs discussion for last.

Sketches and Storyboards

Sketching shots and designs by hand is as old as motion pictures themselves, and the term *storyboards* has been around since at least the 1930s, when it was popularized at Walt Disney Studios as a tool for making animated films. For decades, studio artists there and elsewhere would draw comic-book style panels depicting various scenes in animated movies, and then film them "flipbook style," creating so-called **story reels**, or **animatics**, and even adding music, dialogue, and effects in order to create templates for filmmakers to follow as projects moved along. Over time, the concept was adopted by live-action movies.

Look to Comics

Tip

You can make your storyboards effective by using simple comic-book techniques—speech or thought bubbles, wiggly lines for movement, pencil shading, ovals, coils, cylinders for bodies, and so on. As long as the meaning of your storyboard panels can be understood by merely looking at the pictures, you will have created useful storyboards.

Today, previs options have branched out into numerous areas, including doing everything on a computer. However, one way or another, even if you later plan to digitally previsualize shots or sequences, you will need to incorporate the idea of manually sketching out at least some key ideas into your design approach once you have done meaningful research. There is no single right way to do it, nor is there a requirement to be particularly artistically talented or detailed in your sketches. In fact, some designers warn against overloading storyboards and sketches with minute detail to the point where you've added more than you can feasibly execute or stifled creativity regarding other possible options. Often, professional designers prefer to go with simple hand-drawn pencil or watercolor sketches.

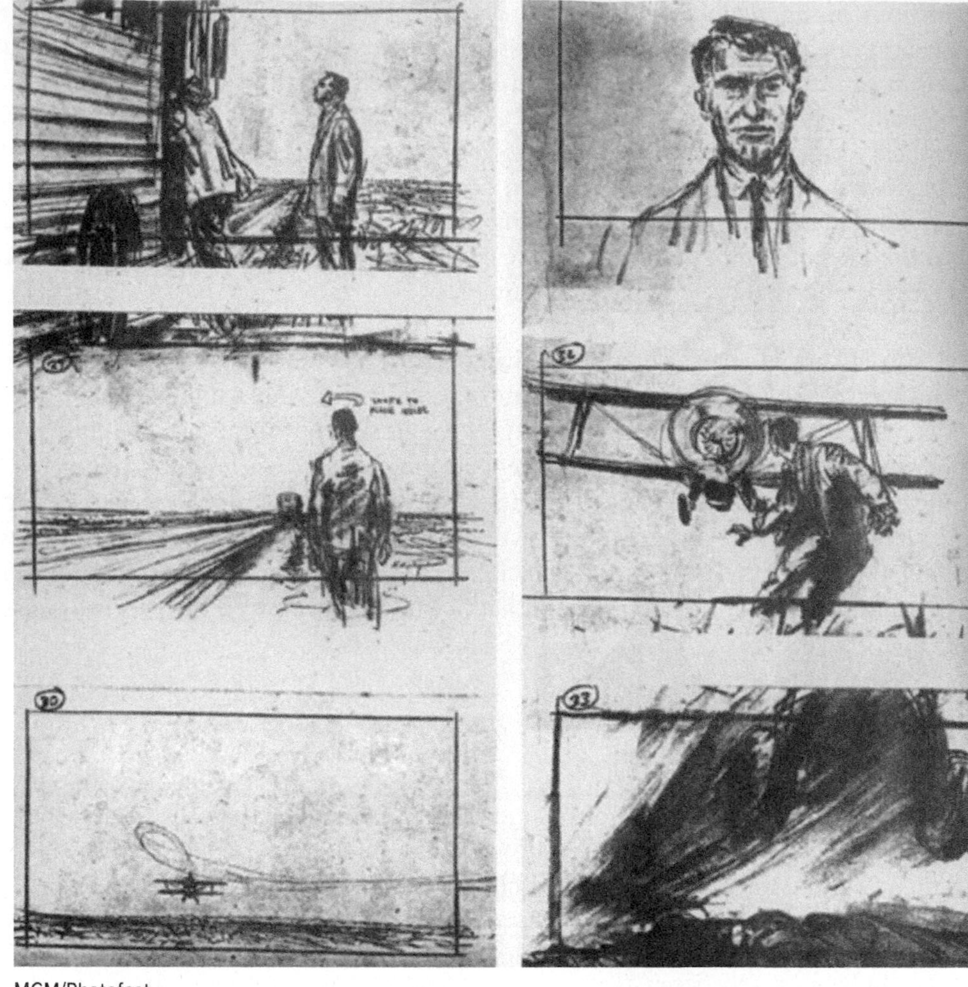

MGM/Photofest.

Figure 4-11. Storyboard panels illustrate visual plans for a sequence in ***North by Northwest*** (1959).

At the prime level, there are two categories of sketches that you will need to concern yourself with. The first is **concept art**. Basically, these are relatively detailed drawings or diagrams that you create as reference templates for costumes or sets for yourself or other artists tasked with building those elements, frequently drawn in pencil, charcoal, or marker. When feasible, create concept art for all major characters, costumes, and sets to help you design the movie more efficiently.

Next, you will want to create storyboards. **Storyboards** are often used to visualize entire films or sequences as individual frames or shots, essentially as hand-drawn panels created to resemble comic books. Depending on your skill, time, and resources, they might be extremely detailed or little more than stick figures or shapes. But either way, their goal is to illustrate how you see characters, sets, and objects interacting in particular environments. This will help you design shots and camera angles and lighting setups later, and it will make it easier to move, solidify, and organize various design ideas along the way. Storyboards will also help you understand what you will and will not actually have to create, because they let you see what area of a set and what backgrounds will be in shots, and which will not.

Walt Disney Pictures/Photofest.

Figure 4-12. Concept art sketches for ***Inside Out*** (2015).

Ideally, after you approve your storyboards, you will be able to make even more detailed drawings or blueprints of sets based on what you've come to understand from your research and your analysis of your storyboards. At that point, you have guides for building sets and set pieces, when necessary. Here is a list of the various storyboard approaches:

- **2D concept drawings.** These are highly detailed hand drawings that specify particular elements in great detail.
- **2D storyboards.** These are essentially hand-drawn, comic-book style panels, with as much detail as you need to plot out shots or sequences.
- **Animatics.** This is the result of 2D storyboard panels being assembled in order and filmed; animatics provide a sense of movement and story order to your previs work.
- **Photomatics, or photo storyboards.** Here, instead of drawings, you use photographs of your actors or people, places, and things that generally resemble your story ideas and assemble them together to give you an idea of designs and concepts you want to implement. You might even take friends or classmates to sets or locations and pose them in key places, photograph them, and use those rough templates as storyboards for some of your shots.
- **3D storyboards.** As with 2D storyboards, these are panels created to plot out your shots and sequences, but they are created on a computer, rather than drawn by hand, and are combined with other panels on the computer.

- **3D animation.** Here, you roughly animate shots or sequences with basic movements and other elements to help you better define how you might design and choreograph a scene. Some form of 3D animated previs is quite common for visual effects sequences.

Use Models

Besides using sketches, you can also benefit by using simple scale models as a previs technique, giving you a three-dimensional view of your design. You don't need expensive materials and deep model-building experience to accomplish this. You can build rough representations of your sets out of cardboard or other readily available materials, and you can paint them to enhance the illusion.

In the next section, we will discuss some of these digital previsualization techniques in more detail. But for hand-drawn storyboards, even if you don't have the artistic talent to produce compelling, professional-level sketches, the web is full of dozens of resources for learning basic drawing and storyboarding skills. Don't let your lack of drawing skills inhibit you from eagerly pursuing concept art and storyboards. As Jack Taylor noted, even rudimentary drawings will "get your mind going" as the design process picks up steam, and that can only help your project.

Digital Previs

Digital previsualization of shots, sequences, even entire movies, has been growing in sophistication and popularity in Hollywood since it first evolved in the late 1980s out of computer-aided design (CAD) technology used in the architecture world and the then-nascent computer-generated imagery (CGI) industry. Today, many filmmakers are commissioning extensive 3D animation to plot out complex sequences down to the last detail. Although you won't have the time, resources, or experience to do that kind of work at first, you will have access to affordable yet powerful 3D tools, with which to do some fairly simple previs work if you put your mind to it (see Tech Talk: "Digital Storyboard Tools"). In some situations, straightforward 3D imagery can give you a better perspective on what the shot's design and technical requirements will be, and how it might work from different angles.

For production design, digital previs can be particularly helpful in allowing you to reach conclusions about what elements you will be able to build and shoot practically and what elements you will need to create on the computer. Particularly for action sequences, car chases and crashes, and explosions, filmmakers have found that they can more safely and affordably create those shots digitally. But even so, they need to design each and every element—from walls and cars to flying glass, smoke, and fire—just as they would for real-world elements, and previs is central to succeeding in that regard.

Figure 4-13. Previsualization (*top*) helps effects-intensive films like ***The Amazing Spider-Man 2*** (2014) map out their action sequences (*final version on the bottom*).

As we've noted, digital previs can also help plot camera moves and lighting placement in great detail. If, for example, you will be shooting actors in front of a green screen on-set, you can figure out long before productions starts what the digital background that will replace that green screen will look like by experimenting with different designs, including colors, textures, and patterns, during the digital previs process.

Indeed, digital previs is crucial in the growing trend toward combining real-world elements with digital elements through "construction" of entirely **virtual sets** or **set extensions**. Virtual sets—used either when productions cannot afford or do not want to travel to locations or build sets, or for stylistic reasons—involve shooting with a green screen and later surrounding the actors with CG environments. Set extensions are used when filmmakers build partial sets, and then combine them with virtual "extensions" that complete the illusion. While the digital age has made this easier to do, the technique of creating matte paintings on glass and combining them with minimal footage from the set is almost as old as the art of filmmaking itself. Like real sets, virtual sets or set extensions require intimate design. The computer allows unprecedented experimenting in this regard. You can change backgrounds, colors, and shapes; add or remove signs, cars, text, and doors; and so much more.

Figure 4-14. The ***Sin City*** films (2005, 2014) use an extreme version of set extension, where most of the settings, sets, and backgrounds are created digitally from bare-bones live-action footage.

Digital previs allows you to view the sets you are designing in three dimensions and in greater detail than a hand-drawn storyboard can provide. As the creator of the film and its production designer, you will hopefully already have a good, three-dimensional vision of the movie in your head. But the ability to work with that image using sophisticated software on a computer, show it to others and get their input, and then revise it rapidly has been a major breakthrough.

Practice

Storyboard Experiment

Identify a shot or sequence from your screenplay, and using techniques discussed in this chapter and any methodology you prefer, create some storyboards or shot sketches. You can hand-draw them, download and use a free version of SketchUp (www.sketchup.com) or a trial version of another digital storyboard tool, or use editing or CG software tools already in your possession. The visceral quality of your artwork is not important at this stage, just its creative usefulness. Experiment with a few different designs and setups; when you come up with something you like, write an essay about your experience—what the challenge of your scene was, what you tried to accomplish with your storyboards, and what you learned about previsualization from the experience.

An added benefit of doing digital previs is that it involves many of the same tools and techniques as visual effects work and, in some cases, will allow you to create portions of digital assets that you will be able to build on later, when you strive to create the eventual 3D image, rather than starting over. If you previs a building, for instance, the basic wire frame and possibly other elements may serve you well when you begin doing visual effects work on the scene involving that building.

Here are the basic steps you will go through if you choose to do digital previs work on your movie:

1. Create a list of scenes or shots that you intend to previsualize, with brief notes about what you need and want from each shot and its significance. If you are previsualizing the entire sequence, you will list every frame you need. If you are conceptualizing it and want to create a digital template for designing the entire scene, you might only list the most crucial shot in the sequence.
2. Doing digital previs does not mean you should forgo storyboards, or at least the use of rough sketches. Start with sketches of key sequences or shots, and then use them as reference material for creating your digital previs material. Alternatively, if sketching is simply not something you feel you can accomplish, go to your locations and photograph environments and specific elements, or even have friends or fellow students roughly act out some blocking for your sequence and take pictures of that, and use those photos as storyboard equivalents.
3. You will use your animation software to create a rough version of the 3D environment you are designing, and block out where characters, elements, and possibly cameras and lights should be placed. If you are previsualizing primarily for blocking and camera movement, your buildings and designs will be rudimentary at best—perhaps even just blobs or blocks. For design specificity, you will need far more detail, but only for the particular elements you are concerned with in a shot. Therefore, you will likely not need to take all the 3D material in each shot through the traditional animation steps.
4. Instead, you will render out CG images as soon as you have the minimal amount of detail you need to previsualize your sequence adequately. Depending on your needs and resources, you may do a rough render and then, after making adjustments, re-render for greater nuance, detail, or other refinements to some elements, such as costumes or architecture. The point, however, is to go only as far as you need to in order to make your design or filming decisions, rather than to pursue near-final-level quality.
5. Eventually, once you have the 3D previs material at the level you need, you will edit the shots together in the order you want to view and share them. But you may also wish to print all or some of them out and mount them on walls or boards in your workspace for easy reference, as is frequently done with hand-drawn storyboards.

Tech TALK

Digital Storyboard Tools

There is now a wide range of useful and affordable computer tools designed specifically to help you create sophisticated storyboards and previsualize action, blocking, lighting, and camera moves, among other things. Here are a few popular ones:

- **SketchUp** (www.sketchup.com). This is a 3D drawing product with a low-end free version, in addition to more powerful versions at reasonable prices. SketchUp is designed for you to use as if you were sketching on paper, and you can certainly do rough blocking and design with it.
- **FrameForge** (www.frameforge3d.com). This tool is specifically designed for moving image previsualization work, and can help you draw rough

storyboards, do layout, and create rough animation and blocking, among other things.

- **StoryBoard Quick** and **StoryBoard Artist** (www.powerproduction.com/index.php). These tools, from the same manufacturer, are both digital storyboard crafting tools. StoryBoard Quick is designed for simple storyboard generation, whereas StoryBoard Artist adds animation and extensive revision tools, among other things.
- **Photoshop** (www.photoshop.com). Long available to consumers and professionals alike, Adobe's famous graphic design software is quite useful for manipulating scanned images, photos, and 3D images, and can be used for storyboard creation, among other design-related tasks.
- **Poser** (http://poser.smithmicro.com). Poser is a well-known tool for simple design and animation of virtual characters, rather than environments.

Designer's Emergency Kit

- Drafting paper/sketchbook
- Pencils and markers
- Tape roll with different kinds of tape
- Dulling spray and other spray paints that can darken surfaces
- Sponges for mottling paint
- Cleaning supplies for cleaning surfaces
- Scissors or X-Acto knife
- Digital still camera
- Camcorder
- Compass
- Maps
- Tape measure
- Laptop with graphics software or CGI software installed

Chapter Essentials

- You need to study the fundamentals of good design and staging. Learn about the use of space, color palette, balance, harmony, lines, textures, shape, form, size, and so on. Then, examine issues related to arranging elements within those spaces—creating things like props and set pieces, developing an overall sense of decor, and figuring out how to place and use those elements wisely.
- Strategically analyze your screenplay—scene by scene, shot by shot—and come up with a design plan for how you want to use the spaces you have available: whether you can use real-world locations or build sets, how you want to arrange elements within those spaces, how you want to design each of those elements, and how you want to light and shoot them. Extensive research is crucial for launching this process.
- Find ways to previsualize how you want to design and arrange things. Methods typically revolve around creating concept art and storyboards for key sequences, and using computer storyboard or animation tools to visualize the shots in three dimensions, allowing you to experiment with design and technical options before you commit to them. This will be useful as you proceed with the construction of sets, the dressing of locations, and the detailed planning of shots.

Telling the Story with the Camera

"Telling the Story with the Camera" from *Filmmaking in Action*, by Adam Leipzig, Barry S. Weiss, and Michael Goldman, pp. 149–176 (Chapter 7, "Telling the Story with the Camera").

"Images, not words, capture feelings."

—Sven Nykvist, Academy Award–winning cinematographer, whose more than 120 films include *Cries and Whispers* (1972), *The Unbearable Lightness of Being* (1988), and *What's Eating Gilbert Grape* (1993)[8]

Figure 4-15. *Skyfall* (2012).

"So why do you need me?" James Bond (played by Daniel Craig) asks Q, the inventor of espionage devices, in the movie *Skyfall* (2012). It's a question Roger Deakins wondered himself when director Sam Mendes asked him to be the cinematographer on the film. Deakins, despite his lengthy resume, had never shot a spy thriller before. "I must say that action is not so much of a thrill as capturing a performance," he said about the experience on his popular website.[9]

But the director didn't want a conventional action movie. The James Bond series is the longest-running franchise in movie history. Could *Skyfall*, its 50th anniversary production, reinvent the main character for a new, global audience?

Deakins, a 10-time Academy Award nominee, came up with a visual answer to this question. He decided to shoot *Skyfall* like a Western,[10] where the action plays out in long takes in the frame, rather than the conventional action-movie approach done with multiple cameras, which, in Deakins's opinion, looks like "an incoherent mess of shots without any particular structure or point of view."[11]

The result? *Skyfall* looks and feels unlike any of its predecessors, and it became the most successful James Bond movie in history, grossing over $1 billion worldwide, with Deakins making a significant visual contribution to that result.

That's why the movie needed him. Or, as Q responded to James Bond's question, "Every now and then a trigger has to be pulled." Indeed, a bit of dialogue fitting for a Western.

In this chapter, you will learn how to use cameras and lenses creatively: how they serve a filmed narrative. As the director of photography, you will work in close collaboration with the director and production designer, or you may be your own director and cinematographer on your class film. The relationship between the cinematographer and the director is the closest of creative marriages—so much so that a few professional directors actually do double duty at times and work as their own DPs, too. Among the well-known directors who have done this for entire movies or sequences within movies are Steven Soderbergh, Stanley Kubrick, James Cameron, Peter Hyams (who began his career as a DP), Ridley Scott, David Fincher, Debra Granik, Chantal Akerman, and Peter Jackson.

When the director and the DP are two different people—which is most often the case in professional productions—they will spend a large part of their time on the set side by side, and the DP's role involves both diplomacy and organization. The DP not only has to find ways to get the shots the director wants with the time and money at hand, but also needs to find the best way to communicate with the director in any given situation.

As the cinematographer, every choice you make affects the moviegoing experience—how the camera moves (or doesn't move), where people and objects are placed in the frame, and how much of the scene you let the audience see (or how much you don't let them see). Even when you are making these choices, you'll be mindful of limiting factors—such as time, budget, scheduling, and what's physically possible where you are shooting—and giving the director and editor plenty of choices for shaping the story when they are in the editing room. In this way, visual storytelling is a skill that combines the most theoretical concepts of imagery with the hard-nosed practicality of getting a day's work done. Few filmmaking tasks combine these realities in as formidable a way, or must balance them so carefully on a minute-by-minute basis.

Although all aspects of filmmaking are related, the interconnection is especially strong between storytelling with images and two other areas: lighting and editorial. Lighting and color determine how we feel about film imagery. To set up your shots effectively, you'll need to light them well. Editorial assemblage of individual shots completes the visual storytelling you begin in this chapter. Taken together, telling the story with the camera, lighting it properly, and editing the shots into sequences form a trio of visual language; you begin your study of it here.

Key Concepts

- The building blocks of film language are a set of basic shots, which cover the action from far and medium distances and at close range.
- Each shot has a particular perspective on the action, which is conveyed through the camera's angle, or viewpoint.
- A good shot is well composed, which means the visual elements are well balanced in the frame and adhere to principles of good aesthetics.
- Visual storytelling functions in close collaboration with picture editing to provide different narrative possibilities as the film is being finished and to preserve continuity—the illusion that everything in a scene is happening in real time—with careful control of lighting.

Basic Shots

Basic shots are the building blocks of visual grammar. If you think of a scene as a sentence, you can consider individual shots the words in the sentence. Each shot must have a reason for being there, and it needs to convey important information to the audience. As a cinematographer, you have a responsibility to get enough shots to make sure there are different ways to assemble the scene in the editing room. Indeed, the entire process of image capture can be thought of as executing your vision while preserving your future options for different editorial and visual effects as the entire story comes together.

Getting the shots you need is called *covering a scene*, or ensuring that you have *coverage*. The cinematographer needs to know the editing style the director will want to achieve before deciding how to cover a scene. What kind of pace should the scene have? Will the scene be intimate or more clinical? Will the actors be moving around or staying in the same position? Different editing styles require different shots; some directors prefer to do scenes in long, single-camera takes, while others like to put together scenes with lots of short bits of imagery. As with every other aspect of filmmaking, the process is outcome-oriented; you start by conceptualizing what you want to finish with.

How can you "see" a scene? First, ask yourself if the audience should experience the scene objectively or subjectively. In an *objective* scene, the camera is a neutral observer, similar to a journalist viewing the action. In a *subjective* scene, the camera experiences the action through the eyes of one of the characters and imparts that character's emotional state to the action. Next, you'll determine the distance from which the camera will see things: from far away, which places the characters and action in the context of their surroundings; from a middle distance, where you can see most of people's bodies as they interact with others; and at close range, where you can see the fine details of faces and motion. These three distances correspond to the three basic shots—long shots, medium shots, and close-ups. We'll look at them as large categories, and examine the variations that provide nuance in the way they convey information. These basic shots comprise the standard approach to making certain a scene is well covered. Although you won't typically use all of them at once, you'll need enough of them to cut the scene together.

Long Shots

Long shots are valuable for setting characters and places in relationship to the world they're in. Images of a person walking down a deserted city street, where you see boarded-up buildings along the sidewalks, is an example of a long shot, as are images of a little house on a wide-open prairie. Following are names and explanations for the three most common long shots:

- **Establishing shot.** The **establishing shot** sets up the location where the ensuing scene will take place. It should be wide enough to capture all the important architectural, or landscape, details. For instance, in a wedding scene, the establishing shot would show the outside (exterior) of the church; for a campfire scene, you'd want to shoot the surrounding countryside, with the campfire visible in the distance. Establishing shots are particularly useful as transitions between scenes or sequences.

- **Wide shot/master shot.** A **wide shot** is a shot that shows all or most of the actors. Typically, the **master shot** is a wide shot of the entire scene, which you can always cut back to or use as reference when you cut in for closer shots. The master is often shown at the start of the scene to establish the geography of the environment and the relative positions of the actors to one another (the *blocking*). Many situation comedies such as *Talladega Nights* (2006), use a wide shot to put characters in the context of everything that's going on around them.

Figure 4-16. A wide shot establishes the dinner-table scene in ***Talladega Nights*** (2006).

Shoot the Master First

Shoot the master shot first; that way, you'll be sure you have captured the entire scene. Later, when you shoot closer shots, you'll match the lighting, action, and blocking in the master shot.

- **Extreme wide shot.** An **extreme wide shot** differs from a wide shot in that the actors will appear much smaller, perhaps taking up as little as 20 percent of the frame. Although it serves much the same function as a wide shot, the extreme wide shot can also be useful in creating a sense that the environment is more of a character in the story, or perhaps to show the powerlessness of the actors against their environment. A science fiction story, in which the actors must grapple with a strange alien world, might make good use of extreme wide shots; they are also staples in epic adventures, as you can see in films like *Lawrence of Arabia* (1962), and traditional Westerns, such as *The Searchers* (1956).

Figure 4-17. An extreme wide shot captures the epic scope of ***Lawrence of Arabia*** (1962).

Medium Shots

Medium shots bring you closer to the action, but not too close—and for that reason, they're the most common shot in films. They let you see the entire action of the scene and some of the background where the action is taking place. A character pulling a cell phone from her pocket, or two characters sitting and talking on a park bench, would both be well-covered in medium shots. There is no hard-and-fast rule for what differentiates a medium shot from a long shot—it's a fuzzy dividing line. In this book, we take the view that long shots emphasize the place more than the characters, and medium shots move in to focus specific attention on the characters and the action. Following are names and explanations for the five most common medium shots:

- **Medium shot.** While everything in this category is a medium shot, a classic **medium shot** is composed to start at the actor's chest and move up to the head. This medium shot feels familiar and objective, because it is how we usually interact with other people—standing or sitting near enough to see their chest and head without getting in their face. You'll use a medium shot to explore an actor's emotional state without the subjective, manipulative quality of a close-up.

Figure 4-18. A medium shot in ***To Kill a Mockingbird*** (1962)

- **MCU, or medium close-up.** Slightly tighter than a medium shot, the **MCU** starts at the middle of the chest and goes up to the top of the head, sometimes cropping the actor's face at the hairline. An MCU doesn't have the forcefulness of a close-up, but it still brings focus to the actor's eyes and facial expression.

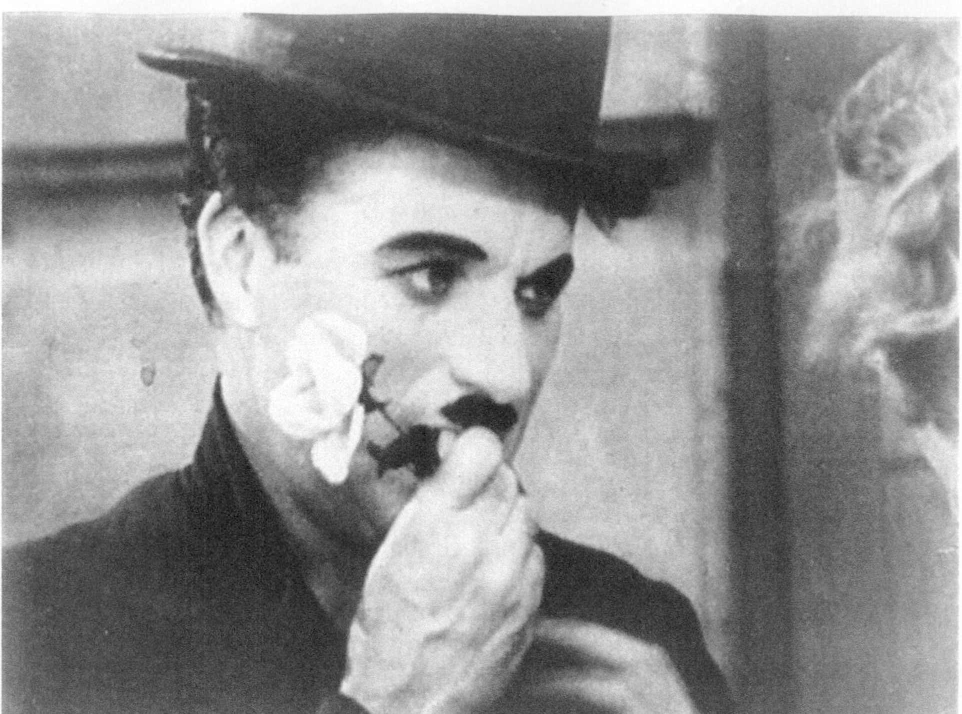

Figure 4-19. MCU in ***City Lights*** (1931)

- **Full shot.** A **full shot** frames a single actor from head to foot. This shot is useful for showing the clothing that the actor is wearing. You might employ a full shot to emphasize a costume change—for example, when a bride-to-be tries on her wedding dress for the first time—but otherwise, full shots should be used sparingly, as they can be difficult to cut to and away from.

Figure 4-20. A full shot in ***Patton*** (1970).

- **Cowboy.** The **cowboy** is *tighter*, or *closer*, than a full shot and will generally cut an actor off just above the knees. It is called a "cowboy" because it is frequently used in Westerns to show someone who is wearing holsters. Because a person's hands hang just above the knees when the arms are at rest, a cowboy shot is useful if you want to emphasize how the actor is using (or not using) hand gestures.

Figure 4-21. A cowboy shot in ***High Noon*** (1952).

- **Two shot/three shot, and so on.** These shots refer to the number of objects— usually actors—in them. Typically, the framing of any of these shots is close to the edges of the actors' backs and will not show as much of the environment as a wide shot or master. It's a good idea to keep the camera at eye level with your actors. A **two shot** or a **three shot** is useful for capturing an intimate discussion in a single shot.

Figure 4-22. A uniquely composed three shot in ***Chinatown*** (1974).

Don't Cut Up Your Actors

Don't frame a shot in which an actor is cut off at the joints (knees, ankles, wrists)—it will look as if part of the body has been cut off.

Close Shots

A close shot brings you right into the action and emotion of a scene; here, the actor's face fills the screen, and you feel deeply, personally connected to the character. In this way, the close shot is the opposite of the long shot: the long shot is *objective*, and the close shot is *subjective*. Directors often choose close shots for the most powerful, impactful moments of storytelling, and they are standard shots in movies that center on relationships. Close shots of actions or objects are narrative devices that tell the story in visual terms, and they often don't need any dialogue to make their point.

Following are names and explanations for the three most common close shots:

- **Close-up** (tight vs. loose). A **close-up (CU)** starts at the top of the shoulders and includes the actor's head. As the shot moves in closer on an actor, it is said to be getting *tighter*. As the shot moves back, it becomes *looser*. Close-ups are especially useful for movies that will play on any screen other than a cinema screen—televisions, tablets, laptops, and mobile devices. When you're shooting for a small screen, close-ups create a sense of intimacy with the actors and convey emotion well. They are also an important tool for emphasizing details and plot points—for example, the close-up of the doorknob turning, the email opening, the money being stuffed into a suitcase, all give the audience essential information so they can follow the story.

Figure 4-23. A loose close-up in ***Django Unchained*** (2012).

Watch the Background

When shooting inserts, make sure the background behind the featured object is consistent with the scene. In the example of someone reading a letter, the insert on the letter should be shot from the actor's perspective, with the actor's fingers visible holding the letter, and perhaps, beyond the letter's edge, a part of the room where the letter is being read. Nothing says "fake" more than an insert that's inconsistent with the rest of the scene.

- **Extreme close-up** ("choker" and "haircut"). An **extreme close-up (ECU)**, or **big close-up (BCU)** will frame out the shoulders and will often not even show the top of an actor's head. It is often called a "choker" when the shot cuts into the actor's neck. When the shot is so tight that it also chops off a bit of the top of the actor's head, it is called giving the actor a "haircut." Some directors use ECUs to convey moments when an actor experiences extreme emotion or must make a big decision. An ECU in a mystery or suspense story may signify that the actor has just figured out an important clue. The shot often focuses on the actor's eyes, which are primary acting tools for conveying emotion.
- **Insert shot.** An **insert shot** (usually a close or a tight shot) captures some important detail in the scene. For instance, if an actor pulls a gun from his or her pocket, the director may want an insert shot of the gun as it is revealed. You should shoot inserts of any physical detail that's significant for the characters—for example, a letter (you'd cut to it as the actor is reading the letter) or a gun (you'd cut to it as the actor pulls out the gun to threaten someone). Inserts can also be used as *cutaways*—shots the editor can use to break up or shorten the main action of a scene.

Practice

Counting the Shots

As you've just learned, every shot takes careful planning to set up. Using a 30-second commercial as an example, count the number of shots (setups). Then, list the kind of shot each one is (master shot, close-up, insert, and so on).

If you think creating all of these shots is time-consuming, you are right! Accomplishing a series of setups for each scene might take anywhere from half a day to two or three days for a particularly long scene. (See "How to Shoot a Scene".)

Another way to cover a scene would be to do it in a single shot. The battlefield scene in *Atonement* (2007) is a good example of a complicated scene shot in a single take. The single shot is thrilling because it conveys a sense of scale and movement, but it also requires a lot of time to rehearse and choreograph and has potential storytelling risks. When you shoot a scene in pieces, you have the ability to shorten or lengthen the scene, and moments within the scene, and to orchestrate its movement in editorial to reflect character and storytelling dynamics. When you shoot a scene in a single shot, you have to live with it as it is.

Camera Angles: How You View the Scene

You've just learned a series of basic shots, each of which is an example of *what* the camera sees. When you decide the angle of each shot, you determine the *viewpoint* from which the camera shows the scene to the audience. Each camera angle, or viewpoint, is part of your visual language that tells the audience about the characters, their story, and the emotion of the scene. Following are the 10 most important shots associated with specific camera angles:

- **Low-angle shot.** A **low-angle shot** is one in which the camera is placed below the characters' eye level. In this shot, the camera must be angled to look *up* to see the action. This gives the appearance of characters looming over the camera and puts them in a position of power. You might choose to shoot dangerous characters from a low angle to emphasize how menacing they are.

Figure 4-24. Low-angle shot in ***Slumdog Millionaire*** (2008).

- **High-angle shot.** A **high-angle shot** is one in which the camera is placed above the characters' eye level. In this shot, the camera looks *down* on the action, often putting a character in a meek or powerless position. High-angle shots can also suggest objectivity and scale by placing the characters in the context of their surroundings.
- **Eye-level shot.** In **eye-level shots**, the camera is placed at eye level with the actors, usually between five and six feet for adult actors. An eye-level shot does not draw attention to itself and conveys the action in a natural, *objective* fashion; it suggests that the audience, as an outsider, is observing the scene. When using eye-level shots, choose between close (*tight*) or far (*loose*) eyelines. A close versus far eyeline refers to how close an actor faces toward the lens while looking at an off-camera subject. An actor with a *close eyeline* looks very close to the lens, as if the off-camera subject were right next to the camera. An actor with a *far eyeline* looks well away from the lens, as if the subject were far away from the camera.
- **Bird's-eye view.** Also referred to as the **overhead shot**, the **bird's-eye view** is shot above the action and looks straight down on it, from a very high angle. It makes the characters appear insignificant in the context of their surroundings.
- **Dutch angle.** Usually the camera is placed parallel to the ground or horizon line; however, the **Dutch angle**, also called the *oblique* or *canted shot*, tilts this view and places the camera at an oblique angle to the horizon—now the images are on a diagonal. Dutch angles suggest instability, danger, strangeness, and suspense. You'll often find them used in horror and suspense films or in a sequence in which a character experiences a physical or psychological change—as when a character is intoxicated or having an emotional breakdown. A classic film that uses Dutch angles to great effect is *The Third Man* (1949). (See Action Steps: "Low-Budget Dutch Angle Trick")

Figure 4-25. Bird's-eye view (overhead) shot in ***Goodfellas*** (1990).

Figure 4-26. Dutch angle in ***The Third Man*** (1949).

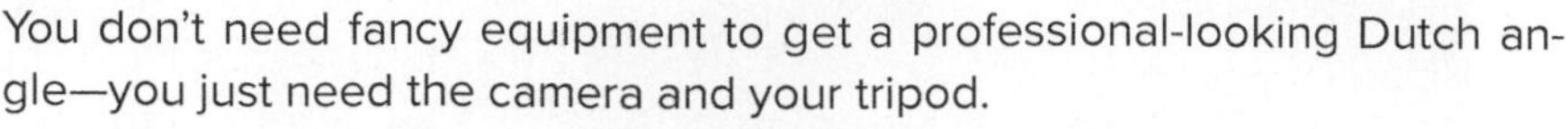

Low-Budget Dutch Angle Trick

You don't need fancy equipment to get a professional-looking Dutch angle—you just need the camera and your tripod.

1. Remove the base plate from the tripod and install it on your camera at a 90-degree angle.
2. Tighten it firmly, and then slide the camera onto your tripod.
3. You can use the tripod's tilt lever to create a Dutch angle.

- **Point-of-view shot.** A **point-of-view (POV) shot** shows what the actor is seeing during the scene. It is often shot with a handheld camera to give a sense of movement that mimics the way a character might be looking at something. POV shots are subjective and must be from the eye level of the character whose point of view it is. POV shots draw the audience into the action and into the mental and emotional state of the characters. They're especially effective in suspense sequences, when a character is looking around corners for possible danger; in dialogue sequences, to "get inside the heads" of the characters as they listen and react to one another; and as inserts and cutaways, to reveal what a character sees or discovers. In the example of the insert shot of the gun (p. 229), you could shoot the same insert with a handheld camera from the subjective angle of another character; in this way, you'd communicate that the character has spotted the gun.

Use POV Correctly

Point-of-view shots must be taken from the perspective of the character whose point of view it is. If you start with a character's POV shot at a wider angle and then move in closer, it tells the audience that the character is observing a detail or noticing something important, or that the filmmaker is emphasizing something.

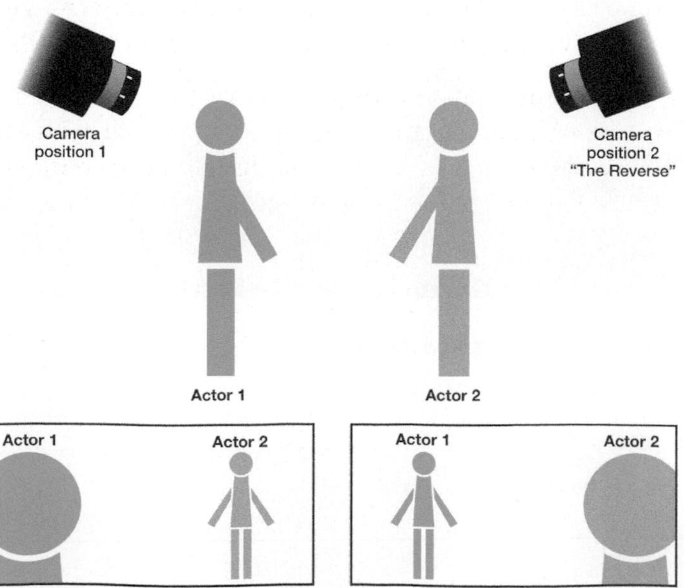

Figure 4-27. Diagram of a reverse shot.

- **Over-the-shoulder.** The **over-the-shoulder (OTS)** is an extremely common shot that includes two actors engaged in dialogue. The actor nearest the camera is called the *foreground*, or downstage, actor; this actor's back will be to the camera (his or her face will not be visible), and the shot will include the actor's shoulder. The actor who is facing the camera (and who is the main subject of the shot) is called the *upstage* actor and is framed in a medium or loose close-up shot. The OTS is an important shot because it can help establish the relationship (both physical and emotional) between two characters by linking them in a single shot. Use OTS for two-person dialogue scenes; just make sure to shoot both sides (over the shoulder of each actor). When you shoot OTS Actor A toward Actor B, then turn around to shoot OTS Actor B toward Actor A, it's called a **reverse shot**, as seen in Figure 4-27. (See also Action Steps: "Dirty vs. Clean")

Practice

Objective and Subjective Scene Work

Using a one- to two-page, two-person scene as material, shoot it two ways: first, in a single shot in which both actors are in the frame; second, with POV shots from the position of each of the actors. The first version is an objective view of the scene, whereas the second version is a subjective view of the scene. Play back the footage and observe how the scene's meaning is altered. What does each variation convey? Decide which angle (objective or subjective) best tells the story and emotion of the scene you've selected.

- **Wide lens close-up vs. long lens (telephoto) close-up.** You can shoot a close-up with different lenses, and the lens choice can make a dramatic difference. A **wide lens close-up** "stretches" the actor's features and exaggerates the distance between the actor and the background. In visual language, this allows the camera to be close on the actor and still emphasize a sense of aloneness or isolation. The **long lens close-up** compresses the actor's facial features and brings the background closer.
- **Profile shot.** A **profile shot** can be a close-up or a wide shot—what's important is profile *image*, which conveys the intensity of the actor's gaze or the sculptural quality of the actor's face. You set up a profile shot by making sure that the actor's eyeline (the actor's look direction to the off-camera subject) is at a 90-degree angle to the lens.
- **Three-quarter back shot.** This shot views the actor from nearly behind; however, the camera will still see part of the actor's eyebrow and ear. (When an actor wears glasses, the shot will often focus on the frames.) The **three-quarter back shot** often conveys that an actor is deep in thought. As with the profile shot, this shot can be a close-up or a wide shot.

Action STEPS

Dirty vs. Clean

A medium or close-up shot that includes a foreground actor, such as an over-the-shoulder, is called *dirty*. A shot that does not include any other actor in the frame is called a *clean* shot. How do you shoot them, and when would you want the shot to be dirty or clean?

1. **For a dirty shot**, focus on the main actor, and include some of the other actor's face or body in the shot (enough so it's clear that the second actor is making the shot "dirty"). This shot emphasizes the emotional or spatial relationship between the two characters.

2. **For a clean shot**, isolate the main actor. No one else should be visible in the frame. This shot emphasizes only the main actor.

3. **Pro camera move:** go from dirty to clean in one shot. This move starts with a dirty shot, then pushes in to the main actor until the shot is clean. Use this move when you want to show that something important is happening to the main character—for example, a moment of revelation, an emotional change, or a glimpse of recognition.

Composition

Whereas camera shots and angles provide a way of seeing what's in a scene, **composition** is the craft of arranging people, architectural details, and objects *inside the frame* so that they look good. Every motion picture image is bound by horizontal and vertical limits, which form the image's frame. In order to compose images inside the frame, you'll need to explore what "looking good" means, discover the core principles of artistic composition when the camera is still or in motion, and learn to use the right lens to get what you're after.

As you learned earlier in this chapter, previsualization can be used to determine the composition of the shot before you arrive on-set, saving valuable time and money by anticipating the setups needed and the best order in which to achieve them. Referencing the previsualization stage will also serve as a way to take into account the visual effects that will be added later, and ensure that the composition on-set accommodates them. However, it is not a substitute for you, as the director, to look through the camera viewfinder on set to make sure the DP is capturing the composition you want.

What Is Good Composition?

There are two answers to this question, one of which can override the other if creative needs require it. The first answer is that a well-composed shot includes well-balanced visual elements and appropriate lighting and color, and occurs when framing, blocking (movement of actors), lens, focus, and movement of the camera all work together in a perfect whole. The second answer is that a good shot can actually be anything, so long as it best tells the story at that particular moment in the film. So, as with other so-called filmmaking rules or principles, the basics of good composition can be altered or skewed if you have a strong enough, story-driven reason for doing so. Most often, though, following the principles of good composition will help your story, so you need to understand and appreciate them in order to properly comprehend when to follow them exactly and when to alter them for well-thought-out creative reasons.

Good composition, then, does have core aesthetic principles—principles that go far back in the history of painting and visual art. Note also that there is a natural connection between many of these principles and some of the fundamentals of production design that you learned about earlier. After all, to compose an orderly image, you need to account for the elements within it individually and collectively. Also, it often takes no more time or money to compose a shot well than it does to shoot haphazardly, with no regard for visual aesthetics. Therefore, one way to make class projects and low-budget movies look superior is to pay attention to these 10 elements of good composition:

1. **Observe the rule of thirds.** Imagine your frame is divided into thirds along both the *x*- and *y*-axes; your subject should be on one of the lines. In a close-up, the eyes should be on the upper horizontal line. The **rule of thirds** will give all of your images a sense of visual balance, because our eyes naturally look first to the upper middle third of the film frame, and then look around to see the rest of the image.

Figure 4-28. A well-composed shot from ***Inception*** (2010) showing the rule of thirds in action.

2. **Give the right amount of headroom. Headroom** is how close the top of the frame is to the actors' heads. A shot will have a lot or a little headroom and will generally (but not always) stay consistent for all actors in a scene. Headroom can convey a lot about a character. When you give characters the right amount of headroom, they will seem to inhabit the scene comfortably; if you purposely give them little headroom, you're suggesting that they are uncomfortable in the scene, and you can use this composition technique for dramatic effect. Although a comedy will usually have more headroom than a drama, there are no hard and fast rules.

3. **Provide negative space.** Frame ahead of your character so that there is **negative space** (space that is not filled) where the character's eyes are looking (this is called giving the character **eye room**, or **look room**), or where the character is walking (this is called giving the character **lead room**). Negative space is important because it allows you to direct the audience's gaze to what's most significant in each shot. In the shot from *The King's Speech*, the audience is naturally directed to King George VI's face; the shot is also artistically composed and looks far more interesting than if his face were dead center in the frame.

Figure 4-29. Just the right amount of headroom in ***Vertigo*** (1958).

Figure 4-30. ***The King's Speech*** (2010).

4. **Use mass and color to your advantage.** The audience's eye will be drawn to a massive object—one that takes up a disproportionate amount of screen space—and an object that's strongly colored. This is sometimes called the Hitchcock Rule, after legendary director Alfred Hitchcock, who framed his shots so that the size of a person or an object in the frame was proportional to its importance at that moment in the story. In a classic shot from *North by Northwest* (1959), the plane is less important than the main character, who is in danger.

Figure 4-31. ***North by Northwest*** (1959).

Figure 4-32. ***The Artist*** (2011).

In the example from *The Artist* (2011), the actor in the foreground attracts attention because of his size, and his mass is balanced with negative space in the rest of the frame. In the example from *Black Swan* (2010), the white dress with pink-hued lighting contrasts with the rest of the frame and focuses the audience on the dancer. Wise costumers choose colors to highlight important characters and important moments (see Chapter 4).

Figure 4-33. ***Black Swan*** (2010).

5. **Avoid center punching** (putting the important subjects directly in the center of the frame), to create a more interesting look. Instead, place the subjects toward the edges of the frame. This is called *weighting* (or *justifying*) the frame to the left or right, and it is a matter of storytelling and personal taste; symmetrical frames are generally less exciting than unsymmetrical frames. That said, there are exceptions that would call for center punching the subject—for example, if you want to emphasize ideas of symmetry and balance.

6. **Decide on foreground elements**—any objects that are positioned between the camera and the main subject of the shot. Although foreground elements can refer to an actor, as in an over-the-shoulder shot, they more commonly take the form of some object or piece of set dressing, such as a window frame or a chain-link fence. The foreground object is generally out of focus, but it can be manipulated through the use of a zoom.

Figure 4-34. ***Hugo*** (2011).

7. **Play the diagonals.** Imagine each shot as a series of lines. Diagonal compositions are more dynamic than flat ones, and they help direct the audience's gaze where you want it to go.

8. **Angle the camera sparingly and always on purpose.** The audience expects the frame of the camera to be level with the ground. If you use a tilted angle, or Dutch angle, tilt the angle approximately 10 to 20 degrees.
9. **Keep composition consistent all the way to the end of the scene.** If the actors are moving and the camera is moving with them, keep the same amount of lead room. If the actors' blocking repositions them during the shot, make sure the shot stays well balanced at both the beginning and the end of their movements. Akira Kurosawa's *High and Low* (1963) is one of the best-composed movies ever. When you watch the film, you will see how the blocking is so carefully staged that no matter how the actors or the camera moves, each shot stays perfectly composed.

Figure 4-35. *High and Low* (1963).

Producer **SMARTS**

Composition Outside the Frame

You've just learned about what you can see inside the frame, but what about what you can't see? A good producer will know how to guide the director and cinematographer to leave some things out of the picture.

Producers generally keep some actions out of the frame for three reasons:

1. It's cheaper. If you only *hear* violence rather than see it, you won't have to make expensive prosthetics and have wardrobe prepare multiple changes of bloody clothes. If you see the train station but only hear the train pulling in, you won't have to find a train.
2. It broadens the audience. On-screen graphic violence and sexuality can be off-putting to some audiences, or it can push a movie to a more restrictive rating. To keep the possibility of a PG or PG-13 rating, instead of an R rating, a producer should always make sure to get shots in which graphic action takes place outside the frame.
3. It's more effective. The imagination is a powerful tool; it's often more compelling to imagine something than to witness it. For example,

you're watching a battle scene: if you see the hero thrust her spear at an opponent who's off-screen, and you *hear* the sickening squish of metal entering flesh, you'll know what happened; your imagination will make it just as violent as you want it to be. Similarly, have you ever noticed that scary movies become scarier when you are seeing the characters in close-up? That's because you can't see what's outside the frame, surrounding them, where the monster may be lurking. What you *think* might be there is scarier than what you see! Hitchcock, of course, was the master of this methodology. Another classic example, indirectly inspired by Hitchcock, is *Jaws* (1975). In the first shark attack you never see the shark, just the terror of its victim. In fact you don't see the entire shark until almost two-thirds of the way into the film. (Of course, director Stephen Spielberg reverted to this approach in part because of technical difficulties he encountered with his mechanical shark, which limited its capabilities, but he has told interviewers over the years that this was a serendipitous problem, because it made the frightful nature of the movie better when he was forced to veer off into a Hitchcockian direction.)

10. **Keep distractions out of the frame.** The exception to this rule is if you want the audience to notice something a character is not aware of (see Producer Smarts: "Composition Outside the Frame").

You won't be required to observe all of these principles in every shot. In fact, almost every movie will use or break each of the rules of good composition at least once. You can also apply these principles to the difference between shooting people and shooting objects (see Action Steps: "Shooting People and Objects").

Action STEPS

Shooting People and Objects

Shooting people is different from shooting things. Most of the time, objects don't move, and they are not the main characters in a story, whereas people generally move and drive the action forward. Because of this difference, you need to be specific about placement and eyelines.

1. **Placement.** It is usually boring to place an actor in the dead center of the frame. Asymmetrical framing—balancing the actor's form with negative space on the other side of the frame—is more appealing. When you do place an actor dead center, it conveys primacy and prominence; this may be combined with a low angle, making the actor appear more powerful and heightening the effect. You can follow the same rule with objects, except that you can place objects at the center of the frame more frequently, especially for cutaways and inserts (see p. 245).
2. **Eyelines.** As previously mentioned, you'll typically shoot actors from eye level or close to eye level—some directors find that exact eye level is too directly challenging for the audience, and in most cases, you get

the best view of the actor's eyes shooting just below them. On the other hand, objects are customarily shot from the eyeline of the actors in the scene.

Composition in the Moving Frame

More often than not, your camera will be in motion—smaller motions as characters engage with one another, and larger motions to cover actions and more complicated scenes. As the camera moves, the framing of the scene moves with it; a good cinematographer will pay attention to composition all the way through every camera move and usually do a rehearsal of the move first.

There are many tools that allow cameras to move—dollies, cranes, Steadicams, and anything with wheels on which a camera can be mounted. Now you will learn to use these camera movement tools for storytelling. Camera moves and setups enhance narrative flow and character development and help convey feelings to the audience. Sometimes, when a camera moves fast alongside action, it creates a sense of speed and power. At other times, when the camera gently comes close to a character's face, the audience might think the character suddenly understands something. In yet another instance, if the camera swoops away or moves higher, expanding the frame wider to give a view of the entire scene, the audience gains a sense of greater perspective.

Use Converging Lines

Use converging lines to make your shots more dynamic. The classic converging-lines shot features railroad tracks disappearing into the distance. A wide-angle lens will emphasize converging lines.

Because camera movements can occur at any speed, they are inextricably linked to *time*. A fast move creates a sense of quickening or an exciting pace, whereas a slow move may enhance suspense; alternately, the move may be so slow and subtle that the audience only perceives it through an unconscious emotional response.

Following are the six most important camera movements, and their visual language meaning for character and plot:

- **Pan.** A **pan** moves the frame on the horizontal axis—from right to left, or left to right. It is useful for following action, for tracking a character that is moving from place to place, and for revealing an important piece of visual information. Mount the camera on a tripod to accomplish a pan.
- **Tilt.** A **tilt** moves the frame along the vertical axis—up or down. You can use a tilt to follow the action from the foreground to the background, or vice versa, or to let the audience notice something significant. Mount the camera on a tripod to accomplish a tilt.
- **Tracking shot.** A tracking shot moves with the characters or the action. Often you'll position the camera ahead of the characters as they walk or run, moving at the same pace and always staying a consistent distance from the characters. Tracking shots should feel effortless; typically the audience won't be aware that the camera is moving because they're focusing on the actors' movements. You can do a tracking shot with or

without actual camera track equipment. You can track actors with a handheld camera or a Steadicam. If you use a camera track and mount the camera on a dolly, the shot can also be called a **dolly shot**.

- **Push in** or **pull out.** These shots move along the depth axis, and they can be accomplished with a dolly and track, a handheld camera, or a Steadicam. A *push in* moves the frame toward the character's face, giving the sense that the character suddenly understands something or is about to take some kind of action. A push in to an object emphasizes the object's importance. A *pull out* creates anticipation that the character is about to do something important, with the frame widening so that the action can take place.

Pan Before Zooming

When combining a pan or tilt with a zoom, start the pan or tilt a fraction of a second before you start the zoom for a more professional look.

- **Zoom.** A zoom pushes in or pulls out along the depth axis, and moves the frame without moving the camera. That's because a zoom is accomplished with a special zoom lens. Due to its special nature, a zoom is able to travel much farther along the z-axis than a camera can move without a zoom lens. Keep in mind there is a crucial storytelling difference between a dolly shot pushing in and a zoom zooming in. A dolly push-in changes the perspective and size relationship between the main actor and the surroundings; a zoom-in does not.
- **Crane.** A *crane shot* uses a crane to move the camera from a high angle to a low angle, or from a low angle to a high angle. If you start at a high angle and then move down into the scene, you set the stage for the action. This shot is often used at the beginning of movies or sequences. If you start at eye level and then move up to a high angle, you convey perspective and completion; this shot is often used at the end of sequences, or as the final shot of a film.

Keep the Horizon Low

Don't let the horizon cut though the actors' heads. Generally, the horizon line should fall at the actors' shoulders or below.

To make the best use of your camera moves, follow these two important steps:

1. Begin with a static frame for a few seconds, perform the camera move, and then end on a static frame, which you should also hold for a few seconds. In editing, you can always cut into or out of the shot while the camera is in motion, but a well-framed, stationary image at the beginning and end of each shot will give you much more flexibility in the editing room (see "Creating Images for Continuity").
2. Begin each camera move from a less comfortable position, and move toward a more comfortable position. This creates a sense of story progression and emotional drive. For example, you may begin the shot on a car door (uncomfortable because of the camera angle and because it doesn't reveal much information), then move up to include the driver coming out of the car (comfortable because the actor is well framed and the

camera move reveals who has been driving the car). In another example, the shot would begin with an open door (uncomfortable because of the suspenseful angle), and then move into the room to discover a writer sitting at her desk (comfortable because we now know who is in the room).

Composition and Lenses

The choice of lens is fundamental to how each shot is composed. Because different lenses will allow you to show more or less of a scene and will place actors in greater or lesser context with their surroundings, you should stick to the following sequence:

1. Set up your preliminary camera position.
2. Select the lens that best conveys the story point or emotion of the scene.
3. Compose the shot by shifting actors and background objects, or by adjusting the camera position to achieve the visual balance you're looking for.
4. In almost all cases, bring the camera to the actor (or the action), instead of bringing the actor to the camera—this feels more cinematic and exciting.

Just as focal length affects composition, so do depth of field and focus choices. When choosing between deep or shallow depth of field, make sure the image is well balanced; obviously, in deep-field focus, you must take into account the balance of the entire scene. In the image from *The Wizard of Oz* (1939), for example, Dorothy is in focus while the rest of the scene is not; the shot is composed so Dorothy has obvious prominence.

Figure 4-36. *The Wizard of Oz* (1939).

Racking focus can also be used to define your composition and to change the audience's attention, revealing new insights or showing something the audience had not noticed before. To accomplish a shot like this, you would use a tape measure to make sure you turn the focus dial accurately to each point that needs to be in focus. On a professional production, this is the focus puller's job. (See Action Steps: "Low-Budget Hacks to Make Your Student Film Look High Budget".)

Action STEPS

Low-Budget Hacks to Make Your Student Film Look High Budget

No money? No problem. With a little resourcefulness and little or no money, you can use these tricks to make your shots look high end.

1. Use a director's viewfinder—an inexpensive handheld zoom lens you can look through—to help visualize the composition.

2. Put a carpenter's level on top of your camera to make sure it is framed straight.

3. Mount small cameras (often called lipstick cameras because they are about as big as a tube of lipstick) on different rigs—a rig is anything you can attach the camera to, such as a broom handle or a helmet. *Actioncams* (such as the GoPro) are designed just for this purpose; some even feature Wi-Fi, so you can monitor the shot on your mobile device.

Practice

Studying Composition

Choose three still frames from any movie or video (a film, a television episode, or a YouTube video), and analyze them according to the principles of good composition you have just learned. Are they well composed? poorly composed? Explain why. If you would like to study some examples of well-composed films, try these: *Citizen Kane* (1941), *Singin' in the Rain* (1952), *Lawrence of Arabia* (1962), *High and Low* (1963), *The Godfather* (1972), *Mother* (2009), and *Winter's Bone* (2010).

Creating Images for Continuity

When the audience watches a scene, it feels as though everything is happening chronologically—the long shot establishes the scene, the medium shots allow them to see the action more clearly, and the cuts back and forth between the actors let them learn more. Of course, in reality, each shot has been carefully set up and shot at different times, sometimes even on different days or at different locations. The process of making every shot in a scene match in time and action is called maintaining **continuity**, and you need to take this into account as you plan your setups so that the editor can cut the scene properly to achieve seamless continuity in your end product.

To make sure your film has continuity, you will want to verify that the lighting matches the master shot—this is crucial, especially when you are shooting outdoors and the sun shifts or the clouds change the light, or if the story sequence involves visual effects. In addition, every time you set up a shot or move the camera, you and the director should consider how the film will be edited. Ask yourself the following:

- Do I need this shot to tell the story?
- Do I have all the coverage I'll need—all the bits and pieces, such as close-ups, reaction shots, and inserts?
- Have I shot enough coverage that the editor will have options in the editing room?
- Or do I want to purposely limit the editor's choices by limiting the coverage?

Deciding how to shoot each scene is the most important day-to-day collaboration between the cinematographer and the director, and in the best films, this relationship is a close, creative marriage. With this relationship in mind, let's learn the classic way to shoot a scene and make sure that your images will cut together properly.

How to Shoot a Scene

There are many ways to shoot a scene. What follows are basic steps for what we might call "classic coverage"—a shooting style that developed in Hollywood decades ago and is still used today because it is practical and efficient, and keeps continuity in mind. Of course, different directors have different approaches, and some choose to break from the classic coverage paradigm; this is fine, as long as the approach you take works for your story.

1. Start with the master shot, which should be a wide shot covering the entire scene, with all of the actors in the scene, and covering all the dialogue and blocking. By definition, a master shot has built-in continuity—because there are no cuts, the action is continuous. Once you have shot your master, your job is to match all action to it. On a professional production, the script supervisor takes careful note of everything that has previously been established to avoid matching or continuity errors. In addition, having your master "in the can" means that you may be able to be cost efficient with your other shots (see Business Smarts: "How Many Shots Do You Need?").
2. Now shoot group shots (two shots and three shots), followed by close-ups, over-the-shoulders, POVs, and reaction shots. Vary the size and angle of each set of shots; this makes your film look more interesting and makes it easier to cut together.
3. As you shoot the closer shots, make sure the action overlaps so that you'll have flexibility in cutting. It is better to leave the camera running on an actor's close-up for the entire scene, even if he or she has only one line; by doing so, you are getting reaction shots and the dialogue shot at the same time, and it will all be in continuity.
4. Avoid brief shots. They take a long time to set up and are difficult to integrate editorially.
5. Always shoot pieces for inserts and cutaways, as well as additional shots of the set from different angles without the cast, to give the visual effects department additional flexibility, when feasible. As you'll recall, inserts are close-ups of important story elements, often taken from the POV of a character—for example, a close-up on a cell-phone screen as someone is reading a text message. Cutaways are shots the editor can liter-

ally cut away to in order to modulate the pace of a scene. For example, good cutaways might be close-ups of food being prepared for dinner, such as the stew simmering on the stove. Hand gestures also make excellent cutaways.

6. When shooting pans, tilts, and zooms of objects, begin with a static shot, do the camera move, and end with a static shot. Without cutting, reverse directions (for example, if you started panning left-to-right, now pan right-to-left), and still without cutting, do the move both slower and faster. This will give the editor maximum flexibility.

Keep Your Editor Close

If possible, have the editor on-set with you when you're shooting key scenes, or at least consult with her or him (if you are not the editor). That way, there will be another perspective to help make sure you get enough coverage to cut the scene together. If you are shooting digitally, the editor can also sometimes do a quick assembly of the scene to make sure there is sufficient coverage.

Don't Cross the Line!

Whenever you shoot a scene, there is an imaginary line that separates the camera and the action. As long as you know where that line is and you stay on your side of it, all the shots will be in continuity because they will have the same screen direction: the actors will maintain the same right-to-left relationship. If you go on the other side of the line, right and left directions will be swapped, and the shots won't cut together any more. This is known as "crossing the line," and the principle is called the **180-degree rule**.

The 180-degree rule sounds confusing, but it is relatively simple in practice. In Figure 4-37, you can see the imaginary line, with actors on one side and the camera on the other. Every camera position on this side of the line will be fine. If the camera operator crosses the line, the shots will be out of continuity.

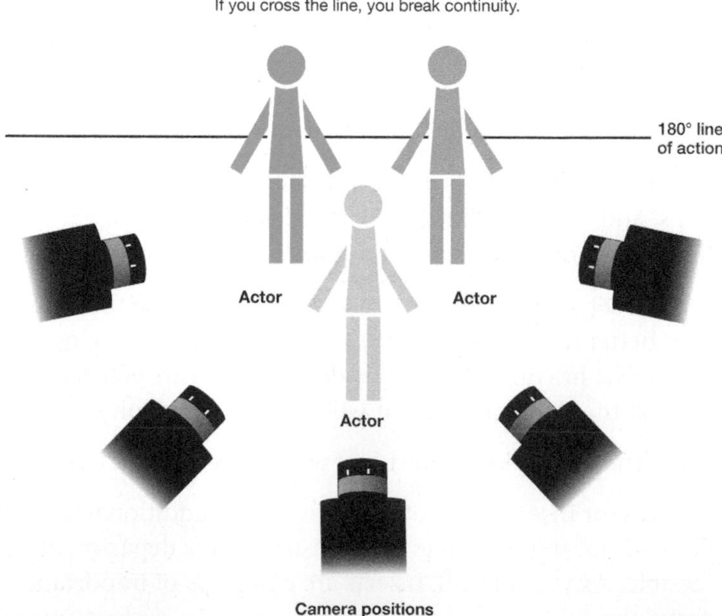

Figure 4-37. The 180-degree line separating the actors and the camera

Eyelines, Visual Effects, and Animation

Sometimes you'll make a movie with visual effects and animation. The visual effect may be a view out a window—a window that's painted green on the set; the animation may be a digital character interacting with the actors. In either case, when you're shooting real actors who appear to be relating to elements that are not really there, you must be scrupulous about keeping your eyelines correct. If you don't, the scene won't work when you get to the editing room because the shots won't match, and the continuity of the scene will be broken.

Virtual Cinematography Is Like Real Cinematography

Everything in this chapter applies to virtual cinematography as well. Virtual cinematography is generally employed in animated films or in visual effects sequences for which most, if not all, of the elements are created in the computer. Camera moves and recomposition are done after completion of shooting, as a result of the editing process.

This process requires careful planning and is one of the reasons we emphasize that post-production actually begins *before* preproduction in well-produced movies. By the time you start shooting your actors performing on set, you need to know, for instance, where the horizon line will be in the window example, or how tall the mouse will be in the case of *Stuart Little* (1999), a technically pioneering film that was among the first to seamlessly introduce an animated character to the live-action world, where he interacted throughout the story with real actors.

James Keivom/NY Daily News Archive/Getty Images

Figure 4-38. Where's Stuart? In this scene from *Stuart Little* (1999), Geena Davis appears to share the frame with Stuart, even though the mouse was a visual effect and was obviously not there when the scene was shot. The visual effects crew, working in collaboration with the camera department, had to make sure the actor's eyeline would be correct, and so they developed two solutions: one high tech, one low tech. In the high-tech solution, the director used a laser pointer synchronized to the camera's shutter to indicate where Stuart would be. The cast learned to "love the dot" since that was their primary frame of reference on set for imagining where Stuart would be. A low-tech solution was to take a stuffed mouse toy about Stuart's size and place him on the end of a stick. A crew member moved the stick and the actors focused on the puppet mouse. The device was affectionately known as "Rod Stuart"!

Practice

Reverse-Engineering How to Cover a Scene

Pick a movie scene that's at least two minutes long. Pretend you are the cinematographer. Make note of each shot (these are the setups you will need to cover the scene). See if you can design how you would set up each shot to replicate what's in the scene.

Business SMARTS

How Many Shots Do You Need?

Every time you set up a shot it takes time—and time is always short on a movie set. There is constant tension between getting every possible shot and getting just enough to finish the scene and move on to the next one. Therefore, every shot is both a creative decision and a business decision.

The number and kinds of shots must be planned for, long before you get to the set—shot planning needs to be part of the budgeting process. The director of photography should have a thorough discussion with the director about what kind of coverage the film needs. Then, the director of photography can make a list of the necessary equipment (cameras and lenses, plus the ways to support and move the camera). If possible, it is generally a good idea to include a bit more equipment than is absolutely necessary, in the event something breaks or someone has a brilliant idea and needs additional tools. In fact, if you have a particularly complicated shot or one that will be nearly impossible to do twice, the director and director of photography will plan for that shot to be done with multiple cameras, if feasible. Each camera will be assigned to cover a different shot type.

During the shooting period, you will work with the director and the first AD to determine the best shooting order of scenes in a given day. It is often good business to get the most important shot first—so you'll know that you have it—and then move down the shot list in priority order. You also have to pick which scenes need the most shots and which ones can be less complicated, to keep your budget and time spent reasonable. For example, a fight scene may require a lot of shots and will therefore take more time to shoot and require more equipment—the close-ups on punches, inserts on bloody noses, and *POV shots* (see p. 232) are all important for the pacing of the scene. A simple "walk and talk" scene that could be covered in one *tracking shot* (see p. 241), may be fast or slow to accomplish, depending on the amount of rehearsal required and the intricacy of camera moves.

Cinematographer's Emergency Kit

- A reference book of imagery that can inspire the look of the film. Images can be from other movies, photographs, graphics, or paintings. When you're not sure how to capture a scene, go back to your image collection for inspiration.
- The editor's cell-phone number, so you can make sure you're getting the coverage you need.
- Your own list of the specific lenses, apertures, light meter readings, and angles you have used to cover a scene, in case you need to go back and do reshoots.

Chapter Essentials

- Every film finds its own visual language to convey character, story, and emotion. Mastering basic shots is essential for understanding filmmaking grammar and telling stories well.
- The camera can be positioned at different angles, with each angle revealing different information and helping to progress the story in a unique way.
- Good shots are aesthetically pleasing because they are well composed. You must take shot composition into account when your camera is stationary and when it is in motion.
- When you're capturing images, you are striving for photographic continuity, and you must provide options for editing. Therefore, get plenty of coverage, and grab inserts and cutaways.

Section 2

Journalism

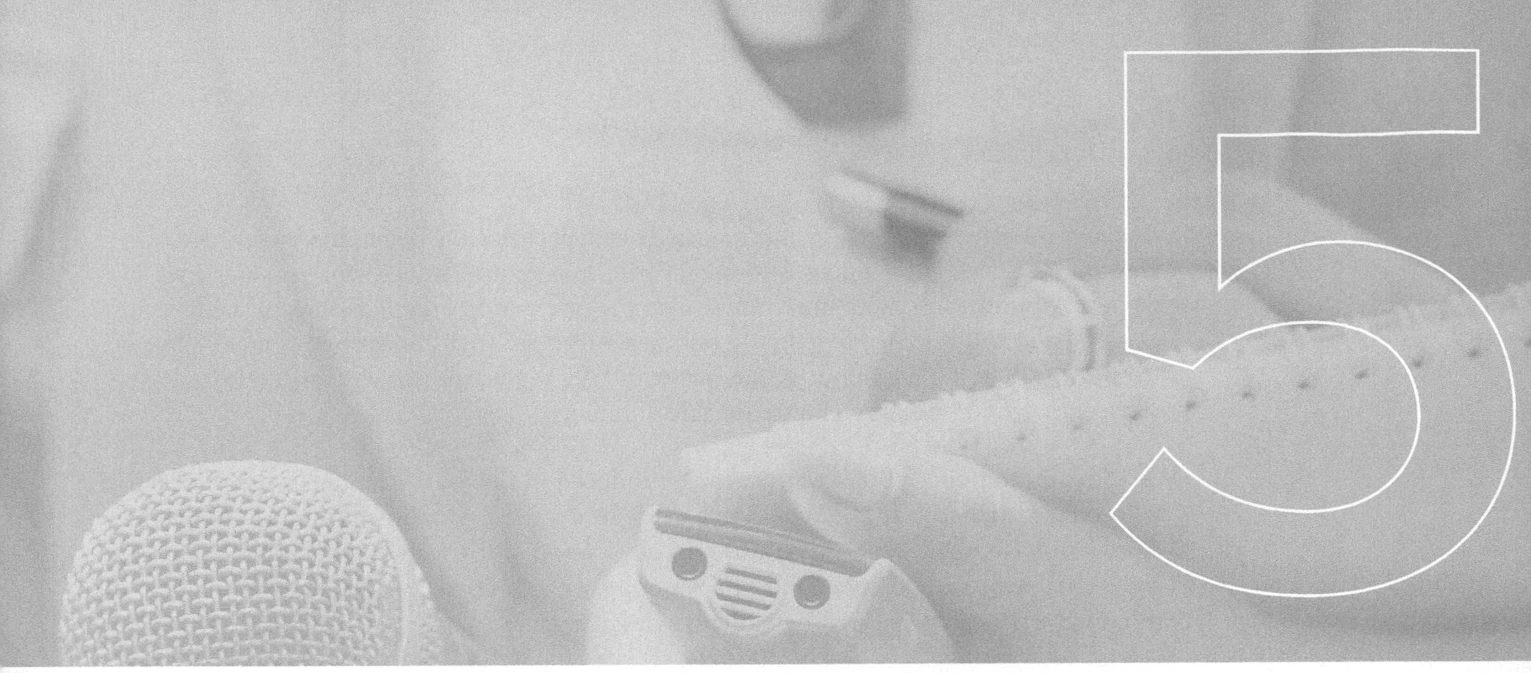

Chapter 5

Basics of Journalism

A History of Communication

"A History of Communication" from *Media & Culture,* Tenth Edition, 2016 update by Richard Campbell, Christopher R. Martin, and Bettina Fabos, pp. 344–348 (Chapter 10), 271–276 (Chapter 8), 311–319 (Chapter 9).

The History of Books, from Papyrus to Paperbacks

Before books, or writing in general, oral cultures passed on information and values through the wisdom and memories of a community's elders or tribal storytellers. Sometimes these rich traditions were lost. Print culture and the book, however, gave future generations different and often more enduring records of authors' words.

Ever since the ancient Babylonians and Egyptians began experimenting with alphabets some five thousand years ago, people have found ways to preserve their written symbols. These first alphabets mark the development stage for books. Initially, pictorial symbols and letters were drawn on wood strips or pressed with a stylus into clay tablets, and tied or stacked together to form the first "books." As early as 2400 BCE, the Egyptians wrote on **papyrus** (from which the word *paper* is derived), made from plant reeds found along the Nile River. They rolled these writings into scrolls, much as builders do today with blueprints. This method was adopted by the Greeks in 650 BCE and by the Romans (who imported papyrus from Egypt) in 300 BCE. Gradually, **parchment**—treated animal skin—replaced papyrus in Europe. Parchment was stronger, smoother, more durable, and less expensive because it did not have to be imported from Egypt.

At about the same time the Egyptians started using papyrus, the Babylonians recorded business transactions, government records, favorite stories, and local history on small tablets of clay. Around 1000 BCE, the Chinese also began creating booklike objects, using strips of wood and bamboo tied together in bundles. Although the Chinese began making paper from cotton and linen around 105 CE, paper did not replace parchment in Europe until the thirteenth century because of questionable durability.

The first protomodern book was probably produced in the fourth century by the Romans, who created the **codex**, a type of book made of sheets of parchment and sewn together along the edge, then bound with thin pieces of wood and covered with leather. Whereas scrolls had to be wound, unwound, and rewound, a codex could be opened to any page, and its configuration allowed writing on both sides of a page.

The Development of Manuscript Culture

During the Middle Ages (400–1500 CE), the Christian clergy strongly influenced what is known as **manuscript culture**, a period in which books were painstakingly lettered, decorated, and bound by hand. This period also marks the entrepreneurial stage in the evolution of books. During this time, priests and monks advanced the art of bookmaking; in many ways, they may be considered the earliest professional editors. Known as *scribes*, they transcribed most of the existing philosophical tracts and religious texts of the period, especially versions of the Bible. Through tedious and painstaking work, scribes became the chief caretakers of recorded history and culture, promoting ideas they favored and censoring ideas that were out of line with contemporary Christian thought.

Many books from the Middle Ages were **illuminated manuscripts**. Often made for churches or wealthy clients, these books featured decorative, colorful designs and illustrations on each page. Their covers were made from leather, and some were embedded with precious gems or trimmed with gold and silver. During this period, scribes developed rules of punctuation, making distinctions between small and capital letters and placing space between words to make reading easier. (Older Roman writing used all capital letters, and the words ran together on a page, making reading a torturous experience.) Hundreds of illuminated manuscripts still survive today in the rare-book collections of museums and libraries.

The Innovations of Block Printing and Movable Type

While the work of the scribes in the Middle Ages led to advances in written language and the design of books, it did not lead to the mass proliferation of books, simply because each manuscript had to be painstakingly created one copy at a time. To make mechanically produced copies of pages, Chinese printers developed **block printing**—a technique in which sheets of paper were applied to blocks of inked wood with raised surfaces depicting hand-carved letters and illustrations—as early as the third century. This constituted the basic technique used in printing newspapers, magazines, and books throughout much of modern history. Although hand-carving each block, or "page," was time consuming, this printing breakthrough enabled multiple copies to be printed and then bound together. The oldest dated printed book still in existence is China's *Diamond Sutra* by Wang Chieh, from 868

CE. It consists of seven sheets pasted together and rolled up in a scroll. In 1295, explorer Marco Polo introduced these techniques to Europe after his excursion to China. The first block-printed books appeared in Europe during the fifteenth century, and demand for them began to grow among the literate middle-class populace emerging in large European cities.

The next step in printing was the radical development of movable type, first invented in China around the year 1000. Movable type featured individual characters made from reusable pieces of wood or metal, rather than entire hand-carved pages. Printers arranged the characters into various word combinations, greatly speeding up the time it took to create block pages. This process, also used in Korea as early as the thirteenth century, developed independently in Europe in the fifteenth century.

The Gutenberg Revolution: The Invention of the Printing Press

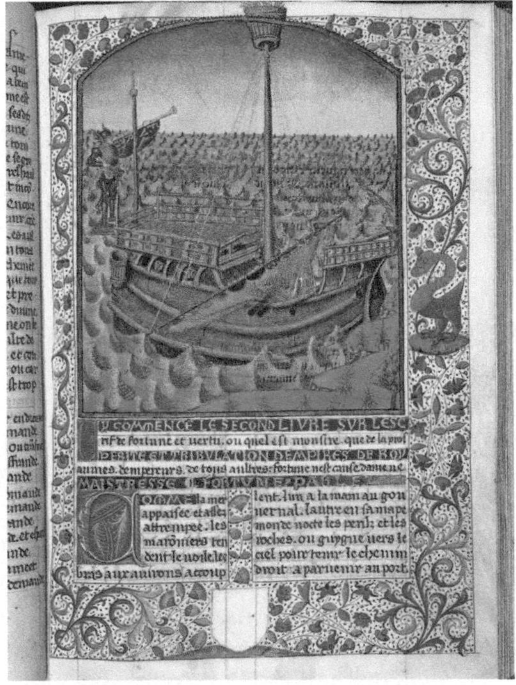

Erich Lessing/Art Resource, NY

Figure 5-1. Illuminated Manuscripts were handwritten by scribes and illustrated with colorful and decorative images and designs.

A great leap forward in printing was developed by Johannes Gutenberg. In Germany, between 1453 and 1456, Gutenberg used the principles of movable type to develop a mechanical **printing press**, which he adapted from the design of wine presses. Gutenberg's staff of printers produced the first so-called modern books, including two hundred copies of a Latin Bible, twenty-one copies of which still exist. The Gutenberg Bible (as it's now known) required six presses, many printers, and several months to produce. It was printed on a fine calfskin-based parchment called vellum. The pages were hand-decorated, and the use of woodcuts made illustrations possible. Gutenberg and his printing assistants had not only found a way to make books a mass medium but also formed the prototype for all mass production.

Printing presses spread rapidly across Europe in the late fifteenth and early sixteenth centuries. Chaucer's *Canterbury Tales* became the first English work to be printed in book form. Many early books were large, elaborate, and expensive, taking months to illustrate and publish. They were usually purchased by aristocrats, royal families, religious leaders, and ruling politicians. Printers, however, gradually reduced the size of books and developed less expensive grades of paper, making books cheaper so that more people could afford them.

The social and cultural transformations ushered in by the spread of printing presses and books cannot be overestimated. As historian Elizabeth Eisenstein has noted, when people could learn for themselves by using maps, dictionaries, Bibles, and the writings of others, they could differentiate themselves as individuals; their social identities were no longer solely dependent on what their leaders told them or on the habits of their families, communities, or social class. The technology of printing presses permitted information and knowledge to spread outside local jurisdictions. Gradually, individuals had access to ideas far beyond their isolated experiences, and this permitted them to challenge the traditional wisdom and customs of their tribes and leaders.[1]

The Birth of Publishing in the United States

In colonial America, English locksmith Stephen Daye set up a print shop in the late 1630s in Cambridge, Massachusetts. In 1640, Daye and his son Matthew printed the first colonial book, *The Whole Booke of Psalms* (known today as *The Bay Psalm Book*), marking the beginning of book publishing in the colonies. This collection of biblical psalms quickly sold out its first printing of 1,750 copies, even though fewer than 3,500 families lived in the colonies at the time. By the mid-1760s, all thirteen colonies had printing shops.

In 1744, Benjamin Franklin, who had worked in printing shops, imported Samuel Richardson's *Pamela; or, Virtue Rewarded* (1740) from Britain, the first novel reprinted and sold in colonial America. Both Pamela and Richardson's second novel, *Clarissa; or, The History of a Young Lady* (1747), connected with the newly emerging and literate middle classes—especially women, who were just starting to gain a social identity as individuals apart from their fathers, husbands, and employers. Richardson's novels portrayed women in subordinate roles; however, they also depicted women triumphing over tragedy, so he is credited as one of the first popular writers to take the domestic life of women seriously.

By the early nineteenth century, the demand for books was growing. To meet this demand, the cost of producing books needed to be reduced. By the 1830s, machine-made paper replaced more expensive handmade varieties, cloth covers supplanted more expensive leather ones, and **paperback books** with cheaper paper covers (introduced from Europe) helped make books more accessible to the masses. Further reducing the cost of books, Erastus and Irwin Beadle introduced paperback **dime novels** (so called because they sold for five or ten cents) in 1860. Ann Stephens authored the first dime novel, *Malaeska: The Indian Wife of the White Hunter*, a reprint of a serialized story Stephens wrote in 1839 for the *Ladies' Companion* magazine.[2] By 1870, dime novels had sold seven million copies. By 1885, one-third of all books published in the United States were popular paperbacks and dime novels, sometimes identified as **pulp fiction**—a reference to the cheap, machine-made pulp paper they were printed on.

In addition, the printing process became quicker and more mechanized. In the 1880s, the introduction of **linotype** machines enabled printers to save time by setting type mechanically using a typewriter-style keyboard, while the introduction of steam-powered and high-speed rotary presses permitted the production of more books at lower costs. In the early 1900s, the development of **offset lithography** allowed books to be printed from photographic plates rather than from metal casts, greatly reducing the cost of color and illustrations and accelerating book production. With these developments, books disseminated further, preserving culture and knowledge and supporting a vibrant publishing industry.

The New York Public Library/Art Resource, NY

Figure 5-2. Pulp Fiction The weekly paperback series *Tip Top Weekly*, which was published between 1896 and 1912, featured stories of the most popular dime novel hero of the day, the fictional Yale football star and heroic adventurer Frank Merriwell. This issue, from 1901, follows Frank's exploits in the wilds of the Florida Everglades.

The Evolution of American Newspapers

The idea of news is as old as language itself. The earliest news was passed along orally from family to family, from tribe to tribe, by community leaders and oral historians. The earliest known written news account, or news sheet, *Acta Diurna* (Latin for "daily events"), was developed by Julius Caesar and posted in public spaces and on buildings in Rome in 59 BCE. Even in its oral and early written stages, news informed people on the state of their relations with neighboring tribes and towns. The development of the printing press in the fifteenth century greatly accelerated a society's ability to send and receive information. Throughout history, news has satisfied our need to know things we cannot experience personally. Newspapers today continue to document daily life and bear witness to both ordinary and extraordinary events.

Colonial Newspapers and the Partisan Press

The novelty and entrepreneurial stages of print media development first happened in Europe with the rise of the printing press. In North America, the first newspaper, *Publick Occurrences, Both Foreign and Domestick*, was published on September 25, 1690, by Boston printer Benjamin Harris. The colonial government objected to Harris's negative tone regarding British rule, and local ministers were offended by his published report that the king of France had an affair with his son's wife. The newspaper was banned after one issue.

In 1704, the first regularly published newspaper appeared in the American colonies—the *Boston News-Letter*, published by John Campbell. Because European news took weeks to travel by ship, these early colonial papers were not very timely. In their more spirited sections, however, the papers did report local illnesses, public floggings, and even suicides. In 1721, also in Boston, James Franklin, the older brother of Benjamin Franklin, started the *New England Courant*. The *Courant* established a tradition of running stories that interested ordinary readers rather than printing articles that appealed primarily to business and colonial leaders. In 1729, Benjamin Franklin, at age twenty-four, took over the *Pennsylvania Gazette* and created, according to historians, the best of the colonial papers. Although a number of colonial papers operated solely on subsidies from political parties, the *Gazette* also made money by advertising products.

Another important colonial paper, the *New-York Weekly Journal*, appeared in 1733. John Peter Zenger had been installed as the printer of the *Journal* by the Popular Party, a political group that opposed British rule and ran articles that criticized the royal governor of New York. After a Popular Party judge was dismissed from office, the *Journal* escalated its attack on the governor. When Zenger shielded the writers of the critical articles, he was arrested in 1734 for *seditious libel*—defaming a public official's character in print. Championed by famed Philadelphia lawyer Andrew Hamilton, Zenger ultimately won his case in 1735. A sympathetic jury, in revolt against the colonial government, decided that newspapers had the right to criticize government leaders as long as the reports were true. After the Zenger case, the British never prosecuted another colonial printer. The Zenger decision would later provide a key foundation—the right of a democratic press to criticize public officials—for the First Amendment to the Constitution, adopted as part of the Bill of Rights in 1791.

By 1765, about thirty newspapers operated in the American colonies, with the first daily paper beginning in 1784. Newspapers were of two general types: political or commercial. Their development was shaped in large part by social, cultural, and political responses to British rule and by its eventual overthrow. The gradual rise of political parties and the spread of commerce also influenced the development of early papers. Although the political and commercial papers carried both party news and business news, they had different agendas. Political papers, known as the **partisan press**, generally pushed the plan of the particular political group that subsidized the paper. The *commercial press*, by contrast, served business leaders, who were interested in economic issues. Both types of journalism left a legacy. The partisan press gave us the editorial pages, while the early commercial press was the forerunner of the business section.

In the eighteenth and early nineteenth centuries, even the largest of these papers rarely reached a circulation of fifteen hundred. Readership was primarily confined to educated or wealthy men who controlled local politics and commerce. During this time, though, a few pioneering women operated newspapers, including Elizabeth Timothy, the first American woman newspaper publisher (and mother of eight children). After her husband died of smallpox in 1738, Timothy took over the *South Carolina Gazette*, established in 1734 by Benjamin Franklin and the Timothy family. Also during this period, Anna Maul Zenger ran the *New-York Weekly Journal* throughout her husband's trial and after his death in 1746.[3]

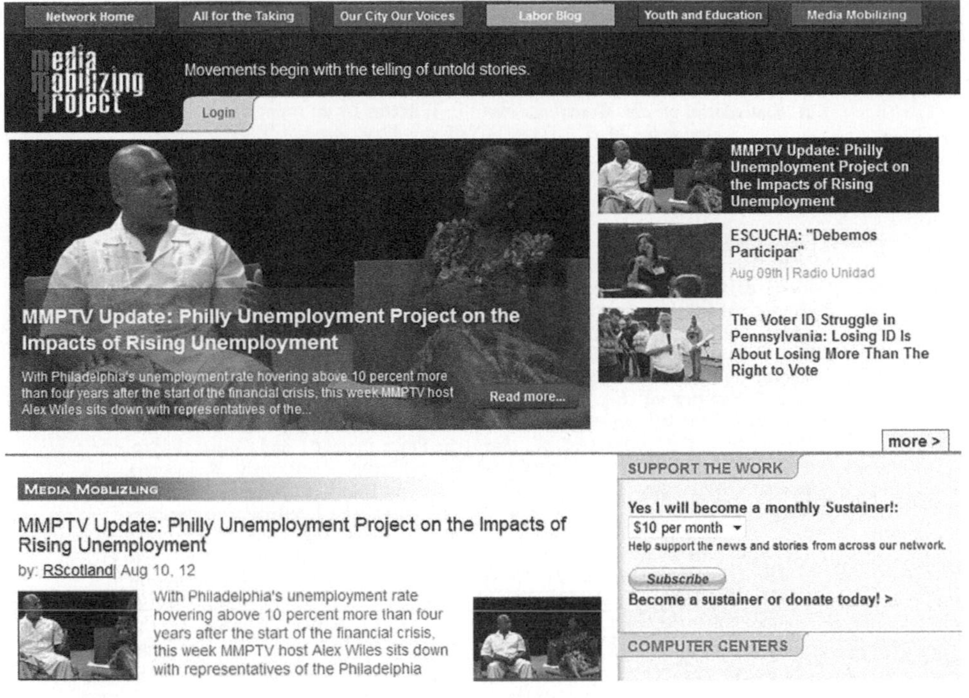

Courtesy of Media Mobilizing

The Penny Press Era: Newspapers Become Mass Media

By the late 1820s, the average newspaper cost six cents a copy and was sold through yearly subscriptions priced at ten to twelve dollars. Because that price was more than a week's salary for most skilled workers, newspaper readers were mostly affluent. By the 1830s, however, the Industrial Revolution made possible the replacement of expensive handmade paper with cheaper machine-made paper. During this time, the rise of the middle class spurred the growth of literacy, setting the stage for a more popular and inclusive press. In addition, breakthroughs in technology, particularly the replacement of mechanical presses by steam-powered presses, permitted publishers to produce as many as four thousand newspapers an hour, which lowered the cost of newspapers. **Penny papers** soon began competing with six-cent papers. Though subscriptions remained the preferred sales tool of many penny papers, they began relying increasingly on daily street sales of individual copies.

Numb. LVI.

THE

New-York Weekly JOURNAL.

Containing the freſheſt Advices, Foreign, and Domeſtick.

MUNDAY December 2d, 1734.

A Continuation of the Proceedings concerning the Preſs.

From the Votes of the Aſſembly.
Die Sab. 9 *ho A. M* 2 *Nov.* 1734.

A Meſſage from the Council by Mr. *Livingſton*, deſiring this Houſe to return by him, to that Board, the ſeveral ſeditious Journals of *Zenger's*, Numb. 7, 47, 48, 49. and *Two Printed Ballads*, which were delivered by a Committee of that board to a Committee of this Houſe, the 17*th* of *October* laſt, together with the Propoſals of the Committee of that Board, delivered therewith, to a Commitee of this Houſe. And then withdrew.

On Tueſday the 5*th of* November, 1734. *The Quarter Seſſions for the City of* New-York *began, when the Sherif delivered to the Court an order which was read by the Clerk in theſe Words.*

At a Council held at Fort George, *in* New-York, *the* 2 Nov. 1734.

Preſent his Excellency *William Coſby*, Captain, General and Governor, in chief, *&c.*

Mr. *Clark*	Mr. Chief Juſtice,
Mr. *Hariſon*,	Mr. *Courtland*,
Dr. *Colden*,	Mr. *Lane*,
Mr. *Livingſton*,	Mr. *Horſmanden*.
Mr. *Kennedy*,	

Whereas by an order of this Board of this Day, ſome of *J. Peter Zenger's* Journalls, entitled the *New-York* weekly *Journall*, containing the freſheſt Advices, Foreign, and Domeſtick, Numb. 7. 47. 48. 49. were ordered to be burnt by the Hands of the common Hangman, or Whipper, near the Pillory in this City, on *Wedneſday* the 6*th* Inſtant, between the Hours of Eleven and Twelve in the Forenoon; as containing in them many Things tending to Sedition and Faction, to bring his Majeſties Government into Contempt, and to diſturb the Peace thereof, and Containing in them likewiſe, not only Reflections upon his Excellency the Governor in particular, the Legiſlature in general, but alſo upon the moſt conſiderable Perſons in the moſt diſtinguiſhed Stations in this Province. It is therefore ordered that the Mayor, and Magiſtrates of this City, do attend at the Burning of the ſeveral Papers or Journals aforeſaid, Numbered as above Mentioned.

Fred. Morris,
Dp. Cl. Conc.

To Robert Lurting, Eſq; *Mayor of the City of* New-York, *and the reſt of the* Magiſtrates *for the ſaid City and County*.

Upon Reading of which, the Court forbid the entring thereof in their Books at that Time, and many of them declared, that

Figure 5-3. Colonial Newspapers During the colonial period, New York printer John Peter Zenger was arrested for seditious libel. He eventually won his case, which established the precedent that today allows U.S. journalists and citizens to criticize public officials. In this 1734 issue, Zenger's *New-York Weekly Journal* reported his own arrest and the burning of the paper by the city's "Common Hangman."

Day and the *New York Sun*

In 1833, printer Benjamin Day founded the *New York Sun* with no subscriptions and the price set at one penny. *The Sun*—whose slogan was "It shines for all"—highlighted local events, scandals, police reports, and serialized stories. Like today's supermarket tabloids, the *Sun* fabricated stories, including the infamous moon hoax, which reported "scientific" evidence of life on the moon. Within six months, the *Sun*'s lower price had generated a circulation of eight thousand, twice that of its nearest New York competitor.

The *Sun*'s success initiated a wave of penny papers that favored **human-interest stories**: news accounts that focus on the daily trials and triumphs of the human condition, often featuring ordinary individuals facing extraordinary challenges. These kinds of stories reveal journalism's ties to literary traditions, such as the archetypal conflicts between good and evil, normal and deviant, or individuals and institutions. Today, these themes can be found in everyday feature stories that chronicle the lives of remarkable people or in crime news that details the daily work of police and the misadventures of criminals. As in the nineteenth century, crime stories remain popular and widely read.

Bennett and the *New York Morning Herald*

The penny press era also featured James Gordon Bennett's *New York Morning Herald*, founded in 1835. Bennett, considered the first U.S. press baron, freed his newspaper from political influence. He established an independent paper serving middle- and working-class readers as well as his own business ambitions. The *Herald* carried political essays, news about scandals, business stories, a letters section, fashion notes, moral reflections, religious news, society gossip, colloquial tales and jokes, sports stories, and eventually reports from the Civil War. In addition, Bennett's paper sponsored balloon races, financed safaris, and overplayed crime stories. Charles Dickens, after returning to Britain from his first visit to America in the early 1840s, used the *Herald* as a model for the sleazy *Rowdy Journal*, the fictional newspaper in his novel *Martin Chuzzlewit*. By 1860, the *Herald* reached nearly eighty thousand readers, making it the world's largest daily paper at the time.

Changing Economics and the Founding of the Associated Press

The penny papers were innovative. For example, they were the first to assign reporters to cover crime, and readers enthusiastically embraced the reporting of local news and crime. By gradually separating daily front-page reporting from overt political viewpoints on an editorial page, penny papers shifted their economic base from political parties to the market—to advertising revenue, classified ads, and street sales. Although many partisan papers had taken a moral stand against advertising some controversial products and "services"—such as medical "miracle" cures, abortionists, and especially the slave trade—the penny press became more neutral toward advertisers and printed virtually any ad. In fact, many penny papers regarded advertising as consumer news. The rise in ad revenues and circulation accelerated the growth of the newspaper industry. In 1830, 650 weekly and 65 daily papers operated in the United States, reaching a circulation of 80,000. By 1840, a total of 1,140 weeklies and 140 dailies attracted more than 300,000 readers.

In 1848, six New York newspapers formed a cooperative arrangement and founded the Associated Press (AP), the first major news wire service. **Wire services** began as commercial

organizations that relayed news stories and information around the country and the world using telegraph lines and, later, radio waves and digital transmissions. In the case of the AP, the New York papers provided access to both their own stories and those from other newspapers. In the 1850s, papers started sending reporters to cover Washington, D.C., and in the early 1860s, more than a hundred reporters from northern papers went south to cover the Civil War, relaying their reports back to their home papers via telegraph and wire services. The news wire companies enabled news to travel rapidly from coast to coast and set the stage for modern journalism.

Library of Congress

Figure 5-4. Newsies sold Hearst and Pulitzer papers on the streets of New York in the 1890s. With more than a dozen dailies competing, street tactics were ferocious, and publishers often made young "newsies"—news boys and girls—buy the papers they could not sell.

The marketing of news as a product and the use of modern technology to dramatically cut costs gradually elevated newspapers from an entrepreneurial stage to the status of a mass medium. By adapting news content, penny papers captured the middle- and working-class readers who could now afford the paper and also had more leisure time to read it. As newspapers sought to sustain their mass appeal, news and "factual" reports about crimes and other items of human interest eventually superseded the importance of partisan articles about politics and commerce.

The Early History of Magazines

The first magazines appeared in seventeenth-century France in the form of bookseller catalogues and notices that book publishers inserted in newspapers. In fact, the word *magazine* derives from the French term *magasin*, meaning "storehouse." The earliest magazines were "storehouses" of writing and reports taken mostly from newspapers. Today, the word **magazine** broadly refers to collections of articles, stories, and advertisements appearing in nondaily (such as weekly or monthly) periodicals that are published in the smaller tabloid style rather than the larger broadsheet newspaper style.

The First Magazines

The first political magazine, called the *Review*, appeared in London in 1704. Edited by political activist and novelist Daniel Defoe (author of *Robinson Crusoe*), the *Review* was printed sporadically until 1713. Like the *Nation*, the *National Review*, and the *Progressive* in the United States today, early European magazines were channels for political commentary and argument. These periodicals looked like newspapers of the time, but they appeared less frequently and were oriented toward broad domestic and political commentary rather than recent news.

Regularly published magazines or pamphlets, such as the *Tatler* and the *Spectator*, also appeared in England around this time. They offered poetry, politics, and philosophy for London's elite, and they served readerships of a few thousand. The first publication to use the term magazine was *Gentleman's Magazine*, which appeared in London in 1731 and consisted of reprinted articles from newspapers, books, and political pamphlets. Later, the magazine began publishing original work by such writers as Defoe, Samuel Johnson, and Alexander Pope.

Magazines in Colonial America

Without a substantial middle class, widespread literacy, or advanced printing technology, magazines developed slowly in colonial America. Like the partisan newspapers of the time, these magazines served politicians, the educated, and the merchant classes. Paid circulations were low—between one hundred and fifteen hundred copies. However, early magazines did serve the more widespread purpose of documenting a new nation coming to terms with issues of taxation, state versus federal power, Indian treaties, public education, and the end of colonialism. George Washington, Alexander Hamilton, and John Hancock all wrote for early magazines, and Paul Revere worked as a magazine illustrator for a time.

THE
GENERAL MAGAZINE,
AND
Historical Chronicle,
For all the British Plantations in America.
[To be Continued Monthly.]
JANUARY, 1741.

VOL. I.
PHILADELPHIA:

Library of Congress

Figure 5-5. Colonial Magazines The first issue of Benjamin Franklin's *General Magazine and Historical Chronicle* appeared in January 1741. Although it lasted only six months, Franklin found success in other publications, like his annual *Poor Richard's Almanac*, which started in 1732 and lasted twenty-five years.

The first colonial magazines appeared in Philadelphia in 1741, about fifty years after the first newspapers. Andrew Bradford started it all with *American Magazine, or A Monthly View of the Political State of the British Colonies*. Three days later, Benjamin Franklin's *General Magazine and Historical Chronicle* appeared. Bradford's magazine lasted only three monthly issues, due to circulation and postal obstacles that Franklin, who had replaced Bradford as Philadelphia's postmaster, put in its way. For instance, Franklin mailed his magazine without paying the high postal rates that he subsequently charged others. Franklin's magazine primarily duplicated what was already available in local papers. After six months it, too, stopped publication.

Nonetheless, following the Philadelphia experiments, magazines began to emerge in the other colonies, beginning in Boston in the 1740s. The most successful magazines simply reprinted articles from leading London periodicals, keeping readers abreast of European events. These magazines included New York's *Independent Reflector* and the *Pennsylvania Magazine*, edited by activist Thomas Paine, which helped rally the colonies against British rule. By 1776, about a hundred colonial magazines had appeared and disappeared. Although historians consider them dull and uninspired for the most part, these magazines helped launch a new medium that caught on after the American Revolution.

U.S. Magazines in the Nineteenth Century

After the revolution, the growth of the magazine industry in the newly independent United States remained slow. Delivery costs remained high, and some postal carriers refused to carry magazines because of their weight. Only twelve magazines operated in 1800. By 1825, about a hundred magazines existed, although about another five hundred had failed between 1800 and 1825. Nevertheless, during the first quarter of the nineteenth century, most communities had their own weekly magazines. These magazines featured essays on local issues, government activities, and political intrigue, as well as material reprinted from other sources. They sold some advertising but were usually in precarious financial straits because of their small circulations.

Northwind Picture Archives

Figure 5-6. Color Illustrations first became popular in the fashion sections of women's magazines in the mid-nineteenth century. The color for this fashion image from *Godey's Lady's Book* was added to the illustration by hand.

As the nineteenth century progressed, the idea of specialized magazines devoted to certain categories of readers developed. Many early magazines were overtly religious and boasted the largest readerships of the day. The Methodist *Christian Journal and Advocate*, for example, claimed twenty-five thousand subscribers by 1826. Literary magazines also emerged at this time. The *North American Review*, for instance, established the work of important writers such as Ralph Waldo Emerson, Henry David Thoreau, and Mark Twain. In addition to religious and literary magazines, specialty magazines that addressed various professions, lifestyles, and topics also appeared, including the *American Farmer*, the *American Journal of Education*, the *American Law Journal*, *Medical Repository*, and the *American Journal of Science*. Such specialization spawned the modern trend of reaching readers who share a profession, a set of beliefs, cultural tastes, or a social identity.

The nineteenth century also saw the birth of the first general-interest magazine aimed at a national audience. In 1821, two young Philadelphia printers, Charles Alexander and Samuel Coate Atkinson, launched the *Saturday Evening Post*, which became the longest-running magazine in U.S. history. Like most magazines of the day, the early *Post* included a few original essays but "borrowed" many pieces from other sources. Eventually, however, the *Post* grew to incorporate news, poetry, essays, play reviews, and more. The *Post* published the writings of such prominent popular authors as Nathaniel Hawthorne and Harriet Beecher Stowe. Although the *Post* was a general-interest magazine, it also was the first major magazine to appeal directly to women, via its "Lady's Friend" column, which addressed women's issues.

National, Women's, and Illustrated Magazines

With increases in literacy and public education, the development of faster printing technologies, and improvements in mail delivery (due to rail transportation), a market was created for more national magazines like the *Saturday Evening Post*. Whereas in 1825 one hundred magazines struggled for survival, by 1850 nearly six hundred magazines were being published regularly. (Thousands of others lasted less than a year.) Significant national magazines of the era included *Graham's Magazine* (1840–1858), one of the most influential and entertaining magazines in the country; *Knickerbocker* (1833–1864), which published essays and literary works by Washington Irving, James Fenimore Cooper, and Nathaniel Hawthorne (preceding such national cultural magazines as the *New Yorker* and *Harper's*); the *Nation* (1865–present), which pioneered the national political magazine format; and *Youth's Companion* (1826–1929), one of the first successful national magazines for younger readers.

Besides the move to national circulation, other important developments in the magazine industry were under way. In 1828, Sarah Josepha Hale started the first magazine directed exclusively to a female audience: the *Ladies' Magazine*. In addition to carrying general-interest articles, the magazine advocated for women's education, work, and property rights. After nine years and marginal success, Hale merged her magazine with its main rival, *Godey's Lady's Book* (1830–1898), which she edited for the next forty years. By 1850, *Godey's*, known for its colorful fashion illustrations in addition to its advocacy, achieved a circulation of 40,000 copies—at the time, the biggest distribution ever for a U.S. magazine. By 1860, circulation swelled to 150,000. Hale's magazine played a central role in educating working- and middle-class women, who were denied access to higher education throughout the nineteenth century.

Figure 5-7. Civil War Photography Famed portrait photographer Mathew Brady commissioned many photographers to help him document the Civil War. (Although all the resulting photos were credited "Photograph by Brady," he did not take them all.) This effort allowed people at home to see and understand the true carnage of the war. Photo critics now acknowledge that some of Brady's photos were posed or reenactments.

The other major development in magazine publishing during the mid-nineteenth century was the arrival of illustration. Like the first newspapers, early magazines were totally dependent on the printed word. By the mid-1850s, drawings, engravings, woodcuts, and other forms of illustration had become a major feature of magazines. During this time, *Godey's Lady's Book* employed up to 150 women to color-tint its magazine illustrations and stencil drawings by hand. Meanwhile, *Harper's New Monthly Magazine*, founded in 1850, offered extensive woodcut illustrations with each issue. During the Civil War, many readers relied on *Harper's* for its elaborate battlefield sketches. Publications like *Harper's* married visual language to the printed word, helping transform magazines into a mass medium. Bringing photographs into magazines took a bit longer. Mathew Brady and his colleagues, whose thirty-five hundred photos documented the Civil War, helped popularize photography by the 1860s. But it was not until the 1890s that magazines and newspapers possessed the technology to reproduce photos in print media.

The Development of Modern American Magazines

In 1870, about twelve hundred magazines were produced in the United States; by 1890, that number had reached forty-five hundred; and by 1905, more than six thousand magazines existed (see Figure 5-8). Part of this surge in titles and readership was facilitated by the Postal Act of 1879, which assigned magazines lower postage rates and put them on an equal footing with newspapers delivered by mail, reducing distribution costs. Meanwhile, faster presses and advances in mass-production printing, conveyor systems, and assembly lines reduced production costs and made large-circulation national magazines possible.[4]

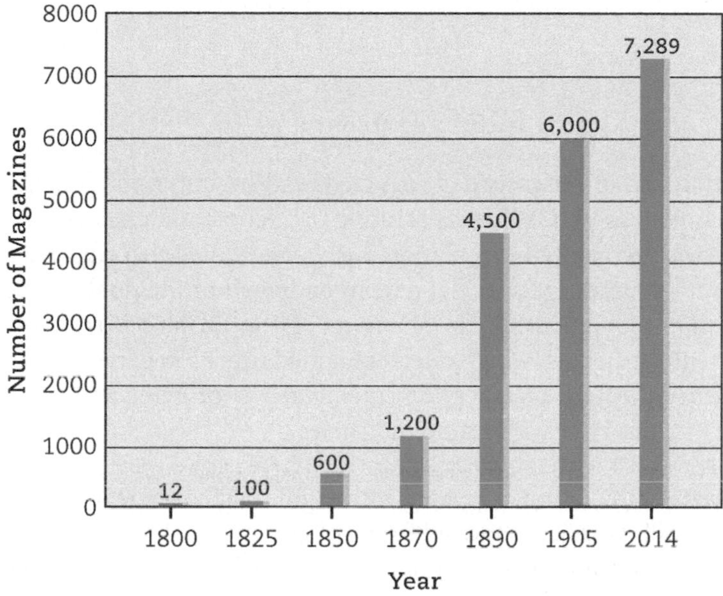

Data from: *Association of Magazine Media*, 2015 Magazine Media Factbook, www.magazine.org/sites/default/files/2015MagazineMediaFactbook.pdf

Figure 5-8. The Growth of Magazines Published in the United States

The combination of reduced distribution and production costs enabled publishers to slash magazine prices. As prices dropped from thirty-five cents to fifteen cents and then to ten cents, the working class was gradually able to purchase national publications. By 1905, there were about twenty-five national magazines, available from coast to coast and serving millions of readers.[5] As jobs and the population began shifting from farms and small towns to urban areas, magazines helped readers imagine themselves as part of a nation rather than as individuals with only local or regional identities. In addition, the dramatic growth of drugstores and dime stores, supermarkets, and department stores offered new venues and shelf space for selling consumer goods, including magazines.

As magazine circulation began to skyrocket, advertising revenue soared. The economics behind the rise of advertising was simple: A magazine publisher could dramatically expand circulation by dropping the price of an issue below the actual production cost for a single copy. The publisher recouped the loss through ad revenue, guaranteeing large readerships to advertisers who were willing to pay to reach more readers. The number of ad pages in

national magazines proliferated. *Harper's*, for instance, devoted only seven pages to ads in the mid-1880s, nearly fifty pages in 1890, and more than ninety pages in 1900.[6]

By the turn of the century, advertisers increasingly used national magazines to capture consumers' attention and build a national marketplace. One magazine that took advantage of these changes was *Ladies' Home Journal*, begun in 1883 by Cyrus Curtis. The women's magazine began publishing more than the usual homemaking tips, including also popular fiction, sheet music, and—most important, perhaps—the latest consumer ads. The magazine's broadened scope was a reflection of the editors' and advertisers' realization that women consumers constituted a growing and lucrative market. *Ladies' Home Journal* reached a circulation of over 500,000 by the early 1890s—the highest circulation of any magazine in the country. In 1903, it became the first magazine to reach a circulation of one million.

Social Reform and the Muckrakers

Better distribution and lower costs had attracted readers, but to maintain sales, magazines had to change content as well. Whereas printing the fiction and essays of the best writers of the day was one way to maintain circulation, many magazines also engaged in one aspect of *yellow journalism*—crusading for social reform on behalf of the public good. In the 1890s, for example, *Ladies' Home Journal* (*LHJ*) and its editor, Edward Bok, led the fight against unregulated patent medicines (which often contained nearly 50 percent alcohol), while other magazines joined the fight against phony medicines, poor living and working conditions, and unsanitary practices in various food industries.

The rise in magazine circulation coincided with rapid social change in America. While hundreds of thousands of Americans moved from the country to the city in search of industrial jobs, millions of new immigrants also poured in. Thus the nation that journalists had long written about had grown increasingly complex by the turn of the century. Many newspaper reporters became dissatisfied with the simplistic and conventional style of newspaper journalism and turned to magazines, where they were able to write at greater length and in greater depth about broader issues. They wrote about such topics as corruption in big business and government, urban problems faced by immigrants, labor conflicts, and race relations.

In 1902, *McClure's Magazine* (1893–1933) touched off an investigative era in magazine reporting with a series of probing stories, including Ida Tarbell's "The History of the Standard Oil Company," which took on John D. Rockefeller's oil monopoly, and Lincoln Steffens's "Shame of the Cities," which tackled urban problems. In 1906, *Cosmopolitan* joined the fray with a series called "The Treason of the Senate," and *Collier's* magazine (1888–1957) developed "The Great American Fraud" series, focusing on patent medicines (whose ads accounted for 30 percent of the profits made by the American press by the 1890s). Much of this new reporting style was critical of American institutions. Angry with so much negative reporting, in 1906 President Theodore Roosevelt dubbed these investigative reporters **muckrakers**, because they were willing to crawl through society's muck to uncover a story. Muckraking was a label that Roosevelt used with disdain, but it was worn with pride by reporters such as Ray Stannard Baker, Frank Norris, and Lincoln Steffens.

A NAUSEATING JOB, BUT IT MUST BE DONE
(President Roosevelt takes hold of the investigating muck-rake himself in the packing-house scandal.)
From the *Saturday Globe* (Utica)

©Bettmann/Contributor/Getty Images

Influenced by Upton Sinclair's novel *The Jungle*—a fictional account of Chicago's meatpacking industry—and by the muckraking reports of *Collier's* and *LHJ*, in 1906 Congress passed the Pure Food and Drug Act and the Meat Inspection Act. Other reforms stemming from muckraking journalism and the politics of the era include antitrust laws for increased government oversight of business, a fair and progressive income tax, and the direct election of U.S. senators.

(Left and right) The Granger Collection

Figure 5-9. Ida Tarbell (1857–1944) is best known for her work "The History of the Standard Oil Company," which appeared as a nineteen-part series in *McClure's Magazine* between November 1902 and October 1904. Tarbell once remarked on why she dedicated years of her life to investigating the company: "They had never played fair, and that ruined their greatness for me." For muckrakers and investigative journalists like Tarbell, exposing such corruption was a driving force behind their work.

The Rise of General-Interest Magazines

The heyday of the muckraking era lasted into the mid-1910s, when America was drawn into World War I. After the war and through the 1950s, **general-interest magazines** were the most prominent publications, offering occasional investigative articles but also covering a wide variety of topics aimed at a broad national audience. A key aspect of these magazines was **photojournalism**—the use of photos to document the rhythms of daily life. High-quality photos gave general-interest magazines a visual advantage over radio, which was the most popular medium of the day. In 1920, about fifty-five magazines fit the general-interest category; by 1946, more than one hundred such magazines competed with radio networks for the national audience.

Saturday Evening Post

Although it had been around since 1821, the *Saturday Evening Post* concluded the nineteenth century as only a modest success, with a circulation of about ten thousand. In 1897, Cyrus Curtis, who had already made *Ladies' Home Journal* the nation's top magazine, bought the *Post* and remade it into the first widely popular general-interest magazine. Curtis's strategy for reinvigorating the magazine included printing popular fiction and romanticizing American virtues through words and pictures (a *Post* tradition best depicted in the three-hundred-plus cover illustrations by Norman Rockwell). Curtis also featured articles that celebrated the business boom of the 1920s. This reversed the journalistic direction of the muckraking era, in which business corruption was often the focus. By the 1920s, the *Post* had reached two million in circulation, the first magazine to hit that mark.

Reader's Digest

The most widely circulated general-interest magazine during this period was *Reader's Digest*. Started in a Greenwich Village basement in 1922 by Dewitt Wallace and Lila Acheson Wallace, *Reader's Digest* championed one of the earliest functions of magazines: printing condensed versions of selected articles from other magazines. In the magazine's early years, the Wallaces refused to accept ads and sold the *Digest* only through subscriptions. With its inexpensive production costs, low price, and popular pocket-size format, the magazine's circulation climbed to over one million during the Great Depression, and by 1946, it was the nation's most popular magazine. By the mid-1980s, it was the most popular magazine in the world, with a circulation of 20 million in America and 10 to 12 million abroad. However, by 2014 it was recovering from bankruptcy, and its circulation base had dropped to about 4.2 million, less than a quarter of its circulation thirty years earlier.

Time

During the general-interest era, national newsmagazines such as *Time* were also major commercial successes. Begun in 1923 by Henry Luce and Briton Hadden, *Time* developed a magazine brand of interpretive journalism, assigning reporter-researcher teams to cover stories, after which a rewrite editor would put the article in narrative form with an interpretive point of view. *Time* had a circulation of 200,000 by 1930, increasing to more than 3 million by the mid-1960s. *Time*'s success encouraged prominent imitators, including *Newsweek* (established in 1933); *U.S. News & World Report* (1948); and, more recently, *The Week*

(2001). By 2014, economic decline, competition from the Web, and a shrinking number of readers and advertisers took their toll on the three top newsweeklies. *Time*'s circulation stagnated at 3.2 million, while *U.S. News* became a monthly magazine in 2008 and switched to an all-digital format in 2010 (and is now most famous for its "America's Best Colleges" reports). *Newsweek*'s circulation peaked in 1991 with 3.3 million readers. As its circulation and revenue sank, it was sold in 2010 for just $1 and the assumption of its debt. After an unsuccessful foray as a digital-only publication, *Newsweek* relaunched as a print publication in 2014 under new ownership and with an uncertain future.

Life

Despite the commercial success of *Reader's Digest* and *Time* in the twentieth century, the magazines that really symbolized the general-interest genre during this era were the oversized pictorial weeklies *Look* and *Life*. More than any other magazine of its day, *Life* developed an effective strategy for competing with popular radio by advancing photojournalism. Launched as a weekly by Henry Luce in 1936, *Life* appealed to the public's fascination with images (invigorated by the movie industry), radio journalism, and advertising and fashion photography. By the end of the 1930s, *Life* had a **pass-along readership**—the total number of people who come into contact with a single copy of a magazine—of more than seventeen million, rivaling the ratings of popular national radio programs.

The LIFE Premium Collection/Getty Images

Figure 5-10. *Life* Magazine published iconic photos during its original 1883–1972 run. Following nearly a century as a weekly, it has since been published as a monthly, an occasional commemorative publication, a newspaper supplement, and an online archive.

Life's first editor, Wilson Hicks—formerly a picture editor for the Associated Press—built a staff of renowned photographer-reporters who chronicled the world's ordinary and extraordinary events from the late 1930s through the 1960s. Among *Life*'s most famous photojournalists were Margaret Bourke-White, the first female war correspondent to fly combat missions during World War II, and Gordon Parks, who later became Hollywood's first African American director of major feature films. Today, *Life*'s photographic archive is hosted online by Google (images. google.com/hosted/life).

(Left and right) Margaret Bourke-White/Time Life Pictures/Getty Images

Figure 5-11. Margaret Bourke-White (1904–1971) was a photojournalist of many "firsts": first female photographer for *Life* magazine, first Western photographer allowed into the Soviet Union, first to shoot the cover photo for *Life*, and first female war correspondent. Bourke-White (*upper right*) was well known for her photos of WWII—including concentration camps—but also for her documentation of the India-Pakistan partition, including a photo of Gandhi at his spinning wheel (*upper left*).

Journalism

"Journalism" from *Telling the Story*, Fifth Edition by the Missouri Group (Brian S. Brooks, George Kennedy, Daryl R. Moen, and Don Ranly), pp. 1–18 (Chapter 1, "The Nature of News").

The late scholar James Carey described journalism as a society's conversation with itself. For a long time, that conversation was one-sided, with professional journalists determining the day's news and delivering it to the public. Today, the public has a voice. The conversation has new participants, new technology, even new language. News spreads via cellphones and iPads as well as through television and newspapers. Nonjournalists engage in **citizen journalism**—joining professionals in blogging, tweeting and posting news on Facebook.

The Project for Excellence in Journalism, in its latest report on the state of the media, summarized the situation: "News organizations—old and new—still produce most of the content audiences consume. But each technological advance has added a new layer of complexity—and a new set of players—in connecting that content to consumers and advertisers."

Those new players include **aggregators** such as Google and HuffingtonPost.com that collect, reorganize and often link to work originally done by others—sometimes without full credit and usually without payment. The new players also include Facebook, a social network that allows participants to exchange news, commentary, gossip and personal information without the involvement of professional journalists.

The professionals have added to their traditional tasks a new role—curator—as they scramble to assess the accuracy and identify the sources of information that is as likely to be announced by the social networking site Twitter as by the Associated Press.

As the *State of the News Media* report concludes, "The result is a news ecology full of experimentation and excitement, but also one that is uneven, has uncertain financial underpinning and some clear holes in coverage."

It's hard to imagine a more interesting, or more confusing, time to be practicing or studying journalism.

Here's just one example of how the news flows through this new conversation of journalism.

In the middle of July 2011, a small alternative magazine based in Vancouver, Canada, posted on the Internet a message calling for protest gatherings of Americans angry about the political and economic dominance of wealthy institutions.

No news organization saw the notice (or, if any did, none thought it was newsworthy). However, individuals did. They began to spread the word through social media. By mid-September, a handful of protesters were camped in a park near Wall Street in New York. Professional reporters took no notice, while Facebook messages attracted more protesters.

Similar groups began to gather in cities across America, but for the most part they remained below the radar of news organizations. Finally, in New York, the Occupy Wall Street crowd clashed with police. With arrests came attention. Within days, the protests were prominent on network and cable television news and on the front pages of newspapers.

Commentators likened Occupy Wall Street to the early days of the conservative tea party movement, which also was nurtured by social media before mainstream journalists caught on.

It's clear, then, that news travels through multiple channels and springs from a confusing array of sources. Still, traditional news organizations remain the most important providers of the news that fulfills what scholar Robert Entman has called the "core democratizing functions" of the media. When researchers ask where citizens get their information about local government, taxes, schools and jobs, the answer is likely to be the most traditional source: the newspaper. For news about the weather, traffic and unfolding events, the leading source is television. Those findings come from a Pew Research Center survey.

That same survey showed that Internet sources are more important for people under age 40, with nearly half of all adults reporting that they used mobile devices to check the news on traditional and nontraditional sites. Nearly one in five said they also get news from social media sites such as Facebook. The oldest form of communication hasn't disappeared either. More than half of those surveyed said they get news by word of mouth from friends, neighbors or co-workers at least once a week.

Journalism has truly become a public conversation.

Convergence in Journalism

Convergence is the term that describes efforts to use the different strengths of different media to reach broader audiences and tell the world's stories in new ways. Convergence demands of journalists new skills and new flexibility. Print reporters find themselves summarizing their stories into a television camera. Videographers find themselves selecting images to be published in the partner newspaper. Both print and broadcast journalists look for Web links to connect their stories to the worldwide audience and nearly infinite capacity of the Internet. **Smartphones**—phones capable of surfing the Web, such as iPhones and BlackBerrys—provide new outlets and require new storytelling techniques.

The technological revolution also has exploded traditional definitions of just who is a journalist. Millions of people across the world have launched **blogs**—online journals or columns. Although one estimate is that only 5 percent of those sites include original reporting, and although most have tiny audiences, many have become influential voices in the public conversation. In an effort to add personality and encourage interactivity with audience members, traditional news organizations are encouraging staff members to write blogs.

Increasingly, members of the public are being invited to respond to stories that are published or broadcast. Citizens are even being enlisted as amateur reporters. **Crowdsourcing**, as it is called, has become a reporting tool at news organizations from North Dakota to Florida. Readers and viewers are invited to submit their own stories, photographs and video. They are sometimes asked to lend their expertise to help solve community problems.

The Public Insight Network takes crowdsourcing to the logical next step. Pioneered by public radio, the Public Insight Network is, as the name suggests, a network of citizens who agree to share their knowledge and their insights with professional reporters. National Public Radio and *The New York Times* have established Public Insight Networks. So have the investigative nonprofit ProPublica and local news organizations, such as the online *St. Louis Beacon*. Network members may be experts in any field of public interest. Some have professional credentials; others have valuable life experience. They join the network as volunteers. Their pay is the satisfaction they derive from enriching the content, and improving the accuracy, of journalism.

Even the fundamentals of journalism are evolving as technology speeds up the communication process, provides new sources for both reporters and audiences, and reshapes journalism from a one-way flow of information to a give-and-take with audiences and competitors. One element that hasn't changed, however, is the importance of accuracy and fairness. And the essential role of journalism in a democratic society remains the one assigned to it by James Madison in 1822: "A popular government without popular information or the means of acquiring it is but a prologue to a farce or a tragedy, or perhaps both."

The basic skills required of every journalist haven't changed either, despite the revolution in technology. Whatever the medium, the skills of news gathering and storytelling are essential to good journalism.

What News Is

The criteria that professional reporters and editors use to decide what news is can be summarized in three words:

- Relevance
- Usefulness
- Interest

Relevance, usefulness and interest for a specific audience are the broad guidelines for judging the news value of any event, issue or personality. These criteria apply generally, but each journalist and each news organization uses them in a specific context that gives them particular meaning. That context is supplied by the audience—the reader, listener or viewer. Journalists always determine newsworthiness with a particular audience in mind.

Elements of a Good News Story

Within the broad news standards of relevance, usefulness and interest, journalists look for more specific elements in each potential story. The most important elements are these:

- *Impact.* The potential impact of a story is another way of measuring its relevance and usefulness. How many people are affected by an event or idea? How seriously does it affect them? The wider and heavier the impact, the better the story. Sometimes, of course, impact isn't immediately obvious. Sometimes it isn't very exciting. The challenge for good journalism is making such dull but important stories lively and interesting. That may require relying on the next three elements.
- *Conflict.* Conflict is a recurring theme in all storytelling, whether the stories told are journalism, literature or drama. Struggles between people, among nations or with natural forces make fascinating reading and viewing. Conflict is such a basic element of life that journalists must resist the temptation to overdramatize or oversimplify it.
- *Novelty.* Novelty is another element common to journalism and other kinds of stories. People or events may be interesting and therefore newsworthy just because they are unusual or bizarre.
- *Prominence.* Names make news. The bigger the name, the bigger the news. Ordinary people have always been intrigued by the doings of the rich and famous. Both prominence and novelty can be, and often are, exaggerated to produce "news" that lacks real relevance and usefulness. For example, in the days following his death, pop star Michael

Jackson received more coverage on network television than did the wars in Iraq and Afghanistan.

- *Proximity*. Generally, people are more interested in and concerned about what happens close to home. When they read or listen to national or international news, they often want to know how it relates to their own community. Some news organizations are turning to hyperlocal coverage as they seek to reconnect with readers by reporting at the neighborhood level, sometimes by soliciting contributions from residents or citizen journalists. Independent websites devoted to this kind of extremely local coverage are springing up across the country. Increasingly, however, journalists and scholars are recognizing that communities organized around a particular interest—a sport, a hobby or an issue—are at least as important as geographic communities.
- *Timeliness*. News is supposed to be new. With the Internet and cable and satellite television, "new" means instantaneous. Events are reported as they happen, and this poses a challenge for journalists. Speed conflicts with thoughtfulness and thoroughness. Opportunities for error multiply. Perspective and context are needed today more than ever, but both are more difficult to supply with little time for thinking. Despite the drawbacks of 24/7 news coverage, it's clear that for news to be relevant and useful, it must be timely. For example, it is much more useful to write about an issue facing the city council before the issue is decided than afterward. Timely reporting can give people a chance to be participants in public affairs rather than remain mere spectators.

The online age, with its often-confusing multitude of sources, splintering of audiences and growing complaints about negative news, has inspired most journalists to add some new criteria for assessing the value of stories:

- *Engagement*. When news was only broadcast or printed on paper, the flow of information was one-way—from journalists to audiences. No more. Today, a news report is often just the beginning of the conversation. Audience members online respond to, correct and criticize the journalism. Many reporters and commentators maintain blogs and invite responses on social networking media such as Twitter and Facebook to encourage such involvement. Increasingly, a goal of both individual journalists and news organizations is to engage the public with the news and with the news provider.
- *Solutions*. Scholars and audiences alike complain that journalists too often report problems and controversies without offering solutions. Political scientist Thomas Patterson has even argued that the negative tone of much coverage of politics and government has the effect of increasing cynicism and decreasing participation in the most basic activities of citizenship, such as voting. More and more journalists are seeking out expert sources and inviting audience members not only to explain complex problems but also to suggest solutions.

How Different Media Present the News

Notice that the preceding list suggests two important things about news. First, not all news is serious, life-and-death stuff. The journalistic conversation that holds a society together includes talk of crime, politics and world affairs, of course, but it also includes talk of everyday life. It includes humor and gossip. All of that can be news. Second, news is more than a collection of facts. Telling the news usually means telling stories. The narrative, the humanity and the drama of storytelling make up the art of journalism. To gather the facts for their stories, journalists use many of the same techniques used by sociologists, political scientists and historians. But to tell their stories so that those facts can be understood, journalists often use the techniques of other storytellers, such as novelists and screenwriters.

The different news media give different weights to the criteria for assessing the value of news stories and require different approaches to telling those stories. For example, newspapers and magazines are better than television or radio for explaining the impact of an issue or the causes of a conflict. Scholars have learned that, although most people say they get most of their news from television, few can remember very much of what they've seen or heard on a newscast. But print can't compete with television in speed or emotional power. The differing strengths and limitations of each medium make it more likely that you'll find a lengthy explanatory story in a newspaper or magazine, while you're more likely to learn of an event from television, radio or the Internet. A newspaper lets you read the details of a budget or a box score, but television shows you the worker whose job was cut or the player scoring the winning basket. The unique power of online journalism is that it brings together the immediacy of television and the comprehensive authority of print, with endless opportunities for users to pursue their interests through the Web. Social media create new communities of interest and allow nonjournalists to join the public conversation.

The Rise of Citizen Journalism

We've already seen how citizen journalists, not employed by traditional news organizations and often not professionally trained, use the new technology and social media to report and comment on the news. Some of these citizen journalists have gone further and have created their own news sites online. The focus may be on local communities, as is the case with YourHub.com. Or it may be broader, as with the activist indymedia.org, an international collective with a strongly anti-establishment approach that publishes online editions in a number of major cities.

Few of these citizen journalism outlets are profitable, and many are deliberately nonprofit. Their goal, whether local or international, is to cover communities and issues that even local newspapers and broadcast stations don't reach. Their staffs are a mix of trained journalists and interested amateurs. Their audiences are people who don't feel adequately served by the traditional media. Some observers have likened them to the pamphleteers who were the pioneers of American journalism two centuries ago.

Some critics of mainstream, traditional journalism hope that these citizen journalists can fill the gaps left by reduced staffs of professionals or even replace the traditional sources altogether. However, research by two University of Missouri scholars shows that few of the new sites are even close to filling either role. The researchers studied citizen journalism sites and sites sponsored by traditional, or legacy, media in 46 randomly selected cities. Their conclusion was that the citizen sites "are much more narrow in their content and focus than the legacy media sites in those cities." Two-thirds of the citizen sites they studied were blogs rather than news sites.

The Role of Journalism

The First Amendment to the U.S. Constitution protects the five freedoms that the nation's founders considered essential to a democracy: the freedom of speech, religion, the press, petition and assembly. In the 1830s, French aristocrat Alexis de Tocqueville came to study the U.S. and wrote his classic *Democracy in America*. He was struck by the central role played by the only journalism available then: the newspapers. "We should underrate their importance if we thought they just guaranteed liberty; they maintain civilization," he wrote.

Challenges to American Journalism

More than 200 years after they were guaranteed, the First Amendment freedoms are still essential and still under threat. After the terrorist attacks of Sept. 11, 2001, a new emphasis on national and personal security tempted government officials and citizens alike to question just how much freedom is compatible with safety. The role of journalism in guaranteeing liberty and maintaining civilization is challenged by those who make news and those who need it.

American journalism is also under threat from growing public skepticism about how well today's journalists are fulfilling their historic roles. National surveys by the Pew Research Center for the People and the Press show, for example, that more than half the public sees bias in the news. About half say that journalists' reports are often inaccurate. Fewer than half say journalism protects democracy, and about one-third say journalism is hurting democracy. In assessing coverage of the 2008 election, voters gave journalists only a grade of C. Views of the press increasingly vary with political affiliation. Republicans are much more critical than Democrats. And those who get their news online rate the major Internet sources—such as Google, Yahoo, AOL and Slate.com—even lower than the traditional media.

On the other hand, the same surveys show that credibility has improved, at least a little, from historic lows. Comfortable majorities say they believe all or most of what they read in newspapers and see on television news. Most people give higher ratings to the particular newspaper or TV station they use than to the news media in general. And two-thirds rate journalists as highly professional. (For regular samplings of public opinion about journalism, visit http://people-press.org, the website of the Pew Research Center.)

Principles of Good Journalism

What these citizens seem to be saying is that the work journalists do is important, but journalists aren't doing it well enough. The past decade has seen the emergence of several major efforts to improve the performance of American journalism.

One of those efforts has been driven by an informal association called the Committee of Concerned Journalists and the related Project for Excellence in Journalism. The project conducts regular research on journalism, and it issues reports that can be accessed on its website, Journalism.org. Among the reports are annual *State of the News Media* assessments, as well as regular reports on the public's news consumption and on journalists' performance. Another product of these reformers is a book that every student and practitioner of journalism should read. Written by two leaders of the committee and the project, Bill Kovach and Tom Rosenstiel, the book is *The Elements of Journalism*.

The book argues that "the purpose of journalism is to provide people with the information they need to be free and self-governing." It proposes 10 principles to achieve this purpose:

1. Journalism's first obligation is to the truth.
2. Its first loyalty is to citizens.
3. Its essence is a discipline of verification.
4. Its practitioners must maintain independence from those they cover.
5. Journalism must serve as an independent monitor of power.
6. It must provide a forum for public criticism and compromise.
7. It must strive to make the significant interesting and relevant.
8. It must keep the news comprehensive and proportional.
9. Its practitioners must be allowed to exercise their personal conscience.
10. Citizens, too, have rights and responsibilities when it comes to the news.

In these principles, you can hear echoes of the Journalist's Creed, written nearly a century before by Walter Williams, founding dean of the world's first journalism school, at the University of Missouri. Williams wrote that "the public journal is a public trust . . . (and) acceptance of a lesser interest than the public interest is a violation of that trust."

Journalists' Responsibilities in a Democracy

The efforts to reform, or restore, journalism recognize these vital functions of journalists in a free society:

- *Journalists report the news.* News reporting, the first and most obvious function, is the foundation of the rest. Reporters cover Congress and council meetings, describe accidents and disasters, and show the horrors of war and the highlights of football games. This reporting takes many forms—**tweets** (Twitter messages), live television, online bulletins, next-day newspaper analyses and long-form magazine narratives. In 2009, the *Houston Chronicle* was a finalist for journalism's highest honor, the Pulitzer Prize, for its staff coverage of a hurricane threatening the city. Nearly all the reporting, plus blogs by staff and citizens, appeared online rather than on paper. No wonder journalism has been called the first rough draft of history.
- *Journalists monitor power.* Most often, Americans are concerned about the power of government. Lately, private power has become more of a worry and more of a source of news. Alexandra Berzon and her colleagues at the *Las Vegas Sun* won the Pulitzer Prize for public service for their investigation of lax inspections that led to high rates of death and injury among construction workers on the Las Vegas Strip. Monitoring is required even if power is used legitimately—when governments raise taxes or take

us to war, for example, or when businesses close plants or cut health care benefits for employees. When the power is used illegally or immorally, another important function comes into play.

- *Journalists uncover injustice.* A television reporter learns that one brand of tires and one model of car are involved in a disproportionate number of fatal accidents. A newspaper discovers that prisoners on death row were convicted unfairly. In those cases and thousands more, journalists bring to light dangerous or illegal abuses that might otherwise go unchecked.
- *Journalists tell compelling stories that delight us and some that dismay us.* For example, the husband-and-wife team of Nicholas Kristof and Sheryl WuDunn told the horrifying and hopeful stories of women struggling to overcome discrimination and abuse in the developing world for *The New York Times* and in a book, *Half the Sky: Turning Oppression into Opportunity for Women Worldwide.* Television's *60 Minutes* and *Frontline* tell the stories of true-life dramas. Bloggers bring firsthand experiences and often great passion to their posts.
- *Journalists sustain communities.* These communities may be small towns, cities or even virtual communities of people connected only by the Internet. Through their reporting, monitoring, revealing and storytelling, journalists serve as the nervous system of the community. They convey information as well as argument.
- *Journalists curate information.* With so much material from so many unknown sources flooding the Internet, an increasingly important role for journalists is that of curator—collecting, sorting and verifying information. Now that professional journalists are not the sole, and sometimes not even the primary, providers of news, their duty has expanded to serving as checker of the facts asserted by others.

Scholars have used other terms for this combination of vital functions. One is "agenda setting," the placing of issues on the public agenda for discussion and decision. Another is "gatekeeping," the process by which some events and ideas become news and others do not. Today the gatekeeping function has been largely succeeded by curating or navigating, guiding readers and viewers through oceans of fact, rumor and fantasy in search of solid meaning. Bloggers such as Matt Drudge and Josh Marshall sometimes serve as agenda setters for mainstream journalists. Entertainers such as Jon Stewart serve as sources not only of laughs but of information. Even in the Internet age, however, the news you read on Google or some other website probably was first reported in one of the traditional newsrooms.

Accuracy, Fairness, and Bias

The goal toward which most journalists strive has seldom been expressed better than in a phrase used years ago by Bob Woodward, then an editor at *The Washington Post.* Woodward was defending in court an investigative story published by *The Post.* The story, he said, was "the best obtainable version of the truth."

A grander-sounding goal would be "the truth," unmodified. But Woodward's phrase, while paying homage to the ideal, recognizes the realities of life and the limitations of journalism. Despite centuries of argument, philosophers and theologians are still unable to agree on what truth is. Even if there were agreement on that basic question, how likely is it that the Roman Catholic Church and the Planned Parenthood organization would agree on the "truth" about abortion, or that a president and an opposition presidential candidate would agree on the "truth" about the state of the American economy?

In American daily journalism, that kind of dispute is left to be argued among the partisans on all sides, on the editorial pages and in commentaries. The reporter's usual role is simply to find and write the facts. The trouble is, that task rarely turns out to be simple.

Sometimes it's hard to get the facts. The committee searching for a new university president announces that the field of candidates has been narrowed to five, but the names of the five are not released. Committee members are sworn to secrecy. What can you do to get the names? Should you try?

Sometimes it's hard to tell what the facts mean. The state supreme court refuses to hear a case in which legislators are questioning the constitutionality of a state spending limit. The court says only that there is no "justiciable controversy." What does that mean? Who won? Is the ruling good news or bad news, and for whom?

Sometimes it's even hard to tell what is fact. After a yearlong study, a presidential commission says there is no widespread hunger in America. Is that conclusion a fact? Or is the fact only what the commission said? And how can you determine whether the commission is correct?

Daily journalism presents still more complications. As a reporter, you usually have only a few hours—or at most a few days—to try to learn as many facts as possible. Then, even in such a limited time, you may accumulate information enough for a story of 2,000 words, only to be told that there is space or time enough for only 1,000 words or fewer. The new media offer more space but no more time for reporting. When you take into account all these realities and limitations, you can see that reaching the best obtainable version of the truth is challenge enough for any journalist.

How can you tell when that goal has been reached? Seldom, if ever, is there a definitive answer. But there are two questions every responsible journalist should ask about every story before being satisfied: Is it accurate? Is it fair?

Accuracy and Fairness

Accuracy is the most important characteristic of any story, great or small, long or short. Every name must be spelled correctly; every quote must be just what was said; every set of numbers must add up. And that still isn't good enough. You can get the details right and still mislead unless you are accurate with context, too. The same statement may have widely different meanings depending on the circumstances in which it was uttered and the tone in which it was spoken. Circumstances and intent affect the meaning of actions as well. You will never have the best obtainable version of the truth unless your version is built on accurate reporting of detail and context.

Nor can you approach the truth without being fair. Accuracy and fairness are related, but they are not the same. Being fair requires asking yourself if you have done enough to uncover all the relevant facts and have delivered those facts in an impartial manner, without favoring one side or another in a story. The relationship between accuracy and fairness—and the differences between them—is shown clearly in this analogy from the world of sports.

The referee in a basketball game is similar, in some ways, to a reporter. Each is supposed to be an impartial observer, calling developments as he or she sees them. (Of course, the referee's job is to make judgments on those developments, while the reporter's job is just to describe them. Rendering judgment is the role of columnists, bloggers and other opinion writers.) Television has brought to sports the instant replay, in which a key play—for example, one in which a player may have been fouled while taking a shot—can be examined again and again, often from an angle different from the referee's view. Sometimes the replay shows an apparent outcome different from the one the official called. Perhaps the players actually didn't make contact. Perhaps what looked like an attempted shot was really a pass. The difference may be due to human error on the official's part, or it may be due to the differences in angle and in viewpoint. Referees recognize this problem. They try to deal with it by obtaining the best possible view of every play and by conferring with their colleagues on some close calls.

Still, every official knows that an occasional mistake will be made. That is unavoidable. What can, and must, be avoided is unfairness. Referees must be fair, and both players and fans must believe they are fair. Otherwise, their judgments will not be accepted; they will not be trusted.

With news, too, there are different viewpoints from which every event or issue can be observed. Each viewpoint may yield a different interpretation of what is occurring and of what it means. There is also, in journalism as in sports, the possibility of human error, even by the most careful reporters.

Fairness requires that you as a reporter try to find every viewpoint on a story. Rarely will there be only one; often there are more than two. Fairness requires that you allow ample opportunity for response to anyone who is being attacked or whose integrity is being questioned in a story. However, neither fairness nor objectivity requires that every viewpoint receive the same amount of time or space. Fairness requires, above all, that you make every effort to avoid following your own biases in your reporting and your writing (see Figure 5-12).

News Stories	Commentaries
Accuracy Make sure facts (events, names, dates, statistics, places, quotes) are correct. Verify facts with multiple sources. Use reliable sources for statistics. Use facts as the substance of the story. Discover and include all necessary facts.	Make sure facts (events, names, dates, statistics, places, quotes) are correct. Include all the facts needed to prove a point of view. Possibly leave out facts that don't support the argument. Provide context for facts. Use facts and reason to persuade the audience of a point of view. Appeal to emotion, but not by distorting the facts. Support personal bias with facts and reasoning. Acknowledge and rebut other points of view. Use civil language, not highly charged language or personal attacks.
Fairness Provide context for facts. Give all relevant sides of a story. Strive for balance.	
Bias Leave personal bias out of the story. Use neutral language.	

Figure 5-12. Accuracy, fairness and lack of bias are essential in news stories. Writers of commentaries (editorials, blogs, written and spoken essays, reviews and letters to the editor) must also be accurate and fair in order to be credible.

Bias

The research summarized earlier in this chapter suggests that citizens don't think journalists do enough to keep bias—conscious or unconscious—out of the news. More than eight out of 10 respondents in a national survey said they see bias at least sometimes. Of those, about twice as many said the bias seemed to be culturally and politically liberal as thought it conservative. A chorus of critics claims that journalists lean to the left. A smaller chorus complains of a rightward tilt. Books and cable television talk shows add heat, if not light, to the criticism. How valid is it?

One answer is that American journalism has many biases built into it. For example, journalists are biased toward conflict. War is a better story than peace. Journalists are biased toward novelty. Airplanes that don't crash are seldom reported. Journalists are biased toward celebrity. The lives and deaths of celebrities are chronicled in detail on the network news as well as in fan magazines.

There's a less obvious but even more important bias, too. This one probably accounts for much of the criticism. It is hidden in the job description of journalism. What do journalists say they do? What are they proudest of? What do they honor?

Journalists describe themselves as the outside agitator, the afflicter of the comfortable and the comforter of the afflicted. They see their job as being the watchdog against the powerful, the voice of the voiceless, the surrogate for the ordinary citizen, the protector of the abused and downtrodden. Journalists expect themselves to be forever skeptical, consistently open-minded, respectful of differences, sensitive to what sociologists call "the other." Neither patriotism nor religion is exempt from their critical examination.

Does that job description seem more "liberal" or more "conservative"?

Conservatives generally are respectful of authority and supportive of the status quo. Is it any surprise, then, that the overwhelming majority of conservatives and many liberals see a liberal bias in journalism? Notice that this bias has little or nothing to do with partisan politics.

Now suppose we had a journalism that wasn't questioning, disrespectful of authority, open to new ideas, dogging the powerful and speaking for the weak. Who would benefit, and who would suffer? Would society and democracy be better or worse off?

At a deeper level, however, American journalism is profoundly conservative. Journalists seldom examine critically the foundation stones on which the American way of life is based. Among these are capitalism, the two-party system, the concepts of the ethnic melting pot and of social mobility. When was the last time you saw any of those ideas questioned seriously in the mainstream press?

One conclusion suggested by this analysis is that in societies that aren't free—such as America before independence—a free press is a revolutionary instrument. In a society such as 21st-century America, which considers itself free and is overall self-satisfied, the free press becomes, at a fundamental level, conservative.

The Issue of Objectivity

The rules that mainstream journalists follow in attempting to arrive at the best obtainable version of the truth—to report accurately, fairly and without bias—are commonly summarized in the concept of objectivity. Objectivity has been and still is accepted as a working credo by most American journalists, as well as by students and teachers of journalism. It has been exalted by leaders of the profession as an essential, if unattainable, ideal. Its critics, by contrast, have attacked objectivity as, in the phrase of sociologist Gaye Tuchman, a "strategic ritual" that conceals a multitude of professional sins while producing superficial and often misleading coverage.

In his classic *Discovering the News*, Michael Schudson traces the rise of objectivity to the post–World War I period, when scholars and journalists alike turned to the methods and the language of science in an attempt to make sense of a world that was being turned upside down by the influence of Sigmund Freud in psychology and Karl Marx in politics, the emergence of new economic forces and the erosion of traditional values. Objectivity was a reliance on observable facts, but it was also a methodology for freeing factual reporting from the biases and values of source, writer or reader. It was itself a value, an ideal.

Schudson writes, "Journalists came to believe in objectivity, to the extent that they did, because they wanted to, needed to, were forced by ordinary human aspiration to seek escape from their own deep convictions of doubt and drift."

Objectivity, then, was a way of applying to the art of journalism the methods of science. Those methods emphasized reliance on observable fact. They also included the use of a variety of transparent techniques for pursuing truth and verifying facts. In science, transparency means that the researchers explain their objectives, their methods, their findings and their limitations. In journalism, only part of that methodology is usually followed. Journalists seldom describe their methods or discuss the limits of their findings. If they did, at least some members of the public might be less suspicious and less critical.

In *The Elements of Journalism*, Kovach and Rosenstiel worry that a kind of phony objectivity has replaced the original concept. The objectivity of science does not require neutrality or the artificial balance of two sides in a dispute. Scientists are free, and expected, to state their conclusions, as long as they report how they reached those conclusions. However, as usually practiced today, journalistic objectivity employs both neutrality and balance, sometimes instead of the kind of openness that is essential in science. This misunderstanding, or misapplication, of the real principles of objectivity has opened the way for critics to call for its abandonment. Journalists would be more honest, these critics argue, if they were open about their biases. In much of Europe, for example, journalists practice, and audiences expect, openly biased reporting.

The problem with that approach is easy to see in European journalism or, closer to home, in the opinionated journalism of partisan publications, cable television or many blogs. One-sided reports appeal to audiences that share the writer's bias, but they repel those who don't. Fairness and accuracy too often are casualties in this journalism of assertion rather than of verification.

Properly understood, objectivity provides the journalistic method most likely to yield the best obtainable version of the truth. True objectivity, Kovach and Rosenstiel argue, would add scientific rigor to journalistic art. Without that, journalists and audiences alike can be misled.

What Is *Not* News

Though there's debate about just how objective a reporter can possibly be, journalists and scholars all agree about one thing: Reporting the news is not the same as expressing an opinion. The primary goal of a news story is to inform. Whether in print, broadcast or online, a reporter's job is to communicate pertinent facts, together with enough background information to help the audience understand those facts. Accuracy and fairness are paramount. By contrast, the primary goal of opinion writers and speakers is to persuade. Accuracy and fairness are still important—though they sometimes get lost in argument. A commentator is expressing a point of view rather than reporting the views of others.

To see for yourself the differences in style and substance, watch Brian Williams deliver the *NBC Nightly News*. Then, later in the evening, switch to MSNBC, a sister network, and listen

to Rachel Maddow discuss the same events. Now move to Fox and Bill O'Reilly. The events of the day, as Williams reported them, haven't changed, but their context and meaning sound very different from the viewpoints of the political left (Maddow) and right (O'Reilly). For another clear example of the differences between reporting and commentary, compare a front-page story in *The New York Times* with an editorial on the same subject on the newspaper's opinion page. The former is seeking to inform you, the latter to persuade you.

Because the aims are different, news stories and commentary approach accuracy, fairness and bias differently.

In 1947, the Hutchins Commission on freedom of the press concluded that what a free society needs from journalists is "a truthful, comprehensive and intelligent account of the day's events in a context which gives them meaning." The goal of this chapter is to show you how the journalists of today and tomorrow understand that need, how they are trying to meet it, and how complex the task is. The rest of the book will help you develop the skills you'll need to take up the challenge. There are few challenges as important or as rewarding.

Suggested Readings

Journalism reviews: Every issue of *Columbia Journalism Review*, *American Journalism Review*, *Quill* and *The American Editor*, the bulletin of the American Society of News Editors, offers reports and analyses of the most important issues of contemporary journalism.

Kovach, Bill, and Tom Rosenstiel. *The Elements of Journalism*. New York: Crown, 2001. This little book is packed with practical advice and inspiration, a kind of applied ethics for journalists in any medium.

Schudson, Michael. *Discovering the News: A Social History of American Newspapers*. New York: Basic Books, 1978. This well-written study traces the development of objectivity in American journalism.

Wurman, Richard Saul. *Information Anxiety*. New York: Doubleday, 1990. This guide for consumers of information can also serve as a guide for journalists as they seek to provide understanding.

Suggested Websites

www.bedfordstmartins.com/newscentral When you visit News Central, you will find up-to-the-moment RSS feeds, research links and exercises to help you improve grammar and AP style usage. In addition, visit the site's *VideoCentral: Journalism* section to find the videos highlighted in this chapter as well as additional clips of leading professionals discussing important media trends.

www.asne.org The American Society of News Editors is the most important of the industry's professional organizations. This website gives you access to the society's landmark credibility project, including the results of a major study of Americans' attitudes toward, and uses of, journalism.

www.cjr.org *Columbia Journalism Review* is the oldest of the magazines devoted to critical analysis of journalists' performance. You'll find critiques of major stories, essays on ethics, book reviews and trade news. *American Journalism Review* (www.ajr.org) offers similar content.

www.journalism.org The site of the Project for Excellence in Journalism contains relevant research and articles on the current state of journalism. See especially the *State of the News Media* reports for the most comprehensive look at the current performance of all the major news media.

www.people-press.org The site of the Pew Research Center for the People and the Press is a reliable source for frequent reports on public attitudes toward journalism, as well as on topics in the news.

www.poynter.org This site is an excellent starting point. The Poynter Institute is the leading center of continuing professional education for journalists. On this site you'll find not only a guide to the services and resources of the institute itself but also links to the sites of every major professional organization and a variety of other useful resources.

The Changing Media Landscape

"The Changing Media Landscape" from *News Reporting and Writing*, Eleventh Edition by the Missouri Group (Brian S. Brooks, George Kennedy, Daryl R. Moen, and Don Ranly), pp. 21–39 (Chapter 2, "The Changing Media Landscape") and 53–55 (Chapter 3, "The Emerging Media").

In this section you will learn:

1. How major changes in news consumption are affecting the U.S. media.
2. How fragmentation hurts the bottom line of legacy media companies.
3. How financial problems affect the gathering of news.
4. Why newspapers are the source of most news.
5. Where journalism fits in our democracy.
6. How people consume news today.
7. Why people distrust the media.
8. Why convergence is a response to media fragmentation.
9. How citizen journalism is changing American journalism.
10. How journalists view the future of their profession.

When a gunman fatally shot 20 children and six adult staff members at Sandy Hook Elementary School in Newtown, Conn., in late 2012, many first got the news through the traditional media. But a record number also got the news on the fastest-growing news platforms in the U.S.: smartphones and tablet computers, often lumped together as **mobile media** or, simply, mobile.

A Pew Research Center study concluded that 27 percent of Americans were regularly turning to mobile devices to get their news by 2012. According to Pew, the age of mobile arrived in 2011—a new era in which "people are connected to the Web wherever they are." Almost nine in 10 Americans now own mobile phones, and 44 percent of those devices are **smartphones**, which enable users to access the Web and its audio and video capabilities. Twenty-two percent of Americans owned **tablet computers** in 2012, up from just 4 percent two years earlier.

News Consumption in the Age of Mobile Devices

According to the Pew study, this new era is encouraging for the news industry. The study found that "mobile devices are adding to people's news consumption, strengthening the lure of traditional news brands and providing a boost to long-form journalism. Eight in 10 who get news on smartphones or tablets . . . get news on personal computers as well. People are taking advantage, in other words, of having easier access to news throughout the day—in their pocket, on their desks and in their laps." At the same time, the news from the survey was mixed: Consumption of traditional media—newspapers, radio and television, in particular—continued to decline.

Mobile's Role in Consumers' Move to the Web

The arrival of mobile as a major force in news adds momentum to the sweeping changes taking place in the media industry. Asked in 2012 to choose whether radio, television, newspapers or the Web was most essential to their lives, a whopping 46 percent of Americans ranked the Web first; newspapers were a distant fourth. Among Americans aged 12 to 34, the response was even more pronounced: 68 percent ranked the Web as most essential. That 2012 study by TV ratings agency Arbitron Inc. and Edison Research seems to depict quite accurately what's happening to media in the U.S.: People increasingly look to the Web to satisfy their need for news, getting there however they can—through personal computers, smartphones and tablets.

Increasing News Audiences

Fueling this change in media consumption is the arrival of faster and easier access to the Web, not only through mobile devices but also within the home. When Arbitron and Edison conducted a similar study 10 years earlier, in 2002, 72 percent of Americans reported being able to access the Web from almost anywhere, but only 13 percent reported having broadband (high-speed) Web access at home. By 2012, the landscape had shifted significantly: 70 percent reported having broadband access, and 76 percent even had their own **Wi-Fi** (wireless Internet access) connection at home. This combination makes access easier and faster, and it allows multiple connections to the Web from within the home. Broadband access also enables the streaming of audio and video over the Web, which has the effect of reducing the market for traditional radio and television while increasing the overall radio and television audience.

Something similar is happening with newspaper companies. Fewer people are buying or subscribing to the traditional print product, but more and more readers access newspaper websites, which has the effect of increasing the overall newspaper audience.

Social media are important to the media mix, too. More than 56 percent of Americans now have a profile on a social networking site such as Facebook or LinkedIn.

Reuters/Lucas Jackson/Landov

Figure 5-13. Newspaper publishers hope that e-readers like the Kindle will spark new interest in newspaper reading.

And while young people dominate the use of social media, the fastest growth rate in social media usage in 2012 was among those 45 and older. Increasingly, people learn about breaking news when someone, often a media company employee, posts about it on Facebook, Twitter or other social media sites.

All that raises the question: What does this mean to those who provide news and news-related information? First, it's quite obvious that both the size of the audience and its appetite for news are growing. Second, it's also true that the way in which that audience wants to receive news is shifting from traditional media toward mobile and online media. It's extremely important, then, for those who produce news to understand this shift and to provide news the way the public wants it. Consumption patterns are shifting so significantly that it's plausible to declare that we are in the midst of nothing less than a media revolution.

Greater Media Fragmentation

Many have misread what's happening. In almost any story about the current state of the media, the recurring theme is likely to be, "Everyone is tuning out." You've heard it: Young people don't consume news. Newspapers are on their deathbeds. Local television will be the next to die. There's just one thing wrong with that conventional wisdom: It isn't true.

What is true is that consuming news is just one of many things people choose to do on their smartphones and tablets. One study of smartphones by comScore Inc. showed that users reported these activities as most important on those devices:

1. Accessing email.
2. Checking the weather.
3. Accessing social networks and blogs.
4. Playing games.
5. Searching for information.
6. Accessing maps.
7. Accessing news.
8. Listening to music.
9. Using instant messaging services.
10. Doing work.

Indications are that consuming news is even more important to users of tablets. Almost one-third of those who buy tablets read more news from more sources than they read before, according to a study conducted by the Pew Research Center's Project for Excellence in Journalism. Consuming news is the second most popular activity for tablet users after email.

So, accessing news is far more important to users than many suggest. That may well account for the dozens of news-based computer applications, or **apps**, for iPhones and iPads found in Apple's online store. Similar apps exist for the Android and Windows markets.

The U.S. population also continues to increase, and the size of the audience for news is growing with it. While audiences decline for newspapers and local television, consumers are flocking to the Web for news—often using smartphones and tablets to access it. The problem for news companies is not that people are tuning out or using media less frequently. Instead, the problem is **media fragmentation**. This proliferation of media outlets has led to smaller audiences for individual media companies. There are many more places to get news today than there were 25 years ago.

Smaller audiences are resulting in less advertising, or reduced prices for it, which has put great financial stress on those media, particularly newspapers and local television. Indeed, in its 2012 report on the State of the News Media, Pew concluded, "The transformation of the nation's news landscape has already taken a heavy toll on print news sources, particularly print newspapers. But there are now signs that television news—which so far has held onto its audience through the rise of the Internet—also is increasingly vulnerable, as it may be losing its hold on the next generation of news consumers." So there's no lack of interest in news, and the audience is increasing. But the news industry has a broken business model.

Financial Challenges to Legacy Media

For the better part of two centuries, owning a newspaper was virtually a license to print money. Great fortunes were made by media barons like William Randolph Hearst, who owned large newspapers, and Donald W. Reynolds, who owned small ones. Their businesses were lucrative: For much of the 20th century, newspapers turned a profit of 20 to 25 cents—sometimes even more—on each dollar that came through the door.

When radio and television came along, those media built on this legacy. Both quickly became profitable, and owning television networks and stations eventually became even more lucrative than owning newspapers. Magazines also found a home in the American media landscape. As advertisers began to covet their ability to deliver targeted audiences, the number of magazines proliferated.

Trouble was brewing, however, and by the end of the 20th century, it became clear that audience fragmentation was becoming a significant problem.

Smaller Audiences as a Result of Media Proliferation

When radio and television came along, they fit into the media landscape with little harm to newspapers and magazines. But by the time the Web and cable television arrived, media outlets were proliferating and media consumption patterns were shifting. Younger people started turning away from newspapers in favor of the Web and its thousands of information sources. Cable television took viewers from local stations. In the end, the proliferation of media outlets began to slice audiences, even growing ones, into smaller and smaller fragments, taking ad revenue from the traditional legacy media.

Today, it's clear that legacy media—newspapers, magazines, radio and broadcast television—are being damaged severely by newer media forms such as cable television, the Web and mobile devices. Newspaper revenues have fallen precipitously, and local television stations are now feeling the pinch caused by a proliferation of cable channels. Magazines are still generally healthy, thanks to their ability to target audiences more efficiently than newspapers or local television. Still, even magazines are threatened by the changes. In late 2012, *Newsweek*, first published in 1933, announced it would quit putting out a print edition and move to all-electronic distribution; the digital edition was later put up for sale. Magazines, like newspapers, suffer from high production and distribution costs. As a result, their long-term prognosis is uncertain. To hedge their bets, magazine publishers, like their newspaper counterparts, are embracing the Web.

Figure 5-14. William Randolph Hearst (1863–1951) made a fortune as the owner of large newspapers.

Lower Advertising Revenues and Higher Debt

Newspapers are costly to produce, and revenue trends are headed in the wrong direction. Classified advertising, long a big moneymaker at newspapers, has been devastated by websites like craigslist.org. Help-wanted advertising, in particular, has plummeted. Newspapers are manufactured products that consume large amounts of expensive paper and ink. They are labor-intensive not only in news reporting but also in printing and distribution. They are, in effect, an increasingly inefficient—and costly—way to deliver news.

Nevertheless, despite what many would have you believe, most newspapers are still profitable. Those that have failed or are suffering mostly fall into two categories: Either they are the second newspaper in a two-newspaper city, or they have been purchased by corporations and have amassed huge debt. Many well-known newspapers have closed, including the *Rocky Mountain News* of Denver and the *Seattle Post-Intelligencer*. Some, like *The (New Orleans) Times-Picayune*, have opted for less-frequent publishing schedules, often three or four days a week. Still others—the *Chicago Tribune*, the *Los Angeles Times* and *The Boston Globe* among them—are in trouble because of heavy debt incurred when they were purchased.

More than 1,700 daily newspapers existed as late as 1980, but today the number hovers around 1,380. Daily newspaper circulation declined almost 29 percent from 1990 to 2011.

More than 15,000 newspaper journalists lost their jobs between 2000 and 2010, and some cities, like Ann Arbor, Mich., home to about 115,000 people and a major university, don't have a daily newspaper anymore.

SUNDAY
Orlando Sentinel
OrlandoSentinel.com OS

NATION & WORLD

3 planets found in 'habitable zones'
It's not too hot or too cold in the "Goldilocks" region. A8

Waco fire survivor remains a believer
He is loyal to teachings of self-styled prophet Koresh. A14

Smithsonian will cut hours to save
Budget woes will close galleries, exhibits on some days. A14

SPORTS

Dwight making most of chance to save L.A.
In the wake of Kobe Bryant's injury, Mike Bianchi, who founded LOATHE (Lakers Officially Are The Hated Enemy) for jilted Magic fans, doesn't like what Howard's up to. C1

READING CAMPAIGN

Time for 'One Book One Community'
Read "The Fast and The Furriest" and enjoy events at libraries. A2

TRAVEL & ARTS

Bok Tower goes from bells to banjo
"Concert Under the Stars" to feature quirky musical guests. F3

SCOTT MAXWELL

Health care: Some yap, some act B1

WEATHER
79°/66° (today/tonight)
50% chance of storms.
Forecast, B8

INDEX
Deaths……B6
Dining……F7
Opinion……A19
Sports……C1
Travel……F1
TV……F9

"Part of being a responsible gun owner is knowing how to shoot and how to avoid situations. It's so much more than owning a gun." *Shirley Hedge*

FLORIDA IN THE CROSS HAIRS

Number of Florida women of all ages with concealed-weapon permits jumps

RED HUBER/STAFF PHOTOGRAPHER

Shirley Hedge, 66, known as "Shotgun Shirley," visits The Gun Shop and Gun Range in Leesburg for target practice recently. She received her concealed-weapon permit 2 weeks ago.

Who are Florida permit holders?
From 2004 to 2013* women have become a bigger portion of the population of Floridians holding concealed-weapon permits.

	2004	2013
Women	15%	21%
Men	85%	79%

*Data reflect the difference between state records for Jan. 7, 2004, and April 10, 2013.
SOURCES: Florida Department of Agriculture and Consumer Services, staff research
STAFF GRAPHIC

BY HENRY PIERSON CURTIS AND SCOTT POWERS | Staff Writers

Shirley Hedge spent more than 40 years saving lives as a nurse.

Now retired, "Shotgun Shirley" represents the biggest increase among Florida's more than 1 million people who have concealed-weapon permits: women 66 and older.

Hedge, 66, is one of 34,937 women in her age bracket licensed to carry a gun almost anywhere they want in Florida and 35 other states. Their numbers have jumped 619 percent since 2004 — the earliest year with available data — when there were 4,856 women licensed in the same age group, according to state records.

The number of women in the youngest age bracket, 21 to 35, jumped 463 percent to 40,386 — four times more than men in the same age group.

After the death of her husband three years ago, Hedge began worrying about her safety.

"I didn't realize how vulnerable I was until I started thinking about it. ... I was in denial," said

Please turn to **PERMITS, A7**

Videos
Women talk about their growing interest in gun ownership. OrlandoSentinel.com

HORROR AT BOSTON MARATHON

A week of terror, tragedy

Americans stunned by bombs at race, blast at Texas plant, ricin-laced letters

D. Tsarnaev

BY JOEL ACHENBACH
The Washington Post

Friday morning America woke up to more mayhem: a manhunt for a terror suspect in suburban Boston. The whole city on lockdown. One suspect dead. Officer slain. Another officer shot. Thousands of officers geared up and ready for battle.

It was utterly captivating. It was also almost unendurable, even at a distance, far from Boston. A person would be forgiven for turning off the television, shutting down the computer and going back to bed to hide under the covers. For those of a gentle disposition, this was all too much like an episode of "24" or a Bruce Willis movie.

Full coverage of marathon case. A3, A6

Please turn to **WEEK, A6**

JIM ROGASH/GETTY IMAGES

Baseball fans at Boston's Fenway Park hold signs Saturday showing support for marathon victims.

Katelyn Wright is a dual-enrollment student at Lake Nona High School. She's taking a Valencia College course.

GEORGE SKENE/STAFF PHOTOGRAPHER

Dual-enrollment programs could face cuts

BY DENISE-MARIE ORDWAY
Staff Writer

Community-college officials say they might have to cut or restrict dual-enrollment programs if the Florida Legislature does not provide more money for the program that allows high-school students to take courses for free at public colleges and universities.

College administrators have become increasingly frustrated about having to absorb the tuition and fees that are not charged to the tens of thousands of teenagers who enroll each year in college courses, mostly at the community colleges.

Higher-education institutions lost $58 million in tuition and fees last school year alone, according to an analysis by the state's Office of Program Policy Analysis and Government Accountability.

College leaders say shortfalls in

Amount of revenue lost. A12

Please turn to **DUAL, A12**

Used with permission of the *Orlando Sentinel* (April 21, 2013).

Figure 5-15. The *Orlando Sentinel* is among the many large-market newspapers still doing well.

Many forecast a similar pending contraction of local television. No one is predicting that local television stations will disappear, but it's likely that fewer stations will offer local news in the years ahead.

Despite all this, the typical U.S. newspaper still turns a nice profit of about 5 cents on the dollar, and most local television stations are still profitable, too. When you consider that many industries operate quite comfortably on much lower profit margins, newspapers and local television are far from dying. The trend, though, is in the wrong direction for legacy media companies, which still derive about 90 percent of their income from their original platforms rather than from the Web because print advertising is more profitable than Web advertising.

Newspapers: The Source of Most News

Although people prefer different news *platforms*, what they are *not* doing is rejecting traditional *sources* of news—news provided by legacy media, companies that specialize in traditional media forms such as newspapers, magazines, radio and broadcast television.

So while it's tempting to dismiss newspapers as a product of a bygone era and suggest that we simply move on to newer and better ways of getting news, the larger problem is that newspapers are the source of most of the news we consume. Indeed, most of the information found on Yahoo or Google News originated with legacy media operations, most often newspapers. The same is true with most other news websites.

In fact, several studies have concluded that the vast majority of all news consumed in the U.S., regardless of where it was consumed, originated with newspapers. The reason? Newspapers have the best news-gathering apparatus in almost every city in the country. They typically employ more journalists than all the radio and television stations in that city combined.

So for more than a century, the legacy media have funded the extensive news-gathering operation that exists in the U.S. and much of the rest of the world. Yet increasingly, because of the diminished audiences for print journalism, newspapers and television companies are trimming the size of their staffs in an effort to survive. Clearly, a new business model is needed.

As we go about this task of creating a new business model for the news media, what we must save is not specific newspapers and television programs, and not the companies that own them, but the high-quality reporting they produce.

Most of that news is **spot news**—breaking news that occurred today. Replacing spot news might not be too tough. After all, if a plane crashes, some blogger or citizen journalist, if no one else, is bound to report it. More problematic is the potential loss of what journalist Alex S. Jones calls "the creation of new awareness provided by either months of investigation or relentlessly regular coverage."

Jones is the Laurence M. Lombard Lecturer in the Press and Public Policy and the director of the Joan Shorenstein Center on the Press, Politics and Public Policy at Harvard University. In his book *Losing the News: The Future of the News That Feeds Democracy*, he praises the technological changes that are altering the journalism landscape, but he fears the loss of the "iron core of news that serves as a watchdog over government, holds the powerful accountable, and gives citizens what they need." He's hopeful and optimistic that the "iron core" can be saved.

In a review of Jones' book in *The New York Times*, Harold Evans, former editor of *The Sunday Times of London* and *The Times of London*, points out what happens when this kind of news doesn't get enough attention: "the insufficiently monitored housing bubble; the neglect in New Orleans, leading to the devastation after Katrina; or the formation of Al Qaeda in Afghanistan, leading to 9/11."

Journalism's Role in a Democracy

While the overall size of the news audience is growing, not all consumers are embracing the new media. Indeed, some young people, in particular, don't consume news at all, and that merely adds to the problems of legacy media.

College student Kendra Logan, 19, is among an increasing number of young people who don't consume news. "I don't read newspapers, I don't watch television news, and I rarely look at news on the Internet," she says. She's among the disengaged, and she's not alone. According to a study by the Pew Research Center, Logan is among the 34 percent of those younger than 25 who get no news daily, up from 25 percent just 10 years earlier.

That's troubling to those who worry about the foundations of U.S. democracy. Ill-informed members of the public can't make good decisions in the voting booth, if indeed they vote at all. They can't possibly understand the big issues of the day— among them conflicts with extremists, health care availability, failing schools, illegal immigration and poverty. In short, they can't be good citizens. To actively participate in democracy requires knowledge of what's going on in the world, the nation, the state and the community.

Logan is one of millions of uninformed Americans who are tuning out the news as the U.S. experiences the biggest shift in media consumption patterns since colonial times. That's bad for the media, but it's also bad for the country, which depends on an informed citizenry to make good decisions in the voting booth. With that in mind, it's important for today's journalist to understand audiences—how and why people decide to consume news and why some choose not to do so.

How People Consume News Today

It's clear that legacy media are falling out of favor at an increasing pace. But if there are losers, there also must be winners. As noted earlier, those winners are the Web and mobile and, to a lesser extent, cable television. According to a 2012 Pew study, television continues to reign as America's favorite news source—55 percent of respondents reported consuming news on television the day before being surveyed. That percentage, however, had dropped from 68 percent in 1991. While cable television audiences remained stable, local television audiences continued to decline.

On THE JOB

Editing Online News

Sarah Rupp graduated with a degree in newspaper journalism but immediately found herself working at online sites.

Right out of school, she landed an internship at msnbc.com in Redmond, Wash. She later worked at other online sites, including ABCNews.com, before landing at seattlepi.com, which operates 24/7.

"I usually work a day shift, which means that I have to keep the site fresh with new articles, story updates, breaking news and photos," Rupp says. "Throughout the day we add new wire stories, staff stories, photo galleries and other Web-only features. . . . Besides doing the daily stuff, I also get to work on special projects like producing video and putting together new content channels for the site."

She enjoys the work: "The great thing about working for a news website is you get the chance to do a little of everything—writing, editing, choosing stories, designing graphics, building Web pages, posting photos and editing audio clips.

"There are a lot of exciting things going on in online journalism. . . . No longer are reporters the only people who report the news. That means the very definition of what 'news' is has changed and will continue to change."

The second most popular source of news? That would be the combination of Web and mobile devices, up to 39 percent in 2012. That's an increase of about 16 percent since 2006. Thirty-three percent listened to radio news, and only 29 percent read a newspaper. So, in that six-year period from 2006 to 2012, Web-based news, whether accessed through computers or mobile devices, passed both radio and newspapers in popularity.

Types of News Audiences

A 2008 Pew study placed news consumers in one of four audience segments. Understanding those segments helps us understand the shifts in news consumption that affect the future of journalism. They are the following:

- **Traditionalists.** This group is older, less affluent and not as well-educated as the typical news consumer. Members of this group are heavy consumers of television news at all times of the day and understand news best by seeing pictures rather than reading or hearing. Traditionalists have a strong interest in the weather and relatively low interest in science and tech news. Most have computers, but few of them get news online on a typical day. This group makes up the largest part of the total audience (46 percent when the study was conducted).
- **Integrators.** These well-educated, affluent and mostly middle-aged people get news from legacy media, the Web and mobile devices. They are more engaged in public af-

fairs than other news consumers are, and they are more sophisticated and sought after by advertisers. Television is a main news source for this group, but most also get news online each day. This group made up 23 percent of the public.

- **Net-Newsers.** This group is affluent, well-educated and relatively young. Members are more likely to read political blogs than watch network news, and their Web use soars during the day. They are frequent online news viewers and heavy technology users, and they have a strong interest in technology news. Fifty-eight percent of them are men, and the group as a whole made up 13 percent of the audience.
- **The Disengaged.** This group stands out for its low levels of news interest and news consumption. This group made up 14 percent of the public.

These segments account for 96 percent of the U.S. public. Of the remaining 4 percent, Pew reported that 2 percent did not name either a traditional source or the Web as their main source of news. An additional 2 percent named the Web as a main source but rarely go online for news.

Can Web-Based News Replace Newspaper Reporting?

Perhaps most telling about those numbers is that no single group of consumers leans toward newspapers as a primary source of news. Television—particularly cable television—and the Web dominate, with the growing Net-Newsers group relying heavily on the Web and its mobile-accessible content. Those who read newspapers or watch network news and local television are older. As that generation starts to die and as younger generations mature into news consumers (or non-news consumers), the Web and mobile stand to be the big winners. Cable television shows resiliency and continues to maintain its market share.

In the view of most journalists, both cable television and many sites on the Web have credibility problems. It's difficult to tell what's news and what's opinion on much of cable television, and determining the veracity of websites is far from easy. Despite that, readers and viewers have spoken. They want to consume news through the new outlets, and, some citizen journalists (nonprofessionals who function as journalists) want to participate in the news-gathering process. Still others may not want to report the news but want to engage professional journalists and others in a discussion of that news. Journalists must determine where they fit in that process and adapt.

Most journalists are reluctantly embracing this changing environment, even while they're troubled by what it portends. Almost certainly, there will be fewer jobs in the legacy media. But almost as certainly, there will be new opportunities in the emerging media, which we will discuss later in this chapter.

This doesn't necessarily mean that newspapers will disappear or that local television will consolidate into one or two stations per market. But the importance of both outlets is declining, and with that decline comes a major transformation of the American media landscape.

Distrust of the Media

At least some of the shift in media consumption patterns can be traced to the public's increasing distrust of the legacy media. According to a Gallup study, in 1998, 55 percent of Americans expressed a great deal or a fair amount of trust and confidence in the media, but by 2012 that had fallen to 40 percent. Fifty-eight percent of Democrats expressed trust in the media, while only 31 percent of independents and 26 percent of Republicans did so.

Journalists are perplexed about the public's attitude, and there are no clear answers about why distrust of the media is growing. Some likely causes have been suggested:

- People fail to distinguish between reporters (who report, as Bob Woodward says, "the best obtainable version of the truth") and columnists (who offer opinion).
- The decline of profitability of newspapers and local television has led to reduced staffing, which in turn has damaged the media's ability to report well and ensure accuracy.
- As newspapers have moved away from fact-based writing in the inverted pyramid format (see Chapter 8), they have given reporters greater license to stylize stories with narrative writing. Descriptive writing is often mistaken for opinion-based journalism.
- On cable television, in particular, the lines blur between news programs and talk shows where opinion, not fact, dominates.
- Cable television and talk radio are dominated by right-wing and left-wing talk-show hosts, many of whom, like Rush Limbaugh and Rachel Maddow, make no pretense of objectivity. Many consumers would consider Limbaugh and Maddow journalists, a description that makes most journalists cringe.
- Some people even argue that news coverage itself is tilted leftward or rightward depending on the political slant of the media outlet. Most journalists deny this, but the public perception remains.

Indeed, Pew studies of press accuracy continue to show that Democrats have the most favorable view of CNN and MSNBC, while Republicans tilt heavily toward Fox News. That doesn't seem to bother any of the three outlets. Nor does it bother their respective viewers. Some have suggested this marks a return to the partisan press that existed in this country before and just after the American Revolution.

There's a major disconnect between how the public and those in the media view various news outlets. Most journalists would consider the reporting and accuracy of *The New York Times* and *The Wall Street Journal* to be far superior to that of CNN, Fox News, MSNBC and network television. The public disagrees. Among those media outlets, network television has the highest favorable ratings, followed by CNN, Fox and MSNBC. *The Times* and *The Journal* are last and next to last, respectively. Even widely respected National Public Radio ranks below CNN, Fox and MSNBC.

Courtesy of *Lawrence Journal-World*

Figure 5-16. In 2001, the *Lawrence (Kan.) Journal-World* became one of the first media organizations to house its print, online and television news reporting groups in one converged newsroom.

In recent years, much of the criticism of the press has come from Republicans, particularly those on the far right, who consider most journalists to be left-wing activists who favor Democratic positions. Now, Democrats are increasingly skeptical, too. But there is good news in all this. Most Americans have favorable views of local television news (73 percent), the daily newspaper they read most often (65 percent) and network television news (64 percent). So while there is great criticism of the press in general, most news consumers have no problem with the media they choose to consume. The prevailing attitude seems to be this: "The media in general are lousy and incompetent, but my newspaper or television station is not so bad."

Convergence as a Response to Media Fragmentation

As shifting media consumption patterns upset the business models of news companies, many are responding by expanding their product offerings and shifting their emphasis away from legacy media and into growth areas, particularly the Web. If the public wants to read news on the Web, or even on tablets or mobile phones, news companies intend to provide that option.

Journalists call this phenomenon—the coordination of print, broadcast and online reporting in a news operation—convergence. It's the transformation of traditional media into something entirely new, a 24/7 news operation where the Web, not the traditional product, comes first. The concept is that consumers should be able to get news on their terms, however and whenever they want it. Radio and television stations put their recorded newscasts online, and some consumers watch them on the Web. Sometimes these Web-based newscasts even contain material that didn't make it into the traditional newscast, including, for example, a full-length video of the mayor's press conference. Sometimes such material is included even on a newspaper website. And the Web, of course, permits users to interact with databases of public information, such as property tax bills, driver's license records and records of the salaries of public officials and schoolteachers. Neither print nor broadcast outlets can provide this information as effectively. The *Tampa Tribune*-WFLA-Tampa Bay Online convergence effort in Florida is one of the oldest experiments in convergence, having started in 2000 (see Figure 5-17).

Courtesy of Tampa Bay Online

Figure 5-17. Tampa Bay Online, started in 2000, is a joint venture of *The Tampa Tribune* and WFLA.

Enhanced Web Coverage

Increasingly, many news operations—even newspapers—think "Web first." An editor of *The Philadelphia Inquirer* wrote, "Let's break as much news as we can online, particularly if it's a story, column or review that readers might get from another source, or that benefits from the strengths of the Web."

Many newspapers have become Web-first, 24-hour-a-day operations that embrace citizen journalism. As news breaks, the reporter writes the story first for the Web and mobile devices and posts it for public consumption as soon as it's ready. Then, when it's time to put together the next morning's newspaper, production efforts shift. If a member of the public comes up with a story before a reporter, so be it.

Without a doubt, more and more media companies are headed in this direction. The Gannett Co. did so with the creation of what it calls Gannett Information Centers. Gannett CEO Craig Dubow described the concept in a letter to Gannett employees:

> The Information Center is a way to gather and disseminate news and information across all platforms, 24/7. The Information Center will let us gather the very local news and information that customers want, then distribute it when, where and how our customers seek it.

In Dubow's opinion, the concept is working:

> Breaking news on the Web and updating for the newspaper draws more people to both those media. Asking the community for help gets it—and delivers the newspaper into the heart of community conversations once again. Rich and deep databases with local, local information gathered efficiently are central to the whole process. The changes impact all media, and the public has approved. Results include stronger newspapers, more popular websites and more opportunities to attract the customers advertisers want.

Synchronized Media Coverage

"Convergence" is the hottest buzzword in the media industry these days, but defining it isn't easy. In the definition of some, convergence occurs when a newspaper or television station starts publishing material on the Web. According to others, convergence occurs when print reporters start carrying digital voice recorders and produce material for radio as well as the newspaper, or when reporters use a video camera to record a press conference for the newspaper's website.

While those may indeed be forms of convergence, in its most complete sense convergence involves the coming together of four communication forms:

- Text.
- Video and audio.
- The Web.
- Mobile phones and other wireless devices such as tablets.

Take a look at newspaper sites on the Web, and you will see this happening. Some of the best uses of video anywhere can be found on the website of *The New York Times*, something you might not expect. Interactive graphics that help readers visualize processes in new ways also dazzle readers on the *Times* site. If *The Times* is often seen as gray and stodgy, its website certainly is not. Want news on your iPhone? *The Times* has an app for that. Want breaking news delivered to your phone through instant messaging? The Associated Press has an app for that.

Newspaper companies aren't the only ones doing convergence. The BBC, CNN, CBS, ESPN and others have created stellar websites that not only give users the news but also add to their understanding of it—often in far more detail than they can provide on their traditional newscasts and sportscasts.

Jeff Greenberg/PhotoEdit, Inc.

Figure 5-18. Anyone with a video camera or smartphone can post observations to a site like CNN's iReport. To combat false reports, media outlets are beginning to moderate what gets posted.

Embracing Citizen Journalism

The best of the legacy media companies are embracing the public's involvement in the news-gathering process and allowing the public to critique stories on the Web. The old "one provider to many consumers" model of newspapers and television is increasingly becoming a thing of the past.

When terrorists planted bombs on a London subway, the first images of the disaster came from survivors who used their mobile phones to take photos and transmit them to the outside world from below ground. When an airplane struck birds during takeoff and was forced to land, nearly miraculously, on New York's Hudson River, some of the first images came from nearby apartment dwellers who took photos and video from their windows. When the Arab Spring uprisings occurred in the Middle East, citizen reporting through social media sometimes was the only source of news as repressive governments banned reporters from the scenes. Social media allowed citizens to provide eyewitness accounts, which were picked up and distributed by mainstream media. This form of citizen journalism—the gathering and reporting of the news by nonjournalists—is cropping up on websites around the world, much of it on sites of established media companies. For example, when the BBC asked users around the world to snap photos of scheduled anti-war protests and send them in, hundreds of photos were submitted. When an F-15 fighter crashed, a citizen in Virginia shot photos that she sent to a local television station. The photo taken immediately following the impact was used in the newscast along with video footage taken later.

Much of the video and still footage taken by people who happen to be on the scene finds its way to moblogs, a form of blogging in which the user publishes blog entries directly to the Web from a mobile phone or tablet. But when it finds its way onto the sites of mainstream media, as the examples above show, citizen journalists effectively serve as an extension of the media outlet's traditional reporting staff.

A notable example of a community-oriented site with citizen-generated blogs is Bluffton-Today.com, produced by the *Bluffton Today* newspaper in South Carolina. BlufftonToday.com contains community blogs, expert blogs and staff blogs. As a result, everyone is part of the dialogue.

> *"Responding to the question, 'Do you ever envision a time when your organization will not publish a print edition,' 62 percent of newspaper publishers replied 'no.' One-third said 'yes' and 5 percent said 'maybe.'"*
>
> **—Mike Jenner, Reynolds Journalism Institute**

Problems with Citizen Journalism

Citizen journalism often works, but occasionally it goes awry, just like professional journalism. Some journalists have devoted a lot of effort to dismissing the idea of citizen journalism, citing the likelihood of inaccuracies. But it may be telling that some 10 years after the advent of citizen journalism, relatively few instances of major errors have been found in national media. One significant one was a false report posted in 2008 on CNN's iReport.cnn.com that Apple CEO Steve Jobs had suffered a heart attack. The erroneous story, which rattled investors, led to a $12 decline in Apple's stock price before the company debunked it three hours later. Jobs later died, but in 2008 he was very much alive.

The iReport site is almost completely open and permits users to post "news"— unedited and unvetted—after a minimal registration process. Observed Scott Karp of Publishing 2.0, a blog that reports on the evolution of media, "The problem is—and this is something that advocates of citizen journalism typically overlook—that if a platform is open, and anyone can participate, that means not only can well-intentioned citizens participate but so can bad actors, spammers, liars, cheats and thieves." Despite such warnings, the 2008 report about Jobs' death remains one of the few examples of false reporting on a national story by a citizen journalist.

Although most mainstream media outlets are allowing citizens to participate, they are moderating what goes onto their sites. As a result, back in the newsroom, journalists often find that their roles have changed. Not only do they perform their traditional roles, but they also edit stories, photos and videos shot by readers and viewers; moderate Web-based discussion forums; write blogs; and post breaking news on Facebook and Twitter. As a result, newsrooms have begun to look different from those of the past, and the websites of traditional media companies are getting more and more attention. That means more and more journalists—even in newspaper newsrooms—are being trained in digital audio and video editing. Some find themselves in front of television cameras to create mini-newscasts that will appear on the website.

Forms of Citizen Journalism

While some citizen journalism finds its way onto the sites of legacy media, today's Web publishing environment makes it easy for citizens to create their own sites and cut out the legacy media entirely. Anyone, it seems, can become a publisher. In an article in *Online Journalism Review*, J.D. Lasica sorted the media forms used in citizen journalism into six types:

- **Audience participation** (user comments attached to news stories, personal blogs, photos or video footage captured from mobile phone cameras, local news written by members of the community). Mainstream media outlets such as msnbc.com give readers the chance to post comments and other items on their sites.
- **Independent news or information websites** (such as the Drudge Report). These sites are published by those not normally associated with traditional media.
- **Participatory news sites** (*Northwest Voice*). Here, readers get to write, take photos and publish their work, perhaps even in newspaper format, with the assistance of professional editors.
- **Collaborative and contributory news sites** (Slashdot.org). These sites, often featuring a specific subject-matter area, are based on reader comments and contributions.
- **Thin media** (mailing lists, email newsletters). Through thin media, targeted news content is directed to those with narrowly defined interests.
- **Personal broadcasting sites** (JustinTV.com). On these sites, the operators provide news-based subject matter in a specific area of interest, such as technology. The result is downloadable audio or video.

There are more sources of information than ever before, and the public is embracing those alternatives. Many websites target specific groups of readers with great precision. Interested in the latest in football recruiting at your favorite university? There's probably a site for that. Interested in a nontraditional take on local politics? There may well be a blog for that. All of these new alternatives are eroding the strength of legacy media.

The Future of Journalism

As we've learned, despite the belief of many that journalism is a dying profession, the audience for journalists' work is actually growing. That reality leads many in the profession to believe that the future of journalism is bright, not dismal.

Even if newspapers—or at least most of them—are indeed destined to die, as some believe, many newspaper companies are almost certain to survive. A 2012 study of U.S. newspaper publishers found that 65 percent were "very optimistic" or "somewhat optimistic" about the future of their industry; 31 percent were neutral on the issue, and only 4 percent said they were "not optimistic." Not a single publisher in that study, conducted by the Reynolds Journalism Institute, reported being "not optimistic at all."

Perhaps that's because many in the newspaper business realize there is still a strong and growing market for the content they produce. In the future, that content may not be delivered on newsprint, but newspaper publishers have high hopes that e-book readers like the Kindle Fire and the growth of tablet computers like the iPad will spark new interest in news consumption. Publishers hope to find a successful business model to support the expensive process of news gathering. Indications are that their hopes have merit. The chore ahead of them, then, is to continue to improve the product and maximize its appeal for delivery on tablets and smartphones while refining the business model.

As mentioned earlier, in almost any city in the U.S., the one newspaper (and usually there is only one) employs more journalists than all the radio and television stations combined. So while the number of newspapers may be declining, newspaper companies are far from dead and are still eager to hire young people who can help them make the transition from print to the Web and mobile phones.

Not all legacy media will disappear—not by a long shot. Some will continue to succeed in their legacy forms, including many newspapers and local television stations, and others will make the transition to the Web and find ways to make it profitable. Still others will create niche sites to create new revenue streams, and others will find totally new models for delivering their content over devices like mobile phones, tablet computers and e-book readers. Meanwhile, information-based Web startups are likely to become increasingly profitable, and foundation-funded, not-for-profit news companies are being tested nationwide. With all this comes the need to hire journalists to create the original content consumers demand.

The way journalism is distributed is changing, but the market for good journalism continues to grow.

Suggested Readings

Croteau, David, and William Hoynes. *The Business of Media: Corporate Media and the Public Interest.* Thousand Oaks, Calif.: Pine Forge Press, 2006. This is a good treatise on the impact of changing economic models on the media industry.

Gillmor, Dan. *Mediactive.* Self-published, 2010. In this book, Gillmor discusses the changes occurring in traditional media and the democratization of new media forms.

Gillmor, Dan. *We the Media: Grassroots Journalism by the People, for the People.* Sebastopol, Calif.: O'Reilly Media, 2006. This book on the value of citizen journalism was written by a longtime newspaper reporter and editor.

Jones, Alex S. *Losing the News: The Future of the News That Feeds Democracy.* New York: Oxford Univ. Press, 2009. This is a superb review of why legacy media are so critical to democracy.

Meyer, Philip. *The Vanishing Newspaper: Saving Journalism in the Information Age.* 2nd ed. Columbia: Univ. of Missouri Press, 2009. In this excellent book, Meyer discusses the importance of newspapers in the news-gathering process.

Wollan, Robert, Nick Smith and Catherine Zhou. *The Social Media Management Handbook: Everything You Need to Know to Get Social Media Working in Your Business.* Hoboken, N.J.: John Wiley and Sons, 2011. This is a good primer on incorporating social media into a business model.

Suggested Websites

www.grady.uga.edu/annualsurveys
The University of Georgia issues an annual report on the employment patterns of journalism graduates nationwide.

www.journalists.org
The Online News Association was organized in 1999.

www.magazine.org
The Association of Magazine Media is the professional organization for magazine journalists.

www.naa.org
The Newspaper Association of America, a leading trade association for the industry, tracks trends in newspaper consumption.

www.nab.org
The National Association of Broadcasters is the primary trade organization of the broadcast industry.

www.people-press.org
The Pew Research Center for the People and the Press is an excellent source that tracks the changing attitudes of the American people toward the press. Pew's research can be found here.

www.rtdna.org
The Radio Television Digital News Association, a leading trade group for broadcast journalists, tracks trends in that field.

Exercises

1. **Team project.** Your instructor will divide the class into groups of three or four. As a team, choose a news aggregator site, such as Google News. On your own, read the top

five stories; then read the top five stories on your local newspaper's site. What are the differences and similarities? What does each site do well? What does each do poorly? Discuss your findings in your group, and rate the sites on how well they fulfill the need for news to be relevant, useful and interesting.

2. Find two newspaper websites that carry staff-generated blogs. Compare and contrast them. Are the writers responsive to readers' comments? Is the discussion lively or slow? What role do readers' comments play on these blogs?
3. Analyze a citizen journalism site in your community or in your area. How does the information in the top three stories compare with the information in the top three stories on the local newspaper's website? If there are no citizen journalism sites in your community, find one in a large city nearby.
4. Provide a revised definition of news using the new realities of citizen journalism. Define it for different audiences, including you and your friends, and your parents.
5. Interview two college students to determine their top three sources of news. Then do the same with two people 40 or older. Write a one-page report on the differences you found in media consumption patterns.
6. The Web, in addition to being a place to publish, is a useful source of information for journalists. Using the Web, locate information on the most recent U.S. census, and report the following:
   a. The population of your state.
   b. The population of your city.
   c. The range of income levels and percentages of population that fall within those income levels in your city.
   d. The demographic breakdown of your city by race.
7. Research two legacy media companies, one that is primarily print-oriented and one that is broadcast-oriented. Using publicly available reports, describe any differences you find in the commitment of those companies to online news.
8. **Journalism blog.** Go to a news site or discussion board, and follow one thread of discussion. Write a post for a blog you set up describing how the information you found on the news site might be useful to a reporter. Also describe how you would verify the information you found there.

Jobs in Journalism

While people like Jim Spencer are forming their own companies in the new media economy, others are finding more traditional types of jobs—sometimes at legacy media companies and sometimes elsewhere. (See Figure 5-19 for insight into the range of jobs and salaries available for journalism graduates.)

When Jenifer Langosch went to journalism school, she thought she'd end up working as a newspaper sports writer. Instead, she found a job covering the Pittsburgh Pirates and St. Louis Cardinals for MLB.com. Troy Wolverton did end up in a legacy media job, writing a personal technology column for the *San Jose Mercury News*. But he did so only after years in Web-based media, including CNET.com.

"I learned a long time ago that the Web was going to open opportunities . . . that never existed before," Jim Spencer says. "There's a whole new world out there. Aspiring journalists have all sorts of jobs to lure them that never even existed a decade ago."

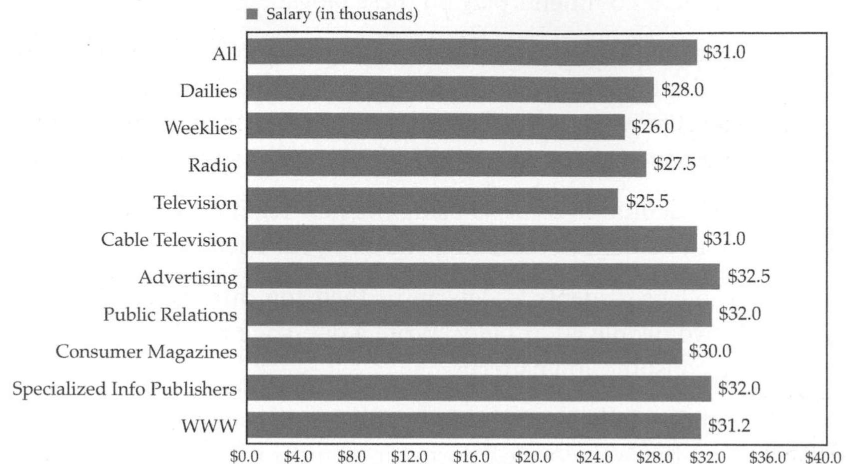

Figure 5-19. Median yearly salaries for 2011 bachelor's degree recipients with full-time jobs.

Source: Lee B. Becker, Tudor Vlad, and Konrad Kaplen, "2011 Annual Survey of Journalism and Communication Graduates," James M. Cox Jr. Center for International Mass Communication Training and Research, Grady College of Journalism and Mass Communication, University of Georgia, 2012. Available at www.grady.uga.edu/annualsurveys.

Training to become a journalist prepares you for many jobs. Some are obvious, some are not. Most jobs, regardless of the medium, fall into one of these categories:

- **Writing and reporting.** Newspaper reporters and magazine writers are examples. At newspapers, most writing jobs are full-time staff positions, but many magazines rely much more heavily on freelance writers who are paid by the story. The skills of reporting and writing go together. No one in journalism can be a good writer without first being a good reporter.
- **Editing.** Great jobs abound for those who can edit well. Newspapers, magazines, radio and television stations and some websites have copy editors, assignment editors and editorial assistants. At newspapers, the entry-level position of copy editor often pays more than the entry-level position of reporter. Copy editors are in greater demand than reporters.

- **Photography and video.** Print publications and websites use lots of photographs and therefore need photographers. At newspapers, most photographers are staff members, but at many magazines freelance photographers are more common. Video is becoming important for all media operations that run websites. No longer is video merely the province of television.
- **Art and design.** Designers are needed in all media. There are jobs for newspaper and magazine designers and Web designers. Even television stations need Web designers. There also is an increasing demand for information graphics specialists—people who produce maps, charts and graphs.
- **Production.** Television producers are in high demand. It's quite possible to become a news producer right out of journalism school. Web producers are also in demand, and additional production jobs exist in the print media, particularly for those who can edit audio and video.
- **Tech support.** Those who combine a knowledge of journalism with computer literacy can find jobs anywhere. Media outlets around the world have a strong interest in computer-literate journalists. To increase their marketability, journalism students should consider a minor or double major in information technology.
- **Advertising and public relations.** Advertising and public relations often are taught within schools and departments of journalism. Jobs in this field abound, and they range from advertising sales and creative design to account management and Internet marketing and promotion.
- **Audience development.** Many websites now have teams of people trained to expand the site's audience. Through the use of viral marketing, audience development specialists post messages on Facebook and Twitter with links to the site. This helps drive traffic and enhances prospects for advertising revenue.
- **Management.** Many who enter journalism eventually become assignment editors, managing editors or executive editors. Those jobs pay more and are part of a natural progression for reporters and copy editors.

As in any period of transition, there are opportunities as well as wrong turns. Those who position themselves to excel in this environment will find success in journalism—even at legacy media companies.

Jobs in Journalism

Jobs in Legacy Media					
Jobs abound for those who seek to enter the legacy media. Here are a few of the possibilities for each medium. Asterisks (*) identify entry-level jobs that beginners are likely to land.					
Newspapers (Daily and Weekly)	**Magazines**	**Television**	**Radio**	**Online Media**	**Other Jobs**
Reporter* Copy editor* Page designer* Information graphics specialist* Photographer* Assignment editor News editor Managing editor Executive editor Columnist	Writer* Fact checker* Editorial assistant* Copy editor* Page designer* Senior writer Senior editor Contributing writer Managing editor Editor Columnist	Reporter* Producer* Desk assistant* Videographer* Anchor News director Executive producer	Reporter* Producer* Anchor News director	Writer* Producer* Graphics specialist* Executive producer (titles vary)	Advertising sales* Advertising copy writer* Advertising account manager* Public relations practitioner* Account executive Art director Media critic Foreign correspondent

Jobs in Emerging Media	
Jobs are rapidly increasing for those who seek work in emerging media. In addition to starting your own website, here are a few of the possibilities for paid jobs in Web-based media. Many jobs listed under "Jobs in Legacy Media" also exist in emerging media. All of the jobs listed below are entry-level jobs that beginners are likely to land.	
Websites	**Entrepreneurial Activities**
Reporter Copy editor Designer Writer Producer Graphics specialist Advertising sales Advertising design	News software designer Ad software designer E-zine editor Multimedia designer Newsletter editor

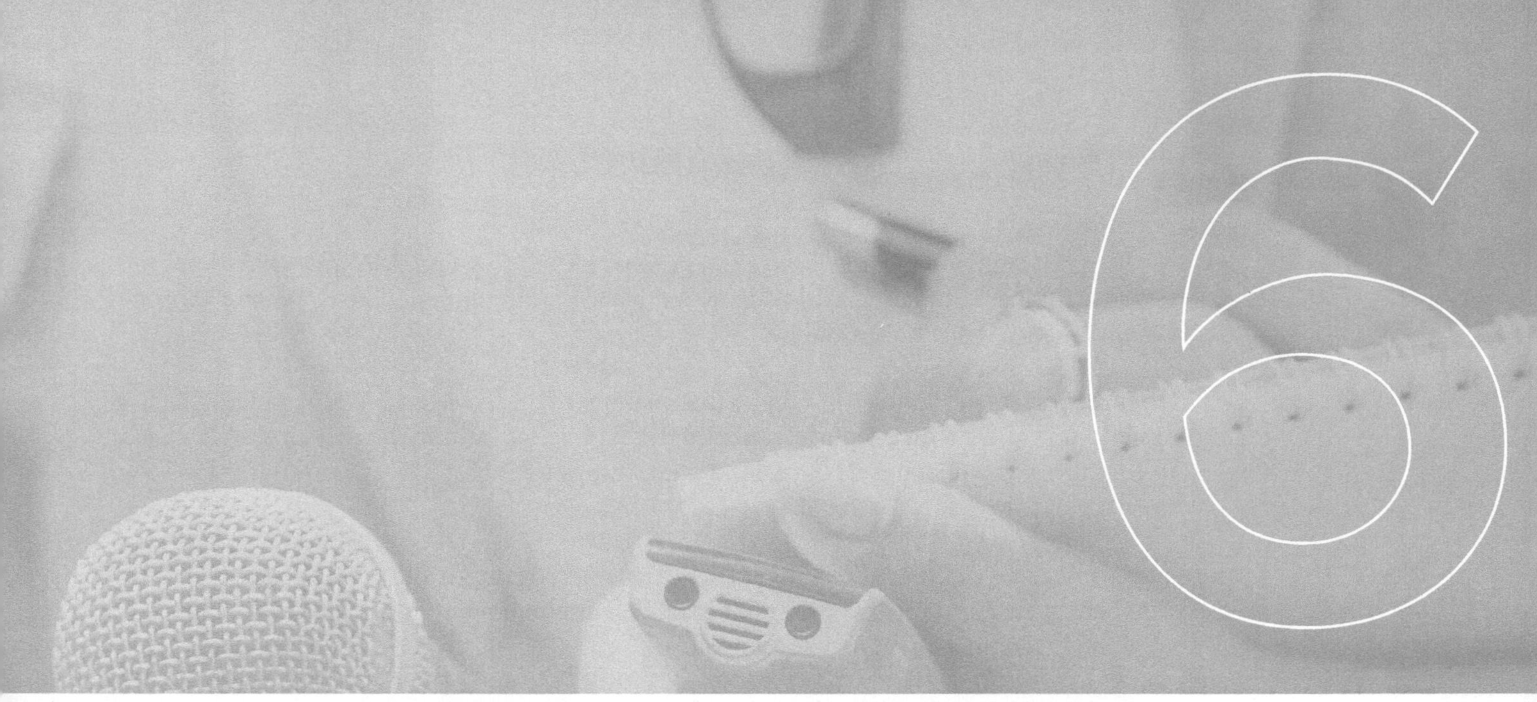

Chapter 6
Gathering Information from People

"Gathering Information from People" from *News Reporting and Writing*, Eleventh Edition by the Missouri Group (Brian S. Brooks, George Kennedy, Daryl R. Moen, and Don Ranly), pp. 59–109 (Chapter 4, "Interviewing" and Chapter 5, "Handling Quotations and Attributions") .

Interviewing

In this section you will learn:

1. How to prepare for an interview for a news story, profile or investigative piece.
2. How to conduct an audio or video interview.
3. How to evaluate the pros and cons of doing interviews by telephone, email, instant messaging or Skype.
4. How to set up an interview.
5. How to prepare your questions.
6. How to establish rapport with a source.
7. How to ensure accuracy.
8. How to end an interview.

Journalists get most of their information by asking people questions. Sometimes, though, the hardest part is just getting a source to agree to talk to you. One of the masters of getting people to open up is Mike McGraw, the Pulitzer Prize–winning projects reporter of *The Kansas City Star*. McGraw is a persistent reporter who has been known to work for months to convince a source to talk with him. "I couldn't get a lawyer to talk to me for the longest time," McGraw says. "I finally learned he was active as an adult leader in the Boy Scouts, as I was. So I brought up our common connection in an email one day. We both valued the organization, he emailed me back, and we began a dialogue that finally ended in an interview."

Persistence is just one of many techniques McGraw uses to get people to talk.

> "I once wanted to talk to workers at a turkey processing plant," McGraw says. "I put my business cards under windshield wipers in the parking lot and asked them to join me for a beer. About 12 showed up."

Often, reporters get sources to talk by first making them feel at ease. Many are not accustomed to speaking with a reporter and find the experience intimidating. "I look for pictures of grandkids on someone's desk and find other things we might have in common," McGraw says.

> "Sometimes I actually start off saying (the conversation) is off the record, which puts them at ease and gets me closer to the truth. I am honest and forthright with them, and I often convince them to go on the record."

McGraw often makes it clear that he's not going to quit working on a story until he gets the interview. "I often tell them, 'Look, I'm going to be looking into this for a long time. I'm going to find the flaws and the positives. Take this journey with me—help educate me—and at the end I promise you a chance to respond to everything I write that affects you. I won't show you the story, but I'll tell you what's in it. No, you won't like all of it, but it won't be lopsided, either.'"

Interviewing—having conversations with sources—is the key to most stories you will write. Your ability to make people feel comfortable with you is often the difference between mediocre reporting and good reporting. A face-to-face interview is always preferable to a telephone interview, which in turn is preferable to having a source answer questions by email. Face-to-face interviews allow you to develop a rapport with a source that is difficult, if not impossible, to achieve over the telephone or by email or instant messaging. If you meet sources in their offices, like McGraw you might find photos or objects that give you a way to break the ice with a nonthreatening conversation.

Of course, when a deadline looms on a breaking news story, you may be forced to settle for a telephone interview. (See "Using the Telephone, Email, Instant Messaging or Skype for Interviews" in this chapter.) That also may be necessary if you and the source are not in the same city or area. Least desirable of all is the email interview, which does not allow any sort of rapport to be established. You'll often get dry and uninformative answers to questions posed by email, and you won't have an opportunity to ask the follow-up questions you may have asked during a face-to-face interview.

Information is the raw material of a journalist. While some of it is gathered from records and some from observation, most is gathered in one-on-one conversations. You try first to talk to **primary sources**, those who witnessed the event or have authority over documents. If you can't get to a primary source, you may be forced to go to a **secondary source**, someone who talked to a witness, such as a public safety official, a lawyer or a next-door neighbor.

Even when you are doing a profile, determine how your source knows your profile subject. Does your source work with the subject? If so, he's probably not much of an authority on the subject's after-hours activities. Does she play poker with the subject? If so, she probably doesn't know the subject in the workplace. Once you know how your source knows what he or she knows, then you can start the conversation. If you're interviewing for television, broadcast or **webcast** (an audio or video report published on the Web), your goals and techniques may be different from those of a print reporter, but the basics are the same.

Preparing for the Interview

How you prepare for an interview depends in part on what kind of story you intend to write. (Table 6-1 shows a checklist you can use in doing interviews.) You may be doing a news story, a personality profile or an investigative piece. In each case, you check the newspaper library and search online databases, talk to other reporters and, if there's enough time, read magazine articles and books. Social media sites such as Facebook offer you information on some people you might not otherwise be able to contact. Don't print information off these sites without verification, though. Interviews are best used to solicit reactions and interpretations, not to gather facts. Good reporters gather their facts before an interview.

To prepare for a news story, you pay more attention to clips about the subject of the story than those about the personality of the interviewee. To prepare for a profile, you look for personality quirks and information about the subject's interests, family, friends, travels and habits. To prepare for an investigative piece, you want to know both your subject matter and the person you are interviewing. In all these stories, do not overlook other reporters and editors who know something about the person or subject. Let's look more closely at each of these types of common stories.

Table 6-1. Successful interviews require careful preparation.

Interviewing Checklist
Before the Interview
1. Know the topic.
• Seek specific information.
• Research the topic.
• List the questions.
2. Know the person.
• Find salient biographical information.
• Understand the person's expertise regarding the topic.
3. Set up the interview.
• Set the time.
• Schedule at the interviewee's convenience, but suggest a time.
• Estimate the length of time needed.
• Ask about possible return visits.
• Set the place.
• Choose the interviewee's turf or neutral turf.
4. Discuss arrangements.
• Will you bring a digital recorder?*
• Will you bring a photographer or a videographer?*
• Will you let the interviewee check the accuracy of quotes?

During the Interview
1. When you arrive
• If possible, control the seating arrangement.
• Place your digital recorder at the optimum spot.
• Warm up the person briefly with small talk.
• Set the ground rules: Everything is on the record once the recorder is turned on.
2. The interview itself.
• Use good interviewing techniques.
• Ask open-ended questions, which require the source to elaborate rather than give simple yes or no answers.
• Allow the person to think and to speak; pause.
• Don't be threatening in voice or manner.
• Control the conversational flow, but be flexible.
• Take good notes
• Be unobtrusive.
• Be thorough.
• Use the digital recorder.
• Make sure it's on and working, but take notes, too.
• Note the number on the digital counter at important parts in the interview so you can find quotes easily.
3. Before You Leave
• Ask if there's anything else the interviewee wants to say.
• Check facts: spellings, dates, statistics and quotes.
• Set a time for rechecking facts and quotes.
• Discuss when and where the interview might appear.
• For a print publication, ask if the interviewee wants extra copies.
After the Interview
1. Organize your notes immediately.
2. Craft a proper lead.
3. Write a coherent story.
4. Check facts for accuracy with the interviewee.

*Some sources may feel uncomfortable being recorded, videotaped or photographed.

The News Story

Usually, reporters don't have much time to prepare to cover a news story. You'll be lucky if you have a few minutes to dig into your newsroom's digital archive for background on the event or the issue. With a few more minutes, you can go online to see what other reporters have written on similar topics. Those hurried searches will provide a bit of background and perhaps some context. Then you're out the door. Still, there are three important mental steps you can take as you chase the news.

First, review in your head what you've turned up in your quick background research. If you're off to meet a political candidate, a public official or a celebrity, when was the person last in the news? For what? What will your audience (or your boss) most likely want to know now? If you're headed for a crime scene or a disaster, what do you know about the neighborhood? Has anything like this happened lately? With what results?

Second, plan your approach. Whom will you seek out at the scene? Who's likely to be in charge? What do you know about that person and her or his attitude toward reporters? Are you alone on this assignment and expected to capture audio or video? If so, double-check your equipment. Will you be reporting live on camera? If so, double-check your appearance.

Finally, plan out your first few questions. Sometimes, those are obvious. If the news is a crime or disaster, you'll want to know what happened. Was anybody hurt? What's the damage? If the story is focused on an issue or a person, you'll have some choices to make. Ideally, your backgrounding has gotten you past the most basic "Who are you?" and "Why are you here?" questions. So you may want to start with something like "What are you hoping to accomplish here?" or "Why do you think this issue is so important?"

Most news interviews aren't adversarial, but if you have tough questions, save them for the end of the conversation. That way, they won't keep you from getting most of what you need.

From there, follow your instincts and your training to find the story.

The Profile

Lane DeGregory, a staff writer for the *Tampa Bay (Fla.) Times*, was writing a profile story about a Largo, Fla., city manager who was fired when he announced he was going to have sex-reassignment surgery. DeGregory's first hurdle was getting the city manager to talk at length with her. The next hurdle was convincing the manager's wife to talk with her. Says DeGregory, "It came to this: 12 days, 10 phone calls, a two-page letter, a note, two stories, immeasurable groveling and a lot of luck."

Sometimes, journalism is hard work.

Describing to Poynter.org how she obtained the key interviews for the remarkable story, DeGregory said she typed a two-page letter to the wife to explain why she wanted to interview her and added a handwritten note and then delivered it to the house. She finally got the interview one evening when she called the former city manager, who handed the phone to the wife. DeGregory said the wife was at first reluctant. She progressed from yes and no answers to sentences. She started to relax. They talked for four hours.

Not every interview is that difficult, time-consuming or important. But every successful interview begins with establishing trust and ends with telling a story.

DeGregory says that writing previous stories on gender issues helped her establish rapport and gain the trust of the city manager. She knew the language, for one thing. She also knew the issues.

> "I knew for most transgendered people, it isn't about who they want to have sex with but about who they feel they really are. So I didn't have to ask any dumb 'I-don't-get-it' questions, and I could speak with some authority on the subject."

If you don't have the background on your subject that DeGregory had on hers, you will need to research the subject and the person you will be profiling. For most profiles, you will be talking not only to your subject but also to his or her friends, family and co-workers. In many cases, you will get their names from your subject. Ask how your subject knows them: co-worker, social acquaintance, recent or lifelong friend? Then ask the co-worker or friend how he or she knows your profile subject. With this information, you won't ask inappropriate questions—you don't want to ask about your subject's love for hunting if the interviewee only knows the person from work, for example—and you can properly evaluate the information you are getting.

On THE JOB

Getting the Tough Interview

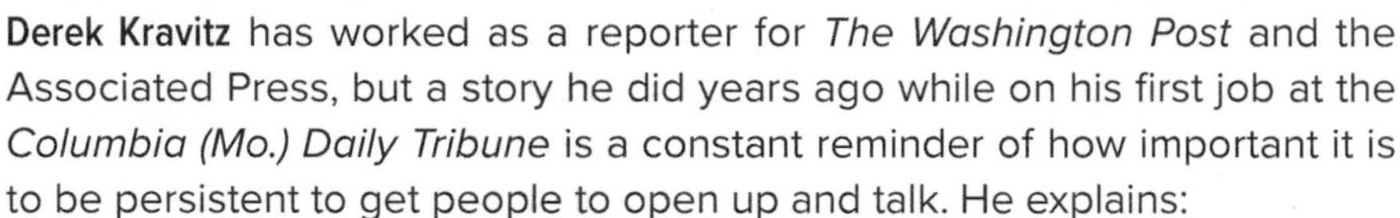

Derek Kravitz has worked as a reporter for *The Washington Post* and the Associated Press, but a story he did years ago while on his first job at the *Columbia (Mo.) Daily Tribune* is a constant reminder of how important it is to be persistent to get people to open up and talk. He explains:

Alan Farha was wanted by Columbia police for scamming area churches, so he was on the move. I found a phone number for his father in Georgetown, Texas, and left a voice mail. Later that night, I got a call from Farha on my cellphone. We spent the next hour discussing why I not only shouldn't interview him (he said he had nothing to say and his case was unimportant) but why we shouldn't focus resources on a larger story on his case (it could affect his fragile sobriety, he said, and he could fall into a deeper hole with his drug addictions).

I told him that many people, not just in Columbia, but across many states and in countless churches, thought he was a con man. He said he wasn't. I gave him the opportunity to tell his story, and after laying out the Police Department's case against him, he described his addictions and how he had resorted to asking people for money to get by. That didn't make him a con man, he said. That made him a beggar. And a Columbia police detective I spoke to agreed.

We ran the story. Farha left Columbia and has been charged with (but not arrested for) scamming churches . . . in Indiana, Texas and New Hampshire.

The *Tribune* story seems to follow him because every time he hits a new town, I get an email or a link from a local newspaper asking about him. He hasn't stopped, but his story is now well-known, mainly thanks to Google.

Oddly enough, I also got a "friend request" from Farha on LinkedIn recently. His profile says he's still struggling with his addictions.

The Investigative Piece

The casual conversations you want to have for profile interviews are not always possible for the investigative reporter. An adversarial relationship determines both the preparation required for an investigative piece and the atmosphere of the interview itself. An investigative reporter is like an attorney in a courtroom. Wise attorneys know in advance what the answers to their questions will be. Investigative reporters often do, too, but they also are open-minded enough to switch gears if sources convince them they are on the wrong track. Regardless, preparation is essential.

Lowell Bergman, a veteran investigative reporter who worked in both print and television, advises, "Learn as much about the subject before you get there, regardless of whether you play dumb because you want them to explain it to you, or whether you just want them to know that you're not going to waste their time."

Gathering Information

In the early stages of the investigation, you conduct some fishing-expedition interviews: Because you don't know how much the source knows, you cast around. Start with people on the fringes. Gather as much as you can from them. Study the records. Only after you have most of the evidence should you confront your central character. You start with a large circle and gradually draw it smaller.

Requesting an Interview

DeGregory had difficulty getting her interview because she wanted to ask questions about a personal topic. Investigative reporters frequently have problems getting the interview because the information they seek is often damaging to the person. Sources who believe you are working on a story that will be critical of them or their friends often try to avoid you. Steve Weinberg, author of an unauthorized biography of industrialist Armand Hammer, had to overcome the suspicion of many former Hammer associates. Their former boss had told them not to talk to Weinberg. Instead of calling, Weinberg approached them by mail. "I sent letters, examples of my previous work, explained what I wanted to cover and why I was doing it without Hammer's blessing," Weinberg says.

He recommends that you use a letter or an email to share some of what you know about the story that might surprise or impress the source. For instance, a reference such as "And last week, when I was checking all the land records . . ." indicates the depth of your research.

In his letter to former Hammer assistants, Weinberg talked about how Hammer was one of the most important people in the history of business. The letters opened doors to all seven of Hammer's former executive assistants whom Weinberg contacted.

Weinberg, like DeGregory, has shown former stories as a way of trying to gain the subject's confidence. Weinberg also offers to show the sources relevant portions of his manuscript as an accuracy check. (An *accuracy check* just verifies the facts. It does not give the source the option of choosing what goes in and what stays out of a story.) He makes it clear in writing that he maintains control of the content.

Requesting an interview in writing can allow you to make your best case for getting it. And an offer to allow your sources to review the story assures them that you are serious about accuracy. Email makes both the request and the offer simpler and faster.

Doing an Audio or Video Interview

When you're interviewing someone in front of a camera, the basic rules of preparation and interviewing don't change. For instance, Bob Schieffer, longtime host of *Face the Nation* on CBS, says the most important thing before every interview is to know as much about the story as possible.

Some of your objectives and techniques, however, do change. Television journalists, at least those who appear on camera, are also performers. Sure, they have to report and write, but they also have to be able to tell their stories with both words and body language to people who are watching and listening—not reading. An important part of the television reporter's performance is the interview.

Reporters who conduct interviews that will appear on radio, in a podcast or online, also are performers. They must ask questions and respond to answers smoothly.

Both print and television reporters often interview to develop information that can be used in further reporting. Interviews conducted on camera usually have a different goal. That goal is the **sound bite**, the few seconds of words with accompanying video that convey not only information but also emotion. Print is a medium that mainly provides information. Television is a medium of emotion. The best interviews for television are those that reveal how a situation feels to the participants or witnesses.

Al Tompkins, the Poynter Institute's group leader for broadcast and online journalism, offers what he calls "a new set of interviewing tools" intended to produce better storytelling for television. You can find these and other tools at www.poynter.org. Here are some tips that show both the similarities and differences between print and television interviewing:

- **Ask both objective and subjective questions.** To gather facts ask objective questions: "When?" "Where?" "How much?" But subjective questions usually produce the best sound bites: "Why?" "Tell me more about . . ." "Can you explain . . . ?"
- **Focus on one issue at a time.** Vague, complicated questions produce vague, complicated, hard-to-follow answers. Remember that readers can reread until they understand, but viewers generally can't rewind an interview. (These days, many broadcast organizations, including PBS, are posting interviews online.) Help viewers follow the story by taking your interviewee through it one step at a time.

- **Ask open-ended questions.** For print, you occasionally want a simple yes or no. That kind of answer stops a television interview. Open-ended questions encourage conversation, and conversation makes for a good interview. (For more on this, see "Open-Ended Questions".)
- **Keep questions short.** Make the interviewee do the talking. Tompkins points out that short questions are more likely to produce focused responses. They also keep the viewer's attention on the person being interviewed and on what she or he has to say.
- **Build to the point.** The best interviews are like the best stories. They don't give away the punch line in the first few words. Ask soft, easy questions to encourage the interviewee to relax and trust you. Then move to the heart of the issue.
- **Be honest.** As true for television as for print and online, the importance of honesty is too often overlooked by rookie reporters. You do neither your source nor yourself a favor if you lead the source to expect an interview about softball when you have an indictment in mind. Tell the source ahead of time that you'll want to ask some tough questions. Say that you want to get the whole story, to be fair—and mean it. Then politely but firmly dig in. As Tompkins notes, honesty has the added benefit of helping you defend yourself against any later accusations of malice.

Using the Telephone, Email, Instant Messaging or Skype for Interviews

Interviews, as noted earlier, are always more successful if conducted in person. But when you have to interview by phone, there are at least three points to remember. These are more important for feature stories, profiles and investigative work than for standard news stories, though some news stories require more time and effort during interviews than others.

First, just as you do in person, if this is the first time you've spoken to the source, attempt to establish rapport. Don't immediately start firing questions. Express your appreciation for the person's time. Explain why you are calling and how important the interviewee is to the story. If you have talked to others who know this person, mention that to help your source relax.

Second, depending on how much time and how important this interview is, you may want to record it. You must seek the permission of the person you are interviewing: "Is it OK to record this conversation? I want to make sure I get it accurately, and this way, I can concentrate more fully on the content." Put the request on the recording. In most states, it is illegal to record a phone conversation without the other person's consent. Remember to take notes even if you are recording an interview. If the recorder malfunctions, you'll still have material for your story.

Third, just as in any other interview, try to have a conversation rather than a Q&A session. (A Q&A—question and answer—story is more or less a verbatim transcript of an interview. The interview material isn't digested and reworked into a story.) React to what is said with affirmations. Laugh when appropriate. Admit when you don't understand, and ask for more explanation.

The phone can be a friend, but it can never replace personal contact. Neither can email, but reporters are using email more frequently because they are facing more deadline pressure than ever as they feed websites, often in addition to another medium.

Email interviews have many weaknesses. They don't permit you to establish rapport. And you need to be certain the person with whom you are corresponding is the person you think he or she is. The classic *New Yorker* cartoon shown below explains the risk.

On the other hand, email is quick and convenient as a follow-up to personal or phone interviews. Email can also be effective for a Q&A story. The email captures the original questions and preserves the responses. Once you've made contact and established identity, an email interview can be useful and even surprisingly revealing.

Some people will say things at a keyboard they wouldn't say face to face. Some get carried away by the power of their own prose. Some, of course, are cryptic and not forthcoming.

Instant messaging has the same strengths and weaknesses as email except that it is faster. You can best use IM for follow-up questions, clarifications and checking information to ensure accuracy.

Don't forget that email and IM are permanent. Don't ask or say anything you wouldn't want to see forwarded to others. Do make your questions clear and grammatically correct. The permanence works *for* you, too. The answers are equally permanent. They can't be taken back or denied later. And it's hard to misquote an email.

Skype **online videoconferencing** offers the advantages of email and eliminates one major drawback. With Skype, you're communicating in real time with someone you can actually see. And you're talking as opposed to typing. So you can be more comfortable that you have the right person on the other end of the link, and you can add the visual information that's missing from an email interview. Soldiers deployed overseas use Skype to stay in touch with families. Reporters can use the same technology to interview sources they might never see in the flesh.

"On the Internet, nobody knows you're a dog."

Peter Steiner/The New Yorker Collection/The Cartoon Bank.

Figure 6-1. You can't be sure who's on the other end of an email message, or that other people aren't helping the interviewee respond to your questions.

Setting Up the Interview

All this homework is important, but something as trifling as your appearance may determine whether you will have a successful interview. You would hardly wear cutoff shorts into a university president's suite, and you wouldn't wear a three-piece suit to talk to underground revolutionaries.

Most interviews are conducted in the source's office. If the story is a profile or a feature, however, it usually is better to get the source away from his or her work. If you are doing a story about a rabbi's hobby of collecting butterflies, seek a setting appropriate to the topic. Suggest meeting where the rabbi keeps the collection.

In some interviews, it is to your advantage to get the source on neutral territory. If you have questions for the provost or a public official, suggest meeting in a coffee shop at a quiet time. A person has more power in his or her official surroundings.

It is important, too, to let the source know how much time you need and whether you expect to return for further information. And if you don't already know how the source might react to a recording device, ask when you are making the appointment.

Source: Robert Kalman/The Image Works

Figure 6-2. This reporter dresses to fit in with the marchers he is interviewing; he gains their confidence by being friendly and attentive.

Preparing Questions

You have now done the appropriate homework. You are properly attired. You have made an appointment and told the source how much time you need. Before you leave to meet your source, you may want to write down a list of questions to ask. They will guide you through the interview and prevent you from missing important topics altogether. The best way to encourage a spontaneous conversation is to have your questions prepared. You'll be more relaxed. Having questions prepared relieves you of the need to be mentally searching for the next question as the source is answering the last one. If you are trying to think of the next question, you cannot pay close attention to what is being said, and you might miss the most important part of the interview.

Researching Questions

Preparing the questions for an interview is hard work, even for veterans. If you are writing for your campus newspaper, seek suggestions from other staff members. You will find ideas in the newspaper's electronic database. If you anticipate a troublesome interview with the chancellor, you might want to seek advice from faculty members, too. What questions would they ask if they were you? Often, they have more background knowledge, or they might have heard some of the faculty talk around campus. Staff members are also valuable sources of information.

Although you may ask all of your prepared questions in some interviews, in most you probably will use only some of them. Still, you will have benefited from preparing the questions in two important ways. First, even when you don't use many, the work you did thinking of the questions helped prepare you for the interview. Second, sources who see that you have a prepared list often are impressed with your seriousness.

On the basis of the information you have gathered already, you know what you want to ask. Now you must be careful about how you phrase the questions.

Phrasing Questions

A young monk who asked his superior if he could smoke while he prayed was rebuked sharply. A friend advised him to rephrase the question. "Ask him if you can pray while you smoke," he said. The young monk was discovering that how questions are structured often determines the answer. Journalists face the same challenge. Reporters have missed many stories because they didn't know how to ask their questions. Quantitative researchers have shown how only a slight wording change affects the results of a survey. If you want to know whether citizens favor a city plan to beautify the downtown area, you can ask the question in several ways:

- Do you favor the City Council's plan to beautify the downtown area?
- The City Council plans to spend $3 million beautifying the downtown area. Are you in favor of this?
- Do you think the downtown area needs physical changes?

- Which of the following actions do you favor?
  - Prohibiting all automobile traffic in an area bounded by Providence Road, Ash Street, College Avenue and Elm Street.
  - Having all the downtown storefronts remodeled to carry out a single theme and putting in brick streets, shrubbery and benches.
  - None of the above.

How you structure that question may affect the survey results by several percentage points. Similarly, how you ask questions in an interview may affect the response.

With the phrasing of the question, many reporters signal the response they expect or the prejudices they have. For instance, a reporter who says, "Don't you think that the City Council should allocate more money to the Parks and Recreation Department?" is not only asking a question but also influencing the source or betraying a bias. Another common way of asking a leading question is this: "Are you going to vote against this amendment like the other City Council members I've talked to?" A neutral phrasing would be "Do you think the City Council should allocate more money to the Parks and Recreation Department?" To avoid leading or even irritating your source, ask neutral questions.

Also ask the interviewee one question at a time. Listen to journalists at press conferences jump up and ask two or three questions at a time. The source then chooses the one he or she wishes to answer and ignores the rest. That can happen in one-on-one interviews, too.

In situations where you have to ask embarrassing or awkward questions, Jeff Truesdell of *People* magazine suggests demonstrating empathy. "Say, 'I'm sorry I have to ask this,' or 'I can't believe I'm asking this but here goes,' or 'My editors will want to know'—editors in absentia make for great fall guys—or 'Let me play devil's advocate here,'" Truesdell suggests. "Acknowledge that there are unpleasant questions, apologize for asking, and then ask."

Sometimes the reporter's phrasing of a question unwittingly blocks a response. A reporter who was investigating possible job discrimination against women conducted several interviews before she told her city editor she didn't think the women with whom she talked were being frank with her. "When I ask them if they have ever been discriminated against, they always tell me no. But three times now during the course of the interviews, they have said things that indicate they have been. How do I get them to tell me about it?" she asked.

"Perhaps it's the way you are asking the question," the city editor replied. "When you ask the women whether they have ever been discriminated against, you are forcing them to answer yes or no. Don't be so blunt. Ask them if others with the same qualifications at work have advanced faster than they have. Ask if they are paid the same amount as men for the same work. Ask them what they think they would be doing today if they were male. Ask them if they know of any qualified women who were denied jobs."

The city editor was giving the reporter examples of both closed- and open-ended questions. Each has its specific strengths.

Open-Ended Questions

Open-ended questions allow the respondent some flexibility. Women may not respond frankly when asked whether they have ever been discriminated against. The question calls for a yes or no response. But an open-ended question such as "What would you be doing at work today if you were a man?" is not as personal. It does not sound as threatening to the respondent. In response to an open-ended question, the source often reveals more than he or she realizes or intends to.

A sportswriter who was interviewing a pro scout at a college football game wanted to know whom the scout was there to see. When the scout diplomatically declined to say, the reporter tried another approach. He asked a series of questions:

- "What kinds of qualities does a pro scout look for in an athlete?"
- "Do you think any of the players here today have those talents?"
- "Who would you put into that category?"

The reporter worked from the general to the specific until he had the information he wanted. Open-ended questions are less direct and less threatening. They are more exploratory and more flexible. However, if you want to know a person's biographical data, don't ask, "Can you tell me about yourself?" That question is too general. Phrase your questions to get information about specific times and places.

Closed-Ended Questions

Eventually, you need to close in on a subject, to pin down details, to get the respondent to be specific. Closed-ended questions are designed to elicit specific responses. Instead of asking the mayor, "What did you think of the conference in Washington, D.C.?" you ask, "What did you learn in the session 'Funds You May Not Know Are Available'?" Instead of asking a previous employee to appraise the chancellor-designate's managerial abilities, you ask, "How well does she listen to the people who work for her?" "Do the people who work for her have specific job duties?" "Does she explain her decisions?"

A vague question invites a vague answer. By asking a specific question, you are more likely to get a specific answer. You are also communicating to your source that you have done your homework and that you are looking for precise details.

Knowing exactly when to ask a closed-ended question or when to be less specific is not something you can plan ahead of time. The type of information you are seeking and the chemistry between you and the source are the determining factors. You must make on-the-spot decisions. The important thing is to keep rephrasing the question until the source answers it adequately. Sports writer Gary Smith wrote in *Intimate Journalism*, "A lot of my reporting comes from asking a question three different ways. Sometimes the third go at it is what produces the nugget, but even if the answers aren't wonderful or the quotes usable, they can still confirm or correct my impressions."

Every reporter seeks anecdotes, and closed-ended questions help elicit them. "What is the funniest thing you've ever done?" "The weirdest?" "What's the saddest thing that ever happened to you?" When the source talks in generalities, ask a closed-ended question to get to specifics. "You say Mary is a practical joker. Can you think of an example of a practical joke she played on someone?" The answers to these types of questions yield the anecdotal nuggets that make your story readable.

Closed-Ended Questions	Open-Ended Questions
Do you like the proposal?	What are the strengths of the proposal? What are the weaknesses?
Did you have trouble coping when your child was in the car accident?	How did you cope after your child was in the car accident? Why did you attend counseling sessions?
Did you keep your promises to exercise today?	What was your exercise routine for today?
Did you give the theater teacher permission to stage that play?	What did you tell the theater teacher when she asked if her group could perform the play?
Do you use iChat in your work?	How do you use iChat in your work?

Establishing Rapport

The most basic requirement of any successful interview is a reasonable degree of trust between reporter and source. Usually, as a reporter you have to earn that trust. Wright Thompson, who worked for *The Kansas City Star* when he wrote this story and now works for ESPN, tells about the time he wanted to do a story about a former college football player named Ernest Blackwell, who had gone on a rampage in his neighborhood, shot a child and almost kicked another to death. He'd collapsed on a police gurney afterward and died en route to the hospital. No one could figure out what had happened. Media outlet after media outlet approached the family for an interview. All got turned down. Thompson tried a unique approach:

> When I called, I had a line. I told them I was going to talk to the cops and was going to do a story about Ernest. The police, I told them, would give me more than enough detail about the last five minutes of Ernest's life. Then I said, "I think there's a lot more to his life than the last five minutes. I think he deserves to be remembered for how he lived and not just how he died."

Thompson's reasoning won him the interview. His conclusion: "Have a plan. You must give someone a reason why it's better if they talk to you than if they don't."

Because he earned the trust of the family, he was able to develop the insights that allowed him to write this:

> *Those who knew him wonder how Blackwell arrived on that day with so much rage in his heart, so much bad intent. Truth is, none of them could peer into the man's soul and see the hate that grew until it reached the breaking point.*

> On Aug. 11, 2004, Blackwell could take no more.
>
> *Lord, why didn't I see the signs?" says his aunt Joyce Strong, who mostly raised Blackwell. "Why didn't I see he was reaching out for help? He must have been a ticking time bomb waiting to go off."*

That's the payoff on the investment in building trust.

You probably won't have many assignments that difficult. It always helps, though, to have a plan. It also helps to have the honesty and empathy that lead strangers to be honest with you. Act like a human being.

Rapport—the relationship between the reporter and the source—is crucial to the success of the interview. It helps a reporter get better story information. The relationship is sometimes relaxed, sometimes strained. Often it is somewhere in between. The type of relationship you try to establish with your source is determined by the kind of story you are doing. Several approaches are possible.

Source: Francis Specker/Landov/MCT

Figure 6-3. Establishing rapport with interview subjects helps a reporter get better story information.

Interview Approaches

For most news stories and personality profiles, the reporter can put the subject at ease by starting with small talk. Ask about a trophy, the plants or an engraved pen. Bring up something humorous you found during your research. Ask about something you know the source will want to talk about. If you think the subject might be skeptical about your knowledge of the field, open with a question that demonstrates your knowledge.

Rapport also depends on where you conduct the interview. Many people, especially those unaccustomed to being interviewed, feel more comfortable in their workplace. Go to them. Talk to the businessperson in the office, to the athlete in the locker room, to the conductor in the concert hall. However, if the source cannot relax at the workplace or is frequently interrupted, you may get a better interview elsewhere. Reporters have talked to politicians during car rides between campaign appearances. They've gone sailing with businesspeople and hunting with athletes. One student reporter doing a feature on a police chief spent a weekend with the chief, who was painting his home. To do a profile, which requires more than one interview, vary the location. New surroundings can make a difference.

There are times when the reporter would rather have the source edgy, nervous or even scared. When you are doing an investigation, you may want the key characters to feel uneasy.

You may pretend you know more than you actually do. You want them to know that the material you have is substantive and serious. Seymour Hersh, a Pulitzer Prize–winning investigative reporter, uses this tactic. *Time* magazine once quoted a government official commenting on Hersh: "He wheedles, cajoles, pleads, threatens, asks a leading question, uses little tidbits as if he knew the whole story. When he finishes you feel like a wet rag."

In some cases, however, it is better even in an investigation to take a low-key approach. Let the source relax. Talk around the subject but gradually bring the discussion to the key issues. The surprise element may work in your favor.

So may the sympathetic approach. When the source is speaking, you may nod or punctuate the source's responses with comments such as "That's interesting." Sources who think you are sympathetic are more likely to volunteer information. Researchers have found, for instance, that a simple "mm-hmmm" affects the length of the answer interviewers get.

> *"I need to create what I call accelerated intimacy. We can't write the beautiful narrative stories that we all dream of unless we can get some things from the mouths of our sources. They must be comfortable enough to tell us* anything. *In journalism school, no one called the interactions between journalists and sources* relationships, *but that's what they are."*
>
> **—Isabel Wilkerson, winner of the Pulitzer Prize for journalism**

On THE JOB

Relating to Your Subject

Scott Nishimura of the *Fort Worth Star-Telegram* has an unusual background for a newspaper reporter, and he takes advantage of it to get sources to talk.

"My wife and I own a small real estate business on the side," Nishimura says. "I found that being in business for myself made me a much more effective business reporter. I include that fact in my LinkedIn and Twitter

profiles, and I usually figure out a way to get that into the initial conversation with new sources. That way, they know they're doing business with someone who knows more about business than your typical reporter."

Nishimura found his knowledge to be of particular help in dealing with small-business owners during his 20 years as a business reporter.

"By demonstrating that I understand their business, and by asking a series of very specific questions, I could often get business owners to disclose financial details they might not otherwise have provided.

"I also use LinkedIn to post some of my best work by embedding stories in blog posts and then linking to those posts from LinkedIn."

Nishimura is now the city hall reporter for his newspaper, but he borrowed the same tactic when he began covering his new beat. He considers it important to let news sources know that he understands the subjects about which he writes.

"I was a school and neighborhood volunteer for years, and people love dealing with me because they know I have context. They know that I understand what happens at city hall because it affects me as a citizen, too."

Other Practical Considerations

Where you sit in relation to the person you are interviewing can be important. Unless you deliberately are trying to make interviewees feel uncomfortable, do not sit directly in front of them. Permit your sources to establish eye contact if and when they wish.

Some people are even more disturbed by the way a reporter takes notes. A digital recorder ensures accuracy of quotes, but it makes many speakers self-conscious or nervous. If you have permission to use a recorder, place it in an inconspicuous spot and ignore it except to make sure it is working properly. Writing notes longhand may interfere with your ability to digest what is being said. But not taking any notes at all is risky. Only a few reporters can leave an interview and accurately write down what was said. Certainly no one can do it and reproduce direct quotes verbatim. You should learn shorthand or develop a note-taking system of your own.

Be sure that you address the people you are interviewing correctly. If you are unsure how they should be addressed—Mrs., Miss, Ms., Dr., Professor—ask them.

Personal Pronouns for Transgender People

The AP Stylebook recommends using the pronoun (he, she) the person prefers. If you don't know the person's preference, use the pronoun that reflects the way the person lives publicly.

If you are interviewing someone from a culture or race different from your own, recognize and avoid your own stereotypes. Perhaps you are uncomfortable in the presence of an Islamic woman wearing a veil when she attends school in the U.S. Instead of letting your feelings influence your actions, respect her beliefs. As a reporter, take pride in your ability to move among people from all cultures. This requires that you read about cultural differences. It might help you to know that in Chinese society, people are generally uncomfortable with too much eye contact. Many Arabs consider it improper for a man to look into a woman's eyes. No one knows everything about every culture, but you can prepare for some situations, and you can also recognize what you don't know. These days, it is easy enough to do a quick search about specific cultural differences before you conduct an interview.

Ensuring Accuracy and Fairness

Accuracy is a major problem in all interviews. Both the question and the answer may be ambiguous. You may not understand what is said. You may write it down incorrectly. You may not remember the context of the remarks. Your biases may interfere with the message.

Using a Recorder

The only way to be sure you capture the content of any interview with word-perfect accuracy is to record it. Careful listening is important, and taking good notes is essential. But using a recorder is the only way you can be certain you've got exactly what was said, both by the source and by you. That's important journalistically. As sources and audiences become increasingly skeptical, absolute accuracy adds to credibility and protects against complaints and even lawsuits.

Today's digital recorders are so small and so powerful that it's often possible to use them while they're in your pocket, purse or briefcase. However, there's seldom a need to be secretive. In fact, it's increasingly common for sophisticated sources to use their own recorders as a form of self-protection from reporters they may not trust. So the best approach usually is just to pull out your recorder, turn it on and place it in sight. If you do that as a matter of routine, chances are the source will take no notice. If there is a question or complaint, explain the importance of accuracy and the benefit to both parties. Then get on with the interview.

Taking Notes

Knowing the background of your sources, having a comfortable relationship with them and keeping good notes are important elements of accuracy. All those were missing when a journalism student, two weeks into an internship at a major daily, interviewed the public information officer for a sheriff's department about criminal activity in and around a shelter for battered women. The reporter had never met the source. She took notes on her phone interview with the deputy and others in whatever notebook happened to be nearby.

She didn't record the time, date or even the source. There were no notes showing context, just fragments of quotes, scrawled in nearly illegible handwriting.

After the story was published, the developer of the shelter sued. Questioned by attorneys, the deputy swore that the reporter misunderstood him and used some of his comments out of context. In several cases, he contended, she completed her fragmentary notes by putting her own words in his mouth. He testified that most reporters come to see him to get acquainted. Many call back to check his quotes on sensitive or complex stories. She did neither.

When the court ordered the reporter to produce and explain her notes, she had trouble reconstructing them. She had to admit on several occasions that she wasn't sure what the fragments meant.

The accuracy of your story is only as good as your notes. David Finkel, whose story on a family's TV-watching habits became a Pulitzer Prize finalist, took extra steps to be certain his material was accurate. Observing what his subjects were watching, he obtained transcripts of the shows so he could quote accurately from them. If he knew transcripts would not be available, he set his recorder near the TV to record the program.

Taking Notes

Here are some helpful guidelines for taking notes during an interview:

- Write the date, the place, and the interviewee's name at the top of the page.
- Develop a consistent shorthand. For example, always use "w/" to mean "with."
- Use a spiral-bound notebook with pages that are easy to turn and that lie flat.
- Make sure you have several working pens or sharpened pencils.
- Leave a wide margin so that you can annotate your writing later on.
- Look up at the interviewee frequently as you write.
- Ask for the spellings of names.
- Always take notes, even if you are using a digital recorder.

Verifying Information

Reporters should do research after an interview to ascertain specific figures when a source provides an estimate. For example, if a restaurant owner says he runs one of 20 pizza parlors in town, check with the city business-license office to get the exact number.

When you finish your interview, go back over the key points in your notes to confirm them. Read back quotes to make sure that you have them right. Realize, too, that you will need to confirm some of the information you get from other, perhaps more authoritative, sources.

And if your interview produces allegations against other people or organizations, you will need to talk to those named.

Some possibilities for making errors or introducing bias are unavoidable, but others are not. To ensure the most accurate and complete reporting possible, you should use all the techniques available to obtain a good interview, including observing and asking follow-up questions. Let's examine these and other techniques.

Observing

Some reporters look but do not see. The detail they miss may be the difference between a routine story and one that is a delight to read. Your powers of observation may enable you to discover a story beyond your source's words. Is the subject nervous? What kinds of questions are striking home? The mayor may deny that he is going to fire the police chief, but if you notice the chief's personnel file sitting on an adjacent worktable, you may have reason to continue the investigation.

Wright Thompson says, "It's all about the scenes. Don't just ask questions. Be an observer." Like any good writer, he offers an example to show what he means:

> I was doing a story about former Heisman Trophy winner Eric Crouch. It was almost exactly one year since he'd won the trophy, and that year had been tough for him. He'd quit pro football and had been forced to ask some hard questions about his life. As we sat in an Omaha bar, a clip of him running the football came on the television. One of the women at the table said, "You're on TV, Eric." I remember he looked up at the screen and spat, "That's not me, man." Then he took a shot of liquor. No amount of interviewing could breathe life into the idea that he had changed like that scene.

Asking Follow-Up Questions

If you understand what the source is saying, you can ask meaningful follow-up questions. There is nothing worse than briefing your city editor on the interview and having the editor ask you, "Well, did you ask . . . ?" Having to say no is embarrassing.

Even if you go into an interview armed with a list of questions, the most important questions will probably be the ones you ask in response to an answer. A reporter who was doing a story on bidding procedures was interviewing the mayor. The reporter asked how bid specifications were written. In the course of his reply, the mayor mentioned that the president of a construction firm had assured him the last bid specifications were adequate. The alert reporter picked up on the statement:

> *"When did you talk to him?"*
> "About three weeks ago," the mayor said.
>
> *"That's before the specifications were published, wasn't it?"*
> "Yes, we asked him to look them over for us."

> *"Did he find anything wrong with the way they were written?"*
> "Oh, he changed a few minor things. Nothing important."
>
> *"Did officials of any other construction firms see the bid specifications before they were advertised?"*
> "No, he was the only one."

Gradually, on the basis of one offhand comment by the mayor, the reporter was able to piece together a solid story on the questionable relationship between the city and the construction firm.

There are three questions that are always useful. One is, "What did you mean by that?" The second is, "How do you know that?" and the last is, "Is there anything I haven't asked that I should?"

Using Other Techniques

Although most questions are designed to get information, some are asked as a delaying tactic. A reporter who is taking notes may fall behind. One good trick for catching up is just to say, "Hold on a second—let me get that" or "Say that again, please." Other questions are intended to encourage a longer response. "Go on with that" or "Tell me more about that" encourages the speaker to add more detail.

You don't have to be stalling for time to say you don't understand. Don't be embarrassed to admit you haven't grasped something. It is better to admit to one person you don't understand something than to advertise your ignorance in newsprint or on the airwaves in front of thousands.

Another device for making the source talk on is not a question at all; it is a pause. You are signaling the source that you expect more. But the lack of a response from you is much more ambiguous than "Tell me more about that." It may indicate that you were skeptical of what was just said, that you didn't understand, that the answer was inadequate or several other possibilities. The source will be forced to react.

> *"Today one has the impression that the interviewer is not listening to what you say, nor does he think it important, because he believes that the tape recorder hears everything. But he's wrong; it doesn't hear the beating of the heart, which is the most important part of the interview."*
>
> **—Gabriel García Márquez, Colombian writer and Nobel laureate**

Ending the Interview

There are two things you should always do when you finish your questions: Check key facts, figures and quotes, and then put away your pen or recorder but keep your ears open. You are not breaching any ethical rule if you continue to ask questions after you have put away your pen or turned off the recorder. Many dull interviews become interesting after they end. That's when some sources loosen up.

Quickly review your notes and check facts, especially dates, numbers, quotes, spellings and titles. Besides helping you get it right, this shows the source you are careful. If necessary, arrange a time when you can call to check other parts of the story or clear up questions you may have as you are writing. Researchers have found that more than half of direct quotations are inaccurate, even when the interview is recorded. That reflects an unacceptable sloppiness. Make sure you are the exception.

As a matter of courtesy, tell the source when the story might appear. You may even offer to send along an extra copy of the article when it's completed. And of course, thank the source for granting the interview in the first place.

Suggested Readings

Adams, Sally, and Wynford Hicks. *Interviewing for Journalists*. 2nd ed. New York: Routledge, 2009. Adams and Hicks offer a useful description of interviewing techniques for journalists.

Kramer, Mark, and Wendy Call, eds. *Telling True Stories*. New York: Plume, 2007. This book contains excellent advice, including how to prepare for and conduct interviews.

Scanlan, Christopher, ed. *America's Best Newspaper Writing*. St. Petersburg, Fla.: Poynter Institute for Media Studies.

Reprints of winners of American Society of News Editors Distinguished Writing Awards and interviews with the writers make this an invaluable resource. It is published annually.

Sedorkin, Gail. *Interviewing: A Guide for Journalists and Writers*. 2nd ed. Crows Nest, New South Wales, Australia: Allen and Unwin, 2011. This is an excellent guide to interviewing skills for reporters and writers.

Suggested Websites

www.journalism.about.com/od/reporting/a/interviewing.htm
This site offers a discussion of basic journalism interviewing techniques.

www.poewar.com
The Writing Career Center offers advice on a variety of writers' concerns, including interviewing.

www.poynter.org/tag/interviewing
Various articles describe interviewing techniques for journalists.

Exercises

1. **Team project.** Your instructor will divide your class into teams to work on questions in preparation for an interview with a high-ranking official on your campus, such as the provost or chancellor. Brainstorm a list of issues that could be addressed in an interview. Choose an issue. Then prepare three open-ended and three closed-ended questions. As a class, rate the issues the teams have chosen in terms of relevance, timeliness and interest. Evaluate the questions. Which are effective, and why?
2. Learn to gather background on your sources. Write a memo of up to two pages about your state's senior U.S. senator. Concentrate on those details that allow you to focus on how the senator views health care issues. Indicate the sources of your information. Do an Internet search on the senator.
3. List five open-ended questions you would ask the senator. Then list five closed-ended questions you would ask.
4. Interview a student enrolled in your reporting class. Write a two- or three-page story focusing on one aspect of the student's life. Ask your classmate to read the story and to mark errors of fact and perception. The instructor will read your story and the critique.
5. **Journalism blog.** In a blog, describe your experience completing Exercise 4. What did you learn about interviewing? Comment on the blog post of the classmate you partnered with. What can you add to each other's assessments of the exercise?
6. Interview a classmate about his or her hobbies. Then switch roles and do the interview again. Write a brief summary of what you learned, and list three additional questions you would ask if you had more time.
7. Interview a faculty or staff member at your college or university and write a profile of that person. Remember to include interviews with others who know the person.

Handling Quotations and Attributions

In this section you will learn:

- How to determine what is worth quoting directly.
- How to ensure accuracy and fairness in quotations.
- Whether, when and how to alter quotations.
- When and how to attribute direct and indirect quotes.
- How to handle both on- and off-the-record information.

At the 2012 Olympics in London, nearly everyone expected 16-year-old gymnast McKayla Maroney to win a gold medal in the vault, especially after performing superbly on her first vault. On her second vault, however, Maroney and all who watched were shocked when she landed on her heels and her feet skidded out from under her.

In an interview after her fall, ESPN quoted Maroney as saying, "I already knew that I pretty much only had the silver medal. I really didn't deserve to win a gold medal if I fall on my butt. I was still happy with a silver, but it's still just sad."

What reporter could resist quoting those exact words of the young star? Not only are they colorful, but they also reveal a good deal about Maroney's character.

AP Photo/Julie Jacobson

Figure 6-4. McKayla Maroney watches the scoreboard after her disappointing finish on the vault in the 2012 Summer Olympics. Quotations from interviews after the event gave insight into her character.

Direct quotes—the exact words that a source says or writes—add color and credibility to your story. By using a direct quote, you put your readers directly in touch with the speaker in your story. Like a handwritten letter, direct quotes are personal. Quotation marks, which always enclose a direct quote, signal to the reader that something special is coming. Direct quotes provide a story with a change of pace, a breath of fresh air.

As Paula LaRoque, former writing coach and assistant managing editor of *The Dallas Morning News*, says, "The right quotes, carefully selected and presented, enliven and humanize a story and help make it clear, credible, immediate and dramatic. Yet many quotations in journalism are dull, repetitive, ill-phrased, ungrammatical, nonsensical, self-serving or just plain dumb."

Now that's a quotation worth quoting!

Not everything people say is worth quoting. You need to learn what to quote directly, when to use partial quotes and when to paraphrase. You also must learn how and how often to at-

tribute quotations and other information. Remember, though, that attributing a remark or some information does not excuse you from a possible libel suit. Finally, you want to be fair.

Being fair sometimes is difficult when sources do not want to be quoted. For that reason you also must learn how to deal with off-the-record quotes and background information.

What to Quote Directly

Crisp, succinct, meaningful **quotes** spice up any story. But you can overdo a good thing. Inexperienced reporters often tend to use too many direct quotations. Even many experienced public relations practitioners use too many quotes.

Remember the wonderful quote from McKayla Maroney at the beginning of this chapter? "I really didn't deserve to win a gold medal if I fall on my butt." Look at the quote used in a story on the official website for USA Gymnastics (USAgym.org):

> "It's really sad that I had to fall on that vault but I'm glad I won a silver medal."
>
> She added, "I know I can do better vaults but I also know I didn't deserve the gold medal because I fell on my second vault. It happens. It's gymnastics."

Which quote do you like better, this one or ESPN's? Which quote conveys more immediacy? More emotion?

You need direct quotes in your stories, but you also need to develop your skill in recognizing what is worth quoting directly. Let's look at the basic guidelines.

> *"I often quote myself. It adds spice to my conversation."*
>
> —**George Bernard Shaw, playwright**

Unique Material

A source sometimes tells you information you would not get in any other way. When you can say, "Ah, I never heard that before," you can be quite sure your readers would like to know exactly what the speaker said. Sometimes it is something surprising, something neither you nor your readers would have expected that person to say.

When singer Dolly Parton was asked how she felt about dumb-blonde jokes, she replied: "I'm not offended by all the dumb blonde jokes because I know I'm not dumb—and I also know that I'm not blond."

Use Good Judgment in Selecting Quotes

Striking statements like Parton's should be quoted, but not always. The *Arizona Daily Star* did a profile of a chef who writes a weekly column. Describing his food philosophy, the chef said, "I have a food philosophy, but it's a kind of an angry one. I'd eat a baby if you cooked it right. Yeah, that's pretty much it."

The *Star*'s reader advocate wrote that at least a half dozen readers objected. Said one, "Shame on the chef for saying it, and shame on the *Star* for printing it."

Don't Use Direct Quotes for Straight Facts

There is no reason to place simple, factual material inside quotation marks. Here is an extract from a story about similarities in the careers of a father and son that needed no quotes at all:

> "My son was born on campus," says the elder Denney.
>
> "In fact, he was born in the same hospital that I met my wife," he says. Since that time, his son has earned his bachelor's degree "technically in agriculture with a major in biological science and conservation."

Although the quoted material is informative, it contains nothing particularly interesting, surprising, disturbing, new or even different.

Avoid quotes that provide statistics. You can usually make a clearer, more succinct presentation by paraphrasing and attributing the information to your source. Save quotes for reaction and interpretation.

When to Use Direct Quotes

- Someone says something unique.
- Someone says something uniquely.
- Someone important says something important.

Use Quotes that Move the Story Forward

A direct quotation should say something significant, and it should not simply repeat what has been said indirectly. It should move the story forward. Here's a passage from a *USA Today* story about a proposed law that would bar health-insurance companies, employers and managed-care plans from discriminating against people because of their genetic makeup:

> Fear of insurance discrimination based on the results of genetic tests has been on the rise for years. "It stops many people cold from getting tested," says Karen Clarke, a genetics counselor at Johns Hopkins University.

The quotation is useful, it is informative, and it moves the story forward.

Consider Using Dialogue to Tell Part of the Story

Sometimes spoken material is unique not because of individual remarks that are surprising or new but because of extended dialogue that can tell the story more effectively than writers

can in their own words. Dialogue is not the same as a quotation. A quotation comes from a source speaking to the reporter. **Dialogue** occurs when two or more sources are speaking to one another.

Here's an example of how dialogue can move the story along and "show" rather than "tell." The story is about the restoration of old cars. A father is passing on a rare technique to his son:

> When the lead is smooth and the irregularities filled to his satisfaction, he reaches for his file.
>
> "How long has it been since you've done this?" his son asks.
>
> "It's been at least 20 years."
>
> "How do you tin it so it won't melt and all run off on the floor?"
>
> "Very carefully."
>
> Before the lesson is finished, a customer and two other shop workers have joined the group watching Larry at work. This is a skill few people know.
>
> "I don't like the way this lead melts," he says.
>
> "That's what it does when there's not enough tin?" his son asks.
>
> "Tin helps it stick."
>
> "Why do you pull the file instead of pushing it?"
>
> "So I can see better."
>
> "I would already have the fiberglass on and be done by now."
>
> "I know, but anything worthwhile you have to work for."

Notice the careful instruction and concerned advice from the father. His last sentence contains one of life's lessons: "Anything worthwhile you have to work for."

The Unique Expression

When you can say, "Ah, I've never heard it said *that* way before," you know you have something quotable. Be on the lookout for the clever, the colorful, the colloquial. For example, an elderly man talking about his organic garden said, "It's hard to tell people to watch what they eat. You eat health, you know."

A professor lecturing on graphic design said, "When you think it looks like a mistake, it is." The same professor once explained that elements in a design should not call attention to themselves: "You don't walk up to a beautiful painting in someone's home and say, 'That's a beautiful frame!'"

A computer trainer said to a reporter: "Teaching kids computers is like leading ducks to water. But teaching adults computers is like trying to teach chickens to swim." Wendy Holden, the co-author of *Uggie, the Artist: My Story*, said about the Jack Russell terrier, "He was born to be a star. The fact he ended up being a dog is sort of by-the-by."

Sometimes something said uniquely is a colloquialism. Colloquialisms and regional usages can add color and life to your copy. A person from Louisiana might say, "I was just fixing to leave when the phone rang." In parts of the South you're apt to hear, "I might could do that." A person from around Lancaster, Pa., might "make the light out" when turning off the lights. In some parts of the U.S., people "redd up" the dishes after a meal, meaning that they wash them and put them away.

Important Quotes by Important People

If citizen Joe Smith says, "Something must be done about this teachers' strike," you might or might not consider it worth quoting. But if the mayor says the same words, many journalists would include the quote. Generally, reporters quote public officials or known personalities in their news stories (although not everything the famous say is worth quoting). Remember, prominence is an important property of news.

Quoting sources whom readers are likely to know lends authority, credibility and interest to your story. Presumably, a meteorologist knows something about the weather, a doctor about health, a chemistry professor about chemicals. However, it is unlikely that a television star knows a great deal about cameras, even if he or she makes commercials about cameras. Important, knowledgeable people are good sources for quotes even if what they say is not unique or said uniquely.

Accuracy and Fairness in Direct Quotations

The first obligation of any reporter is to be accurate. You must learn how to get the exact words of the source.

It's not easy.

Scribbled notes from interviews, press conferences and meetings are often difficult to decipher and interpret. A study by Adrienne Lehrer, now professor emeritus of linguistics at the University of Arizona, found that only 13 of 98 quotations taken from Arizona newspapers proved to be verbatim when compared to recordings. Only twice, however, were the meanings of the nonverbatim quotes considered inaccurate. Your passion for accuracy should compel you to get and record the exact words of your sources. Only then can you decide which words to put between quotation marks.

The following story by *USA Today* marketing reporter Bruce Horovitz uses good quotations and excellent attributions.

1. Note that all the attributions are in the present tense, which gives a sense of immediacy.

2. This strong quote from an authority figure is nonthreatening and inviting.

3. The different point of view expressed here is worth a direct quote.

4. This acceptable, if unexciting, quote is from an authority figure.

5. A more colorful and specific quote: It's important that we hear directly from industry people.

6. This is not a new thought, but it's important to Subway's marketing.

7. This is a good thought that makes for an excellent summary.

ANNOTATED MODEL

USING QUOTES EFFECTIVELY

Ads Put Obese People in Spotlight

By Bruce Horovitz

USA Today, Oct. 4, 2012

Obese people are showing up in the very place that's mostly excluded them for decades: ads.

1 Some of the nation's largest brands—from Nike to Subway to Blue Cross Blue Shield—are featuring images of obese folks in their advertising in a bid to change consumer behavior. Obesity is considered to be anything 20% or more over ideal weight.

The move comes at a time two in three adults are overweight or obese, and diseases caused by obesity cost Americans $145 billion last year. In the past, obese folks in ads were often the butts of jokes. Now, they're increasingly visual images for change.

2 Why is it now acceptable to show obesity? "More of us are overweight, so it's a shared problem," says Valerie Folkes, marketing professor at University of Southern California.

3 It's a generational thing, too, says brand consultant Erich Joachimsthaler. "The new generation doesn't see (obese people) as different. There is a new, democratic world view: Everyone can be a star."

Among those showing obesity:

- **Blue Cross Blue Shield of Minnesota**. The health provider has two new ads with obese actors. In one, an obese father with a tray full of fast food thinks twice when he overhears his large son arguing with a big friend over whose father can eat more. "We want to encourage folks to make healthier choices," says Marc Manley, chief prevention officer. 4
- **Nike.** It launched an ad this summer showing an obese runner jogging. "It's not just championship athletes that aspire to push their limits," spokesman KeJuan Wilkins says. 5
- **Subway**. In March, the sandwich chain celebrates the 15th anniversary of Jared as spokesman. The ads feature photos of him at 425 pounds. "It's hard to lose the weight, but it's even harder to keep it off," says Tony Pace, head of Subway's marketing arm. 6

7 Marketers must avoid stereotypes, warns James Zervios of the Obesity Action Coalition. "So far, they're staying on the positive side of the line, but it's easy to cross over."

Be sure to check the policy of your employer. Chances are, the policy is similar to that of *The Washington Post*: "When we put a source's words inside quotation marks, those exact words should have been uttered in precisely that form."

But no one expects reporters to insert every "huh" or "ya know," and there is almost never cause to embarrass anyone with few English skills.

Radio and television news editors can cut in and out of quotes, and they can certainly insert them out of context. Doing so is not just inaccurate because it distorts the meaning of what the source has said; it is also unethical.

> *"I think of quotes as spices. Spices in themselves have no nutritional value. They make nutritious things taste better, but, like spices, quotes should be used sparingly."*

—Isabel Wilkerson, Pulitzer Prize–winning reporter at *The Washington Post*, quoted in *A Writer's Coach*

Verification

When someone important says something important but perhaps false, putting the material in quotes does not relieve you of the responsibility for the inaccuracies. Citizens, officials and candidates for office often say things that may be partially true or altogether untrue and perhaps even libelous. Quotations need verification, like any other information you gather.

In the interest of balance, fairness and objectivity, many papers leave out, correct or point out the errors and inconsistencies in quotations. They do this in the article itself or in an accompanying story.

If candidate Joe Harkness says that his opponent, Jim McGown, is a member of the Ku Klux Klan, you should check before you print the charge. Good reporters don't stop looking and checking just because someone gives them some information. Look for yourself. Prisoners might have an altogether different account of a riot from the one the prison officials give you. Your story will not be complete unless you talk to all sides.

Quoting from Email, Social Media, the Internet and Chat Rooms

When you quote from email you have received personally, you can usually be sure the sender has written those words. If you have doubts, be sure to check with your correspondent. It's also a good idea to let readers know that you obtained the quote through email and did not speak with the source in person.

If you get a quote from the Web, you need to be much more careful. Try to verify the quote with the source, but if you can't do that, at least be sure to tell readers that the quote comes from the Web, and then cite the URL (Internet address).

Reading what people are saying in chat rooms, blogs and tweets can be useful to reporters. However, quoting what people write in these forums is unwise because some statements might be unverified and even libelous. Nevertheless, if you have verified the information—and identified the

person who is saying it—and if you specifically state where you obtained the information, you might on occasion use such a quote. Identifying the person might well be impossible, though, because some people use screen names, aliases or pseudonyms on the Internet.

Bob Daemmrich/PhotoEdit

Figure 6-5. Although quotes from experts and public figures are generally used to strengthen a story's authority, quotes from ordinary citizens with unique experience in a newsworthy event may also add credibility.

Using Someone Else's Direct Quotations

If you use a direct quotation that you did not personally get from a source, always indicate your source for the quote. Jessica Heslam wrote on BostonHerald.com that a *Boston Herald* review of WBZ-TV political analyst Jon Keller's book *The Bluest State* revealed "almost three dozen instances of direct quotes and other material lifted from numerous newspaper articles without any attribution."

Don't be tempted to use direct quotes you find in news releases. Don't be lazy; get your own quotes. Sources are much less likely to say things that are self-serving if they are talking to a journalist rather than a public relations person.

The Public Relations Society of America doesn't mind if you use material from a news release without attribution. Gerard Corbett, chair and CEO of PRSA, says doing so is not plagiarism, but he does recommend attribution when reporters use direct quotes, facts or figures from releases.

The Kansas City Star obviously disagrees about a reporter using material from news releases. The paper fired 32-year *Star* reporter Steve Penn for using news release materials in his columns dating back four years. Penn is suing McClatchy Co., owner of the newspaper. He says this practice was always OK at *The Star*, and he was not notified of a change in policy.

Practicing Prepublication Review

A decade ago, you would not have had a city editor tell you to check the accuracy of your direct quotations with your source. Today, it is standard practice on many newspapers. Steve Weinberg, a former Missouri School of Journalism professor and former head of Investigative Reporters and Editors, calls it PPR—prepublication review.

Weinberg states candidly that it is not sensitivity to the feelings of his sources that motivates him to support the use of PPR. Rather, he insists that prepublication review loosens the tongues of tight-lipped sources and gets their statements on the record. Prepublication review extends also to checking the facts. Most professional journalists insist it does not make them feel compromised or make them surrender control over their stories or appear as "obsequious lapdogs." *New York Times* Associate Managing Editor for Standards Philip B. Corbett used those words and assured readers they did not apply to reporters at *The New York Times.*

The fact is, however, that too many times journalists get direct quotes wrong. Craig Silverman, an award-winning journalist and author and founder of Regret the Error, a blog that reports on media errors and corrections, has reported on mangled direct quotations from the past and the present. No paper is immune, and neither is history. He writes that while doing research for his book, *Regret the Error: How Media Mistakes Pollute the Press and Imperil Free Speech*, he found that William Randolph Hearst did not say, "You furnish the pictures; I'll furnish the war"; President Lyndon Johnson did not say, "If I've lost Cronkite, I've lost Middle America"; and Vice President Al Gore "sure as hell" never claimed to have invented the Internet.

If you Google "Wikimedia: misquotations," you will find a list of 89 "misattributed, unsourced, unverified or other best guesses." You will also find a list of people who are most commonly misquoted. The name on top of the list? You guessed it. Yogi Berra.

Journalist Philip Weiss offers another reason why more journalists are practicing prepublication review: Reporters are often the subjects of stories. "They have had a taste of their own medicine and they don't like it."

Another reason for prepublication review is that it serves as a defense against libel. Jurors are less likely to find "reckless disregard for the truth" in an article that the source reviewed.

But what happens when sources want to change a quote? Weinberg says he makes it clear that the source is checking only for accuracy. He will consider comments about interpretation, phrasing or tone, but he retains the right to change or not change the quotes.

And what happens if someone denies saying something that is in a direct quote? That possibility is why you need to have good notes, Weinberg says, even if they are in shorthand. Having the interview on tape is even better.

The issue of quote approval is far from settled. In 2012, Poynter reported that *The New York Times*, *The Washington Post*, Bloomberg and Reuters had all agreed to let politicians and campaigns have prior approval on quotations.

But policies can change in a hurry. Just two months later, *New York Times* Executive Editor Jill Abramson wrote a memo to her staff that said:

> So starting now (Sept. 20, 2012), we want to draw a clear line on this. Citing *Times* policy, reporters should say no if a source demands, as a condition of an interview, that quotes be submitted afterwards to the source or a press aide to review, approve or edit.

Note the words "review, approve or edit." What could be wrong with checking the accuracy of a quote? *The Huffington Post* admits that at times it allows sources to edit its quotes. Does "edit" mean change the wording or change the meaning? It surely means something different from checking the accuracy. The Associated Press, McClatchy Co. and *National Journal* have banned checking quotations.

Why? You certainly need to check the accuracy of the facts in your story. Doesn't it make sense to check the accuracy of the quotations? A simple reading of the quotes to the source can accomplish that.

That's a far cry from what *Washington Post* higher education reporter Daniel de Vise did when University of Texas officials were unhappy with his first draft of a story. An email accompanying his second draft included the words, "I'd like to know of any phrases in the piece that you think are too harsh or over-hyped. . . . Everything here is negotiable."

Patrick B. Pexton, ombudsman for *The Washington Post*, writes that de Vise made a mistake. "He forgot that *Post* reporters write for readers, not for sources."

We all need to remember that we write for our readers.

CBS/Landov

Figure 6-6. Getting good quotes in a television interview takes skill and practice.

> *"When you see yourself quoted in print and you're sorry you said it, it suddenly becomes a misquotation."*
>
> —Dr. Laurence J. Peter, author of ***Peter's Quotations*** and ***The Peter Principle***

Altering Quotations

By now you realize that although you should use direct quotations, they present many challenges and problems. Though there is no set number you should strive to include, a story with no quotes often lacks life and substance. Still, including lengthy quotes indiscriminately is a sign that you haven't really digested the material for your audience. Instead of quoting someone at length, look for the effective kernel within a long quotation.

Getting Accurate Quotes

- Use a digital recorder during interviews, and be sure the interviewee knows you are using it.
- Develop a consistent short-hand method for note taking so you can reliably read your own notes.
- Check your written quotes against any available video of the situation.
- Call the source to verify the exact wording of any quote you're unsure of.

Paraphrasing Quotes

Some quotations need verification, others need clarification. Do not quote someone unless you are sure of what that person means. "But that's what the man said" is not a sufficient reason (or excuse) for using an ambiguous quote. It is much better to skip a quotation altogether than to confuse the reader.

The best way to avoid confusing or wordy quotes is to paraphrase. In a **paraphrase** you use your own words to communicate the speaker's meaning. As a reporter, you must have confidence that you will sometimes be able to convey that meaning in fewer words and in better language than the speaker did. Digesting, condensing and clarifying quotes take more effort than simply repeating them word for word. Here is a quote that could be cut drastically:

> "When I first started singing lessons I assumed I would be a public school teacher and maybe, if I was good enough, a voice teacher," he said. "When I graduated from the university, I still thought I would be a teacher, and I wanted to teach."

A paraphrase conveys the meaning more succinctly:

> When he first started singing lessons, and even after he graduated from the university, he wanted to be a public school voice teacher.

Using Partial Quotes

It is much better to paraphrase or to use full quotes than to use fragmentary or partial quotes. Partial quotes often make for choppy, interrupted sentences. Some editors would have you avoid these "orphan quotes" almost altogether. Here is an example of the overuse of partial quotes:

> The mayor said citizens should "turn off" unnecessary lights and "turn down" thermostats "to 65 degrees."

The sentence would be better with no quotation marks at all. Taking out the quotation marks would turn this sentence into an indirect quotation. In an indirect quotation, the reporter uses words and phrases of the speaker's language and includes an attribution but doesn't use quotation marks. Indirect quotations need to meet the same test for accuracy that direct quotations require.

If a particular phrase has special significance or meaning, a partial quote may be justifiable. Sometimes you might want to put a word or phrase in quotation marks to indicate that this was precisely what the speaker said. Look at this use of a one-word quote in a story about genetic engineering in *The Atlantic Monthly*:

> By all but eliminating agricultural erosion and runoff—so Brian Noyes, the local conservation-district manager, told me—continuous no-till could "revolutionize" the area's water quality.

The writer thought it important that readers know that "revolutionize" was not his word but the word of his source. And he was right. "Revolutionize" is a strong word.

When you do use partial quotes, do not put quotation marks around something the speaker could not have said. Suppose a speaker told a student audience at a university, "I am pleased and thrilled with your attendance here tonight." It would be incorrect to write the following:

> The speaker said she was "pleased and thrilled with the students' attendance."

Partial quotes often contain an ellipsis (three periods) to tell the reader that some of the words of the quote are missing. For example:

> "I have come here tonight . . . and I have crossed state lines . . . to conspire against the government."

This practice at times might be justifiable, but you should not keep the reader guessing about what is missing. Sometimes the speaker's actual meaning is distorted when certain words are dropped. If a critic writes about a three-act play, "A great hit—except for the first three acts," an ad that picks up only the first part of that quote is guilty of misrepresentation. A journalist who uses the technique to distort the message is no less guilty.

Capturing Dialect or Accent

Using colorful or colloquial expressions helps the writer capture a person in a particular environment. The same can be true when you write the way people talk:

> "Are you gonna go?" he asked.
>
> "No, I'm not goin'," she replied.

In everyday speech hardly anyone enunciates perfectly. To do so would sound affected. In fiction, therefore, it is common to use spellings that match speech. But when conversation is written down in newspaper reporting, readers expect correct, full spellings. Not only is correct spelling easier to read, it is also less difficult to write. Capturing dialect consistently is difficult, as these passages from a story about a Hollywood actress illustrate:

> "Boy, it's hot out theah," she started. "I could sure use a nice cold beer. How about it, uh? Wanta go get a couple beers?"

If she said "theah," wouldn't she also say "beeah"? Perhaps she said, "How 'bout it, uh?" And if she said "wanta," maybe she also said "geta."

In another passage, the writer has the actress speaking "straight" English:

> "Would you believe I used to dress like that all the time? Dates didn't want to be seen with me. I was always being asked to change clothes before going out."

It is unlikely she is that inconsistent in her speech.

The writer of this story tried to show us something of the character of the actress. If he wanted to convey her speech patterns, he should have either been consistent or simply reported that she talked the same off the set as on it.

Sometimes when a newspaper attempts to quote someone saying something uniquely, it betrays a bias. A Southern politician is more likely to have his quote spelled phonetically than an Eastern politician who says "idee-er" and "Cuber."

However, you should not make everyone's speech the same. Barbara King Lord, former director of editorial training for the Associated Press, laments "our frequent inability to write other than insipid speech" and "our tendency to homogenize the day-to-day speech patterns of the heterogeneous people we write about." She acknowledges that writers worry about exposing to ridicule the immigrant's halting or perhaps unconventional speech while the stockbroker's speech appears flawless.

Lord calls the argument specious. Of course, people should not be exposed to ridicule through their speech. "The point here," she says, "is simply that when the writer's intention in writing dialects, quaint expressions, nonconventional grammar, flowery or showy speech, or the Queen's English is to make a person human, that intention is not only acceptable, it's desirable."

The only way you can make people human is to listen to them. Lord says reporters and writers usually hear but rarely listen. She advises reporters to "listen for expressions, turns of phrase, idiosyncratic talk," and to work these into their stories.

J.R. Moehringer of the *Los Angeles Times* did this in his Pulitzer Prize–winning article:

> "No white man gonna tell me not to march," Lucy says, jutting her chin. "Only make me march harder."

Here the actual speech makes the speaker's determination and passion all the more evident.

You must be especially careful when quoting people for whom English is a second language. Nearly any attempt to quote nonfluent speakers exactly will be looked upon as making fun of their English. Better that you paraphrase their comments or, as some would advise, make them speak good English. Once again, however, if you have audio from baseball star Albert Pujols on your website and have the same quotes in perfect, fluent English in the written text, many would see the discrepancy as a serious problem. Others would say that you are hurting the uniqueness and character of the great slugger, who was born in the Dominican Republic. These problems are as old as radio and television, but convergence of the media has increased their frequency.

> *"The surest way to make a monkey of a man is to quote him."*
>
> **—Robert Benchley, humorist**

Mixing and Matching Questions and Answers

Writers often agonize over whether they must use quotations in the exact order in which the speaker said them.

The primary questions you must ask yourself are these: Why am I changing the order? Am I being fair? Am I distorting the meaning? Am I putting quotes together that change what the speaker intended to say?

Here are two versions of an emotional outburst in a Kansas City Chiefs' locker room after the Chiefs were defeated by Baltimore in 2012 and some Chiefs fans had cheered when quarterback Matt Cassel was knocked unconscious and suffered a concussion.

> "It's 100 percent sickening," Chiefs tackle Eric Winston said. "I've never, ever—and I've been in some rough times on some rough teams—I've never been more embarrassed in my life to play football than at that moment right there. I get emotional about it because these guys, they work their butts off. Matt Cassel hasn't done anything to you people.
>
> "Hey, if he's not the best quarterback, he's not the best quarterback, and that's OK, but he's a person," Winston continued, the big offensive lineman's voice slowly rising. "And he got knocked out in a game and we've got 70,000 people cheering that he got knocked out."

Here's another version of Winston's words in the locker room:

> "But when you cheer, when you cheer somebody getting knocked out, I don't care who it is, and it just so happened to be Matt Cassel—it's sickening. It's 100 percent sickening. I've been in some rough times on some rough teams, I've never been more embarrassed in my life to play football than in that moment right there.

> "I get emotional about it because these guys, they work their butts off. Matt Cassel hasn't done anything to you people, hasn't done anything to you people. Hasn't done anything to the media writers that kill him, hasn't done anything wrong to the people that come out here and cheer him. Hey, if he's not the best quarterback then he's not the best quarterback and that's OK. But he's a person. And he got knocked out in a game and we have 70,000 people cheering that he got knocked out?"

It's obvious that both of these quotes cannot be correct. Neither of them is exact. Other print versions of Winston's words were equally misquoted and out of order. Does it matter?

It should.

By October 2012, more than 80,000 fans heard (and saw) exactly what Winston said on YouTube. In fairness to Winston, he later apologized by acknowledging that he knew that not all 70,000 fans cheered when Cassel was knocked unconscious.

Correcting Grammar in Quotes

Perhaps the most perplexing problem tied to the proper handling of direct quotations is this: When should you correct grammatical errors in a direct quotation? Should you expect people in news conferences or during informal interviews to speak perfect English?

The Case for Correcting Grammar

It is accepted practice at many newspapers to correct mistakes in grammar and to convey a person's remarks in complete sentences. None of us regularly speaks in perfect, grammatical sentences. But if we were writing down our remarks, presumably we would write in grammatically correct English.

Reporters are expected to use standard American written English.

- Standard—News audiences expect to read or hear the most widely and generally accepted English.
- American—Some words have different spellings and meanings in England, Australia and other English-speaking countries.
- Written—Admittedly, people often use words and expressions while speaking that they do not use when writing.

Reporters and editors differ widely on when or even whether to correct quotes. A reporter for the *Rocky Mountain News* quoted an attorney as saying, "Her and John gave each other things they needed and couldn't get anyplace else." The reporter said the quote was accurate but, on second thought, said it might have been better to correct the grammar to "She and John" in the written account.

The Case Against Correcting Grammar

You are most likely to find direct quotations with grammatical errors in the sports pages of daily newspapers. Nevertheless, often you can read an entire newspaper sports section and not find a single grammatical error in a direct quote.

Washington Post reporter Howard Bryant quoted Clinton Portis, then playing for the Washington Redskins, as saying: "I don't know how anybody feels. I don't know how anybody's thinking. I don't know what anyone else is going through. The only thing I know is what's going on in Clinton Portis's life." *Post* columnist Mike Wise quoted Portis as saying: "I don't know how nobody feel, I don't know what nobody think, I don't know what nobody doing, the only thing I know is what's going on in Clinton Portis's life."

Bryant, an African-American then working with ESPN, did not agree with the Post's policy of not changing quotes, a policy that, by the way, he said he never heard of. But Bryant did say, "I am totally convinced—along racial, class and cultural lines—that when it comes to white players from the South, reporters instinctively clean up their language."

Most papers have no written policy on correcting grammatical errors in direct quotations. Because so many variables are involved, these matters are handled on a case-by-case basis. Some argue you should sacrifice a bit of accuracy in the interest of promoting proper English—except for elected officials and public figures.

On the subject of correcting grammar in direct quotations, read what AP says under "Quotations in the News":

> Never alter quotations even to correct minor grammatical errors or word usage. Casual minor tongue slips may be removed by using ellipses but even that should be done with extreme caution. If there is a question about a quote, either don't use it or ask the speaker to clarify.

In this age of convergence, print reporters might also have shot video, and even if they haven't, they know someone has. Correcting quotations is even more unwise for radio and television reporters. Writers and editors for print should remember that the quotation they use might have been heard by millions of people on radio or television. Changing the quote even slightly might make viewers and listeners question the credibility of print reports. Readers might also ask why print writers feel the need to act as press agents who strive to make their subjects look good.

This applies to celebrities of all kinds (actors, sports figures), but it might also apply to political candidates and elected officials. At least, some argue, news agencies should have some consistency. If a reporter quotes a farmer using incorrect grammar, then should the same be done for the mayor or for a college professor?

Removing Redundancies

Another question reporters deal with is whether to remove redundancies and other irrelevant material by using ellipses. Again, there is no agreement in the industry. For most reporters and editors, the answer to the problem of correcting quotes is to take out the quotation marks and to paraphrase. Sometimes you can just remove a phrase or a sentence. However, when you do that, you sometimes lose a lot. The value of quotes often lies in their richness and uniqueness.

When the Columbia *Missourian* quoted University of Missouri basketball star Keon Lawrence after a winning game, it dropped a sentence:

> "That felt good," Keon Lawrence said. "I look forward to doing that again."

The *Columbia Daily Tribune* wrote it this way:

> "Oh, that felt good," Lawrence said a few minutes after the game that hardly anyone thought the Tigers could win. "I didn't never do that. I look forward to doing that again."

Which version do you like better? Which version would you have written?

Deleting Obscenity, Profanity and Vulgarity

Many news organizations never allow some things people say to be printed or broadcast—even if they are said uniquely. Obscenities (words usually referring to sexual parts or functions), profanities (words used irreverently to refer to a deity or to beings people regard as divine) and vulgarities (words referring to excretory matters) are usually deleted or bleeped unless they are essential to the story. Even at major newspapers, policy often demands that an obscenity, for example, be used only with the approval of a top editor.

Of course, there are legitimate reasons to use proper sex-related terms in health stories and in some crime stories, including child molestation stories.

News stories about sexual assaults or accusations sometimes contain words such as these, especially if those involved are noted celebrities or politicians.

Obviously, words such as "God" and "Jesus Christ" used in discussions of religion have always been acceptable to most people.

Nevertheless, the rules are different for what some call "swear" words in direct quotation. Some papers follow *The Associated Press Stylebook* rule: "If a full quote that contains an obscenity, profanity or vulgarity cannot be dropped but there is no compelling reason for the offensive language, replace the letters of the offensive word with hyphens, using only an initial letter."

News is likely to reflect the sensibilities of its audience. Like it or not, language that was once considered vulgar in polite society is now tolerated more widely.

Of course, the Federal Communications Commission regulates the content of radio and television (except for cable) and can still fine a station or suspend its license for indecency. Fining is rare, but audiences are quick to let a station know that it has gone too far.

Individuals and advocacy groups try to curtail the use of profanity in the media. One such group is the Parents Television Council, a U.S.-based advocacy group founded in 1995 by conservative activist L. Brent Bozell III. This group's primary mission is to list television programs and other entertainment products it deems harmful to children. Among other measures, it counts the times profanity is used on a program.

Researchers from the University of Tennessee and Florida State University have kept track of the rapid rise of words such as "jackass" and "sucks." *New York Times* writer Edward Wyatt quotes Timothy Jay, a psychology professor at the Massachusetts College of Liberal Arts, as saying, "Vulgar slang has a way of waxing and waning, where we become desensitized to a word's earlier meanings."

At times you might wish to use vulgarities to show the intensity of someone's anger, terror, frustration or bitterness. Few inside the news media condone the casual, gratuitous use of vulgarities, however.

And neither do most readers and listeners.

Avoiding Made-Up Quotes

Fabricating a direct quote, even from general things that a source has said or from what the source might say if given the chance, is never acceptable. Even seasoned reporters are sometimes tempted to put quotation marks around words that their sources "meant to say," or to clarify or simplify a quote. They reason that it's more important to have a clear and concise quote for the reader than to be a slave to the verbose and unclear words of the source. That's bad reasoning. It's better to paraphrase.

Even worse is fabricating a quote that makes a source look bad or that is defamatory or perhaps even libelous. Doing so can result in a lawsuit. In 1991, in Masson v. Malcolm, the U.S. Supreme Court ruled that suits regarding quotations can proceed to trial if the altered quote "results in a material change in the meaning conveyed by the statement."

Libel or no libel, your credibility as a reporter demands that you be scrupulously exact when you place people's words inside quotation marks. When in doubt, paraphrase.

Attributing Direct and Indirect Quotes

Now that you've learned some of the complexities of using quotations, let's take a look at when and how to attribute them to a source.

When to Attribute

Attribution involves giving the name of, and sometimes other identifying information about, the source of a direct quotation, an indirect quotation or paraphrased material. You should almost always attribute direct quotes—with some exceptions. You would not, for example, attribute a quotation to a 7-year-old who witnessed a gang shooting. You might not wish to attribute a quote to someone who saw a homicide suspect with the victim. To do so in either case could put the source in danger.

You need a good reason to allow an entire paragraph of direct quotations to stand without an attribution. However, if you are quoting from a speech, an interview or a press conference and only the speaker is mentioned in the story, it might be excessive to put an attribution in every paragraph.

Ordinarily you should attribute **indirect quotations**. You should usually have a source for the information you write, and when you do, attribute the information to that source. The source can be a person or a written document. However, there are exceptions.

If you are a witness to damages or injuries, do not name yourself as a source in the story. Attribute this information to the police or to other authorities. But you do not have to attribute the totally obvious. If you are on the scene of an accident and can see that three people were involved, you do not have to write, "'Three people were involved in the accident,' Officer Osbord said." If you are unsure of the information or if there are conclusions or generalities involved, your editor probably will want you to attribute the information to an official or a witness. Avoid, however, attributing factual statements to "officials" or "authorities" or "sources." "Such constructions," writes journalist Jack Hart, "suggest that we are controlled by form and that we have forgotten about function."

If you are quoting from an interview conducted by someone other than yourself, be sure to note that. Do not claim that you obtained the quote yourself by writing, "In an interview, Smith said. . . ." That would make it seem as though you conducted the interview.

Not everyone agrees. Well-known journalist and commentator Fareed Zakaria, who was found guilty of plagiarism, was also found guilty of not attributing sources. In one case he justified his actions by saying that his book was "not an academic work where everything has to be acknowledged and footnoted." He did not wish to "interrupt the flow for the reader."

Zakaria says he feels the same way about attributing quotes from other people's interviews.

He's wrong.

Hart pleads for common sense regarding attributions. "Let's save them for direct quotations or paraphrased quotes laced with opinion," he writes. "Or for assertions likely to be especially sensitive. Or controversial." He says we should attribute only "if it matters."

This is good advice for the veteran. Nevertheless, although it is possible to attribute too often and although you do not always need to attribute, when you have doubts, include an attribution.

That goes for attributing anonymous sources, too. Even though you should seldom use them, you must attribute them. Try to preserve your credibility by giving as much information as you can about the sources without revealing their names. For example, you might report "a source close to the chancellor said." For the second reference to the same source, use "the anonymous source said."

Whether we like them or not, anonymous sources are common, even in the best of newspapers. The figure "Using Anonymous Sources" (on the following page) shows a few paragraphs from an Associated Press story published in the *Columbia Daily Tribune*. The attributions—all anonymous—are highlighted in bold.

Notice how many quotes are attributed to a "criminal complaint" without really saying exactly who was responsible for filing the complaint. Notice also the attribution "family members." The reporter had no reason to name them and invade their privacy.

Sometimes, as in stories about crime victims, you might have to change someone's name and follow the pseudonym with "not her real name" in parentheses to protect the source's privacy or to avoid endangering the source's life or family.

Attribution Not Needed

You need not attribute information to a source if you are a witness or if the information:

- Is a matter of public record.
- Is generally known.
- Is available from several sources.
- Is easily verifiable.
- Makes no assumptions.
- Contains no opinions.
- Is noncontroversial.

ANNOTATED MODEL

USING ANONYMOUS SOURCES

Terror Sting Thwarts Car Bomb Attempt

Attack was planned on Federal Reserve.

NEW YORK (AP)—A Bangladeshi man snared in an FBI terror sting considered targeting President Barack Obama and the New York City Stock Exchange before settling on a car bomb attack on the Federal Reserve, just blocks from the World Trade Center site, a law enforcement official told The Associated Press today.

1 The official, who was not authorized to speak publicly about the investigation and talked to the AP on condition of anonymity, stressed that the suspect never got beyond the discussion stage in considering an attack on the president.

In a September meeting with an undercover agent posing as a fellow jihadist,
2 Quazi Mohammad Rezwanul Ahsan Nafis explained he chose the Federal Reserve as his target "for operational reasons," according to a criminal complaint. Nafis also indicated he knew that choice would "cause a large number of civilian casualties, including women and children," the complaint said.

The bomb was fake, but authorities said that Nafis' admiration of Osama bin Laden and aspirations for martyrdom were not. 3

FBI agents grabbed the 21-year-old Nafis— armed with a cellphone he believed was rigged as a detonator—after he made several attempts to blow up a fake 1,000-pound bomb inside a vehicle parked next to the Federal Reserve yesterday in lower Manhattan, the complaint said. . . .

4 Nafis is a banker's son from a middle-class neighborhood, and family members said today that they were stunned by his arrest. . . .

Sources can be anonymous for a number of reasons. Explaining those reasons improves the credibility of the story.

1. The reporter states the reason for the source's anonymity.

2. The criminal complaint is a matter of public record.

3. The word "authorities" tells the reader the information was confirmed with more than one source.

4. The reporter preserves the sources' privacy.

How to Attribute

In composition and creative writing classes, you may have been told to avoid repeating the same word. You probably picked up your thesaurus to look for a synonym for "to say," a colorless verb. Without much research you may have found 100 or more substitutes. None of them is wrong. Indeed, writers might search long for the exact word they need to convey a particular nuance of meaning. For example:

> The presidential candidate announced the choice of a running mate.
>
> The arrested man divulged the names of his accomplices.
>
> The judge pronounced sentence.

At other times, in the interest of precise and lively writing, you might write:

> "I'll get you for that," she whispered.
>
> "I object!" he shouted.

Nevertheless, reporters and editors prefer forms of "to say" in most instances, even if these are repeated throughout a story. And there are good reasons for this word choice. "Said" is unobtrusive. Rather than appearing tiresome and repetitious, it hides in the news columns and calls no attention to itself. "Said" is also neutral. It has no connotations. To use the word "said" is to be objective.

Some of the synonyms for "said" sound innocent enough, but be careful. If you report that a city official "claimed" or "maintained" or "contended," you are implying that you do not quite believe what the official said. The word "said" is the solution to your problem. If you have evidence that what the official said is incorrect, you should include the evidence or the correct information in your story.

In some newspaper accounts of labor negotiations, company officials always "ask" and labor leaders always "demand." "Demanding" sounds harsh and unreasonable, but "asking" sounds calm and reasonable. A reporter who uses these words in this context is taking an editorial stand—consciously or unconsciously.

Other words you may be tempted to use as a substitute for "said" are simply unacceptable because they represent improper usage. For example:

> "You don't really mean that," he winked.
>
> "Of course I do," she grinned.
>
> "But what if someone heard you say that?" he frowned.
>
> "Oh, you are a fool," she laughed.

You cannot "wink" a word. Similarly, it is impossible to "grin," "frown" or "laugh" words. But you might want to say this:

> "Not again," he said, moaning.
>
> "I'm afraid so," she said with a grin.

This usage is correct. Words like "moaning" or phrases like "with a grin" sometimes are needed to convey the speaker's meaning, but often they are not necessary or even helpful.

Learning the correct words for attribution is the first step. Here are some other guidelines to follow when attributing quotations:

- **If a direct quote is more than one sentence long, place the attribution at the end of the first sentence.** This placement makes the copy flow better and doesn't keep the reader in the dark about the attribution for too long. For example:

  > "The car overturned at least three times," the police officer said. "None of the four passengers was hurt. Luckily, the car did not explode into flames."

  That one attribution is adequate. It would be redundant to write the following:

  > "The car overturned at least three times," the police officer said. "None of the four passengers was hurt," he added. "Luckily, the car did not explode into flames," he continued.

Nor should you write this:

> "The car overturned at least three times. None of the four passengers was hurt. Luckily, the car did not explode into flames," the police officer said.

  Although you should not keep the reader wondering who is being quoted, in most cases you should avoid placing the attribution at the beginning of a quote. Do not write the following:

  > The police officer said: "The car overturned at least three times. None of the four passengers was hurt. Luckily, the car did not explode into flames."

- **If direct quotes from two different speakers follow one another, start the second with its attribution.** This placement avoids confusion for the reader:

  > "The driver must not have seen the curve," an eyewitness said. "Once the car left the road, all I saw was a cloud of dust."
  >
  > The police officer said: "The car overturned at least three times. None of the four passengers was hurt. Luckily, the car did not explode into flames."

  Notice that when an attribution precedes a direct quotation that is more than one sentence long, wire service style requires that a colon follow the attribution.

- **Separate partial quotes and complete quotes.** Avoid constructions like this one:

  > The mayor said the time had come "to turn off some lights. We all must do something to conserve electricity."

The correct form is to separate partial quotes and complete quotes:

> The time has come "to turn off some lights," the mayor said. "We all must do something to conserve electricity."

- **The first time you attribute a direct or an indirect quote, identify the speaker fully.** How fully depends on how well the speaker is known to the readers. In Springfield, Ill., it is sufficient to identify the mayor simply as Mayor Houston. But if a story in the *Chicago Tribune* refers to the mayor of Springfield, the first reference should be "J. Michael Houston, mayor of Springfield"—unless the dateline for the story is Springfield.
- **Attribute direct quotes to only one person.** For example, don't do the following:

  > "Flames were shooting out everywhere," witnesses said.

  If indeed any witnesses made statements like this, all you have to do is eliminate the quotation marks to turn this into an indirect quotation. For example:

  > Several witnesses said that flames were shooting out everywhere.

- **Do not make up a source. Never attribute a statement to "a witness" unless your source is indeed that witness.** At times you might ask a witness to confirm what you have seen, but never invent quotes for anonymous witnesses. Inventing witnesses and making up quotes is dishonest, inaccurate and inexcusable.
- **In stories covering past news events, use the past tense in attributions, and use it throughout the story.** However, features and other stories that do not report on news events might be more effective if the attributions are consistently given in the present tense (see "Using Quotes Effectively", for example). In a feature story like a personality profile, when it is safe to assume that what the person once said, he or she would still say, you might use the present tense. For example, when you write, "'I like being mayor,' she says," you are indicating that the mayor still enjoys her job.
- **Ordinarily, place the noun or pronoun before the verb in attributions:**

  > "Everything is under control," the sheriff said.

  However, if you must identify a person by including a long title, it is better to begin the attribution with the verb:

  > "I enjoy the challenge," says Janet Berry, associate dean for graduate studies and research.

He Said, She Said—Punctuating Direct Quotations

"Always put the comma inside quotation marks," she said. Then she added, "The same goes for the period."

"Does the same rule apply for the question mark?" he asked.

"Only if the entire statement is a question," she replied, "and never add a comma after a question mark. Also, be sure to lowercase the first word of a continuing quote that follows an attribution and a comma.

"However, you must capitalize the first word of a new sentence after an attribution," she continued.

"Do not forget to open and close the sentence with quotation marks."

"Why are there no quotation marks after the word 'comma' at the end of the third paragraph?" he asked.

"Because the same person is speaking at the beginning of the next paragraph," she said. "Notice that the new paragraph does open with quotation marks. Note, too, that a quote inside a quotation needs single quotation marks, as around the word 'comma' in the paragraph above."

Attributing Written Sources

Do not use the word "says" when quoting from written sources. You might be general at times and write, "As *Time* magazine reported last week . . ." or "According to *Time* magazine. . . ." When you know the author of the piece, you might wish to include it: "As Katha Pollitt wrote in the Sept. 21, 2009, issue of *The Nation*. . . ." For a report, survey or study cited in a news story, it's usually enough to identify the authors, the date of publication and the name of the journal or the issuing agency.

Handling On- and Off-the-Record Information

Your job would be easy if all of your sources wished to be "on the record."

Some sources do not want to be named for sound reasons. You must learn to use professional judgment in handling the material they give you. If you agree to accept their information, you must honor their request to remain off the record. Breaching that confidence destroys trust and credibility and may get you in trouble with the law. But it is your obligation to take the information elsewhere to confirm it and get it on the record.

Anonymous sources helped *The New York Times* report the Bush administration's extralegal bugging of international communications. But another *Times* front-page story based on anonymous sources suggesting Sen. John McCain had an extramarital affair with a lobbyist was a great embarrassment.

Problems with Anonymous Sources

Not naming sources is dangerous for three important reasons. First, such information lacks credibility and makes the reporter and the newspaper suspect. Why should readers believe writers who won't cite the sources of their information? Who is to say that the writers didn't simply make things up to suit their stories?

Second, the source might be lying. He or she might be out to discredit someone or might be floating a trial balloon, that is, testing public reaction on some issue or event. Skilled diplomats and politicians know how to use reporters to take the temperature of public opinion. If the public reacts negatively, the sources will not proceed with whatever plans they leaked to the press. In such cases the press has been used—and it has become less credible.

Finally, once you have promised anonymity to a source, you might not change your mind without risking a breach-of-contract suit. In 1991, the U.S. Supreme Court ruled 5-4 in Cohen v. Cowles Media Co. that the First Amendment does not prevent news sources from suing the press for breach of contract when the press makes confidential sources public. That's why at papers such as *The Miami Herald* only a senior editor has authority to commit the paper to a pledge of confidentiality.

The New York Times' Policy on the Use of Anonymous Sources

> *"The policy requires that at least one editor know the identity of every source. Anonymous sources cannot be used when on-the-record sources are readily available. They must have direct knowledge of the information they are imparting; they cannot use the cloak of anonymity for personal or partisan attack; they cannot be used for trivial comment or to make an unremarkable comment seem more important than it is."*
>
> **—From "Culling the Anonymous Sources" by Clark Hoyt, former public editor, *The New York Times***

On THE JOB

Off the Record

T.J. Quinn spent 16 years as a news and sports writer—eight at the New York *Daily News*—before moving to ESPN in 2007. As a reporter for the network's investigative/enterprise unit, most of his work is "cross-platform," with versions of the same stories appearing on television, ESPN.com and ESPN radio. His long-form stories appear primarily on the show "Outside the Lines," for which he is a backup anchor. Quinn's work also appears on "Sports-Center" and other ESPN news platforms, and he works as an adjunct professor at the Columbia University Graduate School of Journalism.

He finds that investigative work requires a lot of off-the-record and not-for-attribution interviews. "Be careful," he says. "Don't be too eager to grant sources anonymity unless they truly won't speak to you otherwise." After a not-for-attribution conversation, he usually asks sources whether they would be comfortable saying the same thing on the record. "They often are," Quinn says.

"If you do go off the record, be absolutely clear about what is on and what is off, and if you agree to stay off the record, respect it," Quinn says. "You'll have no credibility if you don't."

Disagreement about Terminology

Some reporters make these distinctions regarding sources and attribution:

- **Off the record.** You may not use the information.
- **Not for attribution.** You may use the information but with no reference as to its source.
- **Background.** You may use it with a general title for a source (for example, "a White House aide said").
- **Deep background.** You may use the information, but you may not indicate any source.

By no means is there agreement on these terms. For most people "off the record" means not for attribution. For some it means that you cannot use the information in any way. Some find no difference between "background" and "deep background." Journalists are vague about the meaning of the terms, and so are sources. Your obligation is to make sure you and your sources understand each other. Set the ground rules ahead of time. Clarify your terms.

Be careful not to allow a speaker to suddenly claim something is off the record. Sometimes in the middle of an interview a source will see you taking notes and try to change the rules: "Oh, I meant to tell you, that last example was off the record." With all the tact you can muster, try, without losing the source altogether, to change the person's mind. At least, tell the person to try to avoid doing that for the rest of the interview.

Three Reasons to Avoid Anonymous Sources

- You damage your credibility.
- Your source may be lying or floating a trial balloon.
- You may be sued if you later reveal your source.

Background Interviews

If a city manager or police chief wishes to have a background session with you, unless it is against newspaper policy, you should not refuse. Often these officials are trying to be as open as they can under certain circumstances. Without such background sessions the task of reporting complex issues intelligently is nearly impossible. But you must be aware that you are hearing only one point of view and that the information may be self-serving.

Some sources make a habit of saying everything is off the record and of giving commonplace information in background sessions. Although you should not quote a source who asks to remain off the record, you may use the information if one or more of the following is true:

- The information is a matter of public record.
- It is generally known.
- It is available from several sources.
- You are a witness.

So as not to lose credibility with your source, it's a good idea to make it clear that you plan to use the information for one or more of the preceding reasons.

Remember these two important points:

- When possible, set the ground rules with your sources ahead of time.
- Know your newspaper's policy regarding these matters.

Knowing when and how to attribute background information is an art you should continue to develop as a reporter.

Suggested Readings

Brooks, Brian S., James L. Pinson and Jean Gaddy Wilson. *Working with Words: A Handbook for Media Writers and Editors.* 8th ed. New York: Bedford/St. Martin's, 2013. The section on quotations is excellent and follows Associated Press style.

Callihan, E.L. *Grammar for Journalists.* Rev. ed. Radnor, Pa.: Chilton, 1979. This classic text contains a good section on how to punctuate, attribute and handle quotations.

Germer, Fawn. "Are Quotes Sacred?" *American Journalism Review* (September 1995): 34–37. This article presents views from all sides on whether and when to change quotes.

Hart, Jack. "Giving Credit When Credit Isn't Due." *Editor & Publisher* (Sept. 11, 1993): 2. Hart warns against useless attribution.

King, Barbara. "There's Real Power in Common Speech." *Ottaway News Extra*, no. 137 (Winter 1989): 8, 16. The author presents an excellent discussion on using real quotes from real people.

LaRoque, Paula. "People Are Using Quotes More Often—But in Many Cases They Shouldn't Be." *Quill* (March 1, 2004): 32. LaRoque, an excellent writer, writing coach and teacher, provides good advice.

Stein, M.L. "9th Circuit: It's OK to Make Up Quotes." *Editor & Publisher* (Aug. 12, 1989): 16, 30. This article reports reactions from the press and lawyers to the court decision allowing quotes that are not verbatim.

Stimson, William. "Two Schools on Quoting Confuse the Reader." *Journalism Educator* 49, no. 4 (Winter 1995): 69–73. Strong arguments against cleaning up quotes are presented in this article.

Stoltzfus, Duane. "Partial Pre-publication Review Gaining Favor at Newspapers." *Newspaper Research Journal* 27, no. 4 (Fall 2006): 23–37. A practice long thought unconscionable among journalists gains acceptance.

Weinberg, Steve. "So What's Wrong with Pre-publication Review?" *Quill* (May 1990): 26–28. Weinberg answers objections to prepublication review.

Weinberg, Steve. "Thou Shalt Not Concoct Thy Quote." *Fineline* (July/August 1991): 3–4. In this article, Weinberg presents reasons for allowing sources to review quotations before publication.

Weiss, Philip. "Who Gets Quote Approval?" *Columbia Journalism Review* (May/June 1991): 52–54. Weiss discusses the growing practice of allowing sources to check quotations before publication.

Suggested Websites

http://owl.english.purdue.edu/owl/resource/577/1

This site provides an excellent, succinct summary of the rules for using quotation marks.

http://journalism.about.com/od/writing/a/attribution.htm

This page provides an excellent discussion of attribution, including on- and off-the-record attribution and deep background.

Exercises

1. **Team project.** Get together with three other classmates. Each of you should interview a different news reporter or editor working in print, radio or television about his or her policies for handling sources regarding the following types of information:

   a. Off the record

   b. Not for attribution

   c. Background

   d. Deep background

   Then compare what the interviewees said. Which policy or policies seem the most reasonable and effective?

2. Rewrite the following story. Pay special attention to the use of quotations and attribution. Note the sensitive nature of some of the quotations. Delete or paraphrase when you think it's necessary.

   Christopher O'Reilly is a remarkably happy young man, despite a bout with meningitis eight years ago that has left him paralyzed and brain-damaged.

   "I am happy," O'Reilly commented, as he puffed a cigarette. He has much to be happy about. Physical therapy has hastened his recovery since the day he awoke from a 10-week-long coma. He has lived to celebrate his 26th birthday.

   "I had a helluva birthday," he said. "I seen several friends. I had big cake," he added slowly.

   He lives in a house with his mother and stepfather in the rolling, green countryside near Springfield.

O'Reilly's withered legs are curled beneath him now, and his right arm is mostly paralyzed, but he can do pull-ups with his left arm. He can see and hear.

"When he came back, he wasn't worth a damn," his mother said. "The hack doctors told me he would be a vegetable all his life," she claimed.

"He couldn't talk; he could only blink. And he drooled a lot," she smiled.

Now, Chris is able to respond in incomplete sentences to questions and can carry on slow communication. "He don't talk good, but he talks," his mother commented.

It all began when he stole a neighbor's Rototiller. His probation was revoked, and he found himself in the medium-security prison in Springfield. Then came "inadequate medical treatment" in the prison system. O'Reilly's family argued that he received punishment beyond what the Eighth Amendment of the U.S. Constitution calls "cruel and unusual."

"Those prison officials were vicious," they said.

As a result, he was awarded $250,000 from the state, the largest legal settlement in federal court in 10 years. "That sounds like a lot of money. But it really isn't, you know, when you consider what happened and when you consider the worth of a human life, and the way they treated him and all, we thought we should get at least a million," his mother remarked.

O'Reilly contracted the infection of the brain after sleeping "on the concrete floor" of a confinement cell, his mother maintained. He had been placed in solitary confinement because he would not clean his cell. The disease went undiagnosed for eight days, leaving him paralyzed and brain-damaged, she said.

Now O'Reilly likes watching television. "I like TV," he grinned. "And smoking."

His mother said she "never gives up hope" that "one day" her son will "come out of it."

3. Read the following passage by writer and artist John Gerstner. Write a brief story covering what Gerstner said, and use three—and only three—direct quotes.

I believe a magazine should be everything you would like your mate to be: intelligent, adventurous, stimulating, candid, helpful, spirited, nice to look at and full of surprises. I believe a magazine should feast the eye as well as feed the mind. Leafing through a magazine should be an aesthetic as well as an intellectual experience. Each page should be a synthesis of ideas, concepts, words, photographs, illustrations and graphic design that arrests, intrigues and instantly communicates . . . not only the subject of the article but also some of its nuances as well—no small trick.

> I believe a magazine should continually evolve and take risks. About the time a winning formula is found is about the time a new one needs formulating. The best magazines stretch themselves in every issue and surprise both readers and staff.
>
> I believe a magazine should be a team project. No editor is an island, nor should want to be. The editor's job is to set the course and the standard. After that it's a matter of squeezing every ounce of creativity out of himself or herself and others and "arguing, procuring, tinkering and sending things back," as one magazine editor put it. And no editor or publisher should ever underestimate the role human chemistry and magic play in putting out a successful magazine.
>
> Finally, I believe the magazine is one of journalism's highest and noblest forms. The magazine format demands not just good reporting and writing but good communicating, which entails visual as well as verbal sophistication. The best magazines move minds, raise sights and spirits, and make waves to break on distant shores. They aspire to—and sometimes achieve—the level of art.

4. Attend a meeting, a press conference or a speech, and record it. While there, write down the quotes you would use if you were writing the story for your local newspaper. Then listen to the recording, and check the accuracy of your written quotations.
5. **Journalism blog.** Write a blog post explaining when you would feel justified in using an anonymous source. Give examples to support your reasons. If possible, link to one or two news stories that reflect your thinking.
6. Engage a classmate in a half-hour interview about his or her life. Write a story based on the interview, using as many direct quotes as you think are fitting. Then check the accuracy of the quotations with your classmate.
7. Find a story in the sports section of a newspaper, and try to change all or most of the attributions to the present tense. How does this change affect the impact of the story?

Chapter 7
Gathering Information from Archives

"Gathering Information from Archives" from *News Reporting and Writing*, Eleventh Edition by the Missouri Group (Brian S. Brooks, George Kennedy, Daryl R. Moen, and Don Ranly), pp. 110–128 (Chapter 6, "Gathering an Verifying Information").

Gathering and Verifying Information

In this chapter you will learn:

1. How to ensure accuracy in information gathering through the disciplines of multiple sources and verification.
2. How to find and evaluate information from online sources.
3. How to use traditional sources of information to check facts.

During the Syrian uprisings of 2012 and 2013, brave citizen journalists often risked their lives to chronicle a crackdown on dissidents by the government of President Bashar al-Assad. The images of police and military attacks on civilians frequently made their way to YouTube and Facebook, giving the outside world a glimpse of what was transpiring in a brutal dictatorship. Because the regime had blocked outside reporters from entering the country, reports from these citizen journalists were one of the few ways the world could learn about what was happening.

As brutal as the recent attacks were, according to veteran Middle East journalists they were nothing compared to the 1982 massacre of more than 10,000 protesters over a period of three weeks by the same Syrian government. Arguably, social media reporting led the regime to be more restrained 30 years later.

Tweets from both seasoned journalists and citizen reporters keep us informed of developments worldwide. We trust that most of those reports are accurate, but some are not, perhaps because of the confusion of the moment. And just how accurate were those photos coming from Syria? Were they authentic or doctored?

Social media did help some people get the latest news headlines and weather warnings during Hurricane Sandy, which struck the East Coast in 2012. They also helped friends and families stay in touch. Lamar Graham, chief content officer of NJ.com and a former editor of *Parade* magazine, was working hard in New Jersey to cover the storm while his family back in Manhattan hunkered down to survive it. He learned they were safe only when a friend of the family sent him a text of reassurance hours after the storm hit. It was a story akin to those of thousands of others affected by Sandy. Still, while social media offer benefits—getting quick news updates and keeping in touch with loved ones among them—they also have a dark side: Being first with the news is not a good thing when the report is false.

The role of social media in mainstream reporting continues to evolve. Most journalists, even citizen journalists, don't want to report erroneous information, but it's easy for those who want to deceive to doctor photos and put out false reports. For journalists, the need to get breaking news quickly to readers and viewers makes it tempting to put out news that has not been verified. Speed has always been important in journalism, and in the era of Facebook and Twitter, it counts more than ever. But so does accuracy.

What social media do is useful—they almost always report the news first—but what matters even more is sorting through the mass of information, verifying it and making sense of what happened. That's what professional journalists do. It's their job to separate fact from fiction, the good information from the bad. Call this "curating" if you wish. Most journalists simply call it good journalism.

In this chapter, we'll explore the process of not only finding information on the Web, on social media and elsewhere, but also getting it right.

Accurate Information: The Basis of a Good Story

Ask any editor whether a reporter can be a good writer without being good at information gathering, and you're likely to hear a resounding "No!" That's because good writing depends on good reporting. Reporting isn't good unless it is thorough and accurate. To ensure reports are thorough and accurate, journalists employ two main techniques: the discipline of multiple sources and the discipline of verification.

The Discipline of Multiple Sources

Good writing is of course important, as we explore in other chapters, but the quality of writing depends in large part on good fact gathering, which we call good reporting. It's impossible to write a great story without first doing a great job of reporting. Gathering information requires skilled interviewing, as discussed in Chapter 6. It also requires knowing how to use the many sources of information readily available. Make no mistake about it: There are hundreds of places to find information.

Good reporters know that the worst kind of news story is one with a single source. Rarely is such a story worth publishing. Even a personality profile should be based on more than just an interview with the subject. To get a fuller perspective, the journalist also needs to talk with individuals who know the subject. Gathering information from several sources is one of the keys to good writing and good communication. It's also the best way to ensure accuracy because when several sources are used, information is more likely to be verified. When additional sources are checked and cross-checked, the chances of a story being accurate improve greatly.

Imagine how many sources the reporters for the *Milwaukee Journal Sentinel* used in their award-winning series about how the federal government allowed chemical manufacturers to influence the approval of potentially harmful substances in everyday products. Even in the short excerpt from the multipart series, shown in "Integrating Multiple Sources into a Story," it's evident that the reporters used dozens of sources, including peer-reviewed research journals that most reporters seldom touch. Such reporting requires analyzing thousands of pages of data, poring over online and paper records, interviewing dozens of people, and checking, cross-checking and rechecking. Such reporting is both time-consuming and tedious, but work of this sort is exactly what journalists must do as they act as watchdogs over the actions of government agencies and others. Getting it right is of paramount importance.

The Discipline of Verification

Journalists, when operating as they should, follow the same investigative system employed by scientists. They develop a hypothesis and then seek facts to support or reject it. In the 20th century, journalists developed the concept of objectivity—an elusive idea that was often misinterpreted.

As Philip Meyer of the University of North Carolina suggests to journalists Bill Kovach and Tom Rosenstiel in *The Elements of Journalism*: "I think (the) connection between journalism and science ought to emphasize objectivity of method. That's what scientific method is—our humanity, our subjective impulses . . . directed toward deciding what to investigate by objective means."

What objectivity isn't, Kovach and Rosenstiel argue, is blind loyalty to the concepts of fairness and balance. Fairness, they argue, can be misunderstood if it is seen as a goal unto itself. Fairness should mean that a journalist is fair to the facts and to the public's understanding of them. It should not mean, "Am I being fair to my sources, so that none of them will be unhappy?" or "Does my story seem fair?" Those are subjective judgments that lead the journalist away from the task of independent verification.

Similarly, balance should not mean that it's necessary to get an equal number of scientists speaking on each side of the global-warming debate, for example, if an overwhelming number of scientists in fact believe that global warming is a reality.

ANNOTATED MODEL

INTEGRATING MULTIPLE SOURCES INTO A STORY

Chemical Fallout: Bisphenol A Is in You

By Susanne Rust, Cary Spivak and Meg Kissinger

Milwaukee Journal Sentinel

1 For more than a decade, the federal government and chemical-makers have assured the public that a hormone-mimicking compound found in baby bottles, aluminum cans and hundreds of other household products is safe. But a *Journal Sentinel* investigation found that these promises are based on outdated, incomplete government studies and research heavily funded by the chemical industry.

2 In the first analysis of its kind by a newspaper, the *Journal Sentinel* reviewed 258 scientific studies of the chemical bisphenol A, a compound detected in the urine of 93 percent of Americans recently tested. An overwhelming majority of these studies show that the chemical is harmful—causing breast cancer, testicular cancer, diabetes, hyperactivity, obesity, low sperm counts, miscarriage and a host of other reproductive failures in laboratory animals. 3

Studies paid for by the chemical industry are much less likely to find damaging effects or disease.

U.S. regulators so far have sided with industry by minimizing concern about the compound's safety.

4 Last week, a panel commissioned by the National Toxicology Program released a report finding bisphenol A to be of some concern for fetuses and small children. It found that adults have almost nothing to worry about.

Its recommendations could be used by the U.S. Environmental Protection Agency and other regulators to assess federal policies on how much bisphenol A is 5
safe and may have huge ramifications for the multibillion-dollar chemical industry.

The panel said it considered more than 700 studies by university scientists, government researchers and industry-funded chemists. It picked the work it felt was best and threw out the rest.

6 The *Journal Sentinel* found that panel members gave more weight to industry-funded studies and more leeway to industry-funded researchers.

The panel rejected academic studies that found harm—citing inadequate methods. But the panel accepted industry-funded studies using the same methods that concluded the chemical does not pose risks. 7

1. The lead hints at the large number of sources the journalists consulted to counter safety claims.

2. Here the article gets specific about the wide scope of the newspaper's research.

3. The article summarizes the main findings regarding health hazards.

4. The report outlines the most recent finding of toxicity in the chemical compound.

5. The story hints at a possible government change of position and its impact on the chemical industry.

6. The newspaper's investigation finds fault with previous claims of safety.

7. Faulty methodology in government studies is reported.

The panel missed dozens of studies publicly available that the *Journal Sentinel* found online using a medical research Internet search engine. The studies the panel considered were chosen, in part, by a consultant with links to firms that made bisphenol A.

8 More and more university researchers and foreign governments are finding that bisphenol A can do serious damage in small doses. But the panel rejected studies mostly submitted by university and international government scientists that looked at the impact at these levels.

The panel accepted a Korean study translated by the chemical industry's trade group that found bisphenol A to be safe. It also accepted two studies that were not subjected to any peer review—the gold standard of scientific credibility. Both studies were funded by General Electric Co., which made bisphenol A until it sold its plastics division earlier this year.

"This undermines the government's authority," said David Rosner, professor of history and public health at Columbia University. "It makes you think twice about accepting their conclusions." 9

Panel chairman Robert Chapin, a toxicologist who works for Pfizer Inc., the pharmaceutical giant, defended his group's work.

10 "We didn't flippin' care who does the study," said Chapin, who worked as a government scientist for 18 years before joining Pfizer.

If the studies followed good laboratory practices and were backed with strong data, they were accepted, Chapin said. . . .

Using summaries, bulleted lists and quotes, the writers integrated research from a range of sources seamlessly into the story.

8. More reliable university research differs with federal conclusions.

9. An expert finds fault with the government position.

10. The chairman of the government panel defends his group's work.

Kovach and Rosenstiel argue that sharpening the meaning of verification and resisting the temptation to simplify it are essential to improving the credibility of what journalists write. So, while citizen journalists may rush to get out information quickly on Twitter and Facebook without much regard for accuracy, professional journalists seek to get it right—while also producing news as quickly as possible.

The journalistic process of layered editing also helps get facts right. At a good newspaper, magazine, radio or television station, or website, once the reporter writes a story, it may be subjected to extensive review by several editors. Each may find facts to correct or language to clarify in the quest for a story that is as compelling—and accurate—as possible. Thus, as a story flows through the editorial process (see Figure 7-1), the goal is to make it as nearly perfect as possible.

Editors talk about the need to look at a story on both the micro and macro levels. *Microediting* is the process of paying attention to detail:

- Are the facts correct?
- Are the names spelled correctly?
- Is the grammar sound?

Macroediting, on the other hand, looks at the big picture:

- Will readers understand this?
- Are there unanswered questions or inconsistencies in the story?
- Does this agree with what I know from previous stories on the subject?

All of this, and much more, goes into the editorial process of verification. In the end, the goal is to get the story right.

As they strive to get it right, journalists use all types of sources, including interviews, source documents and a variety of other sources ranging from the obvious, such as a Google search, to online sites, computer databases and traditional sources like printed almanacs and encyclopedias. Good reporters make frequent use of all these sources.

Online Sources of Information

Reporters and editors today have a wealth of information available at their fingertips. In addition to making raw data available, computers help reporters organize and analyze information.

From the news library in your local office to national databases of published newspaper, magazine, radio and television stories, the amount of online information is staggering. Primary sources of online information include the following:

- The news archive, or morgue, maintained digitally by your own publication, radio or television station or website. When you're hired, one of the first things you must do is learn to use your organization's archive. The background material you find there will help you provide context for the stories you cover.
- Search engines (Google, Bing, Yahoo, Blekko, DuckDuckGo). Anyone can use Google, right? Well, learning to use search engines wisely is important to a journalist. Some of the tools we use to search the Web have as a main purpose to sell advertising. Page-rank algorithms and filters that personalize search results can yield misleading material. In Google, Bing and Yahoo, search results are ranked based not on quality but on several factors related to audience targeting. These three search engines filter information and rank their results accordingly. A couple of newer search engines, Blekko and DuckDuckGo, claim not to filter or personalize results.
- News sites, social media and content aggregators (USAToday.com, NYTimes.com, msnbc.com, CNN.com, Yahoo News, Google News).

INDIVIDUAL	ACTION
Reporter	Gathers facts, writes story, verifies its accuracy, forwards to city editor.
City Editor*	Edits story, returns to reporter for changes or additional detail (if necessary), forwards story to news editor.
News Editor*	Decides on placement of story in newspaper, forwards story to copy desk chief for implementation of instructions.
Copy Desk Chief	Prepares page dummy that determines story's length, setting and headline size, forwards to copy editor. At some large newspapers, a separate design desk may play this role.
Copy Editor	Polishes writing of story, checks for missing or inaccurate detail, writes headline, returns to copy desk chief for final check.
Copy Desk Chief	Verifies that story is trimmed as necessary and that correct headline is written, transmits story to typesetting equipment.

* Or assistant

Note: At any point in the process, a story may be returned to an earlier editor for clarification, amplification or rewriting.

Figure 7-1. Editing and producing a newspaper is a fast-paced and complex process in which editors at different levels review stories. Shown here is a typical copy-flow pattern for a daily newspaper.

- Other sites on the Web. Millions of organizations maintain websites with useful information.
- Mobile apps (applications for mobile phones and tablets). News apps are available for *The New York Times*, the Associated Press, NPR, CNN, Reuters and Newsy.
- Commercial database services (Factiva, LexisNexis, NewsBank, ProQuest and others).
- Government databases (city, county, state and federal).
- Special-interest databases (those created by organizations with a cause).
- Custom databases and spreadsheets.

Let's explore the usefulness of some of these.

Authoritative Websites

- www.usa.gov
- www.factcheck.org
- www.infoplease.com
- www.people-press.org
- www.politifact.com
- www.snopes.com
- www.webmd.com

News Archives: The Place to Start

Digital archives are a marvel that good reporters and editors have learned to cherish. Before they were available, doing research for a story was a laborious process that involved a trip to the newspaper, magazine or television station library to sift through hundreds or even thousands of tattered, yellowed clippings or old scripts. Too often, clippings and scripts had disappeared, were misfiled or had been misplaced, which made such research a hit-or-miss proposition. Despite those shortcomings, the library was considered a valuable asset. Reporters were routinely admonished to check there first.

You still hear that advice in newsrooms today, but most of today's news libraries are online. This almost ensures that an item will not disappear and will be easy to locate. Typically, you can do a check of the archive from your own computer, sometimes even from a remote location. This makes it easier than ever to do good background work on a story. Your ability to search online databases is limited only by your skill with search techniques and your access to the databases you need.

Digital news archives are full-text databases. All words in the database have been indexed and are searchable. Such capability gives you great flexibility in structuring searches using Boolean search commands. Boolean operators such as AND, OR and NOT allow you to structure the search to find the material most closely related to the subject being researched. For example, if you are interested in finding articles in Factiva on former South African

President Nelson Mandela's visits to the U.S., you might issue this command on the search line:

Mandela AND U.S.

That search command pulls all articles in which both "Mandela" and "U.S." appear, generating almost 40,000 hits. Obviously, that's too many. You need to narrow your search. Try:

Mandela SAME U.S.

That search generates more than 8,000 articles in which both terms appear in the same paragraph. You can then narrow further:

Mandela w/3 U.S.

That command asks for the Mandela-U.S. combination occurring within three words of one another. This yields more than 400 articles, closer to a manageable number. The next step is to narrow by date, region or source to find what you really need.

There are limitations. Some digital archives do not allow you to see photos, nor can you see articles as they appeared in the newspaper or magazine. PressDisplay.com, however, provides PDF files of thousands of newspapers from about 100 countries. (A **PDF file** preserves the formatting of the original document.) Some radio and television stations, including NPR and PBS, have podcasts or vodcasts—downloadable audio or video files—stored on their websites. Factiva also contains audio and video interviews and news clips along with transcripts.

Ten Sources of Story Ideas

- Other people.
- Other publications.
- News releases.
- A social services directory.
- Government reports.
- Stories in your own newspaper.
- Advertisements.
- Wire copy.
- Local news briefs.
- You.

Search Engines

Google is the first stop for many journalists. Indeed, Google and other search engines, such as Yahoo, Bing, Blekko and DuckDuckGo, can be helpful journalistic tools. The key to using them successfully is recognizing whether the information contained on the website to which the search takes you is accurate and therefore usable. Journalists also need to be aware that many search engines like Google, Yahoo and Bing filter information, personalizing it based on the information that they have gathered about the user's previous searches and online purchase history. Good journalists supplement these well-known search engines with newer ones that do not filter, like DuckDuckGo.

Blekko uses crowdsourcing to identify trusted sites, and users can employ slashes (/) to filter results. Typing "/conservative" after a search term yields sites written by right-leaning publications; "/liberal" yields left-leaning sources, for example.

Information from well-known sites may be reliable; information from websites advocating a cause may not be. Be wary of Wikipedia, a user-written and user-edited social encyclopedia. Although much of the information on Wikipedia is excellent, anyone can enter erroneous information into it. Errors or misrepresentations are usually corrected quickly by others, but beware of depending on information from only that source. We discuss how to evaluate such information later in this chapter.

News Sites, Social Media and Content Aggregators

Some might consider it strange to think of news websites, social media and content aggregators as useful sources of information for reporters. Don't tell that to the reporters who use them.

Such sites are accessible to anyone with a computer and an Internet connection. News sites are those published by established media outlets such as *The New York Times*, Microsoft's MSN and CNN.

While mainstream media offer blogs, those found on blog sites such as Google's Blogger or WordPress are usually classified as social media. In part, they are different because their writers answer only to themselves, not to editors. Social media also include Twitter, Facebook and other "friending" sites. Twitter has become so important to journalists that it now has its own journalism and news manager. Many journalists now "tweet their beat." They tweet events live and seek to grow followers for their company's website. Twitter is just one of the social media tools that journalists use to increase "engagement" with their audience.

Not only do journalists often learn about breaking news—such as airplane crashes, fires and shootings—from tweets, but they also communicate with readers through social media. They post links to their stories on Facebook, and they ask Twitter readers to suggest story ideas and sources.

The most popular content aggregators include Yahoo News, Google News and Newsy.com. An aggregator is a website that summarizes a story and links to the originating media for the full report. Newsy does so with the additional benefit of video.

Commercial Database Services

Commercial databases make it easy to see what has been written about a subject in other newspapers and magazines. But there are potential problems with using excerpts from those stories:

- **Copyright laws must be obeyed.** Take care not to use too much material without obtaining permission.

- **Not all articles that appeared in a newspaper can be found in a database.** Wire-service and market reports, death notices, box scores, social announcements and items written by freelancers often are excluded.
- **Publication doesn't ensure accuracy.** History is littered with incidents of newspapers quoting each other's inaccuracies.
- **The reporter might not be credible.** The reporter who wrote the story may not have any real knowledge of the subject matter. Using information from that reporter may introduce an inaccuracy into your story.
- **Databases aren't infallible. The** information is entered by humans, who are susceptible to mistakes. Also, databases are occasionally doctored in an attempt to prove a position or promote a cause.

On many topics, searching your own digital archive will not be sufficient. If U.S. Rep. Michele Bachmann is making her first appearance in your community, your archive probably won't help; little will have been written about her in your city. It probably will be much more useful to search the Web or commercial databases for articles published both in Minnesota, where she resides, and nationally, because she was a candidate for the Republican presidential nomination. This research will arm you with questions to ask about recent events. In such situations, the national commercial databases are invaluable.

The three leading commercial database services are Factiva (see Figure 7-2), NewsBank and ProQuest Newsstand, all of which provide full-text access. If your employer does not subscribe to any of these, see if your local library does. Of course, while you are a student, you have access to many databases through your school's library.

Government Databases

For years, government agencies have maintained large databases of information as a means of managing the public's business. These databases cover almost every conceivable service that government offers, from airplane registration and maintenance records to census data to local court records. They are maintained not only by the federal and state governments but also by even the smallest of city and county agencies.

Now, any reporter with a computer and training can find stories in the numbers. Among the reporters taking advantage of the technology is Penny Loeb, now of ProPublica.org. When she worked for *New York Newsday*, she used a computer analysis of tax and property records to reveal an astounding story: New York City owed $275 million to taxpayers as a result of overpayments on real estate, water and sewer taxes. To get that story, Loeb had to analyze millions of computer records. Doing that by hand would have consumed a lifetime, but with the assistance of a computer, she accomplished the task in a matter of weeks. Still, Loeb cautions against expecting instant stories:

> Don't just (use a computer) and expect a great story. You need a tip that there is a problem that computerized data can confirm. Or you may have seen a problem occur repeatedly, such as sentencing discrimination. The computer can quantify the scope.

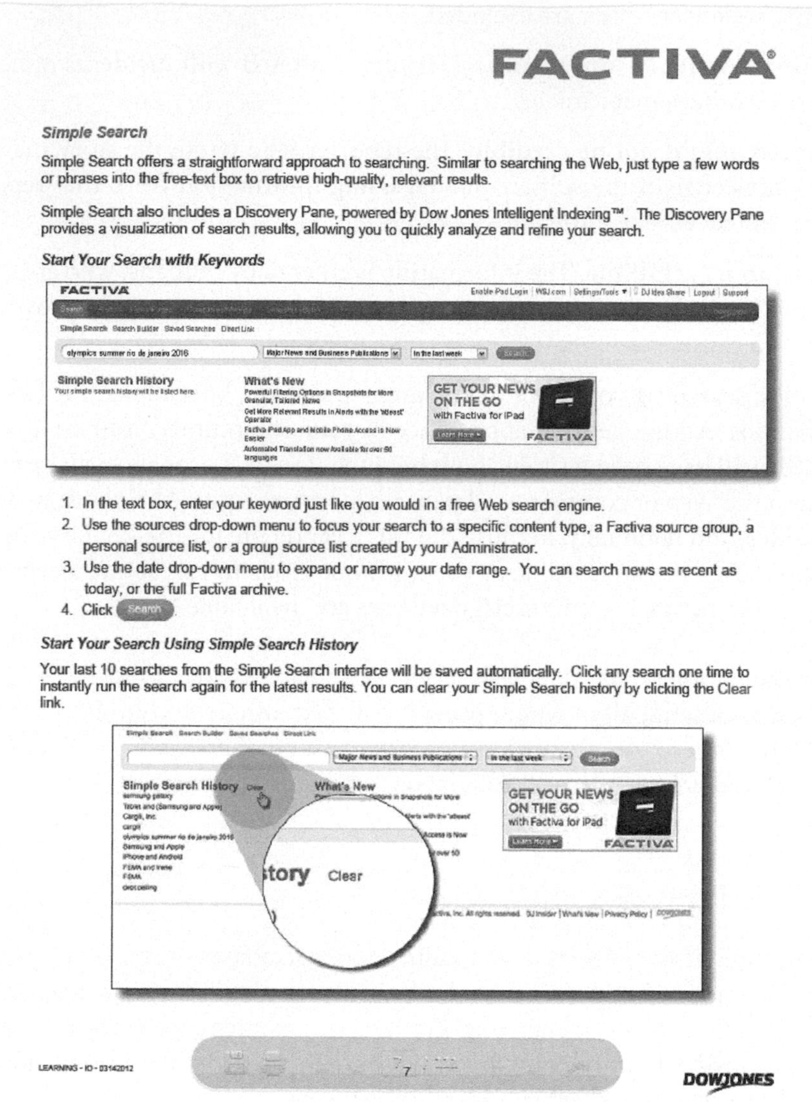

FACTIVA

Simple Search

Simple Search offers a straightforward approach to searching. Similar to searching the Web, just type a few words or phrases into the free-text box to retrieve high-quality, relevant results.

Simple Search also includes a Discovery Pane, powered by Dow Jones Intelligent Indexing™. The Discovery Pane provides a visualization of search results, allowing you to quickly analyze and refine your search.

Start Your Search with Keywords

1. In the text box, enter your keyword just like you would in a free Web search engine.
2. Use the sources drop-down menu to focus your search to a specific content type, a Factiva source group, a personal source list, or a group source list created by your Administrator.
3. Use the date drop-down menu to expand or narrow your date range. You can search news as recent as today, or the full Factiva archive.
4. Click Search.

Start Your Search Using Simple Search History

Your last 10 searches from the Simple Search interface will be saved automatically. Click any search one time to instantly run the search again for the latest results. You can clear your Simple Search history by clicking the Clear link.

LEARNING - ID - 03142012

7

DOWJONES

Figure 7-2. Factiva, owned by Dow Jones & Co., the parent company of *The Wall Street Journal*, allows subscribers to perform in-depth research on "more than 35,000 global news and information sources from 200 countries in 28 languages," according to www.dowjones.com.

Analyses of this type usually are done with relational database programs. **Relational database programs**, unlike simpler **flat-file databases**, permit you to compare one set of data to another. A classic example would be to compare a database of a state's licensed school-bus drivers to another database of the state's drunken-driving convictions. The result would be a list of school-bus drivers found guilty of such offenses.

After the introduction of this technology, investigative reporters were among the first to use it. Reporters can use database programs in their day-to-day work just as easily. For example, you might want to analyze federal records on airplane maintenance to produce a story on the safety record of a particular airline. If the records are maintained in an easily accessible format, the next time an airplane crashes it will be possible to call up the complete maintenance record of the aircraft merely by entering its registration number. Such information can be extremely useful, even in a deadline situation.

Another common use of computers has been to compare bank records on home mortgages to census data. By tracking how many mortgages are issued to homeowners in predominantly black or Hispanic areas, reporters have been able to document the practice of *redlining*, through which banks make it difficult or impossible for minorities to obtain loans.

Again, such records are useful even after the investigation is complete. Access to driver's license records, census data, bank records and other forms of data can be used daily to produce news stories, charts, maps and other graphic devices. Numbers can be valuable in helping to tell a story. They can be particularly effective as the basis for charts that illustrate the impact of the numbers.

Special-Interest Databases

Numerous special-interest groups have discovered the usefulness of placing information in computerized databases, and they are eager to introduce journalists to that information. Some of their material may be quite useful; indeed, it may be unobtainable from other sources. For instance, OpenSecrets.org has databases on campaign contributors that list who is spending what to lobby to whom, among other things. It has proved to be a credible source for news organizations. But other special-interest databases are designed to promote a particular perspective on a topic. Check the "About Us" link, and do a Web search to see how often the group's material appears in other media.

Custom Databases

Journalists Tracy Weber, Charles Ornstein and Maloy Moore had reason to believe the California Board of Registered Nursing was failing in its duty to ensure that nurses are competent, sober and law-abiding. To find out for sure, they had to build their own analysis tool.

Using a database manager, they entered and analyzed all the accusations filed and all the disciplinary actions taken by the board between 2002 and 2008. The print-outs involved more than 2,000 nurses.

The team, representing the online news organization ProPublica and the *Los Angeles Times*, described the task as an enormous amount of work. But in the end, the database enabled the reporters not only to flag the best cases to use as examples but also to highlight a number of weaknesses in the board's oversight. Among the problems they uncovered were nurses involved in multiple disciplinary cases and those with multiple criminal convictions.

The project had immediate impact. The day after their first story ran, California's governor replaced a majority of the nursing board's members. A day later, the board's longtime executive officer resigned.

On THE JOB

The Challenges of Editing for the Web

Eric Ulken is among the journalists who have embraced the digital technologies that are changing journalism. After earning bachelor's and master's degrees, Ulken worked as a news producer at NOLA.com, the website of *The (New Orleans) Times-Picayune*, as well as at *The Columbus Dispatch* and the *Los Angeles Times*. Now he is assistant managing editor–digital at *The Seattle Times*.

Ulken urges would-be journalists to embrace the Web and to think not just about writing jobs but also about editing:

If you take a newspaper job today, chances are much of the work you do won't be for a newspaper at all, but rather for a website. Newsrooms are reorganizing to meet new challenges as their online editions grow in importance. It's still unclear how many duties copy editors ultimately will juggle, but their new responsibilities certainly transcend the traditional role. (Meanwhile, newspaper gigs aren't the only game in town: Broadcast and online-only sites are hiring more copy editors as their Web operations grow.)

In addition to learning basic copy editing skills (which never go out of style), here's how you can prepare yourself:

- Learn how to use content management systems. News organizations use a variety of online content platforms, but there are similarities among them. The simplest content management systems are blogging tools such as WordPress. Learning how they work will help you pick up more complex systems much faster.
- Understand how users find news on the Web. Many come to your site from search engines and aggregator sites such as Google News, which is one reason why Web headlines, optimized for search, are so important.
- Understand audio and video. It's less important to know how to edit in Final Cut Pro than it is to be able to identify what's missing from a multimedia package.
- Be flexible and make an effort to adapt to new technologies. Don't assume that the rules as you've learned them are immutable—even when it comes to style and usage: Technology and indeed language are always evolving.
- Use the Web constantly. The best way to learn how to produce great content for the Web is to experience great content on the Web.

To answer the question I know you're asking: Yes, you'll probably end up doing more work, and doing it faster, than previous generations of copy editors have done. But on the plus side, the greater variety of tasks should keep the routine from getting old.

Evaluating Internet Sources

Journalists always have had to differentiate carefully between fact and fiction on the Web. Lately, however, they have also assumed the task of curating citizen contributions, particularly when citizens are the first to break the news. For instance, after a police officer was shot at Virginia Tech University in late 2011, many media outlets passed along tweets from the editor of the college paper. They determined that the student journalist was a reliable source.

Student editor Zach Crizer told Poynter.org that the college paper monitored tweets from students after the shooting. "For the most part, unless it was something completely unfounded or crazy, we'd try to react and investigate the tweets being sent to us. We wanted to confirm or deny information, and attempt to answer questions if we could."

Evaluating Web sources is not a guessing game. You won't always be correct in your assessment of a website's credibility, but you can dramatically improve your chances.

Journalists have developed methods of gathering and editing news that help ensure, though they don't guarantee, accuracy. Those methods are described in several other chapters in this book. The Web presents its own problems and solutions. How do you differentiate between a credible website and one that has a hidden agenda? Wikipedia is more popular than reputable print encyclopedias, but is it as credible? How do you know if a tweet or a Facebook posting is true? The answer lies in the discipline of verification.

A traditional method of verification relies on the journalistic process of layered editing. At most news media, print and digital, once the reporter writes a story, it is subject to extensive review by one or more editors. Each may find reporting inadequacies, facts to correct or language to clarify. Individual bloggers and those who post on social media outlets aren't edited. That's why curating and editing news posted on social media have become important new functions in newsrooms.

The Web is a great resource for reporters, but determining the credibility of online information can be problematic. If the source is a respected media organization such as *The New York Times* or *The Washington Post*, chances are the information is solid. But if the information was published by an organization promoting a cause, there is ample reason to be wary.

Stan Ketterer, a journalist and journalism professor, tells reporters to evaluate information on the Web by following the same standard journalistic practices that they would use for assessing the credibility and accuracy of any other type of information:

- **Before using information from a website in a story, verify it with a source.** There are exceptions to this rule, including taking information from a highly credible government site like the U.S. Census Bureau. Sometimes you can't contact the source on a breaking story because of time constraints. An editor must clear all exceptions.
- **In most cases, information taken directly from the Web and used in a story must be attributed.** If you have verified the information on a website with a source, you can use the organization in the attribution, for example, "according to the EPA" or "EPA figures show." If you cannot verify the information after trying repeatedly, attribute unverified information to the website—for example, "according to the Voice of America's website." Consult your editor before using unverified information.

- **If you have doubts about the accuracy of the information and you cannot reach the source, get it from another source, such as a book or another person.** When in doubt, omit the information.
- **Check the extension on the site's Web address to get clues as to the nature of the organization and the likely slant of the information.** The most common extensions used in the U.S. are *.gov* (government), *.edu* (education), *.com* (commercial), *.mil* (military), *.org* (not-for-profit organization) and *.net* (Internet administration). Most government and military sites have credible and accurate information. In many cases, you can take the information directly from the site and attribute it to the organization. But consult your editor until you get to know these sites.
- **Treat the sites of colleges and universities as you would other sites.** If college and university sites have source documents, such as the Constitution, attribute the information to the source document. But beware. Personal home pages can have .edu extensions, and the information on them is not always credible.
- **In almost all cases, do not use information directly from the websites of commercial and not-for-profit organizations without verification.**
- **Check the date when the site was last updated.** The date generally appears at the top or bottom of the first page of the site. Although a recent date does not ensure that the information is current, it does indicate that the organization is paying close attention to the site. If no date appears, if the site has not been updated for a while or if it was created some time ago, do not use the information unless you verify it with a source.
- **Check to see if the website is what it appears to be.** The www.martinlutherking.org website was registered in 1999, but if you search its domain registration (whois.net), you'll find it is registered to a white supremacy organization, not the King family. The site ranks high in search results based on its longevity on the Web, its domain name (which includes Martin Luther King's name) and external links to the site. It has not been endorsed by the King family, and in fact, family members have tried many times to have the site removed. However, the domain was registered legitimately, and copyright doesn't protect website domain names. This is an excellent example of poor-quality or fraudulent sites ranking high in search results.

Traditional Sources of Information

Accessing information through computerized sources is quick and easy, but more traditional reference sources also are valuable. In some cases, the sources listed in this section cannot be found on computers.

The Traditional Newsroom Library

Every working reporter gets this advice from an editor early in his or her career: Check the morgue. The morgue, or newsroom library, is often more than a digital archive. Indeed, at most publications and some broadcast stations it's also a physical place with a real librarian. We list it here because many such libraries house bound volumes of old printed editions and clippings of news stories that predate the publication's digital archive. The digital archive is usually the first stop for a reporter on any kind of assignment, but the traditional library also may be of great help, particularly when a reporter needs to understand the historical background of a story.

Covering a speech? Look up background information on the speaker. Covering a sports event? What are the teams' records? Who are the coaches? What's the history of the rivalry? Reporters answer questions like these, and many others, by checking the library, both the digital and analog versions.

One other note on the print or broadcast archive: Here you can find photos of a speaker or coach you haven't met. You'll also find historic photos. A contemporary photo might help you recognize that person for a possible one-on-one interview before the speech or game begins. An old photo may show readers a sports hero who set a record decades ago.

Other Traditional Sources

Traditional sources of information—such as reference books, dictionaries and encyclopedias—still play an important role in the production of the daily news product. Good reporters and editors make a habit of checking every verifiable fact. Here is a list of commonly used references. An increasing number of these are now available online, as noted below, but some are still available only in print form.

- **City directories.** You can find these directories, not to be confused with telephone books, in most cities. They provide the same information as a telephone book but also may include information on the occupations of citizens and the owners or managers of businesses. Useful street indexes provide information on the names of next-door neighbors. City directories usually are found in print form only.
- **Local and area telephone directories.** Use telephone books for verifying the spelling of names and addresses. They usually are reliable, but they are not infallible. Remember that people move and have similar names. Almost all landline telephone numbers in North America are now listed on various Web-based services, including Switchboard.com.
- **Maps of the city, county, state, nation and world.** Local maps usually are posted in the newsroom. Google Maps and Google's street views can help direct you around town. So can MapQuest.com.
- **State manuals.** Each state government publishes a directory that provides useful information on various government agencies. These directories, most of which are online, sometimes list the salaries of state employees.
- ***Bartlett's Familiar Quotations*** (Little, Brown). This writing resource is now available for free at Bartleby.com.
- ***Congressional Directory*** (Government Printing Office). The directory provides profiles of members of Congress. It's available at www.congress.org/congressorg/directory/congdir.tt.
- ***Congressional Record*** (Government Printing Office). The complete proceedings of the U.S. House and Senate are published in the Congressional Record. The *Record* is available at Congress.gov and at www.memory.loc.gov/ammem/amlaw/lwcr.html.

- ***Dictionary of American Biography*** (Scribner's). There are several such biography sources, and this one lists famous deceased people up through 1995. There is no comparable online source for biographies of living people. LexisNexis has a "research people" function that provides biographies from newspapers, magazines and biographical directories.
- ***Facts on File World News Digest*** (Facts on File Inc.). The digest is a weekly compilation of news from metropolitan newspapers.
- ***Guinness Book of World Records*** (Guinness Superlatives). World records in countless categories are listed here. These are also available online at www.guinnessworldrecords.com.
- ***InfoPlease Almanac***. This resource includes biographies and almanac information. It is available at www.infoplease.com.
- ***National Trade and Professional Associations of the United States*** (Columbia Books). USA.gov has an online directory of trade associations at www.usa.gov/directory/tradeassc/index.shtml.
- ***Readers' Guide to Periodical Literature*** (EBSCO). This index to magazine articles on a host of subjects is available online for a fee.
- ***Webster's Biographical Dictionary*** (Merriam-Webster). This dictionary is a good resource for historical biographical information.
- ***Webster's New World College Dictionary***, Fourth Edition (Wiley). This is the primary reference dictionary recommended by both the Associated Press and United Press International.
- ***Webster's Third New International Dictionary*** (Merriam-Webster). AP and UPI recommend this edition of the unabridged dictionary as a backup to *Webster's New World Dictionary*.
- ***Who's Who*** (St. Martin's). This resource contains international listings.
- ***Who's Who in America*** (Marquis). A biennial publication, this resource is reliable for current biographies.
- ***World Almanac and Book of Facts*** (Newspaper Enterprise Association). This almanac is published annually.

These useful publications, and many others like them, enable reporters to verify data and to avoid the embarrassment caused by errors in print. Traditional printed sources of information include government records, business documents, pamphlets published by government and nongovernment agencies, books, newspapers and magazines.

Be careful when using material from a source with which you are not familiar. Some publications come from biased sources promoting a cause. It's the reporter's job to determine whether the information is unbiased and reliable. A good way to do that is to balance information from one source with information from another source with an opposing viewpoint. It may not always be possible for you to determine who's correct. Ensuring balance between two viewpoints is the next best thing.

Suggested Readings

Associated Press Stylebook and Briefing on Media Law. New York: Associated Press, 2013. This is the definitive work on stylistic matters in journalistic writing. It is also available as an online subscription.

Brooks, Brian S., James L. Pinson and Jean Gaddy Wilson. *Working with Words: A Handbook for Media Writers and Edi-tors.* 8th ed. New York: Bedford/St. Martin's, 2013. This is a definitive work on the correct use of language in journalistic writing and editing.

Callahan, Christopher, and Leslie-Jean Thornton. *A Journalist's Guide to the Internet: The Net as a Reporting Tool.* Boston: Allyn and Bacon, 2007. This is a useful guide to using the Internet as a reporting resource.

Houston, Brant. *Computer-Assisted Reporting: A Practical Guide.* New York: Bedford/St. Martin's, 2003. This excellent introduction to computer-assisted reporting was written by the former executive director of Investigative Reporters and Editors.

IRE Journal. This monthly magazine is available from Investigative Reporters and Editors in Columbia, Mo. It offers regular articles on the use of computers in the news-gathering process.

Schlein, Alan M. *Find It Online: The Complete Guide to Online Research.* Edited by Peter Weber and J.J. Newby. Tempe, Ariz.: BRB Publications, 2004. This book offers basic information on the use of Web resources.

Suggested Websites

www.bedfordstmartins.com/newscentral

When you visit News Central, you will find up-to-the-moment RSS feeds, research links and exercises to help you improve your grammar and AP style usage. In addition, the site's Video-Central: Journalism section hosts videos highlighted in this chapter as well as additional clips of leading professionals discussing important media trends.

www.ire.org

Investigative Reporters and Editors maintains an excellent website for anyone interested in investigative reporting.

www.journalism.org

Select "JTools" under "Journalism Resources" to find numerous suggestions for journalists and students.

www.nicar.org

The National Institute for Computer-Assisted Reporting conducts seminars for reporters on data analysis with computers. NICAR is a program of Investigative Reporters and Editors.

Exercises

1. **Team project.** Do an Internet search on a story from your local newspaper. Write a post for your blog explaining how the story could be improved or describing new angles the reporter could explore. List all your sources, or use hyperlinks.
2. If you needed to determine where Apple Inc. is located and the name of its chief financial officer, where would you look? What other sources of information about the company are available?
3. **Journalism blog**. On your blog, post a one-page biographical sketch of your congressional representative, based on information from your library or a database. Send a tweet or a short email to your classmates highlighting a recent important action by the representative.
4. Using the Internet, find the following information:

   The census of Rhode Island (or your home state) in 2010.

   The size of Rwanda in land area.

   The latest grant awards by the U.S. Department of Education.

   The names of universities in Norway that provide information online for the general public.

   The name of a website that contains the complete works of Shakespeare.

   The name of a website that contains federal campaign contribution data.
5. Compile a background dossier on Lance Armstrong, the former Tour de France cycling winner who was stripped of his titles in 2012 as a result of a doping scandal.
6. Go to Google News and attempt to determine where the top three stories originated. Are any of them from the wire services or newspapers?

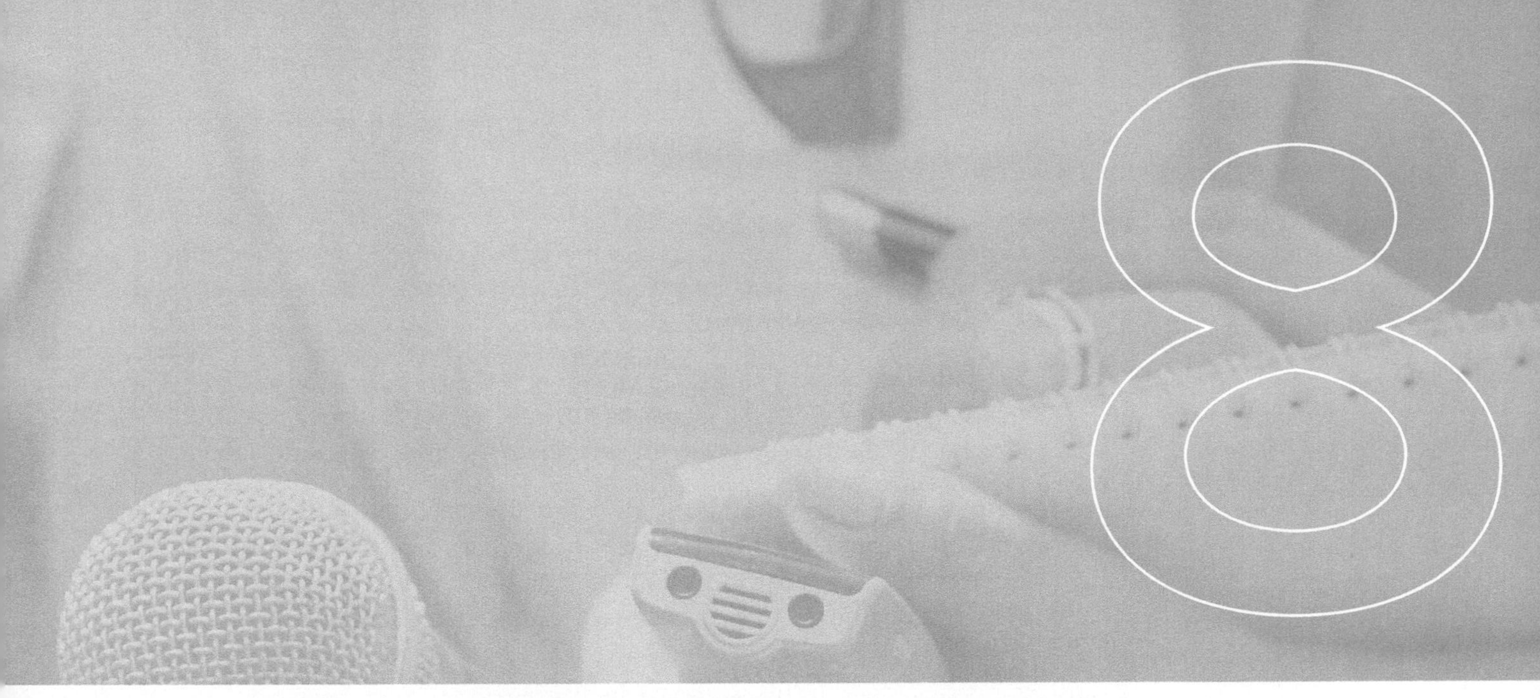

Chapter 8
Writing the News

"Writing the News" from *News Reporting and Writing*, Eleventh Edition by the Missouri Group (Brian S. Brooks, George Kennedy, Daryl R. Moen, and Don Ranly), pp. 167–239 (Chapter 9, "The Inverted Pyramid," Chapter 10, "Writing to be Read," and Chapter 11 "Alternatives to the Inverted Pyramid").

In this section you will learn:

1. Why the inverted pyramid story is important.
2. How to translate news values into leads.
3. How to create variations on the inverted pyramid lead.
4. How to organize a story using the inverted pyramid.
5. How to use the inverted pyramid across media platforms.
6. How to improve your accuracy.

The inverted pyramid—a news story structure that places all the important information in the first paragraph—has been used to write the "first draft of history" in the U.S. for generations. Here is the Associated Press lead on the first use of the atomic bomb in 1945:

> An atomic bomb, hailed as the most destructive force in history and as the greatest achievement of organized science, has been loosed upon Japan.

Twenty-four years later, here is how the AP started its story of the first moon landing:

> Man came to the moon and walked its dead surface Sunday.

And in 2012, when Hurricane Sandy smashed into the East Coast, the AP again used the inverted pyramid:

> NEW YORK (AP)—Stripped of its bustle and mostly cut off from the world, New York was left wondering Tuesday when its particular way of life—carried by subway, lit by skyline and powered by 24-hour deli—would return.

> Mayor Michael Bloomberg and the power company said it could be the weekend before the lights come on for hundreds of thousands of people plunged into darkness by what was once Hurricane Sandy.
>
> Bloomberg said it could also be four or five days before the subway, which suffered the worst damage in its 108-year history, is running again. All 10 of the tunnels that carry New Yorkers under the East River were flooded.

The lead reporting the moonwalk would work within Twitter's 140-character restriction. In fact, citizens who are suddenly thrust into reporting what's happening around them are tweeting inverted pyramid style. Twitter's limitation on the length of tweets neatly reflects the goal of the traditional inverted pyramid news lead: Report the most important news succinctly.

With that goal, citizen journalists have joined specialized financial news services such as Bloomberg News, which relies on the inverted pyramid. So do newspapers, despite many editors' encouragement of new writing forms. So do radio, television, the Internet and newsletters. Businesspeople often use the inverted pyramid in company memos so their bosses don't have to read to the end to find the main point. Public relations professionals use it in news releases to get the attention of news editors.

Importance of the Inverted Pyramid Story

Frequently misdiagnosed as dying, the inverted pyramid has more lives than a cat—perhaps because the more people try to speed up the dissemination of information, the more valuable the inverted pyramid becomes. In the inverted pyramid, information is arranged from most important to least important. The king in *Alice in Wonderland* would never succeed in the electronic news service business. When asked where to start a story, he replied, "Begin at the beginning and go on till you come to the end; then stop." Reporters, however, often begin a story at its end.

> *"Because a story is important, it doesn't follow that it must be long."*
>
> **—Stanley Walker, city editor**

Subscribers to financial services such as Reuters, Dow Jones Factiva and Bloomberg, for instance, react instantly to news about the financial markets to get an edge over other investors. They don't want narration; they want news. This is a typical Bloomberg lead:

> California home prices rose 25 percent in the 12 months through November, the most in eight years, as demand rose in expensive coastal areas, the state Realtors group said.

Many newspaper readers, on average, spend 15 to 25 minutes a day reading the paper. Online readers, who skip around sites as if they were walking barefoot on a hot stove, spend even less time. Both prefer short stories with the news on top. If a reporter were to write an account of a car accident by starting when the driver left the house, many readers would never read far enough to learn that the driver and a passenger had been killed. Instead, such a story starts with its climax:

> Two people died Thursday when a backhoe fell off a truck's flatbed and sliced the top off an oncoming vehicle near Fairchild Air Force Base.

In the inverted pyramid, the lead, which can consist of one or two paragraphs, sits atop other paragraphs arranged in descending order of importance. These paragraphs explain and provide evidence to support the lead. That's why print editors can quickly shorten a story by cutting from the bottom; the paragraphs at the end are the least important. On the Internet, space is not a consideration, but readers' time is. That's why the same inverted pyramid that is used in newspapers is the most common story structure found on such news websites as CNN.com, msnbc.com, CBSNews.com and ABCNews.com. For instance, CNN used the inverted pyramid to report the release of journalists:

> An NBC reporter and his crew spoke Tuesday of their overwhelming relief after being freed from kidnappers in Syria who kept them bound, blindfolded and repeatedly threatened to kill them during a five-day ordeal.
>
> Speaking from Turkey, Richard Engel described on NBC's "Today" show how he and his crew were seized by a group of masked, heavily armed men shortly after crossing into northwest Syria from Turkey on Thursday.

The inverted pyramid does have some shortcomings. Although it delivers the most important news first, it does not encourage people to read the entire story. Stories stop; they don't end. There is no suspense. In a Poynter Institute study, researchers found that half of the 25 percent of readers who started a story dropped out midway through. Interest in an inverted pyramid story diminishes as the story progresses. But the way people use it attests to its value as a quick form of information delivery. Readers can leave a story whenever their needs are met, not when the writer finishes the story. In an age when time is golden, the inverted pyramid still offers value.

Figure 8-1. When exiled Syrian opposition members met in Turkey to demand the resignation of Syrian President Bashar Assad, the *Los Angeles Times* reported the news in an inverted pyramid news story.

The Inverted Pyramid

- Requires the writer to rank the importance of information.
- Puts the most important information first.
- Arranges the paragraphs in descending order of importance.

The day when the inverted pyramid is relegated to journalism history is not yet here and probably never will be. Perhaps 80 percent of the stories in today's newspapers and almost 100 percent of the stories on news services for target audiences such as the financial community are written in the inverted pyramid form. That's changing, but it's changing slowly. Some of the new media highlight other forms of writing, such as narratives and essays. Still, as long as newspaper, electronic and television journalists continue to emphasize the quick, direct, simple approach to communications, the inverted pyramid and its variations will have a role.

There are many other ways to structure a news story. You will learn about some of the options later in this chapter. However, before you explore the alternatives, you should master the inverted pyramid. As you do, you will master the art of making news judgments. The inverted pyramid requires you to identify and rank the most newsworthy elements in each story. This is important work. No matter what kinds of stories you write—whether obituaries, accidents, speeches, press conferences, fires or meetings—you will be required to use the skills you learn here.

Finding the Lead

To determine a **lead**—a simple, clear statement consisting of the first paragraph or two of a news story—you must first recognize what goes into one. You begin by determining the story's relevance, usefulness and interest for readers. One way to measure these standards is to ask "So what?" or "Who cares?" So what if there's a car accident downtown? If it's one of hundreds a month, it may not be news. Any holdup in a community of 5,000 may be news because the "so what" is that holdups are uncommon and some residents probably know the victim. It's unlikely newspapers, radio or television stations would report the holdup in a metropolitan area where holdups are common. But if the holdup appears to be part of a pattern or if someone is killed, the story becomes more significant. One holdup may not be news, but a holdup that authorities believe is one of many committed by the same person may be news. The "so what" is that if the police catch this robber, they stop a crime spree.

To determine the "so what," you have to answer six basic questions: who, what, where, when, why and how. The information from every event you witness and every story you hear can be reduced to answers to these six questions. If the answers add up to a significant "so what," you have a story. Consider this example of an incoming call at fire headquarters.

> "Fire Department," the dispatcher answers.
>
> "Hello. At about 10 o'clock, I was lying on my bed watching TV and smoking," the voice says. "I must have fallen asleep about 10:30 because that's

> when the football game was over. Anyway, I woke up just now, and my bedroom is on fire. . . ."

That dialogue isn't informative or convincing. More likely, our sleepy television viewer awoke in a smoke-filled room, grabbed his cellphone and punched in 9-1-1. The conversation with the dispatcher would more likely have gone like this:

> "9-1-1 call center."
>
> "FIRE!" a voice at the other end yells.
>
> "Where?" the dispatcher asks.
>
> "At 1705 W. Haven St."

When fire is licking at their heels, even nonjournalists know the lead. How the fire started is not important to the dispatcher; that a house is burning—and where that house is located—is.

The journalist must go through essentially the same process to determine the lead. Just as the caller served himself and the fire department, reporters must serve their readers. What is most important to them?

After the fire is over, there is much information a reporter must gather. Among the questions you would routinely ask are these:

- When did it start?
- When was it reported?
- Who reported it?
- How was it reported?
- How long did it take the fire department to respond?
- How long did it take to extinguish the fire?
- How many fires this year have been attributed to smoking in bed?
- How does that compare with figures from previous years?
- Were there any injuries or deaths?
- What was the damage?
- Who owned the house?
- Did the occupant or owner have insurance on the house?
- Will charges be filed against the smoker?
- Was there anything unusual about this case?
- Who cares?

With this information in hand, you can begin to write the story.

The Six Basic Questions

1. Who?
2. What?
3. Where?
4. When?
5. Why?
6. How?

More Questions

So what?

What's next?

Writing the Inverted Pyramid Lead

Start by looking over your notes.

> *Who?* The owner, a smoker, Henry Smith, 29. The age is important. Along with other personal information, such as address and occupation, the age differentiates the subject from other Henry Smiths in the readership area.
>
> *What?* Fire caused damage estimated by the fire chief at $2,500.
>
> *Where?* 1705 W. Haven St.
>
> *When?* The call was received at 10:55 p.m., Tuesday. Firefighters from Station 19 arrived at the scene at 11:04. The fire was extinguished by 11:30. Those times are important to gather even if you don't use them. They show whether the fire department responded quickly.
>
> *Why?* The fire was started by carelessness on the part of Smith, according to Fire Chief Bill Malone.
>
> *How?* Smith told fire officials that he fell asleep in bed while he was smoking a cigarette.

If you had asked other questions, you might have learned more from the fire department:

- This was the eighth fire this year caused by smoking in bed.
- All last year there were four such fires.
- Smith said he had insurance.
- The fire chief said no charges would be filed against Smith.
- It was the first fire at this house.
- Smith was not injured.

Have you figured out the "so what"?

Assume your city editor has suggested you hold the story to about six paragraphs. Your first step is to rank the information in descending order of importance. There are lots of fires in this town, but eight this year have been caused by smoking in bed. Perhaps that's the most important thing about this story. You begin to type:

> A fire started by a careless smoker caused an estimated $2,500 in damage to a home Tuesday.

Only 17 words. You should try to hold every lead to fewer than 25 words unless you use more than one sentence. Maybe it's too brief, though. Have you left anything out? Maybe you should include the time element—to give the story a sense of immediacy. Readers would also want to know where the fire occurred. Is it near their house? Is it someone they know? You rewrite:

> A Tuesday night fire started by a careless smoker caused an estimated $2,500 in damage to a home at 1705 W. Haven St.

Just then the city editor walks by and glances over your shoulder. "Who said it was a careless smoker?" she asks. "Stay out of the story."

You realize you have committed a basic error in news writing: You have allowed an unattributed opinion to slip into the story. You have two choices. You can attribute the "careless smoker" information to the fire chief in the lead, or you can omit it. You choose to rewrite by attributing the opinion. You also revise your sentence to emphasize the cause instead of the damage. You write:

> Fire that caused an estimated $2,500 in damage to a home at 1705 W. Haven St. Tuesday was caused by smoking in bed, Fire Chief Bill Malone said.

Now 28 words have answered the questions "what" (a fire), "where" (1705 W. Haven St.), "when" (Tuesday) and "how" (smoking in bed). And the opinion is attributed. But you have not answered "who" and "why." You continue, still ranking the information in descending order of importance.

> The owner of the home, Henry Smith, 29, said he fell asleep in bed while smoking a cigarette. When he awoke about 30 minutes later, smoke had filled the room.
>
> Firefighters arrived nine minutes after receiving the call. It took them about 26 minutes to extinguish the fire, which was confined to the bedroom of the one-story house.
>
> According to Chief Malone, careless smokers have caused eight fires this year. Smith, who was not injured, said the house was insured.

You take the story to the city editor, who reads through the copy quickly. As you watch, she changes the lead to emphasize the "so what." The lead now reads:

> A smoker who fell asleep in bed ignited a fire that caused minor damage to his home on West Haven Street Tuesday, Fire Chief Bill Malone said. It was the city's eighth fire caused by smokers, twice as many as occurred all last year.

The lead is 44 words, but it is broken into two sentences, which makes it more readable. The importance of the "so what" changed the direction of the story. The fire was minor; there were no injuries. However, the increase in the number of fires smokers caused may force the fire department to start a public safety campaign against careless smoking. The city editor continues:

> The owner of the home, Henry Smith, 29, of 1705 W. Haven St., said he fell asleep in bed while smoking a cigarette. When he awoke about 30 minutes later, smoke had filled the room.

Too many numbers bog down a lead. Focus on the impact of the figures in the lead, and provide details later in the story.

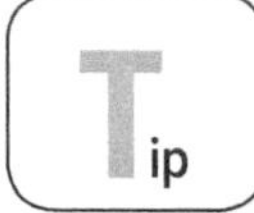

When Writing the Lead, Remember

- Always check names.
- Keep the lead to fewer than 25 words.
- Attribute opinion.
- Find out the who, what, where, when, why and how.
- Tell readers what the news means to them.
- Gather basic information even if it's routine.

When the editor checks the telephone listings and the city directory, she uncovers a serious problem. Both the telephone listings and the city directory give the man who lives at 1705 W. Haven St. as Henry Smyth: S-m-y-t-h. City directories, telephone lists and other sources can be wrong. But at least they can alert you to possible errors. Confirm spellings by going to the original source, in this case, Mr. Smyth.

Never put a name in a story without checking the spelling, even when the source tells you his name is Smith.

Look at the annotated model "A Sample Inverted Pyramid Story" to see the completed fire story. There are several lessons you can learn from this example:

- Always check names.
- Keep the lead short, usually fewer than 25 words, unless you use two sentences.
- Attribute opinion. (Smoking in bed is a fact. That it was careless is an opinion.)
- Find out the who, what, where, when, why and how. However, if any of these elements have no bearing on the story, they may be omitted.
- Write a sentence or paragraph telling readers what the news means to them.
- Report information basic to the story even if it is routine. Not everything you learn is important enough to be reported, but you'll never know unless you gather the information.

When you are learning to write an inverted pyramid story, the process is deliberate. You'll check your notes to be certain you have the six basic questions answered.

> *"Writing is easy; all you do is sit staring at a blank sheet of paper until the drops of blood form on your forehead."*
>
> **—Gene Fowler, author**

Eventually, though, you will mentally check off those questions quickly. Of course, you will not always be able to find answers immediately to "how" and "why." Sometimes, experts need time to analyze accidents, crimes, fires, and so on.

After you've checked your notes, ask yourself, "What else do readers need to know?" Using the news values of relevance, usefulness and interest and figuring out the "so what," decide which answers are the most important so you can put them in the lead.

The rest go in the second and third paragraphs. In the Annotated Model, the news values and "so what" are these:

Relevance	Eight similar fires are more relevant than one minor fire.
Usefulness	Highlighting the number of fires also establishes usefulness by pointing out the bigger problem.
Interest	Multiple fires attract more interest than one minor one.
The "so what"	One minor fire lacks impact, but the fact that eight fires this year were caused by smoking suggests a public safety problem.

In what order are the key questions answered in the fire story? What does that order say about news values?

Emphasizing Different News Values

In the lead reporting the house fire, the "what" (fire) is of secondary importance to the "how" (how the fire started). A slightly different set of facts would affect the news value of the elements and, consequently, your lead. For instance, if Smyth turned out to have been a convicted arsonist, you would probably emphasize that bizarre twist to the story:

> A convicted arsonist awoke Tuesday to find that his bedroom was filled with smoke. He escaped and later said that he had fallen asleep while smoking.
>
> Henry Smyth, 29, who served a three-year term for . . .

That lead emphasizes the news value of novelty. If Smyth were the mayor, you would emphasize prominence:

> Mayor Henry Smyth escaped injury Tuesday when he awoke to find his bedroom filled with smoke. Smyth said he had fallen asleep while smoking in bed.

ANNOTATED MODEL

A SAMPLE INVERTED PYRAMID STORY

A smoker who fell asleep in bed ignited a fire that caused minor damage to his home on West Haven Street Tuesday, Fire Chief Bill Malone said. It was the city's eighth fire caused by smokers, twice as many as occurred all last year.

The owner of the home, Henry Smyth, 29, of 1705 W. Haven St., said he fell asleep in bed while smoking a cigarette. When he awoke about 30 minutes later, smoke had filled the room. 2

3 The fire department, which received the call at 10:55 p.m., had the fire out by 11:30.

Malone said the damage, estimated at $2,500, was confined to the bedroom. The house was insured. 4

Careless smokers caused only four fires last year in the city. Malone said that he is considering a public awareness campaign to try to alert smokers to the hazards. Those four fires caused total damages of $43,000. This year, fires started by careless smoking have caused total damages of $102,500, Malone said.

5 No charges will be filed against Smyth because no one other than the smoker was endangered, Malone said.

1. The identification of "who" is delayed until the next paragraph because the person is not someone readers would recognize and because his name would make the lead unnecessarily long. Also in the lead are the "what," "when," "how" and, most significantly here, the "so what."

2. The "who" is identified. More details on the "how" are given.

3. The performance of the fire department is monitored.

4. Details on the "so what" are given. The impact question is answered with the possible campaign.

5. Least important: If someone else had been endangered and charges had been filed, this information would move higher in the story.

The inverted pyramid structure dictates that the most important information goes in the lead paragraphs. It is the job of the writer and the editor to decide what that information is.

What, So What and What's Next

You know that the answer to "what" is often the lead. The preceding example also illustrates the "so what" factor in news. A $2,500 fire is not news to many people in large communities where there are dozens of fires daily. Even if you crafted a tightly written story about it, your editor probably would not want to print or broadcast it.

In small communities, the story would have more impact because there are fewer fires and because a larger proportion of the community is likely to know the victim.

The "so what" factor grows more important as you add other information. If the fire occurred during a fire-safety campaign, the "so what" would be the need for fire safety even in a community where awareness of the problem had already been heightened. If the fire involved a convicted arsonist or the mayor, the "so what" would be stronger. Oddity or well-known people increase the value of a story. If someone had been injured or if the damage had been $1.2 million instead of $2,500, the "so what" factor might even push the story into the metropolitan press. As discussed, once you have answered all six of the basic questions, it's important to ask yourself what the answers mean to the reader. That answer is your "so what" factor.

In many stories, it is also important to answer the question "What's next?" The city council had its first reading of its budget bill. What's next? *Members will vote on it next month.* Jones was arrested Monday on suspicion of passing bad checks. What's next? *The prosecuting attorney will decide whether there is enough evidence to file charges.*

A reader in a focus group once told researchers that she just wants to be told "what," "so what" and "what's next." That's a good guideline for all journalists to remember.

Variations on the Inverted Pyramid Lead

No journalist relies on formulas to write inverted pyramid leads, but you may find it useful, especially in the beginning, to learn some typical types of leads. The labels in the following sections are arbitrary, but the approaches are not.

The "You" Lead

Regardless of which of these leads journalists use, they are trying to emphasize the relevance of the news to the audience. One good way to highlight the relevance is to speak directly to readers by using "you." This informal, second-person lead—the **"you" lead**—allows the writer to tell readers why they should care. For instance:

> You will find the lowest rates in two years if you are buying a home.
>
> Most Springfield banks yesterday lowered the 15-year loan rate to 2.85 percent, down from 3.9 percent a year ago.

Readers want to know what's in it for them. The traditional approach is less direct:

> The real estate mortgage rate hit a two-year low yesterday.

As with any kind of lead, you can overdo the "you" lead. You don't need to write "You have another choice in the student president's race." Just tell readers who will be running. However, you may use those words in writing for radio or television news as a setup for the story to come. And in tweets and on Facebook, where you are talking to readers one-on-one, "you" is usually appropriate.

The Immediate-Identification Lead

In the **immediate-identification lead**, one of the most important facts is "who," or the prominence of the key actor. Reporters often use this approach when someone important or well-known is making news. Consider the following example:

> NEW YORK (AP)—Lady Gaga is donating $1 million to the Red Cross to aid those affected by Superstorm Sandy.

If Lady Gaga were not well-known, the lead probably would have said that a New York–born singer was donating the money. Names make news.

> *"Language is a very difficult thing to put into words."*
>
> —Voltaire, philosopher

When writing for your campus newspaper or your local newspaper, you would use names in the lead that are known locally but not necessarily nationally. The name of your student body president, the chancellor, the mayor or an entertainer who has a local following would logically appear in the lead. None of these names would be used in a newspaper 50 miles away.

In small communities, names almost always make news. The "who" involved in an accident is usually in the lead. In larger communities, names are not as recognizable. As a rule, if the person's name or position is well-known, it should appear in the lead.

The Delayed-Identification Lead

Usually a reporter uses a **delayed-identification lead** because the person or organization involved has little name recognition among readers. Thus, in fairly large cities, an accident is usually reported like this:

> MADISON, Wis.—A 39-year-old carpenter was killed today in a two-car collision two blocks from his home.
>
> William Domonske of 205 W. Oak St. died at the scene. Mary Craig, 21, of 204 Maple Ave., and Rebecca Roets, 12, of 207 Maple Ave., were taken to Mercy Hospital with injuries.

However, in a smaller community, names almost always make news. Unless a name is nationally recognized, it often appears in the second paragraph:

> LOS ANGELES (AP)—A Southern California insurance broker was arrested Wednesday on allegations he overcharged Tom Hanks, musician Andy Summers and others hundreds of thousands of dollars for insurance premiums.
>
> Jerry B. Goldman, who was arrested at his Thousand Oaks home, remained jailed Wednesday, U.S. attorney's spokesman Thom Mrozek said.

This example demonstrates two things. The name Jerry B. Goldman was not widely known, so his identification was delayed until the second paragraph. However, note that the writer worked two entertainers' names into the lead to attract attention.

A Case Study of Leads

Tina Macias (see On the Job: "Inverted Pyramid—A Basic Tool") covered the news of a school bus driver who was charged with driving while intoxicated. Of course, her stories for *The Daily Advertiser* in Lafayette, La., went into detail, but if you read nothing but the leads, you can follow the essential news. She also posted messages on Twitter while at the school board meeting ("The 3-day suspension for bus driver Kenny Mire approved w/out debate. The policy has been pulled and is about to be debated."). The leads from her series of articles appear below. Leads 3 and 4 begin two stories from the same meeting.

Lead from Story 1

The Lafayette Parish School Board at its meeting tonight could approve a new policy that outlines how to discipline bus drivers if they are charged with drunken driving off duty.

Lead from Story 2

The Lafayette Parish School Bus Drivers Association is "behind the superintendent 100 percent" when it comes to a new policy set to be debated tonight.

Lead from Story 3

The Lafayette Parish School Board tonight voted to suspend bus driver Kenny Joseph Mire for three days without pay.

Lead from Story 4

The Lafayette Parish School Board tonight unanimously approved a new policy that addresses how to discipline bus drivers who are arrested for drunken driving off duty.

Lead from Story 5

Bus drivers who are charged with drug- or alcohol related driving incidents will be suspended with pay until a substance-abuse professional deems them capable of returning to work, according to a policy unanimously approved by the Lafayette Parish School Board on Wednesday.

The new policy puts Lafayette Parish more in line with several other Louisiana school systems.

The Summary Lead

Reporters dealing with several important elements may choose to sum up what happened in a **summary lead** rather than highlighting a specific action. This is one of the few times when a general statement is preferable to specifics.

The Associated Press wrote scores of stories as Hurricane Sandy moved up the East Coast of the U.S. in November 2012. When the worst was over, the AP wrote a summary lead rather than focusing on one impact from the storm:

> Death blew in on the superstorm's wild winds and sea water torrents, claiming 90-year-olds and children with capriciously toppling trees, taking tall-ship adventurers in mountainous Atlantic waves and average folks just trying to deal with a freakish snowstorm. It felled both heroes rushing into harm's way and, ironically, people simply following advice to play it safe at home.
>
> At least 72 died as the shape-shifting hurricane and winter storm ravaged the eastern U.S., and searchers continued looking for victims Wednesday.

Likewise, if a city council rewrites city ordinances, unless one of the changes is of overriding importance, most reporters will use a summary lead:

> MOLINE, Ill.—The City Council replaced the city's 75-year-old municipal code with a revised version Tuesday night.

Summary leads do not appear only in reports of board meetings. A Spokane, Wash., reporter used a summary lead to report a neighborhood dispute:

> An Idaho farmer's fence apparently was cut last week. It set off a chain of events Friday night that landed three people in the hospital, killed a cow and totaled a vehicle in the eastern Spokane Valley.

The basic question you must answer is whether the whole of the action is more important than any of its parts. If the answer is yes, use a summary lead.

The Multiple-Element Lead

In some stories, choosing one theme for the lead is too restrictive. In such cases, you can choose a **multiple-element lead** to work more information into the first paragraph. But you should write the lead within the confines of a clear, simple sentence or sentences. Consider this example:

> PORTLAND, Ore.—The City Council Tuesday ordered three department heads fired, established an administrative review board and said it would begin to monitor the work habits of administrators.

Notice that the actions are parallel, as is the construction of the verb phrases within the sentence. Parallel structures also characterize the following news extract, which presents a visual picture of the scene of a tragedy:

BAY CITY, Mich.—A flash fire that swept through a landmark downtown hotel Saturday killed at least 12 persons, injured 60 more and forced scores of residents to leap from windows and the roof in near-zero cold.

We are told what happened, where it happened and how many were killed and injured.

On **THE JOB**

Inverted Pyramid—A Basic Tool

Tina Macias is an investigative producer at KATC-TV 3 in Lafayette, La. Before she made the jump to TV, she spent nearly five years as a reporter at *The Daily Advertiser* in Lafayette. Macias' time was split between writing human interest stories and breaking news.

Despite all the changes in the industry, she believes the inverted pyramid format still is an essential tool, especially in this 24-hour news age.

Macias says the easiest and most efficient way to organize breaking news on the Web is with the inverted pyramid. Only months out of school, she found herself covering hurricanes. Her job was to get information quickly and put it online and then follow with print stories. Most of the information about school closings, food stamps, curfews and power outages appeared on the Web in the inverted pyramid format. This story was put online the Friday before Labor Day when Hurricane Gustav made landfall:

With Hurricane Gustav edging toward the Gulf, and projections showing Acadiana in its path, public and private schools are preparing for the worst.

One day before she arrived at work, a colleague had reported the bare details of a school bus accident that morning. Macias' job was to update the story.

"As I started to make my phone calls, I thought about the vital information and how I could easily organize it," she says. She produced this inverted pyramid lead:

Nine people, including eight children, were transported to a local hospital Monday morning after a black Impala plowed into the side of a Lafayette Parish school bus.

All were transported for minor or moderate injuries and complaints.

Though then a rookie reporter, Macias was able to be productive immediately, in part because of two internships she held while attending journalism school. Now she is used to covering news quickly for both the Web and print.

Some multiple-element leads consist of two paragraphs. This occurs when the reporter decides that several elements need prominent display. For example:

> The Board of Education Tuesday night voted to lower the tax rate 12 cents per $100 valuation. Members then approved a budget $150,000 less than last year's and instructed the superintendent to decrease the staff by 25 people.
>
> The board also approved a set of student-conduct rules, which include a provision that students with three or more unexcused absences a year will be suspended for a week.

This story, too, could emphasize the "so what" while retaining the multiple elements:

> The Board of Education lowered your real estate taxes Tuesday. Members also approved a budget $150,000 less than last year's and instructed the superintendent to decrease the staff by 25 people.

Simpler leads are preferable. But a multiple-element lead is one of your options. Use it sparingly.

Many newspapers are using graphic devices to take the place of multiple-element leads. They use summary boxes to list other actions. Because the box appears under the headline in type larger than the text, it serves as a graphic summary for the reader who is scanning the page. The box frees the writer from trying to jam too many details into the first few paragraphs. On the Web, such lists are even more common. When Instagram announced that it could sell the photos people post on the site, CNN included four related points in its Story Highlights list to the left of the lead (see Figure 8-2).

Another approach is to break the coverage of a single event into a main story and a shorter story called a **sidebar**. This approach offers the advantage of presenting the information in short, palatable bites. It also allows the writer to elevate more actions into lead positions. Researchers have found that breaking stories into small segments increases readers' comprehension and retention. For instance, in the Board of Education lead above, the angle about the superintendent's having to decrease staff could be spun off into a short sidebar.

"The lead should be a promise of great things to come, and the promise should be fulfilled."

—Stanley Walker, city editor

On the Web, there is an additional advantage. The more stories with separate headlines, the better chance you have to increase the **click-through rate**, the measurement of how many people open the stories.

Instagram backtracks after user privacy revolt

By **Doug Gross**, CNN
updated 6:53 AM EST, Wed December 19, 2012 | Filed under: Social Media

Can Instagram sell your photos?

STORY HIGHLIGHTS

- NEW: Instagram backtracks on controversial privacy language
- Language appeared to let the app sell users' images for advertising
- Facebook CEO Mark Zuckerberg's wedding photographer called it unfair
- NEW: Instagram co-founder: "It is not our intention to sell your photos"

(CNN) -- Faced with a loud and angry backlash from some of its most active users, photo-sharing app Instagram backtracked Tuesday on new language that appeared to give the company ownership of their images.

"The language we proposed ... raised question about whether your photos can be part of an advertisement," Instagram co-founder Kevin Systrom wrote in a blog post. "We do not have plans for anything like this and because of that we're going to remove the language that raised the question."

An update Monday to Instagram's terms of service had stated that data collected through the app can be shared with Facebook. That's not a surprising move, considering Facebook paid an estimated $1 billion for the photo-sharing service earlier this year.

But the language that upset some of the app's more than 100 million users said that "a business or other entity may pay" Instagram for the use of user images and may do so "without any compensation to you."

Figure 8-2. A list, such as CNN's Story Highlights on the left, allows the writer to simplify the lead.

Danger Signals

Here are some leads that understandably raise red flags to editors:

- **Question leads.** Readers don't know the subject, don't know why they are being asked a question and probably couldn't care less. So the next time you are writing a weather story and are tempted to begin with "So, how hot was it yesterday?" lie down until the temptation passes. Either tell readers the temperature or open with an anecdote of a specific roofer sweating on the job. That's showing how hot it is.
- **Leads that say what might happen or what might have happened.** News organizations try to report what happened. Stay away from leads like this: "Springfield residents might be looking forward to warmer weather." Or they might not. Talk to people. Don't speculate.
- **Leads that overreach.** Report what you know. You might think it's harmless to write, "Springfield residents warmly greeted spring yesterday," but you don't know that all Springfield residents were happy about it. Maybe the guy who runs a snow-removal business would rather see winter last longer.

Leads with Flair

Although the inverted pyramid tells readers the news first and fast, not all stories begin with the most important statement. When the news value you want to emphasize is novelty, often the lead is unusual.

> CASTLE SHANNON, Pa. (AP)—This deer wasn't caught in the headlights. It was called on the carpet.
>
> A Pittsburgh-area carpeting store has been cleaning up after the wild animal smashed into the store and ran amok Tuesday.

A less imaginative writer might have written:

> A deer ran through the window of a Pittsburgh-area carpeting store Tuesday.

That approach is like slapping a generic label on a Mercedes-Benz. The inverted pyramid approach is not so rigid that it doesn't permit fun and flair.

Story Organization

Like a theater marquee, the lead is an attention-getter. Sometimes the movie doesn't fulfill the promises of the marquee; sometimes the story doesn't fulfill the promises of the lead. In either case, the customer is dissatisfied.

The inverted pyramid helps you put information in logical order. It forces you to rank, in order of importance, the information you will present.

The One-Subject Story

As we have seen in this chapter, constructing an inverted pyramid news story involves a series of judgments based on classic news values and the specific news outlet. A fire or an accident in a small community is bigger news than a fire or an accident in another, larger area. Earlier events will also influence how you write a story.

The annotated model "A Sample Inverted Pyramid Story"shows a story about the arrest of a suspect in an assault case. Police say drugs were involved. If there had been a string of assaults or a pattern of drug-related violence, the writer probably would have emphasized different aspects of the story. For instance, the writer could have emphasized the suspect's criminal record with this lead:

> A Columbia man who was convicted of assault three times was arrested again Thursday night for an attack on his girlfriend.

The Memo-Structure Story

The memo structure (as illustrated in "A Memo-Structure Story"one of many hybrids journalists are experimenting with as they transition to the Web. It is an effective way to organize information that has no narrative and few voices. You can use it to write an **advance** about upcoming meetings and to update developing stories. The categories can follow the standard who, what, where, when, why, how and so what, or you can create your own subject categories. Reporters can write memo-structure stories quickly, and readers can scan them quickly—a convenient feature for readers using a small-screen device such as a smartphone.

ANNOTATED MODEL

A SINGLE-SUBJECT INVERTED PYRAMID STORY

Man Arrested in Attack, Charged with Child Endangerment

By Elizabeth Phillips
Columbia Missourian

1 Police arrested a Columbia man in connection with an attack on his girlfriend Thursday night.

2 Darrell Vanness Johnson, 37, was arrested on suspicion of second-degree domestic assault, unlawful use of a weapon, felony possession of a controlled substance, misdemeanor possession of a controlled substance and endangering the welfare of a child at about 9 p.m. Thursday in the 1500 block of Greensboro Drive.

3 Johnson and his girlfriend began arguing over drugs Thursday evening, Columbia Police Sgt. Ken Hammond said. Johnson choked her and held a revolver to her head before she was able to escape and call 911 from a neighbor's house, Hammond said. Three children, two 9-year-olds and a 4-year-old, were in the home during the attack, Hammond said.

4 When Columbia police arrived, Johnson was driving away from the Greensboro Drive home with the three children in the car, Hammond said. When police arrested Johnson, they found marijuana and cocaine, Hammond said.

5 The victim was taken to an area hospital by ambulance for treatment of bruises and scratches to the hands, neck and back, Hammond said. Her injuries were not life threatening.

6 According to Missouri Case.net, Johnson has pleaded guilty to third-degree domestic assault three times in the past four years in Boone County Circuit Court, serving close to seven months in jail for those charges. He has also pleaded guilty to theft, first-degree trespass and second-degree property damage in Boone County Circuit Court, serving 75 days in Boone County Jail for the theft charge and receiving two years of unsupervised probation for the trespass and property damage charges.

Johnson violated his probation on the trespass and property damage charges and was scheduled to appear in Boone County Circuit Court for a probation violation hearing in December. He was charged with theft last October in Boone County Circuit Court.

7 He faces up to 40 years in prison and up to a year in jail in connection with the attack.

1. The arrest, not the assault, is the latest development, so it is emphasized. The lead gives "who," "what" and "when."

2. Details of the charges are in the second paragraph because the list is too long to put in the lead. The name is not in the lead because most readers would not recognize it.

3. The writer adds details, attributed to the police, on how the assault occurred. This information includes the "why." "Where" is identified. "When" is made more specific than in the lead. Information about the children is pertinent because it adds to the "so what"—the children were also endangered.

4. This paragraph continues the chronology of the assault and capture.

5. The writer offers evidence of the injuries and attributes this information.

6. Now that the basic facts are established, the writer adds background on the suspect, attributed to a public safety website.

7. Writer gives the "what's next."

This typical one-subject story written in the inverted pyramid form features a delayed-identification lead.

ANNOTATED MODEL

A MEMO-STRUCTURE STORY

Parks and Recreation, City Council Discuss Plans for Parks Tax

By Asif Lakhani
Columbia Missourian

1 COLUMBIA—Earlier this month, Columbia voters approved the extension of the park sales tax. On Monday night, the Columbia City Council and the Parks and Recreation Department attended a work session where they discussed where the tax revenue would go.

2 **What happened:** Mike Hood, director of parks and recreation, presented a proposed five-year plan to council members.

Cost: During the next five years, the one-eighth-cent sales tax is expected to garner about $12 million for Columbia's parks. 3

Timetable: The proposed plan divides projects into four categories: land acquisition and annual park funding, new facility and park development, improvements to existing parks, and trails and greenbelts. . . .

Projects: The five-year plan would be front-loaded with construction projects over a four-year fiscal period between 2011 and 2015, which would leave more room for land acquisition later on, Hood said. Most of the construction projects are listed under new facility and park development and improvements to existing parks. . . .

Comments: First Ward Councilman Paul Sturtz and Sixth Ward Councilwoman Barbara Hoppe voiced concern about front-loading the plan with construction. Both said land acquisition is more important because its value could increase over the next five years. . . .

4 **What's next:** The proposed plan now goes to the Parks and Recreation Commission. After, it will go to the City Council for consideration. The council plans to discuss the suggested land acquisition at an upcoming council meeting.

In a memo-structure story, subheads can reflect the answers to essential questions.

1. The multiple-element lead gives basic facts—the "who," "what" and "when."

2. Subheadings introduce the paragraphs.

3. Subsequent paragraphs organize information by categories, not necessarily by importance. The writer has chosen categories that are relevant to the reader.

4. The last paragraph wraps up the story.

The Multiple-Element Story

Multiple-element stories are most commonly used in reporting on the proceedings of councils, boards, commissions, legislatures and courts. These bodies act on numerous subjects in one sitting. Frequently, their actions are unrelated, and more than one action is often important enough to merit attention in the story. You have four options:

1. **You can write more than one story.** This, of course, requires permission from your editor. There may not be enough space.
2. **You can write a story highlights list.** The list would be displayed along with the story either in print or on the Web. In it you would list the council's major actions or the court's decisions.
3. **You can write a multiple-element lead and story.** Your lead would list all the major actions at the board meeting. The remainder of the story would provide more detail about each action.
4. **You can write a single-element lead and cover the other elements further on in the story.** Your lead would focus on the element you believe readers would find most interesting, relevant and useful.

Let's go back to a multiple-element lead we saw earlier:

> The Board of Education Tuesday night voted to lower the tax rate 12 cents per $100 valuation. Members then approved a budget $150,000 less than last year's and instructed the superintendent to decrease the staff by 25 people.
>
> The board also approved a set of student-conduct rules, which include a provision that students with three or more unexcused absences a year will be suspended for a week.

Four newsworthy actions are mentioned in those two paragraphs: (1) changing the tax rate, (2) approving a budget, (3) cutting staff, (4) adopting student-conduct rules. In stories that deal with several important elements, the writer usually highlights the most important. When this is the case, it is important to summarize the other, lesser actions after the lead.

If you and your editor judge that changing the tax rate was more important than anything else that happened at the school board meeting, you would approach the story like this:

Lead	The Board of Education Tuesday night voted to lower the tax rate 12 cents per $100 valuation.
Support for lead	The new rate is $1.18 per $100 valuation. That means that if your property is assessed at $300,000, your school tax will be $3,540 next year.
Summary of other action	The board also approved a budget that is $150,000 less than last year's, instructed the superintendent to cut the staff by 25 and approved a set of rules governing student conduct.

Notice that the lead is followed by a paragraph that supports and enlarges upon the information in it before the summary paragraph appears. Whether you need a support paragraph before summarizing other action depends on how complete you are able to make the lead.

In every multiple-element story, the first two or three paragraphs determine the order of the rest of the story. To ensure the coherence of your story, you must describe the elements in the order in which you introduce them.

Checklist for Assembling the Rest of the Inverted Pyramid

- Introduce additional important information you were not able to include in the lead.
- If possible, indicate the significance or "so what" factor.
- Elaborate on the information presented in the lead.
- Continue introducing new information in the order in which you have ranked it by importance.
- Develop the ideas in the same order in which you have introduced them.
- Generally, use only one new idea in each paragraph.

Writing A Story Across Media Platforms

The inverted pyramid can serve you throughout the news reporting and writing process, from tweets to online updates. Most breaking news stories are first tweeted and then put on the Web before they are printed in a newspaper or broadcast on television. In fact, the story may never even be printed or broadcast.

The story in the annotated model "The Classic Inverted Pyramid Story" appeared in print. Let's follow its progress from the first tweet to its final form.

Tweeting Breaking News

If you can write a lead, you can write a tweet. The limitation of 140 characters is not much of a problem for journalists. The lead on the accident story is only 95 characters. The difference between writing a lead and writing a tweet is that the journalist often does not know as many details when tweeting. A journalist at the scene of an accident might send this tweet:

> EMT crews are working 4-car accident on I-70 near Stadium Blvd. Exit Missouri 41 to avoid traffic backup.

After the reporter has had a chance to talk to an officer at the scene, she sends the next tweet:

> Police: 4 injured in accident on I-70 near Stadium Blvd. No IDs yet. Exit Missouri 41 to avoid traffic backup both directions.

Initial Online Story

When the reporter is able to get more information, she can post the first blast for online and mobile devices:

> Two people were killed and two others were injured today in a four-car accident on I-70 near Stadium Boulevard, Springfield police said.
>
> Names of the victims were being withheld pending notification of relatives. All four were state residents.
>
> The two injured were taken to Springfield Hospital.
>
> Authorities said a westbound Toyota pickup truck swerved across the median and collided with an Oldsmobile in the eastbound lane.

Full Story with Ongoing Updates

The next version, shown in "The Classic Inverted Pyramid Story", would appear both in print and on the Web. Most publications post the story on the Web immediately, even before the newspaper is printed or the news report is aired. The next day, the reporter is able to update the Web version:

> Two people injured in a four-car accident Sunday were released from Springfield Hospital today. The accident claimed the lives of two others.
>
> William Doolan, 73, of St. Joseph, and Theodore Amelung, 43, of Manchester, were released. Barbara Jones, 41, of St. Louis, and Juanita Doolan, 73, of St. Joseph, died as a result of the collision.

This new lead would replace the first three paragraphs of the existing story. In all versions for all platforms, it is essential to answer and rank the questions that are basic to any inverted pyramid story.

Checking Accuracy and Attributions

All of us can improve our accuracy. Some improvement comes with experience, but most of the errors journalists make involve routine facts. In Chapter 6, you learned the importance of accurately capturing the words that you quote. On page 412 are additional procedures you should use to produce more accurate stories.

ANNOTATED MODEL

THE CLASSIC INVERTED PYRAMID STORY

A four-vehicle accident on eastbound I-70 near Stadium Boulevard ended in two deaths on Sunday. 1

2 Barbara Jones, 41, of St. Louis died at the scene of the accident, and Juanita Doolan, 73, of St. Joseph died at University Hospital, according to a release from Springfield police. Two other people, William Doolan, 73, of St. Joseph and Theodore Amelung, 43, of Manchester, Mo., were injured in the accident.

3 Both lanes of traffic were closed on the eastbound side and limited to one lane on the westbound side as rescue workers cleared the scene.

4 Authorities said a westbound late-model Ford Taurus driven by Lan Wang of Springfield was traveling in the right lane, developed a tire problem and swerved into the passing lane. A Toyota pickup truck in the passing lane, driven by Jones, was forced over the grassy median along with the Taurus. The two vehicles entered eastbound traffic where the truck struck an Oldsmobile Delta 88, driven by Juanita Doolan, head on.

Wang and the one passenger in his car, Kenneth Kuo, 58, of Springfield, were not injured.

5 John Paul, a tractor-trailer driver on his way to Tennessee, said he had to swerve to miss the accident.

"I saw the red truck come across the median and hit the blue car," Paul said. "I just pulled over on the median and called 911."

Jones, who was wearing a seat belt, died at the scene, Officer Stan Williams said. Amelung, a passenger who had been in the truck, was out of the vehicle when authorities arrived, but it was unknown whether he was thrown from the truck or was pulled out by someone else, Williams said.

No charges have been filed, but the investigation continues.

1. The lead identifies the "what," "where" and "when." The "so what" is that people were killed.

2. The second paragraph provides details to support the lead and answers "who."

3. This paragraph shows impact beyond deaths and injuries.

4. The "how" is less important than the "what," "where" and "when," so it appears later in the story.

5. An eyewitness account adds sensory details that make the scene more vivid. What's next? This would be higher if the driver, rather than a tire, appeared to be the cause of the accident.

Note how this story, typical of the inverted pyramid structure, delivers the most important news in the lead and provides less essential details toward the end. It also reflects more complete reporting than an earlier Web version.

These four habits will help you become more accurate:

1. **Go over your notes at the end of every interview.** Read back the quotes and the facts as you have written them down. Don't assume anything. As you read earlier in the chapter, if someone tells you his name is Smith, ask him how to spell it.
2. **Carefully check your story against your notes and the documents you have collected to be certain you didn't introduce any errors while writing.** We all make typing errors. We make errors because of background noise and commotion. If you recognize that you are not infallible, you will be a more accurate journalist.
3. **When sources give you facts, check them if possible.** During an interview, the mayor may tell you that the city has 50 police officers. Check with the police department. The mayor may have the number wrong.
4. **Do a prepublication check.** Some journalists object to prepublication checks because they believe it gives the source too much opportunity to argue over what they will print. Some are afraid sources may approach other media to get their version of the story out even before publication, but those situations are rare.

"Selecting the quotes isn't so hard; it's presenting them that causes the trouble. And the worst place to present them is at the beginning. Quote leads deserve their terrible reputation. Yet they still appear regularly in both print and broadcast journalism.

"We can make three generalizations about quote leads. They're easy, lazy, and lousy. They have no context. The readers don't know who's speaking, why, or why it matters. Without context, even the best quotations are wasted."

—Paula LaRocque, former assistant managing editor, *The Dallas Morning News*

In a study published in the *Newspaper Research Journal*, researcher Duane Stoltzfus found that more newspapers than formerly believed permitted their reporters to check stories or portions of stories with sources before publication. In all cases, sources are told that they are being asked to check the accuracy of the information. No journalist should cede authority for decisions about what goes in and what does not. But no journalist should be afraid to take every step possible to ensure accuracy. Some read back quotes; some read back facts gathered from that source. Some even describe information obtained from other sources. *USA Today*, among many other newspapers, permits its reporters to decide whether to check with sources before publication.

If your publication permits prepublication checks, you will do yourself and your profession a favor by performing them. Verify everything you intend to publish or broadcast. In the online world, where speed is king, verification often is sacrificed in the rush to be first. But being first and wrong is never right, as bloggers will tell you. In an effort to be transparent, some news sites put a note on stories that have been corrected.

Suggested Readings

Brooks, Brian S., James L. Pinson and Jean Gaddy Wilson. *Working with Words: A Handbook for Media Writers and Editors*. 8th ed. New York: Bedford/St. Martin's, 2013. This must-have book provides excellent coverage of grammar and word usage and has a strong chapter on "isms."

Gillman, Timothy. "The Problem of Long Leads in News and Sports Stories." *Newspaper Research Journal* (Fall 1994): 29–39. The researcher found that sentences in leads were longer than sentences in the rest of the story.

Kennedy, George. "Newspaper Accuracy: A New Approach." *Newspaper Research Journal* (Winter 1994): 55–61. The author suggests that journalists do prepublication accuracy checks with proper safeguards in place.

Maier, Scott R. "Accuracy Matters: A Cross-Market Assessment of Newspaper Error and Credibility." *Journalism and Mass Communications Quarterly* (Autumn 2005): 533–51. This study documents the error rates of journalists and the impact on credibility.

Stoltzfus, Duane. "Partial Pre-publication Review Gaining Favor at Newspapers." *Newspaper Research Journal* (Fall 2006): 23–37. The researcher surveyed the 50 largest newspapers to determine their policies toward prepublication review and found that the trend is to permit it.

Suggested Websites

www.poynter.org/category/latest-news/regret-the-error

Regret the Error, housed on the Poynter.org website, chronicles errors made in all media. It is valuable in that it shows that even professional reporters are fallible.

www.stateofthemedia.org

The Pew Research Center's Project for Excellence in Journalism produces an annual "State of the News Media" report that examines journalistic trends and economic trends.

www.public.wsu.edu/~brians/errors/index.html

Paul Brians, a professor of English at Washington State University, will answer your questions about the English language.

Exercises

1. **Team project.** Your professor will divide the class into teams. Read *The Widget Effect*, 2009, a study by the New Teacher Project, which is an organization founded by teachers in 1997 "to address the growing issues of teacher shortages and teacher quality throughout the country." The study reports that teachers are not interchangeable widgets. It can be downloaded at www.widgeteffect.org/downloads /TheWidgetEffect.pdf.

   As you read, annotate your copy of the study with questions and responses, including possible story ideas. Collaborate with your team members to choose four story ideas prompted by the study. Each team member should write a lead for one story idea. As a group, edit the leads to meet the requirements of an inverted pyramid lead. Your teacher may choose to have you report on the best story idea.

2. Identify the who, what, where, when, why and how, if they are present, in the following lead:

The United Jewish Appeal is sponsoring its first-ever walkathon this morning in Springfield to raise money for the Soup Kitchen, a place where the hungry can eat free.

3. Here are four versions of the same lead. Which version answers more of the six questions basic to all stories? Which questions does it answer?

    a. What began 12 years ago with a federal staff investigation and led to hearings and a court fight culminates today with a Federal Trade Commission rule to prevent funeral home rip-offs.

    b. The nation's funeral home directors are required to offer detailed cost statements starting today, a service they say they are now ready to provide despite nearly a dozen years of debate over the idea.

    c. A new disclosure law going into effect today will make it easier for consumers to determine the cost of a funeral.

    d. Twelve years after first being proposed, a federal regulation goes into effect today to require funeral homes to provide an itemized list of services and materials they offer, along with the cost of each item, before a person agrees to any arrangements.

4. Rewrite two of the leads in exercise 3 as "you" leads. Which are better, the third-person or second-person leads? Why are they better?

5. From the following facts, write a tweet of 140 characters or fewer that you could send to tell the story and promote it for a website.

Who:	A nuclear weapon with a yield equivalent to 150,000 tons of TNT
What:	Detonated
Where:	40 miles from a meeting of pacifists and 2,000 feet beneath the surface of Pahute Mesa in the Nevada desert
When:	Tuesday
Why:	To test the weapon
How:	Not applicable

Other information: Department of Energy officials are the source; 450 physicians and peace activists were gathered to protest continued nuclear testing by the U.S.

6. **Journalism blog.** Collect three leads from different Internet news sites. Write a blog post in which you identify each type of lead used and determine what questions each lead answers and what questions it does not. Give your opinion of the effectiveness of each lead. Then review the blog post of at least one other classmate and post a comment in response.

7. From the following facts, write the first two paragraphs of a news article.

Who:	40 passengers
What:	Evacuated from a Northwest Airlines jet, Flight 428
Where:	At the LaCrosse, Wis., Municipal Airport

When:	Monday following a flight from Minneapolis to LaCrosse
Why:	A landing tower employee spotted smoke near the wheels.
How:	Not applicable

Other information: There was no fire or injuries; the smoke was caused by hydraulic fluids leaking onto hot landing brakes, according to Bob Gibbons, a Northwest spokesman.

8. Describe picture and information-graphic possibilities for the story in exercise 5.
9. Collect six leads from newspapers. Determine which basic questions are answered and which are not. Identify the kind of lead used.

Writing to Be Read

In this section you will learn:

1. How the skills of reporting make good writing possible.
2. How to add accurate, specific details.
3. How to write a coherent story.
4. How to write with conciseness and simplicity.
5. How to use correct and effective language.
6. How to use four narrative writing techniques: scenes, dialogue, anecdotes and foreshadowing.

Whether you are writing a newspaper story, a television script, a news release or an article for a website, a good story told well is important to readers and viewers and to the financial success of your company. Many journalists are getting the message. When Hurricane Sandy bore down on the East Coast, *The (Newark, N.J.) Star-Ledger* positioned several reporters to observe the impact of the storm. They filed frequent reports, and just five days after the storm left, Amy Ellis Nutt combined her work with that of several other reporters to create a narrative report on the storm, starting 48 hours before it hit (see Figure 8-3). Until then, the news had been in pieces. These excerpts show you the big story:

> The forecast has hovered like a Sword of Damocles over the state for days. Plenty of time to get ready—shore up windows, move possessions to second floors, purchase batteries and water. That's what New Jersey did last year, right before Irene hit. But this is different—a hurricane buddying with a nor'easter. Almost everyone believes the damage will be substantial and the pain, perhaps unprecedented. But few are prepared for the meteorological time bomb set to explode over New Jersey's coast, or the suddenness of a tidal surge that in the time it takes to watch a movie, will forever change the geography of the state. . . .
>
> In Seaside Heights, Police Chief Thomas J. Boyd studies the forecast on the computer in his office, zeroing in on the radar predicting the storm's path.

> "Follow the map, follow the map," he repeats to himself.
>
> At this moment, with Sandy still only a swirl of color on a meteorologist's computer screen, few up and down New Jersey's 127-mile-long shore could mistake the Atlantic for a monster.
>
> Twenty-four hours later, they will.
>
> Although meteorologists record the first tropical storm-force winds in Cape May at 7 a.m. Sunday, by early afternoon, with Sandy still moving slowly north, there remains a slim possibility it still might skirt New Jersey and turn eastward. That's what Chief Boyd is counting on. But that door out to the east, away from land, is rapidly closing. . . .
>
> When Chief Boyd sees the hurricane make an abrupt left-hand turn on the computer screen, he says to himself, "We're screwed." Immediately he begins calling in more officers and making arrangements to pull cruisers off the island—cars will be useless, and worse, 1-ton missiles in a flood.
>
> The unthinkable is now the inevitable. A storm of historic proportions and intensity is rushing headlong toward one of the most densely populated coastlines in the world. Sixty-five million Americans, 9 million of them in New Jersey, are in her path. And those remaining on the barrier islands are in the bull's-eye.

Readers don't see this type of writing as often as they should, but when they do, they appreciate it. Readers on the website commented: "A fantastic piece of journalism"; "Superbly written"; "A vivid slice of the mayhem we all experienced in so many forms last week."

Stories help people, even those caught in the midst of a storm, make sense of events. Nutt expertly used chronology, built tension, created scenes and reached a resolution. That's the work of a narrative writer.

Writing to inform and entertain is as important for journalists as it is for novelists. Just because newspapers and broadcast reports are finished and gone in a day doesn't mean that we should accept a lower level of skill. Comparing the temporal nature of newspapers to a beach, syndicated columnist James Kilpatrick challenged writers: "If we write upon the sand, let us write as well as we can upon the sand before the waves come in."

If Kilpatrick's challenge to your pride is not enough, then the demands of readers and listeners—and of the editors and news directors who are hiring—should be. Editors are looking for those unusual people who can combine reporting and writing talents. The journalist whose prose jerks around the page like a mouse trapped in a room with a cat has no future in the business. The American Society of News Editors has made the improvement of writing one of its principal long-range goals. Each year, it honors the reporting and writing of journalists in several categories. Some of them go on to win Pulitzer Prizes. Many well-known writers—among them Daniel Defoe, Mark Twain, Stephen Crane, Ernest Hemingway and Alex Haley—began their careers as journalists. At newspapers around the country today, small but growing numbers of journalists are producing literature daily as they deal with everything from traffic accidents to affairs of state. If you have respect for the language, an artist's imagination and the dedication to learn how to combine them, you, too, may produce literature.

Powered by: Suburban News New Jersey

47° 5-day | Satellite

Sign in | Join

N.J. NEWS LOCAL NEWS N.J. POLITICS SPORTS H.S. SPORTS ENTERTAINMENT

All Newspapers | Business | Education | Forums | Lottery | National | Opinion/NJ Voices | Photos | Videos | World

NJPAC Celebrate the holidays at NJPAC with Fred Hammond and D

48 hours: Before, during, and after Hurricane Sandy in Seaside Heights and Cape May

11 comments

By Amy Ellis Nutt/The Star-Ledger
on November 04, 2012 at 8:07 AM, updated November 09, 2012 at 4:24 PM

Tweet 98 Like 337 Share 7 Foursquare Email

Enlarge Star-Ledger Staff

Tom Kowal, left, and Joe Rulli, owners of Joeys Pizza and Pasta, board up their restaurant on Long Beach Blvd as Hurricane Sandy makes its way toward Long Beach Island. They were prepared with their orange sign from previous storms. Beach Haven, NJ 10/28/12 (John

Ancient mariners believed the tides were the angry breathing of a sea creature chained to the ocean floor.

In Cape May on Sunday morning, Oct. 28, with Hurricane Sandy still 300 miles from shore, the tides, instead, beckon surfers, riding wind-driven swells off the Ocean Street beach.

Just inland, residents and business owners take the usual precautions against an impending storm. At the Congress Hall, where Abraham Lincoln once stayed, workers

Courtesy of NJ.com/The Star Ledger

Figure 8-3. After reporting the news of Hurricane Sandy as it happened, reporter Amy Ellis Nutt went back and created a narrative story detailing the impact of the storm. After getting information in fragments, readers could now see the entire story in context.

We should all attempt to bring quality writing, wit and knowledge to our work. If we succeed, our work will be not only informative but also enjoyable, not only educational but also entertaining, and not only bought but also read.

Good Writing Begins with Good Reporting

It was not only Nutt who rode out the storm; nine colleagues were reporting simultaneously throughout the region. Her story, which opened this chapter, is a testament to the power of reporting and writing. (See the link to the full story at the end of this chapter.) Without the proper use of participant accounts, personal observation and detail, the best writer's stories land with a thud. Good writing begins with good reporting. You can settle for a dry police report, or you can go to the scene and gather details. Earlier in this chapter we introduced you to this lead:

> Two people died Thursday when a backhoe fell off a truck's flatbed and sliced the top off an oncoming vehicle near Fairchild Air Force Base.

Now let's look at some of the detail writer Alison Boggs of *The (Spokane, Wash.) Spokesman-Review* collected by being there:

> The top of the Suburban, from about hood height, was shorn off by the backhoe's bucket. The front seats were forced backward, and the dashboard, roof and steering wheel were torn off.
>
> Parts of the car lay in a heap of crumpled metal and glass under the overpass. The silver Suburban was identifiable only by a 1983 owner's manual lying in the dirt nearby.
>
> Both victims wore seat belts, but in this case, that was irrelevant, (Sgt. Jeff) Sale said. Both suffered severe head injuries.
>
> Sleeping bags, a Coleman cooler and fishing equipment scattered on the highway and in the back of the Suburban suggested a camping trip. Unopened cans of Pepsi were jammed behind the front seat of the car.

Notice that the writer built every sentence on concrete detail. Good reporting makes good writing possible.

On **THE JOB**

Setting the Hook in the Opening

Justin Heckert, who lives in Indianapolis and writes for national magazines such as *Sports Illustrated* and *Esquire*, believes one of the most important aspects of writing is the first few sentences of a story:

The experience of reading and being hooked can be because of word play, or rhythm, or a particular style or device. I can recite the first sentences to some of my favorite stories. That's just how they stick with me.

"The madness of an autumn prairie cold front coming through." That's Jonathan Franzen. "It was a pleasure to burn. It was a special pleasure to see things eaten, to see things blackened and changed." That's Ray Bradbury. "Aye, that face. There's a story about that face, you know. About what he was willing to do with it." That's Tom Junod. "Sometimes the silence gets inside of you." That's Gary Smith. "They don't count calories at Fausto's Fried Chicken." That's Wright Thompson. These books/stories are nowhere near me as I write this, but I can remember those sentences, and I know I got them right.

This idea has been a huge part of my own writing. I've done it, or tried to, in pretty much every single story I've ever written, be it a success or failure. A recent example: In 2009, I reported and wrote a story for *Men's Journal*. I was sitting on top of amazing material. I could've, honestly, probably just written it out like I was talking to a third grader, and it still would've been an interesting story. But after I talked to my editor and sat down to write it, I sweated forever about how to begin. I sat on the porch and thought about it. I thought about it driving the car. I thought about how to begin while I was watching a football game, before I was going to bed.

The story was about two people who had been pulled out to the sea and had treaded water for hours. The ocean has been written about more than anything since the beginning of time. It was hard to try and think of something new to say about it, to tie it in to the experience of this guy and his son, victims of the ocean, even though they didn't die. How this situation resolved itself is as esoteric as the nature of writing itself: It just came to me.

"The ocean at night is a terrible dream. There is nothing beyond the water except the profound discouragement of the sky, every black wave another singular misfortune." I had stared at the ocean for hours, had thought about how it affected the characters of the story, thought about everything they said about it. I knew it when the words appeared—they came to me the way ideas come to people, inexplicably. I think those are two good sentences. So did my editor. So have a lot of other people who read it. They were that important to me because I wanted them to hook the readers and then keep them with me.

Accurate, Specific Details

Good writing is accurate when it is built on concrete details. When you use language to communicate those details precisely, you inform and entertain your readers.

Use Concrete Examples

For lawyers, the devil might be in the details, but for writers, clarity is in the details. Echoing your bureaucratic sources, you can write of infrastructures or facilities or learning pods. But try actually touching any of these. By contrast, you ride on a highway, sit in an arena and learn in a reading group.

Be specific. You might write that the speaker is big, but compared to what? Abstractions are ambiguous. To someone who is 6 feet tall, someone big might be 6 feet 6 inches tall. To someone who is 5 feet 2 inches tall, 6 feet is huge.

Note how the concrete details in the following lead from *The Boston Globe* about an employee who killed five co-workers make the story more interesting:

> He was an accountant who had a chip on his shoulder and a bayonet on his kitchen table. He lived with his parents across from a llama farm in a small beige house with a sign informing visitors: "Trespassers will be shot; survivors will be shot again."
>
> As dawn broke over Ledyard yesterday, Matthew Beck, 35, left his folks' home—across town from the casino—got in his car, and drove 1½ hours to his job at Connecticut Lottery headquarters. At some point, he strapped

> a bandolier of bullets across his chest, over his gray pin-striped shirt but concealed by a brown leather jacket. He carried a 9mm pistol and a knife.

Almost every sentence contains specific, concrete detail: "accountant," "bayonet," "across from a llama farm," and so on.

Nutt, whose story opens this chapter, packed specific, concrete details into her story to create this scene describing a harrowing ride during Hurricane Sandy:

> Boyd is in his truck with Fire Chief James Samarelli, who is at the wheel. They turn right onto Sampson Avenue and are nearly hit by a wooden lifeguard boat slicing through the floodwater. A wall of water is headed directly for them, bringing a second lifeguard boat. Samarelli jerks the truck to the right. A large piece of the boardwalk, ripped away by the waves, slams into the front of the flatbed truck. Boyd looks down at his suddenly cold feet. Seawater is rushing into the cab and a 6-foot-tall swell lifts the truck and begins pushing it sideways, into a telephone pole.

To be concrete, you must have facts. And you must describe those facts in a way that makes readers able to touch, feel or smell them. Lazy reporters create puffballs. Poke their stories, and you'll stick your finger clear through them. Instead of saying "some council members," say "five council members." Instead of writing that a business is "downsizing," report that 150 workers will lose their jobs. Avoid abstractions; covet concrete details.

Show, Don't Just Tell

As you chauffeur the reader through the scenes in your story, you can drive down the road or over the green-laced, rolling hills of Kentucky. You can report that a car hit a skunk, or you can convey the nauseating smell. A word here, a phrase there, and you can hear the plane ripping the tin roof off a house, smell the acrid stench of burning tires, feel the boxing glove's leather rasp against the skin. Good writing appeals to one or more of our five senses: sight, hearing, smell, taste and touch.

Reporting for *The Oregonian*, Steve Duin talked to voters standing in the rain while waiting to vote. He observed: "They arrived in wool hats and sweatpants, in Chuck Taylors and hospital scrubs, with borrowed umbrellas and voter guides and 18-month-olds in their arms."

> *"There's a time to sow and a time to reap, but there's never a time for seasonal agricultural activities."*
>
> **—Jack Cappon, Associated Press senior writer and writing coach**

In addition to the years of anecdotal experience journalists have, there is also statistical support for the common advice to show rather than just tell. For instance, researchers constructed 10 sentences telling information and 10 showing information. College students were divided into two groups and asked to read one of the groups of sentences. Then they were asked to rate the sentences on such qualities as interesting-dull, clear-unclear and engaging-unengaging. The researchers concluded, "The experiment found strong evidence that, as many experts have implied, show sentences are seen as more interesting and engaging than tell sentences."

Writer Walt Harrington could simply have told readers that detective V.I. Smith picked up his notebook to leave on a call, but instead he showed us the detective's preparation:

> "Well, here we go," says V.I., in his smooth, lyrical baritone as he palms a radio, unconsciously pats his right breast coat pocket for evidence of his ID wallet, pats his left breast coat pocket for evidence of his notebook and heads out the door in his athlete's saunter, a stylized and liquid stroll, a modern cakewalk.

Readers can see and hear V.I. because the writer is showing, not telling.

A student writer used her sense of touch to gather information: "After 40 years of working outside, his skin is as leathery as an alligator's." Did she actually touch the farmer? "Yes," she says. "I kept looking at his skin. Finally, even though I was embarrassed, I asked him if I could touch his face. He laughed. 'You can tell I don't use no fancy lotions, can't you?'"

The writing is better because the reporters didn't just ask questions and record answers. They looked; they listened; they touched. Readers can see and feel along with the reporters.

Use Words Precisely

Words should mean exactly what you intend them to mean. You should never use "uninterested" when you mean "disinterested." Nor should you use "allude" for "refer," "presume" for "assume," "endeavor" for "try," "fewer" for "less," "farther" for "further." If you report that fire destroyed a house, you mean the home needs rebuilding, not repair. If you say firefighters donned oxygen masks to enter a burning building, you are either impugning their intelligence or revealing your ignorance. (Oxygen is dangerous around fire; firefighters use air tanks.) You can make the mayor "say," "declare," "claim" or "growl"—but only one is accurate.

Coherence

When you write coherently, your writing is understandable. Coherence is built by following a logical order, by matching the content to the appropriate sentence structure, by using the correct coordinating conjunctions and by guiding readers with transitions.

Writing a Coherent Story

- Create logical story structures.
- Express the relationship between ideas properly.
- Use language precisely.
- Use transitions.

Decide on the Order of Elements

Chronology is the most easily understood of story structures. You start at the beginning and go to the end. The story that opens this chapter begins 48 hours before the storm hits and continues until the storm passes and the "sun makes a welcome appearance." (For more on story structure, see later in this chapter.) Journalists, however, often don't have the luxury of readers' time or publication space to use chronology. That's why it is important to outline a story, even if your outline merely lists the three or four points you expect to make. Your outline is your map. If you know where you are going, your readers will be able to follow.

Here's a list you might make about what happened at a city council meeting:

1. Approved one-way streets.
2. Raised parking fines.
3. Bought snowplows.
4. Agreed to study downtown parking facilities.
5. Hired audit firm.

To outline the story, first you rank the actions in order of importance. Then you decide whether to focus on one element or to write a summary lead or a multiple-element lead. Once you have done that, you add detail to your outline:

1. Single-element lead: one-way streets
2. Summary of other actions
   a. Parking fines
   b. Snowplows
   c. Parking study
   d. City audit
3. Support for lead
   a. The vote
   b. Jones quote
   c. Opposition

4. Support for other actions (in order introduced in second paragraph)
    a. Parking fines
        (i) Amount; (ii) reason; (iii) no opposition
    b. Snowplows
        (i) Cost; (ii) when delivered
    c. Parking study
        (i) Define problem; (ii) when study is due; (iii) who will do it; (iv) Dehaven quote; (v) Chamber of Commerce request
    d. City audit
        (i) Who will do it; (ii) cost; (iii) when due

Although outlining might take five minutes, it will save you much more time. The outline also creates a structure that flows logically from one idea to the next. Here's how you could start the story outlined above:

> The Springfield City Council voted Tuesday to make four streets in the downtown area one-way.
>
> The council also raised parking fines to $5, voted to buy two snowplows, ordered a study of downtown parking facilities and hired a firm to audit the city.
>
> Effective March 1, the four streets that will be one- way are . . .

Select the Proper Sentence Structure

Within each sentence, you must express the proper relationships between ideas. One way to do this is to think about your sentence structure. Simple sentences express one idea. Compound sentences express two or more ideas of equal importance. Complex sentences subordinate one idea to another. Here are some examples.

Simple	The mayor scolded the council.
Compound	The mayor scolded the council, and she insisted on a vote.

Compound sentences equate two or more ideas without commenting on them. Complex sentences allow you to show sequence and cause and effect, among other things:

Complex	After the mayor scolded the council, she insisted on a vote. (Shows sequence.)
Complex	Because the mayor was angry, she insisted on a vote. (Shows cause and effect.)

Both sentences are correct, but the meaning of each is slightly different.

Use the Precise Conjunction

Subordinating conjunctions—such as "if," "since," "while," "after" and "until"—each carry a different and precise meaning. Choose the subordinating conjunction that expresses the idea you want.

Coordinating conjunctions ("and," "or," "but," "for," "nor," "so," "yet") also require careful selection. Observe how the meaning changes with the conjunction in these examples:

> The mayor insisted that the council vote, and the members ignored her.
>
> The mayor insisted that the council vote, but the members ignored her.

The second example is more coherent because it expresses the council members' reaction more logically.

Use Transitions

Transitions are words, phrases, sentences or paragraphs that show the logical progression of the story structure and the ideas within the structure. Transitions are road signs directing readers through a story. The annotated model "Using Transitions"shows how transitions can be used in a story.

> Mr. and Mrs. Lester Einbender are using their memory to project life as it might have been.
>
> *That memory* centers around a son named Michael, a rheumatic disease called lupus and a desire to honor one while conquering the other.

The use of the word "That" at the beginning of the second paragraph is subtle, but its impact is dramatic. If you wrote "A memory," you would not link the reader to the memory already mentioned. If you wrote "The memory," you would be more specific, but by writing "That memory," you point directly to the memory mentioned in the preceding paragraph. Because "a" is good only for general references, "a" is called an *indefinite modifier*. Because "the" is more specific, "the" is called a *definite modifier*. Because "that" is most specific, it is a *demonstrative adjective*; it demonstrates precisely the word or phrase to which you are referring when you couple it with the noun ("memory"). When you move from indefinite to definite modifier and then to demonstrative adjective, you climb the ladder of coherence.

> *"But I obsess during writing to the point where I can lose sleep over the right word."*
>
> **—Madeleine Blais, writer**

Transitions help you achieve coherence, the logical connection of ideas. They guide you from one sentence to the next, from one paragraph to the next. Writers unfamiliar with transitions merely stack paragraphs, like pieces of wood, atop one another. Transitions keep the story, if not the woodpile, from falling apart.

ANNOTATED MODEL

USING TRANSITIONS

1 On a Monday afternoon, Dr. Glenn Billman pulled back from the autopsy he was performing on a dead girl and stared at the sight before him.

In his seven years at Children's Hospital, he had never seen anything like it. The girl's colon was severely hemorrhaged, ravaged by bacteria that normally lived in a cow's intestine.

Puzzled and quietly alarmed, Billman notified local health officials. It was the first indication that the lethal strain of bacteria E. coli 0157:H7 was on the loose.

2 But Billman didn't make his discovery at Children's Hospital in Seattle. He made it at Children's Hospital in San Diego, and he made it three weeks before the E. coli epidemic struck the Northwest, killing three children and sickening about 500 people.

In December, San Diego was hit by a small E. coli outbreak that killed the 6-year-old girl and made at least seven other people sick.

3 It is now being linked to the Seattle outbreak, but in its early stages, San Diego health officials were slow to recognize the crisis, and they have been sharply criticized for failing to notify the public about the E. coli death and illnesses.

"I really believe we need to be safe and not sorry, and the fact is, a girl died in San Diego," said San Diego County Supervisor Dianne Jacob. "I was outraged. The only way I found out was by reading it in the newspaper" after the Northwest outbreak. 4

When the first Washington cases were reported in mid-January, authorities there immediately queried neighboring states, including California, but were not told about the E. coli death of the San Diego girl. That information would have alerted them about the bacteria's severity and might have pointed them sooner to the source of the contamination.

5 Like the patients here, the San Diego girl had eaten a hamburger at a Jack in the Box restaurant days before she got sick and died. The seven other E. coli patients had all eaten hamburgers at fast-food restaurants, among them Jack in the Box.

6 That information was available in early January, according to Dr. Michele Ginsberg, San Diego County epidemiologist. She would not say how many of the seven patients had eaten at Jack in the Box.

"A variety of restaurants were mentioned," she said. "Naming any one of them would create public reaction and perhaps avoidance of those restaurants."

7 That reticence angers Jacob, the San Diego County supervisor. "I had a follow-up meeting with county health officials, and I have to tell you, very honestly, I was not pleased with their attitude," she said. . . .

1. The first four paragraphs focus on Billman, which makes the story easy to follow. Billman's name or a pronoun links the paragraphs.

2. "But" is a transition that shows the writer is introducing another angle.

3. Time reference used as a transition: "It is now . . ." links the Northwest outbreak to the earlier San Diego outbreak ("In December . . .").

4. Time references ("after the Northwest outbreak" and "When the first . . .") link these paragraphs.

5. The phrase "Like the patients here" links this paragraph to the preceding one.

6. The word "that" is a demonstrative adjective that points to the preceding paragraph.

7. "That" again creates a transition from the preceding paragraph.

Transitions, like road signs, help readers understand where they have been and where they are going.

Repeating a word or phrase also helps to keep the story from falling apart. In the preceding example, the writer used a demonstrative adjective and repeated a word. (Other demonstrative adjectives are "this," "these" and "those.")

Parallelism, repetition of a word or grammatical form, is another way to guide readers through a story. Writers frequently use parallelism to achieve coherence.

Writing about the complicated subject of nuclear-waste disposal in America, Donald Barlett and James Steele, then of *The Philadelphia Inquirer*, relied on parallelism for coherence and emphasis. Notice the parallel use of "They said . . ." to start sentences—and the repeated variations of "It cannot."

> This assessment may prove overly optimistic. For perhaps in no other area of modern technology have so many experts in the government, industry and science been so wrong so many times over so many years as have those involved in radioactive waste.
>
> They said, repeatedly, that radioactive waste could be handled like any other industrial refuse. It cannot.
>
> They said that science had most of the answers, and was on the verge of getting the few it did not have, for dealing with radioactive waste permanently. It did not, and it does not.
>
> They said that some of it could be buried in the ground, like garbage in a landfill, and that it would pose no health hazard because it would never move. It moved.
>
> They said that liquid radioactive waste could be put in storage tanks, and that rigorous safety systems would immediately detect any leaks. The tanks leaked for weeks and no one noticed.

Barlett and Steele's use of parallelism sets up the story. In the following case, the writer repeated the word "waiting" for emphasis:

> Realized or not, we live in constant anticipation. We're always waiting. Waiting to drive. Waiting to turn 21. Waiting for winter break. Waiting to graduate. Waiting for a significant other to come along.

Chronology and references to time provide other ways to tie a story together. Words and phrases such as "now," "since then" and "two days later" are invaluable in helping readers understand where they have been and where they are going. Chronology is important in everything from reports of automobile accidents (which car entered the intersection first?) to recaps of events that occurred over months or even hours, as in the Hurricane Sandy story at the beginning of this chapter.

Conciseness and Simplicity

Conciseness is a virtue, particularly in newspapers and broadcasting where space and time constraints are severe—as well as on Twitter and Facebook feeds. However, even when you write longer online stories, you have to respect readers' time. No one has unlimited time or attention to give you.

Be Concise

Being concise means saying what you need to say in as few words as possible. Some subjects require more details than others. Here are four ways to shorten your stories. (See also the annotated model "Editing for Conciseness".)

1. **Eliminate some subject areas.** Always ask yourself whether all of the subjects need to be included. No doubt, your editor will have a more dispassionate view of what's needed than you will.
2. **Eliminate redundancies.** One way to achieve conciseness is to rid your sentences of cabooses, unneeded words or phrases that hitch themselves, like barnacles, onto other words. Delete the barnacles in italics: remand *back*; gather *together*; consensus *of opinion*; *totally* destroyed; *excess* verbiage; open *up*; fall *down*; my own *personal* favorite; strangled *to death*.
3. **Challenge intensive and qualifying adverbs.** Your job is to select the right word so you don't need two or more. Instead of "really unhappy," perhaps you mean "sad." Instead of "very cold," perhaps you mean "frigid." "Really" and "very" are examples of intensive adverbs. When you say "almost there," you are using a qualifying adverb. You might be near, or you might be a mile away. Be specific.
4. **Train yourself to value brevity.** Some of the most notable writing in history is brief: Lincoln's Gettysburg Address contains 272 words; the Ten Commandments, 297; and the American Declaration of Independence, 300.

You will use fewer words when you figure out what you want to say and then express it positively. Enter the following negatively phrased thicket of verbiage at your own risk:

> The Missouri Gaming Commission has 30 days to appeal a judge's temporary order reversing the commission's decision not to grant a gaming license to a firm that wanted to dock a riverboat casino in Jefferson City.

The writer is lost in a maze of reversals of negative findings. The lead tries to cover too much territory. Express it in the positive and strip it to its essential information:

> The state has 30 days to persuade a judge it should not have to license a firm that wants to open a riverboat casino in Jefferson City.

The writer of this sentence also failed to think clearly:

> Amtrak, formally the National Passenger Railroad Corp., was created in 1970 to preserve declining passenger train service.

Does the writer really mean that Amtrak was created to preserve declining passenger train service?

Writing Clearly

- Keep sentences short.
- Limit each sentence to one idea.
- Favor subject-verb-object sentences.
- Avoid using more than three prepositional phrases in one sentence.
- Avoid using more than three numbers in one sentence.
- Use plain and simple words instead of jargon, journalese, or clichés.

—Paula LaRocque, writing consultant

ANNOTATED MODEL

EDITING FOR CONCISENESS

Bartholow is ~~currently~~ working on other projects, but he has plans to continue ~~with~~ his video game research. ~~In the future~~, he hopes to recruit female subjects—a difficult task because far fewer women than men play violent video games. He's also interested in examining how a person's prior *people's* gaming history affects ~~his or her~~ *their* response to a single exposure to a violent video game.

Pumpkins are everywhere ~~during the fall season~~ *in fall*. They ~~serve as a way to~~ help families and friends ~~to get closer~~ *bond* during the ~~holiday season~~ *holidays*. Whether you're ~~taking a trip~~ *traveling* to the local pumpkin patch ~~to search for the perfect pumpkin~~, or baking ~~up some delicious~~ treats ~~for people to enjoy~~, pumpkins are a ~~strong~~ reminder that comfort isn't ~~too~~ far away.

"Currently" is usually redundant because the verb tense implies it.

Change "has plans" to "plans" to strengthen the verb.

"With" is unnecessary.

"In the future" is already implied in the verb.

The plural form gets around the wordy "his or her."

No information is lost by eliminating "serve as a way to."

"Season" isn't required in either sentence in this paragraph.

"Traveling" says "taking a trip" in one word.

"Strong" and "too" are unnecessary intensifiers.

"Up" is an unnecessary caboose on "baking." Treats are delicious. Whom else do you bake treats for?

To be concise, challenge every word or phrase you write. These examples show how to eliminate 36 of the 127 words. (The replacement words are in italics.)

Keep It Simple

The readers of one newspaper confronted the following one-sentence paragraph:

> "Paradoxically, cancer-causing mutations often result from the repair of a cell by error-prone enzymes and not the 'carcinogenic' substance's damage to the cell," Abe Eisenstark, director of biological sciences at the university, said at a meeting of the Ad Hoc Council of Environmental Carcinogenesis Wednesday night at the Cancer Research Center.

If there is a message in those 53 words, it would take a copy editor, a lexicologist and a Nobel Prize–winning scientist to decipher it. The message simply is not clear. Although the sentence is not typical of newspaper writing, it is not unusual either.

> *"Short is beautiful. Short and simple is more beautiful. Short, simple and interesting is most beautiful."*
>
> **—Don Gibb, educator**

The scientist is using the vocabulary of science, which is inappropriate for a general audience. The reporter should say, "I don't understand that exactly. Can you translate it for my readers?" The response may produce an understandable quote, but if it doesn't, paraphrase the statement and check back with your source to be sure you have paraphrased it accurately.

Too much of what is written is mumbo jumbo. For instance:

> Approximately 2 billion tons of sediment from land erosion enters our nation's waters every year. While industrial waste and sewage treatment plants receive a great deal of attention, according to the Department of Agriculture the No. 1 polluter of our waterways is "non-point" pollution.

The writer of that lead contributed some linguistic pollution of his own. The message may have been clear in his mind, but it is not clear in print. Here's another way to approach this story:

> Soil carried into the water by erosion, not industrial waste or sewage from treatment plants, is the No. 1 polluter of U.S. waterways, according to the Department of Agriculture.

One remedy for unclear writing is the short sentence. The following examples introduce the same subject:

> From measurements with high-precision laser beams bounced off reflectors left at three lunar sites by Apollo astronauts, plus one atop an unmanned Soviet lunar vehicle, scientists believe that the moon is still wobbling from a colossal meteorite impact 800 years ago.
>
> Scientists believe the moon is still wobbling from a colossal meteorite impact 800 years ago.

The writer of the first example drags the reader through some prickly underbrush full of prepositional phrases. The writer of the second has cleared the brush to expose the flowers.

Correct and Effective Language

Writing to be read is not easy. Reporters become writers by the sweat of their brows. John Kenneth Galbraith, a best-selling author who was able to make economics understandable to the lay reader, commented on the difficulty of writing well. "There are days when the result is so bad that no fewer than five revisions are required," he wrote. "In contrast, when I'm inspired, only four revisions are needed."

Trying the techniques discussed in this chapter is the first step. Mastering them will be the result of repeated practice.

Figures of Speech

Good writers understand how to use literary devices known as figures of speech. Similes and metaphors, two common figures of speech, permit writers to show similarities and contrasts. *Similes* show similarities by comparing one thing to another, often using the word "like" or "as." Describing her roommate's reaction to the news that she was moving, one writer said, "She stared into space for a few moments, scowling, *as if she were squaring large numbers in her head*." Writing about a high school girls' basketball coach, Madeleine Blais wrote, "At 6 feet 6 inches, Moyer looms over his players. With a thick cap of graying brown hair and bangs that flop down over his forehead, *he resembles a grizzly bear on spindly legs*."

Metaphor is the first cousin of simile. A simile says one thing is *like* another, but a metaphor says one thing *is* another: "Michael is a lion with gazelle legs." A metaphor is a stronger analogy than a simile. Describing the radio personality and writer Garrison Keillor, a reporter once wrote, "And there he is. A sequoia in a room full of saplings." The metaphor works on two levels. Keillor is tall enough to tower over most others in the room. Because he is known internationally, his work towers over that of others, too.

With similes and metaphors, writers draw word pictures. These techniques turn the pages of a scrapbook of images in each reader's mind.

Careful Word Choice

Freedom in word choice is exhilarating when the result is a well-turned phrase. Here's how one student described the weather in fresh terms: "I rushed off the bus into a downpour of beaming sunlight." Here's Julie Sullivan of *The Spokesman-Review*: "Hand him a soapbox, he'll hand you a homily."

Freedom in word choice is dangerous when it results in nouns masquerading as verbs (*prioritize, impact, maximize*) or jargon masquerading as respectable English (*input, output, throughput*).

Precision, however, means more than knowing the etymology of a word; it means knowing exactly what you want to say. Instead of saying, "The City Council wants to locate the landfill three blocks from downtown," to be precise, you say, "Some members of the City Council . . ." or, better yet, "Five members of the City Council. . . ."

Precision also means using the conditional mood (*could, might, should, would*) when discussing proposals:

Incorrect The bill will make it illegal . . .

Correct The bill would make it illegal . . .

The use of "will" is imprecise because the legislation has not been passed. By using "would," you are saying, "If the legislature passes the bill, it would. . . ."

> *"The real problem is that misplaced modifiers and similar glitches tend to distract readers. Introduce blunders to an otherwise smoothly flowing story and it's as though a drunk stumbled through a religious procession.*
>
> *"What's more, while those errors due to carelessness may not permanently damage the language, they can damage a paper's credibility. Botching a small job sows mistrust about the larger enterprise."*
>
> —Jack Cappon, Associated Press senior writer and writing coach

Bias-Free Language

Even when used innocently, sexist and racist language, besides being offensive and discriminatory, is imprecise. Doctors aren't always "he," nor are nurses always "she." Much of our language assumes people are male unless they are identified as female.

Precise writers avoid "policeman" ("police officer"), "ad man" ("advertising representative"), "assemblyman" ("assembly member") and "postman" ("postal worker"). In some situations, you can use the plural to eliminate the need for a gender-specific word: "Doctors treat their patients."

Check *The AP Stylebook* to see whether to identify a person's race or ethnicity. Then try to follow the person's own preference and be as specific as possible: "Asian-American" is acceptable but "Chinese-American" may be preferable. "Black" is acceptable for any nationality, but use "African-American" only for an American black person of African descent.

Avoiding Carelessness in Word Choice

- Know precisely what you want to say.
- Use the conditional mood ("could," "might," "should," "would") when discussing proposals.
- Choose the correct sentence structure to communicate explicitly what you mean.

Some words, perfectly precise when used correctly, are imprecise when used in the wrong context. "Boy" is not interchangeable with "young man," and "girl" is not interchangeable with "young woman." Not all active retired people are "spry," which implies that the writer is surprised to find that the person is active. "Grandmotherly" fails when you describe people in their 40s who are grandmothers. It also fails when you use it indiscriminately. When Nancy Pelosi became the first female speaker of the U.S. House of Representatives, many accounts identified her as a grandmother. While it is true that she's a grandmother, accounts of new male leaders seldom mention that they are grandfathers. Pelosi's wardrobe also became a subject of stories, something seldom found in accounts of male leaders.

"Dumb," as in "deaf and dumb," is imprecise and derogatory. Instead, use "speech-impaired." When the terms are used in tandem, use "hearing-impaired and speech-impaired" for parallelism. Because alcoholism is a disease, use "recovering alcoholic" instead of "reformed alcoholic." "Handicapped" is imprecise; "disabled" is preferred.

The Associated Press recommends "gay" and "lesbian" and sometimes allows "homosexual" but does not permit "queer" and other derogatory terms. AP suggests consulting the National Lesbian and Gay Journalists Association (www.nlgja.org/Toolbox) for background on this issue. The battle over abortion extends to the terms used in news. One side wants to be described as "pro-life"; the other wants to be described as "pro-choice." The Associated Press prescribes the terms "anti-abortion" and "pro-abortion rights" in an attempt to be neutral.

> *"I once lost a job I dearly wanted because I had misspelled the name of the publisher of the publication I was about to go to work for. Not very smart, but I learned a brutal lesson that has stayed with me."*
>
> **—David Carr,** *New York Times* **columnist**

Some dismiss this concern for language as overly zealous political correctness. That attitude implies that we are afraid to tell the truth. What is the truth about ethnic slang? The truth is that many words historically applied to groups of people were created in ignorance or hate or fear. During the world wars, American citizens of German descent were called "krauts" to depersonalize them. Over the years, pejorative terms have been applied to immigrants from Ireland, Poland, China and Africa. We see the same thing happening to more recent immigrants from Latin America, the Caribbean and the Middle East. The adjective "Muslim" is seldom seen or heard in news reports except to modify "terrorists" or "fundamentalists." As writers concerned with precision of the language, we should deal with people, not stereotypes.

Words are powerful. When used negatively, they define cultures, create second-class citizens and reveal stereotypical thinking. They also change the way people think about and treat others. Writers have the freedom to choose precisely the right word. That freedom can be both exhilarating and dangerous.

Avoiding Sexism in Language

- Use a generic term ("flight attendant," "firefighter").
- Participate in the movement to drop feminine endings. (Use "comedian," "hero," "actor" and "poet" for both genders.)
- Make the subject plural. ("Reporters must not reveal their opinions.")
- Drop the gender-specific pronoun and replace it with an article. ("A reporter must not form *a* judgment.")
- Rewrite to eliminate the gender-specific pronoun. ("A reporter must not judge.")
- Write the sentence in the second person. ("You should not form *your* judgment.")

Correct Grammar and Punctuation

Far too often, grammar and punctuation errors obscure meaning. Consider this example:

> Watching his parents struggle in low-paying jobs, a college education looked desirable to him.

Because the participial phrase ("Watching . . .") is dangling, the sentence seems to mean that the college education did the watching. Write the sentence this way:

> Watching his parents struggle in low-paying jobs, he realized he wanted a college education.

No one who aspires to be a writer will succeed without knowing the rules of grammar. Dangling participles, subject-verb disagreement, pronoun-antecedent disagreement and misplaced modifiers are like enemy troops: They attack sentences and destroy their meaning, as the authors of a survey discovered.

The personnel director of an Inglewood, Calif., aerospace company had to fill out a government survey form that asked, among other things, "How many employees do you have, broken down by sex?" After considering the sentence for a few moments, she wrote, "Liquor is more of a problem with us."

Here are some typical errors and ways to correct them:

Pronoun-antecedent disagreement	Each of the boys brought *their* sleeping bags.
Correct	Each of the boys brought *his* sleeping bag.

Subject-verb disagreement	The *mayor* together with the city council *oppose* collective bargaining by the firefighters.
Correct	The *mayor* together with the city council *opposes* . . .
	The *mayor* and city council *oppose* . . .
Misplaced modifier	*Despite his size*, the coach said Jones would play forward.
Correct	The coach said that Jones, *despite his size*, would play forward.

Improper punctuation creates ambiguities at best and inaccuracies at worst. For instance:

> Giving birth to Cynthia five years earlier had been difficult for Mrs. Davenport and the two parents decided they were content with the family they had.

Without the required comma before "and," the sentence can easily be misunderstood. A person reading quickly misses the pause and sees this: "Giving birth to Cynthia had been difficult for Mrs. Davenport and the two parents." That's a lot of people in the delivery room.

Most newspapers have two or three people who read each story to catch these and other errors. However, the writer's responsibility is to get it right in the first place.

The Tools of Narration

The tools of narration allow you to build interest in stories. When we use scenes, dialogue and anecdotes, we are using narrative tools that help make our stories as entertaining as they are interesting. In exposition, the writer clearly stands between the reader and the information: Journalists have sources, who tell them things. Journalists then tell the reader what they heard and saw. Scenes, dialogue and anecdotes allow the reader to see the action. If you also learn to tease this good stuff with foreshadowing, readers will be more likely to read it. But more about foreshadowing later.

Scenes

"The most important thing to any writing, and especially profile writing, is the telling detail."

—Jacqui Banaszynski, Pulitzer Prize winner

Gene Roberts, former managing editor of *The New York Times,* tells about his first job at a daily newspaper. His publisher, who was blind, had someone read the newspaper to him each morning. One day, the publisher called Roberts into his office and complained, "Roberts, I can't see your stories. Make me see."

We should all try to make readers see, smell, feel, taste and hear. One way to do that is to write using scenes as much as possible. To write a scene, you have to be there. You need to capture the pertinent details. Think of yourself as a playwright, not as a narrator standing on a stage. Leave the stage and let your readers see the action and hear the dialogue. You can see and hear what is happening in the following excerpt. Put yourself in a theater watching the actors on stage:

> She was in her office getting ready to attend a doctoral candidate's prospectus defense when the call came that would turn her life upside down. The surgeon told her she was very sorry, but it was invasive breast cancer.
>
> "Am I going to die?" Carver asked her.
>
> "Well, I certainly hope not," the surgeon said.
>
> She hung up the phone in a daze but refused to go home. Somehow, she managed to get through the defense. Then she went to see her husband, Bill Horner, an MU political science professor. She walked into his office and shut the door. Horner knew before she had uttered a word.

A student reporter at South Dakota State University was on the farm to capture this opening scene:

> Don Sheber's leathery, cracked hands have been sculpted by decades of wresting a living from the earth.
>
> But this year, despite work that often stretches late into the evening, the moisture-starved soil has yielded little for Sheber and his family.
>
> Sheber's hands tugged at the control levers on his John Deere combine last week as rotating blades harvested the thin stands of wheat that have grown to less than a foot high.

The writer allows the reader to visit Sheber on the farm. We can see and feel the farmer's hands. We can touch the John Deere combine and the stunted wheat.

David Bacon/The Image Works

Figure 8-4. "Don Sheber's leathery, cracked hands have been sculpted by decades of wresting a living from the earth." Use descriptive language to paint a vivid picture for readers and to bring a story to life.

To create such scenes, you must use all your senses to gather information, and your notebook should reflect that reporting. Along with the results of interviews, your notebook should bulge with details of sights and smells, sounds and textures. David Finkel, winner of the American Society of News Editors Distinguished Writing Award in 1986 and a Pulitzer Prize in 2006, says, "Anything that pertains to any sense I feel at any moment, I write down." Gather details indiscriminately. Later, you can discard those that are not germane. Because you were there, you can write the scene as if you were writing a play.

Because Bartholomew Sullivan of *The (Memphis) Commercial Appeal* was observing and listening closely at a trial, his readers were able to sit in the courtroom with him:

> Helfrich banged an index finger on the rail of the jury box as he recalled Thursday's testimony in which a string of Bowers's Jones County friends testified that he was a solid businessman, a Christian—"a gentleman." One of the witnesses was Nix, who called Bowers a "real, real nice man."
>
> "They talk of gentlemen," Helfrich whispered. Then, shouting, he said: "These people don't have a gentle bone in their bodies. They were nightriders and henchmen. They attacked a sleeping family and destroyed all they owned."

Analyze the detail: the banging of an index finger, the whisper, the shout. We can see and we can hear. By creating a scene, the writer transported us to the courtroom rather than just telling us what he saw.

Dialogue

The use of *dialogue*—conversation between two or more people, not including the reporter—allows the reporter to recede and the characters to take center stage. When you use quotations, you—the writer—are repeating for the reader what the source said, and the reader listens to you relating what was said. But when you use dialogue, you disappear, and the reader listens directly to the characters. Dialogue is a key element in creating scenes. Compare these examples:

> During the public hearing, Henry Lathrop accused the council of wasting taxpayers' money. "If you don't stop voting for all this spending, I am going to circulate a recall petition and get you all kicked off the council," he said.
>
> Mayor Margorie Gold told Lathrop he was free to do as he wished. "As for us," she said, "we will vote in the best interests of the city."

That is the traditional way of presenting quotations. The reporter uses quotes but also paraphrases some of what was said. That's telling readers instead of taking them to the council chambers and letting them listen. Here is how that account would sound handled as dialogue:

> When Henry Lathrop spoke to the City Council during the public hearing, he pounded on the podium. "You folks are wasting taxpayers' money. If you don't stop voting for all this spending, I am going to circulate a recall petition and get you all kicked off the council."

> Mayor Margorie Gold slammed her gavel on her desk.
>
> "Mr. Lathrop," she said as she tried to control the anger in her voice. She looked at him directly. "You are free to do as you wish. As for us, we will vote in the best interests of the city."

At the hearing, Lathrop and Gold were speaking to each other. The second version captures the exchange without the intercession of the writer.

Here's another example of dialogue. This conversation took place between Cindy Martling, a rehabilitation nurse, and Mary Jo, a patient's wife, after Martling scolded the patient for feeling sorry for himself:

> She wandered around a bit, then saw Mary Jo standing in the hallway. The two women went to each other and embraced. "I'm sorry," Martling said through more tears. "I didn't mean to lose control. I hope I didn't offend you."
>
> "What you did was wonderful," Mary Jo said. "He needed to hear that. Dan is going to work through it, and we're all going to be OK."

Anecdotes

The ultimate treats, **anecdotes** are stories embedded in stories. They can be happy or sad, funny or serious. Whatever their tone, they should illustrate a point. Readers are likely to remember the anecdotes more readily than anything else in a story. You probably remember the stories that your professors tell regardless of whether you remember the rest of the lecture. Long after you've forgotten this chapter, you will probably remember some of the examples from it. Facts inform. Anecdotes inform and entertain.

If history were taught in the form of stories, it would never be forgotten."

—Rudyard Kipling, English writer

"As befits something so valuable, anecdotes are hard to obtain. You can't get them by asking your source, "Got any good anecdotes?" But you can get them by asking for examples so you can re-create the scene. To do this, be alert to the possibilities that an anecdote might be lurking in the details. One reporter gathered this quote:

> "We had one of those coaching nights where we sat up until I don't know when trying to figure it out," Richardson says. "We refer to that as the red-letter day in Spartan football, and since that day, we are 33-15, with three district titles and a conference championship."

The editor pointed out to the reporter that if it was a red-letter day, the reporter should have asked more questions about that coaching meeting. He did, and he ended up with an anecdote about how the coaches figured out a new strategy that turned out to be successful.

Here's another example. Your source says: "Darren is like a one-man entertainment committee. He's always got something going on. And if nothing is going on, he'll hike up his pants really high and dance to the Jonas Brothers."

To turn this dry quote into an anecdote, you need to ask, "Can you give me an example of when he acted like an entertainment committee?" or "Tell me about the time he danced to the Jonas Brothers."

Some anecdotes come from phrasing questions in the superlative: "What's the funniest thing that ever happened to you while you were standing in front of an audience?" "What's the worst case you've ever seen come into this emergency room?" "People tell me Rodney is always the first one they call when they need help on a project. Has he ever helped you? Can you give me an example?"

When leading bankers were summoned to the Treasury Department to discuss the financial meltdown, journalists were not allowed in the meeting. Yet some were able to reconstruct the scene inside. Here's an anecdote set in a scene:

> **Drama Behind a $250 Billion Banking Deal**
>
> By Mark Landler and Eric Dash
>
> WASHINGTON—The chief executives of the nine largest banks in the United States trooped into a gilded conference room at the Treasury Department at 3 p.m. Monday. To their astonishment, they were each handed a one-page document that said they agreed to sell shares to the government, then Treasury Secretary Henry M. Paulson Jr. said they must sign it before they left.
>
> The chairman of JPMorgan Chase, Jamie Dimon, was receptive, saying he thought the deal looked pretty good once he ran the numbers through his head. The chairman of Wells Fargo, Richard M. Kovacevich, protested strongly that, unlike his New York rivals, his bank was not in trouble because of investments in exotic mortgages, and did not need a bailout, according to people briefed on the meeting.
>
> But by 6:30, all nine chief executives had signed—setting in motion the largest government intervention in the American banking system since the Depression and retreating from the rescue plan Mr. Paulson had fought so hard to get through Congress only two weeks earlier.

Use anecdotes to entertain while you are informing. If the relevance of the anecdote to the larger story isn't obvious, tell in the transition into the anecdote or at the end of it.

Foreshadowing

Foreshadowing is the technique of giving hints about what's coming. Moviemakers tease you with the scenes they think will encourage you to buy a ticket. Broadcasters use foreshadowing to keep you from leaving during a commercial: "Coming up, there's a burglar prowling your neighborhood." Every lead foreshadows the story. The leads that not only tell but promise more good stuff to come are the most successful. Tom Koetting, then of *The Wichita Eagle*, spent nine months observing the recovery of a doctor who had nearly lost his life in a farm accident. He produced a story of about 100,000 words. The simple lead promised great things to come: "Daniel Calliendo Jr. had not expected to meet death this calmly."

A student at Florida A&M University used the same technique to invite readers to continue reading the story:

> A North Carolina family thought the worst was behind them when they were robbed Saturday morning at a gas station just off Interstate 95.

The worst was yet to come.

The worst was yet to come. That's another way of saying, "Read on; the story gets even better."

In the next example, the long opening is packed with promises of great things to come:

> Deena Borman's relationship with her roommate, Teresa, during her freshman year in college had shattered long before the wine bottle.
>
> Weeks had gone by with Teresa drawing further and further away from Deena. Finally, after repeatedly hearing Teresa talk about suicide, Deena says, "I kept telling her how silly she was to want to die."
>
> That made Teresa angry, so she threw a full wine bottle at Deena. It shattered against the wall and broke open the simmering conflict between them. That was when Deena tried to find out what had gone wrong with Teresa's life, and that was when Teresa told Deena that she wanted to do something to get rid of her.
>
> And that was when Deena began to be scared of her own roommate.

The writer is promising a great story. What is wrong with Teresa? Does Teresa really try to hurt Deena? Does Deena really have something to be scared about? There is a promise of great things to come. Would you keep reading?

Moving Your Story Along

- Create vivid scenes.
- Let the actors speak to one another through dialogue. (When the source tells the reporter who tells the reader, you have a *quotation*. When the reporter records the conversation of two or more people speaking not to the reporter but to one another, you have *dialogue*.)
- Relate memorable anecdotes.
- Foreshadow important events.

Suggested Readings

Hart, Jack. *A Writer's Coach: The Complete Guide to Writing Strategies That Work*. New York: Pantheon, 2006. This guide helps you understand the "how" and "why" of sentence, paragraph and story construction.

Kramer, Mark, and Wendy Call, eds. *Telling True Stories*. New York: Plume, 2007. This book offers the collected wisdom of many writers, gathered in short bits. You can jump around easily to pick out applicable bits of advice.

Osborn, Patricia. *How Grammar Works: A Self-Teaching Guide*. New York: John Wiley and Sons, 1999. This book will do for you what it promises: It will guide you, step by step, through the basics of English grammar. Its goal is to make you feel comfortable with grammar and the way words work.

Strunk, William, and E.B. White. *The Elements of Style*. 3rd ed. Boston: Allyn and Bacon, 1995. This little book practices what it preaches. For the beginner, it is a good primer; for the pro, it is a good review of writing rules and word meanings.

Tankard, James, and Laura Hendrickson. "Specificity, Imagery in Writing: Testing the Effects of 'Show, Don't Tell.'" *Newspaper Research Journal* (Winter/Spring 1996): 35–48. The authors found that participants in a test said that examples of "show" writing were more interesting and believable.

Suggested Websites

www.papyr.com/hypertextbooks/comp1/coherent.htm
Daniel Kies of the Department of English at the College of DuPage explains how to achieve coherence in your writing.

www.nieman.harvard.edu/narrative/home.aspx
The Nieman Foundation at Harvard has a "Narrative Digest" site that offers narrative stories and, often, interviews with writers.

www.nj.com/news/index.ssf/2012/11/48_hours_before_during_and_aft.html#
Go to this website to see the full version of the hurricane story that opens this chapter.

Exercises

1. **Team project.** Your instructor will divide the class into three groups. On the Internet, find at least three versions of the same news event written on the same day. Each group should compare the sentence lengths. Look for transitions. Find figures of speech and analogies. Which, in your opinion, is the most readable? The least readable? Why?

2. **Journalism blog.** In the following paragraph from earlier in this chapter, identify the concrete details and the similes. Evaluate what they add to your understanding of the scene. Then list and evaluate the verbs. Write a blog post about your analysis of the paragraph.

> Boyd is in his truck with Fire Chief James Samarelli, who is at the wheel. They turn right onto Sampson Avenue and are nearly hit by a wooden lifeguard boat slicing through the floodwater. A wall of water is headed directly for them, bringing a second lifeguard boat. Samarelli jerks the truck to the right. A large piece of the boardwalk, ripped away by the waves, slams into the front of the flatbed truck. Boyd looks down at his suddenly cold feet. Seawater is rushing into the cab and a 6-foot-tall swell lifts the truck and begins pushing it sideways, into a telephone pole.

3. Choose precisely the right word:
   a. We need to (ensure, insure) a victory.
   b. Stop (annoying, irritating) your friend.
   c. The attorney won because she (refuted, responded to) the allegations.
   d. The prisoner was able to produce (mitigating, militating) evidence.
4. Rewrite Barlett and Steele's story on nuclear-waste disposal (p. 426) to take out the parallelism. Which version, the original or yours, is better? Why?
5. Punctuate the following sentences:
   a. Government officials have come under a newly enacted censorship system and several foreign speakers have been denied permission to enter the country.
   b. It was a Monday night and for the next two days he teetered between life and death.
   c. The council approved the manager's proposals and rejected a tax increase.
6. Use a simile to explain the following numbers:

   > The student council's budget is $350,000. The university has 19,000 students. The local city budget is $3 million. The city has 70,000 residents.

7. Calculate the readability levels of a couple of paragraphs you have written and stories from *The New York Times* and the Associated Press. Compare the readability scores, and account for scoring differences and similarities. You can get the calculation at www.standards-schmandards.com/exhibits/rix.

Alternatives to the Inverted Pyramid

In this section you will learn:

1. How to construct a chronology.
2. How to construct a news narrative story.
3. How to construct a focus structure story.
4. How to deliver information in service journalism formats.

Newspapers, magazines and websites publish some stories that are not suited for the inverted pyramid structure. Here's the opening to a story written as if it were a novel, except that it is all true.

Ill-Fated Train Ride Tears Indian Boy from Mother, Sparks 25-Year Worldwide Hunt for Home

By Kristen Gelineau and Ravi Nessman

KHANDWA, India—Saroo's eyes snapped open and everything was suddenly, horribly, wrong.

The 5-year-old's tiny body was still curled up on the hard wooden seat of the Indian train, just as it was when he'd drifted off to sleep. The rattle of the train was loud and steady, just as it always was when he rode home with his big brother, Guddu.

But Guddu was not there. And the alien landscape flashing past the window looked nothing like home.

Saroo's heart began to pound. The train car was empty. His brother should have been there, sweeping under the seats for loose change. Where was Guddu?

Where was Saroo?

It was 1987 and Saroo knew only that he was alone on the train.

Soon, he would find himself alone in the world. He wouldn't know for decades that this fateful train ride was setting into motion a chain of events both fantastic and horrific—events that would tear him away from his family and join him with a new one. Events that would spark the determined hunt of a mother for her son and a son for his mother, brought together only to realize that you can never really go home again.

In the beginning, though, all Saroo knew was that nothing was as it should be. "MA!" he screamed, wild with fear as he ran up and down the empty compartment, tears streaming down his face. "GUDDU!"

Only the relentless hum of the train answered his cries. Outside the window, the remains of his old life had faded into the distance. The train was thundering down the track toward a destination—and a destiny—unknown.

Fatima Munshi was frantic. When she returned to her cramped house after a hard day of work on a construction site, her two young sons still hadn't arrived. They should have been back hours earlier.

Fatima lived for her children. She had little else to live for. . . .

When night fell and her boys still weren't home, Fatima panicked. She took a neighbor she called Uncle Akbar to the station to look for them, but most

> of the trains had already come and gone. They searched the nearby market where the boys would beg. She went to the fountain where they liked to play.
>
> By morning, her body felt like it was on fire. Her mind raced.
>
> Maybe they had been kidnapped.
>
> Maybe they were lost.
>
> Maybe they were dead.
>
> She had never been on a train before, but she and Uncle Akbar rode to Burhanpur and Bhusawal, asking police if they had seen her sons. She widened her search to bigger and further cities.
>
> She cried and prayed for their safe return at the holy crypt of the Sufi Muslim saint Tekri Wale Baba. She approached another mystic said to channel the dead saint's spirit.
>
> "There are no longer two flowers," he said. "One flower has fallen, the other has gone to a far off place. He doesn't remember where he is from. He will come back, but only after a long, long time."
>
> She didn't believe him. Her boys were going to be fine.
>
> Then she ran into a police officer she knew.
>
> Guddu was dead, he said.
>
> The boy had either fallen off the train or been pushed. Police took photos of the mangled but still identifiable body found by the tracks, and then cremated him.
>
> Fatima fainted.

AP writers Gelineau and Nessman used chronology to reconstruct the story of a young boy's separation from his family and his search, which ended successfully 25 years later. Earlier you learned how to rank information from most important to least important. That inverted pyramid structure serves news, particularly breaking news, well. Other structures support other types of stories better. Like the standard formula for telling fairy tales, chronology works best when characters encounter complications in bringing the story to a resolution. Writers focus on the people involved in issues to tell important stories—health care, cancer research, prayer in schools—in an interesting and informative way.

If time, detail and space are available, consider the alternative structures we describe in this chapter and summarize in Table 8-1 and Table 8-2. Whether you are writing about a car accident, the Boy Scouts' jamboree or the campaign for student government president, writing the story will be easier if you know how to use some of the alternative story forms: the chronology, news narrative, focus structure and service journalism formats.

Chronology

Stories that work best as a chronology are those that have complications or tension and a resolution worth waiting for. Saroo Brierley was separated from his family. That's a complication. Fortunately, he ended up in an orphanage, was adopted by a family in Australia and grew up healthy and educated. But there was another complication. Brierley wondered about his family in India. So the next complication is how to find his family when he didn't know his Indian name or the city in which he lived. That part of the story reaches a resolution when he returns to India and finds his mother.

Complications are present even in events like meetings. When a city council faces a contentious issue, such as a proposed smoking ban in public places, you are presented with controversy (supporters and opponents testifying), tension (weighing health and economic interests) and a resolution (the vote). Time constraints and tradition often dictate an inverted pyramid structure. But you have other options:

- You could summarize the vote in a sidebar and use chronology to tell the story of the meeting.
- You could write an inverted pyramid version of the story for both the website and the newspaper and then write a chronological version for the Web to replace the earlier version.
- You might use news narrative (see the next section) to report the results and then move to chronology.

Where to Start

Oddly enough, when you use chronology, you don't have to begin at the beginning. Instead, you look for a key moment you can use in the lead to engage readers. To get started, writers often jot down a timeline. In the case of the council meeting, it might look like this:

7:00 p.m.	Opponents and supporters of the smoking ban begin testifying before the council.
	Jones, an opponent, angrily denounces the proposal.
	Smith, a supporter, relates a story about her cancer.
8:15	Council members begin debate.
	Mayor pounds the gavel to break up an out-of-control argument between two council members.
	Council member Rodriguez is nearly in tears as he urges the council to pass the ordinance.
	Council member Jackson says merchants will face financial ruin.
8:47	Solinski, a member of the audience, interrupts the debate and is escorted out of the chambers by city police. Several in the audience boo, but some cheer.
9:10	During a recess, no council members mingle with the public, which irritates several of those who are attending.
9:30	The council votes 5-4 in favor of the smoking ban. There are both jeers and cheers.

A Sample Outline

You could begin at the beginning of the timeline given above, with the chamber filling with members of the public, but this lead would not attract attention. You need a dramatic scene that captures emotion, is short and does not give away the outcome. The removal of a member of the audience has potential; so does the heated argument within the council.

Table 8-1. Different structures are useful for different types of news stories.

New Story Structures		
	Inverted Pyramid	**Chronology**
What is it?	The lead paragraphs have the most important information, and succeeding paragraphs give details in descending order of importance.	Starting at a particular point of interest, the paragraphs tell a story in chronological order.
When should it be used?	It's best used for hard news, where timeliness is essential and the reader wants to know the important facts right away.	It's good for reporting a detailed sequence of events in a story with controversy or tension and resolution, especially as a follow-up to a news story.
How is it structured?	**Traditional news lead** • Give who, what, when, where, why and how. • Frame the story.	**Narrative lead** • Describe a dramatic point in the story. • Create narrative suspense with foreshadowing.
	Body: support paragraphs in descending order of importance • Give additional details about the lead. • Summarize other significant actions or elements relevant to the lead. • Give the impact or effect of the event. • Give the "so what"—the story's importance to the reader. • Give background and history. • Describe relevant physical details. • Narrate relevant sequences of events. • Use quotations from relevant sources. • Give sources of additional information, including links to websites.	**Nut paragraph** Give the theme of the story. **Body: narrative support paragraphs** • Use foreshadowing. • Pick up story with a transition back to the beginning of the narrative. • Tell the story in chronological order, highlighting key events found in the timeline. • Describe relevant physical details. • Use narrative techniques like dialogue, flashback and foreshadowing.
	Ending • End with the least significant information, not with a conclusion, summary or tie-back to the beginning. The story can be cut from the bottom up without compromising its effectiveness.	**Ending** • Give a conclusion to the story. • Resolve the tension or conflict in the story.

Table 8-2.

New Story Structures		
	News Narrative	**Focus Structue**
What is it?	The story combines elements of inverted pyramid and chronology formats, with an emphasis on either news or narrative.	The story follows one individual as a representative of a larger group.
When should it be used?	It's useful for stories where timeliness is somewhat important, but the hard news element is not prominent.	It's useful for making complex or abstract stories meaningful to readers.
How is it structured?	**Narrative lead** • Open with an interesting scene or twist that teases the story. or **Traditional news lead** • Give who, what, when, where, why and how. **Support paragraphs** • Briefly add whatever helps the reader understand the story summarized in the lead. **Body: narrative support paragraphs** • Go back to the beginning, and tell the story in chronological order. **Ending** • Give a conclusion to the story. • Resolve the tension or conflict in the story.	**Narrative lead** • Introduce the subject and describe the person's problem. **Transition** • Create a bridge from the subject to the theme of the story. **Nut paragraph** • Give the theme of the story. **Support paragraphs** • Foreshadow. • Give the "so what"—the story's importance to the reader. • Give the "to be sure"—opposing perspectives. **Body: narrative and expository support paragraphs** • Interweave narrative about the subject with facts about the theme to tell the story. **Ending** • Conclude the story, with a summary or with a tie-back that refers to the beginning of the story.

Here is a typical outline for a story using chronology:

1. The lead (the scene with Rodriguez).
2. The nut (theme) paragraph.
3. Foreshadowing.
4. A transition back to the beginning of the meeting to pick up the story from that point.
5. The body, highlighting key events found in the timeline. (As with any news story, much of the action is left out; this is a news story, not a secretary's report.)
6. An ending that highlights the vote and the audience reaction.

The Nut Paragraph, Foreshadowing and the "To Be Sure"

Like the lead in an inverted pyramid story, a **nut paragraph** (or *nut graf*) is a paragraph that gives the theme of the story and summarizes the key facts. Unlike the lead in the inverted pyramid format, however, the nut paragraph is not the first paragraph in the story. For the council story, after the first (or lead) paragraph describing the scene with Rodriguez, the nut paragraph might look like this:

> In a meeting filled with emotional, sometimes angry testimony, citizens and the City Council debated the proposed smoking ban for nearly three hours. Citizens urged—sometimes threatened—council members. The mayor pounded his gavel to bring the council to order several times when some members engaged in heated, personal arguments. In the end, council members voted on the landmark legislation amid jeers and cheers and then left through a back door.
>
> From the beginning, it was clear that emotions were running high. . . .

The nut paragraph both defines the story and foreshadows the heated debate. Even though readers will know the results, many will want to read the blow-by-blow account. It also establishes the "so what": This is a divisive issue, involving landmark legislation, that people care about. Notice that the last line, "From the beginning . . . ," creates a transition back to the start of the story narrative.

In the story that opened this chapter, the nut paragraph and foreshadowing start in paragraph 5:

> Where was Saroo?
>
> It was 1987 and Saroo knew only that he was alone on the train.
>
> Soon, he would find himself alone in the world. He wouldn't know for decades that this fateful train ride was setting into motion a chain of events both fantastic and horrific—events that would tear him away from his family and join him with a new one. Events that would spark the determined hunt of a mother for her son and a son for his mother, brought together only to realize that you can never really go home again.

In some stories, you might also need to include a **"to be sure" paragraph**. This paragraph, which gives opposing points of view, is a must when you are focusing on one side of an issue. Before the council vote, you could do a story about a restaurant shift from the perspective of a server. You could follow that with a story from the perspective of a smoker at a bar. In both cases, you would include a paragraph acknowledging that others disagree, especially if that opposing viewpoint is not included elsewhere in the story. For instance:

> Not everyone agrees with Megan Addison that smoking should be banned. Others, including smokers and business owners, believe that the proposal infringes on their right to smoke or to run their business as they please. But Addison and her fellow servers at the Sports Grill want to work in a smoke-free environment.

You do not need a "to be sure" paragraph in the council meeting story because all sides are represented in the debate.

The Ending

Stories written chronologically need strong endings. After the tearful reunion with his family, Saroo Brierley returned to Australia, where he had another family, a girlfriend and a job. His Indian mother wanted him to live in India. The resolution is not a simple, happy ending. Instead, both parties accept the separation reluctantly:

> Saroo doesn't want to overthink it. He wants to revel in the joy of their remarkable reunion. For him, it has been a miracle punctuated by a happy ending.
>
> "It's sort of taken a weight off my shoulders," he says. "Instead of going to bed at night and thinking, 'How is my family? Are they still alive?' I know in my head now I can let those questions rest."
>
> He hopes to visit India once or twice a year, but he cannot move back. He has other responsibilities, other family and a whole other life in Tasmania.
>
> He is Australian now.
>
> "This is where I live," he says. "When I come back, whether it's sooner or later, then we can start building our relationship again."
>
> Fatima is confused and frustrated.
>
> She doesn't want him to move back here, where there is nothing. But she wants to be with him. Maybe she can move to Australia, she says. She adds sternly that she would ban all girlfriends from his house.
>
> A few minutes later she softens. She couldn't really move away from her life here to an unfamiliar place where no one can talk with her, she says.
>
> At least, and at last, Saroo's return has brought her "mental peace," she says. She tries to understand that he has new parents, new expectations and a new life a world away.
>
> She just wants him to see her once in a while, to call her occasionally, even if they can only speak a few sentences to each other.
>
> "For the moment," she says, "it's enough for me that I went to him. And he called me Amma."
>
> Mother.

For both the hypothetical council story and the real story of the reunion, readers want to know the outcome of the narrative. In the council story, how did the meeting end? How heated was it? The reunion story was framed through the eyes of Saroo, searching for his mother, and Fatima, searching for her son. Readers read a chronology to the end because they want to know the conclusion of the story.

News Narrative

Earlier in this chapter you saw examples of inverted pyramid stories that didn't have the news in the first paragraph (see "The 'You' Lead" and "Leads with Flair") but as soon as the writer teased the reader, the news lead appeared. Then the writer arranged the rest of the story in the traditional descending order of importance. Further modification, though, offers writers more choices. The **news narrative** structure combines the inverted pyramid and chronology. Here is an outline of its basic elements:

1. An opening with an interesting scene or twist that teases the story.
2. A traditional news lead.
3. Brief paragraphs that add whatever help readers need to understand the story summarized in the traditional lead.
4. A transition back to the beginning to tell the story in chronological order.

The "news" in "news narrative" implies that the story has a time element and that the story is not a feature. **Features**, sometimes called "soft stories," are those that can run nearly any time, such as a profile of a stamp collector, a story on a volunteer at the local food bank or an article about riding with a police officer for a shift. A story with a time element usually has to be tweeted, posted on the Web and published in the next issue of the newspaper. The "narrative" in "news narrative" means that you can use chronology, one of the most important tools of narrative writing. In the news narrative, you will often find other narrative tools, such as those discussed earlier: scenes, dialogue, anecdotes and foreshadowing.

News Narrative with News Emphasis

When the local sheriff's department broke an unusual burglary ring, Jane Meinhardt of the *St. Petersburg (Fla.) Times* elected to use the news narrative structure. In the annotated model "News Narrative with News Emphasis," you can read her story, which follows the outline above. Notice that the story is a news narrative with news emphasis. This format works well for news that is significant but not earth-shattering. You probably wouldn't use it to report during the first few hours or perhaps even the first couple of days after a major news event like a mass shooting. You need to be able to get all the details of how something happened to relate the chronology. Immediately following a disaster or other major event, the authorities don't have all the information, and the reporter might not have access to witnesses or documents.

1. The opening paragraphs set the scene with information that informs and is interesting.

2. A traditional news lead gives "who," "what" and "when."

3. The writer supports the lead with a quote.

4. The story continues with the breaking news for the next four paragraphs.

5. Now that the news has been established, instead of continuing to present the information in order of importance, the writer presents the rest of the story in chronological fashion. Note the important transition from inverted pyramid to chronology: "The burglary ring unraveled Tuesday, Tita said."

6. The story ends with a quote rather than a tie-back or summary.

In news narratives with a news emphasis, the writer needs to establish the facts before giving the chronology. This format is associated with breaking news of significance, such as crime.

In news narratives with a narrative emphasis, less space is devoted to the news, and more narrative techniques are used than in the inverted pyramid format. These types of narratives use fewer quotes and save important information for a strong ending.

Source: Jane Meinhardt, "Mother Accused of Being Criminal Ringleader," *St. Petersburg Times*, Oct. 21, 1994.

ANNOTATED MODEL

NEWS NARRATIVE WITH NEWS EMPHASIS

1

PALM HARBOR—They carried knapsacks and bags to tote loot. They had a screwdriver to pry open doors and windows.

They used latex gloves.

They acted like professional criminals, but officials say they were teenage burglars coached and directed by a Palm Harbor woman whose son and daughter were part of her gang.

2 Pinellas County Sheriff's deputies arrested Rovana Sipe, two of her children and two other teens Wednesday after a series of home burglaries.

"She was the driver," said Sheriff's Sgt. Greg Tita. "She pointed out the houses. She's the one who said 'Do these.'" 3

4 Sipe, 38, of 2333 State Road 584, was charged with two counts of being a principal in burglary. She was held Thursday in lieu of $20,000 bail.

Her daughter, Jackie Shifflet, 16, was charged with grand theft. Her son, Ryan Shifflet, 15, was charged with two counts of burglary.

Charles Ruhe, 17, of 1600 Ensley Ave., in Safety Harbor, and Charles Taylor, 16, of 348 Jeru Blvd. in Tarpon Springs, also were held on four counts of burglary each.

"They were very well-prepared to do burglaries, especially with the guidance they were given," Tita said. "We recovered thousands of dollars of stolen items. Anything that could be carried out, was."

5 The burglary ring unraveled Tuesday, Tita said. A Palm Harbor woman saw a large, yellow car driven by a woman drop off three boys, he said. The three went to the back of her house.

They put on gloves and started to pry open a window with a screwdriver, she said. When she tapped on a window, they ran.

She called 911. As she waited for deputies, other neighbors saw the boys walk through a nearby neighborhood carrying bags.

Deputies chased the boys and caught two. The third got into a large yellow car driven by a woman.

The bags contained jewelry, a shotgun and other items deputies say were taken from another house in the neighborhood.

Tita said the boys, later identified as Taylor and Ruhe, told detectives about other burglaries in Dunedin and Clearwater and who else was involved.

At Sipe's house, detectives found stolen VCRs, televisions, camcorders and other valuables. They arrested the other two teens and Sipe.

6 "We're very familiar with this family and its criminal history," Tita said. "We have found stolen property at the house in the past and made juvenile arrests.

News Narrative with Narrative Emphasis

When the news is less important, the news narrative structure is also useful, but the emphasis is on narrative rather than news. John Tully, a reporter for the *Columbia Missourian*, was asked to look for a story at a horse-riding competition one Sunday afternoon. Because most of the competitors were not from the newspaper's local area, reporting the results of the competition was not as important as finding a good story.

Tully knew nothing about horse-riding competitions, so he first found people who could explain the judging. He also asked people to suggest interesting competitors. A youth coordinator told him that Cara Walker was competing for the first time since her accident. After gathering more information from the coordinator, Tully found Walker and her mother—and a story that lent itself to news narrative. Through Tully's story (see the annotated model "News Narrative with News Emphasis"), readers learned that Walker, who had been seriously injured in a car accident, was able to recover enough to ride again. What they didn't find out until the end was that she won the competition. Because he had less news to report, Tully was able to go to the chronological format more quickly than Meinhardt. He used the outcome of the competition to reward readers who completed the story.

Focus Structure

For centuries, writers have used the focus structure to tell the story of an individual or a group that represents a bigger population. This approach allows the writer to make large institutions, complex issues and seven-digit numbers meaningful. Not many of us can understand—let alone explain—the marketing system for wheat, but we could more easily do so if we followed a crop of wheat from the time it was planted until a consumer bought a loaf of bread.

Applying the Focus Structure

- Focus on the individual.
- Transition to the larger issue.
- Report on the larger issue.
- Return to the opening focus.

The Wall Street Journal knew that not many of us would be attracted to a story about the interaction between pesticides and prescription drugs. That's why a reporter focused on one person to tell a story of pesticide poisoning:

> Thomas Latimer used to be a vigorous, athletic man, a successful petroleum engineer with a bright future.
>
> Then he mowed the lawn.

Does this opening make you want to read on?

In a quip attributed to him, the Soviet dictator Josef Stalin summed up the impact of focusing on a part of the whole: "A single death is a tragedy; a million deaths is a statistic." Think about that the next time you hear that a plane crash killed 300 people. Some events, such as mass shootings or earthquakes, are horrific enough to attract attention in and of themselves. However, when readers have digested the news, you can reach them again by creating a narrative told through the eyes of participants.

1. The first two paragraphs reveal the news of the injury and the twist that even though doctors were unsure, she recovered enough to compete. The horse show is the news event that generated the story. Note that the second paragraph reveals that she competed but only foreshadows how she did.

2. "Last July" is the transition to chronology after the news lead.

3. Note that there are no quotes to break the narrative flow. "My spurs got caught on the bar under my seat" and "She first started walking, and going to the mailbox wore her out" (paragraph 8) are paraphrased to stay in storytelling mode.

4. This background helps establish that she isn't just any rider and that she had more to lose in this accident than most riders.

5. The story has a surprise ending, which is possible in a chronology. In a straight news story, this would have been the lead.

In news narratives with a narrative emphasis, less space is devoted to the news, and more narrative techniques are used than in the inverted pyramid format. These types of narratives use fewer quotes and save important information for a strong ending.

Source: John Tully, "Horse Power," *Missourian*, Nov. 27, 2006.

ANNOTATED MODEL

NEWS NARRATIVE WITH NARRATIVE EMPHASIS

1 About five months ago, Cara Walker, 17, was lying in a hospital recovering from the spinal injury she received when she lost control of her car, rolled the vehicle and was thrown halfway through the side window.

Doctors weren't sure she would ever ride again. On Sunday, in a remarkable turnaround, Walker competed in the Midway Fall Classic Quarter Horse Show at the Midway Expo Center. The results were surprising.

2 Last July, Walker, a junior at Rock Bridge High School, was taking a lunch break from riding in preparation for the Fort Worth Invitational, where she qualified in five events. Driving with three passengers on a back road near Moberly, she rolled her car at 50 mph where the paved road turned to gravel without warning. Walker was the only one not wearing a seat belt. Her head and upper body smashed through the side window.

3 Fortunately, she was still in her riding boots. Her spurs got caught on the bar under the seat, which Walker says may have saved her life.

At the time of the accident, Walker was nationally ranked in the trail-riding event.

Doctors fused her neck in surgery. During the next couple of weeks, she was able to shed her full upper-body cast. Walker returned home to her parents and twin sisters two days after surgery, but her mother, Jane Walker, said doctors told her to stay away from her sport for a few months until she healed.

4 For Walker, the top all-around youth rider in Missouri and the president of the American Quarter Horse Youth Association, the four months following the accident was her first time away from riding.

After returning home she worked to regain strength and mobility from the accident that initially left her right side paralyzed. She walked short distances. Going to the mailbox at the end of the driveway wore her out, her mother recalls.

5 Walker had to work almost every muscle in her body back into shape. After the accident, the family brought her 10-year-old quarter horse to their barn in Columbia. That motivated Walker to at first walk to the barn and then to start caring for the horse and eventually ride again.

Sunday, the rehabilitation was complete. With ramrod posture and strict horse control, she won first place in the horsemanship class.

Writing the Lead

Issues like health care, budget deficits and sexual harassment don't have much emotional appeal in the abstract. You make them relevant if you discuss the issue by focusing on someone affected by it. For instance, the college student who wrote the following story spoke to Karen Elliott, who willingly told her story to help others with the same disease. The key word is "story." You write articles about diseases; you write stories about people. The lead paragraphs focus on one person in an anecdote that shows her as a character we can relate to:

> Karen Elliott, 44, remembers the phone call from Dr. Jonathen Roberts, a general surgeon, as if it had happened yesterday. Dr. Roberts' nurse called one afternoon two years ago and told Karen to hold the line. She froze. She had just had a biopsy on her right breast because of a new lump. It's never good news when the doctor calls at home. Dr. Roberts cut to the chase.
>
> "You have atypical hyperplasia," he said.
>
> Being a nurse, Karen knew exactly what he meant. No number of breast self-exams could have detected this. Atypical hyperplasia is a life-long condition characterized by abnormal cells. Affecting only 4 percent of the female population, it puts Karen and others at an increased risk for breast cancer. With her family history of the disease, her risk of breast cancer jumps sky-high.

Reporters working on local stories have just as many opportunities to apply this approach as those writing national and international stories. For example, instead of keeping score on the United Way fund drive, focus on the people who will benefit— or will fail to benefit—from the campaign. If the streets in your city jar your teeth when you drive, write about the problem from the point of view of a driver. If a disease is killing the trees in your city, concentrate on a homeowner who has lost several. The focus structure offers the writer a powerful method of reducing institutions, statistics and cosmic issues to a level that readers can relate to and understand.

Advertising agencies use the technique, too. That's why instead of being solicited for money to help the poor and starving, you are asked to support one child for only pennies a day. The technique gives poverty and hunger a face. A starving population is an abstraction; one starving child is a tragedy.

Writing the Setup

Once you've completed the opening, you must finish the setup to the story. The **setup** consists of the transition to the nut paragraph, foreshadowing, the "so what" and the "to be sure." Let's look at each of these elements.

The Transition and the Nut Paragraph

When you open with a scene or an anecdote, you must construct a transition that explicitly makes the connection to the nut, or theme, paragraph. "Explicitly" is the key word. If you fail to help readers understand the point of the opening, however interesting it is, you risk losing them. The transition in this example is in italics:

> Anita Poore hit the rough pavement of the parking lot with a thud. She had never felt such intense, stabbing pain and could barely lift her heavy head. When she reached for the car door, a police officer stared at her and asked her husband, "Is she drunk?" A wave of nausea swept over her, and she vomited.
>
> "That's it. Get her out of here!" the officer demanded.
>
> Poore was not drunk. She avoided jail, but she faces a life sentence of pain.
>
> Now 25, she has suffered migraine headaches since she was in seventh grade.
>
> *Not that it is much comfort, but she's not alone.* Health officials estimate that Americans miss 157 million workdays a year because of migraines and spend more than $2 million a year on over-the-counter painkillers for migraine, tension and cluster headaches. Researchers haven't found a cure, but they have found methods to lessen the pain.

The italicized transition explicitly places Anita Poore among those who miss work, buy painkillers and are waiting for a cure. The material that follows the transition is the theme.

Let's return to the story of Karen Elliott, who was diagnosed with atypical hyperplasia. Here is the nut paragraph, the part of the story that states the theme:

> What Karen didn't know was that her pleasant life in New Bloomfield would become a roller coaster of ups and downs for the next two years, a ride that nearly destroyed her. Her husband of 19 years, Bob, and their two children, Bethany, 6, and Jordan, 8, could only watch as she struggled with the decision of whether to voluntarily have her breasts removed because Karen, and only Karen, could make that choice.

This is where the writer tells readers what the story is about—in this case, Karen's struggle with her decision. There are many other themes the writer could have pursued.

The nut paragraph, says Jacqui Banaszynski, Pulitzer Prize-winning writer, "is like a secret decoder ring—it lets the hapless reader know what your story is about and why they should read it." When you have involved the reader and successfully written the explicit transition to the nut paragraph, you are ready to build the rest of the setup.

Foreshadowing

Foreshadowing can be done in a single line: "The killing started early and ended late." Or you can foreshadow events over several paragraphs. The goal is to assure readers they will be rewarded if they continue reading.

This is what Erik Larson of *The Wall Street Journal* promised readers of his fire investigation story:

> And so began what may well be the most intensive scientific investigation in the history of arson—not a whodunit, exactly, but a whatdunit. So far the inquiry has taken Seattle investigators places arson squads don't typically go, even to the Navy's weapons-testing grounds at China Lake in California. Along the way, the investigation has attracted a team of scientists who, likewise ensnared by the "Twilight Zone" nature of the mystery, volunteered time and equipment. At one point the investigators themselves torched a large building just to test a suspected fuel.

The "So What"

The "so what" tells readers explicitly why they should care. Thomas Latimer was poisoned when he mowed his lawn. Karen Elliott has to decide whether to have surgery. Anita Poore almost got arrested for having a migraine headache. Interesting, but so what? Reporters and editors know the "so what" or they wouldn't spend time on the story. Too often, however, they fail to tell it to readers. Latimer's story is interesting, but it's much more important because the writer added the "so what" (in italics):

> The makers of the pesticide, diazinon, and of Tagamet firmly deny that their products had anything to do with Mr. Latimer's condition. The pesticide maker says he doesn't even believe he was exposed to its product. And in fact, Mr. Latimer lost a lawsuit he filed against the companies. *Even so, the case intrigues scientists and regulators because it illustrates the need for better understanding of the complex interactions between such everyday chemicals as pesticides and prescription drugs.*
>
> *Neither the Food and Drug Administration nor the Environmental Protection Agency conducts routine tests for such interactions. Indeed, the EPA doesn't even evaluate the synergy of two or more pesticides commonly used together. "We have not developed ways to test any of that," says an EPA spokesman. "We don't know how to do it." And a new congressional report says the FDA lacks both the resources and the enforcement powers to protect Americans from all kinds of poisons.*

The "so what" is the impact—the relevance—for people who have no warning that pesticides and prescription drugs may interact to poison them.

In other cases, the "so what" may be included in the theme statement. Let's look at the migraine story again:

> [1] Not that it is much comfort, but she's not alone.
>
> [2] Health officials estimate that Americans miss 157 million workdays a year because of migraines and spend more than $2 million a year on over-the-counter painkillers for migraine, tension and cluster headaches.
>
> [3] Researchers haven't found a cure, but they have found methods to lessen the pain.

Sentence 1 is the transition. Sentence 2 is the "so what." The reporter is writing about Anita Poore, but the problem is widespread. Sentence 3 is the theme, which includes foreshadowing. The search for a cure, and the intermediate discovery of ways to lessen the pain, will be the focus of the story. The "so what" establishes the dimensions of the problem. When you define the "so what," you are establishing the story's impact.

Types of Journalistic Writing	
News Writing	**Feature (Soft News) Writing**
• News stories emphasize facts and current events. • Timeliness is especially important. • Typical news stories cover government, politics, international events, disasters, crime, important breakthroughs in science and medicine, and sports.	• Feature stories go into depth about a generally newsworthy situation or person. • Timeliness is relevant but not critical. • Typical feature stories are profiles, day-in-the-life stories, how-to stories, and background stories.

The "To Be Sure"

To maintain an evenhanded approach, writers must acknowledge that there are two or more sides to a story. We call this the "to be sure," as in "to be sure, there are other opinions." We've seen in the pesticide story that the drug and pesticide makers "firmly deny that their products had anything to do with Mr. Latimer's condition." We see the technique again in an article about the impact of gambling on Tunica, Miss. Writer Jenny Deam opens with a scene in the mayor's store. The mayor says gambling is the best thing that ever happened to the town. At the front counter, a woman is asking for the $85 back she paid on furniture last week because she lost her grocery money gambling. What comes next is a combination theme and "to be sure" statement, highlighted in italics:

> And so is the paradox of this tiny Mississippi Delta county, now that the casinos have come to call.
>
> On the one hand, unemployment in a place the Rev. Jesse Jackson once called "America's Ethiopia" has dropped from nearly 24 percent to a low last fall of 5 percent. Anyone who wants a job has one with the casinos. There are more jobs than people to fill them. In a county of about 8,100 people, the number of food stamp recipients fell from 4,218 before the casinos to 2,907 now.
>
> *But there is another side. New problems never before seen.*
>
> Since the first casino opened in 1992, the number of DUI arrests has skyrocketed by 400 percent. U.S. Highway 61 leading to Memphis is constantly jammed. On a busy weekend as many as 28,000 cars head toward the nine casinos now open. The criminal court system is just as overloaded. In 1992, there were 1,500 cases filed. A year later, 2,400. As of last month there had already been 6,800 cases filed for this year.

> "Well," says the mayor, "it's just like anything else in life: You got to take the evil with the good."

The story of Tunica's economic rebirth had been told before. This story focused on the problems that inevitably follow gambling. To be sure, there are benefits, but this story also examined the costs.

Now that you have constructed the setup, you are ready to enter the body of the story.

On THE JOB

Tips for Writing

Wright Thompson, a senior writer at *ESPN The Magazine*, concentrates on long-form stories built around characters, complications and resolutions in both print and television documentaries. This is how he describes his approach:

In his book *Writing for Story*, Jon Franklin details the most important element in storytelling: conflict and resolution. Every story has characters, is laced through with a strong sense of place, and the character faces a challenge that reveals something. That's such a standard definition that now that I've typed it, I'm sure it's stolen from somewhere. It's that essential and universal. There must be conflict, and there must be resolution. So how do you turn the theory of characters facing challenges into an actual story?

For me, it's through religious and detailed outlining, whether you're doing a 10,000-word profile for print or an hourlong documentary for television. Stories are all about arc, and when there are multiple and supportive arcs in a story, it has more muscle and driving force. So when you're outlining, make sure you see that your story moves with determined but steady pace. Figure out the micro arc of chronology, and the macro arc of understanding. We go from, say, Monday to Tuesday, or 1980 to 2012, while we are also going from nothing to something, mystery to knowledge, light to dark.

Remember to ask a question in the beginning that is answered at the end. Use scenes as the engine of a story. Use backstory as the mechanism to give the action meaning, not as the story itself. Remember, the facts are the tool for the job, not the job itself.

When I'm outlining, thinking about these principles of asking a question and answering it, and about scenes, I start by reading through the notes with a pen and a highlighter. I do this once or twice. Then I transfer these notes to note cards, laying them out so I can see them visually, and see the story start to take shape. I read and reread the cards. Then when I know where everything goes, I begin to write, hopefully without notes. I want to know the story, know the scenes and the characters and the setting, know the conflict and the resolution, and just relax and tell a story.

Writing the Body

Think of readers as people antsy to do something else. To maintain their interest, offer them frequent examples to support your main points. Use anecdotes, scenes and dialogue to move the story line. Mix *exposition* (the facts) with narration (the story line). Let's return to Karen Elliott, who just learned that she has atypical hyperplasia. The writer, Tina Smithers, has been dealing in exposition for a few paragraphs, so she shares an anecdote set in the following scene to keep the readers' interest:

> Karen was walking downstairs to get the beach ball out of the summer box for Bethany's Hawaiian swim party at Kindercare. Suddenly, Karen fainted and fell down the stairs. She knew she had broken something. Coming to, she blindly made her way upstairs and lay on the bed.
>
> "The cat was staring me in the eyes," she mumbled as Bob, fresh from the shower, grabbed ice and a pillow.
>
> Karen noticed Bethany crying in the doorway. At this point, Karen realized she had been shouting, "Call 9-1-1! Call 9-1-1!" She didn't want her daughter to see her lose control. She quieted down and told Bethany to come to her bed.
>
> "It's okay, honey. Mommy broke her arm, but they'll be over soon to fix it." Later, in the ambulance, one of the paramedics tried to cut off her yellow Tommy Hilfiger sweater.
>
> "It's brand new," Karen shouted. "Can't you pull it off?"
>
> They gave one small yank, and Karen immediately changed her mind. Every bump along the way was agonizing. Karen pleaded for more morphine. Her wrist, it turned out, was broken in 20 places.

Writing the Ending

As in the chronology structure, you need a strong ending in the focus structure. The difference is that in chronology, you end with the resolution or outcome. In the focus structure, one device is the **tie-back**, a reference to something that appears at or near the beginning of the story. Here is the lead from a *Wall Street Journal* story:

> ETHEL, Mo.—Kristin Gall can't look at an old tractor without wondering about the lives it's rolled through. "There's a story behind every one if you can find it," says the 36-year-old farmer. In 2000, he began trying to track down one that belonged to his late grandfather.
>
> By then, Leonard Gall had been dead for 11 years and the tractor had been gone from the family for nearly twice that long. But Kristin Gall's memories were stirred after he stumbled across a tattered notebook in which his grandfather had jotted down the vehicle's serial number, along with the dates of each oil change.

Ending the Story

- Use anecdotes, dialogue, scenes and good quotes to end the story.
- Be sure the ending wraps up the whole story, not just the last section of the story.

The story goes on to detail Gall's successful search. It even mentions, high in the story, that his grandfather sometimes bought his grandchildren pedal-driven toy tractors. The story ends with this tie-back to the lead and that anecdote:

> Mr. Gall's hopes are clearer. Aiming to keep his grandfather's tractor in the family for at least one more generation, he revived a tradition his grandfather started: He bought his toddler son a pedal-driven 1206 for Christmas this year.

The goal in the focus structure is to summarize the theme of the story or tie back to the top of the story. Anecdotes, dialogue, scenes and good quotes can all end the story. Don't just stop writing; construct an ending.

Service Journalism

One of the criteria for news is usefulness. Many, if not most, magazines you find on the racks appeal to readers by presenting information they might find useful. More than that, they attempt to present this useful information in the most usable way. This approach to presenting information has been called **service journalism**. You often see it labeled "news you can use." One way to think of this is "refrigerator journalism," information presented in such a way that people can cut it out and put it on their refrigerator or bulletin board. (See Figure 8-5, pages 460–461.)

Service Journalism

In today's digital world, in-a-hurry readers want practical information presented in the most efficient and effective way.

What this means is that you must think not just of a message—the words. You also must think of how those words will appear on the page or screen—the presentation.

Basics

Service journalism is:

- **Useful.** You must inform people, but if you also find ways to demonstrate how your audience can use the information, you will be more successful. Emphasize WIIFM: "What's in it for me?" See how often you can get "you" in the first sentence of your copy.

- **Usable.** Whenever you can, make a list. Lists get more attention and are better understood and more easily retained. You don't have to write sentences. "Tips" is a magical word.

- **Used.** People stop paying attention to information they never use. You should be able to prove that your audience acts on information. To get people to respond, promise them something. Offer a prize; give them something free.

• *Refrigerator Journalism* •

10 tips to serve audiences today

1. Save them time.
2. Help them make more money, save money or get something free.
3. Address different levels of news interest.
4. Address niche audiences more effectively.
5. Become more personally useful.
6. Make information more immediately usable.
7. Become more accessible. Give people your name, phone number, fax number, Web address and email address.
8. Become easier to use. Learn to layer the news, use cross-references and links, put things in the same place, color-code, tell people where to find things, use page numbers on contents blurbs, use glossaries and show readers where to find more information.
9. Make effective use of visuals and graphics. Use photos, videos, slide presentations, interactive graphics, maps, cartoons, comics and other visuals.
10. Become more engaging and interactive. Use contests, quizzes, crosswords, games. People remember better if they do something. Give awards to those who send in answers. Give a coffee mug to the person with the best tip or post of the month.

Refrigerator journalism—giving people printouts they can post in a handy place — invites access and participation.

Other Devices of Service Journalism

1. **Use blurbs.** After a title and before the article begins, write a summary/contents/benefit blurb. David Ogilvy says no one will read the small type without knowing the benefit upfront. Use the same benefit blurb in a table of contents or menu or briefs column. The best word in a benefit blurb is "how." How to, how you, how I do something. Be personal. Use people in your messages. Also, use internal blurbs, little summaries, pull quotes and tips to tease and coax readers into the story.

2. **Use subheads.** Before you write, outline. Put the main points of the outline into the copy. Perhaps a better word than subhead is "entry point." Let readers enter the copy where they find something interesting.

3. **Have a FAQ page or question-and-answer column.** A Q&A format allows readers to skip over things they already know or are not interested in.

4. **Repeat things in different ways for different people.** Don't be afraid to say something in a box or a graphic that you have said elsewhere. Reinforcing a message aids retention.

5. **Think more visually.** Include pictures and graphics that contain information and are not purely decorative. Remember, being effective and efficient is the only thing that matters. We used to write articles and then look for graphics or photos to enhance the message. Now we put the information in the graphic (where it will get more attention and have more impact) and write a story to enhance the graphic.

"Never be above a gimmick."
—Dave Orman, ARCO

The power of the box

When you can, put some information in a box. Like lists, boxes or sidebars (1) get more attention, (2) increase comprehension, and (3) aid retention. On the Web, these kinds of boxes can be linked from the main story:

1. **A reference box.** "For more information, see, read, call, click . . ."
2. **A note box.** Take notes from your articles as if you were studying for an exam. Give them to your readers to complement your message.
3. **A glossary box.** Put unfamiliar or technical terms in a glossary box. Use color or another graphic treatment to indicate which words are defined. Also, teach your audience how to pronounce difficult words.
4. **A bio box.** When you need to say something about where a person lived, went to school and worked, put this information in a box or on a separate linked Web page so that your main story is not interrupted.

The 4 goals of the service journalist:

In a nutshell

1. Attention
2. Comprehension
3. Retention
4. Action

PR Tip

Newspapers, magazines, newsletters and websites are doing more and more service journalism. "News You Can Use" and "Tips & Tactics" have become familiar heads. Both newspapers and magazines are becoming more visual. Yet most news releases sent out by PR professionals look the same as they did five and 50 years ago. Why not try refrigerator journalism techniques in your next news release, whether it's sent by mail or digitally?

Figure 8-5. Employing the common presentation devices of service journalism, such as boxes and sidebars, this example shows how to highlight information so readers can easily find it and use it.

When Hurricane Sandy combined with a winter storm to hit parts of the East Coast, news media across the region used Twitter to send information about where to get shelter and supplies, posted how-to and where-to-go information on their websites and used service journalism techniques in their print products to help residents cope. The *Star-Gazette* in Elmira, N.Y., was typical in carrying news about help coming from the military and the Red Cross. A box on its front page listed ways readers could donate money and explained how to sign up for text alerts.

A pioneer in service journalism, James Autrey of the Meredith Corp., liked to call service journalism "action journalism." Its goal is to get readers to use the information. Magazine publishers know that people are more likely to resubscribe to a magazine if they do some of the things the magazine suggests they do.

All media produce service journalism. Many newspapers have sections dedicated to travel, food and entertainment. Providing tips on how to save money on travel is service journalism. A recipe is service journalism. Telling people when and where an upcoming event is and how much tickets are is service journalism. Front-page news stories, too, often contain elements of service journalism, even if it's just a box listing a sequence of events or directing readers to more information. Service journalism is even easier to do on the Web. You can provide links to lists, how-to information, time-date-place of events, and relevant websites.

In this textbook, you see examples of service journalism in the marginal elements that list the learning objectives for each chapter or that highlight important points. The techniques of service journalism require that you think about content and presentation even as you are reporting. Ask yourself, "What do readers need so they can act on this information?" The answer might range from a Web address to a phone or fax number to instructions on how to fix a lawnmower or make a loaf of bread. It might include directions on how to travel to a festival or information on where and when to buy tickets. As these examples illustrate, you move from simply talking about something to providing the information the reader needs to act on your story.

Much of the basic service journalism information can be presented as sidebars or lists or boxed material. Figure 8-5 uses common service journalism devices to present more information about this topic.

Suggested Readings

Franklin, Jon. *Writing for Story: Craft Secrets of Dramatic Nonfiction by a Two-Time Pulitzer Prize Winner*. New York: Plume, 1994. If you want to write nonfiction narratives, this book will show you the structure and explain all the elements.

Harrington, Walt, and Mike Sager, eds. *Next Wave: America's New Generation of Great Literary Journalists*. The Sager Group at Smashwords, 2012. E-book. This is a collection of literary journalism written by authors under 40. They are practicing what we describe in this chapter of this textbook.

LaRocque, Paula. *The Book on Writing: The Ultimate Guide to Writing Well*. Oak Park, Ill.: Marion Street Press, 2003. This great book for new writers covers three main topics:

mechanical and structural guidelines; creative elements of storytelling; and grammar, usage and punctuation.

Stewart, James B. *Follow the Story: How to Write Successful Nonfiction.* New York: Touchstone, 1998. Stewart, formerly of *The Wall Street Journal*, won a Pulitzer Prize in 1988 for his reporting on the stock market crash and insider trading. He uses his work to illustrate how to write narration.

Suggested Websites

www.gangrey.com
Gangrey compiles stories primarily written in narrative style, usually using chronology.

www.longreads.com
Longreads offers a selection of stories using the structures described in this chapter.

www.niemanstoryboard.org/2012/07/20/the-aps-kristen-gelineau-ravi-nessman-and-mary-rajkumar-on-the-saroo-brierley-saga
This is an interview with the writers and editor of the story of Saroo Brierley, which opens this chapter. It also contains a link to the complete story.

www.writersandeditors.com
This site offers everything from advice to freelancers to how-to material for writers and editors to great links to related content.

Exercises

1. **Team project.** Your instructor will organize the class into four teams. Each team selects a different story structure to analyze and locates at least three stories using that structure. (The focus structure is often found in *The Wall Street Journal* and *USA Today*, among other publications.) Identify the elements of the setup. Find all the anecdotes. Identify any dialogue. Then discuss the impact of the story. How does the story structure suit, or not suit, the subject? Report your findings to the class.
2. From the first seven paragraphs of the following story, identify:
    a. The nut paragraph
    b. Foreshadowing
    c. How chronology is used

Web Plays Incendiary Role in Ohio High School Rape Case

By Matt Pearce, LATimes.com

The two high school football players accused of rape will get their day in court. The city of Steubenville, Ohio, however, will have to fight some of its battles online, where news of the case began.

It's the story of a horrifying accusation met with small-town side-taking and blown up into a national scandal. Trent Mays and Ma'lik Richmond, both 16,

are accused of raping a drunk and unconscious 16-year-old girl at a party on the night of Aug. 11 while other partygoers tweeted and Instagrammed about the attack.

On Aug. 14, the incident was reported to the Steubenville police, and on Aug. 22, the boys were arrested and charged. As they await trial, their attorneys have asserted their innocence, saying the girl was conscious enough to consent to sex.

The viral nature of the news was not limited to tweets on the night of the incident. The high-profile criminal case spotlighted by social media has put not only the defendants on trial but the culture surrounding them. Some town residents have compared the attention to a public lynching; others have said that without the attention, nothing would have been done.

Steubenville, a city of about 18,000 on the Ohio River, dotes on its Big Red high school sports teams.

A blogger and a native of Steubenville, Alexandria Goddard, was among the first to flag the attack, saving screen shots from social media at the party and using students' names. Others have wondered why more students at the party weren't charged; the county sheriff said investigators interviewed 59 people and decided that only the two boys were responsible.

But the scandal has entangled more than those two. Hacker collective Anonymous recently posted video of youths who were said to be Steubenville High School students and alumni joking about the rape victim. Someone also hacked and defaced a website dedicated to Steubenville High School athletics, drawing scorn and the promise of litigation.

3. **Journalism blog.** Write four to eight paragraphs about how you and your classmates learned to be reporters. Use narrative tools. For instance, re-create a scene from one of your classes. Provide the transition into the body of the story, and then stop. Invite your classmates to comment on your story—how closely does it match their recollection of events?
4. Attend a local school board or city council meeting, and write the story as either news narrative or chronology focusing on a key agenda item.
5. Using a chronology, write about eight paragraphs of a story about some aspect of your experience in your reporting class.
6. Create a news narrative opening for either a story based on your own reporting or an inverted pyramid story that has already been published.
7. Find two examples of service journalism in newspapers or magazines, and analyze them. Find an example of a story that would have benefited from service journalism techniques. Tell what you would have done to make the information more usable for readers.
8. Write the first two pages of a story describing an event in your life. Try to include as many parts of the setup as you can: scenes, dialogue, foreshadowing and the "so what" statement.

Section 3

Mass Communication

Chapter 9
Mass Communication

"Mass Communication" from *Media & Culture*, Tenth Edition, 2016 Update by Richard Campbell, Christopher R. Martin, and Bettina Fabos, pp. 1–35 (Chapter 1).

A Critical Approach

Unlike any national election in recent memory, the 2016 presidential race started with a bang: a political campaign packaged as a reality show. With billionaire businessman Donald Trump taking the early lead in the crowded Republican field, the former host of NBC's *The Apprentice* seemed inoculated from the scrutiny most politicians face when they say things that cause voters to question their sanity, like "The beauty of me is that I'm very rich".[1] In Trump's case, his standing as a reality-show celebrity seemed to elevate, rather than sink, him in the early polls.

One of the appeals of reality TV, of course, is that viewers expect blunt opinions, outrageous actions, and crazy plot twists—and that's exactly what Donald Trump delivered to the 2016 campaign. He criticized other candidates for taking "special interest" money (including from him); he denigrated legal and illegal immigrants, promising to build a wall between the United States and Mexico—and make Mexico pay for it; and he retweeted comments labeling Fox News anchor Megyn Kelly a "bimbo." She had asked him tough questions during the first debate of the season—which, thanks to Trump's celebrity, drew a record twenty-four million viewers.

Particularly disheartening to many of the other Republican presidential candidates was the need to spend money on campaign ads to counter the Trump juggernaut. In response to Trump's critical remarks about him, fellow GOP candidate Jeb Bush had to pay for ads reminding voters that Trump used to be a Democrat. Trump's retort that President Ronald

Reagan also started out as a Democrat, though, cost him nothing; his social media and TV interviews received so much attention that he didn't need to repeat his assertions in paid ads. Instead, his shocking comments about other candidates were picked up and recirculated—for free—by CNN, CBS, Fox News, NBC, the *New York Times*, and the *Wall Street Journal*, among others. at one point early in the campaign, the conservative Media Research Center reported in a study that "Donald Trump [had] received almost three times the network TV news coverage than all the other [sixteen] GOP candidates combined. . . ."[2]

Trump's candidacy demonstrated the power of social media to gain free publicity and cheap access. Recently, office seekers have depended on their parties and outside partisan groups to afford the expensive TV ads campaigning usually requires. Following the *Citizens United v. Federal Election Commission* ruling by the Supreme Court in 2010, election campaigns now benefit from unlimited funds raised by wealthy individuals, corporations, and other groups, causing partisan pundits and concerned citizens alike to fret about rich donors dictating election outcomes.

For the 2016 election cycle, Donald Trump used social media to share his own criticisms of political ads and the "big money" that pays for them, thereby making candidates beholden to special interest groups. Though most media today communicate primarily to niche markets, Trump seemed to offer broad appeal at the time—even Democrats who said they would not vote for him enjoyed watching him make other GOP candidates squirm. So will Trump's TV strategies reshape political campaigning by forging a link with the sensibilities of reality television?

The fate of elections in the end increasingly rests with young voters and a candidate's ability to draw them into the election, which could make the rawness of reality TV enticing to some strategists. In election year cycles, news media often reduce the story of an election to two-dimensional narratives, obscuring or downplaying complex policy issues like climate change, economic recovery, campaign financing, immigration reform, and worldwide terrorism. To his credit, Trump's candid and controversial ideas during the 2016 presidential campaign forced the news media to pay closer attention. In a democracy, we depend on media to provide information to help us make decisions about our leaders. Despite their limitations, the media continue to serve as watchdogs for us over government and business. We must hope they are not too easily distracted by the power of celebrity to generate ratings and readers. As media watchdogs ourselves, we can point a critical lens back at the media and describe, analyze, and interpret news stories, reality TV shows, and political ads, arriving at informed judgments about the media's performance. This textbook offers a map to help us become more *media literate*, critiquing the media not as detached cynics or rabid partisans, but as informed citizens with a stake in the outcome.

So What Exactly Are the Responsibilities of Newspapers and Media in General?

In an age of highly partisan politics, economic and unemployment crises, and upheaval in several Arab nations, how do we demand the highest standards from our media to describe and analyze such complex events and issues—especially at a time when the business models for newspapers and most other media are in such flux? At their best, in all their various forms—from mainstream newspapers and radio talk shows to blogs—the media try to help us understand the events that affect us. But at their worst, the media's appetite for telling and selling stories leads them not only to document tragedy but also to misrepresent or exploit it. Many viewers and critics disapprove of how media, particularly TV and cable, hurtle from one event to another, often dwelling on trivial, celebrity-driven content.

In this part of the book, we examine the history and business of mass media and discuss the media as a central force in shaping our culture and our democracy. We start by examining key concepts and introducing the critical process for investigating media industries and issues. In later chapters, we probe the history and structure of media's major institutions. In the process, we will develop an informed and critical view of the influence these institutions have had on national and global life. The goal is to become media literate—to become critical consumers of mass media institutions and engaged participants who accept part of the responsibility for the shape and direction of media culture. In this chapter, we will:

- Address key ideas, including communication, culture, mass media, and mass communication
- Investigate important periods in communication history: the oral, written, print, electronic, and digital eras
- Examine the development of a mass medium from emergence to convergence
- Learn about how convergence has changed our relationship to media
- Look at the central role of storytelling in media and culture
- Discuss two models for organizing and categorizing culture: a skyscraper and a map
- Trace important cultural values in both modern and postmodern societies
- Study media literacy and the five stages of the critical process: description, analysis, interpretation, evaluation, and engagement

As you read through this chapter, think about your early experiences with the media. Identify a favorite media product from your childhood—a song, book, TV show, or movie. Why was it so important to you? How much of an impact did your early taste in media have on your identity? How has your taste shifted over time? What do your current preferences indicate about your identity now? Do your current media preferences reveal anything about you? For more questions to help you think about the role of media in your life, see "Questioning the Media" in the Chapter Review.

Culture and the Evolution of Mass Communication

One way to understand the impact of the media on our lives is to explore the cultural context in which the media operate. Often, culture is narrowly associated with art, the unique forms of creative expression that give pleasure and set standards about what is true, good, and beautiful. Culture, however, can be viewed more broadly as the ways in which people live and represent themselves at particular historical times. This idea of culture encompasses fashion, sports, literature, architecture, education, religion, and science, as well as mass media.

Krzysztof Dydynski/Getty Images

Figure 9-1. Cultural Values and Ideals are transmitted through the media. Many fashion advertisements show beautiful people using a company's products; such images imply that anyone who buys the products can obtain such ideal beauty. What other societal ideas are portrayed through the media?

Although we can study discrete cultural products, such as novels or songs from various historical periods, culture itself is always changing. It includes a society's art, beliefs, customs, games, technologies, traditions, and institutions. It also encompasses a society's modes of **communication**: the creation and use of symbol systems that convey information and meaning (e.g., languages, Morse code, motion pictures, and one-zero binary computer codes).

Culture is made up of both the products that a society fashions and, perhaps more important, the processes that forge those products and reflect a culture's diverse values. Thus **culture** may be defined as the symbols of expression that individuals, groups, and societies use to make sense of daily life and to articulate their values. According to this definition, when we listen to music, read a book, watch television, or scan the Internet, we are usually not asking "Is this art?" but are instead trying to identify or connect with something or someone. In other words, we are assigning meaning to the song, book, TV program, or Web site. Culture, therefore, is a process that delivers the values of a society through products or other meaning-making forms. The American ideal of "rugged individualism"—depicting heroic characters overcoming villains or corruption, for instance—has been portrayed on television for decades through a tradition of detective stories like HBO's *True Detective* and crime procedurals like CBS's *NCIS*. This ideal has also been a staple in movies and books, and even in political ads.

Culture links individuals to their society by providing both shared and contested values, and the mass media help circulate those values. The **mass media** are the cultural industries—the channels of communication—that produce and distribute songs, novels, TV shows, newspapers, movies, video games, Internet services, and other cultural products to large numbers of people. The historical development of media and communication can be traced through several overlapping phases or eras in which newer forms of technology disrupted and modified older forms—a process that many academics, critics, and media professionals began calling *convergence* with the arrival of the Internet.

These eras, which all still operate to some degree, are oral, written, print, electronic, and digital. The first two eras refer to the communication of tribal or feudal communities and agricultural economies. The last three phases feature the development of **mass communication**: the process of designing cultural messages and stories and delivering them to large and diverse audiences through media channels as old and distinctive as the printed book and as new and converged as the Internet. Hastened by the growth of industry and modern technology, mass communication accompanied the shift of rural populations to urban settings and the rise of a consumer culture.

Oral and Written Eras in Communication

In most early societies, information and knowledge first circulated slowly through oral traditions passed on by poets, teachers, and tribal storytellers. As alphabets and the written word emerged, however, a manuscript—or written—culture began to develop and eventually overshadowed oral communication. Documented and transcribed by philosophers, monks, and stenographers, the manuscript culture served the ruling classes. Working people were generally illiterate, and the economic and educational gap between rulers and the ruled was vast. These eras of oral and written communication developed slowly over many centuries. Although exact time frames are disputed, historians generally consider these eras as part of Western civilization's premodern period, spanning the epoch from roughly 1000 B.C.E. to the beginnings of the Industrial Revolution.

Early tensions between oral and written communication played out among ancient Greek philosophers and writers. Socrates (470–399 B.C.E.), for instance, made his arguments through public conversations and debates. Known as the Socratic method, this dialogue style of communication and inquiry is still used in college classrooms and university law schools. Many philosophers who believed in the superiority of the oral tradition feared that the written word would threaten public discussion. In fact, Socrates' most famous student, Plato (427–347 B.C.E.), sought to banish poets, whom he saw as purveyors of ideas less rigorous than those generated in oral, face-to-face, question-and-answer discussions. These debates foreshadowed similar discussions in our time in which we ask whether TV news, Twitter, or online comment sections cheapen public discussion and discourage face-to-face communication.

The Print Revolution

While paper and block printing developed in China around 100 C.E. and 1045, respectively, what we recognize as modern printing did not emerge until the middle of the fifteenth century. At that time in Germany, Johannes Gutenberg's invention of movable metallic type and the printing press ushered in the modern print era. Printing presses and publications spread rapidly across Europe in the late fifteenth century and early sixteenth century. Early on, the size and expense of books limited them to an audience of wealthy aristocrats, royal families, church leaders, prominent merchants, and powerful politicians. Gradually, printers reduced the size and cost of books, making them available and affordable to more people. Books eventually became the first mass-marketed products in history because of the way the printing press combined three necessary elements.

Scala/Art Resource, NY

Figure 9-2. Early Books Before the invention of the printing press, books were copied by hand in a labor-intensive process. This beautifully illuminated page is from an Italian Bible made in the early fourteenth century.

First, machine duplication replaced the tedious system in which scribes hand-copied texts. Second, duplication could occur rapidly, so large quantities of the same book could be reproduced easily. Third, the faster production of multiple copies brought down the cost of each unit, which made books more affordable to less-affluent people.

Since mass-produced printed materials could spread information and ideas faster and farther than ever before, writers could use print to disseminate views counter to traditional civic doctrine and religious authority—views that paved the way for major social and cultural changes, such as the Protestant Reformation and the rise of modern nationalism. People started to resist traditional clerical authority and also began to think of themselves not merely as members of families, isolated communities, or tribes but as part of a country whose interests were broader than local or regional concerns. While oral and written societies had favored decentralized local governments, the print era supported the ascent of more centralized nation-states.

Eventually, the machine production of mass quantities that had resulted in a lower cost per unit for books became an essential factor in the mass production of other goods, which led to the Industrial Revolution, modern capitalism, and the consumer culture of the twentieth century. With the revolution in industry came the rise of the middle class and an elite business class of owners and managers who acquired the kind of influence formerly held only by the nobility or the clergy. Print media became key tools that commercial and political leaders used to distribute information and maintain social order.

As with the Internet today, however, it was difficult for a single business or political leader, certainly in a democratic society, to gain exclusive control over printing technology (although the king or queen did control printing press licenses in England until the early nineteenth century, and even today, governments in many countries control presses, access to paper, advertising, and distribution channels). Instead, the mass publication of pamphlets, magazines, and books in the United States helped democratize knowledge, and literacy rates rose among the working and middle classes. Industrialization required a more educated workforce, but printed literature and textbooks also encouraged compulsory education, thus promoting literacy and extending learning beyond the world of wealthy upper-class citizens.

Just as the printing press fostered nationalism, it also nourished the ideal of individualism. People came to rely less on their local community and their commercial, religious, and political leaders for guidance. By challenging tribal life, the printing press "fostered the modern idea of individuality," disrupting "the medieval sense of community and integration."[3] In urban and industrial environments, many individuals became cut off from the traditions of rural and small-town life, which had encouraged community cooperation in premodern times. By the mid-nineteenth century, the ideal of individualism affirmed the rise of commerce and increased resistance to government interference in the affairs of self-reliant entrepreneurs. The democratic impulse of individualism became a fundamental value in American society in the nineteenth and twentieth centuries.

The Electronic Era

In Europe and the United States, the impact of industry's rise was enormous: Factories replaced farms as the main centers of work and production. During the 1880s, roughly 80 percent of Americans lived on farms and in small towns; by the 1920s and 1930s, most had moved to urban areas, where new industries and economic opportunities beckoned. The city had overtaken the country as the focal point of national life.

The gradual transformation from an industrial, print-based society to one grounded in the Information Age began with the development of the telegraph in the 1840s. Featuring dot-dash electronic signals, the telegraph made four key contributions to communication. First, it separated communication from transportation, making media messages instantaneous—unencumbered by stagecoaches, ships, or the pony express.[4] Second, the telegraph, in combination with the rise of mass-marketed newspapers, transformed "information into a commodity, a 'thing' that could be bought or sold irrespective of its uses or meaning."[5] By the time of the Civil War, news had become a valuable product. Third, the telegraph made it easier for military, business, and political leaders to coordinate commercial and military operations, especially after the installation of the transatlantic cable in the late 1860s. Fourth, the telegraph led to future technological developments, such as wireless telegraphy (later named radio), the fax machine, and the cell phone, which ironically resulted in the telegraph's demise: In 2006, Western Union telegraph offices sent their final messages.

The rise of film at the turn of the twentieth century and the development of radio in the 1920s were early signals, but the electronic phase of the Information Age really boomed in the 1950s and 1960s with the arrival of television and its dramatic impact on daily life. Then, with the coming of ever more communication gadgetry—personal computers, cable TV, DVDs, DVRs, direct broadcast satellites, cell phones, smartphones, PDAs, and e-mail—the Information Age passed into its digital phase, where old and new media began to converge, thus dramatically changing our relationship to media and culture.

The Digital Era

In **digital communication**, images, texts, and sounds are converted (encoded) into electronic signals (represented as varied combinations of binary numbers—ones and zeros) that are then reassembled (decoded) as a precise reproduction of, say, a TV picture, a magazine article, a song, or a telephone voice. On the Internet, various images, texts, and sounds are all digitally reproduced and transmitted globally.

New technologies, particularly cable television and the Internet, developed so quickly that traditional leaders in communication lost some of their control over information. For example, starting with the 1992 presidential campaign, the network news shows (ABC, CBS, and NBC) began to lose their audiences, first to MTV and CNN, and later to MSNBC, Fox News, Comedy Central, and partisan radio talk shows. By the 2012 national elections, Facebook, Twitter, and other social media sites had become key players in news and politics, especially as information resources for younger generations who had grown up in an online and digital world.

Moreover, e-mail—a digital reinvention of oral culture—has assumed some of the functions of the postal service and is outpacing attempts to control communications beyond national borders. A professor sitting at her desk in Cedar Falls, Iowa, sends e-mail or Skype messages routinely to research scientists in Budapest. Moreover, many repressive and totalitarian regimes have had trouble controlling messages sent out over the borderless Internet, as opposed to hard copy "snail mail."

Oral culture has been further reinvented by the emergence of *social media*—such as Twitter and, in particular, Facebook, which now has nearly one billion users worldwide. Social media allow people from all over the world to have ongoing online conversations, share stories and interests, and generate their own media content. This turn to digital media forms has fundamentally overturned traditional media business models, the ways we engage with and consume media products, and the ways we organize our daily lives around various media choices.

The Linear Model of Mass Communication

The digital era also brought about a shift in the models that media researchers have used over the years to explain how media messages and meanings are constructed and communicated in everyday life. In one of the older and more enduring explanations of how media operate, mass communication has been conceptualized as a linear process of producing and delivering messages to large audiences. **Senders** (authors, producers, and organizations) transmit **messages** (programs, texts, images, sounds, and ads) through a **mass media channel** (newspapers, books, magazines, radio, television, or the Internet) to large groups of **receivers** (readers, viewers, and consumers). In the process, **gatekeepers** (news editors, executive producers, and other media managers) function as message filters. Media gatekeepers make decisions about what messages actually get produced for particular receivers. The process also allows for **feedback**, in which citizens and consumers, if they choose, return messages to senders or gatekeepers through phone calls, e-mail, Web postings, talk shows, or letters to the editor.

But the problem with the linear model is that in reality, media messages—especially in the digital era—do not usually move smoothly from a sender at point A to a receiver at point Z. Words and images are more likely to spill into one another, crisscrossing in the daily media deluge of ads, TV shows, news reports, social media, smartphone apps, and—of course—everyday conversation. Media messages and stories are encoded and sent in written and visual forms, but senders often have very little control over how their intended messages are decoded or whether the messages are ignored or misread by readers and viewers.

A Cultural Model for Understanding Mass Communication

A more contemporary approach to understanding media is through a cultural model. This concept recognizes that individuals bring diverse meanings to messages, given factors and

differences such as gender, age, educational level, ethnicity, and occupation. In this model of mass communication, audiences actively affirm, interpret, refashion, or reject the messages and stories that flow through various media channels. For example, when controversial singer Lady Gaga released her nine-minute music video for the song "Telephone" in 2010, fans and critics had very different interpretations of the video. Some saw Lady Gaga as a cutting-edge artist pushing boundaries and celebrating alternative lifestyles—and the rightful heir to Madonna. Others, however, saw the video as tasteless and cruel, making fun of transsexuals and exploiting women—not to mention celebrating the poisoning of an old boyfriend.

While the linear model may demonstrate how a message gets from a sender to a receiver, the cultural model suggests the complexity of this process and the lack of control that "senders" (such as media executives, moviemakers, writers, news editors, and ad agencies) often have over how audiences receive messages and interpret their intended meanings. Sometimes, producers of media messages seem to be the active creators of communication while audiences are merely passive receptacles. But as the Lady Gaga example illustrates, consumers also shape media messages to fit or support their own values and viewpoints. This phenomenon is known as **selective exposure**: People typically seek messages and produce meanings that correspond to their own cultural beliefs, values, and interests. For example, studies have shown that people with political leanings toward the left or the right tend to seek out blogs or news outlets that reinforce their preexisting views.

The rise of the Internet and social media has also complicated the traditional roles in both the linear and the cultural models of communication. While there are still senders and receivers, the borderless, decentralized, and democratic nature of the Internet means that anyone can become a sender of media messages—whether it's by uploading a video mashup to YouTube or by writing a blog post. The Internet has also largely eliminated the gatekeeper role. Although some governments try to control Internet servers, and some Web sites have restrictions on what can and cannot be posted, for the most part, the Internet allows senders to transmit content without first needing approval from, or editing by, a gatekeeper. For example, some authors who are unable to find a traditional book publisher for their work turn to self-publishing on the Internet. And musicians who don't have deals with major record labels can promote, circulate, and sell their music online.

The Development of Media and Their Role in Our Society

The mass media constitute a wide variety of industries and merchandise, from moving documentary news programs about famines in Africa to shady infomercials about how to retrieve millions of dollars in unclaimed money online. The word *media* is, after all, a Latin plural form of the singular noun *medium*, meaning an intervening substance through which something is conveyed or transmitted. Television, newspapers, music, movies, magazines, books, billboards, radio, broadcast satellites, and the Internet are all part of the media, and they are all quite capable of either producing worthy products or pandering to society's worst desires, prejudices, and stereotypes. Let's begin by looking at how mass media develop, and then at how they work and are interpreted in our society.

The Evolution of Media: From Emergence to Convergence

The development of most mass media is initiated not only by the diligence of inventors, such as Thomas Edison, but also by social, cultural, political, and economic circumstances. For instance, both telegraph and radio evolved as newly industrialized nations sought to expand their military and economic control and to transmit information more rapidly. The Internet is a contemporary response to new concerns: transporting messages and sharing information more rapidly for an increasingly mobile and interconnected global population.

Media innovations typically go through four stages. First is the *emergence*, or *novelty*, *stage*, in which inventors and technicians try to solve a particular problem, such as making pictures move, transmitting messages from ship to shore, or sending mail electronically. Second is the *entrepreneurial stage*, in which inventors and investors determine a practical and marketable use for the new device. For example, early radio relayed messages to and from places where telegraph wires could not go, such as military ships at sea. Part of the Internet also had its roots in the ideas of military leaders, who wanted a communication system that was decentralized and distributed widely enough to survive nuclear war or natural disasters.

The third phase in a medium's development involves a breakthrough to the *mass medium stage*. At this point, businesses figure out how to market the new device or medium as a consumer product. Although the government and the U.S. Navy played a central role in radio's early years, it was commercial entrepreneurs who pioneered radio broadcasting and figured out how to reach millions of people. In the same way, Pentagon and government researchers helped develop early prototypes for the Internet, but commercial interests extended the Internet's global reach and business potential.

Finally, the fourth and newest phase in a medium's evolution is the *convergence stage*. This is the stage in which older media are reconfigured in various forms on newer media. However, this does not mean that these older forms cease to exist. For example, you can still get the *New York Times* in print, but it's also now accessible on laptops and smartphones via the Internet. During this stage, we see the merging of many different media forms onto online platforms, but we also see the fragmenting of large audiences into smaller niche markets. With new technologies allowing access to more media options than ever, mass audiences are morphing into audience subsets that chase particular lifestyles, politics, hobbies, and forms of entertainment.

Media Convergence

Developments in the electronic and digital eras enabled and ushered in this latest stage in the development of media—**convergence**—a term that media critics and analysts use when describing all the changes that have occurred over the past decade, and are still occurring, in media content and within media companies. The term actually has two meanings—one referring to technology and one to business—and describes changes that have a great impact on how media companies are charting a course for the future.

The Dual Roles of Media Convergence

The first definition of media convergence involves the technological merging of content across different media channels—the magazine articles, radio programs, songs, TV shows, video games, and movies now available on the Internet through laptops, tablets, and smartphones.

H. Armstrong Roberts/ClassicStock/Getty Images

© The Toronto Star/ZUMApress.com

Figure 9-3. Media Convergence In the 1950s, television sets— like radios in the 1930s and 1940s—were often encased in decorative wood and sold as stylish furniture that occupied a central place in many American homes. Today, using our computers, we can listen to a radio talk show, watch a movie, or download a favorite song—usually on the go—as older media forms now converge online.

Such technical convergence is not entirely new. For example, in the late 1920s, the Radio Corporation of America (RCA) purchased the Victor Talking Machine Company and introduced machines that could play both radio and recorded music. In the 1950s, this collaboration helped radio survive the emergence of television. Radio lost much of its content to TV and could not afford to hire live bands, so it became more dependent on deejays to play records produced by the music industry. However, contemporary media convergence is much broader than the simple merging of older and newer forms. In fact, the eras of communication are themselves reinvented in this "age of convergence." Oral communication, for example, finds itself reconfigured, in part, in e-mail and social media. And print communication is re-formed in the thousands of newspapers now available online. Also, keep in mind the wonderful ironies of media convergence: The first major digital retailer, Amazon, made its name by selling the world's oldest mass medium—the book—on the world's newest mass medium—the Internet.

A second definition of media convergence—sometimes called **cross platform** by media marketers—describes a business model that involves consolidating various media holdings, such as cable connections, phone services, television transmissions, and Internet access, under one corporate umbrella. The goal is not necessarily to offer consumers more choice in their media options but to better manage resources and maximize profits. For example, a company that owns TV stations, radio outlets, and newspapers in multiple markets—as well as in the same cities—can deploy a reporter or producer to create three or four versions of the same story for various media outlets. So rather than having each radio station, TV station, newspaper, and online news site generate diverse and independent stories about an issue, a media corporation employing the convergence model can use fewer employees to generate multiple versions of the same story.

Media Businesses in a Converged World

The ramifications of media convergence are best revealed in the business strategies of digital age companies like Amazon, Facebook, Apple, and especially Google—the most profitable company of the digital era so far. Google is the Internet's main organizer and aggregator because it finds both "new" and "old" media content—like blogs and newspapers—and delivers that content to vast numbers of online consumers. Google does not produce any of the content, and most consumers who find a news story or magazine article through a Google search pay nothing to the original media content provider or to Google. Instead, as the "middleman," or distributor, Google makes most of its money by selling ads that accompany search results. But not all ads are created equal; as writer and journalism critic James Fallows points out, Google does not necessarily sell ads on the news sites it aggregates: Almost all of the company's money comes from shopping-related searches, rather than from the information searches it is best known for. In fact, Fallows writes that Google, which has certainly done its part in contributing to the decline of newspapers, still has a large stake in seeing newspapers succeed online.[6] Over the last few years, Google has undertaken a number of experiments to help older news media make the transition into the converged world. Google executives believe that since they aren't in the content creation business, they are dependent on news organizations to produce the quality information and journalism that healthy democracies need—and that Google can deliver.

Today's converged media world has broken down the old definitions of distinct media forms like newspapers and television—both now available online and across multiple platforms. And it favors players like Google, whose business model works in a world where customers expect to get their media in multiple places—and often for free. But the challenge ahead in the new, converged world is to resolve who will pay for quality content and how that system will emerge. In the upcoming industry chapters, we take a closer look at how media convergence is affecting each industry in terms of both content production and business strategies.

Media Convergence and Cultural Change

The Internet and social media have led to significant changes in the ways we consume and engage with media culture. In the pre-Internet days (say, back in the late 1980s), most people would watch popular TV shows like *Dallas*, *Cheers*, or *Roseanne* at the time they originally aired. Such scheduling provided common media experiences at specific times within our culture. While we still watch TV shows, we are increasingly likely to do so at our own convenience through Web sites like Hulu and Netflix or DVR/On-Demand options. We are also increasingly making our media choices on the basis of Facebook, YouTube, or Twitter recommendations from friends. Or we upload our own media—from photos of last night's party to homemade videos of our lives, pets, and hobbies—to share with friends instead of watching "mainstream" programming. While these options allow us to connect with friends or family and give us more choices, they also break down shared media experiences in favor of our individual interests and pursuits.

The ability to access many different forms of media in one place is also changing the ways we engage with and consume media. In the past, we read newspapers in print, watched TV on our televisions, and played video games on a console. Today, we are able to do all these things on a computer, tablet, or smartphone, making it easy—and very tempting—to multitask. Media multi-tasking has led to growing media consumption, particularly for young people. A recent Kaiser Family Foundation study found that today's youth—now doing two or more things at once—packed ten hours and forty-five minutes worth of media content into the seven and a half hours they spent daily consuming media.[7] But while we might be consuming more media, are we really engaging with it? And are we really engaging with our friends when we communicate with them by texting or posting on Facebook? Some critics and educators feel that media multitasking means that we are more distracted, that we engage less with each type of media we consume, and that we often pay closer attention to the media we are using than to people immediately in our presence.

However, media multitasking could have other effects. In the past, we would wait until the end of a TV program, if not until the next day, to discuss it with our friends. Now, with the proliferation of social media, and in particular Twitter, we can discuss that program with our friends—and with strangers—as we watch the show. Many TV shows now gauge their popularity with audiences by how many people are "live-tweeting" it and by how many related trending topics they have on Twitter. In fact, commenting on a TV show on social media grew by 194 percent between April 2011 and April 2012.[8] This type of participation could indicate that audiences are in fact engaging more with the media they consume, even though they are multitasking. Some media critics even posit that having more choice actually makes us more engaged media consumers, because we have to actively choose the media we want to consume from the growing list of options.

Stories: The Foundation of Media

The stories that circulate in the media can shape a society's perceptions and attitudes. Throughout the twentieth century and during the recent wars in Afghanistan and Iraq, for instance, courageous professional journalists covered armed conflicts, telling stories that helped the public comprehend the magnitude and tragedy of such events. In the 1950s and 1960s, network television news stories on the Civil Rights movement led to crucial legislation that transformed the way many white people viewed the grievances and aspirations of African Americans. In the late 1960s to early 1970s, the persistent media coverage of the Vietnam War ultimately led to a loss of public support for the war. In the late 1990s, news and tabloid magazine stories about the President Clinton–Monica Lewinsky affair sparked heated debates over private codes of behavior and public abuses of authority. In each of these instances, the stories told through a variety of media outlets played a key role in changing individual awareness, cultural attitudes, and public perception.

While we continue to look to the media for narratives today, the kinds of stories we seek and tell are changing in the digital era. During Hollywood's Golden Age in the 1930s and 1940s, as many as ninety million people each week went to the movies on Saturday to take in a professionally produced double feature and a newsreel about the week's main events. In the 1980s, during TV's Network Era, most of us sat down at night to watch the polished evening news or the scripted sitcoms and dramas written by paid writers and performed by seasoned actors. But in the digital age, where reality TV and social media now seem to dominate storytelling, many of the performances are enacted by "ordinary" people. Audiences are fascinated by the stories of couples finding love, relationships gone bad, and backstabbing friends on shows like the *Real Housewives* series and its predecessors, like *Jersey Shore*. Other reality shows—like *Pawn Stars*, *Deadliest Catch*, and *Duck Dynasty*—give us glimpses into the lives and careers of everyday people, while amateurs entertain us in singing, dancing, and cooking shows like *The Voice*, *So You Think You Can Dance*, and *Top Chef*. While these shows are all professionally produced, the performers are almost all ordinary people (or celebrities and professionals performing alongside amateurs), which is part of the appeal of reality TV—we are better able to relate to the characters, or compare our lives against theirs, because they seem just like us.

Online, many of us are entertaining each other with videos of our pets, Facebook posts about our achievements or relationship issues, photos of a good meal, or tweets about a funny thing that happened at work. This cultural blending of old and new ways of telling stories—told by both professionals and amateurs—is just another form of convergence that has disrupted and altered the media landscape in the digital era. More than ever, ordinary citizens are able to participate in, and have an effect on, the stories being told in the media. For example, when the Russian government took control of Crimea and threatened the borders of other parts of the Ukraine in 2014, many ordinary people caught between allegiances to different nations got their stories out via videos, tweets, social media, and blog posts. They were able to communicate in an online world that was much harder for autocratic leaders to control, and their messages allowed the more traditional media to find and report stories that in another age would not have been told. Our varied media institutions and outlets are basically in the **narrative**—or storytelling—business. Media stories put events in context, helping us to better understand both our daily lives and the larger world. As psychologist Jerome Bruner argues, we are storytelling creatures, and as children we acquire language to tell the stories we have inside us. In his book *Making Stories*, he says, "Stories, finally, provide models of the world."[9] The common denominator, in fact, between our entertainment and information cultures is the narrative. It is the media's main cultural currency—whether it's Michael Jackson's "Thriller" video, a post on a gossip blog, a Fox News "exclusive," a *New York Times* article, a tweet about a bad breakfast, or a funny TV commercial. The point is that the popular narratives of our culture are complex and varied. Roger Rosenblatt, writing in *Time* magazine during the 2000 presidential election, made this observation about the importance of stories: "We are a narrative species. We exist by storytelling—by relating our situations—and the test of our evolution may lie in getting the story right."[10]

The Power of Media Stories in Everyday Life

The earliest debates, at least in Western society, about the impact of cultural narratives on daily life date back to the ancient Greeks. Socrates, himself accused of corrupting young minds, worried that children exposed to popular art forms and stories "without distinction" would "take into their souls teachings that are wholly opposite to those we wish them to be possessed of when they are grown up."[11] He believed art should uplift us from the ordinary routines of our lives. The playwright Euripides, however, believed that art should imitate life, that characters should be "real," and that artistic works should reflect the actual world—even when that reality is sordid.

Figure 9-4. Vietnam War Protests On October 21, 1967, a crowd of 100,000 protesters marched on the Pentagon demanding the end of the Vietnam War. Sadly, violence erupted when some protesters clashed with the U.S. Marshals protecting the Pentagon. However, this iconic image from the same protest appeared in the *Washington Post* the next day and went on to become a symbol for the peaceful ideals behind the protests. When has an image in the media made an event "real" to you?

In *The Republic*, Plato developed the classical view of art: It should aim to instruct and uplift. He worried that some staged performances glorified evil and that common folk watching might not be able to distinguish between art and reality. Aristotle, Plato's student, occupied a middle ground in these debates, arguing that art and stories should provide insight into the human condition but should entertain as well.

The cultural concerns of classical philosophers are still with us. In the early 1900s, for example, newly arrived immigrants to the United States who spoke little English gravitated toward cultural events (such as boxing, vaudeville, and the emerging medium of silent film) whose enjoyment did not depend solely on understanding English. Consequently, these popular events occasionally became a flash point for some groups, including the Daughters of the American Revolution, local politicians, religious leaders, and police vice squads, who not only resented the commercial success of immigrant culture but also feared that these "low" cultural forms would undermine what they saw as traditional American values and interests.

In the United States in the 1950s, the emergence of television and rock and roll generated several points of contention. For instance, the phenomenal popularity of Elvis Presley set the stage for many of today's debates over hip-hop lyrics and television's influence, especially on young people. In 1956 and 1957, Presley made three appearances on the *Ed Sullivan Show*. The public outcry against Presley's "lascivious" hip movements was so great that by the third show the camera operators were instructed to shoot the singer only from the waist up. In some communities, objections to Presley were motivated by class bias and racism.

Many white adults believed that this "poor white trash" singer from Mississippi was spreading rhythm and blues, a "dangerous" form of black popular culture.

Today, with the reach of print, electronic, and digital communications and the amount of time people spend consuming them (see Figure 9-5), mass media play an even more controversial role in society. Many people are critical of the quality of much contemporary culture and are concerned about the overwhelming amount of information now available. Many see popular media culture as unacceptably commercial and sensationalistic. Too many talk shows exploit personal problems for commercial gain, reality shows often glamorize outlandish behavior and dangerous stunts, and television research continues to document a connection between aggression in children and violent entertainment programs or video games. Children, who watch nearly forty thousand TV commercials each year, are particularly vulnerable to marketers selling junk food, toys, and "cool" clothing. Even the computer, once heralded as an educational salvation, has created confusion. Today, when kids announce that they are "on the computer," many parents wonder whether they are writing a term paper, playing a video game, chatting on Facebook, or peering at pornography.

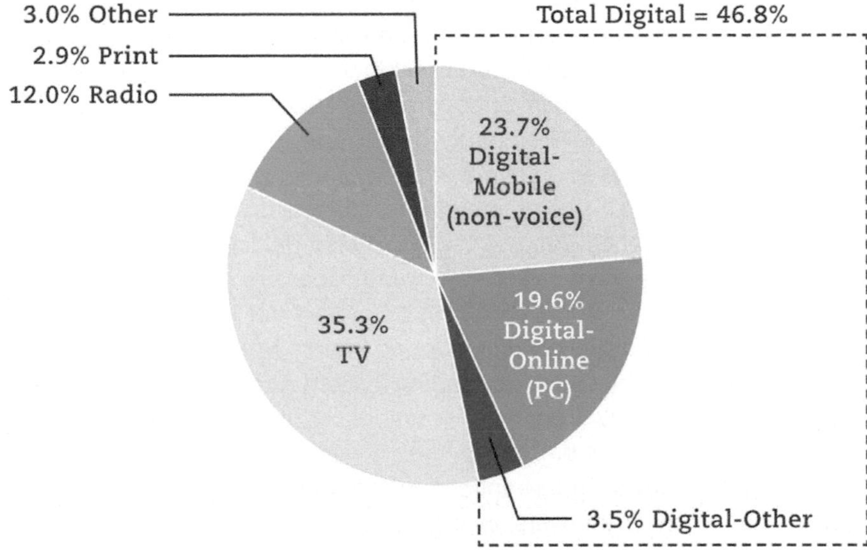

Figure 9-5. Daily Media Consumption by Platform, 2015

Data from: "U.S. Adults' Media Consumption Estimates: Marketing Charts, www.marketingcharts.com/traditional/US-adults-daily-major-media-consumption-estimates-2011-2015-53783

Yet how much the media shape society—and how much they simply respond to existing cultural issues—is still unknown. Although some media depictions may worsen social problems, research has seldom demonstrated that the media directly cause our society's major afflictions. For instance, when a middle-school student shoots a fellow student over designer clothing, should society blame the ad that glamorized clothes and the network that carried the ad? Or are parents, teachers, and religious leaders failing to instill strong moral values? Are economic and social issues involving gun legislation, consumerism, and income disparity at work as well? Even if the clothing manufacturer bears responsibility as

a corporate citizen, did the ad alone bring about the tragedy, or is the ad symptomatic of a larger problem?

With American mass media industries earning more than $200 billion annually, the economic and societal stakes are high. Large portions of media resources now go toward studying audiences, capturing their attention through stories, and taking their consumer dollars. To increase their revenues, media outlets try to influence everything from how people shop to how they vote. Like the air we breathe, the commercially based culture that mass media help create surrounds us. Its impact, like the air, is often taken for granted. But to monitor that culture's "air quality"—to become media literate—we must attend more thoughtfully to diverse media stories that are too often taken for granted. (For further discussion, see Examining Ethics: "Covering War")

Examining **ETHICS**

Covering War

By 2014, the United States withdrew most of its military forces from Afghanistan—from a war that was in its thirteenth year (making it the longest war in U.S. history)—journalistic coverage of Middle East war efforts had declined dramatically. This was partly due to the tendency of news organizations to lose interest in an event when it drags on for a long time and becomes "old news." The news media are often biased in favor of timeliness and "current events." But war reporting also declined because of the financial crisis—more than twenty thousand reporters lost their jobs or took buyouts between 2009 and 2013 as papers cut staff to save money. In fact, most news organizations stopped sending reporters to cover the wars in Iraq and Afghanistan, depending instead on wire service reporters, foreign correspondents from other countries, or major news organizations like the *New York Times* or CNN for their coverage. Despite the decreasing coverage, the news media continue to confront ethical challenges about the best way to cover the wars, including reporting on the deaths of soldiers; documenting drug abuse or the high suicide rate among Iraq and Afghanistan war veterans; dealing with First Amendment issues; and knowing what is appropriate for their audiences to view, read, or hear.

Images of War The photos and images that news outlets choose to show greatly influence their audience members' opinions. In each of the photos below, what message about war is being portrayed? How much freedom do you think news outlets should have in showing potentially controversial scenes from war?

Wissam al-Okaili/AFP/Getty Images

ZUMApress.com

When President Obama took office in 2009, he suspended the previous Bush administration ban on media coverage of soldiers' coffins returning to U.S. soil from the Iraq and Afghanistan wars. First Amendment advocates praised Obama's decision, although after a flurry of news coverage of these arrivals in April 2009, media outlets grew less interested as the wars dragged on. Later, though, the Obama administration upset some of the same First Amendment supporters when it withheld more prisoner and detainee abuse photos from earlier in the wars, citing concerns for the safety of current U.S. troops and fears of further inflaming anti-American opinion. Both issues—one opening up news access and one closing it down—suggest the difficult and often tense relationship between presidential administrations and the news media.

In May 2011, these issues surfaced again when U.S. Navy SEALs killed Osama bin Laden, long credited with perpetrating the 9/11 tragedy. As details of the SEAL operation began to emerge, the Obama administration weighed the appropriateness of releasing photos of bin Laden's body and video of his burial at sea. While some news organizations and First Amendment advocates demanded the release of the photos, the Obama administration ultimately decided against it, saying that the government did not want to spur any further terrorist actions against the United States and its allies.

How much freedom should the news media have to cover a war?

Back in 2006, President George W. Bush criticized the news media for not showing enough "good news" about U.S. efforts to bring democracy to Iraq. Bush's remarks raised ethical questions about the complex relationship between the government and the news media during times of war: How much freedom should the news media have to cover a war? How much control, if any, should the military have over reporting a war? Are there topics that should not be covered?

These kinds of questions have also created ethical quagmires for local TV stations that cover war and its effects on communities where soldiers have been called to duty and then injured or killed. In one extreme case, the nation's largest TV station owner—Sinclair Broadcast Group—would not air the ABC News program *Nightline* in 2004 because it devoted an episode to reading the names of all U.S. soldiers killed in the Iraq War up to that time. Here is an excerpt from a *New York Times* account of that event:

Sinclair Broadcast Group, one of the largest owners of local television stations, will preempt tonight's edition of the ABC News program "Nightline," saying the program's plan to have Ted Koppel [who then anchored the program] read aloud the names of every member of the armed forces killed in action in Iraq was motivated by an antiwar agenda and threatened to undermine American efforts there.

The decision means viewers in eight cities, including St. Louis and Columbus, Ohio, will not see "Nightline." ABC News disputed that the program carried a political message, calling it "an expression of respect which simply seeks to honor those who have laid down their lives for their country."

But Mark Hyman, the vice president of corporate relations for Sinclair, who is also a conservative commentator on the company's newscasts, said tonight's edition of "Nightline" is biased journalism. "Mr. Koppel's reading of the fallen will have no proportionality," he said in a telephone interview, pointing out that the program will ignore other aspects of the war effort.

Mr. Koppel and the producers of "Nightline" said earlier this week that they had no political motivation behind the decision to devote an entire show, expanded to 40 minutes, to reading the names and displaying the photos of those killed. They said they only intended to honor the dead and document what Mr. Koppel called "the human cost" of the war.[1]

Given such a case, how might a local TV news director today—under pressure from the station's manager or owner—formulate guidelines to help negotiate such ethical territory? While most TV news divisions have ethical codes to guide journalists' behavior in certain situations, could ordinary citizens help shape ethical discussions and decisions? Following is a general plan for dealing with an array of ethical dilemmas that media practitioners face and for finding ways in which nonjournalists might participate in this decision-making process.

Arriving at ethical decisions is a particular kind of criticism involving several steps. These include (1) laying out the case; (2) pinpointing the key issues; (3) identifying the parties involved, their intents, and their potentially competing values; (4) studying ethical models and theories; (5) presenting strategies and options; and formulating a decision or policy.[2]

As a test case, let's look at how local TV news directors might establish ethical guidelines for war-related events. By following the six steps above, our goal is to make some ethical decisions and to lay the groundwork for policies that address TV images or photographs—for example, those of protesters, supporters, memorials, or funerals—used in war coverage.

Examining Ethics Activity

As a class or in smaller groups, design policies that address one or more of the issues raised here. Start by researching the topic; find as much information as possible. For example, you can research guidelines that local stations already use by contacting local news directors and TV journalists.

Do the local stations have guidelines? If so, are they adequate? Are there certain types of images they will not show? If the Obama administration had released photographic evidence of bin Laden's death, would a local station have shown it? Finally, if time allows, send the policies you designed to various TV news directors or station managers; ask for their evaluations, and ask whether they would consider implementing the policies.

Surveying the Cultural Landscape

Some cultural phenomena gain wide popular appeal, and others do not. Some appeal to certain age groups or social classes. Some, such as rock and roll, jazz, and classical music, are popular worldwide; other cultural forms, such as Tejano, salsa, and Cajun music, are popular primarily in certain regions or ethnic communities. Certain aspects of culture are considered elite in one place (e.g., opera in the United States) and popular in another (e.g., opera in Italy). Though categories may change over time and from one society to another, two metaphors offer contrasting views about the way culture operates in our daily lives: culture as a hierarchy, represented by a *skyscraper* model, and culture as a process, represented by a *map* model.

Culture as a Skyscraper

Throughout twentieth-century America, critics and audiences perceived culture as a hierarchy with supposedly superior products at the top and inferior ones at the bottom. This can be imagined, in some respects, as a modern skyscraper. In this model, the top floors of the building house **high culture**, such as ballet, the symphony, art museums, and classic literature. The bottom floors—and even the basement—house popular or **low culture**, including such icons as soap operas, rock music, radio shock jocks, and video games (see Figure 9-6). High culture, identified with "good taste" and higher education, and supported by wealthy patrons and corporate donors, is associated with "fine art," which is available primarily in libraries, theaters, and museums. In contrast, low or popular culture is aligned with the "questionable" tastes of the masses, who enjoy the commercial "junk" circulated by the mass media, such as reality TV, celebrity-gossip Web sites, and violent action films. Whether or not we agree with this cultural skyscraper model, the high–low hierarchy often determines or limits the ways we view and discuss culture today.[12] Using this model, critics have developed at least five areas of concern about so-called low culture: the depreciation of fine art, the exploitation of high culture, the disposability of popular culture, the driving out of high culture, and the deadening of our cultural taste buds.

An Inability to Appreciate Fine Art

Some critics claim that popular culture, in the form of contemporary movies, television, and music, distracts students from serious literature and philosophy, thus stunting their imagination and undermining their ability to recognize great art.[13] This critical view pits popular culture against high art, discounting a person's ability to value Bach and the Beatles or Shakespeare and *The Simpsons* concurrently. The assumption is that because popular forms of culture are made for profit, they cannot be experienced as valuable artistic experiences in the same way as more elite art forms, such as classical ballet, Italian opera, modern sculpture, or Renaissance painting—even though many of what we regard as elite art forms today were once supported and even commissioned by wealthy patrons.

A Tendency to Exploit High Culture

Another concern is that popular culture exploits classic works of literature and art. A good example may be Mary Wollstonecraft Shelley's dark Gothic novel *Frankenstein*, written in 1818 and ultimately transformed into multiple popular forms. Today, the tale is best remembered by virtue of two movies: a 1931 film version starring Boris Karloff as the towering and tragic monster, and the 1974 Mel Brooks comedy *Young Frankenstein*. In addition to the many cinematic versions, television turned the tale into *The Munsters*, a mid-1960s situation comedy. The monster was even resurrected as sugarcoated Franken Berry cereal. In the recycled forms of the original story, Shelley's powerful themes about abusing science and judging people on the basis of appearances are often lost or trivialized in favor of a simplistic horror story, a comedy spoof, or a form of junk food.

A Throwaway Ethic

Unlike an Italian opera or a Shakespearean tragedy, many elements of popular culture have a short life span. The average newspaper circulates for about twelve hours, then lands in a recycling bin; a hit song might top the charts for a few weeks at a time; and most new Web sites or blogs are rarely visited and doomed to oblivion. Although endurance does not necessarily denote quality, many critics think that so-called better or higher forms of culture have more staying power. In this argument, lower or popular forms of culture are unstable and fleeting; they follow rather than lead public taste. In the TV industry in the 1960s and 1970s, for example, network executives employed the "least objectionable programming" (or LOP) strategy, which critics said pandered to mediocrity with bland, disposable programs that a "regular" viewer would not find objectionable, challenging, or disturbing.

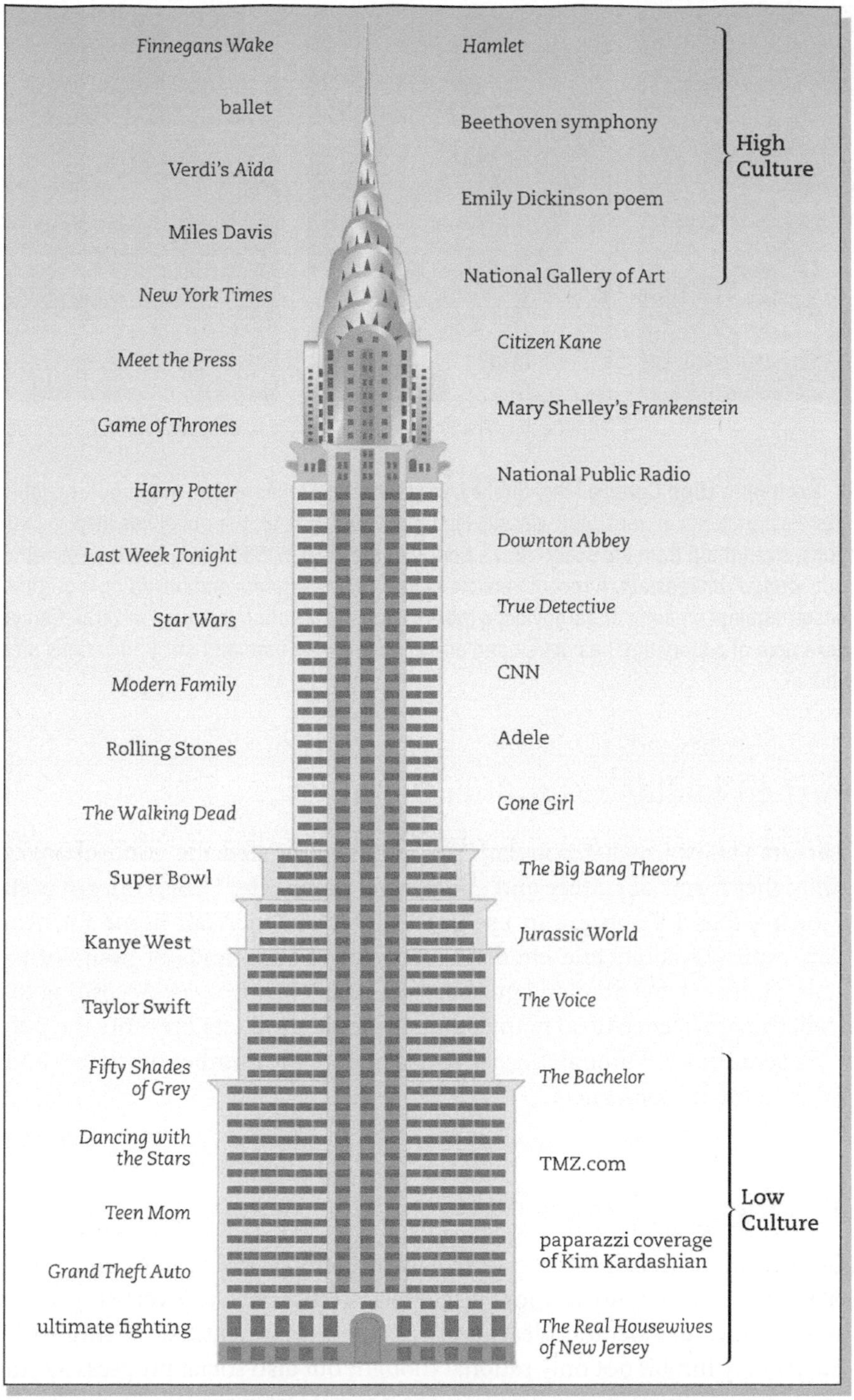

Finnegans Wake
ballet
Verdi's *Aïda*
Miles Davis
New York Times
Meet the Press
Game of Thrones
Harry Potter
Last Week Tonight
Star Wars
Modern Family
Rolling Stones
The Walking Dead
Super Bowl
Kanye West
Taylor Swift
Fifty Shades of Grey
Dancing with the Stars
Teen Mom
Grand Theft Auto
ultimate fighting

Hamlet
Beethoven symphony
Emily Dickinson poem
National Gallery of Art
High Culture
Citizen Kane
Mary Shelley's *Frankenstein*
National Public Radio
Downton Abbey
True Detective
CNN
Adele
Gone Girl
The Big Bang Theory
Jurassic World
The Voice
The Bachelor
TMZ.com
paparazzi coverage of Kim Kardashian
The Real Housewives of New Jersey
Low Culture

Figure 9-6. Culture as a Skyscraper Culture is diverse and difficult to categorize. Yet throughout the twentieth century, we tended to think of culture not as a social process but as a set of products sorted into high, low, or middle positions on a cultural skyscraper. Look at this highly arbitrary arrangement and see if you agree or disagree. Write in some of your own examples. Why do we categorize or classify culture in this way? Who controls this process? Is control of making cultural categories important? Why or why not?

Photofest

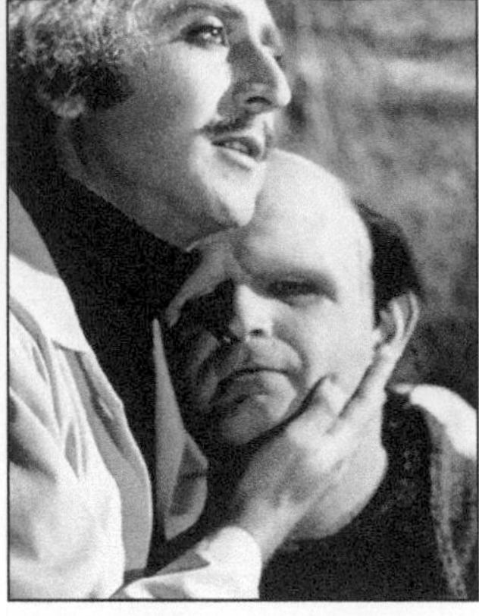

20th Century Fox/Photofest

© Lionsgate/Everett Collection

Figure 9-7. Exploiting High Culture Mary Shelley, the author of *Frankenstein*, might not recognize our popular culture's mutations of her Gothic classic. First published in 1818, the novel has inspired numerous interpretations, everything from the scary—Boris Karloff in the classic 1931 movie—to the silly—the Mel Brooks spoof *Young Frankenstein*. A recent version, called *I, Frankenstein* and based on a graphic novel, pits the monster against an army of gargoyles; a more serious adaptation followed in 2015. Can you think of another example of a story that has developed and changed over time and through various media transformations?

A Diminished Audience for High Culture

Some observers also warn that popular culture has inundated the cultural environment, driving out higher forms of culture and cheapening public life.[14] This concern is supported by data showing that TV sets are in use in the average American home for nearly eight hours a day, exposing adults and children each year to thousands of hours of trivial TV commercials, violent crime dramas, and superficial reality programs. According to one story critics tell, the prevalence of so many popular media products prevents the public from experiencing genuine art—though this view fails to note the number of choices and options now available to media consumers.

Dulling Our Cultural Taste Buds

One cautionary story, frequently recounted by academics, politicians, and pundits, tells how popular culture, especially its more visual forms (such as TV advertising and YouTube videos), undermines democratic ideals and reasoned argument. According to this view, popular media may inhibit not only rational thought but also social progress by transforming audiences into cultural dupes lured by the promise of products. A few multinational conglomerates that make large profits from media products may be distracting citizens from examining economic disparity and implementing change. Seductive advertising images showcasing the buffed and airbrushed bodies of professional models, for example, frequently contradict the actual lives of people who cannot hope to achieve a particular "look" or may not have the money to obtain the high-end cosmetic or clothing products offered. In this environment, art and commerce have become blurred, restricting the audience's ability to make cultural and economic distinctions. Sometimes called the "Big Mac" theory, this view suggests that people are so addicted to mass-produced media menus that they lose their discriminating taste for finer fare and, much worse, their ability to see and challenge social inequities.

Case **STUDY**

Is *Anchorman* a Comedy or a Documentary?

One fascinating media phenomenon of the first few decades of the twenty-first century is that fictional storytelling has changed dramatically over this time while TV news stories, especially local TV news, have hardly changed at all.

Why is this?

They are both media products that depend on storytelling to draw audiences and make money. But while complex and controversial TV narratives like HBO's *Game of Thrones* and *True Detective*, Showtime's *Penny Dreadful*, FX's *Fargo* and *The Americans*, AMC's *Better Call Saul*, Netflix's *Orange Is the New Black*, and Fox's *Empire* were not possible in the 1960s, when just three networks—careful not to offend or challenge viewers—dominated, the lead crime story on most local TV newscasts around the country looks pretty much like it did decades earlier. In the film *Anchorman 2*, Will Ferrell and Adam McKay follow up their satire of small-minded local news anchors in the 1970s with a story about the birth of pandering twenty-four-hour news coverage in the 1980s. The film points out that nonfictional storytelling on television remains locked in narrative patterns from the 1960s and 1970s—making Ferrell's newscaster comedies, at times, seem more like documentaries.

Gemma LaMana/© Paramount Pictures/Everett Collection

The reason for the lack of advances in news narratives is itself a story—one that's about money, and which stories sell and why.

American filmmakers from D. W. Griffith and Orson Welles to Steven Spielberg and Wes Anderson have understood the allure of narrative. But narrative is such a large category—encompassing everything from poetry and novels to movies and TV shows to TV newscasts and political ads—that it demands subdivisions. So over time we developed the idea of genre as a way to differentiate the vast array of stories. In Poetics, Aristotle first talked about generic categories in his analysis of poetry, which he divided into three basic types: "Epic poetry and Tragedy, Comedy also and Dithyrambic poetry, and the music of the flute and of the lyre." Fast-forwarding to more contemporary takes on popular genres, literary scholar John Cawelti, in his book Adventure, Mystery, and Romance, identified five popular literary formulas: adventure, romance, mystery, melodrama, and "alien beings or states."[1]

In fact, most local and national TV news stories function as a kind of melodrama as defined by Cawelti and others. In the melodrama, "the city" is often the setting—as it is in most TV newscasts—and has degenerated into a corrupt and mysterious place, full of crime and mayhem. Historically, heroes of fictional melodramas are small-town sheriffs and big-city cops who must rise above the corruption to impose their individual moral values to defeat various forms of evil. In today's popular culture, cities like Los Angeles and New York are portrayed as places that conceal evil terrorist cells, corrupt cops, maniacal corporate bosses, and other assorted "bad guys," until the strong cops or triumphant lawyers conquer evil and restore order through the convictions of their strong individual characters. Variations on these melodramatic themes can be found as the major organizing structure in everything from cop shows like *NCIS*, *The Good Wife*, and *Justified* to newsmagazines like *60 Minutes* or cable TV shows like Fox News' *The O'Reilly Factor* and *Hannity*. Even the 2015 stories about Brian Williams, who lost his real NBC anchor job by exaggerating his news exploits, play as a melodrama in the news. This is not surprising given that individualism is probably our most persistent American value and that the melodrama generally celebrates the rugged tenacity and moral virtue of tough-minded heroes and condemns characters who fail to meet their standards—whether they are gunfighters, cops, reporters, or even news anchors.

The appropriation of these narratives by news shows has been satirized by the likes of *Anchorman*; *Saturday Night Live*; the long-running *Daily Show* and *Nightly Show*, both on Comedy Central; and John Oliver's *Last Week Tonight*, on HBO. These satires often critique the way news producers repeat stale formulas rather than invent dynamic new story forms for new generations of viewers. As much as the world has changed since the 1970s (when SNL's "Weekend Update" debuted), local TV news story formulas have gone virtually unaltered. Modern newscasts still limit reporters' stories to two minutes or less and promote stylish male–female anchor teams, a sports "guy," and a certified meteorologist as personalities, usually leading with a dramatic local crime story and teasing viewers to stay tuned for a possible weather disaster.

© NBC/Photofest

By indulging these formulas, TV news continues to address viewers not primarily as citizens and members of communities but as news consumers who build the TV ratings that determine the ad rates for local stations and the national networks. In the book *The Elements of Journalism*, Bill Kovach and Tom Rosenstiel argue that "journalists must make the significant interesting and relevant."[2] Too often, however, on cable, the Internet, and local news, we are awash in news stories that try to make something significant out of the obviously trivial, voyeuristic, or narrowly relevant—like stories about troubled celebrities, attention-seeking politicians, or decontextualized stock-market numbers.

In fictional TV, however, storytelling has evolved over time, becoming increasingly dynamic and complex with shows like *Mad Men*, *Game of Thrones*, *The Good Wife*, *Fargo*, *Homeland*, and *Girls*. In *Everything Bad Is Good for You*, Steven Johnson argues that in contrast to popular 1970s programs like *Dallas* or *Dynasty*, the best TV stories today layer "each scene with a thick network of affiliations. You have to focus to follow the plot, and in focusing you're exercising the parts of your brain that map social networks, that fill in missing information, that connect multiple narrative threads."[3] Johnson says that younger audiences today—brought up in an era of the Internet and complicated interactive visual games—bring high expectations to other kinds of popular culture as well, including television. "The mind," he writes, "likes to be challenged; there's real pleasure to be found in solving puzzles, detecting patterns or unpacking a complex narrative system."[4]

This evolution of fictional storytelling has not yet happened with its nonfictional counterparts; TV news remains entrenched in old formulas and time constraints. The reasons for this, of course, are money and competition. Whereas national networks today have begun to adjust their programming decisions to better compete against cable services like AMC and HBO and new story "content" providers like Netflix and Amazon, local TV news still competes against just three or four other news stations and just one (if any) local newspaper. Even with diminished viewership (most local TV stations

have lost half their audience over the past ten to fifteen years), local TV news still draws enough viewers in a fragmented media landscape to attract top ad dollars.

But those viewership levels continue to decline as older audiences give way to new generations more likely to comb social media networks for news and information. Perhaps younger audiences crave news stories that match the more complicated storytelling that surrounds them in everything from TV dramas to interactive video games to their own conversations. Viewers raised on the irony of *Saturday Night Live*, *The Simpsons*, *Family Guy*, *South Park*, *The Daily Show*, *Inside Amy Schumer*, and *Broad City* are not buying—and not watching—news stories that seem as if they still belong to their grandparents' generation.

Culture as a Map

While the skyscraper model is one way to view culture, another way to view it is as a map. Here, culture is an ongoing and complicated process—rather than a high–low vertical hierarchy—that allows us to better account for our diverse and individual tastes. In the map model, we judge forms of culture as good or bad based on a combination of personal taste and the aesthetic judgments a society makes at particular historical times. Because such tastes and evaluations are "all over the map," a cultural map suggests that we can pursue many connections from one cultural place to another and can appreciate a range of cultural experiences without simply ranking them from high to low.

Lionsgate/Photofest

Figure 9-8. The Popular *Hunger Games* book series, which has also become a blockbuster film franchise, mixes elements that have, in the past, been considered "low" culture (young-adult stories, science fiction) with the "high" culture of literature and satire. It also doubles as a cautionary story about media used to transform and suppress its audience: In the books and films, the media, controlled by a totalitarian government, broadcast a brutal fight to the death between child "tributes," fascinating the population while attempting to quash any hope of revolution.

Our attraction to and choice of cultural phenomena—such as the stories we read in books or watch at the movies—represent how we make our lives meaningful. Culture offers plenty of places to go that are conventional, familiar, and comforting. Yet at the same time, our culture's narrative storehouse contains other stories that tend toward the innovative, unfamiliar, and challenging. Most forms of culture, however, demonstrate multiple tendencies. We may use online social networks because they are both comforting (an easy way to keep up with friends) and innovative (new tools or apps that engage us). We watch televised sporting events for their familiarity and conventional organization, and because the unknown outcome can be unpredictable or challenging. The map offered here (see Figure 9-9) is based on a familiar subway grid. Each station represents tendencies or elements related to why a person may be attracted to different cultural products. Also, more popular culture forms congregate in more congested areas of the map, while less popular cultural forms are outliers. Such a large, multidirectional map may be a more flexible, multidimensional, and inclusive way of imagining how culture works.

The Comfort of Familiar Stories

The appeal of culture is often its familiar stories, pulling audiences toward the security of repetition and common landmarks on the cultural map. Consider, for instance, early television's *Lassie* series, about the adventures of a collie named Lassie and her owner, young Timmy. Of the more than five hundred episodes, many have a familiar and repetitive plotline: Timmy, who arguably possessed the poorest sense of direction and suffered more concussions than any TV character in history, gets lost or knocked unconscious. After finding Timmy and licking his face, Lassie goes for help and saves the day. Adult critics might mock this melodramatic formula, but many children found comfort in the predictability of the story. This quality is also evident when children night after night ask their parents to read them the same book, such as Margaret Wise Brown's *Goodnight Moon* or Maurice Sendak's *Where the Wild Things Are*, or when they want to watch the same DVD, such as *Snow White* or *The Princess Bride*.

Innovation and the Attraction of "What's New"

Like children, adults also seek comfort, often returning to an old Beatles or Guns N' Roses song, a William Butler Yeats or an Emily Dickinson poem, or a TV rerun of *Seinfeld* or *Andy Griffith*. But we also like cultural adventure. We may turn from a familiar film on cable's AMC to discover a new movie from Iran or India on the Sundance Channel. We seek new stories and new places to go—those aspects of culture that demonstrate originality and complexity. For instance, James Joyce's *Finnegans Wake* (1939) created language anew and challenged readers, as the novel's poetic first sentence illustrates: "riverrun, past Eve and Adam's, from swerve of shore to bend of bay, brings us by a commodius vicus of recirculation back to Howth Castle and Environs." A revolutionary work, crammed with historical names and topical references to events, myths, songs, jokes, and daily conversation, Joyce's novel remains a challenge to understand and decode. His work demonstrated that part of what culture provides is the impulse to explore new places, to strike out in new directions, searching for something different that may contribute to growth and change.

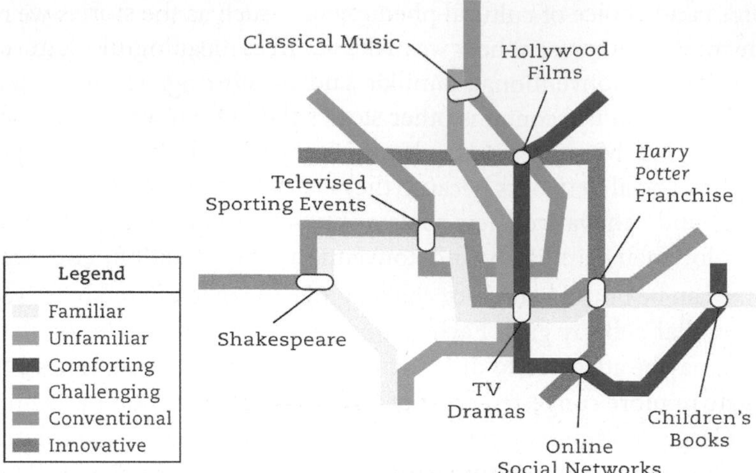

Figure 9-9. Culture as a Map In this map model, culture is not ranked as high or low. Instead, the model shows culture as spreading out in several directions across a variety of dimensions. For example, some cultural forms can be familiar, innovative, and challenging, like the *Harry Potter* books and movies. This model accounts for the complexity of individual tastes and experiences. The map model also suggests that culture is a process by which we produce meaning—that is, make our lives meaningful—as well as a complex collection of media products and texts. The map shown is just one interpretation of culture. What cultural products would you include in your own model? What dimensions would you link to, and why?

A Wide Range of Messages

We know that people have complex cultural tastes, needs, and interests based on different backgrounds and dispositions. It is not surprising, then, that our cultural treasures, from blues music and opera to comic books and classical literature, contain a variety of messages. Just as Shakespeare's plays—popular entertainments in his day—were packed with both obscure and popular references, TV episodes of *The Simpsons* have included allusions to the Beatles, Kafka, *Teletubbies*, Tennessee Williams, Apple, *Star Trek*, *The X-Files*, Freud, *Psycho*, and *Citizen Kane*. In other words, as part of an ongoing process, cultural products and their meanings are "all over the map," spreading out in diverse directions.

Challenging the Nostalgia for a Better Past

Some critics of popular culture assert—often without presenting supportive evidence—that society was better off before the latest developments in mass media. These critics resist the idea of reimagining an established cultural hierarchy as a multidirectional map. The nostalgia for some imagined "better past" has often operated as a device for condemning new cultural phenomena. This impulse to criticize something that is new is often driven by fear of change or of cultural differences. Back in the nineteenth century, in fact, a number of intellectuals and politicians worried that rising literacy rates among the working class would create havoc: How would the aristocracy and intellectuals maintain their authority and status if everyone could read? A recent example includes the fear that some politicians, religious leaders, and citizens have expressed about the legalization of same-sex marriage, claiming that it will violate older religious tenets or the sanctity of past traditions.

Throughout history, a call to return to familiar terrain, to "the good old days," has been a frequent response to new, "threatening" forms of popular culture or to any ideas that are different from what we already believe. Yet over the years many of these forms—including the waltz, silent movies, ragtime, and jazz—have themselves become cultural "classics." How can we tell now what the future has in store for such cultural expressions as rock and roll, soap operas, fashion photography, dance music, hip-hop, tabloid newspapers, graphic novels, reality TV, and social media?

Cultural Values of the Modern Period

To understand how the mass media have come to occupy their current cultural position, we need to trace significant changes in cultural values from the modern period until today. In general, U.S. historians and literary scholars think of the **modern period** as beginning with the Industrial Revolution of the nineteenth century and extending until about the mid-twentieth century. Although there are many ways to define what it means to be "modern," we will focus on four major features or values that resonate best with changes across media and culture: efficiency, individualism, rationalism, and progress.

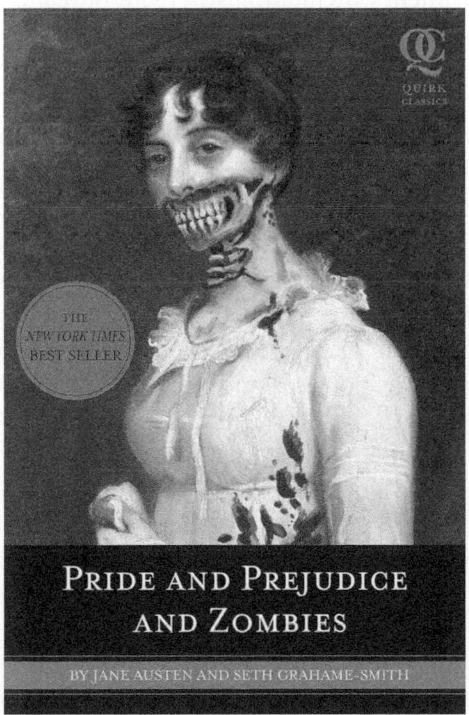

Reprinted with permission of Quirk Books

Figure 9-10. ***Pride and Prejudice and Zombies*** is a famous "mash-up"—a new creative work made by mixing together disparate cultural pieces. In this case, the classic novel by Jane Austen is reimagined as taking place among zombies and ninjas, mixing elements of English literature and horror and action films. Usually intended as satire, such mash-ups allow us to enjoy an array of cultural elements in a single work and are a direct contradiction to the cultural hierarchy model. A feature-film version of *Zombies* was released in 2016.

Modernization involved captains of industry using new technology to create efficient manufacturing centers, produce inexpensive products to make everyday life better, and make commerce more profitable. Printing presses and assembly lines made major contributions in this transformation, and then modern advertising spread the word about new gadgets to American consumers. In terms of culture, the modern mantra has been "form follows function." For example, the growing populations of big cities placed a premium on space, creating a new form of building that fulfilled that functional demand by building upward. Modern skyscrapers made of glass, steel, and concrete replaced the supposedly wasteful decorative and ornate styles of premodern Gothic cathedrals. This new value was echoed in journalism, where a front-page style rejected decorative and ornate adjectives and adverbs for "just the facts." To be lean and efficient, modern news de-emphasized complex analysis and historical context and elevated the new and the now.

Cultural responses to and critiques of modern efficiency often manifested themselves in the mass media. For example, in *Brave New World* (1932), Aldous Huxley created a fictional world in which he cautioned readers that the efficiencies of modern science and technology posed a threat to individual dignity. Charlie Chaplin's film *Modern Times* (1936), set in a futuristic manufacturing plant, also told the story of the dehumanizing impact of modernization and machinery. Writers and artists, in their criticisms of the modern world, have often pointed to technology's ability to alienate people from one another, capitalism's tendency to foster greed, and government's inclination to create bureaucracies whose inefficiency oppresses rather than helps people.

While the values of the premodern period (before the Industrial Revolution) were guided by a strong belief in a natural or divine order, modernization elevated individual self-expression to a more central position. Modern print media allowed ordinary readers to engage with new ideas beyond what their religious leaders and local politicians communicated to them. Modern individualism and the Industrial Revolution also triggered new forms of hierarchy in which certain individuals and groups achieved higher standing in the social order. For example, those who managed commercial enterprises gained more control over the economic ladder, while an intellectual class of modern experts acquired increasing power over the nation's economic, political, and cultural agendas.

To be modern also meant valuing the ability of logical and scientific minds to solve problems by working in organized groups and expert teams. Progressive thinkers maintained that the printing press, the telegraph, and the railroad, in combination with a scientific attitude, would foster a new type of informed society. At the core of this society, the printed mass media—particularly newspapers—would educate the citizenry, helping to build and maintain an organized social framework.[15]

A leading champion for an informed rational society was Walter Lippmann, who wrote the influential book *Public Opinion* in 1922. Lippmann distrusted both the media and the public's ability to navigate a world that was "altogether too big, too complex, and too fleeting for direct acquaintance," and to reach the rational decisions needed in a democracy. Instead, he advocated a "machinery of knowledge" that might be established through "intelligence bureaus" staffed by experts. While such a concept might look like the modern think tank, Lippmann saw these as independent of politics, unlike think tanks of today, such as the Brookings Institution or the Heritage Foundation, which have strong partisan ties.[16]

Walter Lippmann's ideas were influential throughout the twentieth century and were a product of the **Progressive Era**—a period of political and social reform that lasted roughly from the 1890s to the 1920s. On both local and national levels, Progressive Era reformers championed social movements that led to constitutional amendments for both Prohibition and women's suffrage, political reforms that led to the secret ballot during elections, and economic reforms that ushered in the federal income tax to try to foster a more equitable society. Muckrakers—journalists who exposed corruption, waste, and scandal in business and politics—represented media's significant contribution to this era.

Influenced by the Progressive movement, the notion of being modern in the twentieth century meant throwing off the chains of the past, breaking with tradition, and embracing progress. For example, twentieth-century journalists, in their quest for modern efficiency, focused on "the now" and the reporting of timely events. Newly standardized forms of front-page journalism that championed "just the facts" and events that "just happened yesterday" did help reporters efficiently meet tight deadlines. But realizing one of Walter Lippmann's fears, modern newspapers often failed to take a historical perspective or to analyze sufficiently the ideas and interests underlying these events.

Shifting Values in Postmodern Culture

For many people, the changes occurring in the **postmodern period**—from roughly the mid-twentieth century to today—are identified by a confusing array of examples: music videos, remote controls, Nike ads, shopping malls, fax machines, e-mail, video games, blogs, *USA Today*, YouTube, iPads, hip-hop, and reality TV (see Table 9-1). Some critics argue that post-modern culture represents a way of seeing—a new condition, or even a malady, of the human spirit. Although there are many ways to define the postmodern, this textbook focuses on four major features or values that resonate best with changes across media and culture: populism, diversity, nostalgia, and paradox.

Table 9-1. Trends Across Historical Periods

Trend	Premodern (pre-1800s)	Modern Industrial Revolution (1800s–1950s)	Postmodern (1950s–present)
Work hierarchies	peasants/merchants /rulers	factory workers/managers /national CEOs	temp workers/global CEOs
Major work sites	field/farm	factory/office	office/home/"virtual" or mobile office
Communication reach	local	national	global
Communication transmission	oral/manuscript	print/electronic	electronic/digital
Communication channels	storytellers/elders/ town criers	books/newspapers/magazines/ radio	television/cable/ Internet/multimedia
Communication at home	quill pen	typewriter/office computer	personal computer/ laptop/smartphone/ social networks
Key social values	belief in natural or divine order	individualism/rationalism/efficiency/ antitradition	antihierarchy/skepticism (about science, business, government, etc.)/diversity/ multiculturalism/irony & paradox
Journalism	oral & print-based/ partisan/ controlled by political parties	print-based/"objective"/efficient/ timely/controlled by publishing families	TV- & Internet-based/opinionated/ conversational/ controlled by global entertainment conglomerates

As a political idea, *populism* tries to appeal to ordinary people by highlighting or even creating an argument or conflict between "the people" and "the elite." In virtually every campaign, populist politicians often tell stories and run ads that criticize big corporations and political favoritism. Meant to resonate with middle-class values and regional ties, such narratives generally pit southern or midwestern small-town "family values" against the supposedly coarser, even corrupt, urban lifestyles associated with big cities like Washington or Los Angeles.

In postmodern culture, populism manifests itself in many ways. For example, artists and performers, like Chuck Berry in "Roll Over Beethoven" (1956) or Queen in "Bohemian Rhapsody" (1975), intentionally blur the border between high and low culture. In the visual arts, following Andy Warhol's 1960s pop art style, advertisers borrow from both fine art and street art, while artists appropriate styles from commerce and popular art. Film stars, like Angelina Jolie and Ben Affleck, often champion oppressed groups while appearing in movies that make the actors wealthy global icons of consumer culture.

Other forms of postmodern style blur modern distinctions not only between art and commerce but also between fact and fiction. For example, television vocabulary now includes infotainment (such as *Entertainment Tonight* and *Access Hollywood*) and infomercials (such as fading celebrities selling antiwrinkle cream). On cable, reality programs—such as MTV's *The Real World* and *16 and Pregnant*—blur boundaries between the staged and the real, mixing serious themes and personal challenges with comedic interludes and romantic entanglements. Fake news programs, like *Last Week Tonight with John Oliver*, combine real, insightful news stories with biting satires of traditional broadcast and cable news programs.

Closely associated with populism, another value (or vice) of the postmodern period is the emphasis on *diversity* and fragmentation, including the wild juxtaposition of old and new cultural styles. In a suburban shopping mall, for instance, Gap stores border a food court with Vietnamese, Italian, and Mexican options, while techno-digitized instrumental versions of 1960s protest music play in the background to accompany shoppers. Part of this stylistic diversity involves borrowing and transforming earlier ideas from the modern period. In music, hip-hop deejays and performers sample old R&B, soul, and rock classics, both reinventing old songs and creating something new. Critics of postmodern style contend that such borrowing devalues originality, emphasizing surface over depth and recycled ideas over new ones. Throughout the twentieth century, for example, films were adapted from books and short stories. More recently, films often derive from old popular TV series: *Mission Impossible*, *Charlie's Angels*, and *The A-Team*, to name just a few. Video games like the *Resident Evil* franchise and *Tomb Raider* have been made into Hollywood blockbusters. In fact, by 2015, more than forty video games, including *BioShock* and the *Warcraft* series, were in various stages of script or film development.

Another tendency of postmodern culture involves rejecting rational thought as "the answer" to every social problem, reveling instead in *nostalgia* for the premodern values of small communities, traditional religion, and even mystical experience. Rather than seeing science purely as enlightened thinking or rational deduction that relies on evidence, some artists, critics, and politicians criticize modern values for laying the groundwork for dehumanizing technological advances and bureaucratic problems. For example, in the renewed debates over evolution, one cultural narrative that plays out often pits scientific evidence against religious belief and literal interpretations of the Bible. And in popular culture, many TV programs—such as *The X-Files*, *Buffy the Vampire Slayer*, *Charmed*, *Angel*, *Lost*, and *Fringe*—emerged to offer mystical and supernatural responses to the "evils" of our daily world and the limits of science and the purely rational.

Lastly, the fourth aspect of our postmodern time is the willingness to accept *paradox*. While modern culture emphasized breaking with the past in the name of progress, postmodern culture stresses integrating—or converging—retro beliefs and contemporary culture. So at the same time that we seem nostalgic for the past, we embrace new technologies with a vengeance. For example, fundamentalist religious movements that promote seemingly outdated traditions (e.g., rejecting women's rights to own property or seek higher education) still embrace the Internet and modern technology as recruiting tools or as channels for spreading messages. Culturally conservative politicians, who seem most comfortable with the values of the 1950s nuclear family, welcome talk shows, Twitter, Facebook, and Internet and social media ad campaigns as venues to advance their messages and causes.

Chaplin/Zuma Press

© Warner Bros./Photofest

Figure 9-11. Films Often Reflect the Key Social Values of an era—as represented by the modern and postmodern movies pictured. Charlie Chaplin's *Modern Times* (1936, above left) satirized modern industry and the dehumanizing impact of a futuristic factory on its overwhelmed workers. Similarly, Ridley Scott's *Blade Runner* (1982, above right), set in futuristic Los Angeles in 2019, questioned the impact on humanity when technology overwhelms the natural world. In *Pop Culture Wars*, author William Romanowski suggested that *Blade Runner* managed to "capture some postmodern themes" that were not fully recognized at the time by "trying to balance the promise of technology with the threats of technology." [17]

Although, as modernists warned, new technologies can isolate people or encourage them to chase their personal agendas (e.g., a student perusing his individual interests online), new technologies can also draw people together to advance causes; to solve community problems; or to discuss politics on radio talk shows, Facebook, or smartphones. For example, in 2011 and 2012, Twitter made the world aware of protesters in many Arab nations, including Egypt and Libya, when governments there tried to suppress media access. Our lives today are full of such incongruities.

Critiquing Media and Culture

In contemporary life, cultural boundaries are being tested; the arbitrary lines between information and entertainment have become blurred. Consumers now read newspapers on their computers. Media corporations do business across vast geographic boundaries. We are witnessing media convergence, in which televisions, computers, and smartphones easily access new and old forms of mass communication. For a fee, everything from magazines to movies is channeled into homes through the Internet and cable or satellite TV.

Considering the diversity of mass media, to paint them all with the same broad brush would be inaccurate and unfair. Yet that is often what we seem to do, which may in fact reflect the distrust many of us have of prominent social institutions, from local governments to daily newspapers. Of course, when one recent president leads us into a long war based on faulty intelligence that mainstream news failed to uncover, or one of the world's leading media companies—with former editors in top government jobs—engages in phone hacking and privacy invasion, our distrust of both government and media may be understandable. It's ultimately more useful, however, to replace a cynical perception of the media with an attitude of genuine criticism. To deal with these shifts in how we experience media and culture, as well as their impact, we need to develop a profound understanding of the media, focused on what they offer or produce and what they downplay or ignore.

Media Literacy and the Critical Process

Developing **media literacy**—that is, attaining an understanding of mass media and how they construct meaning—requires following a critical process that takes us through the steps of description, analysis, interpretation, evaluation, and engagement (see "Media Literacy and the Critical Process" on pages 506–508). We will be aided in our critical process by keeping an open mind, trying to understand the specific cultural forms we are critiquing, and acknowledging the complexity of contemporary culture.

Just as communication cannot always be reduced to the linear sender-message-receiver model, many forms of media and culture are not easily represented by the high–low model. We should, perhaps, strip culture of such adjectives as *high*, *low*, *popular*, and *mass*. These modifiers may artificially force media forms and products into predetermined categories. Rather than focusing on these worn-out labels, we might instead look at a wide range of issues generated by culture, from the role of storytelling in the mass media to the global influences of media industries on the consumer marketplace. We should also be moving toward a critical perspective that takes into account the intricacies of the cultural landscape. A fair critique of any cultural form, regardless of its social or artistic reputation, requires a working knowledge of the particular book, program, or music under scrutiny. For example, to understand W. E. B. Du Bois's essays, critics immerse themselves in his work and in the historical context in which he wrote. Similarly, if we want to develop a meaningful critique of TV's *Ray Donovan* (in which the protagonist is a professional "fixer") or Rush Limbaugh's radio program or a gossip magazine's obsession with Justin Bieber, it is essential to understand the contemporary context in which these cultural phenomena are produced.

To begin this process of critical assessment, we must imagine culture as richer and more complicated than the high–low model allows. We must also assume a critical stance that enables us to get outside our own preferences. We may like or dislike hip-hop, R&B, pop, or country, but if we want to criticize these musical genres intelligently, we should understand what the various types of music have to say and why their messages appeal to particular audiences that may be different from us. The same approach applies to other cultural forms. If we critique a newspaper article, we must account for the language that is chosen and what it means; if we analyze a film or TV program, we need to slow down the images in order to understand how they make sense and create meaning.

Benefits of a Critical Perspective

Developing an informed critical perspective and becoming media literate allow us to participate in a debate about media culture as a force for both democracy and consumerism. On the one hand, the media can be a catalyst for democracy and social progress. Consider the role of television in spotlighting racism and injustice in the 1960s; the use of video technology to reveal oppressive conditions in China and Eastern Europe or to document crimes by urban police departments; the impact of TV coverage of both business and government's slow response to the 2010 Gulf oil spill on people's understanding of the event; and the role of blogs and Twitter in debunking bogus claims or protesting fraudulent elections. The media have also helped to renew interest in diverse cultures around the world and other emerging democracies (see "Global Village: "Bedouins, Camels, Transistors, and Coke").

Global **VILLAGE**

Bedouins, Camels, Transistors, and Coke

Upon receiving the Philadelphia Liberty Medal in 1994, President Václav Havel of the Czech Republic described postmodernism as the fundamental condition of global culture, "when it seems that something is on the way out and something else is painfully being born." He described this "new world order" as a "multicultural era" or state in which consistent value systems break into mixed and blended cultures:

For me, a symbol of that state is a Bedouin mounted on a camel and clad in traditional robes under which he is wearing jeans, with a transistor radio in his hands and an ad for Coca-Cola on the camel's back. . . . New meaning is gradually born from the . . . intersection of many different elements.[1]

Many critics, including Havel, think that there is a crucial tie between global politics and postmodern culture. They contend that the people who overthrew governments in the former Yugoslavia and the Soviet Union were the same people who valued American popular culture—especially movies, pop music, and television—for its free expression and democratic possibilities.

Back in the 1990s, as modern communist states were undermined by the growth and influence of transnational corporations, citizens in these nations capitalized on the developing global market, using portable video cameras, digital cameras and phones, and audio technology to smuggle out recordings of repression perpetrated by totalitarian regimes. Thus it was difficult for political leaders to hide repressive acts from the rest of the world. In *Newsweek*, former CBS news anchor Dan Rather wrote about the role of television in the 1989 student uprising in China:

Television brought Beijing's battle for democracy to Main Street. It made students who live on the other side of the planet just as human, just as vulnerable as the boy on the next block. The miracle of television is that the triumph and tragedy of Tiananmen Square would not have been any more vivid had it been Times Square.[2]

> This trend continues today through the newer manifestations of our digital world, like Facebook, Twitter, and YouTube. as protesters sent out messages and images on smartphones and laptops during the Arab Spring uprisings in 2011 and 2012, they spread stories that could not be contained by totalitarian governments.
>
> At the same time, we need to examine the impact on other nations of the influx of U.S. popular culture (movies, TV shows, music, etc.), our second-biggest export (after military and airplane equipment). Has access to an American consumer lifestyle fundamentally altered Havel's Bedouin on the camel? What happens when Westernized popular culture encroaches on the mores of Islamic countries, where the spread of American music, movies, and television is viewed as a danger to tradition? These questions still need answers. A global village, which through technology shares culture and communication, can also alter traditional customs forever.
>
> To try to grasp this phenomenon, we might imagine how we would feel if the culture from a country far away gradually eroded our own established habits. This, in fact, is happening all over the world, as U.S. culture has become the world's global currency. Although newer forms of communication—such as tweeting and texting—have in some ways increased citizen participation in global life, in what ways have they threatened the values of older cultures?
>
> Our current postmodern period is double-coded: It is an agent both for the renewed possibilities of democracy and, even in tough economic times, for the worldwide spread of consumerism and American popular culture.

On the other hand, competing against these democratic tendencies is a powerful commercial culture that reinforces a world economic order controlled by relatively few multinational corporations. For instance, when Poland threw off the shackles of the Soviet Union in the late 1980s, one of the first things its new leadership did was buy and dub the American soap operas *Santa Barbara* and *Dynasty*. For some, these shows were a relief from sober Soviet political propaganda, but others worried that Poles might inherit another kind of indoctrination—one starring American consumer culture and dominated by large international media companies.

This example illustrates that contemporary culture cannot easily be characterized as one thing or another. Binary terms such as *liberal* and *conservative* or *high* and *low* have less meaning in an environment where so many boundaries have been blurred, so many media forms have converged, and so many diverse cultures coexist. Modern distinctions between print and electronic culture have begun to break down largely because of the increasing number of individuals who have come of age in what is both a print and an electronic culture.[18] Either/or models of culture, such as the high–low approach, are giving way to more inclusive ideas, like the map model for culture discussed earlier.

What are the social implications of the new, blended, and merging cultural phenomena? How do we deal with the fact that public debate and news about everyday life now seem as likely to come from Facebook, Twitter, John Oliver, *SNL*, or bloggers as from the *Wall Street Journal*, the *NBC Nightly News*, or *Time* magazine?[19] Clearly, such changes challenge us to

reassess and rebuild the standards by which we judge our culture. The search for answers lies in recognizing the links between cultural expression and daily life. The search also involves monitoring how well the mass media serve democracy, not just by providing us with consumer culture but by encouraging us to help improve political, social, and economic practices. A healthy democracy requires the active involvement of everyone. Part of this involvement means watching over the role and impact of the mass media, a job that belongs to every one of us—not just the paid media critics and watchdog organizations.

Media Literacy and THE CRITICAL PROCESS

It is easy to form a cynical view about the stream of TV advertising, reality programs, video games, celebrities, gossip blogs, tweets, and news tabloids that floods the cultural landscape. But cynicism is no substitute for criticism. To become literate about media involves striking a balance between taking a critical position (developing knowledgeable interpretations and judgments) and becoming tolerant of diverse forms of expression (appreciating the distinctive variety of cultural products and processes).

A cynical view usually involves some form of intolerance and either too little or too much information. For example, after enduring the glut of news coverage and political advertising devoted to the 2008 and 2012 presidential elections, we might easily become cynical about our political system. However, information in the form of "factual" news bits and knowledge about a complex social process such as a national election are not the same thing. The critical process stresses the subtle distinctions between amassing information and becoming media literate.

Developing a media-literate critical perspective involves mastering five overlapping stages that build on one another:

Description: paying close attention, taking notes, and researching the subject under study

Analysis: discovering and focusing on significant patterns that emerge from the description stage

Interpretation: asking and answering "What does that mean?" and "So what?" questions about one's findings

Evaluation: arriving at a judgment about whether something is good, bad, or mediocre, which involves subordinating one's personal taste to the critical "bigger picture" resulting from the first three stages

Engagement: taking some action that connects our critical perspective with our role as citizens to question our media institutions, adding our own voice to the process of shaping the cultural environment

Let's look at each of these stages in greater detail.

1 **DESCRIPTION.** If we decide to focus on how well the news media serve democracy, we might critique the fairness of several programs or individual stories from, say, *60 Minutes* or the *New York Times*. We start by describing the programs or articles, accounting for their reporting strategies, and noting those featured as interview subjects. We might further identify central characters, conflicts, topics, and themes. From the notes taken at this stage, we can begin comparing what we have found to other stories on similar topics. We can also document what we think is missing from these news narratives—the questions, viewpoints, and persons that were not included—and other ways to tell the story.

2 **ANALYSIS.** In the second stage the critical process, we isolate patterns that call for closer attention. At this point, we decide how to focus the critique. Because *60 Minutes* has produced thousands of hours of programs in its nearly fifty-year history, our critique might spotlight just a few key patterns. For example, many of the program's reports are organized like detective stories, reporters are almost always visually represented at a medium distance, and interview subjects are generally shot in tight close-ups. In studying the *New York Times*, in contrast, we might limit our analysis to social or political events in certain countries that get covered more often than events in other areas of the world. Or we could focus on recurring topics chosen for front-page treatment, or the number of quotes from male and female experts.

3 **INTERPRETATION.** In the interpretation stage, we try to determine the meanings of the patterns we have analyzed. The most difficult stage in criticism, interpretation demands an answer to the "So what?" question. For instance, the greater visual space granted to *60 Minutes* reporters—compared with the close-up shots used for interview subjects—might mean that the reporters appear to be in control. They are given more visual space in which to operate, whereas interview subjects have little room to maneuver within the visual frame. As a result, the subjects often look guilty and the reporters look heroic—or, at least, in charge. Likewise, if we look again at the *New York Times*, its attention to particular countries could mean that the paper tends to cover nations in which the United States has more vital political or economic interests, even though the *Times* might claim to be neutral and evenhanded in its reporting of news from around the world.

4 **EVALUATION.** The fourth stage of the critical process focuses on making an informed judgment. Building on description, analysis, and interpretation, we are better able to evaluate the fairness of a group of *60 Minutes* or *New York Times* reports. At this stage, we can grasp the strengths and weaknesses of the news media under study and make critical judgments measured against our own frames of reference—what we like and dislike, as well as what seems good or bad or missing, in the stories and coverage we analyzed.

This fourth stage differentiates the reviewer (or previewer) from the critic. Most newspaper reviews, for example, are limited by daily time or space

constraints. Although these reviews may give us key information about particular programs, they often begin and end with personal judgments—"This is a quality show" or "That was a piece of trash"—that should be saved for the final stage in the critical process. Regrettably, many reviews do not reflect such a process; they do not move much beyond the writer's own frame of reference or personal taste.

5 **ENGAGEMENT.** To be fully media literate, we must actively work to create a media world that helps serve democracy. So we propose a fifth stage in the critical process—engagement. In our *60 Minutes* and *New York Times* examples, engagement might involve something as simple as writing a formal letter or an e-mail to these media outlets to offer a critical take on the news narratives we are studying.

But engagement can also mean participating in Web discussions, contacting various media producers or governmental bodies like the Federal Communications Commission with critiques and ideas, organizing or participating in public media literacy forums, or learning to construct different types of media narratives ourselves—whether print, audio, video, or online—to participate directly in the creation of mainstream or alternative media. Producing actual work for media outlets might involve writing news stories for a local newspaper (and its Web site), producing a radio program on a controversial or significant community issue, or constructing a Web site that critiques various news media. The key to this stage is to challenge our civic imaginations, to refuse to sit back and cynically complain about the media without taking some action that lends our own voices and critiques to the process.

Chapter Review

Common Threads

In telling the story of mass media, several plotlines and major themes recur and help provide the big picture—the larger context for understanding the links between forms of mass media and popular culture. Under each thread that follows, we pose a set of questions that we will investigate together to help you explore media and culture:

- **Developmental stages of mass media.** How did the media evolve, from their origins in ancient oral traditions to their incarnation on the Internet today? What discoveries, inventions, and social circumstances drove the development of different media? What roles do new technologies play in changing contemporary media and culture?
- **The commercial nature of mass media.** What role do media ownership and government regulation play in the presentation of commercial media products and serious journalism? How do the desire for profit and other business demands affect and change the media landscape? What role should government oversight play? What role do we play as ordinary viewers, readers, students, critics, and citizens?

- **The converged nature of media**. How has convergence changed the experience of media from the print to the digital era? What are the significant differences between reading a printed newspaper and reading the news online? What changes have to be made in the media business to help older forms of media, like newspapers, transition to an online world?
- **The role that media play in a democracy.** How are policy decisions and government actions affected by the news media and other mass media? How do individuals find room in the media terrain to express alternative (nonmainstream) points of view? How do grassroots movements create media to influence and express political ideas?
- **Mass media, cultural expression, and storytelling.** What are the advantages and pitfalls of the media's appetite for telling and selling stories? As we reach the point where almost all media exist on the Internet in some form, how have our culture and our daily lives been affected?
- **Critical analysis of the mass media.** How can we use the critical process to understand, critique, and influence the media? How important is it to be media literate in today's world? at the end of each chapter, we will examine the historical contexts and current processes that shape media products. By becoming more critical consumers and more engaged citizens, we will be in a better position to influence the relationships among mass media, democratic participation, and the complex cultural landscape that we all inhabit.

Review Questions

Culture and the Evolution of Mass Communication

1. Define culture, mass communication, and mass media, and explain their interrelationships.
2. What key technological breakthroughs accompanied the transition to the print and electronic eras? Why were these changes significant?
3. Explain the linear model of mass communication and its limitations.

The Development of Media and Their Role in Our Society

4. Describe the development of a mass medium from emergence to convergence.
5. In looking at the history of popular culture, explain why newer and emerging forms of media seem to threaten status quo values.

Surveying the Cultural Landscape

6. Describe the skyscraper model of culture. What are its strengths and limitations?
7. Describe the map model of culture. What are its strengths and limitations?
8. What are the chief differences between modern and postmodern values?

Critiquing Media and Culture

9. What are the five steps in the critical process? Which of these is the most difficult, and why?

10. What is the difference between cynicism and criticism?
11. Why is the critical process important?

Questioning the Media

1. Drawing on your experience, list the kinds of media stories you like and dislike. You might think mostly of movies and TV shows, but remember that news, sports, political ads, and product ads are also usually structured as stories. Conversations on Facebook can also be considered narratives. What kinds of stories do you like and dislike on Facebook, and why?
2. Cite some examples in which the media have been accused of unfairness. Draw on comments from parents, teachers, religious leaders, friends, news media, and so on. Discuss whether these criticisms have been justified.
3. Pick an example of a popular media product that you think is harmful to children. How would you make your concerns known? Should the product be removed from circulation? Why or why not? If you think the product should be banned, how would you do so?
4. Make a critical case either defending or condemning Comedy Central's *South Park*, a TV or radio talk show, a hip-hop group, a soap opera, or TV news coverage of the ongoing wars in the Middle East. Use the five-step critical process to develop your position.
5. Although in some ways postmodern forms of communication, such as e-mail, MTV, smartphones, and Twitter, have helped citizens participate in global life, in what ways might these forms harm more traditional or native cultures?

Chapter 10

Advertising

The Shape of U.S. Advertising Today

"Advertising" from *Media & Culture*, Tenth Edition, 2016 Update by Richard Campbell, Christopher R. Martin, and Bettina Fabos, pp. 383–409 (Chapter 11, "Advertising and Commercial Culture").

Until the 1960s, the shape and pitch of most U.S. ads were determined by a **slogan**, the phrase that attempts to sell a product by capturing its essence in words. With slogans such as "A Diamond Is Forever" (which De Beers first used in 1948), the visual dimension of ads was merely a complement. Eventually, however, through the influence of European design, television, and (now) multimedia devices such as the iPad, images asserted themselves, and visual style became dominant in U.S. advertising and ad agencies.

The Influence of Visual Design

Just as a postmodern design phase developed in art and architecture during the 1960s and 1970s, a new design era began to affect advertising at the same time. Part of this visual revolution was imported from non-U.S. schools of design; indeed, ad-rich magazines such as *Vogue* and *Vanity Fair* increasingly hired European designers as art directors. These directors tended to be less tied to U.S. word-driven radio advertising because most European countries had government-sponsored radio systems with no ads.

By the early 1970s, agencies had developed teams of writers and artists, thus granting equal status to images and words in the creative process. By the mid-1980s, the visual techniques of MTV, which initially modeled its style on advertising, influenced many ads and most agencies. MTV promoted a particular visual aesthetic—rapid edits, creative camera angles, compressed narratives, and staged performances. Video-style ads soon saturated television and featured such prominent performers as Paula Abdul, Ray Charles, Michael Jackson, Elton John, and Madonna. The popularity of MTV's visual style also started a trend in the 1980s to license hit songs for commercial tie-ins. By the twenty-first century, a wide range of short, polished musical performances and familiar songs—including the work of Train (Samsung), the Shins (McDonald's), LMFAO (Kia Motors), and classic Louis Armstrong (Apple iPhone)—were routinely used in TV ads to encourage consumers not to click the remote control.

Jaimie Trueblood/© AMC/Everett Collection

Figure 10-1. *Mad Men* AMC's hit series *Mad Men* depicts the male-dominated world of Madison Avenue in the 1960s, as the U.S. consumer economy kicked into high gear and agencies developed ad campaigns for cigarettes, exercise belts, and presidential candidates. The show ended its run in 2015 after seven seasons and many awards.

Most recently, the Internet and multimedia devices, such as computers, mobile phones, and portable media players, have had a significant impact on visual design in advertising. As the Web became a mass medium in the 1990s, TV and print designs often mimicked the drop-down menu of computer interfaces. In the twenty-first century, visual design has evolved in other ways, becoming more three-dimensional and interactive as full-motion, 3-D animation becomes a high-bandwidth multimedia standard. At the same time, design is also simpler, as ads and logos need to appear clearly on the small screens of smartphones and portable media players, and more international, as agencies need to appeal to the global audiences of many companies and therefore need to reflect styles from around the world.

Types of Advertising Agencies

About fourteen thousand ad agencies currently operate in the United States. In general, these agencies are classified as either **mega-agencies**—large ad firms that formed by merging several agencies and that maintain regional offices worldwide—or small **boutique agencies** that devote their talents to only a handful of select clients. With the economic crisis, both types of ad agencies suffered revenue declines in 2008 and 2009 but had slowly improved within about five years.

Mega-Agencies

Mega-agencies provide a full range of services, from advertising and public relations to operating their own in-house radio and TV production studios. In 2014, the four global mega-agencies were WPP, Omnicom, Publicis, and Interpublic (see Figure 10-2).

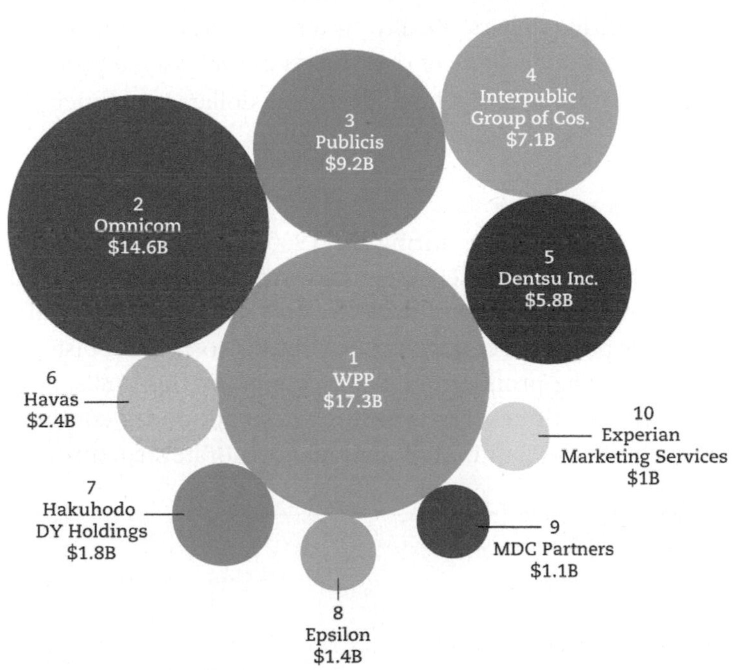

Data from: Advertising Age Marketing Fact Pack 2015, *pp. 26–27*.

Figure 10-2. Global revenue for the world's largest agencies (in billions of dollars).

In 2013, Omnicom and Publicis announced a merger that would have created the world's largest mega-agency. But that plan fell apart in 2014, according to the *New York Times*, over a "mix of clashing personalities, disagreements about how the companies would be integrated and complications over legal and tax issues."[1] Based in New York, Omnicom in 2015 had more than 74,000 employees operating in more than 100 countries and currently owns the global advertising firms BBDO Worldwide, DDB Worldwide, and TBWA Worldwide. The company also owns three leading public relations agencies: Fleishman-Hillard, Ketchum, and Porter

Novelli. The Paris-based Publicis Groupe has a global reach through agencies like Leo Burnett Worldwide, the British agency Saatchi & Saatchi, DigitasLBi, and the public relations firm MSL Group. Publicis employed more than 63,000 people worldwide in 2015.

The London-based WPP Group grew quickly in the 1980s with the purchases of J. Walter Thompson, the largest U.S. ad firm at the time; Hill & Knowlton, one of the largest U.S. public relations agencies; and Ogilvy & Mather Worldwide. In the 2000s, WPP Group continued its growth and acquired Young & Rubicam and Grey Global—both major U.S. ad firms. By 2013, WPP had 179,000 employees in 111 countries. The Interpublic Group, based in New York with 47,400 employees worldwide, holds global agencies like McCann Erickson (the top U.S. ad agency), FCB, and Lowe and Partners, and public relations firms Golin and Weber Shandwick.

This mega-agency trend has stirred debate among consumer and media watchdog groups. Some consider large agencies a threat to the independence of smaller firms, which are slowly being bought out. An additional concern is that these four firms now control more than half the distribution of advertising dollars globally. As a result, the cultural values represented by U.S. and European ads may undermine or overwhelm the values and products of developing countries. (See Figure 10-3 for a look at how advertising dollars are spent by medium.)

Boutique Agencies

The visual revolutions in advertising during the 1960s elevated the standing of designers and graphic artists, who became closely identified with the look of particular ads. Breaking away from bigger agencies, many of these creative individuals formed small boutique agencies. Offering more personal services, the boutiques prospered, bolstered by innovative ad campaigns and increasing profits from TV accounts. By the 1980s, large agencies had bought up many of the boutiques. Nevertheless, these boutiques continue to operate as fairly autonomous subsidiaries within multinational corporate structures.

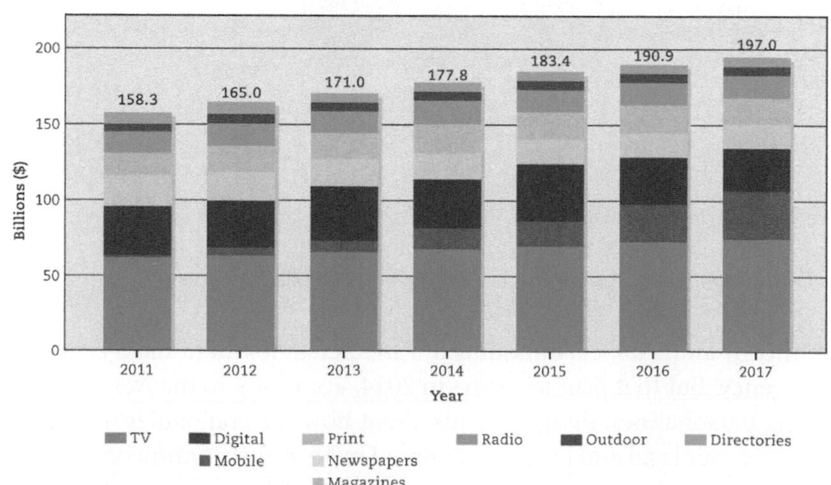

Figure 10-3. Where Will the Advertising Dollars Go?*

*Years 2015–2017 are projections. Data from: eMarketer, "US Total Media Ad Spend Inches Up, Pushed by Digital," August 22, 2013.

One independent boutique agency in Minneapolis, Peterson Milla Hooks (PMH), made its name with a boldly graphic national branding ad campaign for Target department stores. Target moved its business to another agency in 2011, but PMH—which employs only about sixty people—rebounded. By 2015, the agency's client list included Gap, Kohl's, Nine West, Mattel, Kmart, Sephora, Rooms To Go, Sleep Number, JCPenney, Target, and Chico's.[2]

The Structure of Ad Agencies

Traditional ad agencies, regardless of their size, generally divide the labor of creating and maintaining advertising campaigns among four departments: account planning, creative development, media coordination, and account management. Expenses incurred for producing the ads are part of a separate negotiation between the agency and the advertiser. As a result of this commission arrangement, it generally costs most large-volume advertisers no more to use an agency than it does to use their own staff.

Account Planning, Market Research, and VALS

The account planner's role is to develop an effective advertising strategy by combining the views of the client, the creative team, and consumers. Consumers' views are the most difficult to understand, so account planners coordinate **market research** to assess the behaviors and attitudes of consumers toward particular products long before any ads are created. Researchers may study everything from possible names for a new product to the size of the copy for a print ad. Researchers also test new ideas and products with consumers to get feedback before developing final ad strategies. In addition, some researchers contract with outside polling firms to conduct regional and national studies of consumer preferences.

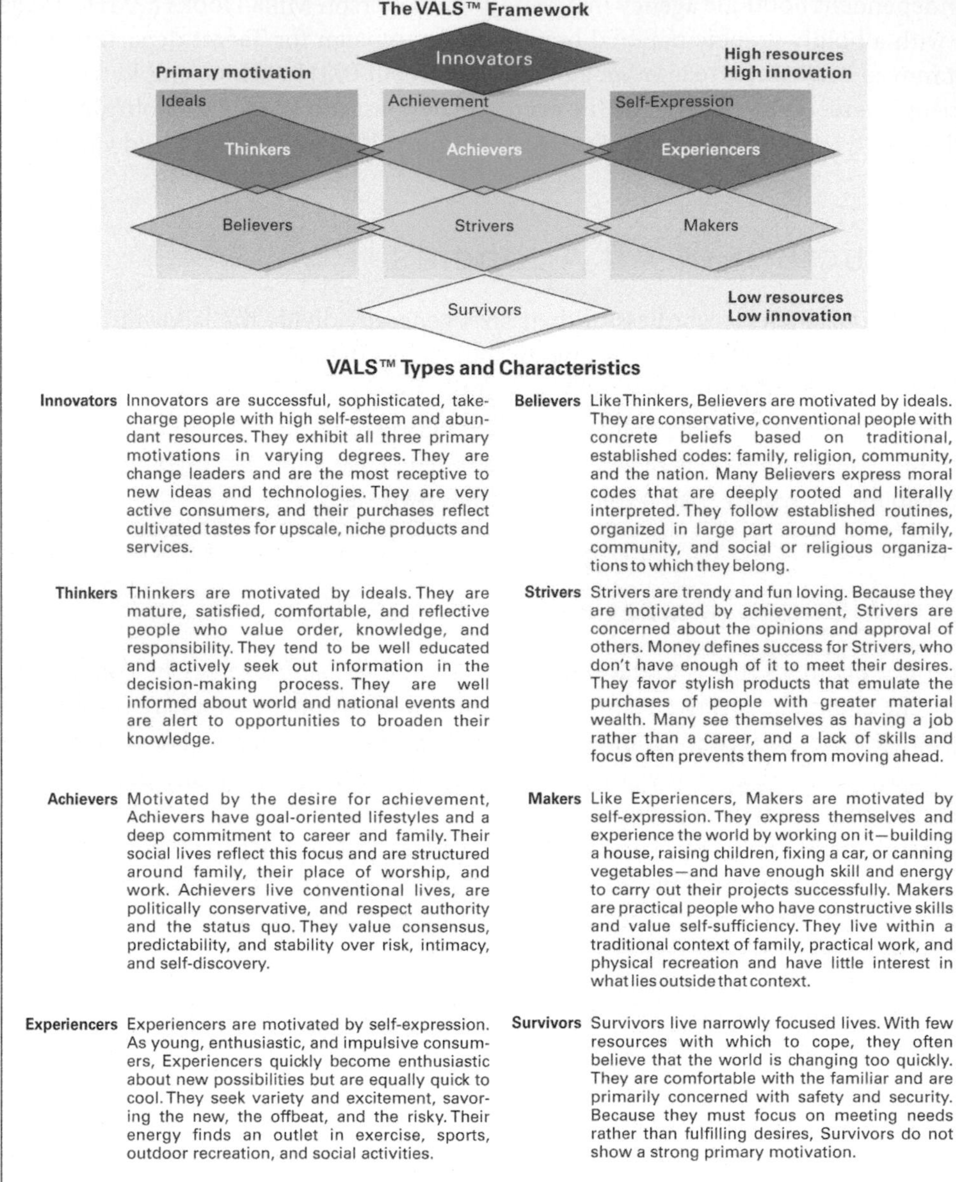

Data from: Strategic Business Insights, 2010, http://strategicbusinessinsights.com/vals/ustypes.shtml.

Figure 10-4. VALS Types and Characteristics

Agencies have increasingly employed scientific methods to study consumer behavior. In 1932, Young & Rubicam first used statistical techniques developed by pollster George Gallup. By the 1980s, most large agencies retained psychologists and anthropologists to advise them on human nature and buying habits. The earliest type of market research, **demographics**, mainly studied and documented audience members' age, gender, occupation, ethnicity, education, and income. Today, demographic data are much more specific. They make it possible to locate consumers in particular geographic regions—usually by zip code. This enables advertisers and product companies to target ethnic neighborhoods or affluent suburbs for direct mail, point-of-purchase store displays, or specialized magazine and newspaper inserts.

Demographic analyses provide advertisers with data on people's behavior and social status but reveal little about feelings and attitudes. By the 1960s and 1970s, advertisers and agencies began using **psychographics**, a research approach that attempts to categorize consumers according to their attitudes, beliefs, interests, and motivations. Psychographic analysis often relies on **focus groups**, a small-group interview technique in which a moderator leads a discussion about a product or an issue, usually with six to twelve people. Because focus groups are small and less scientific than most demographic research, the findings from such groups may be suspect.

In 1978, the Stanford Research Institute (SRI), now called Strategic Business Insights (SBI), instituted its **Values and Lifestyles (VALS)** strategy. Using questionnaires, VALS researchers measured psychological factors and divided consumers into types. VALS research assumes that not every product suits every consumer and encourages advertisers to vary their sales slants to find market niches.

Over the years, the VALS system has been updated to reflect changes in consumer orientations (see Figure 10-4). The most recent system classifies people by their primary consumer motivations: ideals, achievement, or self-expression. The ideals-oriented group, for instance, includes *thinkers*—"mature, satisfied, comfortable, and reflective people who value order, knowledge, and responsibility." VALS and similar research techniques ultimately provide advertisers with microscopic details about which consumers are most likely to buy which products.

Agencies and clients—particularly auto manufacturers—have relied heavily on VALS to determine the best placement for ads. VALS data suggest, for example, that *achievers* and *experiencers* watch more sports and news programs; these groups prefer luxury cars or sport-utility vehicles. *Thinkers*, on the other hand, favor TV dramas and documentaries and like the functionality of minivans or the gas efficiency of hybrids.

VALS researchers do not claim that most people fit neatly into a category. But many agencies believe that VALS research can give them an edge in markets where few differences in quality may actually exist among top-selling brands. Consumer groups, wary of such research, argue that too many ads promote only an image and provide little information about a product's price, its content, or the work conditions under which it was produced.

Creative Development

Teams of writers and artists—many of whom regard ads as a commercial art form—make up the nerve center of the advertising business. The creative department outlines the rough sketches for print and online ads and then develops the words and graphics. For radio, the creative side prepares a working script, generating ideas for everything from choosing the narrator's voice to determining background sound effects. For television, the creative department develops a **storyboard**, a sort of blueprint or roughly drawn comic-strip version of the potential ad. For digital media, the creative team may develop Web sites, interactive tools, flash games, downloads, and **viral marketing**—short videos or other content that (marketers hope) quickly gains widespread attention as users share it with friends online or by word of mouth.

Often the creative side of the business finds itself in conflict with the research side. In the 1960s, for example, both Doyle Dane Bernbach (DDB) and Ogilvy & Mather downplayed research; they championed the art of persuasion and what "felt right." Yet DDB's simple ads for Volkswagen Beetles in the 1960s were based on weeks of intensive interviews with VW workers as well as on creative instincts. The campaign was remarkably successful in establishing the first niche for a foreign car manufacturer in the United States. Although sales of the VW Bug had been growing before the ad campaign started, the successful ads helped Volkswagen preempt the Detroit auto industry's entry into the small-car field.

Both the creative and the strategic sides of the business acknowledge that they cannot predict with any certainty which ads and which campaigns will succeed. Agencies say ads work best by slowly creating brand-name identities—by associating certain products over time with quality and reliability in the minds of consumers. Some economists, however, believe that much of the money spent on advertising is ultimately wasted because it simply encourages consumers to change from one brand name to another. Such switching may lead to increased profits for a particular manufacturer, but it has little positive impact on the overall economy.

Media Coordination: Planning and Placing Advertising

Ad agency media departments are staffed by media planners and **media buyers**: people who choose and purchase the types of media that are best suited to carry a client's ads, reach the targeted audience, and measure the effectiveness of those ad placements. For instance, a company like Procter & Gamble, currently the world's leading advertiser, displays its more than three hundred major brands—most of them household products like Crest toothpaste and Pampers diapers—on TV shows viewed primarily by women. To reach male viewers, however, media buyers encourage beer advertisers to spend their ad budgets on cable and network sports programming, evening talk radio, or sports magazines.

Along with commissions or fees, advertisers often add incentive clauses to their contracts with agencies, raising the fee if sales goals are met and lowering it if goals are missed. Incentive clauses can sometimes encourage agencies to conduct repetitive **saturation advertising**, in which a variety of media are inundated with ads aimed at target audiences. The initial Miller Lite beer campaign ("Tastes great, less filling"), which used humor and retired athletes to reach its male audience, became one of the most successful saturation campaigns in media history. It ran from 1973 to 1991 and included television and radio spots, magazine and newspaper ads, and billboards and point-of-purchase store displays. The excessive repetition of the campaign helped light beer overcome a potential image problem: being viewed as watered-down beer unworthy of "real" men.

The cost of advertising, especially on network television, increases each year. The Super Bowl remains the most expensive program for purchasing television advertising, with thirty seconds of time costing on average $4.5 million in 2015 on Fox—up from $4 million in 2014. (The network also reported that in 2015, the big game generated 24.4 million tweets.) Running a thirty-second ad during a national prime-time TV show can cost from $50,000 to more than $500,000, depending on the popularity and ratings of the program. The prime-time average for a thirty-second TV spot was $107,000 in 2015, down from an all-time high of $129,600 in the prerecession year 2005.[3] (See Case Study: "Hey, Super Bowl Sponsors: Your Ads Are Already Forgotten")

Account and Client Management

Client liaisons, or **account executives**, are responsible for bringing in new business and managing the accounts of established clients, including overseeing budgets and the research, creative, and media planning work done on their campaigns. This department also oversees new ad campaigns in which several agencies bid for a client's business, coordinating the presentation of a proposed campaign and various aspects of the bidding process, such as determining what a series of ads will cost a client. Account executives function as liaisons between the advertiser and the agency's creative team. Because most major companies maintain their own ad departments to handle everyday details, account executives also coordinate activities between their agency and a client's in-house personnel.

Figure 10-5. Creative Advertising The New York ad agency Doyle Dane Bernbach created a famous series of print and television ads for Volkswagen beginning in 1959 (*above, left*) and helped usher in an era of creative advertising that combined a single-point sales emphasis with bold design, humor, and honesty. Arnold Worldwide, a Boston agency, continued the highly creative approach with its clever, award-winning "Drivers wanted" campaign for the New Beetle (*above*).

The advertising business is volatile, and account departments are especially vulnerable to upheavals. One industry study conducted in the mid-1980s indicated that client accounts stayed with the same agency for about seven years on average, but since the late 1980s, clients have changed agencies much more often. Clients routinely conduct **account reviews**, the process of evaluating and reinvigorating a product's image by reviewing an ad agency's existing campaign or by inviting several new agencies to submit new campaign strategies, which may lead the product company to switch agencies. For example, when General Motors restructured its business in 2010, it put its advertising account for Chevrolet under review. Campbell Ewald (a subsidiary of Interpublic) had held the Chevy account since 1919, creating such campaigns as "The Heartbeat of America" and "Like a Rock," but after the review, it lost the $30 million account to Publicis.[4]

Trends in Online Advertising

The earliest form of Web advertising appeared in the mid-1990s and featured *banner ads*, the printlike display ads that load across the top or side of a Web page. Since that time, other formats have emerged, including video ads, sponsorships, and "rich media"—like pop-up ads, pop-under ads, flash multimedia ads, and **interstitials**, which pop up in new screen windows as a user clicks to a new Web page. Other forms of Internet advertising include classified ads and e-mail ads. Unsolicited commercial e-mail—known as **spam**—accounted for more than 85 percent of e-mail messages by 2010.

Paid search advertising has become the dominant format of Web advertising. Even though their original mission was to provide impartial search results, search sites such as Google, Yahoo!, and Bing have quietly morphed into advertising companies, selling sponsored links associated with search terms and distributing online ads to affiliated Web pages.[5]

Back in 2004, digital ads accounted for just over 4 percent of global ad spending. By 2012, the Internet had gained an 18 percent share of worldwide ad spending, and in 2014, it was the second-largest global advertising medium behind only television. In the United States, the Internet accounted for 19.1 percent of ad spending in 2012, making it the second-largest advertising medium, behind television.[6] According to *Adweek*, spending on digital ads globally grew to 16 percent in 2014.[7]

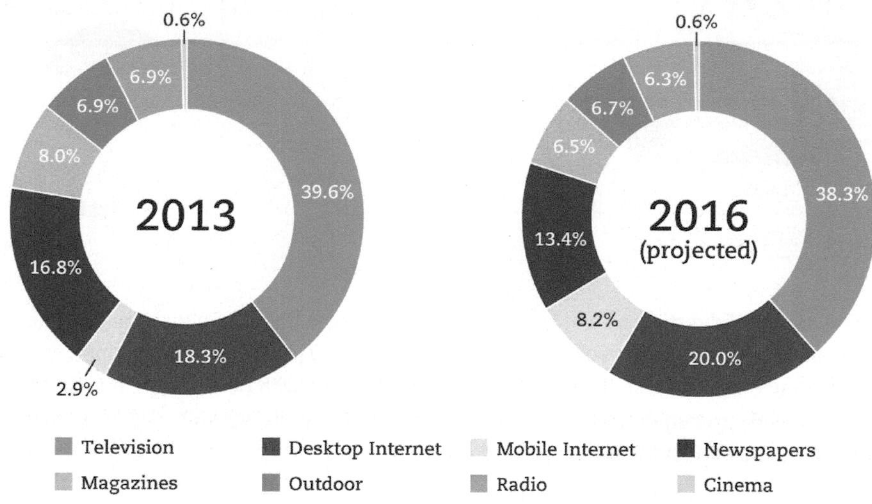

Data from: ZenithOptimedia, in Ricardo Bilton, "The Surprising State of Digital Ad Spending in 5 Charts," Digiday, June 17, 2014, http://digiday.com/brands/present-future-digital-ad-spending-5-charts/.

Figure 10-6. Share of Global Ad Spending by Medium

Online Advertising Challenges Traditional Media

Because Internet advertising is the leading growth area, advertising mega-agencies have added digital media agencies and departments to develop and sell ads online. For example, WPP has 24/7 Media and Xaxis, Omnicom owns Proximity Worldwide, Publicis has Digitas LBi and Razorfish, and Interpublic operates R/GA. Realizing the potential of their online ad businesses, major Web services have also aggressively expanded into the advertising market by acquiring smaller Internet advertising agencies. Google bought DoubleClick, the biggest online ad server; Yahoo! purchased Right Media, which auctions online ad space; and Microsoft acquired aQuantive, an online ad server and network that enables advertisers to place ads on multiple Web sites with a single buy. Google, as the top search engine, has surpassed the traditional mega-agencies in revenue, earning $66 billion in 2014, with almost all of that coming from advertising. Facebook, the top social networking site, is not yet in Google's league but remains poised to become a bigger advertising threat with an audience of over 1.4 billion users worldwide in 2015. Facebook earned $12.4 billion in 2014, most of that profit also coming from ads.[8]

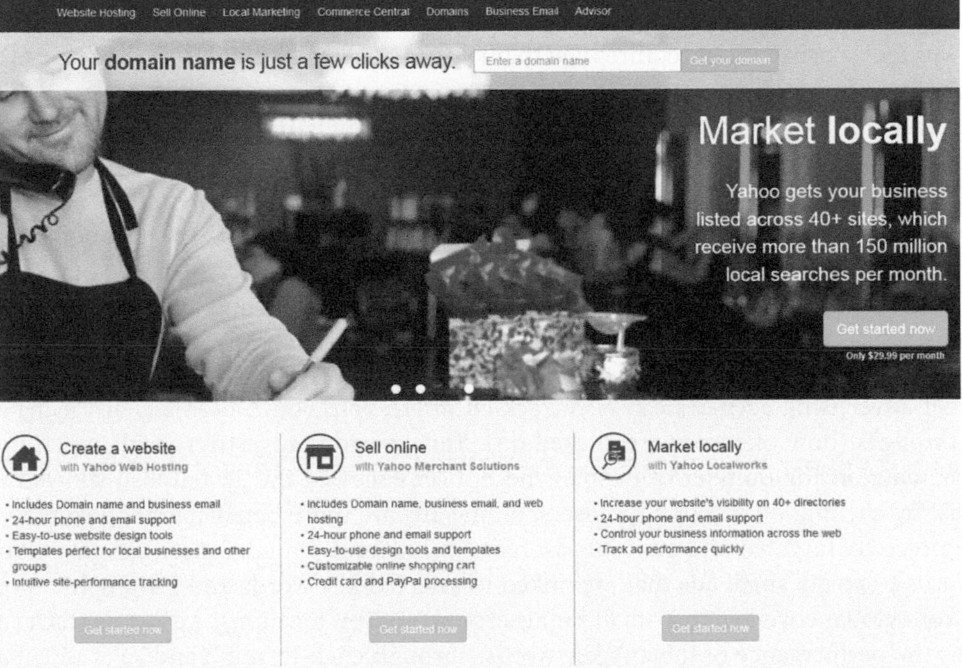

Figure 10-7. Online Ads are mostly placed by large Internet companies like Google, Yahoo!, Microsoft, and AOL. Such services have allowed small businesses access to more customers than traditional advertising because the online ads are often cheaper to produce and are shown only to targeted users.

Facebook has made its biggest strides in mobile advertising. While Google accounted for nearly 32 percent of all online global ad spending in 2013—over $120 billion—Facebook finished in second place, with roughly 6 percent of the total spent on online global advertising that year. In 2014, the *New York Times* reported that Facebook was closing the mobile gap, noting that the social media site accounted for nearly 16 percent of mobile advertising dollars in the previous year, while Google's share had dropped.[9]

As the Internet draws people's attention away from traditional mass media, leading advertisers are moving more of their ad campaigns and budget dollars to digital media. For example, the CEO of consumer product giant Unilever, a company with more than four hundred brands (including Dove, Hellmann's, and Lipton) and a multibillion-dollar advertising budget, doubled its spending on digital media back in 2010, since customers were spending much more time on the Internet and mobile phones. "I think you need to fish where the fish are," the Unilever CEO said. "So I've made it fairly clear that I'm driving Unilever to be at the leading edge of digital marketing."[10]

Online Marketers Target Individuals

Internet ads offer many advantages to advertisers, compared to ads in traditional media outlets like newspapers, magazines, radio, or television. Perhaps the biggest advantage—and potentially the most disturbing part for citizens—is that marketers can develop consumer profiles that direct targeted ads to specific Web site visitors. They do this by collecting information about each Internet user through cookies and online surveys. For example, when an ESPN.com contest requires you to fill out a survey to be eligible to win sports tickets, or when washingtonpost.com requires that you create an account for free access to the site, marketers use that information to build a profile about you. The cookies they attach to your profile allow them to track your activities on a certain site. They can also add to your profile by tracking what you search for and even by mining your profiles and data on social networking sites. Agencies can also add online and retail sales data (what you bought and where) to user profiles to create an unprecedented database, largely without your knowledge. Such data mining is a boon to marketers, but it is very troubling to consumer privacy advocates.

Internet advertising agencies can also track ad *impressions* (how often ads are seen) and *click-throughs* (how often ads are clicked on). This provides advertisers with much more specific data on the number of people who not only viewed the ad but also showed real interest by clicking on it. For advertisers, online ads are more beneficial because they are more precisely targeted and easily measured. For example, an advertiser can use Google AdWords to create small ads that are linked to selected key words and geographic targeting (from global coverage to a small radius around a given location). AdWords tracks and graphs the performance of the ad's key words (through click-through and sales rates) and lets the advertiser update the campaign at any time. This kind of targeted advertising enables smaller companies with a $500 ad budget, for example, to place their ads in the same location as larger companies with multimillion-dollar ad budgets.

Beyond computers, smartphones—the "third screen" for advertisers—are of increasing importance. Smartphones offer effective targeting to individuals, as does Internet advertising, but they also offer advertisers the bonus of tailoring ads according to either a specific geographic location (e.g., a restaurant ad goes to someone in close proximity) or the user demographic, since wireless providers already have that information. Google has also developed unique applications for mobile advertising and searching. For example, the Google Goggles smartphone app enables the user to take a photo of an object—such as a book cover, a landmark, a logo, or text—and then have Google return related search results. Google's Voice Search app lets users speak their search terms. Such apps are designed to maintain Google's dominant search engine position (which generates most of its profits) on the increasingly important mobile platform.

Advertising Invades Social Media

Social media, such as Facebook, Twitter, and Foursquare, provide a wealth of data for advertisers to mine. These sites and apps create an unprecedented public display of likes, dislikes, locations, and other personal information. And advertisers are using such information to further refine their ability to send targeted ads that might interest users. Facebook and other sites (like Hulu) go even further by asking users if they liked the ad or not. For example, clicking off a display ad in Facebook results in the question "Why didn't you like it?" followed by the choices "uninteresting," "misleading," "offensive," "repetitive," and "other." All that information goes straight back to advertisers so they can revise their advertising and try to engage you the next time. Beyond allowing advertisers to target and monitor their ad campaigns, most social media encourage advertisers to create their own online identity. For example, Ben & Jerry's Ice Cream's Facebook page has more than seven million "friends." Despite appearances, such profiles and identities still constitute a form of advertising and serve to promote products to a growing online audience for virtually no cost.

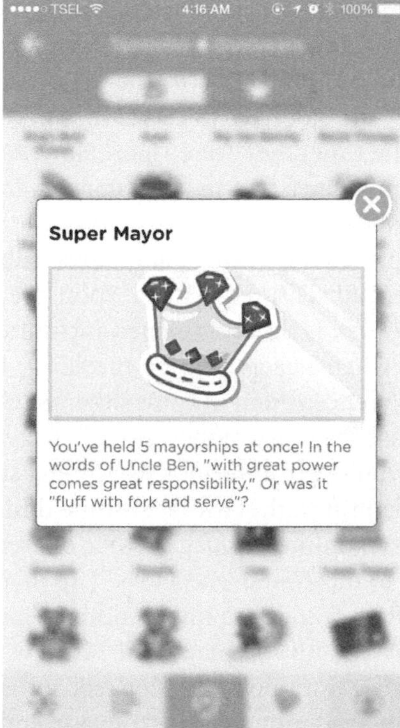

Figure 10-8. Foursquare is using its recent popularity to increase revenues by partnering with businesses to provide "specials" to Foursquare users and "mayors." While it may seem like a great deal to offer free snacks or drinks to users, what Foursquare is really offering to businesses ("venues") is the chance to mine data and "be able to track how your venue is performing over time thanks to [Foursquare's] robust set of venue analytics."

Companies and organizations also buy traditional paid advertisements on social media sites. A major objective of their *paid media* is to get *earned media*, or to convince online consumers to promote products on their own. Imagine that the environmental group the National Resources Defense Council buys an ad on Facebook that attracts your interest. That's a successful paid media ad for the council, but it's even more effective if it becomes earned media—that is, when you mark that you "Like" it, you essentially give the organization a personal endorsement. Knowing you like the ad, your friends view it; as they pass it along, it gets more earned media and eventually becomes viral—an even greater advertising achievement. As the Nielsen Media rating service says about online earned media, "Study after study has shown that consumers trust their friends and peers more than anyone else when it comes to making a purchase decision."[11] Social media are helping advertisers use such personal endorsements to further their own products and marketing messages—basically, letting consumers do the work for them.

A recent controversy in online advertising is whether people have to disclose if they are being paid to promote a product. For example, bloggers often review products or restaurants as part of their content. Some bloggers with large followings have been paid (either directly or by "gifts" of free products or trips) to give positive reviews or promote products on their site. When such instances, dubbed "blog-ola" by the press, came to light in 2008 and 2009, the bloggers argued that they did not have to reveal that they were being compensated for posting their opinions. At the time, they were right. However, in 2009, the Federal Trade Commission released new guidelines that require bloggers to disclose when an advertiser is compensating them to discuss a product. In 2010, a similar controversy erupted when it was revealed that many celebrities were being paid to tweet about their "favorite" products. One of Facebook's more recent ad ventures is called "sponsored stories." The way this works, according to the *New York Times*, is that companies, including Amazon, "pay Facebook to generate . . . automated ads" when a user clicks on the "Like" button for a Facebook participating brand partner or "references them in some other way." Sponsors and product companies like this service because they save money, since "no creative work is involved." However, in 2012, this practice resulted in Facebook's settling a state of California class action suit out of court. The lead plaintiff in the case, a costume designer from Seattle, innocently clicked the "Like" button for an online language course offered by Rosetta Stone. Then several months later, according to the *Times*, "she showed up in an ad for Rosetta Stone on her friends' Facebook pages."[12] Part of the case involved her resentment about not consenting to be used in an ad or receiving any compensation. As new ways to advertise or sponsor products through social media continue to develop, consumers need to keep a careful eye out for what is truly a friendly recommendation from a friend and what is advertising.

Persuasive Techniques in Contemporary Advertising

Ad agencies and product companies often argue that the main purpose of advertising is to inform consumers about available products in a straightforward way. Most consumer ads, however, merely create a mood or tell stories about products without revealing much else. A one-page magazine ad, a giant billboard, or a thirty-second TV spot gives consumers little information about how a product was made, how much it costs, or how it compares with similar brands. In managing space and time constraints, advertising agencies engage in a variety of persuasive techniques.

Conventional Persuasive Strategies

One of the most frequently used advertising approaches is the **famous-person testimonial**, in which a product is endorsed by a well-known person. Famous endorsers include Justin Timberlake for Bud Light, Taylor Swift for Diet Coke, and Beyoncé for Pepsi. Athletes earn some of the biggest endorsement contracts. For example, Chicago Bulls player Derrick Rose has a $185 million thirteen-year deal with Adidas, the same shoe company that has a $160 million deal with now-retired soccer star David Beckham. Tiger Woods remains one of the leading endorsers, despite his personal scandals in 2009. Although some sponsors—including Accenture, Gatorade, and Gillette—dropped him, companies such as Nike and Rolex either stayed with him or sought him out in deals that still totaled over $60 million a year in 2014—down from $80 million in 2012.

Figure 10-9. Famous-Person Testimonials Major stars used to be somewhat wary of appearing in ads (at least in the United States), but many brands now use celebrity endorsements. A recent Revlon campaign featured both Emma Stone and Olivia Wilde.

Another technique, the **plain-folks pitch**, associates a product with simplicity. Over the years, Volkswagen ("Drivers wanted"), General Electric ("We bring good things to life"), and Microsoft ("I'm a PC and Windows 7 was my idea") have each used slogans that stress how new technologies fit into the lives of ordinary people. In a way, the Facebook technique of sponsored stories fits this model, since it depends on friends' endorsements of products rather than the words or images of stars or athletes.

By contrast, the **snob-appeal approach** attempts to persuade consumers that using a product will maintain or elevate their social status. Advertisers selling jewelry, perfume, clothing, and luxury automobiles often use snob appeal. For example, the pricey bottled water brand Fiji ran ads in *Esquire* and other national magazines that said, "The label says Fiji because it's not bottled in Cleveland"—a jab intended to favorably compare the water bottled in the South Pacific to the drinking water of an industrial city in Ohio. (Fiji ended up withdrawing the ad after the Cleveland Water Department released test data showing that its water was more pure than Fiji water.)

Another approach, the **bandwagon effect**, points out in exaggerated claims that *everyone* is using a particular product. Brands that refer to themselves as "America's favorite" or "the best" imply that consumers will be left behind if they ignore these products. A different technique, the **hidden-fear appeal**, plays on consumers' sense of insecurity. Deodorant, mouthwash, and shampoo ads frequently invoke anxiety, pointing out that only a specific product could relieve embarrassing personal hygiene problems and restore a person to social acceptability.

Case **STUDY**

Hey, Super Bowl Sponsors: Your Ads Are Already Forgotten

by Eric Chemi

With Super Bowl ad rates averaging $4.5 million per 30 seconds, total spending for commercials during this year's game approached $337 million. Here's the problem: Most of those commercials have already been forgotten. A survey of audience respondents conducted by marketing-research firm Db5 for *Bloomberg Businessweek* suggests they remembered less than 10 percent of Sunday's commercials. Despite what some so-called expert panels say about why certain ads are more successful than others, it's likely those results are too biased or subjective to tell us which ads were truly memorable. Db5 surveyed 504 people who watched the game in its entirety, and the results are surprising.

When asked to recall as many companies as possible that had ads during the big game, the average viewer in the survey could name only 5.4 brands. With more than 50 companies buying ads, that means less than 10 percent were recalled. The top winners were Budweiser, Doritos, Coca-Cola, PepsiCo, and GoDaddy—the only brands with viewer recall rates of more than 25 percent. Just 12 companies saw more than 10 percent recollection rates; the vast majority saw less than 10 percent recall. Even when viewers were given a sample list of advertisers and asked whether they remembered seeing an ad for each company, only 49 percent of those ads were recalled on average.

Daniel Goldstein, Db5's chief strategy officer, is a former ad executive who has worked on several major Super Bowl campaigns (Pepsi, Doritos, Visa). He says everybody is trying to copy the one-hit-wonder approach of Apple's famous "1984" ad. Apple was the first to prove you could air a commercial only one time, during the Super Bowl, and have it bring you a ton of follow-up attention, praise, and sales," he says. Since then, that phenomenon has created a monster. Talking animals, talking babies, talking animal babies, big celebrities, bikinis, big-name Hollywood directors—the list of gimmicks is endless. Most of the audience can't keep up with all the tricks, and almost all the ads are quickly forgotten.

Some trends could have made a difference. Consistency may have been a factor; the most-remembered commercials came from companies who buy Super Bowl ads on an annual basis, such as Budweiser, Doritos, Coke, Pepsi, and GoDaddy. Another theory says that ads can be remembered better with advanced viewings, because they would give audiences more chances to see and process the spot. According to the data, however, that did not turn out to be the case. Ads that were seen for the first time did just as well as previously viewed ads.

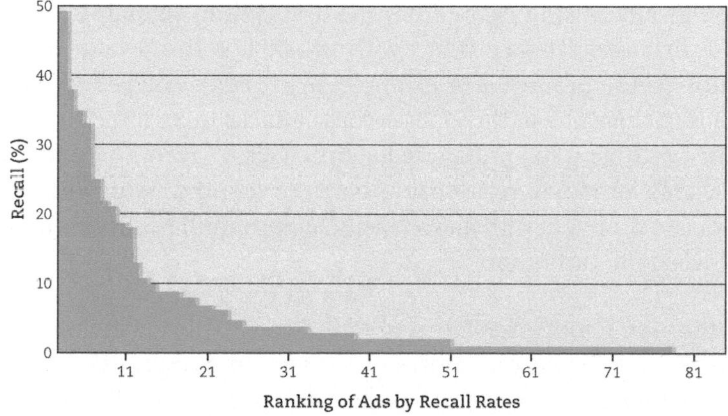

Data from: Eric Chemi, "Hey, Super Bowl Sponsors: Your Ads Are Already Forgotten," *Bloomberg Businessweek*, February 3, 2014, www.businessweek.com/articles/2014-02-03/hey-super-bowl-sponsors-your-ads-are-already-forgotten.

The mathematical question for companies: Is 10 percent recall among 100 million people worth $4.5 million? With the increase of media fragmentation, there are so few opportunities to reach so many viewers at once. Goldstein says that this is not a knock against the Super Bowl as a platform for advertisers, but rather a signal that advertisers should not waste such a big opportunity for which they paid big bucks. The one trend that does seem to work is consistently showing up year after year, making the money a worthwhile investment in the long run. If companies want to go big, they should be going big every year.

A final ad strategy, used more in local TV and radio campaigns than in national ones, has been labeled **irritation advertising**: creating product-name recognition by being annoying or obnoxious. Although both research and common sense suggest that irritating ads do not work very well, there have been exceptions. In the 1950s and 1960s, for instance, an aspirin company ran a TV ad illustrating a hammer pounding inside a person's brain. Critics and the product's own agency suggested that people bought the product, which sold well, to get relief from the ad as well as from their headaches. On the regional level, irritation ads are often used by appliance discount stores or local car dealers, who dress in outrageous costumes and yell at the camera.

The Association Principle

Historically, American car advertisements have shown automobiles in natural settings—on winding roads that cut through rugged mountain passes or across shimmering wheat fields—but rarely on congested city streets or in other urban settings where most driving actually occurs. Instead, the car—an example of advanced technology—merges seamlessly into the natural world.

This type of advertising exemplifies the **association principle**, a widely used persuasive technique that associates a product with a positive cultural value or image even if it has little connection to the product. For example, many ads displayed visual symbols of American patriotism in the wake of the 9/11 terrorist attacks in an attempt to associate products and companies with national pride. Media critic Leslie Savan noted that in trying "to convince us that there's an innate relationship between a brand name and an attitude," advertising may associate products with nationalism, happy families, success at school or work, natural scenery, freedom, or humor.[13]

One of the more controversial uses of the association principle has been the linkage of products to stereotyped caricatures of women. In numerous instances, women have been portrayed either as sex objects or as clueless housewives who, during many a daytime TV commercial, need the powerful off-screen voice of a male narrator to instruct them in their own homes.

Another popular use of the association principle is to claim that products are "real" and "natural"—possibly the most familiar adjectives associated with advertising. For example, Coke sells itself as "the real thing," and the cosmetics industry offers synthetic products that promise to make women look "natural." The adjectives *real* and *natural* saturate American ads yet almost always describe processed or synthetic goods. Green marketing has a similar problem, as it is associated with goods and services that aren't always environmentally friendly.

Philip Morris's Marlboro brand has used the association principle to completely transform its product image. In the 1920s, Marlboro began as a fashionable women's cigarette. Back then, the company's ads equated smoking with a sense of freedom, attempting to appeal to women who had just won the right to vote. Marlboro, though, did poorly as a women's product, and new campaigns in the 1950s and 1960s transformed the brand into a man's cigarette. Powerful images of active, rugged men dominated the ads. Often, Marlboro associated its product with nature, displaying an image of a lone cowboy roping a calf, building a fence, or riding over a snow-covered landscape. In 2014, the branding consultancy BrandZ (a division of WPP) named Marlboro the world's ninth "most valuable global brand," having an estimated worth of $67 billion. (Google, Apple, IBM, Microsoft, McDonald's, Coca-Cola, Visa, and AT&T ranked ahead of Marlboro.)

Disassociation as an Advertising Strategy

As a response to corporate mergers and public skepticism toward impersonal and large companies, a *disassociation corollary* emerged in advertising. The nation's largest winery, Gallo, pioneered the idea in the 1980s by establishing a dummy corporation, Bartles & Jaymes, to sell jug wine and wine coolers, thereby avoiding the use of the Gallo corporate image in ads and on its bottles. The ads featured Frank and Ed, two low-key, grandfatherly types, as "co-owners" and ad spokesmen. On the one hand, as a *BusinessWeek* article observed, the ad was "a way to connect with younger consumers who yearn for products that are handmade, quirky, and authentic."[14] On the other hand, this technique, by concealing the Gallo tie-in, allowed the wine giant to disassociate from the negative publicity of the 1970s—a period when labor leader Cesar Chavez organized migrant workers in a long boycott of Gallo.

In the 1990s, General Motors also used the disassociation strategy, according to the same *BusinessWeek* report. Reeling from a declining corporate reputation, GM tried to package the Saturn as "a small-town enterprise, run by folks not terribly unlike Frank and Ed," who provide caring, personal service.[15] In 2009, however, GM shut down its struggling Saturn brand during the economic recession. As an ad strategy, disassociation often links new brands in a product line to eccentric or simple regional places rather than to images conjured up by big cities and multinational conglomerates.

Advertising as Myth and Story

Another way to understand ads is to use **myth analysis**, which provides insights into how ads work at a general cultural level. Here, the term *myth* does not refer simply to an untrue story or outright falsehood. Rather, myths help us define people, organizations, and social norms. According to myth analysis, most ads are narratives with stories to tell and social conflicts to resolve. Three common mythical elements are found in many types of ads:

1. Ads incorporate myths in mini-story form, featuring characters, settings, and plots.
2. Most stories in ads involve conflicts, pitting one set of characters or social values against another.
3. Such conflicts are negotiated or resolved by the end of the ad, usually by applying or purchasing a product. In advertising, the product and those who use it often emerge as the heroes of the story.

Even though the stories that ads tell are usually compressed into thirty seconds or onto a single page, they still include the traditional elements of narrative. For instance, many SUV ads ask us to imagine ourselves driving out into the raw, untamed wilderness, to a quiet, natural place that only, say, a Jeep can reach. The audience implicitly understands that the SUV can somehow, almost magically, take us out of our fast-paced, freeway-wrapped urban world, plagued with long commutes, traffic jams, and automobile exhaust. This implied conflict between the natural world and the manufactured world is apparently resolved by the image of the SUV in a natural setting. Although SUVs typically clog our urban and suburban highways, get low gas mileage, and create tons of air pollution particulates, the ads ignore those facts. Instead, they offer an alternative story about the wonders of nature, and the SUV amazingly becomes the vehicle that negotiates the conflict between city/suburban blight and the unspoiled wilderness.

Most advertisers do not expect consumers to accept without question the stories or associations they make in ads. As media scholar Michael Schudson observed in his book *Advertising: The Uneasy Persuasion*, they do not "make the mistake of asking for belief."[16] Instead, ads are most effective when they create attitudes and reinforce values. Then they operate like popular fiction, encouraging us to suspend our disbelief. Although most of us realize that ads create a fictional world, we often get caught up in their stories and myths. Indeed, ads often work because the stories offer comfort about our deepest desires and conflicts—between men and women, nature and technology, tradition and change, the real and the artificial. Most contemporary consumer advertising does not provide much useful information about products. Instead, it tries to reassure us that through the use of familiar brand names, everyday tensions and problems can be managed.

Product Placement

Product companies and ad agencies have become adept in recent years at *product placement*: strategically placing ads or buying space in movies, TV shows, comic books, video games, blogs, and music videos so that products appear as part of a story's set environment. For example, a 2015 episode of *Modern Family* was told entirely through a character's MacBook Pro and apps filmed on Apple devices, though the idea came from the show rather than from Apple. In 2013, the Superman movie *Man of Steel* had the most product placements ever for a film up to that time, with two-hundred-plus marketing partners in deals worth $160 million, including those with Hardee's, Gillette, Sears, Nikon, Nokia, 7-Eleven, IHOP, and the National Guard.

David Giesbrecht/© Netflix/Everett Collection

Figure 10-10. Product Placement in movies and television is more prevalent than ever. On television, placement is often most visible in reality shows, while scripted series and films tend to be more subtle—at least some of the time. Apple products are so ubiquitous in movies and television that many viewers have probably become accustomed to the prominent display of its glowing, familiar logo on shows like *House of Cards*.

For many critics, product placement has gotten out of hand. What started out as subtle appearances in realistic settings—like Reese's Pieces in the 1982 movie *E.T.*—has turned into Coca-Cola's being almost an honorary cast member on Fox's *American Idol* set. The practice is now so pronounced that it was a subject of Hollywood parody in the 2006 film *Talladega Nights: The Ballad of Ricky Bobby*, starring Will Ferrell.

In 2005, watchdog organization Commercial Alert asked both the FTC and the FCC to mandate that consumers be warned about product placement on television. The FTC rejected the petition, whereas the FCC proposed product placement rules but had still not approved them by the fall of 2015. In contrast, in 2007 the European Union approved product placement for television but requires programs to alert viewers of such paid placements. In Britain, for example, the letter *P* must appear in the corner of the screen at commercial breaks and at the beginning and end of a show to signal product placements.[17]

Examining ETHICS

Do Alcohol Ads Encourage Binge Drinking?

With clear evidence that cigarettes caused lung cancer, the tobacco industry in the early 1970s chose to pull all TV ads for cigarettes, in part to ward off the planned increase in public service ads that the government and nonprofit agencies were airing about the dangers of smoking. Similarly, for decades ads for hard liquor (called "distilled spirits" by the industry) were not shown in TV markets across the United States for fear of igniting anti-alcohol public service spots warning about alcoholism and heavy drinking, and countering TV commercials. Some ads for hard liquor have reappeared in recent years, but not all channels or shows will air them; often they appear on late-night or specialized programming.

Beer ads, however, have never been interrupted and remain ubiquitous, usually associating beer drinking with young people, sex appeal, and general good times. As such, the debates over alcohol ads continue, especially in light of the ritual of binge drinking that has bedeviled universities throughout the United States. According to the Centers for Disease Control and Prevention, more than 4,500 deaths annually result from underage and binge drinking, the latter of which is generally defined as six drinks or more in one sitting.

A Dartmouth University study released in 2015 and published in the medical journal *JAMA Pediatrics* demonstrated that "alcohol ads have led to a risk in underage drinking and binge drinking."[1] The study, "Cued Recall of Alcohol Advertising on Television and Underage Drinking Behavior," surveyed more than 2,500 young people between the ages of fifteen and twenty-three in 2011 and then reinterviewed 1,500 of them in 2013.

In 2013, 66 percent of high school students said they had tried alcohol, whereas only 21 percent said they had engaged in binge drinking. However, 29 percent of the fifteen- to seventeen-year-olds reinterviewed after exposure to alcohol ads reported binge drinking. One coauthor of the study said, "It's very strong evidence that underage drinkers are not only exposed to television advertising, but they also assimilate the messages. That process moves them forward in their drinking behavior."[2] Although the study argues that the efforts by hard liquor advertisers to protect young people from the messages in their ads are ineffective, the Distilled Spirits Council disagrees and said the Dartmouth study was "driven by advocacy, not science."[3]

One ethical question raised by the 2015 study has to do with those who work in the ad business and the work they are asked to do. Many reputable ad agencies will ask new or potential employees if there are clients and products that they would not represent. Some agencies might specifically ask newly hired account executives if they would be willing to work for a tobacco or liquor company or if, given what they know about childhood obesity and the low nutrition content in many fast foods, sugared cereals, and popular sodas, they could represent those products.

It might be a useful exercise, then, to ask yourself, Are their products or companies you would not work for or represent in some capacity? Why or why not? Would you be willing to represent tobacco companies that wanted to place ads in magazines or a hard liquor product that wanted to advertise on TV? Why or why not?

Media Literacy and THE CRITICAL PROCESS

The Branded You

To what extent are you influenced by brands?

1 **DESCRIPTION.** Take a look around your home or dormitory room and list all the branded products you've purchased, including food, electronics, clothes, shoes, toiletries, and cleaning products.

2 **ANALYSIS.** Now organize your branded items into categories. For example, how many items of clothing are branded with athletic, university, or designer logos? What patterns emerge, and what kind of psychographic profile do these brands suggest about you?

3 **INTERPRETATION.** Why did you buy each particular product? Was it because you thought it was of superior quality? Because it was cheaper? Because your parents used this product (so it was tried, trusted, and familiar)? Because it made you feel a certain way about yourself and you wanted to project this image toward others? Have you ever purchased items without brands or removed logos once you bought the product? Why?

4 **EVALUATION.** As you become more conscious of our branded environment (and your participation in it), what is your assessment of U.S. consumer culture? Is there too much conspicuous branding? What is good and bad about the ubiquity of brand names in our culture? How does branding relate to the common American ethic of individualism?

5 **ENGAGEMENT.** Visit Adbusters (www.adbusters.org) and read about action projects that confront commercialism, including Buy Nothing Day, Media Carta, TV Turnoff, the Culturejammers Network, the Blackspot nonbrand sneaker, and Unbrand America. Also visit the home page for the advocacy organization Commercial Alert (www.commercialalert.org) to learn about the most recent commercial incursions into everyday life and what can be done about them. Or write a letter to a company about a product or ad that you think is a problem. How does the company respond?

Commercial Speech and Regulating Advertising

In 1791, Congress passed and the states ratified the First Amendment to the U.S. Constitution, promising, among other guarantees, to "make no law . . . abridging the freedom of speech, or of the press." Over time, we have developed a shorthand label for the First Amendment, misnaming it the free-speech clause. The amendment ensures that citizens and journalists can generally say and write what they want, but it says nothing directly about **commercial speech**—any print or broadcast expression for which a fee is charged to organizations and individuals buying time or space in the mass media.

Whereas freedom of speech refers to the right to express thoughts, beliefs, and opinions in the abstract marketplace of ideas, commercial speech is about the right to circulate goods, services, and images in the concrete marketplace of products. For most of the history of mass media, only very wealthy citizens established political parties, and multinational companies could routinely afford to purchase speech that reached millions. The Internet, however, has helped level that playing field. Political speech, like a cleverly edited mash-up video, or entertaining speech, like a music video by California teenager Rebecca Black singing about the weekend (the infamous "Friday" video on YouTube), can go viral and quickly reach millions, rivaling the most expensive commercial speech.

Although the mass media have not hesitated to carry product and service-selling advertisements and have embraced the concepts of infomercials and cable home-shopping channels, they have also refused certain issue-based advertising that might upset their traditional advertisers. For example, although corporations have easy access in placing paid ads, many labor unions have had their print and broadcast ads rejected as "controversial." The nonprofit Adbusters Media Foundation, based in Vancouver, British Columbia, has had difficulty getting networks to air its "uncommercials." One of its spots promotes the Friday after Thanksgiving (traditionally, the beginning of the holiday shopping season) as Buy Nothing Day.

Courtesy of adbusters.org

Figure 10-11. Adbusters Media Foundation This nonprofit organization based in Canada says its spoof ads, like the one shown here, are designed to "put out a better product and beat the corporations at their own game" (see www.adbusters.org). Besides satirizing the advertising appeals of the fashion, tobacco, alcohol, and food industries, the Adbusters Media Foundation sponsors Buy Nothing Day, an anticonsumption campaign that annually falls on the day after Thanksgiving—one of the busiest shopping days of the year.

Critical Issues in Advertising

In his 1957 book *The Hidden Persuaders*, Vance Packard expressed concern that advertising was manipulating helpless consumers, attacking our dignity, and invading "the privacy of our minds."[18] According to this view, the advertising industry was all-powerful. Although consumers have historically been regarded as dupes by many critics, research reveals that the consumer mind is not as easy to predict as some advertisers once thought. In the 1950s, for example, Ford could not successfully sell its midsize car, the oddly named Edsel, which was aimed at newly prosperous Ford customers looking to move up to the latest in push-button window wipers and antennas. After a splashy and expensive ad campaign, Ford sold only 63,000 Edsels in 1958 and just 2,000 in 1960, when the model was discontinued.

One of the most disastrous campaigns ever featured the now-famous "This is not your father's Oldsmobile" spots, which began running in 1989 and starred celebrities like former Beatles drummer Ringo Starr and his daughter. Oldsmobile (which became part of General Motors in 1908) and its ad agency, Leo Burnett, decided to market to a younger generation after sales declined from a high of 1.1 million vehicles in 1985 to only 715,000 in 1988. But the campaign backfired, apparently alienating its older loyal customers (who may have felt abandoned by Olds and its catchy new slogan) and failing to lure younger buyers (who probably still had trouble getting past the name Olds). In 2000, Oldsmobile sold only 260,000 cars, and GM had phased out its Olds division by 2005.[19]

As these examples illustrate, most people are not easily persuaded by advertising. Over the years, studies have suggested that between 75 and 90 percent of new consumer products typically fail because they are not embraced by the buying public.[20] But despite public resistance to many new products, the ad industry has made contributions, including raising the American standard of living and financing most media industries. Yet serious concerns over the impact of advertising remain. Watchdog groups worry about the expansion of advertising's reach, and critics continue to condemn ads that stereotype or associate products with sex appeal, youth, and narrow definitions of beauty. Some of the most serious concerns involve children, teens, and health.

Children and Advertising

Children and teenagers, living in a culture dominated by TV ads, are often viewed as "consumer trainees." For years, groups such as Action for Children's Television (ACT) worked to limit advertising aimed at children. In the 1980s, ACT fought particularly hard to curb program-length commercials: thirty-minute cartoon programs (such as *G.I. Joe*, *My Little Pony and Friends*, *The Care Bear Family*, and *He-Man and the Masters of the Universe*) developed for television syndication primarily to promote a line of toys. This commercial tradition continued with programs such as *Pokémon* and *SpongeBob SquarePants*.

In addition, parent groups have worried about the heavy promotion of products like sugar-coated cereals during children's programs. Pointing to European countries, where children's advertising is banned, these groups have pushed to minimize advertising directed at children. Congress, hesitant to limit the protection that the First Amendment offers to commercial speech, and faced with lobbying by the advertising industry, has responded weakly.

The Children's Television Act of 1990 mandated that networks provide some educational and informational children's programming, but the act has been difficult to enforce and has done little to restrict advertising aimed at kids.

Because children and teenagers influence nearly $500 billion a year in family spending—on everything from snacks to cars—they are increasingly targeted by advertisers.[21] A Stanford University study found that a single thirty-second TV ad can influence the brand choices of children as young as age two. Still, methods for marketing to children have become increasingly seductive as product placement and merchandising tie-ins become more prevalent. Most recently, companies have used seemingly innocuous online games to sell products like breakfast cereal to children.

Advertising in Schools

A controversial development in advertising was the introduction of Channel One into thousands of schools during the 1989–90 school year. The brainchild of Whittle Communications, Channel One offered "free" video and satellite equipment (tuned exclusively to Channel One) in exchange for a twelve-minute package of current events programming that included two minutes of commercials. Public pressure managed to get most junk-food ads removed from Channel One schools by 2006.

Over the years, the National Dairy Council and other organizations have also used schools to promote products, providing free filmstrips, posters, magazines, folders, and study guides adorned with corporate logos. Teachers, especially in underfunded districts, have usually been grateful for the support. Early on, however, Channel One was viewed as a more intrusive threat, violating the implicit cultural border between an entertainment situation (watching commercial television) and a learning situation (going to school). One study showed that schools with a high concentration of low-income students were more than twice as likely as affluent schools to receive Channel One.[22]

Texas and Ohio contain the highest concentrations of Channel One contracts, but many individual school districts and some state systems, including New York and California, have banned Channel One News. These school systems have argued that Channel One provides students with only slight additional knowledge about current affairs, and fear that students deem the products advertised—sneakers, clothing, cereal, and controversial sugar-flavored juices like SunnyD—more worthy of purchase because they are advertised in educational environments.[23] A 2006 study found that students remember "more of the advertising than they do the news stories shown on Channel One."[24] Though it has changed owners several times over the past ten years, Channel One is still in business.

Health and Advertising

Eating Disorders. Advertising has a powerful impact on the standards of beauty in our culture. A long-standing trend in advertising is the association of certain products with ultra-thin female models, promoting a style of "attractiveness" that girls and women are invited to emulate. Even today, despite the popularity of fitness programs, most fashion models are much thinner than the average woman. Some forms of fashion and cosmetics advertising actually pander to individuals' insecurities and low self-esteem by promising the ideal body. Such advertising suggests standards of style and behavior that may not only be unattainable but also be harmful, leading to eating disorders such as anorexia and bulimia and an increase in cosmetic surgeries.

If advertising has been criticized for promoting skeleton-like beauty, it has also been blamed for the tripling of obesity rates in the United States since the 1980s, with more than two-thirds of adult Americans identified in 2015 as being overweight or obese. Corn syrup–laden soft drinks, fast food, and processed food are the staples of media ads and are major contributors to the nationwide weight problem. More troubling is that an obese nation is good for business (creating a multibillion-dollar market for diet products, exercise equipment, and self-help books), so media outlets see little reason to change current ad practices. The food and restaurant industry at first denied any connection between ads and the rise of U.S. obesity rates, instead blaming individuals who make bad choices. Increasingly, however, some fast-food chains offer healthier meals and calorie counts on various food items.

Figure 10-12. As American Obesity Continues to Rise, ads touting fast food and soft drinks have been countered by health advocacy, as in this ad on the New York City subway warning riders about the sugar content of their morning coffee drinks.

Tobacco. One of the most sustained criticisms of advertising is its promotion of tobacco consumption. Opponents of tobacco advertising have become more vocal in the face of grim statistics: Each year, an estimated 400,000 Americans die from diseases related to nicotine addiction and poisoning. Tobacco ads disappeared from television in 1971, under pressure from Congress and the FCC. However, over the years, numerous ad campaigns have targeted teenage consumers of cigarettes. In 1988, for example, R. J. Reynolds, a subdivision of RJR Nabisco, updated its Joe Camel cartoon character, outfitting him with hipper clothes and sunglasses. Spending $75 million annually, the company put Joe on billboards and store posters and in sports stadiums and magazines. One study revealed that before 1988, fewer than 1 percent of teens under age eighteen smoked Camels. After the ad blitz, however, 33 percent of this age group preferred Camels.

In addition to young smokers, the tobacco industry has targeted other groups. In the 1960s, for instance, the advertising campaigns for Eve and Virginia Slims cigarettes (reminiscent of ads during the suffrage movement in the early 1900s) associated their products with women's liberation, equality, and slim fashion models. And in 1989, Reynolds introduced a cigarette called Uptown, targeting African American consumers. The ad campaign fizzled due to public protests by black leaders and government officials. When these leaders pointed to the high concentration of cigarette billboards in poor urban areas and the high mortality rates among black male smokers, the tobacco company withdrew the brand.

The government's position regarding the tobacco industry began to change in the mid-1990s, when new reports revealed that tobacco companies had known that nicotine was addictive as early as the 1950s and had withheld that information from the public. In 1998, after four states won settlements against the tobacco industry and the remaining states threatened to bring more expensive lawsuits against the companies, the tobacco industry agreed to an unprecedented $206 billion settlement that carried significant limits on advertising and marketing tobacco products.

The agreement's provisions banned cartoon characters in advertising, thus ending the use of the Joe Camel character; prohibited the industry from targeting young people in ads and marketing and from giving away free samples, tobacco-brand clothing, and other merchandise; and ended outdoor billboard and transit advertising. The agreement also banned tobacco company sponsorship of concerts and athletic events, and it strictly limited other corporate sponsorships by tobacco companies. These agreements, however, do not apply to tobacco advertising abroad.

Alcohol. In 2013, 88,000 people died from alcohol-related diseases, and another 10,000 died in car crashes involving drunk drivers. As you can guess, many of the same complaints regarding tobacco advertising are also being directed at alcohol ads. (The hard liquor industry has voluntarily banned TV and radio ads for decades.) For example, one of the most popular beer ad campaigns of the late 1990s, featuring the Budweiser frogs (which croak "Budweis-errrr"), has been accused of using cartoonlike animal characters to appeal to young viewers. In fact, the Budweiser ads would be banned under the tough standards of the tobacco industry settlement, which prohibits the attribution of human characteristics to animals, plants, or other objects.

The Advertising Archives

Figure 10-13. Lifestyle Ad Appeals TBWA (now a unit of Omnicom) introduced Absolut Vodka's distinctive advertising campaign in 1980. The campaign marketed a little-known Swedish vodka as an exclusive lifestyle brand, an untraditional approach that parlayed it into one of the world's best-selling spirits. The long-running ad campaign ended in 2006, with more than 1,450 ads having maintained the brand's premium status by referencing fashion, artists, and contemporary music.

Alcohol ads have also targeted minority populations. Malt liquors, which contain higher concentrations of alcohol than beers do, have been touted in high-profile television ads for such labels as Colt 45 and Magnum. There is also a trend toward marketing high-end liquors to African American and Hispanic male populations. In a recent marketing campaign, Hennessy targeted young African American men with ads featuring hip-hop star Nas and sponsored events in Times Square and at the Governors Ball and Coachella music festivals. Hennessy also sponsored VIP parties with Latino deejays and hip-hop acts in Miami and Houston.

College students, too, have been heavily targeted by alcohol ads, particularly by the beer industry. Although colleges and universities have outlawed "beer bashes" hosted and supplied directly by major brewers, both Coors and Miller still employ student representatives to help "create brand awareness." These students notify brewers of special events that might be sponsored by and linked to a specific beer label. The images and slogans in alcohol ads often associate the products with power, romance, sexual prowess, or athletic skill. In reality, though, alcohol is a chemical depressant; it diminishes athletic ability and sexual performance, triggers addiction in roughly 10 percent of the U.S. population, and factors into many domestic abuse cases. A national study demonstrated "that young people who see more ads for alcoholic beverages tend to drink more."[25]

Global Village

Smoking Up the Global Market

By 2000, the status of tobacco companies and their advertising in the United States had hit a low point. A $206 billion settlement in 1998 between tobacco companies and state attorneys general ended tobacco advertising on billboards and severely limited the ways in which cigarette companies can promote their products in the United States. Advertising bans and antismoking public service announcements contributed to tobacco's growing disfavor in America, with smoking rates dropping from a high of 42.5 percent of the population in 1965 to just 18 percent fifty years later.

© John van Hasselt – Corbis/Getty Images

As Western cultural attitudes have turned against tobacco, the large tobacco multinationals have shifted their global marketing focus, targeting Asia in particular. Of the world's more than 1 billion smokers, 120 million adults smoke in India, 125 million adults smoke in Southeast Asia (Indonesia, Malaysia, the Philippines, Singapore, Thailand, Brunei, Burma, Cambodia, Laos, and Vietnam), and 350 million people smoke in China.[1] Underfunded government health programs and populations that generally admire American and European cultural products make Asian nations ill-equipped to resist cigarette marketing efforts. For example, in spite of China's efforts to control smoking (several Chinese cities have banned smoking in public places), recent studies have shown that nearly two-thirds of Chinese men and 10 percent of Chinese women are addicted to tobacco. Chinese women, who are now starting to smoke at increasing rates, are associating smoking with slimness, feminism, and independence.[2]

Advertising bans have actually forced tobacco companies to find alternative and, as it turns out, better ways to promote smoking. Philip Morris, the largest private tobacco company, and its global rival, British American Tobacco (BAT), practice "brand stretching"—linking their logos to race-car events, soccer leagues, youth festivals, concerts, TV shows, and popular cafés. The higher price for Western cigarettes in Asia has increased their prestige and has made packs of Marlboros symbols of middle-class aspiration.

The unmistakable silhouette of the Marlboro Man is ubiquitous throughout developing countries, particularly in Asia. In Hanoi, Vietnam, almost every corner boasts a street vendor with a trolley cart, the bottom half of which carries the Marlboro logo or one of the other premium foreign brands. Vietnam's Ho Chi Minh City has two thousand such trolleys. Children in Malaysia are especially keen on Marlboro clothing, which, along with watches, binoculars, radios, knives, and backpacks, they can win by collecting a certain number of empty Marlboro packages. (It is now illegal to sell tobacco-brand clothing and merchandise in the United States.)

Sporting events have proved to be an especially successful brand-stretching technique with men. In addition to Philip Morris's sponsorship of the Marlboro soccer league in China in the mid- to late 1990s, cigarette ads flourished on Chinese television (in the U.S., such ads have been banned by FCC rules since 1971). For the last twenty years, however, cigarette ads have been banned in China on TV and radio and in newspapers and magazines. But in 2014, the powerful government-controlled Chinese tobacco industry blocked a complete ban, according to Reuters, still permitting "cigarette product launches, and tobacco sponsorship for sporting events and schools."[3]

Critics suggest that the same marketing strategies will make their way into the United States and other Western countries, but that's unlikely. Tobacco companies are mainly interested in developing regions like Asia for two reasons. First, the potential market is staggering: Only one in twenty cigarettes now sold in China is a foreign brand, and women are just beginning to develop the habit. Second, many smokers in countries like China are unaware that smoking causes lung cancer. In fact, a million Chinese people die each year from tobacco-related health problems—around 50 percent of Chinese men will die before they are sixty-five years old, and lung cancer among Chinese women has increased by 30 percent in the past few years.[4] Smoking is projected to cause about eight million deaths a year by 2030.[5]

Prescription Drugs. Another area of concern is the surge in prescription drug advertising. Spending on direct-to-consumer advertising for prescription drugs increased from $266 million in 1994 to $4.5 billion in 2014—largely because of growth in television advertising, which today accounts for about two-thirds of such ads. The ads have made household names of prescription drugs such as Nexium, Claritin, Paxil, and Viagra. The ads are also very effective: Another survey found that nearly one in three adults has talked to a doctor, and one in eight has received a prescription in response to seeing an ad for a prescription drug.[26] Between 2007 and 2011, direct-to-consumer TV advertising for prescription drugs dropped 23 percent—from $3.1 billion in 2007 to $2.3 billion in 2011—due both to doctors' concerns about being pressured by patients who see the TV ads for new drugs and to notable recalls of heavily advertised drugs like Vioxx, a pain reliever that was later found to have harsh side effects. Still, in 2011, Pfizer spent $156 million on TV ads for Lipitor (a cholesterol-lowering drug that reduces the risk of heart attack and stroke), the highest amount spent for any prescription drug that year. But then, in 2012, spending rose again to over $3 billion.[27]

Ben Gabbe/Getty Images

Figure 10-14. Celebrity Spokespeople Tennis champion Serena Williams recently endorsed the sleep supplement Sleep Sheets, an over-the-counter sleep aid that promises to combat insomnia and promote natural sleep. Although it is available without a prescription, Williams's vigorous ad campaign for the supplement, which she co-owns, attests to the persistence of prescription drug ads and the vulnerability of their audience.

The tremendous growth of prescription drug ads brings the potential for false and misleading claims, particularly because a brief TV advertisement can't possibly communicate all the relevant cautionary information. More recently, direct-to-consumer prescription drug advertising has appeared in text messages and on Facebook. Pharmaceutical companies have also engaged in "disease awareness" campaigns to build markets for their products. As of 2014, the United States and New Zealand were the only two nations to allow prescription drugs to be advertised directly to consumers.

Watching Over Advertising

A few nonprofit watchdog and advocacy organizations—Commercial Alert, as well as the Better Business Bureau and the National Consumers League—compensate in many ways for some of the shortcomings of the Federal Trade Commission and other government agencies in monitoring the excesses of commercialism and false and deceptive ads.

Excessive Commercialism

Since 1998, Commercial Alert, a nonprofit organization founded in part by longtime consumer advocate Ralph Nader and based in Portland, Oregon, has been working to "limit excessive commercialism in society" by informing the public about the ways that advertising has crept out of its "proper sphere." For example, Commercial Alert highlights the numerous deals for cross-promotion made between Hollywood studios and fast-food companies. These include Warner Brothers' partnership with Hardee's for *Man of Steel*, and DreamWorks Animation's partnership with McDonald's for family-friendly flicks like *The Croods* and *How to Train Your Dragon 2*.

These deals not only helped movie studios make money as DVD sales declined but also helped movies reach audiences that traditional advertising can't. As Jeffrey Godsick, president of consumer products at 21st Century Fox, has said, "We want to hit all the lifestyle points for consumers. Partners get us into places that are nonpurchasable (as media buys). McDonald's has access to tens of millions of people on a daily basis—that helps us penetrate the culture."[28]

Commercial Alert is a lonely voice in checking the commercialization of U.S. culture. Its other activities have included challenges to specific marketing tactics, such as HarperCollins Children's Books' creation of the Mackenzie Blue series, which included "dynamic corporate partnerships," or product placements woven into the stories, written by the founder of a marketing group aimed at teens. In constantly questioning the role of advertising in democracy, the organization has aimed to strengthen noncommercial culture and limit the amount of corporate influence on publicly elected government bodies.

The FTC Takes on Puffery and Deception

Since the days when Lydia Pinkham's Vegetable Compound promised "a sure cure for all female weakness," false and misleading claims have haunted advertising. Over the years, the FTC, through its truth-in-advertising rules, has played an investigative role in substantiating the claims of various advertisers. A certain amount of *puffery*—ads featuring hyperbole and exaggeration—has usually been permitted, particularly when a product says it is "new and improved." However, ads become deceptive when they are likely to mislead reasonable consumers based on statements in the ad or because they omit information. Moreover, when a product claims to be "the best," "the greatest," or "preferred by four out of five doctors," FTC rules require scientific evidence to back up the claims.

A typical example of deceptive advertising is the Campbell Soup ad in which marbles in the bottom of a soup bowl forced more bulky ingredients—and less water—to the surface. In another instance, a 1990 Volvo commercial featured a monster truck driving over a line of cars and crushing all but the Volvo; the company later admitted that the Volvo had been specially reinforced and the other cars' support columns had been weakened. A more subtle form of deception featured the Klondike Lite ice cream bar—"the 93 percent fat-free dessert with chocolate-flavored coating." The bars were indeed 93 percent fat-free, but only after the chocolate coating was removed.[29]

Rudi Von Briel/Photo Edit

Figure 10-15. Green Advertising In response to increased consumer demand, companies have been developing and advertising green, or environmentally conscious, products to attract customers who want to lessen their environmental impact. How effective is this ad for you? What shared values do you look for or respond to in advertising?

In 2003, the FTC brought enforcement actions against companies marketing the herbal weight-loss supplement ephedra. Ephedra has a long-standing connection to elevated blood pressure, strokes, and heart attacks and has contributed to numerous deaths. Nevertheless, companies advertised ephedra as a safe and miraculous weight-loss supplement and, incredibly, as "a beneficial treatment for hypertension and coronary disease." According to the FTC, one misleading ad said: "Teacher loses 70 pounds in only eight weeks. . . . This is how over one million people have safely lost millions of pounds! No calorie counting! No hunger! Guaranteed to work for you too!" As the director of the FTC's Bureau of Consumer Protection summed up, "There is no such thing as weight loss in a bottle. Claims that you'll lose substantial amounts of weight and still eat everything you want are simply false."[30] In 2004, the United States banned ephedra.

When the FTC discovers deceptive ads, it usually requires advertisers to change them or remove them from circulation. The FTC can also impose monetary civil penalties for companies, and it occasionally requires an advertiser to run spots to correct the deceptive ads.

Alternative Voices

One of the provisions of the government's multibillion-dollar settlement with the tobacco industry in 1998 established a nonprofit organization with the mission to counteract tobacco marketing and reduce youth tobacco use. That mission became a reality in 2000, when the American Legacy Foundation, now Truth Initiative®, launched its youth smoking prevention/anti-tobacco industry campaign called **truth**®.

Working with a coalition of ad agencies, a group of teenage consultants, and a $300 million budget, initial **truth** ads were stylish, gritty print and television ads that deconstructed the images that have long been associated with cigarette ads—macho horse country, carefree beach life, sexy bar scenes, and daring skydives. Iconic **truth** ads include "Body Bags," a commercial where teens drag and pile up body bags outside a major tobacco company building; "Singing Cowboy," a spot portraying a cowboy with a breathing stoma (opening) in his neck singing about losing a lung; and "Shards O' Glass," a commercial featuring an executive for a popsicle company warning about the dangers of their product—a popsicle with shards of glass in it—in much the same way tobacco companies warn about their products.

The TV and print ads prominently reference the campaign's website, www.thetruth.com, which offers opportunities for teens to take action and a "vault" of statistics. For example, the site provides facts about addiction (e.g., "people recovering from substance abuse are twice as likely to relapse within three years if they are a smoker") and tobacco industry marketing (e.g., "in the U.S. alone, every day the tobacco industry spends enough money marketing its products to buy 150,000 10-karat gold grillz) and urges site visitors to "join the cause" and "enlist."

By 2007, with its jarring messages and cross-media platform, **truth** was recognized by 80 percent of teens and was ranked in the Top 10 "most memorable teen brands."31 The **truth** campaign at least partly explains the reported decline in teen smoking. Back in 2000, according to University of Michigan studies, 23 percent of all teens said they smoked. In 2017, that figure was down to 6 percent.[32]

Courtesy TRUTH Initiative

Figure 10-16. Alternative Ads In 2005, **truth**, A national youth smoking prevention campaign, won an Emmy Award in the National Public Service Announcement category. **truth** ads were initiated by the ad firms of Arnold Worldwide of Boston and Crispin Porter & Bogusky of Miami and are now produced by 72 & Sunny of Los Angeles.

Advertising, Politics, and Democracy

Advertising as a profession came of age in the twentieth century, facilitating the shift of U.S. society from production-oriented small-town values to consumer-oriented urban lifestyles. With its ability to create consumers, advertising became the central economic support system for our mass media industries. Through its seemingly endless supply of pervasive and persuasive strategies, advertising today saturates the cultural landscape. Products now blend in as props or even as "characters" in TV shows and movies. In addition, almost every national consumer product now has its own Web site to market itself to a global audience 365 days a year. With today's digital technology, ad images can be made to appear in places where they don't really exist. For example, advertisements can be superimposed on the backstop wall behind the batter during a nationally televised baseball broadcast. Viewers at home see the ads, but fans at the game do not.

Advertising's ubiquity, especially in the age of social media, raises serious questions about our privacy and the ease with which companies can gather data on our consumer habits. But an even more serious issue is the influence of ads on our lives as democratic citizens. With fewer and fewer large media conglomerates controlling advertising and commercial speech, what is the effect on free speech and political debate? In the future, how easy will it be to get heard in a marketplace where only a few large companies control access to that space?

Advertising's Role in Politics

Since the 1950s, political consultants have been imitating market-research and advertising techniques to sell their candidates, giving rise to **political advertising**, the use of ad techniques to promote a candidate's image and persuade the public to adopt a particular viewpoint. In the early days of television, politicians running for major offices either bought or were offered half-hour blocks of time to discuss their views and the issues of the day. As advertising time became more valuable, however, local stations and the networks became reluctant to give away time in large chunks. Gradually, TV managers began selling thirty-second spots to political campaigns, just as they sold time to product advertisers.

During the 1992 and 1996 presidential campaigns, third-party candidate Ross Perot restored the use of the half-hour time block when he ran political infomercials on cable and the networks. Barack Obama also ran a half-hour infomercial in 2008, and in the 2012 presidential race, both major candidates and various political organizations supporting them ran many online infomercials that were much longer than the standard thirty- to sixty-second TV spot. However, only very wealthy or well-funded candidates can afford such promotional strategies, and television does not usually provide free airtime to politicians. Questions about political ads continue to be asked: Can serious information on political issues be conveyed in thirty-second spots? Do repeated attack ads, which assault another candidate's character, so undermine citizens' confidence in the electoral process that they stop voting?[33] And how does a democratic society ensure that alternative political voices, which are not well financed or commercially viable, still receive a hearing?

Although broadcasters use the public's airwaves, they have long opposed providing free time for political campaigns and issues, since political advertising is big business for television stations. TV broadcasters earned $400 million in political ad revenue in 1996 and took in more than $1.5 billion (of $4.14 billion total spending) from political ads during the presidential and congressional elections in 2004. In the historic 2008 election, more than $5.28 billion was spent on advertising by all presidential and congressional candidates and interest groups. In 2012 (with a total of $6.28 billion spent on all elections), more than $1.1 billion alone went to local broadcast TV stations in the twelve most highly contested states, with local cable raking in another $200 million in those states.[34]

Digital JOB OUTLOOK

Media Professionals Speak about Jobs in the Advertising Industry

Paul Ten Haken, President and Chief Online Strategist, Click Rain, Inc.

If you want to work in the online space, you'll want to have an online footprint to match. Start a blog, polish up your social profiles, and make sure who Google says you are is who *you* say you are.

Winston Binch, Partner/Chief Digital Officer, Deutsch LA

Do your homework. Research the hell out of the place you want to work. Learn the history and facts about the people you're meeting with. Take it further. Come with questions. A lot of them. This is a great way to start a dialogue with someone you're interviewing with. And it proves you really want the job. If people don't know anything about my company, it's generally an immediate pass.

Jonathan Goldhill, CEO and Head Marketing Coach, The Goldhill Group

The world will always need great storytellers (i.e., copy writers) and visual types (i.e., graphic designers). People who can turn abstract concepts and execute these complex programs will succeed because they can harness the creative ideas and concepts and see them through to execution. The industry will also always need good managers.

Debra Murphy, Marketing Coach and Founder, Masterful Marketing

Creativity is needed to develop the messages and determine the right set of strategies to implement for achieving your goals. You also need to be flexible in order to take on whatever is needed to execute the strategy. And likeability is needed for the transparency that is critical in today's online marketing environment.

Nadja Bellan-White, Senior Partner and Managing Director, Ogilvy & Mather

I think for me, the best advice I've been given, and what I try to do, is really be good to the people around you—people you're competing against [and] your clients. Because the people that you see who you may think are your enemies could be your friends the next day. So be good to everybody. I try to tell that particularly to the younger folks coming in. They think you can be so competitive that you cut people off. You've got to be really, really good to the people around you.

The Future of Advertising

Although commercialism—through packaging both products and politicians—has generated cultural feedback that is often critical of advertising's pervasiveness, the growth of the industry has not diminished. Ads continue to fascinate. Many consumers buy magazines or watch the Super Bowl just for the advertisements. Adolescents decorate their rooms with their favorite ads and identify with the images certain products convey. In 2014, the fifth straight year of increases, advertising spending in the United States totaled more than $140 billion.[35]

A number of factors have made possible advertising's largely unchecked growth. Many Americans tolerate advertising as a "necessary evil" for maintaining the economy, but many dismiss advertising as not believable and trivial. As a result, unwilling to admit its centrality to global culture, many citizens do not think advertising is significant enough to monitor or reform. Such attitudes have ensured advertising's pervasiveness and suggest the need to escalate our critical vigilance.

As individuals and as a society, we have developed an uneasy relationship with advertising. Favorite ads and commercial jingles remain part of our cultural world for a lifetime, yet we detest irritating and repetitive commercials. We realize that without ads, many mass media would need to reinvent themselves. At the same time, we should remain critical of what advertising has come to represent: the overemphasis on commercial acquisitions and images of material success, and the disparity between those who can afford to live comfortably in a commercialized society and those who cannot.

Chapter 11
Public Relations

"Public Relations" from *Media & Culture*, Tenth Edition, 2016 Update by Richard Campbell, Christopher R. Martin, and Bettina Fabos, pp. 421–436 (Chapter 12, "Public Relations and Framing the Message").

The Practice of Public Relations

Today, there are more than seven thousand PR firms in the United States, plus thousands of additional PR departments within corporate, government, and nonprofit organizations.[1] Since the 1980s, the formal study of public relations has grown significantly at colleges and universities. By 2014, the Public Relations Student Society of America (PRSSA) had more than eleven thousand members and over three hundred chapters in colleges and universities. As certified PR programs have expanded (often requiring courses or a minor in journalism), the profession has relied less and less on its traditional practice of recruiting journalists for its workforce. At the same time, new courses in professional ethics and issues management have expanded the responsibility of future practitioners. In this section, we discuss the differences between public relations agencies and in-house PR services and the various practices involved in performing PR.

Approaches to Organized Public Relations

The Public Relations Society of America (PRSA) offers this simple and useful definition of PR: "Public relations helps an organization and its publics adapt mutually to each other." To carry out this mutual communication process, the PR industry uses two approaches. First, there are independent PR agencies whose sole job is to provide clients with PR services. Second, most companies, which may or may not also hire independent PR firms, maintain their own in-house PR staffs to handle routine tasks, such as writing press releases, managing various media requests, staging special events, and dealing with internal and external publics.

Many large PR firms are owned by, or are affiliated with, multinational communications holding companies, such as Publicis, Omnicom, WPP, and Interpublic (see Table 11-1). Three of the largest PR agencies—Burson-Marsteller, Hill+Knowlton Strategies, and Ogilvy Public Relations—generated part of the $17.4 billion in revenue earned by their parent corporation, the WPP Group, in 2014. Founded in 1953, Burson-Marsteller has 158 offices and affiliate partners in 110 countries and lists Facebook, IKEA, Coca-Cola, Ford, Sony, and the United Arab Emirates among its clients. Hill+Knowlton, founded in 1927, has 90 offices in 52 countries and includes Johnson & Johnson, Nestlé, Proctor & Gamble, Canon, Splenda, and Latvia on its client list. Most independent PR firms are smaller and operate locally or regionally. New York–based Edelman, the largest independent firm, is an exception, with global operations and clients like Starbucks, Microsoft, Hewlett-Packard, Samsung, and Unilever.

Table 11-1. The Top 10 Public Relations Firms, 2013 (by Worldwide Revenue, in Millions of U.S. Dollars)

Rank	Agency	Parent Firm	Headquarters	Revenue
1	Edelman	Independent	New York/Chicago	$741
2	Weber Shandwick	Interpublic	New York	$567
3	Fleishman-Hillard	Omnicom	St. Louis	$551
4	MSL Group	Publicis	Paris	$501
5	Burson-Marsteller	WPP	New York	$466
6	Ketchum	Omnicom	New York	$464
7	Hill+Knowlton Strategies	WPP	New York	$390
8	Ogilvy Public Relations	WPP	New York	$296
9	BlueDigital	BlueFocus Communication Group	Beijing	$271
10	Brunswick Group	Independent	London	$231

Data from: "CRM/Direct and PR," *Advertising Age*, April 28, 2014, p. 31.

In contrast to these external agencies, most PR work is done in-house at companies and organizations. Although America's largest companies typically retain external PR firms, almost every company involved in the manufacturing and service industries has an in-house PR department. Such departments are also a vital part of many professional organizations, such as the American Medical Association, the AFL-CIO, and the National Association of Broadcasters, as well as large nonprofit organizations, such as the American Cancer Society, the Arthritis Foundation, and most universities and colleges.

Performing Public Relations

Public relations, like advertising, pays careful attention to the needs of its clients—politicians, small businesses, industries, and nonprofit organizations—and to the perspectives of its targeted audiences: consumers and the general public, company employees, shareholders, media organizations, government agencies, and community and industry leaders. To do so, PR involves providing a multitude of services, including publicity, communication, public affairs, issues management, government relations, financial PR, community relations, industry relations, minority relations, advertising, press agentry, promotion, media relations, social networking, and propaganda. This last service, **propaganda**, is communication strategically placed, either as advertising or as publicity, to gain public support for a special issue, program, or policy, such as a nation's war effort.

Figure 11-1. World War II was a time when the U.S. government used propaganda and other PR strategies to drum up support for the war. One of the more iconic posters at the time asked women to join the workforce.

In addition, PR personnel (both PR technicians, who handle daily short-term activities, and PR managers, who counsel clients and manage activities over the long term) produce employee newsletters, manage client trade shows and conferences, conduct historical tours, appear on news programs, organize damage control after negative publicity, analyze complex issues and trends that may affect a client's future, manage Twitter and other social media accounts, and much more. Basic among these activities, however, are formulating a message through research, conveying the message through various channels, sustaining public support through community and consumer relations, and maintaining client interests through government relations.

Research: Formulating the Message

One of the most essential practices in the PR profession is doing research. Just as advertising is driven today by demographic and psychographic research, PR uses similar strategies to project messages to appropriate audiences. Because it has historically been difficult to determine why particular PR campaigns succeed or fail, research has become the key ingredient in PR forecasting. Like advertising, PR makes use of mail, telephone, and Internet surveys and focus group interviews—as well as social media analytics tools, such as Google Analytics, Twtrland, and Twitter Analytics—to get a fix on an audience's perceptions of an issue, a policy, a program, or a client's image.

Research also helps PR firms focus the campaign message. For example, the Department of Defense hired the PR firm Fleishman-Hillard International Communications to help combat the rising rates of binge drinking among junior enlisted military personnel. The firm first verified its target audience by researching the problem, finding from the Department of Defense's triennial Health Related Behaviors Survey that eighteen- to twenty-four-year-old servicemen had the highest rates of binge drinking. It then conducted focus groups to refine the tone of its antidrinking message and developed and tested its Web site for usability. The finalized campaign concept and message—"Don't Be *That Guy*!"—has been successful: It has shifted binge drinkers' attitudes toward less harmful drinking behaviors through a Web site (www.thatguy.com) and multimedia campaign that combines humorous videos, mobile games, and cartoons with useful resources. By 2015, the award-winning campaign had been implemented in over eight hundred military locations across twenty-three countries, and had expanded to a poster series (including "That Girl"-specific materials), playing cards, magnets, and PSAs on a "That Guy" YouTube channel.[2]

Conveying the Message

One of the chief day-to-day functions in public relations is creating and distributing PR messages for the news media or the public. There are several possible message forms, including press releases, VNRs, and various online options.

Press releases, or news releases, are announcements written in the style of news reports that give new information about an individual, a company, or an organization and pitch a story idea to the news media. In issuing press releases, PR agents hope that their client information will be picked up by the news media and transformed into news reports.

Through press releases, PR firms manage the flow of information, controlling which media get what material in which order. (A PR agent may even reward a cooperative reporter by strategically releasing information.) News editors and broadcasters sort through hundreds of releases daily to determine which ones contain the most original ideas or are the most current. Most large media institutions rewrite and double-check the releases, but small media companies often use them verbatim because of limited editorial resources. Usually, the more closely a press release resembles actual news copy, the more likely it is to be used. Twitter has also become a popular format for releasing information—140 characters or less—to the news media.

Doug Pensinger/Getty Images

Figure 11-2. Twitter Makes a News Story Less than 10 percent of U.S. adults get their news directly from Twitter, but more than half of journalists follow Twitter to get news tips. A tweet can be just as successful as a complete press release in gaining news media coverage. In this example, Priority Sports, a leading sports management firm based in Chicago and Los Angeles, tweeted that its client, NBA forward Robbie Hummel, had just re-signed with the Minnesota Timberwolves. This resulted in dozens of news stories, including one by *Sports Illustrated* online that incorporates an image of the tweet in its story, as well as Robbie Hummel's tweet that he's "excited to be back in Minneapolis for another season."

Since the introduction of portable video equipment in the 1970s, PR agencies and departments have also been issuing **video news releases (VNRs)**—thirty- to ninety-second visual press releases designed to mimic the style of a broadcast news report. Although networks and large TV news stations do not usually broadcast VNRs, news stations in small TV markets regularly use material from VNRs. On occasion, news stations have been criticized for using video footage from a VNR without acknowledging the source. In 2005, the FCC mandated that broadcast stations and cable operators must disclose the source of the VNRs they air. As with press releases, VNRs give PR firms some control over what constitutes "news" and a chance to influence what the general public thinks about an issue, a program, or a policy.

The equivalent of VNRs for nonprofits are **public service announcements (PSAs)**: fifteen- to sixty-second audio or video reports that promote government programs, educational projects, volunteer agencies, or social reform. As part of their requirement to serve the public interest, broadcasters have been encouraged to carry free PSAs. Since the deregulation of broadcasting began in the 1980s, however, there has been less pressure and no minimum obligation for TV and radio stations to air PSAs. When PSAs do run, they are frequently scheduled between midnight and 6:00 a.m., a less commercially valuable time slot.

Today, the Internet is an essential avenue for distributing PR messages. Companies upload or e-mail press releases, press kits, and VNRs for targeted groups. Social media has also transformed traditional PR communications. For example, a social media press release pulls together "remixable" multimedia elements, such as text, graphics, video, podcasts, and hyperlinks, giving journalists ample material to develop their own stories.

Case **STUDY**

The NFL's Concussion Crisis

The stylized violence of hard-hitting is a favored American football tradition. Broadcasts of games repeat the most violent tackles with instant replay, often using slow motion to enhance the drama of the hit. Over the years, NFL Films has created several video collections featuring hours of player collisions, with titles like *Crunch Course*, *Moment of Impact*, and *NFL's Hardest Hits*.

But this celebration of big hits has begun to seem callous and cruel, as decades of professional football popularity have produced retired players in their thirties, forties, fifties, and older who are experiencing the trauma of brain damage. The diagnosis is CTE, chronic traumatic encephalopathy, which can leave its victims with problems like hearing loss, memory loss, aggression, depression, and overall dementia. The concussion problem for football players is caused not only by the big concussions that knock them unconscious but also by what researchers call "subconcussions"—the hits to the head that happen many times during a game, and that can number in the hundreds and thousands over the course of a career.

Chris Sweda/Chicago Tribune/MCT via Getty Images

CTE can best be confirmed upon death, when the interior of the brain can be examined to show the buildup of a protein that strangles neurons—not unlike what happens in much older patients with Alzheimer's disease. Several distraught players suffering the symptoms of CTE have committed suicide. Dave Duerson, who played in the NFL in the 1980s and 1990s, killed himself in 2011 at age fifty, leaving a message to his family requesting that his brain be studied for CTE; researchers verified that he had the condition. In 2012, just two years after he retired from the field, NFL star Junior Seau committed suicide at age forty-three; as with Duerson, researchers checked his brain and confirmed that he had CTE.

In the 2013 book *League of Denial: The NFL, Concussions, and the Battle for Truth*, ESPN investigative reporters (and brothers) Mark Fainaru-Wada and Steve Fainaru explain that the NFL spent years responding to the crisis of concussions with dubious public relations tactics: first covering it up, then denying it, and then generating their own scientific studies to dispute the independent research. The NFL's response mirrors the deceptive tactics used by big tobacco companies for decades to deny smoking's link to cancer.

The NFL has a lot to protect. Their business is a $10 billion industry, and the very nature of the game requires hulking players to knock their heads and bodies into other very large players, often running at full speed.[1] As a result, more than four thousand retired players are suing the NFL to cover their head trauma expenses. These stories have begun to change the country's attitude toward the game. News stories about the effects of football concussions are increasingly common, and youth football league participation has dropped nearly 10 percent in the past two years, as parents have grown scared of the impact of the game on their children's health.

More recently, the NFL has responded by trying to change the conversation, acknowledging a concussion problem but emphasizing that the game has always evolved toward more safety in rules and technology (suggesting, perhaps, that it's just a matter of time before this forward march solves the concussion crisis). Indeed, the NFL hired a public relations counsel to help develop the NFLevolution.com site (motto: Forever Forward Forever Football). NFL's Corporate Communications Department also courted "mommy bloggers" to promote football as a healthy, safe activity for their children.

Yet as players continue to come forward with fears or diagnoses of CTE, and as long as the game (and business) of football continues to be played this way, the NFL's public relations crisis will likely persist. As Fainaru-Wada and Fainaru write, "There has never been anything like this in the history of sports: a public health crisis that emerged from the playing fields of our twenty-first-century pastime."[2]

Media Relations

PR managers specializing in media relations promote a client or an organization by securing publicity or favorable coverage in the news media. This often requires an in-house PR person to speak on behalf of an organization or to direct reporters to experts who can provide information. Media-relations specialists also perform damage control or crisis management when negative publicity occurs. Occasionally, in times of crisis—such as a scandal at a university or a safety recall by a car manufacturer—a PR spokesperson might be designated as the only source of information available to news media. Although journalists often resent being cut off from higher administrative levels and leaders, the institution or company wants to ensure that rumors and inaccurate stories do not circulate in the media. In these situations, a game often develops between PR specialists and the media in which reporters attempt to circumvent the spokesperson and induce a knowledgeable insider to talk off the record, providing background details without being named directly as a source.

PR agents who specialize in media relations also recommend advertising to their clients when it seems appropriate. Unlike publicity, which is sometimes outside a PR agency's control, paid advertising may help focus a complex issue or a client's image. Publicity, however, carries the aura of legitimate news and thus has more credibility than advertising. In addition, media specialists cultivate associations with editors, reporters, freelance writers, and broadcast news directors to ensure that press releases or VNRs are favorably received.

Special Events and Pseudo-Events

Another public relations practice involves coordinating *special events* to raise the profile of corporate, organizational, or government clients. Since 1967, for instance, the city of Milwaukee has run Summerfest, a ten-day music and food festival that attracts about a million people each year and now bills itself as "The World's Largest Music Festival." As the festival's popularity grew, various companies sought to become sponsors of the event. Today, Milwaukee's Miller Brewing Company sponsors one of the music festival's stages, which carries the Miller name and promotes Miller Lite as the "official beer" of the festival. Briggs & Stratton and Harley-Davidson are also among the local companies that sponsor stages at the event. In this way, all three companies receive favorable publicity by showing a commitment to the city in which their corporate headquarters are located.[3]

More typical of special-events publicity is a corporate sponsor's aligning itself with a cause or an organization that has positive stature among the general public. For example, John Hancock Financial has been the primary sponsor of the Boston Marathon since 1986 and funds the race's prize money. The company's corporate communications department also serves as the PR office for the race, operating the pressroom and creating the marathon's media guide and other press materials. Eighteen other sponsors, including Adidas, Gatorade, PowerBar, and JetBlue Airways, also pay to affiliate themselves with the Boston Marathon. At the local level, companies often sponsor a community parade or a charitable fundraising activity.

Jemal Countess/Stringer/Getty Images

Figure 11-3. Leonardo DiCaprio established the nonprofit Leonardo DiCaprio Foundation in 1998 to raise awareness of, and donate money to, environmental causes. In addition to conservation, the foundation addresses humanitarian issues, such as access to clean water.

In contrast to a special event, a **pseudo-event** is any circumstance created for the sole purpose of gaining coverage in the media. Historian Daniel Boorstin coined the term in his influential book *The Image* when pointing out the key contributions of PR and advertising in the twentieth century. Typical pseudo-events are press conferences, TV and radio talk-show appearances, or any other staged activity aimed at drawing public attention and media coverage. The success of such events depends on the participation of clients, sometimes on paid performers, and especially on the media's attention to the event. In business, pseudo-events extend back at least as far as P. T. Barnum's publicity stunts, such as parading Jumbo the Elephant across the Brooklyn Bridge in the 1880s. In politics, Theodore Roosevelt's administration set up the first White House pressroom and held the first presidential press conferences in the early 1900s. By the twenty-first century, presidential pseudo-events involved a multimillion-dollar White House Communications Office. One of the most successful pseudo-events in recent years was a record-breaking space-diving project. On October 14, 2012, a helium balloon took Austrian skydiver Felix Baumgartner twenty-four miles into the stratosphere. He jumped from the capsule and went into a free dive for about four minutes, reaching a speed of 833.9 mph before deploying his parachute. Red Bull sponsored the project, which took more than five years of preparation.

Examining **ETHICS**

Public Relations and Bananas

Doing public relations on behalf of bananas doesn't sound particularly necessary. After all, bananas are the number-one fresh fruit eaten in the United States, having long ago displaced apples in the top position. Yet the seemingly uncomplicated banana figures into the history of public relations, and not always in a good way.

ROMEO GACAD/AFP/Getty Images

In the early twentieth century, huge banana plantations were established in Colombia, Ecuador, Peru, Costa Rica, Guatemala, and Honduras. United Fruit (the predecessor of today's Chiquita Brands) was the dominant grower and importer of bananas, and was particularly powerful in the small nations of Central America—in fact, too powerful. In 1951, Jacobo Árbenz, the new democratically elected president of Guatemala, proposed a number of reforms to raise the status of poor agrarian Guatemalans. One of the reforms included redistributing idle, cultivatable lands to peasants to lift them from poverty. United Fruit owned some of those lands (which it had been given years earlier and on which it didn't pay property taxes). Unwilling to tolerate any limits on its control, United Fruit hired public relations pioneer Edward Bernays to work behind the scenes to build U.S. public opinion against the liberal Árbenz government, branding it as "communist." In one of the worst moments for public relations and U.S. foreign policy, the CIA led a covert operation that deposed Guatemala's democratically elected administration in 1954 and installed a right-wing military dictator that was more to United Fruit's liking. Guatemala then endured decades of war, while the CIA repeated similar covert interventions on behalf of U.S. business interests in several Latin American countries, giving rise to the term *banana republic*—a country in which a single dominant industry controls business and politics.

In another black eye for the banana industry, Dole and Del Monte, two of today's largest banana producers, were sued in 2012 by more than one thousand banana plantation workers for using a pesticide that had been banned in the United States in 1979. Bloomberg reported that the pesticide, dibromochloropropane (DBCP), "has been linked to sterility, miscarriages, birth defects, cancer, eye problems, skin disorders and kidney damage," and that workers argued they had not been informed of the dangers or issued protective equipment.[1]

Now the good news for bananas and public relations: In 2001, Dole Food Company responded to increasing consumer interest by producing organic bananas for the first time. Although it still produces bananas that are not certified as organic, it is now the leading producer of organic bananas in the world. In 2007, Dole improved communication of its organic program with the launch of doleorganic.com, and began labeling each bunch of organic bananas sold with a sticker that identifies the farm that produced the bananas. The sticker reads, "Visit the Farm at doleorganic.com," and includes the country of origin and a three-digit banana farm code. The Web site includes information about the farm in question; a Google map (viewers can zoom in on the satellite view to see the expanse of the farm); and photo albums containing shots of workers, plants, and facilities. The company says its doleorganic.com site "reflects Dole's dedication to transparency, sustainability and corporate responsibility."[2] Considering the lack of transparency in the history of public relations for bananas, this is a good thing—for the countries where Dole does business, the company's workers, and its consumers.[3]

As powerful companies, savvy politicians, and activist groups became aware of the media's susceptibility to pseudo-events, these activities proliferated. For example, to get free publicity, companies began staging press conferences to announce new product lines. During the 1960s, antiwar and Civil Rights protesters began their events only when the news media were assembled. One anecdote from that era aptly illustrates the principle of a pseudo-event: A reporter asked a student leader about the starting time for a particular protest; the student responded, "When can you get here?" Today, politicians running for office are particularly adept at scheduling press conferences and interviews to take advantage of television's appetite for live remote feeds and breaking news.

Community and Consumer Relations

Another responsibility of PR is to sustain goodwill between an agency's clients and the public. The public is often seen as two distinct audiences: communities and consumers.

Companies have learned that sustaining close ties with their communities and neighbors not only enhances their image and attracts potential customers but also promotes the idea that the companies are good citizens. As a result, PR firms encourage companies to participate in community activities, such as hosting plant tours and open houses, making donations to national and local charities, and participating in town events like parades and festivals. In addition, more progressive companies may also get involved in unemployment and job-retraining programs, or donate equipment and workers to urban revitalization projects, such as Habitat for Humanity.

EPA/Uwe Ansbach/Newscom

Figure 11-4. JP Morgan organizes the JPMorgan Chase Corporate Challenge each year, a series of road races that raise money for several not-for-profit organizations around the world. Taking place in twelve major cities, including New York, Frankfurt, and Shanghai, these races, which are owned and operated by JPMorgan Chase, also allow the financial firm to gain valuable publicity.

In terms of consumer relations, PR has become much more sophisticated since 1965, when *Unsafe at Any Speed*, Ralph Nader's groundbreaking book, revealed safety problems concerning the Chevrolet Corvair. Not only did Nader's book prompt the discontinuance of the Corvair line, but it also lit the fuse that ignited a vibrant consumer movement. After the success of Nader's book, along with a growing public concern over corporate mergers and corporations' lack of accountability to the public, consumers became less willing to readily accept the claims of corporations. As a result of the consumer movement, many newspapers and TV stations hired consumer reporters to track down the sources of customer complaints and embarrass companies by putting them in the media spotlight. Public relations specialists responded by encouraging companies to pay more attention to customers, establish product service and safety guarantees, and ensure that all calls and mail from customers were answered promptly. Today, PR professionals routinely advise clients that satisfied customers mean not only repeat business but also new business, based on a strong word-of-mouth reputation about a company's behavior and image.

Government Relations and Lobbying

While sustaining good relations with the public is a priority, so is maintaining connections with government agencies that have some say in how companies operate in a particular community, state, or nation. Both PR firms and the PR divisions within major corporations are especially interested in making sure that government regulation neither becomes burdensome nor reduces their control over their businesses.

Government PR specialists monitor new and existing legislation, create opportunities to ensure favorable publicity, and write press releases and direct-mail letters to persuade the public about the pros and cons of new regulations. In many industries, government relations has developed into **lobbying**: the process of attempting to influence lawmakers to support and vote for an organization's or industry's best interests. In seeking favorable legislation, some lobbyists contact government officials on a daily basis. In Washington, D.C., alone, there are about twelve thousand registered lobbyists—and thousands more government-relations workers who aren't required to register under federal disclosure rules. Lobbying expenditures targeting the federal government were at $3.24 billion in 2014, far above the $2.18 billion spent ten years earlier (see Figure 11-5).[4]

Lobbying can often lead to ethical problems, as in the case of earmarks and astroturf lobbying. *Earmarks* are specific spending directives that are slipped into bills to accommodate the interests of lobbyists and are often the result of political favors or outright bribes. In 2006, lobbyist Jack Abramoff (dubbed "the Man Who Bought Washington" in *Time*) and several of his associates were convicted of corruption related to earmarks, leading to the resignation of leading House members and a decline in the use of earmarks.

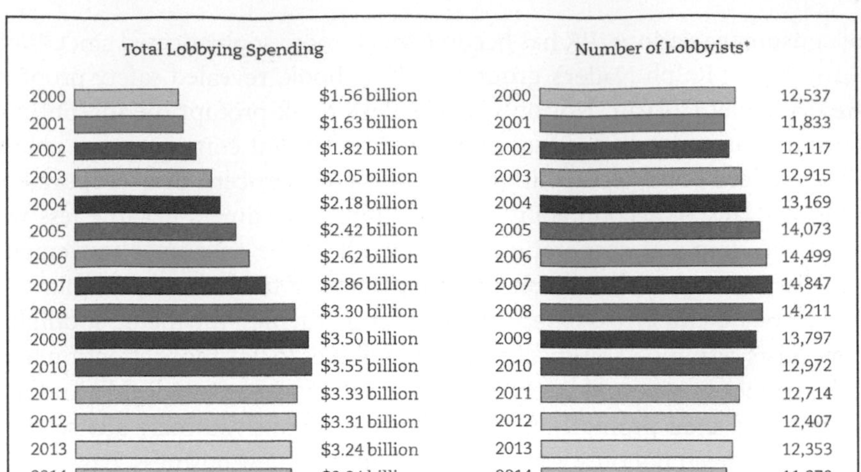

Data from: Figures are calculations by the Center for Responsive Politics based on data from the Senate Office of Public Records, accessed August 20, 2015, www.opensecrets.org/lobby.

*The number of unique, registered lobbyists who have actively lobbied.

Figure 11-5. Total Lobbying Spending and Number of Lobbyists (2000–2013)

Astroturf lobbying is phony grassroots public affairs campaigns engineered by public relations firms. PR firms deploy massive phone banks and computerized mailing lists to drum up support and create the impression that millions of citizens back their client's side of an issue. For instance, the Center for Consumer Freedom (CCF), an organization that appears to serve the interests of consumers, is actually a creation of the Washington, D.C.–based PR firm Berman & Co. and is funded by the restaurant, food, alcohol, and tobacco industries. According to SourceWatch, which tracks astroturf lobbying, anyone who criticizes tobacco, alcohol, processed food, fatty food, soda pop, pharmaceuticals, animal testing, overfishing, or pesticides "is likely to come under attack from CCF."[5]

Public relations firms do not always work for the interests of corporations, however. They also work for other clients, including consumer groups, labor unions, professional groups, religious organizations, and even foreign governments. In 2005, for example, the California Center for Public Health Advocacy—a nonpartisan, nonprofit organization—hired Brown-Miller Communications, a small California PR firm, to rally support for landmark legislation that would ban junk food and soda sales in the state's public schools. Brown-Miller helped state legislators see obesity not as a personal choice issue but as a public policy issue, cultivated the editorial support of newspapers to compel legislators to sponsor the bills, and ultimately succeeded in getting a bill passed.

Presidential administrations also use public relations—with varying degrees of success—to support their policies. From 2002 to 2008, the Bush administration's Defense Department operated a "Pentagon Pundit" program, secretly cultivating more than seventy retired military officers to appear on radio and television talk shows and shape public opinion about the Bush agenda. In 2008, the *New York Times* exposed the unethical program, and its story earned a Pulitzer Prize.[6] President Obama pledged to be more transparent on day one of his administration, but in 2014, an Associated Press analysis concluded that "the administration has made few meaningful improvements in the way it releases records."[7]

Public Relations Adapts to the Internet Age

Historically, public relations practitioners have tried to earn news media coverage (as opposed to buying advertising) to communicate their clients' messages to the public. While that is still true, the Internet, with its instant accessibility, offers public relations professionals a number of new routes for communicating with the public.

A company or an organization's Web site has become the home base of public relations efforts. Companies and organizations can upload and maintain their media kits (including press releases, VNRs, images, executive bios, and organizational profiles), giving the traditional news media access to the information at any time. And because everyone can access these corporate Web sites, the barriers between the organization and the groups that PR professionals ultimately want to reach are broken down.

The Web also enables PR professionals to have their clients interact with audiences on a more personal, direct basis through social media tools like Facebook, Twitter, YouTube, Wikipedia, and blogs. Now people can be "friends" and "followers" of companies and organizations. Corporate executives can share their professional and personal observations and seem downright chummy through a blog (e.g., Whole Foods Market's blog by CEO John Mackey). Executives, celebrities, and politicians can seem more accessible and personable through a Twitter feed. But social media's immediacy can also be a problem, especially for those who send messages into the public sphere without considering the ramifications.

Kevin Winter/Getty Images for PCA

Figure 11-6. PR and Social Media More companies are using social media tools like Twitter and Facebook to interact with their customers on a more personal level, which can be engaging but precarious. DiGiorno Pizza, for example, erred in 2014 by adopting the trending hashtag "#WhyIStayed" (used for a domestic violence conversation) for a promotional joke to promote its pizza on Twitter. DiGiorno then used its account to apologize to many outraged followers.

Another concern about social media is that sometimes such communications appear without complete disclosure, which is an unethical practice. Some PR firms have edited Wikipedia entries for their clients' benefit, a practice Wikipedia founder Jimmy Wales has repudiated as a conflict of interest. A growing number of companies also compensate bloggers to subtly promote their products, unbeknownst to most readers. Public relations firms and marketers are particularly keen on working with "mom bloggers," who appear to be independent voices in discussions about consumer products but may receive gifts in exchange for their opinions. In 2009, the Federal Trade Commission instituted new rules requiring online product endorsers to disclose their connections to companies.

As noted earlier, Internet analytics tools enable organizations to monitor what is being said about them at any time. However, the immediacy of social media also means that public relations officials might be forced to quickly respond to a message or an image once it goes viral. For example, when one diner posted a review of a restaurant in Chicago that delivered her ginger salad with a small cockroach, the word spread quickly on Yelp, where she had more than eight hundred friends. The owner wisely apologized on Yelp (six months later—perhaps after he noticed a downturn in business), explained that the bug likely came from the paper bag that contained the order, not their kitchen, and urged the customer to contact the restaurant to make amends.

Public Relations during a Crisis

Since the Ludlow strike, one important duty of PR has been helping a corporation handle a public crisis or tragedy, especially if the public assumes the company is at fault. Disaster management may reveal the best and the worst attributes of the company and its PR firm (see Case Study: "The NFL's Concussion Crisis"). Let's look at two contrasting examples of crisis management and the different ways they were handled.

One of the largest environmental disasters so far in the twenty-first century occurred in 2010. BP's Deepwater Horizon oil rig exploded on April 10 of that year, killing eleven workers. The oil gushed from the ocean floor for months, spreading into a vast area of the Gulf of Mexico, killing wildlife, and washing tar balls onto beaches. Although the company, formerly British Petroleum, officially changed its name to BP in 2001, adopting the motto Beyond Petroleum and a sunny new yellow and green logo in an effort to appear more "green-friendly," the disaster linked the company back to the hazards of its main business in oil. BP's many public relations missteps included its multiple underestimations of the amount of oil leaking, the chairman's reference to the "small people" of the Gulf region, the CEO's wish that he could "get his life back," and the CEO's attendance at an elite yacht race in England even as the oil leak persisted. In short, many people felt that BP failed to show enough remorse or compassion for the affected people and wildlife. BP tried to salvage its reputation by vowing to clean up the damaged areas, establishing a $20 billion fund to reimburse those economically affected by the spill, and creating a campaign of TV commercials to communicate its efforts. Nevertheless, harsh criticism persisted, and BP's ads were overwhelmed by online parodies and satires of its efforts. Years later, entire communities of fishermen and rig workers continue to be affected, and BP made its first $1 billion payment for Gulf restoration projects.

A decidedly different approach was taken in the 1982 tragedy involving Tylenol pain-relief capsules. Seven people died in the Chicago area after someone tampered with several bottles and laced them with poison. Discussions between the parent company, Johnson & Johnson, and its PR representatives focused on whether or not withdrawing all Tylenol capsules from store shelves might send a signal that corporations could be intimidated by a single deranged person. Nevertheless, Johnson & Johnson's chairman, James E. Burke, and the company's PR agency, Burson-Marsteller, opted for full disclosure to the media and the immediate recall of the capsules nationally, costing the company an estimated $100 million and cutting its market share in half. As part of its PR strategy to overcome the negative publicity and to restore Tylenol's market share, Burson-Marsteller tracked public opinion nightly through telephone surveys and organized satellite press conferences to debrief the news media. In addition, emergency phone lines were set up to take calls from consumers and health-care providers. When the company reintroduced Tylenol three months later, it did so with tamper-resistant bottles that were soon copied by almost every major drug manufacturer. Burson-Marsteller, which received PRSA awards for its handling of the crisis, found that the public thought Johnson & Johnson had responded admirably to the crisis and did not hold Tylenol responsible for the deaths. In less than three years, Tylenol recaptured its former (and dominant) share of the market.

Doug Mills/The New York Times/Redux Pictures

Figure 11-7. Ralph Lauren attracted media scrutiny when it was discovered that the 2012 U.S. Olympic Team uniforms the company designed were manufactured in China. After lawmakers publicly chastised the decision to outsource the uniforms, Lauren released a statement promising to produce the 2014 U.S. Olympic Team's uniforms in the United States.

Tensions between Public Relations and the Press

In 1932, Stanley Walker, an editor at the *New York Herald Tribune*, identified public relations agents as "mass-mind molders, fronts, mouthpieces, chiselers, moochers, and special assistants to the president."[8] Walker added that newspapers and PR firms would always remain enemies, even if PR professionals adopted a code of ethics (which they did in the 1950s) to "take them out of the red-light district of human relations."[9] Walker's tone captures the spirit of one of the most mutually dependent—and antagonistic—relationships in all of mass media.

Much of this antagonism, directed at public relations from the journalism profession, is historical. Journalists have long considered themselves part of a public service profession, but some regard PR as having emerged as a pseudo-profession created to distort the facts that reporters work hard to gather. Over time, reporters and editors developed the derogatory term **flack** to refer to a PR agent. The term, derived from the military word *flak*, meaning an antiaircraft artillery shell or a protective military jacket, symbolizes for journalists the protective barrier PR agents insert between their clients and the press. Today, the Associated Press manual for editors defines *flack* simply as "slang for *press agent*." Yet this antagonism belies journalism's dependence on public relations. Many editors, for instance, admit that more than half of their story ideas each day originate with PR people. In this section, we take a closer look at the relationship between journalism and public relations, which can be both adversarial and symbiotic.

Elements of Professional Friction

The relationship between journalism and PR is important and complex. Although journalism lays claim to independent traditions, the news media have become ever more reliant on public relations because of the increasing amount of information now available. Newspaper staff cutbacks, combined with television's need for local news events, have expanded the news media's need for PR story ideas.

Another cause of tension is that PR firms often raid the ranks of reporting for new talent. Because most press releases are written to imitate news reports, the PR profession has always sought good writers who are well connected to sources and savvy about the news business. For instance, the fashion industry likes to hire former style or fashion news writers for its PR staff, and university information offices seek reporters who once covered higher education. However, although reporters frequently move into PR, public relations practitioners seldom move into journalism; the news profession rarely accepts prodigal sons or daughters back into the fold once they have left reporting for public relations. Nevertheless, the professions remain codependent: PR needs journalists for publicity, and journalism needs PR for story ideas and access.

Public relations, by making reporters' jobs easier, has often enabled reporters to become lazy. PR firms now supply what reporters used to gather for themselves. Instead of trying to get a scoop, many journalists are content to wait for a PR handout or a good tip before following up on a story. Some members of the news media, grateful for the reduced workload that occurs when they are provided with handouts, may be hesitant to criticize a particular PR firm's clients. Several issues shed light on this discord and on the ways in which different media professions interact.

Undermining Facts and Blocking Access

Journalism's most prevalent criticism of public relations is that it works to counter the truths reporters seek to bring to the public. Modern public relations redefined and complicated the notion of what "facts" are. PR professionals demonstrated that the facts can be spun in a variety of ways, depending on what information is emphasized and what is downplayed. As Ivy Lee noted in 1925: "The effort to state an absolute fact is simply an attempt to achieve what is humanly impossible; all I can do is to give you my interpretation of the facts."[10] With practitioners like Lee showing the emerging PR profession how the truth could be interpreted, the journalist's role as a custodian of accurate information became much more difficult.

Journalists have also objected that PR professionals block press access to key business leaders, political figures, and other newsworthy people. Before the prevalence of PR, reporters could talk to such leaders directly and obtain quotable information for their news stories. Now, however, journalists complain that PR agents insert themselves between the press and the newsworthy, thus disrupting the journalistic tradition in which reporters would vie for interviews with top government and business leaders. Journalists further argue that PR agents are now able to manipulate reporters by giving exclusives to journalists who are likely to cast a story in a favorable light or by cutting off a reporter's access to one of their newsworthy clients altogether if that reporter has written unfavorably about the client in the past.

Promoting Publicity and Business as News

Another explanation for the professional friction between the press and PR involves simple economics. As Michael Schudson noted in his book *Discovering the News: A Social History of American Newspapers*, PR agents help companies "promote as news what otherwise would have been purchased in advertising."[11] Accordingly, Ivy Lee wrote to John D. Rockefeller after he gave money to Johns Hopkins University: "In view of the fact that this was not really news, and that the newspapers gave so much attention to it, it would seem that this was wholly due to the manner in which the material was 'dressed up' for newspaper consumption. It seems to suggest very considerable possibilities along this line."[12] News critics worry that this type of PR is taking media space and time away from those who do not have the financial resources or the sophistication to become visible in the public eye. There is another issue: If public relations can secure news publicity for clients, the added credibility of a journalistic context gives clients a status that the purchase of advertising cannot offer.

Another criticism is that PR firms with abundant resources clearly get more client coverage from the news media than their lesser-known counterparts. For example, a business reporter at a large metro daily sometimes receives as many as a hundred press releases a day—far outnumbering the fraction of handouts generated by organized labor or grassroots organizations. Workers and union leaders have long argued that the money that corporations allocate to PR leads to more favorable coverage for management positions in labor disputes. Therefore, standard news reports may feature subtle language choices, with "rational, cool-headed management making offers" and "hotheaded workers making demands." Walter Lippmann saw such differences in 1922 when he wrote, "If you study the way many a strike is reported in the press, you will find very often that [labor] issues are rarely in the headlines, barely in the leading paragraph, and sometimes not even mentioned anywhere."[13] This imbalance is particularly significant in that the great majority of workers are neither managers nor CEOs, and yet these workers receive little if any media coverage on a regular basis. Most newspapers now have business sections that focus on the work of various managers, but few have a labor, worker, or employee section.[14]

Shaping the Image of Public Relations

Dealing with both a tainted past and journalism's hostility has often preoccupied the public relations profession, leading to the development of several image-enhancing strategies. In 1948, the PR industry formed its own professional organization, the PRSA (Public Relations Society of America). The PRSA functions as an internal watchdog group that accredits PR agents and firms, maintains a code of ethics, and probes its own practices, especially those pertaining to its influence on the news media. Most PRSA local chapters and national conventions also routinely invite reporters and editors to speak to PR practitioners about the news media's expectations of PR. In addition to the PRSA, independent agencies devoted to uncovering shady or unethical public relations activities publish their findings in publications like *Public Relations Tactics*, *PR Week*, and *PRWatch*. Ethical issues have become a major focus of the profession, with self-examination of these issues routinely appearing in public relations textbooks as well as in various professional newsletters (see Table 11-2).

Over the years, as PR has subdivided itself into specialized areas, it has used more positive phrases—such as *institutional relations*, *corporate communications*, and *news and information services*—to describe what it does. Public relations' best press strategy, however, may be the limitations of the journalism profession itself. For most of the twentieth century, many reporters and editors clung to the ideal that journalism is, at its best, an objective institution that gathers information on behalf of the public. Reporters have only occasionally turned their pens, computers, and cameras on themselves to examine their own practices or their vulnerability to manipulation. Thus, by not challenging PR's more subtle strategies, many journalists have allowed PR professionals to interpret "facts" to their clients' advantage.

Table 11-2. **Public Relations Society of America Ethics Code** In 2000, the PRSA approved a completely revised Code of Ethics, which included core principles, guidelines, and examples of improper conduct. Here is one section of the code.

Data from: The full text of the PRSA Code of Ethics is available at www.prsa.org.

PRSA Member Statement of Professional Values
This statement presents the core values of PRSA members and, more broadly, of the public relations profession. These values provide the foundation for the Member Code of Ethics and set the industry standard for the professional practice of public relations. These values are the fundamental beliefs that guide our behaviors and decision-making process. We believe our professional values are vital to the integrity of the profession as a whole.
Advocacy We serve the public interest by acting as responsible advocates for those we represent. We provide a voice in the marketplace of ideas, facts, and viewpoints to aid informed public debate.
Honesty We adhere to the highest standards of accuracy and truth in advancing the interests of those we represent and in communicating with the public.
Expertise We acquire and responsibly use specialized knowledge and experience. We advance the profession through continued professional development, research, and education. We build mutual understanding, credibility, and relationships among a wide array of institutions and audiences.
Independence We provide objective counsel to those we represent. We are accountable for our actions.
Loyalty We are faithful to those we represent, while honoring our obligation to serve the public interest.
Fairness We deal fairly with clients, employers, competitors, peers, vendors, the media, and the general public. We respect all opinions and support the right of free expression.

Alternative Voices

Because public relations professionals work so closely with the press, their practices are not often the subject of media reports or investigations. Indeed, the multibillion-dollar industry remains virtually invisible to the public, most of whom have never heard of Burson-Marsteller, Hill+Knowlton, or Edelman. The Center for Media and Democracy (CMD) in Madison, Wisconsin, is concerned about the invisibility of PR practices and has sought to expose the hidden activities of large PR firms since 1993. Its *PRWatch* publication reports on the PR industry, with the goal of "investigating and countering PR campaigns and spin by corporations, industries and government agencies."[15] (See "Media Literacy and the Critical Process: "The Invisible Hand of PR")

CMD staff members have also written books targeting public relations practices having to do with the Republican Party's lobbying establishment (*Banana Republicans*), U.S. propaganda on the Iraq War (*The Best War Ever*), industrial waste (*Toxic Sludge Is Good for You!*), mad cow disease (*Mad Cow USA*), and PR uses of scientific research (*Trust Us, We're Experts!*). Their work helps bring an alternative angle to the well-moneyed battles over public opinion. "You know, we feel that in a democracy, it's very, very critical that everyone knows who the players are, and what they're up to," said CMD founder and book author John Stauber.[16]

Reprinted by permission of Little, Brown Book Group.

Figure 11-8. The Invisibility of Public Relations is addressed in a series of books by John Stauber and Sheldon Rampton.

Public Relations and Democracy

From the days of PR's origins in the early twentieth century, many people—especially journalists—have been skeptical of communications originating from public relations professionals. The bulk of the criticism leveled at public relations argues that the crush of information produced by PR professionals overwhelms traditional journalism. However, PR's most significant impact may be on the political process, especially when organizations hire spin doctors to favorably shape or reshape a candidate's media image. In one example, former president Richard Nixon, who resigned from office in 1974 to avoid impeachment hearings regarding his role in the Watergate scandal, hired Hill & Knowlton to restore his postpresidency image. Through the firm's guidance, Nixon's writings, mostly on international politics, began appearing in Sunday op-ed pages. Nixon himself started showing up on television news programs like *Nightline* and spoke frequently before such groups as the American Newspaper Publishers Association and the Economic Club of New York. In 1984, after a media blitz by Nixon's PR handlers, the *New York Times* announced, "After a decade, Nixon is gaining favor," and *USA Today* trumpeted, "Richard Nixon is back." Before his death in 1994, Nixon, who never publicly apologized for his role in Watergate, saw a large portion of his public image shift from that of an arrogant, disgraced politician to that of a revered elder statesman.[17] Many media critics have charged that the press did not counterbalance this PR campaign and treated Nixon too reverently. In 2014, on the fortieth anniversary of the Watergate scandal, former CBS news anchor Dan Rather remembered Nixon's administration as a "criminal presidency" but added, "There has been an effort to change history, and in some ways it has been successful the last 40 years, saying well, it wasn't all that bad."[18]

Media Literacy and THE CRITICAL PROCESS

The Invisible Hand of PR

John Stauber, founder of the Center for Media and Democracy and its publication *PRWatch*, has described the PR industry as "a huge, invisible industry . . . that's really only available to wealthy individuals, large multinational corporations, politicians and government agencies."[1] How true is this? Is the PR industry so invisible?

1 **Description.** Test the so-called invisibility of the PR industry by seeing how often, and in what way, PR firms are discussed in the print media. Using LexisNexis, search U.S. newspapers—over the last six months—for any mention of three prominent PR firms: Edelman, Weber Shandwick, and Fleishman-Hillard.

2 **Analysis.** What patterns emerge from the search? Possible patterns may have to do with personnel: Someone was hired or fired. (These articles may be extremely brief, with only a quick mention of the firms.) Or these personnel-related articles may reveal connections between politicians or corporations and the PR industry. What about specific PR campaigns or articles that quote "experts" who work for Edelman, Weber Shandwick, or Fleishman-Hillard?

3 **Interpretation.** What do these patterns tell you about how the PR industry is covered by the news media? Was the coverage favorable? Was it critical or analytical? Did you learn anything about how the industry operates? Is the industry itself, its influencing strategies, and its wide reach across the globe visible in your search?

4 **Evaluation.** PR firms—such as the three major firms in this search—have enormous power when it comes to influencing the public image of corpora-

tions, government bodies, and public policy initiatives in the United States and abroad. PR firms also have enormous influence over news content. Yet the U.S. media are silent on this influence. Public relations firms aren't likely to reveal their power, but should journalism be more forthcoming about its role as a publicity vehicle for PR?

5 **Engagement.** Visit the Center for Media and Democracy's Web site (prwatch.org) and begin to learn about the unseen operations of the public relations industry. (You can also visit SpinWatch.org for similar critical analyses of PR in the United Kingdom.) Follow the CMD's Twitter feed. Read some of the organization's books, join forum discussions, or attend a *PRWatch* event. Visit the organization's wiki site, SourceWatch (sourcewatch.org), and if you can, do some research of your own on PR and contribute an entry.

In terms of its immediate impact on democracy, the information crush delivered by public relations is at its height during national election campaigns. The 2012 presidential election was the most expensive in history, with President Barack Obama's and Republican candidate Mitt Romney's campaigns spending a combined $2.34 billion. Although much of that money was spent on television advertising, public relations helped hone each campaign's message. PR professionals assembled by *PR Week* magazine generally agreed that Obama's reelection campaign succeeded because it was able to change the focus of the campaign from a referendum on Obama's first term (the Romney campaign's goal) to a choice between candidates with two very different philosophies. They also acknowledged that there were unexpected events that aided Obama with his message. One was Romney's infamous comment at a private $50,000-a-person fund-raiser. Romney told his supporters, "There are 47 percent of the people who will vote for the president no matter what" because they are "dependent on government," "believe that they are victims," and "believe that they are entitled to health care, to food, to housing. . . . My job is not to worry about those people." His comments were secretly videotaped by a bartender, and when they became a viral sensation, Romney had difficulty recovering from it. As public relations firm owner Carolyn Grisko noted, "The words that come out of a candidate's own mouth are ultimately the ones that resonate."[19] The other unexpected event was Superstorm Sandy, a hurricane that hit the Atlantic coast a week before the election. As president and commander in chief, Obama dominated news headlines in responding to the storm and received praise for his actions from Republican New Jersey governor Chris Christie. Christie later experienced his own public relations nightmare with the George Washington Bridge lane closure scandal. Several of his staff members and appointees ended up losing their jobs for conspiring to close lanes on a busy New Jersey toll plaza for several days in 2013, creating huge traffic jams. Christie denied any involvement in the bridge lane closings and hired a law firm that produced a report exonerating him, but the continuing cloud of scandal followed him as he announced his 2016 presidential candidacy.

Another critical area for public relations and democracy is how organizations integrate environmental claims into their public communications. In 1992, the Federal Trade Commission first issued its "Green Guides"—guidelines to ensure that environmental marketing practices don't run afoul of its prohibition against unfair or deceptive acts or practices, sometimes called **greenwashing**. As concern about global warming has grown in recent years, green marketing and public relations now extend into nearly every part of business and industry: product packaging (buzzwords include *recyclable*, *biodegradable*, *compostable*, *refillable*, *sustainable*, and *renewable*), buildings and textiles, renewable energy certificates, carbon offsets (funding projects to reduce greenhouse gas emissions in one place to offset carbon emissions produced elsewhere), labor conditions, and fair trade. Although there have been plenty of companies that make claims of green products and services, only some have infused environmentally sustainable practices throughout their corporate culture, and being able to tell the difference is essential to the public's understanding of environmental issues.

Though public relations often provides political information and story ideas, the PR profession bears only part of the responsibility for "spun" news; after all, it is the job of a PR agency to get favorable news coverage for the individual or group it represents. PR professionals police their own ranks for unethical or irresponsible practices, but the news media should also monitor the public relations industry as they do other government and business activities. Journalism itself also needs to institute changes that will make it less dependent on PR and more conscious of how its own practices play into the hands of spin strategies. A positive example of change on this front is that many major newspapers and news networks now offer regular critiques of the facts and falsehoods contained in political advertising. This media vigilance should be on behalf of citizens, who are entitled to robust, well-rounded debates on important social and political issues.

Like advertising and other forms of commercial speech, PR campaigns that result in free media exposure raise a number of questions regarding democracy and the expression of ideas. Large companies and PR agencies, like well-financed politicians, have money to invest to figure out how to obtain favorable publicity. The question is not how to prevent that but how to ensure that other voices, less well financed and less commercial, also receive an adequate hearing. To that end, journalists need to become less willing conduits in the distribution of publicity. PR agencies, for their part, need to show clients that participating in the democratic process as responsible citizens can serve them well and enhance their image.

Digital JOB OUTLOOK

Media Professionals Speak about Jobs in the Public Relations Industry

Alex T. Williams, Pew Research Center

One factor behind the increase in public relations jobs has been digital technology. Agencies and companies are now able to reach out directly to the public in any number of ways and are hiring public relations specialists to help them do so.

Lindsay Groepper, Vice President, Blastmedia

When I first began my career in PR more than a decade ago, we would e-mail or fax (gasp!) the full press release text to the press. What we see now is new methods of distributing the info, driven by social media. Rather than e-mailing a press release, PR people are sending journalists to custom landing pages created just for that specific announcement, contacting them via Twitter with a BudURL link to the release, or even directing them to a YouTube video with a message from the CEO making the announcement.

Cara Stewart, Founder and Principal, Remarx Media

The most important platforms for PR pros in the future will be the ones most targeted for their clients. Twitter, LinkedIn, and Facebook are "fun"; getting nitty-gritty into community sites that are industry-specific is less "fun," because PR pros have to really understand clients' technologies, business models, services, and more. Really, it's more about PR pros becoming better PR pros and understanding their clients' businesses, as well as what their clients do. . . . Social media is not a one-size-fits-all solution.

Erica Swallow, Owner, Southern Swallow Productions

There is also a growing demand for social platforms that make it easier for journalists and PR reps to contact one another. Help a Reporter Out (HARO), PRNewswire's ProfNet, NewsBasis, and Media Kitty are all enabling the communication lines to run in both directions. Rather than having PR reps make the first moves all the time, now members of the media can put out requests for pitches from particular types of experts.

Chapter 12

Theories of Communication

"Theories of Communication" from *Media & Culture*, Tenth Edition, 2016 Update by Richard Campbell, Christopher R. Martin, and Bettina Fabos, pp. 511–532 (Chapter 15, "Media Effects and Cultural Approaches to Research").

Media Effects and Cultural Approaches to Research

In 1966, NBC showed the Rod Serling made-for-television thriller *The Doomsday Flight*, the first movie to depict an airplane hijacking. In the story, a man plants a bomb and tries to extract ransom money from an airline. In the days following the telecast, the nation's major airlines reported a dramatic rise in anonymous bomb threats, some of them classified as teenage pranks. The network agreed not to run the film again.

In 1985, the popular heavy-metal band Judas Priest made headlines when two Nevada teenagers shot themselves after listening to the group's allegedly subliminal suicidal message on their 1978 *Stained Class* album. One teen died instantly; the other lived for three more years, in constant pain from severe facial injuries. The teenagers' parents lost a civil product liability suit against the British metal band and CBS Records.

In 1995, an eighteen-year-old woman and her boyfriend went on a killing spree in Louisiana after reportedly watching Oliver Stone's 1994 film *Natural Born Killers* more than twenty times. The family of one of the victims filed a lawsuit against Stone and Time Warner, charging that the film—starring Juliette Lewis and Woody Harrelson as a demented, celebrity-craving young couple on a murderous rampage—irresponsibly incited real-life violence. Stone and Time Warner argued that the lawsuit should be dismissed on the grounds of free speech, and the case was finally thrown out in 2001. There was no evidence, according to the judge, that Stone had intended to incite violence.

In 1999, two heavily armed students wearing trench coats attacked Columbine High School in Littleton, Colorado. They planted as many as fifty bombs and murdered twelve fellow students and a teacher before killing themselves. In the wake of this tragedy, many people blamed the mass media, speculating that the killers had immersed themselves in the dark lyrics of shock rocker Marilyn Manson and were desensitized to violence by "first-person-shooter" video games such as *Doom*.

In April 2007, a student massacred thirty-two people on the Virginia Tech campus before killing himself. Gunman Seung-Hui Cho was mentally disturbed and praised "martyrs like Eric and Dylan," the infamous Columbine killers. But Cho's rampage included a twist: During the attack, he sent a package of letters, videos, and photos of himself to NBC News. The images and ramblings of his "multimedia manifesto" became a major part of the news story (as did ethical questions about the news media broadcasting clips of his videos) while the country tried to make sense of the tragedy.

Yet another tragic shooting occurred in 2012 in Aurora, Colorado, at a midnight screening of *The Dark Knight Rises*. A shooter opened fire in the darkened theater, killing twelve people and injuring fifty-eight. The gunman was identified as James Holmes, a twenty-four-year-old wearing a gas mask and trench coat and carrying several semiautomatic firearms. Holmes repeatedly identified himself as "the Joker" to police. Holmes was sentenced to life in prison in 2015, right around the time of another movie theater shooting, this time at a screening of *Trainwreck*—suggesting these acts might be driven less by the content of films than by their ability to gather together crowds in a public space.

Later in 2015, Vester Lee Flanagan, a former TV news reporter, killed a TV anchor and a photographer and injured their guest during a live interview on location for television station WDBJ in Roanoke, Virginia. Flanagan, who had been fired from the same station two years earlier, was mentally troubled, but was able to legally buy guns and ammunition for the attack. He fled the scene of the murders and committed suicide, but not before posting his own video of the shooting on Twitter and Facebook. In a rambling document he sent to ABC News, Flanagan cited as motivating factors the Virginia Tech shooting, the Columbine shooting, and the racially motivated Charleston, South Carolina, shooting in which Dylann Roof killed nine people earlier that year.

Each of these events and recent political battles over the need for gun control laws have renewed long-standing cultural debates over the suggestive power of music, visual imagery, and screen violence. Since the emergence of popular music, movies, television, and video games as influential mass media, the relationship between make-believe stories and real-life imitation has drawn a great deal of attention. Concerns have been raised not only by parents, teachers, and politicians but also by several generations of mass communication researchers.

As these tragic tales of violence illustrate, many believe that media have a powerful effect on individuals and society. This belief has led media researchers to focus most of their efforts on two types of research: media effects research and cultural studies research.

Media effects research attempts to understand, explain, and predict the effects of mass media on individuals and society. The main goal of this type of research is to uncover whether there is a connection between aggressive behavior and violence in the media, particularly in children and teens. In the late 1960s, government leaders—reacting to the social upheavals of that decade—first set aside $1 million to examine this potential connection. Since that time, thousands of studies have told us what most teachers and parents believe instinctively: Violent scenes on television and in movies stimulate aggressive behavior in children and teens—especially young boys.

The other major area of mass media research is **cultural studies**. This research approach focuses on how people make meaning, apprehend reality, articulate values, and order experience through their use of cultural symbols. Cultural studies scholars also examine the way status quo groups in society, particularly corporate and political elites, use media to circulate their messages and sustain their interests. This research has attempted to make daily cultural experience the focus of media studies, keying on the subtle intersections among mass communication, history, politics, and economics.

In this chapter, we will:

- Examine the evolution of media research over time
- Focus on the two major strains of media research, investigating the strengths and limitations of each
- Conclude with a discussion of how media research interacts with democratic ideals

As you get a sense of media effects and cultural studies research, think of some research questions of your own. Consider your own Internet habits. How do the number of hours you spend online every day, the types of online content you view, and your motivations for where you spend your time online shape your everyday behavior? Also, think about the ways your gender, race, sexuality, or class play into other media you consume—like the movies and television you watch and the music you like.

Early Media Research Methods

In the early days of the United States, philosophical and historical writings tried to explain the nature of news and print media. For instance, the French political philosopher Alexis de Tocqueville, author of *Democracy in America*, noted differences between French and American newspapers in the early 1830s:

> *In France the space allotted to commercial advertisements is very limited, and . . . the essential part of the journal is the discussion of the politics of the day. In America three quarters of the enormous sheet are filled with advertisements and the remainder is frequently occupied by political intelligence or trivial anecdotes; it is only from time to time that one finds a corner devoted to the passionate discussions like those which the journalists of France every day give to their readers.*[1]

During most of the nineteenth century, media analysis was based on moral and political arguments, as demonstrated by the de Tocqueville quote.[2]

More scientific approaches to mass media research did not begin to develop until the late 1920s and 1930s. In 1920, Walter Lippmann's *Liberty and the News* called on journalists to operate more like scientific researchers in gathering and analyzing factual material. Lippmann's next book, *Public Opinion* (1922), was the first to apply the principles of psychology to journalism. Described by media historian James Carey as "the founding book in American media studies,"[3] it led to an expanded understanding of the effects of the media, emphasizing data collection and numerical measurement. According to media historian Daniel Czitrom, by the 1930s "an aggressively empirical spirit, stressing new and increasingly sophisticated research techniques, characterized the study of modern communication in America."[4] Czitrom traces four trends between 1930 and 1960 that contributed to the rise of modern media research: propaganda analysis, public opinion research, social psychology studies, and marketing research.

Propaganda Analysis

After World War I, some media researchers began studying how governments used propaganda to advance the war effort. They found that during the war, governments routinely relied on propaganda divisions to spread "information" to the public. According to Czitrom, though propaganda was considered a positive force for mobilizing public opinion during the war, researchers after the war labeled propaganda negatively, calling it "partisan appeal based on half-truths and devious manipulation of communication channels."[5] Harold Lasswell's important 1927 study *Propaganda Technique in the World War* focused on propaganda in the media, defining it as "the control of opinion by significant symbols, . . . by stories, rumors, reports, pictures and other forms of social communication."[6] **Propaganda analysis** thus became a major early focus of mass media research.

Public Opinion Research

Researchers soon went beyond the study of war propaganda and began to focus on more general concerns about how the mass media filtered information and shaped public attitudes. In the face of growing media influence, Walter Lippmann distrusted the public's ability to function as knowledgeable citizens as well as journalism's ability to help the public separate truth from lies. In promoting the place of the expert in modern life, Lippmann celebrated the social scientist as part of a new expert class that could best make "unseen facts intelligible to those who have to make decisions."[7]

Today, social scientists conduct *public opinion research*, or citizen surveys; these have become especially influential during political elections. On the upside, public opinion research on diverse populations has provided insights into citizen behavior and social differences, especially during election periods or following major national events. For example, a 2015 Pew Research poll confirmed what many other polls reported: a majority of Americans support same-sex marriage, made legal in June 2015 by the Supreme Court. Since the late 1980s, when the majority of Americans opposed same-sex marriage, the balance has been shifting toward support—gradually at first and more rapidly since 2009.[8]

Scott Olson/Getty Images

Figure 12-1. Public Opinion Research Public opinion polls suggest that the American public's attitude toward same-sex marriage has evolved. Just weeks before the Supreme Court ruled same-sex marriage legal nationwide, a 2015 Pew Research poll reported that 57 percent of Americans were in favor of it—the same percentage of people who opposed it in a poll back in 2001.

On the downside, journalism has become increasingly dependent on polls, particularly for political insight. Some critics argue that this heavy reliance on measured public opinion has begun to adversely affect the active political involvement of American citizens. Many people do not vote because they have seen or read poll projections and have decided that their votes will not make a difference. Furthermore, some critics of incessant polling argue that the public is just passively responding to surveys that mainly measure opinions on topics of interest to business, government, academics, and the mainstream news media. A final problem is the pervasive use of unreliable **pseudo-polls**, typically call-in, online, or person-in-the-street polls that the news media use to address a "question of the day." The National Council of Public Opinion Polls notes that "unscientific pseudo-polls are widespread and sometimes entertaining, but they never provide the kind of information that belongs in a serious report," and discourages news media from conducting them.[9]

Social Psychology Studies

While opinion polls measure public attitudes, *social psychology studies* measure the behavior and cognition of individuals. The most influential early social psychology study, the Payne Fund Studies, encompassed a series of thirteen research projects conducted by social psychologists between 1929 and 1932. Named after the private philanthropic organization that funded the research, the Payne Fund Studies were a response to a growing national concern about the effects of motion pictures, which had become a particularly popular pastime for young people in the 1920s. These studies, which were later used by some politicians to attack the movie industry, linked frequent movie attendance to juvenile delinquency, promiscuity, and other antisocial behaviors, arguing that movies took "emotional possession" of young filmgoers.[10]

Photofest

Figure 12-2. Social and Psychological Effects of Media Concerns about film violence are not new. The 1930 movie *Little Caesar* follows the career of gangster Rico Bandello (played by Edward G. Robinson, shown), who kills his way to the top of the crime establishment and gets the girl as well. The Motion Picture Production Code, which was established a few years after this movie's release, reined in sexual themes and profane language, set restrictions on film violence, and attempted to prevent audiences from sympathizing with bad guys like Rico.

In one of the Payne studies, for example, children and teenagers were wired with electrodes and galvanometers, mechanisms that detected any heightened response via the subject's skin. The researchers interpreted changes in the skin as evidence of emotional arousal. In retrospect, the findings hardly seem surprising: The youngest subjects in the group had the strongest reaction to violent or tragic movie scenes, while the teenage subjects reacted most strongly to scenes with romantic and sexual content. The researchers concluded that films could be dangerous for young children and might foster sexual promiscuity among teenagers. The conclusions of this and other Payne Fund Studies contributed to the establishment of the Motion Picture Production Code, which tamed movie content from the 1930s through the 1950s. As forerunners of today's TV violence and aggression research, the Payne Fund Studies became the model for media research. (See Figure 12-3 for one example of a contemporary policy that has developed from media research. Also see "Case Study: "The Effects of TV in a Post-TV World")

The following categories apply to programs designed solely for children:

TV Y — All Children
This program is designed to be appropriate for all children. Whether animated or live-action, the themes and elements in this program are specifically designed for a very young audience, including children from ages 2–6. This program is not expected to frighten young children.

TV Y7 FV — Directed to Older Children—Fantasy Violence
For those programs where fantasy violence may be more intense or more combative than other programs in this category, such programs will be designated **TV-Y7-FV**.

TV Y7 — Directed to Older Children
This program is designed for children age 7 and above. It may be more appropriate for children who have acquired the developmental skills needed to distinguish between make-believe and reality. Themes and elements in this program may include mild fantasy violence or comedic violence, or may frighten children under the age of 7. Therefore, parents may wish to consider the suitability of this program for their very young children.

The following categories apply to programs designed for the entire audience:

TV G — General Audience
Most parents would find this program suitable for all ages. Although this rating does not signify a program designed specifically for children, most parents may let younger children watch this program unattended. It contains little or no violence, no strong language and little or no sexual dialogue or situations.

TV PG — Parental Guidance Suggested
This program contains material that parents may find unsuitable for younger children. Many parents may want to watch it with their younger children. The theme itself may call for parental guidance and/or the program may contain one or more of the following: some suggestive dialogue (D), infrequent coarse language (L), some sexual situations (S), or moderate violence (V).

TV 14 — Parents Strongly Cautioned
This program contains some material that many parents would find unsuitable for children under 14 years of age. Parents are strongly urged to exercise greater care in monitoring this program and are cautioned against letting children under the age of 14 watch unattended. This program may contain one or more of the following: intensely suggestive dialogue (D), strong coarse language (L), intense sexual situations (S), or intense violence (V).

TV MA — Mature Audiences Only
This program is specifically designed to be viewed by adults and therefore may be unsuitable for children under 17. This program may contain one or more of the following: crude indecent language (L), explicit sexual activity (S), or graphic violence (V).

Data from: TV Parental Guidelines Monitoring Board, accessed November 24, 2014, www.tvguidelines.org.

Figure 12-3. TV Parental Guidelines The TV industry continues to study its self-imposed rating categories, promising to fine-tune them to ensure that the government keeps its distance. These standards are one example of a policy that was shaped in part by media research. Since the 1960s, research has attempted to demonstrate links between violent TV images and increased levels of aggression among children and adolescents.

Marketing Research

A fourth influential area of early media research, *marketing research*, developed when advertisers and product companies began conducting surveys on consumer buying habits in the 1920s. The emergence of commercial radio led to the first ratings systems that measured how many people were listening on a given night. By the 1930s, radio networks, advertisers, large stations, and advertising agencies all subscribed to ratings services. However, compared with print media, whose circulation departments kept careful track of customers' names and addresses, radio listeners were more difficult to trace. This problem precipitated the development of increasingly sophisticated marketing research methods to determine consumer preferences and media use, such as direct-mail diaries, television meters, phone surveys, telemarketing, and Internet tracking. In many instances, product companies paid consumers nominal amounts of money to take part in these studies.

Case **STUDY**

The Effects of TV in a Post-TV World

Since TV's emergence as a mass medium, there has been persistent concern about the effects of violence, sex, and indecent language seen in television programs. The U.S. Congress had its first hearings on the matter of television content in 1952 and has held hearings in every subsequent decade.

In its coverage of congressional hearings on TV violence in 1983, the *New York Times* accurately captured the nature of these recurring public hearings: "Over the years, the principals change but the roles remain the same: social scientists ready to prove that television does indeed improperly influence its viewers, and network representatives, some of them also social scientists, who insist that there is absolutely nothing to worry about."[1]

One of the central focuses of the TV debate has been television's effect on children. In 1975, the major broadcast networks (then ABC, CBS, and NBC) bowed to congressional and FCC pressure and agreed to a "family hour" of programming in the first hour of prime-time television (8–9 p.m. eastern or 7–8 p.m. central). Shows such as *Happy Days*, the *Cosby Show*, and *Little House on the Prairie* flourished in that time slot. By 1989, Fox had arrived as a fourth major network and successfully counterprogrammed in the family hour with dysfunctional family shows like *Married . . . with Children*.

The most prominent watchdog monitoring prime-time network television's violence, sex, and indecent language has been the Parents Television Council (PTC), formed in 1995. The lobbying group's primary mission is to "promote and restore responsibility and decency to the entertainment industry in answer to America's demand for positive, family-oriented television programming. The PTC does this by fostering changes in TV programming to make the early hours of prime time family-friendly and suitable for viewers of all ages."[2] The PTC (through its Web campaign) played a leading role in inundating the FCC with complaints and getting the FCC to approve a steep increase in its fines for broadcast indecency.

Jason LaVeris/FilmMagic/Getty Images

Figure 12-4. MTV's Video Music Awards, an annual televised music special that sometimes includes sexually tinged or irreverent performances, often catches the ire of the PTC.

Yet to address the ongoing concerns of parent groups and Congress, it's worth asking: What are the effects of TV in what researchers now call a "post-TV" world? In just the past few years, digital video recorders have become common, and services like Hulu, YouTube, Netflix, iTunes, and on-demand cable viewing mean that viewers can access TV programming of all types at any time of the day. Although Americans are watching more television than ever before, it's increasingly time-shifted programming. How should we consider the possible harmful effects of prime-time network television given that most American families are no longer watching during the appointed broadcast network prime-time hours? Does the American public care about such media effects in this post-TV world?

These days, the Parents Television Council still releases its weekly "Family Guide to Prime Time Television" on its Web site. A sample of its guide from summer 2015, for example, listed only one show as "family-friendly" (*Are You Smarter Than a Fifth Grader?),* while shows as diverse as *The Big Bang Theory*, *2 Broke Girls*, *America's Got Talent*, and *Arrow* received a red-light designation for sexual content, language, and violence.

Of course, as television viewers move away from broadcast networks and increasingly watch programming from multiple sources on a range of devices, the PTC's traditional concern about prime-time network viewing can seem outdated. In recent years, the PTC announced it was giving its seal of approval to the Inspiration Network cable channel "for programming that embraces time-honored values."[3] The channel's lineup features shows like *The Waltons*; *Dr. Quinn, Medicine Woman*; *Little House on the Prairie*; and *The Big Valley*—all shows from an era decades before our post-TV world.

Research on Media Effects

As concern about public opinion, propaganda, and the impact of the media merged with the growth of journalism and mass communication departments in colleges and universities, media researchers looked more and more to behavioral science as the basis of their research. Between 1930 and 1970, as media historian Daniel Czitrom has noted, "Who says what to whom with what effect?" became the key question "defining the scope and problems of American communications research."[11] In addressing this question specifically, media effects researchers asked follow-up questions such as this: If children watch a lot of TV cartoons (stimulus or cause), will this repeated act influence their behavior toward their peers (response or effect)? For most of the twentieth century, media researchers and news reporters used different methods to answer similar sets of questions—who, what, when, and where—about our daily experiences (see "Media Literacy and the Critical Process: "Wedding Media and the Meaning of the Perfect Wedding Day").

Early Theories of Media Effects

A major goal of scientific research is to develop theories or laws that can consistently explain or predict human behavior. The varied impacts of the mass media and the diverse ways in which people make popular culture, however, tend to defy predictable rules. Historical, economic, and political factors influence media industries, making it difficult to develop systematic theories that explain communication. Researchers developed a number of small theories, or models, that help explain individual behavior rather than the impact of the media on large populations. But before these small theories began to emerge in the 1970s, mass media research followed several other models. Developing between the 1930s and the 1970s, these major approaches included the hypodermic-needle, minimal-effects, and uses and gratifications models.

The Hypodermic-Needle Model

One of the earliest media theories attributed powerful effects to the mass media. A number of intellectuals and academics were fearful of the influence and popularity of film and radio in the 1920s and 1930s. Some social psychologists and sociologists who arrived in the United States after fleeing Germany and Nazism in the 1930s had watched Hitler use radio, film, and print media as propaganda tools. They worried that the popular media in America also had a strong hold over vulnerable audiences. The concept that powerful media affect weak audiences has been labeled the **hypodermic-needle model**, sometimes also called the *magic bullet theory* or the *direct-effects model*. It suggests that the media shoot their potent effects directly into unsuspecting victims.

One of the earliest challenges to this theory involved a study of Orson Welles's legendary October 30, 1938, radio broadcast of *War of the Worlds*, which presented H. G. Wells's Martian invasion novel in the form of a news report and frightened millions of listeners who didn't realize it was fictional. In a 1940 book-length study of the broadcast, *The Invasion from Mars: A Study in the Psychology of Panic*, radio researcher Hadley Cantril argued that contrary to expectations based on the hypodermic-needle model, not all listeners thought the radio program was a real news report. Instead, Cantril—after conducting personal interviews and a nationwide survey of listeners, and analyzing newspaper reports and listener mail to CBS Radio and the FCC—noted that although some did believe it to be real (mostly those who missed the disclaimer at the beginning of the broadcast), the majority reacted out of collective panic, not out of a gullible belief in anything transmitted through the media. Although the hypodermic-needle model over the years has been disproved by social scientists, many people still attribute direct effects to the mass media, particularly in the case of children.

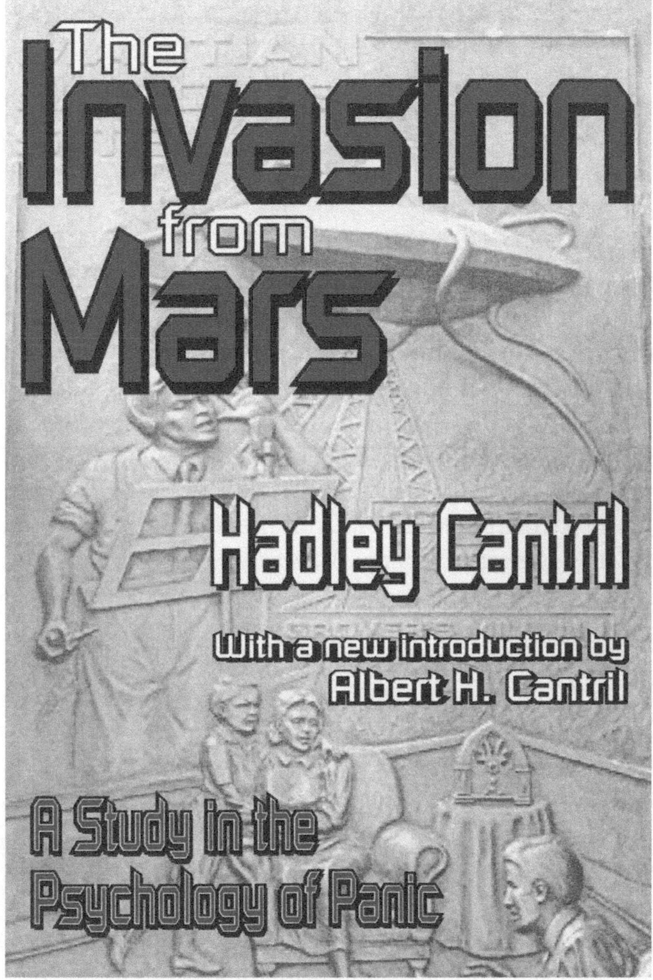

Figure 12-5. Media Effects? In *The Invasion from Mars: A Study in the Psychology of Panic*, Hadley Cantril (1906–1969) argued against the hypodermic-needle model as an explanation for the panic that broke out after the *War of the Worlds* radio broadcast. A lifelong social researcher, Cantril also did a lot of work in public opinion research, even working with the government during World War II.

The Minimal-Effects Model

Cantril's research helped lay the groundwork for the **minimal-effects model**, or *limited model.* With the rise of empirical research techniques, social scientists began discovering and demonstrating that media alone cannot cause people to change their attitudes and behaviors. Based on tightly controlled experiments and surveys, researchers argued that people generally engage in **selective exposure** and **selective retention** with regard to the media. That is, people expose themselves to the media messages that are most familiar to them, and they retain the messages that confirm the values and attitudes they already hold. Minimal-effects researchers have argued that in most cases, mass media reinforce existing behaviors and attitudes rather than change them. The findings from the first comprehensive study of children and television—by Wilbur Schramm, Jack Lyle, and Edwin Parker in the late 1950s—best capture the minimal-effects theory:

> *For some children, under some conditions, some television is harmful. For other children under the same conditions, or for the same children under other conditions, it may be beneficial. For most children, under most conditions, most television is probably neither particularly harmful nor particularly beneficial.*[12]

In addition, Joseph Klapper's important 1960 research study, *The Effects of Mass Communication*, found that the mass media only influenced individuals who did not already hold strong views on an issue and that the media had a greater impact on poor and uneducated audiences. Solidifying the minimal-effects argument, Klapper concluded that strong media effects occur largely at an individual level and do not appear to have large-scale, measurable, and direct effects on society as a whole.[13]

The minimal-effects theory furthered the study of the relationship between the media and human behavior, but it still assumed that audiences were passive and were acted upon by the media. Schramm, Lyle, and Parker suggested that there were problems with the position they had taken on effects:

> *In a sense the term "effect" is misleading because it suggests that television "does something" to children. The connotation is that television is the actor, the children are acted upon. Children are thus made to seem relatively inert; television, relatively active. Children are sitting victims; television bites them. Nothing can be further from the fact. It is the children who are most active in this relationship. It is they who use television, rather than television that uses them.*[14]

Indeed, as the authors observed, numerous studies have concluded that viewers—especially young children—are often *actively* engaged in using media.

The Uses and Gratifications Model

A response to the minimal-effects theory, the **uses and gratifications model** was proposed to contest the notion of a passive media audience. Under this model, researchers—usually using in-depth interviews to supplement survey questionnaires—studied the ways in which people used the media to satisfy various emotional or intellectual needs. Instead of asking, "What effects do the media have on us?" researchers asked, "Why do we use the media?" Asking the *why* question enabled media researchers to develop inventories cataloguing how people employed the media to fulfill their needs. For example, researchers noted that some individuals used the media to see authority figures elevated or toppled, to seek a sense of community and connectedness, to fulfill a need for drama and stories, and to confirm moral or spiritual values.[15]

Although the uses and gratifications model addressed the *functions* of the mass media for individuals, it did not address important questions related to the impact of the media on society. Once researchers had accumulated substantial inventories of the uses and functions of media, they often did not move in new directions. Consequently, uses and gratifications never became a dominant or an enduring theory in media research.

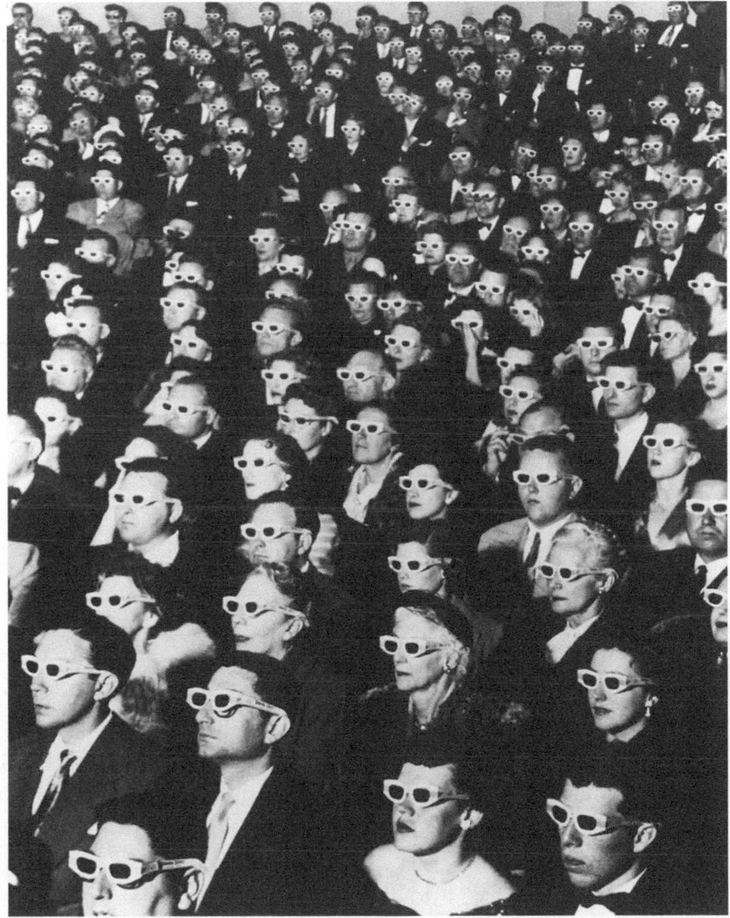

J.R. Eyerman/Getty Images

Figure 12-6. Uses and Gratifications In 1952, audience members at the Paramount Theater in Hollywood donned 3-D glasses for the opening-night screening of *Bwana Devil*, the first full-length color 3-D film. The uses and gratifications model of research investigates the appeal of mass media, such as going out to the movies.

Conducting Media Effects Research

Media research generally comes from the private or public sector, and each type has distinguishing features. *Private research*, sometimes called *proprietary research*, is generally conducted for a business, a corporation, or even a political campaign. It is usually applied research in the sense that the information it uncovers typically addresses some real-life problem or need. *Public research*, in contrast, usually takes place in academic and government settings. It involves information that is often more *theoretical* than applied; it tries to clarify, explain, or predict the effects of mass media rather than to address a consumer problem.

Most media research today focuses on the effects of the media in such areas as learning, attitudes, aggression, and voting habits. This research employs the **scientific method**, a blueprint long used by scientists and scholars to study phenomena in systematic stages. The steps in the scientific method include the following:

1. Identifying the research problem
2. Reviewing existing research and theories related to the problem
3. Developing working hypotheses or predictions about what the study might find
4. Determining an appropriate method or research design
5. Collecting information or relevant data
6. Analyzing results to see if the hypotheses have been verified
7. Interpreting the implications of the study to determine whether they explain or predict the problem

The scientific method relies on *objectivity* (eliminating bias and judgments on the part of researchers); *reliability* (getting the same answers or outcomes from a study or measure during repeated testing); and *validity* (demonstrating that a study actually measures what it claims to measure).

In scientific studies, researchers pose one or more **hypotheses**: tentative general statements that predict the influence of an *independent variable* on a *dependent variable*. For example, a researcher might hypothesize that frequent TV viewing among adolescents (independent variable) causes poor academic performance (dependent variable). Or another researcher might hypothesize that playing first-person-shooter video games (independent variable) is associated with aggression in children (dependent variable).

Broadly speaking, the methods for studying media effects on audiences have taken two forms—experiments and survey research. To supplement these approaches, researchers also use content analysis to count and document specific messages that circulate in mass media.

Experiments

Like all studies that use the scientific method, **experiments** in media research isolate some aspect of content; suggest a hypothesis; and manipulate variables to discover a particular medium's impact on attitude, emotion, or behavior. To test whether a hypothesis is true, researchers expose an *experimental group*—the group under study—to a selected media program or text. To ensure valid results, researchers also use a *control group*, which serves as a basis for comparison; this group is not exposed to the selected media content. Subjects are picked for each group through **random assignment**, which simply means that each subject has an equal chance of being placed in either group. Random assignment ensures that the independent variables researchers want to control are distributed to both groups in the same way.

For instance, to test the effects of violent films on preadolescent boys, a research study might take a group of ten-year-olds and randomly assign them to two groups. Researchers expose the experimental group to a violent action movie that the control group does not see. Later, both groups are exposed to a staged fight between two other boys so that the researchers can observe how each group responds to an actual physical confrontation. Researchers then determine whether or not there is a statistically measurable difference between the two groups' responses to the fight. For example, perhaps the control subjects tried to break up the fight but the experimental subjects did not. Because the groups were randomly selected and the only measurable difference between them was the viewing of the movie, researchers may conclude that under these conditions, the violent film caused a different behavior (see the "Bobo doll" experiment photos in Figure 12-7).

When experiments carefully account for independent variables through random assignment, they generally work well to substantiate direct cause-effect hypotheses. Such research takes place both in laboratory settings and in field settings, where people can be observed using the media in their everyday environments. In field experiments, however, it is more difficult for researchers to control variables. In lab settings, researchers have more control, but other problems may occur. For example, when subjects are removed from the environments in which they regularly use the media, they may act differently—often with fewer inhibitions—than they would in their everyday surroundings.

Experiments have other limitations as well. First, they are not generalizable to a larger population; they cannot tell us whether cause-effect results can be duplicated outside of the laboratory. Second, most academic experiments today are performed on college students, who are convenient subjects for research but are not representative of the general public. Third, while most experiments are fairly good at predicting short-term media effects under controlled conditions, they do not predict how subjects will behave months or years later in the real world.

Survey Research

In the simplest terms, **survey research** is the collecting and measuring of data taken from a group of respondents. Using random sampling techniques that give each potential subject an equal chance to be included in the survey, this research method draws on much larger populations than those used in experimental studies. Surveys may be conducted through direct mail, personal interviews, telephone calls, e-mail, and Web sites, enabling survey researchers to accumulate large amounts of information by surveying diverse cross sections of people. These data help researchers examine demographic factors such as educational

background, income level, race, ethnicity, gender, age, sexual orientation, and political affiliation, along with questions directly related to the survey topic.

Two other benefits of surveys are that they are usually generalizable to the larger society and that they enable researchers to investigate populations in long-term studies. For example, survey research can measure subjects when they are ten, twenty, and thirty years old to track changes in how frequently they watch television and what kinds of programs they prefer at different ages. In addition, large government and academic survey databases are now widely available and contribute to the development of more long-range or **longitudinal studies**, which make it possible for social scientists to compare new studies with those conducted years earlier.

Like experiments, surveys have several drawbacks. First, survey investigators cannot account for all the variables that might affect media use; therefore, they cannot show cause-effect relationships. Survey research can, however, reveal **correlations**—or associations—between two variables. For example, a random questionnaire survey of ten-year-old boys might demonstrate that a correlation exists between aggressive behavior and watching violent TV programs. Such a correlation, however, does not explain what is the cause and what is the effect—that is, do violent TV programs cause aggression, or are more aggressive ten-year-old boys simply drawn to violent television? Second, the validity of survey questions is a chronic problem for survey practitioners. Surveys are only as good as the wording of their questions and the answer choices they present. For example, as NPR reported, "If you ask people whether they support or oppose the death penalty for murderers, about two-thirds of Americans say they support it. If you ask whether people prefer that murderers get the death penalty or life in prison without parole, then you get a 50-50 split."[16]

Content Analysis

Over the years, researchers recognized that experiments and surveys focused on general topics (violence) while ignoring the effects of specific media messages (gun violence, fistfights). As a corrective, researchers developed a method known as **content analysis** to study these messages. Such analysis is a systematic method of coding and measuring media content.

Although content analysis was first used during World War II for radio, more recent studies have focused on television, film, and the Internet. Probably the most influential content analysis studies were conducted by George Gerbner and his colleagues at the University of Pennsylvania. Beginning in the late 1960s, they coded and counted acts of violence on network television. Combined with surveys, their annual "violence profiles" showed that heavy watchers of television, ranging from children to retired Americans, tend to overestimate the amount of violence that exists in the actual world.[17]

The limits of content analysis, however, have been well documented. First, this technique does not measure the effects of the messages on audiences, nor does it explain how those messages are presented. For example, a content analysis sponsored by the Kaiser Family Foundation that examined more than eleven hundred television shows found that 70 percent featured sexual content.[18] But the study didn't explain how viewers interpreted the content or the context of the messages.

Second, problems of definition occur in content analysis. For instance, in the case of coding and counting acts of violence, how do researchers distinguish slapstick cartoon aggression from the violent murders or rapes in an evening police drama? Critics point out that such varied depictions may have diverse and subtle effects on viewers that are not differentiated by content analysis. Third, critics point out that as content analysis grew to be a primary tool in media research, it sometimes pushed to the sidelines other ways of thinking about television and media content. Broad questions concerning the media as a popular art form, as a measure of culture, as a democratic influence, or as a force for social control are difficult to address through strict measurement techniques. Critics of content analysis, in fact, have objected to the kind of social science that reduces culture to acts of counting. Such criticism has addressed the tendency by some researchers to favor measurement accuracy over intellectual discipline and inquiry.[19]

Media Literacy and THE CRITICAL PROCESS

Wedding Media and the Meaning of the Perfect Wedding Day

According to media researcher Erika Engstrom, the bridal industry in the United States generates $50 to $70 billion annually, with more than two million marriages a year.[1] Supporting that massive industry are books, magazines, Web sites, reality TV shows, and digital games (in addition to fictional accounts in movies and music) that promote the idea of what a "perfect" wedding should be. What values are wrapped up in these wedding narratives?

1 **Description.** Select three or four bridal media and compare them. Possible choices include magazines such as *Brides*, *Bridal Guide*, and *Martha Stewart Weddings*; reality TV shows like *My Fair Wedding*, *Bridezillas*, *Say Yes to the Dress*, *My Big Fat American Gypsy Wedding*, and *Four Weddings*; Web sites like the Knot, Southern Bride, and Project Wedding; and games like *My Fantasy Wedding*, *Wedding Dash*, and *Imagine Wedding Designer*.

2 **Analysis.** What patterns do you find in the wedding media? (Consider what isn't depicted as well.) Are there limited ways in which femininity is defined? Do men have an equal role in the planning of wedding events? Are weddings depicted as something just for heterosexuals? Do the wedding media presume that weddings are first-time experiences for the couple getting married? What seem to be the standards in terms of consumption—the expense, size, and number of things to buy and rent to make a "perfect" day?

3 **Interpretation.** What do the wedding media seem to say about what it is to be a woman or a man on her or his wedding day? What do these gender roles for the wedding suggest about the appropriate gender roles for married life after the wedding? What do the wedding media infer about the appropriate level of consumption? In other words, consider the role of wedding media in constructing *hegemony*: In their depiction of what makes a perfect wedding, do the media stories attempt to get us to accept the dominant cultural values relating to things like gender relations and consumerism?

4 **Evaluation.** Come to a judgment about the wedding media analyzed. Are they good or bad on certain dimensions? Do they promote gender equality? Do they promote marriage equality (that is, gay marriage)? Do they offer alternatives to having a "perfect" day without buying all the trappings of so many weddings?

5 **Engagement.** Talk to friends about what weddings are supposed to celebrate, and whether an alternative conception of a wedding would be a better way of celebrating a union of two people. (In real life, if there is discomfort in talking about alternative ways to celebrate a wedding, that's probably the pressure of hegemony. Why is that pressure so strong?) Share your criticisms and ideas on wedding Web sites as well.

Contemporary Media Effects Theories

By the 1960s, the first departments of mass communication began graduating Ph.D.-level researchers schooled in experiment and survey research techniques, as well as content analysis. These researchers began documenting consistent patterns in mass communication and developing new theories. Five of the most influential contemporary theories that help explain media effects are social learning theory, agenda-setting, the cultivation effect, the spiral of silence, and the third-person effect.

Courtesy of Albert Bandura

Figure 12-7. Social Learning Theory These photos document the "Bobo doll" experiments conducted by Albert Bandura and his colleagues at Stanford University in the early 1960s. Seventy-two children from the Stanford University Nursery School were divided into experimental and control groups. The "aggressive condition" experimental group subjects watched an adult in the room sit on, kick, and hit the Bobo doll with hands and a wooden mallet while saying such things as "Sock him in the nose," "Throw him in the air," and "Pow." (In later versions of the experiment, children watched filmed versions of the adult with the Bobo doll.) Afterward, in a separate room filled with toys, the children in the "aggressive condition" group were more likely than the other children to imitate the adult model's behavior toward the Bobo doll.

Social Learning Theory

Some of the most well-known studies that suggest a link between the mass media and behavior are the "Bobo doll" experiments, conducted on children by psychologist Albert Bandura and his colleagues at Stanford University in the 1960s. Bandura concluded that the experiments demonstrated a link between violent media programs, such as those on television, and aggressive behavior. Bandura **developed social learning theory** as a four-step process: *attention* (the subject must attend to the media and witness the aggressive behavior), *retention* (the subject must retain the memory for later retrieval), *motor reproduction* (the subject must be able to physically imitate the behavior), and *motivation* (there must be a social reward or reinforcement to encourage modeling of the behavior).

Supporters of social learning theory often cite real-life imitations of media aggression (see the beginning of the chapter) as evidence of social learning theory at work. Yet critics note that many studies conclude just the opposite—that there is no link between media content and aggression. For example, millions of people have watched episodes of *Criminal Minds* and *Breaking Bad* without subsequently exhibiting aggressive behavior. As critics point out, social learning theory simply makes television, film, and other media scapegoats for larger social problems relating to violence. Others suggest that experiencing media depictions of aggression can actually help viewers let off steam peacefully through a catharsis effect.

Agenda-Setting

A key phenomenon posited by contemporary media effects researchers is **agenda-setting**: the idea that when the mass media focus their attention on particular events or issues, they determine—that is, set the agenda for—the major topics of discussion for individuals and society. Essentially, agenda-setting researchers have argued that the mass media do not so much tell us what to think as *what to think about*. Traceable to Walter Lippmann's notion in the early 1920s that the media "create pictures in our heads," the first investigations into agenda-setting began in the 1970s.[20]

AP Photo/Baba Ahmed

Figure 12-8. Mali The West African nation of Mali has been in the midst of a political crisis since its northern region was seized by rebel forces in 2012. One of the most devastating outcomes of the country's political strife is the recruitment of child soldiers, as desperate, poor families often give up their children to rebels in exchange for food and money. Despite the devastation in Mali, many feel the international response to Mali's crisis has been woefully inadequate and the mass media's coverage equally insufficient.

Over the years, agenda-setting research has demonstrated that the more stories the news media do on a particular subject, the more importance audiences attach to that subject. For instance, when the media seriously began to cover ecology issues after the first Earth Day in 1970, a much higher percentage of the population began listing the environment as a primary social concern in surveys. When *Jaws* became a blockbuster in 1975, the news media started featuring more shark attack stories; even landlocked people in the Midwest began ranking sharks as a major problem, despite the rarity of such incidents worldwide. More recently, extensive news coverage about the documentary *An Inconvenient Truth* and its companion best-selling book in 2006 sparked the highest-ever public concern about global warming, according to national surveys. But in the following years, the public's sense of urgency faltered somewhat as stories about the economy and other topics dominated the news agenda.

The Cultivation Effect

Another mass media phenomenon—the **cultivation effect**—suggests that heavy viewing of television leads individuals to perceive the world in ways that are consistent with television portrayals. This area of media effects research has pushed researchers past a focus on how the media affects individual behavior and toward a focus on larger ideas about the impact on perception.

The major research in this area grew from the attempts of George Gerbner and his colleagues to make generalizations about the impact of televised violence. The cultivation effect suggests that the more time individuals spend viewing television and absorbing its viewpoints, the more likely their views of social reality will be "cultivated" by the images and portrayals they see on television.[21] For example, Gerbner's studies concluded that although fewer than 1 percent of Americans are victims of violent crime in any single year, people who watch a lot of television tend to overestimate this percentage. Such exaggerated perceptions, Gerbner and his colleagues argued, are part of a "mean world" syndrome, in which viewers with heavy, long-term exposure to television violence are more likely to believe that the external world is a mean and dangerous place.

According to the cultivation effect, media messages interact in complicated ways with personal, social, political, and cultural factors; they are one of a number of important factors in determining individual behavior and defining social values. Some critics have charged that cultivation research has provided limited evidence to support its findings. In addition, some have argued that the cultivation effects recorded by Gerbner's studies have been so minimal as to be benign and that when compared side by side, the perceptions of heavy television viewers and nonviewers in terms of the "mean world" syndrome are virtually identical.

The Spiral of Silence

Developed by German communication theorist Elisabeth Noelle-Neumann in the 1970s and 1980s, the **spiral of silence** theory links the mass media, social psychology, and the formation of public opinion. The theory proposes that those who believe that their views on controversial issues are in the minority will keep their views to themselves—that is, become silent—for fear of social isolation, which diminishes or even silences alternative perspectives. The theory is based on social psychology studies, such as the classic conformity research studies of Solomon Asch in 1951. In Asch's study on the effects of group pressure, he demonstrated that a test subject is more likely to give clearly wrong answers to questions about line lengths if all other people in the room unanimously state the incorrect answers. Noelle-Neumann argued that mass media, particularly television, can exacerbate this effect by communicating real or presumed majority opinions widely and quickly.

According to the theory, the mass media can help create a false, overrated majority; that is, a true majority of people holding a certain position can grow silent when they sense an opposing majority in the media. One criticism of the theory is that some people may fail to fall into a spiral of silence either because they don't monitor the media or because they mistakenly perceive that more people hold their position than really do. Noelle-Neumann acknowledges that in many cases, "hard-core" nonconformists exist and remain vocal even in the face of social isolation and can ultimately prevail in changing public opinion.[22]

The Third-Person Effect

Identified in a 1983 study by W. Phillips Davison, the **third-person effect** theory suggests that people believe others are more affected by media messages than they are themselves.[23] In other words, it proposes the idea that "we" can escape the worst effects of media while still worrying about people who are younger, less educated, more impressionable, or otherwise less capable of guarding against media influence.

Under this theory, we might fear that other people will, for example, take tabloid newspapers seriously, imitate violent movies, or get addicted to the Internet, while dismissing the idea that any of those things could happen to us. It has been argued that the third-person effect is instrumental in censorship, as it would allow censors to assume immunity to the negative effects of any supposedly dangerous media they must examine.

Evaluating Research on Media Effects

The mainstream models of media research have made valuable contributions to our understanding of the mass media, submitting content and audiences to rigorous testing. This wealth of research exists partly because funding for studies on the effects of the media on young people remains popular among politicians and has drawn ready government support since the 1960s. Media critic Richard Rhodes argues that media effects research is inconsistent and often flawed but continues to resonate with politicians and parents because it offers an easy-to-blame social cause for real-world violence.[24] (For more on real-world gun violence in the United States, see "Case Study: "Our Masculinity Problem".)

Funding restricts the scope of some media effects and survey research, particularly if government, business, or other administrative agendas do not align with researchers' interests. Other limits also exist, including the inability to address how media affect communities and social institutions. Because most media research operates best when examining media and individual behavior, fewer research studies explore media's impact on community and social life. Some research has begun to address these deficits and also to turn more attention to the increasing impact of media technology on international communication.

Cultural Approaches to Media Research

During the rise of modern media research, approaches with a stronger historical and interpretive edge developed as well, often in direct opposition to the scientific models. In the late 1930s, some social scientists began to warn about the limits of "gathering data" and "charting trends," particularly when these kinds of research projects served only advertisers and media organizations and tended to be narrowly focused on individual behavior, ignoring questions like "Where are institutions taking us?" and "Where do we want them to take us?"[25]

In the United States in the 1960s, an important body of research—loosely labeled *cultural studies*—arose to challenge mainstream media effects theories. Since that time, cultural studies research has focused on how people make meaning, understand reality, and order experience by using cultural symbols that appear in the media. This research has attempted to make everyday culture the centerpiece of media studies, focusing on how subtly mass communication shapes and is shaped by history, politics, and economics. Other cultural studies work examines the relationships between elite individuals and groups in government and politics and how media play a role in sustaining the authority of elites and, occasionally, in challenging their power.

Early Developments in Cultural Studies Research

In Europe, media studies have always favored interpretive rather than scientific approaches; in other words, researchers there have approached the media as if they were literary or cultural critics rather than experimental or survey researchers. These approaches were built on the writings of political philosophers such as Karl Marx and Antonio Gramsci, who investigated how mass media support existing hierarchies in society. They examined how popular culture and sports distract people from redressing social injustices, and they addressed the subordinate status of particular social groups, something emerging media effects researchers were seldom doing.

In the United States, early criticism of media effects research came from the Frankfurt School, a group of European researchers who emigrated from Germany to America to escape Nazi persecution in the 1930s. Under the leadership of Max Horkheimer, T. W. Adorno, and Leo Lowenthal, this group pointed to at least three inadequacies of traditional scientific approaches to media research, arguing that they (1) reduced large "cultural questions" to measurable and "verifiable categories"; (2) depended on "an atmosphere of rigidly enforced neutrality"; and (3) refused to place "the phenomena of modern life" in a "historical and moral context."[26] The researchers of the Frankfurt School did not completely reject the usefulness of measuring and counting data. They contended, however, that historical and cultural approaches were also necessary to focus critical attention on the long-range effects of the mass media on audiences.

Since the time of the Frankfurt School, criticisms of the media effects tradition and its methods have continued, with calls for more interpretive studies of the rituals of mass communication. Academics who have embraced a cultural approach to media research try to understand how media and culture are tied to the actual patterns of communication in daily life. For example, in the 1970s, Stuart Hall and his colleagues studied the British print media and the police, who were dealing with an apparent rise in crime and mugging incidents. Arguing that the close relationship between the news and the police created a form of urban surveillance, the authors of *Policing the Crisis* demonstrated that the mugging phenomenon was exacerbated, and in part created, by the key institutions assigned the social tasks of controlling crime and reporting on it.[27]

Conducting Cultural Studies Research

Cultural studies research focuses on the investigation of daily experience, especially on issues of race, gender, class, and sexuality, and on the unequal arrangements of power and status in contemporary society. Such research emphasizes how some social and cultural groups have been marginalized and ignored throughout history. Consequently, cultural studies have attempted to recover lost or silenced voices, particularly among African American; Native American; Asian and Asian American; Arab; Latino; Appalachian; lesbian, gay, bisexual, and transgender (LGBT); immigrant; and women's cultures. The major analytical approaches in cultural studies research today are textual analysis, audience studies, and political economy studies.

Textual Analysis

In cultural studies research, **textual analysis** highlights the close reading and interpretation of cultural messages, including those found in books, movies, and TV programs. It is the equivalent of measurement methods like experiments and surveys and content analysis. While media effects research approaches media messages with the tools of modern science—replicability, objectivity, and data—textual analysis looks at rituals, narratives, and meaning. One type of textual analysis is *framing research*, which looks at recurring media story structures, particularly in news stories. Media sociologist Todd Gitlin defines media frames as "persistent patterns of cognition, interpretation, and presentation, of selection, emphasis, and exclusion, by which symbol-handlers routinely organize discourse, whether verbal or visual."[28]

Although textual analysis has a long and rich history in film and literary studies, it became significant to media in 1974, when Horace Newcomb's *TV: The Most Popular Art* became the first serious academic book to analyze television shows. Newcomb studied why certain TV programs and formats became popular, especially comedies, westerns, mysteries, soap operas, news reports, and sports programs. Newcomb took television programs seriously, examining patterns in the most popular programs at the time, such as the *Beverly Hillbillies*, *Bewitched*, and *Dragnet*, which traditional researchers had usually snubbed or ignored. Trained as a literary scholar, Newcomb argued that content analysis and other social science approaches to popular media often ignored artistic traditions and social context. For Newcomb, "the task for the student of the popular arts is to find a technique through which many different qualities of the work—aesthetic, social, psychological—may be explored" and to discover "why certain formulas . . . are popular in American television."[29]

Before Newcomb's work, textual analysis generally focused only on "important" or highly regarded works of art—debates, films, poems, and books. But by the end of the 1970s, a new generation of media studies scholars, who had grown up on television and rock and roll, began to study less elite forms of culture. They extended the concept of what a "text" is to include architecture, fashion, tabloid magazines, pop icons like Madonna, rock music, hip-hop, soap operas and telenovelas, movies, cockfights, shopping malls, reality TV, Martha Stewart, and professional wrestling—trying to make sense of the most taken-for-granted aspects of everyday media culture. Often the study of these seemingly minor elements of popular culture provides insight into broader meanings within our society. By shifting the focus to daily popular culture artifacts, cultural studies succeeded in focusing scholarly attention not just on significant presidents, important religious leaders, prominent political speeches, or military battles but on the more ordinary ways that "normal" people organize experience and understand their daily lives.

Audience Studies

Cultural studies research that focuses on how people use and interpret cultural content is called **audience studies**, or *reader-response research*. Audience studies differs from textual analysis because the subject being researched is the audience for the text, not the text itself. For example, in *Reading the Romance: Women, Patriarchy, and Popular Literature*, Janice Radway studied a group of midwestern women who were fans of romance novels. Using her training in literary criticism and employing interviews and questionnaires, Radway investigated the meaning of romance novels to the women. She argued that reading romance novels functions as personal time for some women, whose complex family and work lives leave them very little time for themselves. The study also suggested that these particular romance-novel fans identified with the active, independent qualities of the romantic heroines they most admired. As a cultural study, Radway's work did not claim to be scientific, and her findings are not generalizable to all women. Rather, Radway was interested in investigating and interpreting the relationship between reading popular fiction and ordinary life.[30]

Radway's influential cultural research used a variety of interpretive methods, including literary analysis, interviews, and questionnaires. Most important, these studies helped define culture in broad terms—as being made up of both the *products* a society fashions and the *processes* that forge those products.

Political Economy Studies

A focus on the production of popular culture and the forces behind it is the topic of **political economy studies**, which specifically examine interconnections among economic interests, political power, and how that power is used. Among the major concerns of political economy studies is the increasing conglomeration of media ownership. The increasing concentration of ownership means that the production of media content is being controlled by fewer and fewer organizations, investing those companies with more and more power. In addition, the domination of public discourse by for-profit corporations may mean that the bottom line for all public communication and popular culture is money, not democratic expression.

The Granger Collection

Figure 12-9. Public Sphere Conversations in eighteenth-century English coffeehouses (like the one shown) inspired Jürgen Habermas's public-sphere theory. However, Habermas expressed concerns that the mass media could weaken the public sphere by allowing people to become passive consumers of the information distributed by the media instead of entering into debates with one another about what is best for society. What do you think of such concerns? Has the proliferation of political cable shows, Internet bloggers, and other mediated forums decreased serious public debate, or has it just shifted the conversation to places besides coffeehouses?

Political economy studies work best when combined with textual analysis and audience studies, which provide context for understanding the cultural content of a media product, its production process, and how the audience responds. For example, a major media corporation may, for commercial reasons, create a film and market it through a number of venues (political economy), but the film's meaning or popularity makes sense only within the historical and narrative contexts of the culture (textual analysis), and it may be interpreted by various audiences in ways both anticipated and unexpected (audience studies).

Case STUDY

Our Masculinity Problem

There have been at least seventy mass shootings in the United States since 1982, and nearly half of them have happened since 2006.[1] Just some of those that made headlines include the Washington Navy Yard in 2013 (13 dead, 8 injured); Sandy Hook Elementary in Newtown, Connecticut, in 2012 (28 dead, 2 injured); the movie theater in Aurora, Colorado, in 2012 (12 dead, 58 injured); and Virginia Tech in 2007 (33 dead, 23 injured).

What are the reasons? Our news media respond with a number of usual suspects: the easy availability of guns in the United States; influential movies, television shows, and video games; mental illness; bad parenting. But Jackson Katz, educator, author, and filmmaker (of *Tough Guise* and *Tough Guise 2*), sees another major factor. The least-talked-about commonality in all the shootings is the one so obvious most of us miss it: Nearly all the mass murderers are male (and usually white).

What would psychologists, pundits, and other talking heads be saying if women were responsible for nearly every mass shooting for more than three decades? "If a woman were the shooter," Katz says, "you can bet there would be all sorts of commentary about shifting cultural notions of femininity and how they might have contributed to her act, such as discussions in recent years about girl gang violence."[2]

But a woman was responsible for only one of the seventy mass shootings; all the others had a man (or men) behind the trigger. "Because men represent the dominant gender, their gender is rendered invisible in the discourse about violence," Katz says.[3] In fact, the dominance of masculinity is the norm in our mainstream mass media. Dramatic content is often about the performance of heroic, powerful masculinity (e.g., many action films, digital games, and sports). Similarly, humorous content often derives from calling into question the standards of masculinity (e.g., a man trying to cook, clean, or take care of a child). The same principles apply for the advertising that supports the content. How many automobile, beer, shaving cream, and food commercials peddle products that offer men a chance to maintain or regain their rightful masculinity?

Rachel Kalish and Michael Kimmel, sociologists at SUNY Stonybrook, analyzed the problem of mass shootings that usually end in suicide. They found that males and females have similar rates of suicide attempts. "Feeling aggrieved, wronged by the world—these are typical adolescent feelings, common to many boys and girls," they report.

The result of these attempts, though, differ by gender. Female suicide behaviors are more likely to be a cry for help. Male suicide behaviors, informed by social norms of masculinity, often result in a different outcome: "aggrieved entitlement." Kalish and Kimmel define this as "a gendered emotion, a fusion of that humiliating loss of manhood and the moral obligation and entitlement to get it back. And its gender is masculine."[4] Retaliation, which is considered acceptable in lesser forms (think of all the cultural narratives in which the weak or aggrieved character finally gets his revenge), becomes horrifying when combined with the immediacy and lethal force of assault firearms.

Archive Photos/Getty Images

Elliot Rodger, the Isla Vista shooter in 2014, posted similar thoughts on a YouTube video titled "Retribution" before gunning down students at the University of California in Santa Barbara:

Tomorrow is the day of retribution, the day in which I will have my revenge. You girls have never been attracted to me. I don't know why you girls aren't attracted to me, but I will punish you all for it.[5]

There is some evidence that the gun industry understands the sense of masculine entitlement but uses that knowledge to sell guns, not to consider how they might be misused. A marketing campaign begun in 2010 for the Bushmaster .223-caliber semiautomatic rifle showed an image of the rifle with the large tagline "Consider Your Man Card Reissued." The Bushmaster was the same civilian assault rifle used by the shooter who massacred twenty-eight people at the Newtown elementary school in 2012.

How do we find a way out of this cultural cycle? "Make gender—specifically the idea that men are gendered beings—a central part of the national conversation about rampage killings," Katz says. "It means looking carefully at how our culture defines manhood, how boys are socialized, and how pressure to stay in the 'man box' not only constrains boys' and men's emotional and relational development, but also their range of choices when faced with life crises."[6]

Cultural Studies' Theoretical Perspectives

Developed as an alternative to the predictive theories of social science research (e.g., if X happens, the result will be Y), cultural studies research on media is informed by more general perspectives about how the mass media interact with the world. Two foundational concepts in cultural studies research are (1) the public sphere, and (2) the idea of communication as culture.

The Public Sphere

The idea of the **public sphere**, defined as a space for critical public debate, was first advanced by German philosopher Jürgen Habermas in 1962.[31] Habermas, a professor of philosophy, studied late-seventeenth-century and eighteenth-century England and France, and he found those societies to be increasingly influenced by free trade and the rise of the printing press. At that historical moment, an emerging middle class began to gather to discuss public life in coffeehouses, meeting halls, and pubs and to debate the ideas of novels and other publications in literary salons and clubs. In doing so, this group (which did not yet include women, peasants, the working classes, and other minority groups) began to build a society beyond the control of aristocrats, royalty, and religious elites. The outcome of such critical public debate led to support for the right to assembly, free speech, and a free press.

Habermas's research is useful to cultural studies researchers when they consider how democratic societies and the mass media operate today. For Habermas, a democratic society should always work to create the most favorable communication situation possible—a public sphere. Basically, without an open communication system, there can be no democratically functioning society. This fundamental notion is the basis for some arguments on why an open, accessible mass media system is essential. However, Habermas warned that the mass media could also be an enemy of democracy; he cautioned modern societies to beware of "the manipulative deployment of media power to procure mass loyalty, consumer demand, and 'compliance' with systematic imperatives" of those in power.[32]

Communication as Culture

As Habermas considered the relationship between communication and democracy, media historian James Carey considered the relationship between communication and culture. Carey rejected the "transmission" view of communication—that is, that a message goes simply from sender to receiver. Carey argued that communication is more of a cultural ritual; he famously defined communication as "a symbolic process whereby reality is produced, maintained, repaired, and transformed."[33] Thus communication creates our reality and maintains that reality in the stories we tell ourselves. For example, think about novels; movies; and other stories, representations, and symbols that explicitly or tacitly supported discrimination against African Americans in the United States prior to the Civil Rights movement. When events occur that question reality (like protests and sit-ins in the 1950s and 1960s), communication may repair the culture with adjusted narratives or symbols, or it may completely transform the culture with new dominant symbols. Indeed, analysis of media culture in the 1960s and afterward (including books, movies, TV, and music) suggests a U.S. culture undergoing repair and transformation.

Carey's ritual view of communication leads cultural studies researchers to consider communication's symbolic process as culture itself. Everything that defines our culture—our language, food, clothing, architecture, mass media content, and the like—is a form of symbolic communication that signifies shared (but often still-contested) beliefs about culture at a point in historical time. From this viewpoint, then, cultural studies is tightly linked with communication studies.

Evaluating Cultural Studies Research

In opposition to media effects research, cultural studies research involves interpreting written and visual "texts" or artifacts as symbolic representations that contain cultural, historical, and political meaning. For example, the wave of police and crime TV shows that appeared in the mid-1960s can be interpreted as a cultural response to concerns and fears people had about urban unrest and income disparity. Audiences were drawn to the heroes of these dramas, who often exerted control over forces that, among society in general, seemed out of control. Similarly, people today who participate in radio talk shows, Internet forums, and TV reality shows can be viewed, in part, as responding to their feelings of disconnection from economic success or political power. Taking part in these forums represents a popular culture avenue for engaging with media in ways that are usually reserved for professional actors or for the rich, famous, and powerful. As James Carey put it, the cultural approach, unlike media effects research, which is grounded in the social sciences, "does not seek to explain human behavior, but to understand it. . . . It does not attempt to predict human behavior, but to diagnose human meanings."[34] In other words, a cultural approach does not provide explanations for laws that govern how mass media behave. Rather, it offers interpretations of the stories, messages, and meanings that circulate throughout our culture.

Figure 12-10. Cultural Studies researchers are interested in the production and meaning of a wide range of elements within communication culture, as well as audiences' responses to these. Some researchers have focused on the meaning of the recent trend of dark subject matter in young-adult novels like the *Twilight* series by Stephenie Meyer, the *Hunger Games* trilogy by Suzanne Collins, and *Wintergirls* by Laurie Halse Anderson. As such books are made into movies, researchers may also study the cultural fascination with actors who appear in them (like Jennifer Lawrence, the star of the *Hunger Games* films, shown here).

One of the main strengths of cultural studies is the freedom it affords researchers to broadly interpret the impact of the mass media. Because cultural work is not bound by the precise control of variables, researchers can more easily examine the ties between media messages and the broader social, economic, and political world. For example, media effects research on politics has generally concentrated on election polls and voting patterns, while cultural research has broadened the discussion to examine class, gender, and cultural differences among voters and the various uses of power by individuals and institutions in authority. Following Horace Newcomb's work, cultural investigators have expanded the study of media content beyond "serious" works. They have studied many popular forms, including music, movies, and prime-time television.

Just as media effects research has its limits, so does cultural studies research. Sometimes cultural studies have focused exclusively on the meanings of media programs or texts, ignoring their effect on audiences. Some cultural studies, however, have tried to address this deficiency by incorporating audience studies. Both media effects and cultural studies researchers today have begun to look at the limitations of their work more closely, borrowing ideas from one another to better assess the complexity of the media's meaning and impact.

Notes

Chapter 2

1. Peter Thai Larsen, "Comcast Looks to Snatch Disney with $66 Billion Bid," Fi*nancial Times*, February 12, 2004, p. 1; and Geraldine Fabricant, "Comcast Pulls Disney Bid Off the Table," *New York Times*, April 29, 2004, pp. C1, C6.
2. For alternative methodologies see *International Encyclopedia of the Social & Behavioral Sciences*, ed. Neil J. Smelser and Paul B. Baltes (New York: Elservier, 2001), s.vv. "Film and Video Industry" and "Television: Industry," by Douglas Gomery.
3. Karl Marx, preface to *A Contribution to the Critique of Political Economy* (1859; repr., London: Beekman, 1972).
4. Terry Eagleton, *Marxism and Literary Criticism* (Berkeley: University of California Press, 1976), 5.
5. See Adam Smith, *An Inquiry into the Nature and Causes of the Wealth of Nations* (1776; repr., New York: Oxford University Press, 2008).
6. For more on the free-market approach, see Benjamin M. Compaine and Douglas Gomery, *Who Owns the Media?*, 3rd ed. (Mahwah, N.J.: Lawrence Erlbaum Associates, 2001).
7. "All Time Box Office," Box Office Mojo, accessed May 23, 2013, http://boxofficemojo.com/alltime/world/.
8. Denis McQuail, Media Performance: Mass Communication and the Public Interest (London: Sage, 1992).
9. See *Frontline*, "News War" (Boston: Frontline/WGBH, 2007), PBS Video, 270 min., www.pbs.org/wgbh/pages/frontline/newswar/view/.
10. Robert G. Picard, *Media Economics* (London: Sage, 1989), 80.
11. U.S. Government Accounting Office, *Telecommunications: The Changing Status of Competitions to Cable Television* (Washington, D.C.: GAO, July 1999).
12. Epigraph: All Tim Moore quotes from in-person interview with author on 1/24/14.
13. All Jon Gunn quotes from author interview on 1/19/14.
14. Steven Ascher and Edward Pincus, *The Filmmaker's Handbook* (New York: Plume, 2012), 358.
15. Ibid.

Chapter 3

1. Epigraph: Quote and source information for opener derived from the *Hollywood Reporter*, July 2002: www.wga.org/subpage_newsevents.aspx?id=1907

Chapter 4

1. Epigraph: www.interviewmagazine.com/film/steve-mcqueen-1/#_
2. www.youtube.com/yt/press/statistics.html
3. Backstage interview with author at the ACE Eddie Awards, 2/7/14, at the Beverly Hilton Hotel. Audio of interview available from link in story on *Post* magazine website: www.postmagazine.com/Press-Center/Daily-News/2014/ACE-celebrates-the-craft-of-Editing.aspx
4. www.filmclass.net/ElementsFilm.htm
5. Epigraph: All Oppewall quotes from author interview on 12/2/13.
6. All Jack Taylor quotes from author interview on 11/23/13 or from updated material supplied by Jack Taylor in April 2014.
7. Vincent LoBrutto, *The Filmmaker's Guide to Production Design* (New York: Allworth Press, 2002), 1.
8. Epigraph:www.moviemaker.com/articles-directing/50-memorable-quotes-from-our-first-50-issues-3248
9. www.rogerdeakins.com/forum2/viewtopic.php?f=2&t=2128&sid=7007765867af39c79b2cb1a2cdbf01b2
10. www.hollywood.com/news/movies/43958072/roger-deakins-on-shooting-skyfall-like-a-western-not-an-action-movie?page=all
11. www.rogerdeakins.com/forum2/viewtopic.php?f=2&t=2039&sid=7007765867af39c79b2cb1a2cdbf01b2

Chapter 5

1. See Elizabeth Eisenstein, *The Printing Press as an Agent of Change* (Cambridge: Cambridge University Press, 1980).
2. See Quentin Reynolds, *The Fiction Factory: From Pulp Row to Quality Street* (New York: Street & Smith/Random House, 1955), 72–74.
3. See Kay Mills, *A Place in the News: From the Women's Pages to the Front Page* (New York: Dodd, Mead, 1988).
4. See Theodore Peterson, *Magazines in the Twentieth Century* (Urbana: University of Illinois Press, 1964), 5.
5. See Richard Ohmann, *Selling Culture: Magazines, Markets, and Class at the Turn of the Century* (New York: Verso, 1996).
6. See Peterson, *Magazines*, 5.

Chapter 9

1. For Trump quotes, see Daniel Kurtzman, "Donald Trump Quotes," http://politicalhumor.about.com/od/Donald-Trump/a/Donald-Trump-Quotes.htm, accessed September 5, 2015.
2. Eddie Scarry, "Trump Gets Almost Three Times the TV Coverage of All Other GOP Candidates," Washington Examiner, August 25, 2015, http://www.washingtonexaminer.com/trump-gets-almost-three-times-the-tv-coverage-of-all-other-gop-candidates/article/2570782.
3. Neil Postman, *Amusing Ourselves to Death: Public Discourse in the Age of Show Business* (New York: Penguin Books, 1985), 19.
4. James W. Carey, *Communication as Culture: Essays on Media and Society* (Boston: Unwin Hyman, 1989), 203.
5. Postman, *Amusing Ourselves to Death*, 65. See also Elizabeth Eisenstein, *The Printing Press as an Agent of Change*, 2 vols. (Cambridge: Cambridge University Press, 1979).
6. James Fallows, "How to Save the News," *Atlantic*, June 2010, http://www.theatlantic.com/magazine/archive/2010/06/how-to-save-the-news/8095/.
7. "Generation M2: Media in the Lives of 8- to 18-Year-Olds," A Kaiser Family Foundation Study, p. 2, accessed May 24, 2010, http://www.kff.org/entmedia/upload/8010.pdf.
8. Jefferson Graham, "For TV Networks, Social Is Hugely Important," *USA Today*, May 3, 2012, http://www.usatoday.com/tech/columnist/talkingtech/story/2012-05-02/social-media-tv/54705524/1.
9. Jerome Bruner, *Making Stories: Law, Literature, Life* (New York: Farrar, Straus & Giroux, 2002), 8.
10. Roger Rosenblatt, "I Am Writing Blindly," *Time*, November 6, 2000, p. 142.
11. See Plato, *The Republic*, Book II, 377B.
12. For a historical discussion of culture, see Lawrence Levine, *Highbrow/Lowbrow: The Emergence of Cultural Hierarchy in America* (Cambridge, Mass.: Harvard University Press, 1988).
13. For an example of this critical position, see Allan Bloom, *The Closing of the American Mind: How Higher Education Has Failed Democracy and Impoverished the Souls of Today's Students* (New York: Simon & Schuster, 1987).
14. For overviews of this position, see Postman, *Amusing Ourselves to Death*; and Stuart Ewen, *Captains of Consciousness: Advertising and the Social Roots of the Consumer Culture* (New York: McGraw-Hill, 1976).
15. See James W. Carey, *Communication as Culture: Essays on Media and Society* (Boston: Unwin Hyman, 1989).
16. Walter Lippmann, *Public Opinion* (New York: Free Press, 1922), 11, 19, 246–247.

17. See William Romanowski, *Pop Culture Wars: Religion & the Role of Entertainment in American Life* (Downers Grove, Ill.: InterVarsity Press, 1996).
18. For more on this idea, see Cecelia Tichi, *Electronic Hearth: Creating an American Television Culture* (New York: Oxford University Press, 1991), 187–188.
19. See Jon Katz, "Rock, Rap and Movies Bring You the News," *Rolling Stone*, March 5, 1992, p. 33.

EXAMINING ETHICS—Covering War

1. Bill Carter, "Some Stations to Block 'Nightline' War Tribute," New York Times, April 30, 2004, p. A13.
2. For reference and guidance on media ethics, see Clifford Christians, Mark Fackler, and Kim Rotzoll, *Media Ethics: Cases and Moral Reasoning*, 4th ed. (White Plains, N.Y.: Longman, 1995); and Thomas H. Bivins, "A Worksheet for Ethics Instruction and Exercises in Reason," *Journalism Educator* (Summer 1993): 4–16.

CASE STUDY—Is Anchorman a Comedy or a Documentary?

1. John Cawelti, *Adventure, Mystery, and Romance: Formula Stories as Art and Popular Culture* (Chicago: University of Chicago Press, 1976), 39.
2. Bill Kovach and Tom Rosenstiel, *The Elements of Journalism: What People Should Know and the Public Should Expect* (New York: Three Rivers Press, 2007), 187.
3. Steven Johnson, *Everything Bad Is Good for You: How Today's Popular Culture Is Actually Making Us Smarter* (New York: Riverhead Books, 2005), 115.
4. Steven Johnson, "Watching TV Makes You Smarter," *New York Times Magazine*, April 24, 2005, http://www.nytimes.com/2005/04 /24/magazine/24TV.html.

GLOBAL VILLAGE—Bedouins, Camels, Transistors, and Coke

1. Václav Havel, "A Time for Transcendence," *Utne Reader*, January/February 1995, p. 53.
2. Dan Rather, "The Threat to Foreign News," *Newsweek*, July 17, 1989, p. 9.

Chapter 10

1. David Gelles, "At Odds, Omnicom and Publicis End Merger, *New York Times*, May 8, 2014, chttp://dealbook.nytimes.com/2014/05/08 /ad-agency –giants-said-to-call-off -35-billion-merger/.
2. Natalie Zmuda, "Peterson Milla Hooks Is Ad Age's Comeback Agency of the Year," January 28, 2013, *Advertising Age*, http://adage .com/article/special-report-agency-alist-2013/

comeback-agency-year-peterson-milla-hooks/239306/. See also PMH Web site at http://www.pmhadv.com/about/.

3. See TVB, "TV Cost & CPM Trends—Network TV Primetime (M–Su), accessed September 19, 2014, http://www.tvb.org/trends/4718/4709.
4. Andrew McMains and Noreen O'Leary, "GM Shifts Chevy Biz to Publicis from C-E," *Adweek*, April 23, 2010, http://www.adweek.com /aw/content_display/news/account-activity/e3i091074075f7ed276cf 510b1df8dddbcd.
5. Bettina Fabos, "The Commercialized Web: Challenges for Libraries and Democracy," *Library Trends* 53, no. 4 (Spring 2005): 519–523.
6. "Share of Ad Spending by Medium: U.S.," *Advertising Age*, December 31, 2012, p. 16.
7. Lauren Johnson, "Digital to Pass 25% of Global Media Spend for First Time," *Adweek*, July 9, 2014, http://www.adweek.com/news/technology/digital-pass-25-global-media-spend-first-time-158815.
8. Google, "Form 10-K for the Fiscal Year Ended December 31, 2012," http://www.sec.gov/Archives/edgar/data/1288776/000119312513028362/d452134d10k.htm; eMarketer, "Google Takes Home Half of Worldwide Mobile Internet Ad Revenues," June 13, 2013, http://www.emarketer.com/Article/Google -Takes-Home-Half-of-Worldwide-Mobile-Internet-Ad-Revenues/1009966; Facebook, "Form 10-K for the Fiscal Year Ended December 31, 2012," http://investor.fb.com/secfiling.cfm?filingID=1326801-13-3.
9. See Mike Isaac, "Google's Quarterly Results Show Its Continuing Struggle with Mobile Advertising," *New York Times*, July 17, 2014, http://www.nytimes.com/2014/07/18/technology/googles-earnings -show-its-struggle-with-mobile-ads.html.
10. Jack Neff, "Unilever to Double Digital Spending This Year," Advertising Age, June 25, 2010, http://adage.com/cannes2010/article?article_id=144672.
11. Jon Gibs and Sean Bruich, "Advertising Effectiveness: Understanding the Value of a Social Media Impression," Nielsen, April 2010, http://www.iab.net/media/file/Nielsen-FacebookValueof SocialMediaImpressions.pdf.
12. See Somini Sengupta, "Like It or Not, His Face Is on Ad," *New York Times*, June 1, 2012, p. A1.
13. Leslie Savan, "Op Ad: Sneakers and Nothingness," *Village Voice*, April 2, 1991, p. 43.
14. See Mary Kuntz and Joseph Weber, "The New Hucksterism," *BusinessWeek*, July 1, 1999, 79.
15. Ibid.
16. Schudson, *Advertising*, 210.
17. Eric Pfanner, "Your Brand on TV for a Fee, in Britain," *New York Times*, March 6, 2011, http://www.nytimes.com/2011/03/07/business /media/07iht-adco.html.
18. Vance Packard, *The Hidden Persuaders* (New York: Basic Books, 1957, 1978), 229.
19. See Eileen Dempsey, "Auld Lang Syne," *Columbus Dispatch*, December 28, 2000, p. 1G; John Reinan, "The End of the Good Old Days," *Minneapolis Star Tribune*, August 31, 2004, p. 1D.

20. See Schudson, *Advertising*, 36–43; Andrew Robertson, *The Lessons of Failure* (London: MacDonald, 1974).

21. Kim Campbell and Kent Davis-Packard, "How Ads Get Kids to Say, I Want It!" *Christian Science Monitor*, September 18, 2000, p. 1.

22. See Jay Mathews, "Channel One: Classroom Coup or a 'Sham'?" *Washington Post*, December 26, 1994, p. A1ff.

23. See Michael F. Jacobson and Laurie Ann Mazur, *Marketing Madness: A Survival Guide for a Consumer Society* (Boulder, Colo.: Westview Press, 1995), 29–31.

24. Ads Beat News on School TVs," *Pittsburgh Post-Gazette*, March 6, 2006, p. A7.

25. Hilary Waldman, "Study Links Advertising, Youth Drinking," *Hartford Courant*, January 3, 2006, p. A1.

26. Alix Spigel, "Selling Sickness: How Drug Ads Changed Health-care," National Public Radio, October 13, 2009, http://www.npr.org /templates/story/story.php?storyid=113675737.

27. PorCon.org, "Should Prescription Drugs Be Advertised Directly to Consumers?" updated March 2014, http://prescriptiondrugs.procon.org/view.answers.php?questionID=001603.

28. Jeffrey Godsick, quoted in T. L. Stanley, "Hollywood Continues Its Fast-Food Binge," *Adweek*, June 6, 2009, http://www.adweek.com/news /advertising-branding/hollywood-continues-its-fast-food-binge-105907.

29. Douglas J. Wood, "Ad Issues to Watch for in '06," *Advertising Age*, December 19, 2005, p. 10.

30. Associated Press, "Two Ephedra Sellers Fined for False Ads," *Washington Post*, July 2, 2003, p. A7.

31. Beth Harskovits, "Corporate Profile: Legacy's Truth Finds Receptive Audience," *PR Week*, June 12, 2006, p. 9.

32. Robin Koval, "Monitoring the Future Reveals Good and Bad News Underscoring the Need for Education and Regulation," December 14, 2017, https://truthinitiative.org/news/monitoring-future-reveals-good-and-bad-news-underscoring-need-education-and-regulation.

33. See Stephen Ansolabehere and Shanto Iyengar, *Going Negative: How Attack Ads Shrink and Polarize the Electorate* (New York: Free Press, 1996).

34. Center for Responsive Politics, "The Money behind the Elections," accessed June 14, 2013, http://www.opensecrets.org/bigpicture/.

35. Kantar Media, "KM Reports U.S. Advertising Expenditures Increased 0.9 Percent in 2013, Fueled by Larger Advertisers," March 25, 2014, http://kantarmedia.us/press/kantar-media-reports-us-advertising-expenditures-increased-09-percent-2013.

EXAMINING ETHICS—Do Alcohol Ads Encourage Binge Drinking?

1. Amanda Stewart, "Alcohol Ads Have Heavy Impact on Underage Binge Drinking," Design & Trends, January 20, 2015, http://www .designntrend.com/articles/35740/20150120/alcohol-ads-heavy-impact-underage-binge-drinking.htm. See also FoxNews.com, "Children's Health: TV Alcohol Ad Exposure Linked to Greater Chance of Underage Drinking," January 20, 2015, http://www.foxnews.com/health/2015/01/20/tv-alcohol-ad-exposure-linked-to-greater-chance-underage-drinking/.
2. Stewart, "Alcohol Ads Have Heavy Impact."
3. FoxNews.com, "Children's Health."

GLOBAL VILLAGE—Smoking Up the Global Market

1. Peh Shing Huei, "7 Chinese Cities All Fired Up to Curb Smoking," *Straits Times*, January 23, 2010, p. 4.
2. Cheng Yingqi, "Women Now Main Target of Tobacco Firms," *China Daily*, May 19, 2010, http://www.chinadaily.com.cn/china/2010-05/19/content_9865347.htm.
3. See Li Hui and Ben Blanchard, "China Tobacco Monopoly Blocks Full Ban on Tobacco," Reuters, September 4, 2014, http://www.reuters.com/article/2014/09/05/us-china-smoking-idUSKBN0H001 N20140905.
4. Cheng Yingqi, "Women Now Main Target of Tobacco Firms," *China Daily*, May 19, 2010, http://www.chinadaily.com.cn/china/2010-05/19/content_9865347.htm.
5. National Institutes of Health, "Fact Sheet: Global Tobacco Research," October 2010, http://report.nih.gov/nihfactsheets/Pdfs /GlobalTobaccoResearch%28FIC%29.pdf.

Chapter 11

1. PRSA, "PR by the Numbers," accessed June 12, 2013, http://media.prsa.org/pr-by-the-number/.
2. Fleishman Hillard, "Department of Defense/TRICARE: That Guy," accessed June 12, 2013, http://fleishmanhillard.com/work/department-of-defensetricare-management-activity-that-guy/.
3. The lead author of this book, Richard Campbell, worked briefly as the assistant PR director for Milwaukee's Summerfest in the early 1980s.
4. Center for Responsive Politics, "Lobbying Database," accessed August 26, 2012, http://opensecrets.org/lobby.

5. SourceWatch, "Center for Consumer Freedom," accessed August 20, 2014, http://www.sourcewatch.org/index.php?title=Center_for _Consumer_Freedom.
6. David Barstow, "Message Machine: Behind TV Analysis, Pentagon's Hidden Hand," *New York Times*, April 20, 2008, http://www.nytimes.com/2008/04/20/us/20generals.html.
7. Associated Press, "Open Government Study: Secrecy Up," *Politico*, March 16, 2014, http://www.politico.com/story/2014/03/open-government-study-secrecy-up-104715.html.
8. Stanley Walker, "Playing the Deep Bassoons," *Harper's*, February 1932, p. 365.
9. Ibid., p. 370.
10. Ivy Lee, *Publicity* (New York: Industries Publishing, 1925), 21.
11. Schudson, *Discovering the News*, 136.
12. Ivy Lee, quoted in Ray Eldon Hiebert, *Courtier to the Crowd: The Story of Ivy Lee and the Development of Public Relations* (Ames: Iowa State University Press, 1966), 114.
13. See Walter Lippmann, *Public Opinion* (New York: Free Press, 1922, 1949), 221.
14. Christopher R. Martin, *Framed! Labor and the Corporate Media* (Ithaca, N.Y.: Cornell University Press, 2003).
15. *PRWatch*, "About Us," accessed August 26, 2012, http://www.prwatch.org/cmd.
16. John Stauber, "Corporate PR: A Threat to Journalism?" *Background Briefing: Radio National*, March 30, 1997, http://www.abc.net .au/radionational/programs/backgroundbriefing/corporate-pr-a-threat-to-journalism/3563876.
17. See Alicia Mundy, "Is the Press Any Match for Powerhouse PR?" in Ray Eldon Hiebert, ed., *Impact of Mass Media* (White Plains, N.Y.: Longman, 1995), 179–188.
18. Dan Rather, interviewed in "Forty Years after Watergate: Carl Bernstein & Dan Rather with CNN's Candy Crowley," *State of the Union with Candy Crowley*, CNN, August 3, 2014, http://cnnpressroom .blogs.cnn.com/2014/08/03/forty-years-after-watergate-carl-bernstein-dan-rather-with-cnns-candy-crowley/.
19. "PR Pros Call the 2012 Election in Advance for Obama," *PR Week*, November 6, 2012, http://www.prweek.com/article/1277656 /pr-pros-call-2012-election-advance-obama.

EXAMINING ETHICS—Public Relations and Bananas

1. Peter Chapman, *Bananas: How the United Fruit Company Shaped the World* (New York: Canongate, 2008), p. 2.
2. Phil Milford, "Dole, Del Monte, Dow Chemical Sued Over Banana Pesticide," Bloomberg-Business, June 4, 2012, http://www.bloomberg.com/news/articles/2012-06-04/dole-del-monte-dow-chemical-sued-over-banana-pesticide.
3. Dole Organic Program, "Nazira Farm," accessed May 11, 2015, http://www.doleorganic.com/index.php?option=com_content&view =article&id=110&Itemid=210&phpMyAdmin=101ec4fece409t7349 8e50.

CASE STUDY—The NFL's Concussion Crisis

1. Brent Schrotenboer, "NFL Takes Aim at $25 Billion, but at What Price?" *USA Today*, February 5, 2014, http://www.usatoday.com/story/sports/nfl/super/2014/01/30/super-bowl-nfl-revenue-denver-broncos-seattle-seahawks/5061197/.
2. Mark Fainaru-Wada and Steve Fainaru, *League of Denial: The NFL, Concussions, and the Battle for Truth* (New York: Crown, 2013), 6.

MEDIA LITERACY AND THE CRITICAL PROCESS—The Invisible Hand of PR

1. John Stauber, "Corporate PR: A Threat to Journalism?" *Background Briefing: Radio National*, March 30, 1997, http://www.abc.net .au/radionational/programs/background-briefing/corporate-pr-a-threat-to-journalism/3563876.

Chapter 12

1. Alexis de Tocqueville, *Democracy in America* (New York: Modern Library, 1835, 1840, 1945, 1981), 96–97.
2. Steve Fore, "Lost in Translation: The Social Uses of Mass Communications Research," *Afterimage*, no. 20 (April 1993): 10.
3. James Carey, *Communication as Culture: Essays on Media and Society* (Boston: Unwin Hyman, 1989), 75.
4. Daniel Czitrom, *Media and the American Mind: From Morse to McLuhan* (Chapel Hill: University of North Carolina Press, 1982), 122–125.
5. Ibid., 123.
6. Harold Lasswell, *Propaganda Technique in the World War* (New York: Alfred A. Knopf, 1927), 9.
7. Walter Lippmann, *Public Opinion* (New York: Macmillan, 1922), 18.
8. Jon Cohen, "Gay Marriage Support Hits New High in *Post*–ABC Poll," *Washington Post*, March 18, 2013, http://www.washingtonpost.com/blogs/the-fix/wp/2013/03/18/gay-marriage-support-hits-new-high-in-post-abc-poll/.
9. Sheldon R. Gawiser and G. Evans Witt, "20 Questions a Journalist Should Ask about Poll Results," 2nd ed., http://www.ncpp.org/qajsa.htm.
10. See W. W. Charters, *Motion Pictures and Youth: A Summary* (New York: Macmillan, 1934); and Garth Jowett, *Film: The Democratic Art* (Boston: Little, Brown, 1976), 220–229.

11. Czitrom, *Media and the American Mind*, 132. See also Harold Lasswell, "The Structure and Function of Communication in Society," in Lyman Bryson, ed., *The Communication of Ideas* (New York: Harper and Brothers, 1948), 37–51.
12. Wilbur Schramm, Jack Lyle, and Edwin Parker, *Television in the Lives of Our Children* (Stanford, Calif.: Stanford University Press, 1961), 1.
13. See Joseph Klapper, *The Effects of Mass Communication* (New York: Free Press, 1960).
14. Schramm, Lyle, and Parker, *Television*, 1.
15. For an early overview of uses and gratifications, see Jay Blumler and Elihu Katz, *The Uses of Mass Communication* (Beverly Hills, Calif.: Sage, 1974).
16. National Public Radio, "Death-Penalty Option Varies Depending on Question," *Weekend Edition*, July 2, 2006.
17. See George Gerbner et al., "The Demonstration of Power: Violence Profile No. 10," *Journal of Communication* 29, no. 3 (1979): 177–196.
18. Kaiser Family Foundation, *Sex on TV 4* (Menlo Park, Calif.: Henry C. Kaiser Family Foundation, 2005).
19. Robert P. Snow, *Creating Media Culture* (Beverly Hills, Calif.: Sage, 1983), 47.
20. See Maxwell McCombs and Donald Shaw, "The Agenda-Setting Function of Mass Media," *Public Opinion Quarterly* 36, no. 2 (1972): 176–187.
21. See Nancy Signorielli and Michael Morgan, *Cultivation Analysis: New Directions in Media Effects Research* (Newbury Park, Calif.: Sage, 1990).
22. John Gastil, *Political Communication and Deliberation* (Beverly Hills, Calif.: Sage, 2008), 60.
23. W. Phillips Davison, "The Third-Person Effect in Communication," *Public Opinion Quarterly* 47, no. 1 (1983): 1–15, doi:10.1086/268763.
24. Richard Rhodes, *The Media Violence Myth*, 2000, http://www.abffe.com/myth1.htm.
25. Robert Lynd, *Knowledge for What? The Place of Social Science in American Culture* (Princeton, N.J.: Princeton University Press, 1939), 120.
26. Czitrom, *Media and the American Mind*, 143; and Leo Lowenthal, "Historical Perspectives of Popular Culture," in Bernard Rosenberg and David White, eds., *Mass Culture: The Popular Arts in America* (Glencoe, Ill.: Free Press, 1957), 52.
27. See Stuart Hall et al., *Policing the Crisis: Mugging, the State, and Law and Order* (London: Macmillan, 1978).
28. Todd Gitlin, *The Whole World Is Watching* (Berkeley: University of California Press, 1980), 7.
29. Horace Newcomb, *TV: The Most Popular Art* (Garden City, N.Y.: Anchor Books, 1974), 19, 23.
30. See Janice Radway, *Reading the Romance: Women, Patriarchy, and Popular Literature* (Chapel Hill: University of North Carolina Press, 1984).

31. Jürgen Habermas, *The Structural Transformation of the Public Sphere* (Cambridge, Mass.: MIT Press, 1962/1994).
32. Craig Calhoun, ed., *Habermas and the Public Sphere* (Cambridge, Mass.: MIT Press, 1994), 452.
33. James W. Carey, *Communication as Culture* (New York: Routledge, 1989), 23.
34. James Carey, "Mass Communication Research and Cultural Studies: An American View," in James Curran, Michael Gurevitch, and Janet Woollacott, eds., *Mass Communication and Society* (London: Edward Arnold, 1977), 418, 421.

CASE STUDY—The Effects of TV in a Post-TV World

1. Frank J. Prial, "Congressmen Hear Renewal of Debate over TV Violence," *New York Times*, April 16, 1983, http://www.nytimes.com/1983/04/16/arts/congressmen-hear-renewal-of-debate-over-tv-violence.html.
2. Parents Television Council, "What Is the PTC's Mission?" accessed May 15, 2011, http://www.parentstv.org/PTC/faqs/main.asp#What%20is%20the%20PTCs%20mission.
3. Parents Television Council, "INSP Network Earns PTC Seal of Approval," May 23, 2012, http://www.parentstv.org/PTC/news/release/2012/0523.asp.

MEDIA LITERACY AND THE CRITICAL PROCESS—Wedding Media and the Meaning of the Perfect Wedding Day

1. Erika Engstrom, *The Bride Factory: Mass Media Portrayals of Women and Weddings* (New York: Peter Lang, 2012).

CASE STUDY—Our Masculinity Problem

1. Mark Follman, Gavin Aronsen, and Deanna Pan, "A Guide to Mass Shootings in America," *Mother Jones*, May 24, 2014, http://www.motherjones.com/politics/2012/07/mass-shootings-map. See also John Wihbey, "Mass Murder, Shooting Sprees and Rampage Violence: Research Roundup," Journalist's Resource, April 3, 2014, http://journalistsresource.org/studies/government/criminal-justice/mass-murder-shooting-sprees-and-rampage-violence-research-roundup.
2. Jackson Katz, "Memo to Media: Manhood, Not Guns or Mental Illness, Should Be Central in Newtown Shooting," *Huffington Post*, updated February 17, 2013, http://www.huffingtonpost.com/jackson-katz/men-gender-gun-violence_b_2308522.html.
3. Ibid.

4. Rachel Kalish and Michael Kimmel, “Suicide by Mass Murder: Masculinity, Aggrieved Entitlement, and Rampage School Shootings,” *Health Sociology Review* 19, no. 4 (2010): 451–464.
5. Elliot Rodger, quoted in ibid.
6. See Ralph Ellis and Sara Sidner, “Deadly California Rampage: Chilling Video, but No Match for Reality,” CNN, May 27, 2014, http://www.cnn.com/2014/05/24/justice/california-shooting-deaths/.

Acknowledgments

Chapter 1

Greg Smith. "'It's Just a Movie': A Teaching Essay for Introductory Media Classes" by Greg M. Smith, first published in *Cinema Journal*, Volume 41 Issue 1, pp. 127–134. Copyright © 2001 by the University of Texas Press. Reprinted with permission of the University of Texas Press.

Chapter 5

J. D. Lasica, "Six Types of Citizen Journalism" from "What Is Participatory Journalism?," *Online Journalism Review*, August 7, 2003. J. D. Lasica/Socialmedia.biz. Reprinted by permission of the author.

Sarah Rupp, "On the Job" Interview. Reprinted by permission of Sarah Rupp.

Chapter 6

Wright Thompson, "Comments on a story about a former college football player and a memorable interview with Heisman Trophy winner Eric Crouch." Reprinted by permission of the author.

Associated Press, "Terror Sting Thwarts Car Bomb Attempt," as appeared in *Columbia Daily Tribune*, October 18, 2012. Reprinted by permission of Associated Press.

Bruce Horovitz, "Advertisement Put Obese People in Spotlight," *USA Today*, October 4, 2012. Copyright © 2012 Gannett. Reprinted by permission.

T. J. Quinn, "On the Job" Interview. Reprinted by permission of T. J. Quinn.

Chapter 7

Erik Ulken, "On the Job" Interview. Reprinted by permission of Erik Ulken.

Stan Ketterer, journalist and journalism professor. "Guidelines for Evaluating Information of the Web." Reprinted by permission of the author.

Susanne Rust, Meg Kissinger and Cary Spivak, "Chemical Fallout: Bisphenol A Is in You," *Milwaukee Journal Sentinel*, December 2, 2007. Copyright © 2007 by Journal/Sentinel, Inc. Reprinted by permission of Journal/Sentinel, Inc.

Chapter 8

AP Leads, excerpts from several Associated Press leads. Reprinted with permission of The Associated Press.

Asif Lakhami, "Parks and Recreation, City Council discuss plans for parks tax," *Columbia Missourian*, November 29, 2010. Reprinted by permission of the Columbia Missourian.

Tina Macias, "On the Job" Interview. Reprinted by permission of Tina Macias.

Tina Macias, education reporter. "A Case Study of Leads." Reprinted by permission of the author.

Elizabeth Phillips, "Man Arrested in Attack, Charged with Child Endangerment," *Columbia Missourian*, November 17, 2006. Copyright © 2006 Columbia Missourian. Reprinted by permission.

Mark Landler and Eric Dash, "Drama Behind a $250 Billion Banking Deal," *The New York Times*, October 15, 2008 Issue, p. A1. Copyright © 2008 New York Times. All rights reserved. Reprinted by permission.

Justin Heckert, "On the Job" Interview. Reprinted by permission of Justin Heckert.

Amy Ellis Nutt, "48 hours: Before, during, and after Hurricane Sandy in Seaside Heights and Cape May," *The Star-Ledger*, November 4, 2012. Copyright © 2012. Reprinted by permission.

Kristen Gelineau and Ravi Nessman, "Ill-fated train ride tears Indian boy from mother, sparks 25-year worldwide hunt for home," Associated Press, June 11, 2012. Reprinted by permission of Associated Press.

John Tully. "Horse Power" from *Columbia Missourian*, November 27, 2006, p. 1. Copyright © 2006 *Columbia Missourian.* Reprinted by permission of the Columbia Missourian.

Jane Meinhardt, "Mother Accused of Being Criminal Ring-leader," *St. Petersburg Times*, October 21, 1994. Copyright © 1994 by St. Petersburg Times. Reprinted by permission.

Matt Pearce, "Web plays incendiary role in Ohio high school rape case," *Los Angeles Times*, January 7, 2013. Reprinted by permission of the Los Angeles Times.

Chapter 11

Public Relations Society of America, Ethics Code. Used by permission of the Public Relations Society of America.